CONTEMPORARY CHINA

A RESEARCH GUIDE

現代中國研究指南

CONTEMPORARY
CHINA

A RESEARCH GUIDE

CONTEMPORARY CHINA

A RESEARCH GUIDE

by

Peter Berton and Eugene Wu

Edited by Howard Koch, Jr.

Prepared for the Joint Committee on Contemporary China
of the American Council of Learned Societies
and the Social Science Research Council

Hoover Institution Bibliographical Series: XXXI

The Hoover Institution on War, Revolution and Peace
Stanford University
Stanford, California

1967

The Hoover Institution on War, Revolution and Peace, founded at Stanford University in 1919 by the late President Herbert Hoover, is a center for advanced study and research on public and international affairs in the twentieth century. The views expressed in its publications are entirely those of the authors and do not necessarily reflect the views of the Hoover Institution.

The Hoover Institution on War, Revolution and Peace
Stanford, California
Library of Congress Catalog Card Number: 67–14235
Printed in Hong Kong

TO MICHELE AND NADINE

FOREWORD

Twenty years ago, contemporary China did not appear to most of the outside world to pose a major intellectual or political challenge. Scholars and statesmen alike, after a perfunctory bow in formal recognition of the problem, could turn their attention elsewhere. Serious study was handicapped by limited access to the country, by a severe shortage of specialists, and by the thinness of the written material reaching the outside. Inevitably we were dependent on the informed guesswork either of specialists on communism who knew little about China or of specialists on earlier periods of Chinese history who were ill-prepared to analyze the cataclysmic changes that were occurring. In the years since 1949 there has been little access to the Mainland for scholarly purposes, but a beginning has been made in the training of specialists on contemporary China, and the volume of materials has quickly become so vast that an entirely different problem is posed: Where should one begin? This book, begun by Peter Berton and Eugene Wu several years ago on the initiative of a number of American scholars, is an attempt to answer this question. The completion of the work was made possible through an allocation of funds by the Joint Committee on Contemporary China of the American Council of Learned Societies and the Social Science Research Council. The activities of the Joint Committee are supported by a grant from the Ford Foundation.*

The Joint Committee is grateful to the Hoover Institution for publishing this volume as part of its long-standing program not only of collecting source materials on the Chinese Revolution, but of encouraging their use by scholars through the production and publication of numerous research aids. Although Messrs. Berton and Wu have investigated the resources of libraries throughout the world, the Hoover Institution's own excellent collections have provided the core of the materials described. Both authors and several others associated with the preparation of this Research Guide have been at some time members of the staff of the Hoover Institution since the Chinese Collection was founded during World War II by Dr. Harold H. Fisher, then Director of the Institution. His successors, Dr. C. Easton Rothwell and, more recently, Dr. W. Glenn Campbell have continued to emphasize and to support research on contemporary China based on the Hoover Institution's material resources.

Mr. Berton and Mr. Wu have performed a signal service for academic communities outside China, in preparing a guide to the unwieldy mass of sources now available. Even the most experienced scholars now engaged in research on contemporary China will find here new suggestions for locating the information they need. More important, such a guide should encourage more young scholars to enter this field; it should also make it possible for scholars in other fields to include China in comparative studies.

* The members of the Joint Committee (1966–67) are A. Doak Barnett, Columbia University; Alexander Eckstein, University of Michigan; John K. Fairbank, Harvard University; Albert Feuerwerker, University of Michigan; Walter Galenson, Cornell University; John M. H. Lindbeck, Harvard University; Robert A. Scalapino, University of California, Berkeley; George E. Taylor, University of Washington; and Arthur P. Wolf, Cornell University; *staff*, Bryce Wood, Social Science Research Council. Mary C. Wright was member of the committee, 1963–66.

Further, the social scientist who does not know Chinese can now begin to use a research assistant effectively, because both he and his translator will know where to find what may be available in Chinese on the point at issue. And by no means of least importance, scholars who have been trained in other fields of Chinese studies may now acquaint themselves with the voluminous documentation available on China since 1949 and give this period something more than the perfunctory treatment which has often been unavoidable in the past.

This Guide introduces the reader to the study of Nationalist China as well as of Communist China. The former is more complex than is sometimes realized. The volume of documentary material issued by the Kuomintang, the National Government, the Taiwan Provincial Government, local governments, and numerous research organizations is substantial and deserves more attention than it has received. The meticulous listings provided in this book should lead to monographs which may transform our dull generalizations, from several viewpoints, into genuinely interesting controversies.

For the study of Communist China the most important sources are Mainland publications in Chinese. The torrent of periodicals and newspapers, and the number that are now indexed indicate the feasibility of research on many important subjects of which we now know very little. Subject bibliographies listed in the *Guide* provide an introduction to books, pamphlets, and articles. Even though some items are very difficult to obtain, it is clear that we now have available materials of sufficient quality and quantity to permit considerable verification through cross-checking, according to the criteria of credibility used by the various disciplines.

An important additional resource is the substantial body of Mainland documentation collected and reproduced for limited distribution by government agencies on Taiwan. Even the existence of these collections has not hitherto been widely known. In the few instances where they have been checked, the Mainland and the Taiwan texts have corroborated each other. Taiwan agencies, as the listings in this book indicate, have also compiled useful reference works concerning the Mainland, notably in the field of biography.

Our major problem with the Chinese sources is therefore to understand what a particular piece of information really means, rather than to authenticate the text. This of course does not hold true for the English language pro-Communist publications from the Mainland, or for the English language anti-Communist publications from Taiwan. Since both are intended for foreign consumption, they lack the built-in limits on falsification which characterize the Chinese texts intended primarily for internal use.

Translations of Chinese sources into other languages, principally English, should be clearly distinguished from materials intended from the beginning for foreign consumption. On some problems, the translations are as useful as the originals. On others, important sources have not been selected for translation, or important sections may have been omitted. Some translations are full of errors and all translations distort to some degree. Nonetheless, the voluminous translation services of the Peking government, of the American Consulate General in Hong Kong, of the Union Research Institute, of the U.S. Joint Publications Research Service, and of other organizations are a major scholarly resource. Mr. Berton and Mr. Wu deserve our thanks for describing them and for telling us how to use them efficiently. In addition to the flow of translation, there are available in English essential reference books whose counterparts are not known to exist in Chinese.

The Japanese sources for the study of Communist China, comprehensively described for the first time in this volume, deserve particular attention because they are often ignored by Chinese and Western scholars. Some of them of course are mainly intended for the use of Japanese scholars, but many add substantially to what is available in either Chinese or Western languages. The biographical dictionaries, handbooks and chronologies prepared by the Japanese Foreign Office and by the Cabinet Research Office are especially noteworthy. Anyone who can read Chinese can learn to use these.

The materials on contemporary China in other languages, including Russian, are primarily conveniences for scholars in those countries, and add less substance than the materials in English and Japanese. It is nonetheless useful to have them listed.

Every college and university library, and major public libraries as well, will find this volume indispensable both in acquiring materials and in helping readers to use them. Confronted with a flood of paper, even the major research libraries have found it difficult to maintain systematic programs of acquisitions adequate to their users' needs. The result inevitably has been omission of major sources in random buying. This Guide will be no less useful to the numerous new centers of Chinese studies, with their smaller libraries. It will enable them with a minimum of funds and specialized staff to identify, acquire, and make available to readers the most important sources. For the liberal arts colleges, where students now want to write papers relating to contemporary China, these descriptions of the English-language sources should be a great help both to the bewildered general college librarian and to the hard-pressed undergraduate teacher.

Thus far, the normal interplay between research and library development has been sluggish in the contemporary Chinese field: scholars have neglected the subject because of the unwieldy character of the sources; because of this neglect, library development has lagged; and this lag has further discouraged research. The publication of this Guide is an important step in reversing the direction of this interplay: as the sources come under better control, research should increase, and this research in turn should further stimulate library development.

The real lesson of this volume, however, is that we can do a great deal more than we have been doing with the available materials, and that we are foolish to waste our time debating over the impressions of travelers or scoops in spot news when the sources exist for basic research of enduring value.

MARY C. WRIGHT
Professor of History

Yale University
July 1, 1965

CONTENTS

ANALYTICAL TABLE OF CONTENTS

PART ONE
BIBLIOGRAPHIES AND INDEXES

PART THREE

PART FOUR
SELECTED SERIAL PUBLICATIONS 333

APPENDIX A

RESEARCH LIBRARIES AND INSTITUTIONS:
SURVEYS, DIRECTORIES, CATALOGS, AND REFERENCES

APPENDIX B
DISSERTATIONS AND THESES

PREFACE

The purpose of this Guide is to facilitate research on contemporary China by providing descriptions of the most significant bibliographical and reference works, selected documentary compilations, and listings of series, dissertations and theses.

The temporal scope of the Guide is limited almost exclusively to post-1949 Mainland China and post-1945 Taiwan. The material covered originated primarily on the Mainland, in Taiwan, Hong Kong, Japan, the United States, Great Britain, and the Soviet Union, and in a number of languages, notably Chinese, Japanese, English and Russian. In terms of content, heavy emphasis has been placed on the humanities and social sciences. Coverage of the natural sciences and technology is extended only to bibliographies, indexes, glossaries and a few periodicals. The systematic collection of materials for this volume ended with publications issued in 1963, and, in the case of series, theses and dissertations, 1964. A number of important works published beyond these cut-off dates (such as the *Index Sinicus*) have been included, as have indications of revised editions and collateral references. Parenthetically, while many of the works listed in the Guide are to be found in the major East Asian libraries in the United States, the institutions most likely to have extensive holdings are the Library of Congress and the Hoover Institution and, in Japan, the National Diet Library in Tokyo.

It should be emphasized that the Guide is not a conventional subject bibliography on contemporary China. Secondary sources do not receive attention except in the form of publications in series, and dissertations and theses, listed in Chapter XXII and Appendix B respectively. The volume is essentially a reference work keyed to those materials providing *access* to sources on contemporary China and, to a lesser extent, to the sources themselves.

Governing all questions of organization has been our central concern that the most significant materials, irrespective of language or place of origin, be brought together to facilitate the study of a given subject. The Guide is organized, therefore, according to category of material and by subject, and normally without distinction as to language or place of publication. By way of illustration, in discussing yearbooks concerned with mainland China we have incorporated those from the Mainland together with those from Taiwan, Japan, the United States and the Soviet Union, in whatever languages they may have been published. In listing indexes to Mainland newspapers, we have attempted to bring together *all* such tools, again without reference to place or language. It is perhaps inevitable that any organizational scheme will fail to meet all contingencies, especially when called upon to deal with materials of exceedingly diverse character. Many sources, for example, fit into more than one category or cover more than a single subject, and their location in the volume has been more or less arbitrarily determined. The reader is therefore cautioned to read with care the introductory remarks preceding each section which identify other sections of the Guide that should be consulted.

Part One contains bibliographies—general and topical, of books, pamphlets and periodicals—and indexes to newspaper and periodical articles as well as to laws and treaties. The second part is given over to general reference works, such as yearbooks, statistical handbooks, directories, biographies, chronologies, atlases and dictionaries. Part Three is documentary, providing some of the basic primary sources for the study of present-day China. Part Four consists of a selection of roughly four hundred newspapers and periodicals and a list of over five hundred serial publications (which are either directly concerned with or contain material on contemporary China) in Chinese, English, Japanese, Russian and other languages. Catalogs, directories, surveys and related publications concerning the resources of research libraries and institutions in the United States and abroad are provided in Appendix A. The volume concludes with a list of dissertations and theses on contemporary China accepted by American universities.

Each of the four parts, each chapter, and most of the sections and subsections, are preceded by introductions. In addition to giving an overview of the sections themselves, the introductions provide a discussion of some of the more important entries (frequently offering comparisons), and list cross references to other sources of information in the Guide as well as, occasionally, to some not listed in this volume.

Within a particular section, the organization of items is entirely arbitrary and follows the order best suited to the materials contained in the section. As a general rule, however, the more important as well as the more general sources have been listed first, followed by those of lesser importance or those narrower in scope.

The entries themselves provide full bibliographical citations, including Chinese characters. The annotations are largely descriptive, although critical evaluations have been provided whenever possible and appropriate. It is realized that a specialist in any given field might have been able to provide a more meaningful evaluation of materials within his field, but the enlistment of a battery of specialists in a collaborative venture was not practicable. Nonetheless, the advice of many scholars in diverse fields has been solicited, and we feel that the evaluative statements that appear in these pages will facilitate the use of the materials described.

The planning of the present Guide had its inception among interested scholars at the 1959 annual meeting of the Association for Asian Studies. A further step was the preparation of a preliminary report on the problem for the Gould House Conference on Contemporary Chinese Studies, sponsored by the Ford Foundation; this was prepared by Peter Berton with the collaboration of Chün-tu Hsüeh, Tamotsu Takase and Eugene Wu, and was entitled *The Control of Sources for the Study of Contemporary China: A Preliminary Bibliographic Survey*. In 1960 the ACLS-SSRC Joint Committee on Contemporary China commissioned Peter Berton and Eugene Wu to undertake the preparation of the present Guide. In its compilation, beyond the utilization of the resources of the Hoover Institution, the authors spent considerable periods of time on field trips, Eugene Wu searching the major libraries in the United States and Peter Berton the collections in Japan, Taiwan and Hong Kong. The result is that over ninety per cent of the contents of this volume is new material gathered during the past several years, while the remainder has in most cases been revised, expanded or up-dated. Work at all stages of the project has been characterized by continual consultation and cooperation.

ACKNOWLEDGMENTS

In an undertaking of this magnitude, it is inevitable that we should have reached out for assistance to a wide circle of persons and institutions, academic and non-academic. The list of those who have at one time or another during these several years helped us with advice, information, criticism and suggestion is lengthy indeed.

We should like to begin this long list of acknowledgments with a tribute to our editor, Howard E. Koch, Jr. Not only did he perform in his capacity at the highest professional level, but his contribution to this book was far beyond that which can be defined as strictly editorial, difficult as it was involving the work of two authors. Almost since the inception of this undertaking, he has been our trusted friend and critic, who has in the end cheerfully assumed the additional responsibility of seeing the project to its conclusion. For all this we are most grateful.

We wish to thank next Professors Mary C. Wright and John K. Fairbank for their interest, encouragement and critical readings of the manuscript. Mary Wright also graciously wrote a preface to this publication.

For placing behind this project the rich human and material resources of the Hoover Institution, we wish to express our indebtedness to its Director, Dr. W. Glenn Campbell. Dr. Campbell also granted leaves of absence to Eugene Wu during the various stages of compilation. We are also indebted to Karol Maichel, Director of Publications and Curator of the East European Collection for his generous assistance in seeing the manuscript through the press.

We now turn to thank the persons who have in other ways contributed to our project. First we would like to salute Chün-tu Hsüeh, now with the University of Maryland, and Tamotsu Takase, both of whom collaborated with us on the preliminary survey. As Deputy Curator of the East Asian Collection at the Hoover Institution, Mr. Takase, however, remained in association with the project and gathered much information, especially on his numerous trips to Japan, and particularly with respect to Japanese-language periodicals. He also supervised the checking of the Japanese-language portion of the manuscript. Dr. Shōzō Fujii of the Japan Institute for the Study of International Problems, Dr. Shigeaki Uno, formerly with the China Section of the Japanese Foreign Office, and Mr. Wan Wei-ying, Curator, East Asian Collections, Yale University Library, assisted in the search for Japanese and Chinese sources and contributed material that was incorporated into the manuscript. Professors Lyman P. Van Slyke and Mark Mancall of Stanford, Harold L. Kahn of the London School of Oriental and African Studies, Stuart R. Schram of the Fondation Nationale des Sciences Politiques, and Herbert Franke of the University of Munich contributed descriptions of research libraries and institutions in Taiwan, the Soviet Union, Great Britain, France and Germany respectively. These descriptions, originally scheduled for inclusion in the Guide, will now for reasons of space appear separately.

John Ma, Library Curator of the Hoover Institution's East Asian Collection and Dennis J. Doolin, Research Curator, provided invaluable assistance in the preparation of the manuscript for publication. In addition, Dr. Doolin read the manuscript critically and made a number of substantive suggestions. Together with Howard Koch, he supervised the indexing.

Many scholars have provided information, counsel and criticism. We should like very sincerely to thank A. Doak Barnett, Eugene Boardman, Howard L. Boorman, Joseph Chen, Theodore H. E. Chen, J. Chester Cheng, Anne B. Clark, Allan B. Cole, John F. Howes, Joyce K. Kallgren, Paul F. Langer, Charleton M. Lewis, Kurt L. London, Theodore McNelly, Franz Michael, David Mozingo, James W. Morley, George R. Packard, Klaus H. Pringsheim, Alvin Z. Rubinstein, Richard Sorich, Peter S. H. Tang, C. Martin Wilbur, Bernhard Wilhelm, Hellmut Wilhelm and Y. L. Wu.

Librarians and administrators in various academic and research institutions in the United States and abroad have from the very beginning exhibited genuine interest in this project. They have without exception been most cooperative during our visits, have patiently answered many of our queries by correspondence, and in some cases have prepared special statements on the holdings of their collections or publication programs which have contributed immeasurably to the compilation of this work. We wish to thank the following persons, their colleagues, and the institutions with which they are affiliated: Dr. Edwin G. Beal, Jr., Assistant Chief, Orientalia Division of the Library of Congress and Dr. Ruth Krader, Librarian, Far Eastern Library of the University of Washington, who commented on the preliminary survey; Teg C. Grondahl, Executive Director, American Universities Field Staff; William C. Cromwell, Assistant Dean, School of International Service, the American University; Dr. Elizabeth Huff, Head, East Asiatic Library, University of California at Berkeley; Mrs. Man-Hing Yue Mok, Head, Oriental Library of the University of California at Los Angeles; Dr. T. H. Tsien, Curator, Far Eastern Library, University of Chicago; Dr. T. K. Tong and Dr. Philip Yampolsky, East Asian Library, Columbia University; Miss Gussie E. Gaskill, former Curator and Dr. Richard C. Howard, Curator, Wason Collection, Cornell University Library; Mr. Norman Jacobs, Editor, Foreign Policy Association; Professor G. Raymond Nunn of the University of Hawaii; Dr. A. Kaiming Chiu, University Librarian, Chinese University of Hong Kong; Dr. Paul L. Horecky, Assistant Chief, Slavic and Central European Division, the late Dr. Osamu Shimizu, Head of the Japanese Section, Dr. Warren M. Tsuneishi, Chief, Orientalia Division; and Dr. K. T. Wu, Head of the Chinese Section, Orientalia Division of the Library of Congress; Mrs. Bernadette P. N. Shih, formerly of the Chinese Science Project, Massachussets Institute of Technology; Mr. Yukihisa Suzuki, Librarian, Asia Library, University of Michigan; Dr. Herbert C. Jackson, Director, and Mrs. Elizabeth H. Rempson, Reference Assistant, Missionary Research Library; Dr. Wallace C. Merwin, Executive Secretary, Far Eastern Office, National Council of Churches; Mr. Kay I. Kitagawa of the National Science Foundation; Dr. Scott Adams, Deputy Director, and Samuel Lazerow of the National Library of Medicine; Mr. Benjamin Cheng, the Van Pelt Library, University of Pennsylvania; Mr. Shih-kang Tung, Curator, the Gest Oriental Library, Princeton University; Mr. Theodore E. Kyriak, Executive Director, Research and Microfilm Publications, Inc.; Dr. Leslie T. C. Kuo, Chief, Oriental Project, National Agricultural Library; Dr. Robert

D. Barendsen, Far Eastern Specialist, U.S. Office of Education; Messrs. Daniel Fendrick, Acting Chief, and Walter F. Cronin of the External Research Division of the U.S. Department of State; and Miss Chou-ming Hsia, University of Southern California Library.

Japanese experts on China have been most gracious in offering assistance. A debt of gratitude is due Professor Ichiko Chūzō of Ochanomizu Women's University and Toyo Bunko's Seminar on Modern China, who shared his own outstanding bibliographical files; Professor Ueda Toshio, formerly with the Institute for Oriental Culture of the University of Tokyo, who provided introductions to various centers of Chinese studies in Japan; Professors Muramatsu Yūji and Uchida Naosaku who, during their stay at Stanford, shared their wide knowledge and proved extremely helpful in the preparation of the preliminary survey; Professors Banno Masataka of Tokyo Metropolitan University, Etō Shinkichi of Tokyo University and Ishikawa Tadao of Keio University; the staff of the Asian and African Reference Section of the National Diet Library, which has the most extensive collection on contemporary China in Chinese, Japanese and Western languages in Japan—Nakata Yoshinobu, Head of Section, and Messrs. the late Kuramochi Tokuichirō, Ōnishi Hiroshi, and especially Taira Kazuhiko who also provided a special list of Chinese reference works for the preliminary survey, and Messrs. Suzuki Heihachirō and Tanaka Azusa of the Library's administrative staff; Mr. Endō Matao, formerly head of the China Section of the Gaimusho and Mr. Tanabe Shin'ichi, the Foreign Ministry's librarian; Okazaki Osamu of the Cabinet Research Office; Colonel Kōtani Etsuo, formerly Counsellor of the Public Security Investigation Agency and currently Director of the KDK Kojimachi Institute; Dr. Tōbata Seiichi, President of the Institute of Asian Economic Affairs; Professors Kawasaki Ichirō, Noma Kiyoshi, Suzuki Chūsei and Suzuki Takurō of Aichi University; Miyashita Tadao and Hara Toshio of Kobe University; Chikusa Masaaki of Kyoto University's Research Institute for Humanistic Studies; Amano Motonosuke of Osaka Municipal University; Sawada Mizuho of Tenri University; and finally, Miss Fukuda Naomi, Librarian of the International House of Japan, who is ever ready to help the foreign scholar in Tokyo.

In Taiwan we are especially indebted to Dr. Chiang Fu-ts'ung, formerly Director of the National Central Library and currently Director of the National Palace Museum, and Professor Lai Yung-hsiang of the Library of the National Taiwan University; Mr. Li Nien-hsüan of Academia Sinica; Mr. Edgar N. Pike, formerly Representative of the Asia Foundation; Mr. Ku Cheng-kang, President, Asian Peoples' Anti-Communist League; Messrs. Ch'en Ch'iang and Wu Mu-feng of the Bureau of Investigation Library; the late Professor Pu Tao-min, Mr. Wu Chen-tsai and Mr. Wong Hsüeh-wen of the Institute of International Relations; General Lo Ying-te, Deputy Chief of Staff for Intelligence, Ministry of National Defense, and Messrs. Yeh Hsiang-chih and Hsiang Nai-kuang, Director and Research Director respectively of the Bureau of Intelligence; Professor Sung Shee and Mr. Lin Tze-hsiun of the National War College; Mr. Ch'en Chien-chung, Director of the Sixth Section of the Kuomintang Central Committee; and Professor Albert E. Dien, formerly Director, Inter-University Program for Chinese Language Studies.

In Hong Kong we wish to thank particularly Anderson Shih, former Director of the Union Research Institute, Geoffrey Chiang of the same institution; Stephen Uhalley, Jr. of the Asia Foundation, and Fenton Babcock and Donald Klein, formerly with the Foundation; Mr. Chow Ching-wen, Director, Continental Research Institute; Dr. Francis Pan and Mr. David Ting of the Mencius Educational Foundation; Professor E. Stuart Kirby, formerly of the University of Hong Kong; Jack Friedman and Linwood R. Starbird, at the time stationed with the U.S. Consulate-General, and Wallace E. Gibson of the U.S. Information Service.

In other parts of the world thanks are due to Professor Vidya Prakash Dutt, Head of the Department of East Asian Studies of the Indian School of International Studies; Mr. Sidney O. Fosdick of the University of British Columbia; Mr. E. D. Grinstead of the British Museum; Dr. Bernhard P. Grossmann, Director of the Institut für Asienkunde in Hamburg; General Jacques Guillermaz, formerly of the École Pratique des Hautes Études; Professor Lionello Lanciotti of the Istituto Italiano per il Medio ed Estremo Oriente in Rome; Mr. John Lust and Mr. J. D. Pearson of the London School of Oriental and African Studies; M. Roger Pelissier of the École Pratique des Hautes Études; and Miss Ruth Pryor, formerly with the Royal Institute of International Affairs in London.

The staff of the East Asian Collection of the Hoover Institution has contributed to this volume in more than one way—from constant checking of innumerable Chinese and Japanese books and periodicals to the answering of countless questions, reviewing romanization and providing expert calligraphy. We wish to thank David Tseng, T. Y. Wu, Keiko Farrer, Toru Goto (on leave from the National Diet Library in Tokyo), Margaret Lee, Allan Paul and Linda Tsou; also Kimiko Vorhees and Patricia Stea, who are no longer connected with the Institution.

The Reference Department of the Hoover Institution under the able direction of Mrs. Arline Paul has been most helpful and cooperative. Mrs. Dolores Kason, Miss Laverne Marcotte, and particularly Mrs. Naomi Penaat typed and retyped innumerable drafts and the final copy.

Maryann Doolin prepared the author-title index. Janet Colson and Raissa Berstein collated the drafts. Miss Lise Hofmann, in addition to typing portions of the manuscript, provided invaluable assistance to Howard Koch in the preparation of the subject index. We also drew on the extensive experience of James McSherry, former editor of the Hoover Institution, in a number of technical matters. His successor, Mrs. Carole Norton, went over the entire manuscript several times for technical copy-editing, and much credit for the resultant consistency is due to her efforts.

It remains to acknowledge the assistance of the Joint Committee on Contemporary China of the American Council of Learned Societies and the Social Science Research Council, which made the entire project possible, and the Hoover Institution which undertook the publication of the Guide. Here special thanks are due to the chairmen of the Commitee, Dr. George E. Taylor and Dr. John M. H. Lindbeck and Dr. Bryce Wood, Executive Associate of SSRC, for administrative support.

Needless to say, none of the many persons listed above is to be held responsible for errors of fact or interpretation to be found in the Guide. We alone are responsible.

Finally, this enterprise, which lasted several years and necessitated our frequent absences from home, has been particularly trying for our families. Our wives, Michele and Nadine, have been most patient and understanding, and it is fitting that this work be dedicated to them.

PETER BERTON
School of International Relations
University of Southern California

EUGENE WU
Harvard-Yenching Library
Harvard University

December 1966

EXPLANATORY NOTES

The following remarks are intended to facilitate the use of the Guide, to account for certain stylistic preferences, and to explain a number of the procedures employed in the handling of bibliographical detail.

In consulting the annotations of the works listed in the Guide, the reader is cautioned not to overlook the introduction preceding each of the subsections. Further, introductions to sections, chapters and parts contain much relevant information and additional, general references. Although the entries themselves are frequently cross-referenced, the introductions, together with the indexes, pull together the full range of collateral references.

The terms 'Mainland' and 'Taiwan' are widely used throughout the volume as general terms to designate geographical entities only. The terms 'Republic of China' and 'People's Republic of China' are reserved for materials or organizations possessing a formal legalistic character—constitutions, laws, organs of government, etc. In referring to the Peking regime, Taiwan publications generally employ such terms as 'puppet' or 'bandit'. Expressions of this nature have been translated literally.

Translation of names of organizations. Uniformity has been attempted in the translation of the names of Chinese and Japanese organizations and government agencies. The official translation is followed when available, except in the case of translations having more common usage in the United States. However, supplied translations of titles and names appearing on the title pages of foreign publications have not been altered in any way.

Romanization. With few exceptions, the Wade-Giles system has been applied to Chinese romanization, and Kenkyūsha to the Japanese.

Diacritical marks. Long vowels in Japanese have been indicated by a macron, except for such well known place names as Tokyo, Osaka and the like. In Chinese only the umlaut is used.

Numbering. The bibliographical entries in the Guide are numbered consecutively from 1 through 2226, letters accompanying numbers in the case of additions made after the numerical order was fixed. A bold-face figure, wherever it may appear, represents an entry number for a work listed in this volume.

Bibliographical entries. Each entry consists of a bibliographical heading and an annotation containing both descriptive and evaluative comments. The bibliographical heading encompasses all of the facts of publication known to the compilers: author, title, place and date of publication, publisher and pagination (pagination of prefatory material under ten pages is not indicated). Information in the heading supplied by the compilers is enclosed in brackets.

Characters are provided for all Chinese and Japanese names, titles, etc., in the bibliographical headings, and in the annotations where deemed necessary. Well known translated titles, such as People's Daily or Red Flag appear without characters or italics (inasmuch as the translated title was not supplied by the publisher). An English translation is provided for all Chinese and Japanese titles and names of corporate authors and publishers.

Entries are listed by author, or by title when no author is given. Periodicals are listed by title rather than publisher. Government publications, including official serial publications, are usually entered under the issuing agency. Authors, joint authors included, are listed last name first. In the case of corporate authors, the order of listing is from the most general to the most specific (e.g., from ministry, to bureau, to section; from university, to school, to department).

All titles are italicized in the customary manner unless they are English translations supplied by the compilers. The latter appear unitalicized in parentheses. For easier identification, titles in English, as well as those translated into English, are placed on a separate line in the heading of each entry. Proper names are capitalized in romanized Chinese, Japanese and Russian titles. Common usage has been followed in titles in Western languages.

Theses and Dissertations (Appendix B). In doctoral dissertations, the last names of the authors have been set in block capital letters for easier identification.

Two additional details should be noted. First, Chinese Communist and Soviet periodicals generally use both a calendar year and a cumulative numbering system, and both have been included in the Guide. Thus '1959 No. 1 (No. 13)' means that the issue is the first issue of 1959 and cumulatively No. 13. Second, translations provided by the Joint Publications Research Service have been indicated in the following manner (e.g.): J.P.R.S. No. 1730, June 18, 1961, 43p. (U.S.G.P.O. Monthly Catalog, 1962, No. 3451). The foregoing listing provides not only the Joint Publications Research Service number and date, but also the number in the *Monthly Catalog of U.S. Government Publications* for the year indicated, and thus allows additional access to the translated material through the microprint edition of non-depository U.S. Government documents.

PART ONE

BIBLIOGRAPHIES AND INDEXES

This is in a sense the core of the present work. The chapters which follow provide access to the voluminous documentation available for the study of contemporary China—each, in effect, a different guide. The first chapter contains bibliographies of books (and pamphlets) and of books and articles. Chapter II describes the various lists of periodicals. The last chapter covers indexes to periodical literature and to laws and treaties.

We distinguish three kinds of indexes: (1) an index to periodical literature on a given *subject*—e.g., education or foreign relations; (2) an index to a number of periodicals, listing *all* the articles in the periodicals under review without regard to subject matter; and (3) an index to a *single* newspaper or periodical, again without regard to subject matter. The indexes in the first category are, in fact, subject bibliographies and, as such, are included in the bibliography chapter (Chapter I). The general indexes to periodicals are treated in the chapter on indexes (Chapter III), whereas indexes to individual newspapers and periodicals are grouped for convenience with the respective newspapers or periodicals in Part Four. Thus, in attempting to locate material on any given topic, it is necessary to consult the bibliographies and general indexes as well as the indexes to individual newspapers and periodicals.

Since materials in this Guide are generally arranged by subject or by type, rather than by language or place of origin, it may be useful at the outset to provide the reader with an overview of the most important bibliographical sources within the framework of language.

For Chinese-language material, the two national bibliographies are enormously important in that they provide a record not only of all sources bearing on Mainland China and Taiwan, but of all their book-publishing activities as well. Peking issues both a current (*Ch'üan-kuo hsin shu-mu*, **8**) and a cumulative (*Ch'üan-kuo tsung shu-mu*, **9**) bibliography. Taiwan publications can be followed through the current bibliography appearing in *The Monthly List of Chinese Books* (**11**), as well as through the national bibliographies (*Chung-hua min-kuo ch'u-pan t'u-shu mu-lu*, **10**) and a special compilation of selected books (*Chung-hua min-kuo ch'u-pan t'u-shu hsüan-mu* **12**). Chinese-language books and periodical articles available outside the Mainland are listed in the bibliography section of *Contemporary China*, published by the University of Hong Kong (**14**), and in the annual bibliography of Kyoto University (**30**), which carries extensive lists of Chinese-language sources. They may also be found in the accession list of Chinese books issued by the National Diet Library in Tokyo and other research libraries and institutions (see Appendix A).

Chinese-language periodical literature is more adequately indexed for the last ten years than for any previous period. The Mainland index to the major newspapers and periodicals (*Ch'üan-kuo chu-yao pao-k'an tzu-liao so-yin*, **184**) is without question the basic source for the Mainland, while two Taiwan indexes cover Taiwan periodicals (*Chung-wen ch'i-k'an lun-wen fen-lei so-yin*, **192**, and *Ch'i-k'an lun-wen so-yin*, **193**), and another (*Chung-wen pao-chih lun-wen fen-lei so-yin*, **194a**) covers the newspapers. In addition, individual Mainland newspapers carry their own monthly indexes, as do a select number of both Mainland and Taiwan periodicals.

Mainland periodical literature can also be surveyed from the comprehensive catalog prepared by the Shanghai Library (**172**), and that available outside the Mainland from the lists of international holdings of Chinese periodicals compiled by Raymond Nunn (**1709**) and by Bernadette Shih and Richard Snyder (**1708**).

Although the various regions of China are unevenly covered in the section on regional bibliographies, the latter should nonetheless be consulted in conjunction with the national and general bibliographies.

Another important source of Chinese-language materials are the various subject bibliographies. Of these, several are recommended as being particularly solid: (1) the Mainland-produced bibliography on economic geography (**115**), (2) Professor Ichiko's compilation of Chinese works on the Chinese economy (**109**), (3) Professor Noma's bibliography on the communes (**125**), (4) Feuerwerker and Cheng's *Chinese Communist Studies of Modern Chinese History* (**79**), (5) the current bibliography of Chinese-language books and articles in the *Journal of Chinese Literature* published by Kyoto University (**90**), (6) Mainland bibliographies on the 'People's Liberation Army' (**130**), and (7) on library science (**147** and **148**), and Taiwan bibliographies on (8) education (**99**), (9) agriculture (**151**), and (10) Overseas Chinese (**135** and **136**).

It should be noted here that the standard American bibliographies—such as those of Teng and Biggerstaff, Fairbank-Liu and Fairbank-Teng, which cover an earlier period than is the concern of this Guide—are not listed here.

English-language literature on China is comprehensively treated in T. L. Yuan's and J. Lust's bibliographies (**16** and **16a**), and, more critically and selectively, in Professor Hucker's bibliography (containing both books and articles; **17**). The most comprehensive listing is, of course, the annual 'Bibliography of Asian Studies' (**15**). The indexes to the compilations of the American Consulate General in Hong Kong (**1043** ff.) and the bibliography of and indexes to the Joint Publications Research Services reports (**1047** ff.) are indispensable guides to the mass of translated material on contemporary China.

Japanese-language bibliographical works on China deserving of special mention are the ten-year bibliography compiled under the direction of Mr. Taira (**31**), the two lists of articles prepared by Professor Ishikawa (**35** and **36**), the bibliography section in the recent editions of the *Chūgoku seiji keizai sōran* (**33** and **34**), and the current bibliography of Japanese-language books and articles in Kyoto University's *Journal of Chinese Literature* mentioned above. Current books and articles on China can be traced through the annual bibliography of Kyoto University (**30**), as well as through the national bibliography of Japan *(Zen Nihon shuppambutsu sōmokuroku)*, the publishers' annual *(Shuppan nenkan)*, and the monthly index to Japanese periodical literature *(Zasshi kiji sakuin)*, which is published, together with the national bibliography, by the National Diet Library.

Through the year 1957, Russian-language publications (books as well as articles) on China are amply covered by the Skachkov bibliography (**42**). More current publications can be located through the general Soviet bibliographical sources, such as the weekly book annals *(Knizhnaia letopis')* and the indexes to newspapers, periodicals and book reviews. The two bibliographies of Russian-language books and pamphlets compiled in the United States by T. L. Yuan **(43)** and Peter Berton **(44)** should be noted in this connection. The former is also useful for Russian-language publications issued outside the Soviet Union.

Publications on China in languages other than Chinese, Japanese, English and Russian can be traced through the special language bibliographies listed below for German, Italian, Czech, Hungarian and Polish. Other languages, as well as more current publications in all these languages, must be traced through the respective national bibliographies of the countries concerned. Some coverage of non-English language material on China also can be found in the annual 'Bibliography of Asian Studies' **(15)**.

Bibliographical material is also to be found in such reference works as the yearbooks in Part Two and in the documentary materials in Part Three. The indexes to individual newspapers and periodicals as well as to translated material are located in Part Four, and lists of research reports, library catalogs, union catalogs and accession lists in Appendix A.

BIBLIOGRAPHIES

The contents of Chapter I, which are strictly bibliographical, are arranged within the following main sections:

A further breakdown of the subject bibliographies (which comprise roughly one-half of the entries in the chapter) is given at the beginning of that section. It must be stressed that the various parts of this chapter should be consulted in conjunction with one another, as well as with other bibliographical sources.

A. BIBLIOGRAPHIES OF BIBLIOGRAPHIES

The most elaborate bibliography of bibliographies is the first entry in this section. Listing bibliographies, catalogs, indexes and related works compiled by libraries in Communist China, the volume, in terms of sheer comprehensiveness, has no peer. Unfortunately, most of its contents are unavailable outside Mainland China.

For available Chinese bibliographies, indexes and other reference works, consult the bibliography compiled by Professor Ichiko of the Seminar on Modern China at the Tōyō Bunko (4). The compilation of Mrs. Clark (5) is restricted largely to English-language publications.

1 **Feng, Ping-wen** 馮秉文, **comp.** *Ch'üan-kuo t'u-shu kuan shu-mu hui-pien* 全國圖書館書目滙編
(A Bibliography of Bibliographies Compiled by Chinese Libraries). Peking: Chung-hua shu-chü 中華書局, 1958. 144p.

A bibliography of 2,409 bibliographies, catalogs, indexes, reading lists, etc., compiled or planned by Mainland libraries from 1949 to 1957. The volume excludes those prepared during the same period by individuals and non-library corporate authors. The 2,409 titles include 188 in process and 239 planned as of

October 1958. It should be noted, however, that most of the entries in the bibliographies do not necessarily deal with post-1949 China.

Arranged topically, entries are numbered consecutively with full bibliographical citations given in most cases. A detailed subject index is provided, as is an index to names of libraries, arranged by the number of strokes. Works cited in this volume are largely mimeographed compilations, and, with a few exceptions, none have been available outside Mainland China.

This is undoubtedly the most comprehensive bibliography of its kind.

2　**Pei-ching t'u-shu kuan, Shu-mu so-yin tsu** 北京圖書館書目索引組 (National Library of Peking, Bibliography and Index Section). 'Shu-mu kung-tso pao-kao' 書目工作報告
(Report on Bibliographical Work), *T'u-shu kuan hsüeh t'ung-hsün* 圖書館學通訊 (Library Science Bulletin), No. 1, 1960 (January 20, 1960), pp. 51–57; No. 2, 1960 (February 20, 1960), pp. 47–49; No. 3, 1960 (March 20, 1960), pp. 51–52; No. 4, 1960 (April 20, 1960), pp. 47–49.

A bibliography of about 630 bibliographies issued by various libraries in Communist China from January 1959 to March 1960. Brief annotations are given for some items.

A good supplement to the preceding work.

3　**'Chūgoku hakkō shomoku ichiran hyō'** 中國發行書目一覽表
(A List of Chinese Publications), *Ajia keizai jumpō* アジア經濟旬報 (Ten-Day Report on Asian Economy), Tokyo, Nos. 417, 421, 424, 426 (December 1959–March 1960).

A bibliography of 360 Chinese-language bibliographies, indexes and catalogs published or slated for publication in Communist China between 1949 and 1959. Based on *T'u-shu kuan hsüeh t'ung-hsün* 圖書館學通訊 (Library Science Bulletin) from its first issue in 1957 to September issue 1959, and on other sources, the bibliography is classified by subject (general, philosophy, religion, technology, natural science, industry, etc.). The general section is in turn divided into general bibliographies, library science, collectanea, general, general and special catalogs of periodicals, etc. The entries show title, author and, when ascertained, the date or frequency of publication. Holdings of the Library of the China Research Institute (Chūgoku Kenkyūjo), which publishes *Ajia keizai jumpō*, are marked with an asterisk.

Most of the entries are included in the preceding bibliography of bibliographies published in 1958 (1).

A rough translation of the first three issues appears in J.P.R.S.: No. 5244, August 3, 1960, 35p. (U.S.G.P.O. Monthly Catalog, 1960, No. 15,810), under the title *A List of Catalogues of Books Published in Communist China*.

4 Ichiko, Chūzō, 市古宙三 **comp.** *Kindai Chūgoku kankei bunken mokuroku ihen*
近代中國關係文獻目錄彙編
(A List of Bibliograpies and Catalogs on Modern China). Tokyo: Tōyō Bunko
nai Kindai Chūgoku Kenkyū Iinkai 東洋文庫內近代中國研究委員會, 1960. 44p.

A list of some 300 bibliographies, catalogs and related reference works on
nineteenth and twentieth century China published since August 1945, based on
the Japanese library holdings in the Tokyo and Kyoto areas. The works—both
Chinese and Japanese books and parts thereof, and periodical articles—are arranged
in seventeen categories: library science, publishers' catalogs, union catalogs and
library catalogs, general bibliographies, translations, indexes to newspaper and
periodical literature, and various subject divisions (history, language and literature, industry-economics, etc.). Chapter 18 lists twenty-six similar Western-
language works in alphabetical order. In each category the arrangement is from
the general to the more specific works. Entries provide full bibliographical
information, including pagination and location symbols. Mimeographed.

5 Clark, Anne B., comp.
*A Checklist of Bibliographies and Reference Tools on Communist China for the
Use of the Center for East Asian Studies.* Revised. Cambridge, Mass.: Harvard
University, Center for East Asian Studies, 1961. 20p.

An annotated guide to some of the more important reference tools for research
on Communist China available at the Center for East Asian Studies and other
Harvard libraries. While most of the entries are in the English language, a few bibliographies are in Chinese, Japanese or Russian. In five main sections: (1) general
bibliographies of monographs and periodical literature; (2) bibliographies of the
holdings on Communist China in American university libraries and in the
Library of Congress; (3) bibliographies on special topics; (4) special guides,
catalogs, handbooks; and (5) general reference tools. Mimeographed. The original
checklist was published in 1960. Conveniently arranged.
Good coverage, though not exhaustive.

6 Garde, P. K.
Directory of Reference Works Published In Asia. Paris: United Nations Educational,
Scientific and Cultural Organization, 1956. 27;139p.

Contains the titles of general and special encyclopedias; linguistic and technical
dictionaries; collections of biographies, travel guides, atlases and geographical
dictionaries; chronologies and other compendia of historical facts. Also contains
reference works relating to economic and social, artistic and literary, scientific
and technical questions published in more than fifteen countries of Asia. Publications are arranged initially by subject in accordance with the Universal Decimal
Classification. (An abridged schedule of U.D.C. classes is included in the directory.)
Within each subject group, publications are arranged according to country of

publication; within each country group, the arrangement is alphabetical by author, or by title where authorship could not be determined.

The 'China' section list works (mostly Chinese, some English) published before 1949; those published after 1949 in Taiwan are entered under 'China (Formosa).' (No post-1949 Mainland Chinese publications are included.) The 'China (Formosa)' section contains a number of very useful reference works, most of which have been annotated for the present Guide. There are three indexes: author or title, subject, and index of language dictionaries.

7 Tōyōgaku Infuōmēshon Sentā 東洋學インフオーメーシヨン センター The Information Centre of Asian Studies. *Ajia ni kansuru shoshi mokuroku—jimbun kagaku, shakai kagaku, 1957 nendo* アジアに關する書誌目錄ー人文科學社會科學 1957 年度
Bibliography of Japanese Bibliographies Concerning Asia and Asian Studies on Humanities and Social Sciences for the Year 1957. Tokyo: Tōyō Bunko nai Kindai Chūgoku Kenkyū Iinkai 東洋文庫內近代中國研究委員會, 1960. 47p.

The first issue in a series of projected annual surveys of Japanese bibliographies on Asia in the field of the humanities and social sciences (including the history of natural science). Coverage is extended to general and special bibliographies, periodical indexes, union lists, catalogs, and similar reference tools appearing as books, parts of books or as articles. The first issue covers works published in Japan during 1957, primarily in Japanese, together with a few in Chinese and European languages. Entries include full bibliographical citations.

Arranged in two parts—Japan, and the rest of Asia—with many subdivisions. The section on China is further subdivided into China–general, history–general, special bibliographies, Chinese language and literature, bibliographies on individuals, and Chinese studies abroad. Items on China in the first issue number some twenty-four, of which all pertinent ones on contemporary China have been included in the present Guide.

B. National Bibliographies

The national bibliographies of both the Nationalist government on Taiwan and the Communist government on the Mainland provide a continuous record of what has been published in China since 1949 (no comparable compilations are available for the pre-1949 period). Aside from the obvious fact that they constitute the basic listing of primary sources for the study of contemporary China, the national bibliographies provide insights into the policies of the two governments in the fields of education and information, and further into the intellectual climate of the Mainland and Taiwan.

I. PEOPLE'S REPUBLIC OF CHINA

The Chinese Communists have stressed the fact that the publication of printed material on the Mainland has increased many-fold since their assumption of power. As in the Soviet Union, however, much ephemera finds its way into the national bibliography, inflating the overall figures. Nevertheless, the level of book production in Communist China is impressive. The total output is reported to have increased from some 1,000 items in 1950 to almost 30,000 in the short period of nine years ending 1958. (An analysis of Chinese publishing is currently being done under the supervision of Professor G. Raymond Nunn of the University of Hawaii.)

Using Soviet library practice as their model, and borrowing heavily on Soviet experience (indeed, many Chinese librarians have studied under Russian tutelage since 1949), Chinese librarians have made significant progress in centralizing and refining the methods of control of this burgeoning literature. As yet, understandably, Mainland bibliographical work does not equal in comprehensiveness that of the Soviet Union, but the existence of such a gap does not detract from what is to date a rather remarkable record.

Publication of the National Bibliography began in August 1951 with a volume entitled *Ch'üan-kuo hsin shu-mu* (**8**), covering publications of the period October 1949–December 1950. It has been kept up-to-date by a publication of the same title now issued twice a month.

In addition to this current bibliography, there is also published an annual cumulative volume, *Ch'üan-kuo tsung shu-mu* (**9**), beginning with the year 1955. A special volume was issued covering the years 1949–1954 inclusive. The two editions of the Chinese Communist national bibliography are dealt with in detail in the following pages.

Parenthetically, the reader is directed to the following periodicals described in Chapter XVII: *Ch'u-pan hsiao-hsi* (Publishing News, **865**), *T'u-shu* (Book Readers, **910**), and the library journals (**911–913**).

8 Ch'üan-kuo hsin shu-mu, 1950— 全國新書目
(National Bibliography, 1950—). Peking: Wen-hua pu ch'u-pan shih-yeh kuan-li chü t'u-shu kuan 文化部出版事業管理局圖書館, 1951—. Frequency varies.

The national bibliography of Communist China. It includes all books (new titles and reprints), pamphlets, pictorials, etc., published during the period under review (see table below). Arrangement has been topical (twenty-one topics) according to the 'Classification Scheme for Medium and Small Size Libraries' (*Chung-hsiao hsing t'u-shu kuan t'u-shu fen-lei piao* 中小型圖書館圖書分類表) since 1958, similar to a prior scheme. A statistical table of works listed was included in each issue through 1957, but omitted thereafter.

Beginning with No. 19, 1958 (November 1958), a new format was adopted which comprised a 'Special Topics Section' (*chuan-t'i mu-lu* 專題目錄) and a 'General Section' (*i-pan mu-lu* 一般目錄). The 'Special Topics Section' consisted of topics of current interest, such as 'Study Chairman Mao's Works', 'Socialist and Communist Education', 'People's Communes', 'Critique of Reactionary Deviationist and Capitalist Thought and Academic Viewpoints', 'Works by Workers and Peasants', and others. This feature appeared through 1959 but was omitted from publication beginning with No. 1, 1960. For the first six issues of 1960 a brief, insignificant 'Index to Special Topics' (*Chuan-t'i so-yin*

專題索引) was included, only to be dropped from publication beginning with No. 7, 1960.

The National Bibliography was compiled and published by the General Bureau of Publications (全國出版總署) from 1951 to 1953. It has been published since 1954 by the Acquisitions Library of the Bureau of Publications of the Ministry of Culture, successor to the General Bureau of Publications.

The following table contains other bibliographical information on this publication:

NO. AND FREQUENCY	COVERAGE	DATE OF PUBLICATION
1950 (Annual, 1 vol.)	Oct. 1949–Dec. 1950	Aug. 1951
1951 (Quarterly, 2 issues)	1951 with Addendum (Oct. 1949–Apr. 1951)	Oct. and Dec. 1951
1952 (3 times a month, 65 issues)	1952	Jan.–Dec. 1952
(Also Semi-annual 2 vols.)	Jan.–Jun., Jul.–Dec. 1952 with Addendum (Oct. 1949–Jan. 1951; Nov. 1950–Jun. 1952)	Mar. and Jul. 1953
1953 (3 times a month, 29 issues)	1953	Jan.–Sep. 1953
(3 issues monthly)	1953	Oct.–Dec. 1953
(Also Annual, 1 vol.)	1953	Aug. 1954
1954 (Monthly, 12 issues)	1954	Jan. 1954–Jan. 1955
1955 (Monthly, 12 issues)	1955	Jan.–Dec. 1955 (?)
1956 (Monthly, 11 issues)	1956	Jan.–Dec. 1956
1957 (Monthly, 12 issues)	1957	Jan.–Dec. 1957
1958 (Monthly, 7 issues)	Jan.–Jul. 1958	Jan.–Jul. 1958
(3 times a month, 15 issues)	Aug.–Dec. 1958	Aug.–Dec. 1958
1959 (3 times a month, 36 issues)	1959	Jan.–Dec. 1959
1960 (3 times a month, 20 issues)	1960	Jan.–Jul. 1960
1962 (2 times a month, 24 issues)	1962	Jan.–Dec. 1962
1963 (2 times a month, 24 issues)	1963	Jan–Dec. 1963

The cumulative editions (see next entry) do not reproduce all the items in the monthly or ten-day issues. Reprints and ephemera are excluded.

9 Ch'üan-kuo tsung shu-mu, 1949-1954— 全國總書目
(Cumulative National Bibliography, 1949-1954—). Peking: Chung-hua shu-chü 中華書局, 1956—. Annual.

An annual cumulation of the *Ch'üan-kuo hsin shu-mu* (see preceding entry). The first two volumes (1949–1954 and 1955) were compiled and published by the Peking Hsin-hua shu-tien (新華書店) in 1956 and 1957 respectively. With the publication of the 1956 volume in 1957, the bibliography has been compiled by the Library of the Bureau of Publications of the Ministry of Culture and published annually by the Peking Chung-hua shu-chü. The last volume examined was the 1958 volume (published in 1959).

The arrangement is topical according to a modified classification scheme of the Chinese People's University Library. Each volume consists of a 'General Section' (*fen-lei tsung mu-lu* 分類總目錄) of nineteen topics; a 'Special Features Section' (*chuan-men mu-lu* 專門目錄) containing juvenile literature, art works, foreign-language publications, etc.; and an 'Appendix' which lists all elementary and secondary school textbooks and current newspapers and periodicals. (The last feature is not included in the 1957 volume.) There is also a publishers' list and a title index at the end of each volume.

The 1949–1954 volume (published in 1956) covers nearly all publications, including reprints, published between October 1949 and December 1954 which were sold by the Hsin-hua shu-tien in addition to Chinese titles published by the Moscow Foreign Languages Press and Western-language titles published by the Peking Foreign Languages Press. The textbooks are those published between 1955 and 1956. Newspapers and periodicals to October 1955 are arranged by region. The total number of titles included in this volume is 21,809.

The 1955 volume (published in 1957) covers all 1955 publications including reprints with revised texts. Chinese titles published by the Moscow Foreign Languages Press have been omitted from the 'Special Features Section', and a new category of Chinese Communist 'Internal Publications' (*nei-pu k'an-wu* 內部刊物) has been added. The textbooks are 1955–1957 imprints, and the list of newspapers and periodicals covers those titles published between November 1955 and December 1956. There is an addendum which lists titles left out of the 1949–1954 edition. The total number of titles included in this volume is 12,767.

The 1956 volume (published in 1957) covers all 1956 publications including reprints with revised texts. The textbooks are 1957 imprints; the newspapers and periodicals list contains only new titles published in 1957. The total number of titles included in this volume is 18,108.

The 1957 volume (published in 1958) covers all 1957 imprints and earlier publications left out of previous editions; reprints are included only when there are significant revisions. 'Internal Publications' no longer form a category in the 'Special Section'. Individual titles are integrated into the 'Topical Section' with the designation *nei-pu k'an-wu*. A new category of 'Books for the Blind' is added to the 'Special Section'. The lists of textbooks, newspapers and periodicals which would all have been 1958 imprints were temporarily withheld from publication in this edition and included in the 1958 volume. Also, beginning with this volume, only Chinese titles are given for Western-language publications of the Peking Foreign Languages Press. They are now grouped by language instead of by subject matter as in previous editions. The total number of titles included in this volume is 17,245.

The 1958 volume (published in 1959) covers all 1958 publications including reprints with revised texts. 'Internal Publications' are no longer listed. The 1958 textbooks are now listed in the 'Special Section' instead of in the Appendix. The newspapers and periodicals list contains new titles published in 1958. The total number of titles included in this volume is 28,090.

The main differences between this cumulated edition and the *Ch'üan-kuo hsin shu-mu* should be noted. (1) The cumulated edition lists fewer titles than the *Hsin shu-mu*, mainly because of its selectiveness in listing reprints. For instance, the 1956 cumulated edition gives a total of 18,108 titles (including selected reprints with revised texts), whereas the eleven issues of the *Hsin shu-mu* for the same year give a total of 28,092 titles. (It should be noted, however, that there were 15,917 reprints of all kinds published in 1956.) (2) The useful newspapers and periodical lists and the title index of the cumulated edition are not available in the *Hsin shu-mu*. (3) *Hsin shu-mu* carries more bibliographical and publishing data than the cumulated edition. In addition to the bibliographical data on author title, date, and place of publication, price and number of copies printed which are available in both editions, the *Hsin shu-mu* also provides information on the size, number of pages and number of characters for every title listed. (4) Different classification schemes have been employed. The cumulated edition uses the scheme devised by the Chinese People's University Library, while the *Hsin shu-mu* uses the 'Classification Scheme for Medium and Small Size Libraries' (another scheme was used before 1958). The main topical divisions of these two schemes are similar, except that the People's University Library scheme is more refined and carries more subdivisions.

These two editions are undoubtedly the most important bibliographical tools published in Communist China. Not only do they contain a wealth of factual information on publishing activities on the Mainland, but they also provide a gauge with which to measure the direction and degree of intensity of the Chinese Communist attempt to inform, educate, and indoctrinate the Mainland population through the medium of the printed word. (For a preliminary statistical analysis of the cumulated edition, see G. Raymond Nunn, *Chinese Publishing Statistics, 1949–1959*, Preliminary Data Paper 1, Ann Arbor, Michigan, December 1960.)

Microfilm copies of the 1949–1954, 1955, 1956, and 1957 volumes can be purchased from the Photoduplication Service, The Library of Congress, Washington 25, D.C. Microfilm copies of the 1958 volume are obtainable from University Microfilms, Ann Arbor, Michigan.

2. REPUBLIC OF CHINA

The National Central Library in Taipei commenced publication of a national bibliography in 1956, covering the years 1949 through June 1955, and has continued with cumulative volumes, the coverage of which has varied from six months to two years. Since September 1960, a current national bibliography has appeared in *The Monthly List of Chinese Books*.

The National Central Library has also published a cumulative listing of publications from 1949 through 1963, and two selected bibliographies covering the periods 1949–1956 and 1958–1960.

10 Chung-yang t'u-shu kuan 中央圖書館 (National Central Library). *Chung-hua min-kuo ch'u-pan t'u-shu mu-lu* 中華民國出版圖書目錄
(National Bibliography of the Republic of China). Taipei: Chung-hua wen-hua ch'u-pan shih-yeh wei-yüan hui 中華文化出版事業委員會, 1956—.

The National Bibliography of the Republic of China lists Chinese books published in Taiwan since late 1949 and submitted to the National Central Library in accordance with the copyright law. Included also are gifts to the National Central Library of books published in Hong Kong. Five volumes, averaging 2,000 titles, had been published to 1961. Vol. 1 contains books published to June 1955 (1956); Vol. 2, July to December 1955 (1956); Vol. 3, 1956 (1958); Vol. 4, 1957 (1959); and Vol. 5, 1958–1960 (in two parts; 1961).

The arrangement of the bibliography is topical under the following headings: general, philosophy, religion, natural sciences, applied sciences, social sciences, history and geography, language and literature, and fine arts. Under each heading items are listed by title with full bibliographical information arranged according to the Nanking University Classification Scheme (modified Dewey Decimal Classification). Beginning with Vol. 2, textbooks have also been included in an appendix. No index.

The most comprehensive listing of Taiwan publications.

The National Central Library published in 1964 *Chung-hua min-kuo ch'u-pan t'u-shu mu-lu hui-pien* 中華民國出版圖書目錄彙編 (Cumulative National Bibliography of the Republic of China) in two volumes (846p.) containing 15,000 titles for the years 1949 through 1963.

11 Chung-yang t'u-shu kuan 中央圖書館 (National Central Library).
The Monthly List of Chinese Books. Taipei, Vol. 1—, September 1960—.

A monthly English-language publication containing in each issue (beginning with Vol. 2, No. 3/4) abstracts, a selected list of Chinese publications, and a monthly list of Chinese publications. The abstracts consist of lengthy annotations on a few important publications such as the China Yearbook, the Statistical Abstract of the Republic of China, etc. The selected list of Chinese publications is classified according to the Chinese decimal classification scheme and provides full bibliographical information in Chinese and English for a number of Taiwan publications recommended for purchase by the staff of the National Central Library. The monthly list of Chinese publications covers all Taiwan publications in Chinese issued during the month under review as known to the editorial staff of the Library. Some issues contain an occasional review article, or an article of bibliographical interest. (The first six numbers were issued in mimeographed form in Chinese and contain in each number some sixty selected titles for the preceding month without annotations. Two pages are given over to a few annotations in English.)

The first systematic report of current Taiwan publications.

12 **Chung-yang t'u-shu kuan** 中央圖書館 (National Central Library). *Chung-hua min-kuo ch'u-pan t'u-shu hsüan-mu* 中華民國出版圖書選目 *Selected Bibliography of the Republic of China.* Taipei, 1957. 59p.

A selection of some 1,200 titles published in Taiwan in Chinese between 1949 and 1956, arranged under the following headings: general works, philosophy, religion, the social sciences, natural sciences, applied sciences, history and geography, language and literature, and fine arts. A directory of publishers in English is appended to the volume. The titles are given in English translation with full bibliographical information, including price, but with no apparent system of arrangement. Chinese characters are given only for author and title. The lack of an index detracts from the usefulness of the bibliography.

13 **Chung-yang t'u-shu kuan** 中央圖書館 (National Central Library). *A Selected and Annotated Bibliography of the Republic of China.* Taipei: National Central Library, 1960–1962. 2 vols.

Covers a representative selection of scholarly books and articles published in Taiwan. The first volume deals with the years 1958–1959 (128 titles); the second, 1959–1960 (132 titles). The number of books and articles are just about equal. With a heavy emphasis on the humanities and social sciences, the bibliography provides only small coverage of pure and applied science. In two parts: books, and periodical literature. The entries are listed alphabetically under broad categories such as bibliography, philosophy and religion, political science, economics and industries, literature, history, Communism, and Overseas Chinese. Each entry is given in English translation, followed by title, author, and publisher in Chinese characters. (There are also English-language works.) Annotations are in English. Both volumes carry an alphabetical author index. A list of Chinese classics reprinted in Taiwan during the period July 1958–June 1959 is appended to the first volume.

A useful general bibliography.

C. CHINA—GENERAL

The present section contains general bibliographies exclusively or partially devoted to China, without distinction as to Mainland or Taiwan. While certain of the entries described in these pages are restricted to the coverage of the contemporary period, the majority are somewhat broader in scope.

The bibliograpies listed here have, for convenience, been divided by language: Chinese, English, Japanese, Russian and other languages. In cases where a given bibliography contains works in more than one language, the dominant linguistic group determines its location in the section. Thus, 'Bibliography of Asian Studies' is listed in the English section, although it also contains, in addition to English, works in French, German and other European languages; the Kyoto University bibliography, listed in the Japanese section, contains Chinese and Western-language works; the Hong Kong University compilation, listed in the Chinese section, also includes titles in English, etc.

Reference should be made to other sections in this chapter, especially those on the national bibliographies, subject bibliographies and China—Regional.

I. BIBLIOGRAPHIES OF WORKS IN CHINESE

The Hong Kong University compilation listed below constitutes the only available bibliography of Chinese-language books and articles dealing with current Chinese developments (emphasis is on the Mainland).

For other guides to Chinese-language sources, the reader is directed to the national bibliographies listed above, and to the entries listed elsewhere in the present chapter (for example, the catalog of the Science Publishing House, **154**). Reference should also be made to the various indexes to Chinese-language periodical literature in Chapter III, especially the Index to Major Newspapers and Periodicals published on the Mainland (**184**).

14 Kirby, E. Stuart, ed.
Contemporary China. Hong Kong: Hong Kong University Press, Vol. 1—, 1956—. Irregular.

In addition to articles on contemporary economic and social conditions on Mainland China (with occasional articles on Taiwan), each volume of *Contemporary China* also contains selected Mainland documents and statistics, together with a fairly detailed chronology of major events and a bibliography. The bibliography section, arranged by subject (general, economic, political, social, cultural and educational, youth and intellectuals, people's communes, etc.) consists almost exclusively of Chinese-language publications issued on the Mainland and in Taiwan, and Hong Kong—periodical articles in particular (it also lists a few articles from English-language periodicals). A full bibliographical citation is provided, including a translation of the title and Chinese characters for both the author and title. In the five volumes published to date, more than five thousand entries have appeared.

The following is a summary of coverage and dates of publications of the five volumes:

VOLUME NO.	COVERAGE	DATE OF PUBLICATION
Vol. 1	1955	1956
Vol. 2	1956–1957	1958
Vol. 3	1958–1959	1960
Vol. 4	1959–1960	1961
Vol. 5	1961–1962	1963

Particularly useful for locating Chinese periodical articles.

2. BIBLIOGRAPHIES OF WORKS IN ENGLISH

Of the fifteen bibliographies of English-language works on China contained in this section, the first four should be singled out for special mention. The best coverage of current monographic and periodical literature is provided by the 'Bibliography of Asian Studies' (**15**). The most comprehensive listing of books and pamphlets in English and other European languages (Russian excepted) is T. L. Yuan's *China in Western Literature* (**16**), and of periodical literature, John Lust's *Index Sinicus* (**16a**). Professor Hucker's compilation (**17**) is perhaps the most useful selected and critically annotated bibliography of books and articles.

15 The Association for Asian Studies, comp.
'Bibliography of Asian Studies' in *The Journal of Asian Studies*. Ann Arbor, Mich., 1941—. Annual.

An annual bibliography of the Association for Asian Studies, comprising monographic and periodical literature on Asia largely in Western languages and predominantly in English. Formerly published under the titles 'Bulletin of Far Eastern Bibliography' (Earl E. Pritchard, ed., 1936–1940) and 'Far Eastern Bibliography' in the *Far Eastern Quarterly* (Earl E. Pritchard, Gussie E. Gaskill, John J. Nolde, Howard P. Linton, eds., 1941–1955), the bibliography assumed its present name in 1956 and continued under the general editorship of Howard P. Linton to 1961. The 1961 bibliography was edited by Dorothea Scott. The present editor is Richard C. Howard.

Under 'China', the entries are listed by author in alphabetical order with full bibliographical citations under a number of subjects, such as bibliography and reference, history, biography, politics and government, Communism, law, foreign relations, economics, agriculture, industry, press and radio, social conditions and welfare, Overseas Chinese, literature, etc.

This is the most extensive current bibliography on China in Western languages and is particularly useful for its coverage of periodical literature in English.

The following is a summary of the volumes issued to date:

> 1936 (Vol. 1). 5 numbers. Index.
> 1937 (Vol. 2). 5 numbers. Index.
> 1938 (Vol. 3). 5 numbers. Index.
> 1939 (Vol. 4). 5 numbers. Index.
> 1940 (Vol. 5). 5 numbers in 2 parts. Index.
> 1941. Nov. 1941, Feb., May 1942 *FEQ*. No index.
> 1942. Aug., Nov. 1942, Feb., May 1943 *FEQ*. No index.
> 1943. Aug., Nov. 1943, Feb. 1944 *FEQ*. No index.
> 1944. May, Aug., Nov. 1944, Feb. 1945 *FEQ*. No index.
> 1945. May, Nov. 1945, May 1946 *FEQ*. No index.
> 1946. May 1947 *FEQ*. Index.
> 1947. May, Nov. 1947. Feb., May 1948 *FEQ*. No index.
> 1948. Aug., Nov. 1948, Feb., May, Nov. 1949 *FEQ*. No index.

1949. Aug. 1950 *FEQ*. Index.
1950. Aug. 1951 *FEQ*. Index.
1951. Aug. 1952 *FEQ*. Index.
1952. Aug. 1953 *FEQ*. Index.
1953. Aug. 1954 *FEQ*. Index.
1954. Sep. 1955 *FEQ*. Index.
1955. Sep. 1956 *FEQ*. Index.
1956. Sep. 1957 *JAS*. Index.
1957. Sep. 1958 *JAS*. Index.
1958. Sep. 1959 *JAS*. Index.
1959. Sep. 1960 *JAS*. Index.
1960. Sep. 1961 *JAS*. Index.
1961. Sep. 1962 *JAS*. Index.
1962. Sep. 1963 *JAS*. Index.
1963. Sep. 1964 *JAS*. Index.

16   Yuan, Tung-li, comp.
China in Western Literature: A Continuation of Cordier's Bibliotheca Sinica.
New Haven, Conn.: Far Eastern Publications, 1958. 19; 802p.

A bibliography of approximately 18,000 books and pamphlets on China published in English, French, German, and Portuguese from 1921 to 1957, excluding periodical articles except for those issued subsequently as independent monographs. Arranged under the following twenty-eight broad subject headings: (1) bibliography and reference, (2) general works, (3) geography and travel, (4) history, (5) biography, (6) politics and government, (7) army, navy and air force, (8) law and legislation, (9) foreign relations, (10) economics, industry and commerce, (11) social conditions and problems, (12) philosophy, (13a–b) religion, (14) education, (15) language, (16) literature, (17) archeology and fine arts, (18) music and sports, (19) natural science, (20) agriculture and forestry, (21) medicine and public health, (22) Northeastern Provinces (Manchuria), (23) Mongolia and Mongols (including Tannu Tuva), (24) Tibet, (25) Sinkiang, (26) Taiwan (Formosa), (27) Hong Kong, (28) Macao. Entries are arranged alphabetically by author under each subsection with full bibliographical data including Chinese characters for Chinese authors' names. There are no annotations.

There are two appendices: (1) serial publications, and (2) addenda. Appendix 1 lists about 540 Western-language serials with bibliographical data and is arranged under the following topics (and within each topic alphabetically by title): (1) general, (2) China at war [1937–1945], (3) Chinese studies, (4) Communist and anti-Communist, (5) economics and foreign trade, (6) law and international relations, (7) religion, (8) education and psychology, (9) literature, (10) art, (11) library science and bibliography, (12) general science, (13) mathematics, physics and chemistry, (14) astronomy and meteorology, (15) biology, (16) botany, (17) zoology, (18) geography and ethnology, (19) geology and paleontology, (20) medicine and public health, (21) agriculture and forestry, (22) engineering,

(23) Manchuria, (24) Tibet, (25) Taiwan. Appendix 2 contains addenda to the bibliography proper, containing about 240 titles arranged under appropriate sections by author. There is an author index, and an index to Chinese titles (in Wade-Giles romanization) in the bibliography.

This work, compiled by the former director of the National Library of Peking, is the most important and comprehensive listing of Western books and pamphlets on China for the period covered.

For periodical literature, see next entry.

16a Lust, John, comp.
Index Sinicus: A Catalogue of Articles Relating to China in Periodicals and Other Collective Publications, 1920–1955. Cambridge, England: Heffer, 1964. 663p.

Contains 20,000 entries in European languages taken from 700 periodicals and 150 symposia, memorial volumes, proceedings of congresses and conferences, etc., in the field of humanities and the social sciences (including the history of science). Classification follows substantially that of Dr. Yuan's bibliography (**16**) which it supplements. Author index, index of names, place names, titles of articles and books discussed in articles.

Together with the preceding entry, this provides basic bibliographical control of Western literature on China for the period covered.

17 Hucker, Charles O., comp.
China: A Critical Bibliography. Tucson, Ariz.: The University of Arizona Press, 1962. 125p.

A selected and annotated list of 2,285 books, articles and individual chapters or sections of books considered to be significant contributions to knowledge on traditional, modern and contemporary China (some titles appear more than once). Priority in selection is given to books published in English since 1940 and articles in standard English-language journals. Works in Oriental languages are not included, but works in French and German are listed if they are standard references not substantially duplicated or superseded by English publications.

There are seven major sections: (1) introduction; (2) lands and peoples; (3) history; (4) intellectual and aesthetic patterns; (5) political patterns; (6) social patterns; and (7) economic patterns. Under each section, entries are divided among subsections, some arranged chronologically and some topically. Items are numbered consecutively throughout the text, and a short introduction precedes each section and some subsections. Of relevance to the contemporary period are the following subsections: 'Nationalist China in Taiwan' (pp. 44–45); 'The People's Republic: General' (pp. 47–50), 'Personal Accounts' (pp. 50–51), 'Foreign Relations—General' (pp. 51–52), 'Relations with Tibet and India' (p. 52), 'Relations with the Soviet Union' (p. 52), and 'American Policy Toward Communist China' (pp. 52–53).

A good, well annotated selection.

18   U.S. Department of the Army, Headquarters.
Communist China: Ruthless Enemy or Paper Tiger? A Bibliographic Survey.
Washington, D.C.: U.S. Government Printing Office, 1962. 137p.

An annotated bibliography mainly of English-language books, pamphlets and
periodical articles on Communist China published between 1948 and 1961,
excluding translations of Chinese Communist materials. The volume also contains
a number of Russian, Japanese, French, and German works, as well as a few in
Korean and Swedish. The items listed and annotated range from serious research
studies to articles in *Newsweek, Look, Reader's Digest* and other popular magazines.
Arranged under the following topics with subsections: (1) general information;
(2) Chinese Communist state: government and party; (3) national policy, strategy,
and objectives; (4) sources of strength and weaknesses; (5) armed forces; (6) other
significant factors contributing to success or failure; (7) progress and failures as
reported by visitors and eye-witnesses; (8) Nationalist China vs. Communist
China; (9) United States actions and proposed measures to contain Chinese
Communist ambitions; (10) historical factors; (11) bibliographies, indexes and
other documentation. The appendices contain maps, charts, a bibliography of
Russian works on the Chinese Communist Army (see **133**), and a bibliography
of Western-language publications on the Korean War (see **145**).
The bibliography is extensive but not exhaustive, and it suffers from the lack
of an index.

18a Whelan, Joseph G., comp.
World Communism: A Selected Annotated Bibliography. Washington, D.C.:
U.S. Government Printing Office, 1964. 394p. (88th Congress, Second Session,
Senate Document No. 69).

Contains over 3,000 books, pamphlets, articles, and government documents
and reports, of which over 200 deal with Communist China (see particularly B.,
Communist China, pp. 237–263, in Chapter 9, Communism in Asia and Oceania).
The section on China is further subdivided into general; political affairs; foreign
relations; problems of war, defense and military strategy; economic affairs;
and cultural, social and religious affairs; and under each category into books,
articles and pamphlets, and government publications. Most entries are accompanied by a descriptive annotation or a contents note. Author index.
This bibliography is particularly valuable for its listing of government publications.

19   Henderson, Martha T.
'A Selected Bibliography [of Communist China] in Western Languages' in
Walter W. Rostow, *The Prospects for Communist China* (Cambridge, Mass.:
The Technology Press of Massachusetts Institute of Technology, 1954), pp.
327–374.

A detailed bibliography of Western-language materials (mostly English and some French) on Communist China, with concise annotations, especially useful for references to newspaper and periodical articles and government publications. Arranged under three broad categories: sources, subjects, and appendices. Under 'Sources' are listed (1) other bibliographies; (2) press, radio, and other translations and commentaries; (3) newspapers; (4) periodicals (American, French, and non-Communist Chinese and Communist Chinese published in English, and others). Under 'Subject' are (1) history, 1848–1949 (selected list); (2) Communist period, 1949–1954 (including certain background sources; emphasis on 1951–1954); (3) Sino-Soviet relations; (4) Chinese society; and (5) Chinese economy. The three appendices include (1) papers from the Center for International Studies, M.I.T.; (2) papers on China from the Regional Studies Seminars, Committee on International and Regional Studies, Harvard University; (3) papers prepared for the Chinese Documents Project, Human Resources Institute, Air University, Maxwell Air Force Base, Montgomery, Alabama.

For updated listings, see Chapter XXII of this Guide.

A useful compilation though partially outdated.

20 American Universities Field Staff.
A Select Bibliography: Asia, Africa, Eastern Europe, and Latin America. New York, 1960. 534p.

An annotated bibliography of books and journals in Western languages on Asia, Africa, Eastern Europe and Latin America for college and general use. Of the nearly 6,000 titles included, 1,049 are on East Asia, including 559 titles on China, of which 104 are grouped under a subsection entitled 'Communist China: Origins and Development'.

A very selective list, thin on reference and bibliographical materials. (T. L. Yuan's *China in Western Literature*, and *China News Analysis*, *The China Quarterly*, *The Peking Review*, as well as English translations of Communist newspaper and periodical extracts, are not mentioned.)

Supplements appeared in 1961 (75p.) and 1963 (66p.).

21 American Institute of Pacific Relations.
China: A Selected List of References. Second edition. New York, 1957. 26p.

A mimeographed list of approximately 350 English-language books on China, including two or three French works, published between 1945 and 1957. Supersedes the earlier bibliography, *Recent Books on China, 1945–1951*, prepared originally by Professor Knight Biggerstaff of Cornell University for the I.P.R. in 1947 and up-dated in 1951 by S. B. Thomas. One section contains 107 titles on Communist China, all post-1949 publications except two. A section on Taiwan contains fourteen titles published since 1949. An addendum, listing books published between March and November 1957, appears at the end of the volume.

Though titles appearing in this volume are now included in T. L. Yuan's *China in Western Literature* (see **16**), this remains a very useful reference.

22 Cole, Allan B.
Forty Years of Chinese Communism, Selected Readings with Commentary. Washington, D.C.: American Historical Association, Service Center for Teachers of History, 1962. 43p. (Publication No. 47).

A bibliographical essay on the Chinese Communist movement intended mainly for teachers in secondary schools. The works included—all in English and most of them books—are analyzed under the following topical headings: (1) main periods in the movements; (2) general works; (3) early history to the schism in 1927; (4) civil war and the Kiangsi Republic to the United Front in 1937; (5) war against Japan and expansion of Communist-led 'liberated areas'; (6) failure of coalition and civil war resumed; and (7) studies of mainland China under the Communists. The last section is further divided under (1) government and politics; (2) economic planning and development; (3) basic revolution in an ancient society; (4) education and intellectual affairs; (5) foreign relations of the People's Republic of China; and (6) policies of the United States toward Communist China. There are three appendices: (1) a list of bibliographies of works in English on Communist China, 1949–1962, and on the Communist movement in China prior to 1949; (2) works of salient importance for teachers; (3) current serials in English on the People's Republic of China: documentation, abstracts, surveys, analyses.

An informative review providing a good analysis of the literature surveyed. For a more comprehensive annotated bibliography of books and serials, see Charles O. Hucker, comp., *China, A Critical Bibliography* (**17**).

23 Harris, Richard.
Modern China. London: Cambridge University Press, 1961. 32p. (The National Book League, Reader's Guides, Fourth Series No. 5).

A bibliography of 121 selected works on China in English (some translations) covering the period since 1840, arranged under the following chapter headings: (1) general; (2) conflict with the West and fall of the Empire, 1840–1912; (3) nationalism and the rise of Communism; (4) international relations; (5) sociology; (6) travel; (7) China under Communist rule; (8) 'the periphery and beyond'. Titles are listed alphabetically by author's name in each chapter. Thirty-one titles are included in Chapter 6, 'China Under Communist Rule.' Polemic literature—both pro- and anti-Communist—is excluded. Short but critical annotations, from a British point of view, are provided for each title. Index of authors and editors.

For a supplement, see 'Recent Books on China', *Arts and Sciences in China*, Vol. 1, No. 3 (July–September 1963), pp. 30–35, bringing the coverage up to early 1963.

24 Chao, Kuo-chün 趙國鈞**, comp.**
Selected Works in English for a Topical Study of Modern China, 1840–1952.
Cambridge, Mass.: Harvard University, Regional Studies Program on East Asia,
1952. 38p.

A bibliography containing 497 works in English on modern China arranged
under sixty-nine topical headings in seven parts: (1) general reference works,
(2) political thought and political institutions since 1840, (3) international relations,
(4) economic institutions and problems, (5) social and educational topics, (6)
major movements, (7) leading personalities since 1840. Though works on the
pre-1949 period constitute the predominant part of this bibliography, there are
a number of important items on the Chinese Communist movement to 1952.
Mimeographed.

25 Nolde, John J., comp.
Chinese Communism. Ithaca, N.Y.: Cornell University [1949?]. 12p.

A selected bibliography on Chinese Communism including both books and
periodical articles published in English prior to 1949. Full bibliographical
citations are given, but entries are unannotated. Mimeographed.

Good coverage of periodical literature on the postwar period between 1945
and 1949.

26 Pundeff, Marin, comp.
*Recent Publications on Communism—A Bibliography of Non-periodical Literature,
1957–1962.* Los Angeles: University of Southern California, 1962. 66p.

A list of 947 English-language books and pamphlets on Communism published
since 1958, with over 100 titles on China, including paperbacks (Nos. 681–793
in the bibliography). Author index. Mimeographed.

27 Quan, L. King.
Introduction to Asia: A Selective Guide to Background Reading. Washington, D.C.:
The Library of Congress, 1955. 214p.

An annotated bibliography, mainly of English-language works on Asia. Works
on China fall under Section 2 (The Far East). A total of twenth-three titles—
mostly post-1949 publications including articles—are on Communist China;
seven are on Taiwan; all are post-1949 imprints except one.

For a somewhat more extensive bibliography of English-language books and
periodicals on China, see **1700a.**

28 Indian Council of World Affairs Library.
Documents on Asian Affairs, Select Bibliography. New Delhi, Vol. 1—, 1959—.

A bibliography of documents and speeches reflecting significant trends in the political, economic and social affairs of Asian countries, selected from sources available in the English language. Arranged by country or region, the bibliography covers both Communist China and Taiwan. Useful references to speeches, statements and reports on foreign affairs. Two volumes have appeared thus far: Vol. 1—1957 (1959), 150p. (Bibliographical Series No. 5); and Vol. 2—1958 (1961), 174p. (Bibliographical Series No. 9).

29   Loon, Piet van der, ed.
Revue bibliographique de Sinologie. Paris: Mouton, Vol. 1—, 1957—. Irregular.

The *Revue* provides annotations for books and articles in Sinology published in all languages during the preceding year. Although the emphasis is not on contemporary China, the bibliography contains good reviews of scholarly works currently published in Communist China and Taiwan. Annotations are largely in English, some in French. Three volumes have appeared thus far: Vol. 1—1955 (1957); Vol. 2—1956 (1959); Vol. 3—1957 (1962).

3. BIBLIOGRAPHIES OF WORKS IN JAPANESE

The most comprehensive bibliography of Japanese books on China published in the postwar period is the second entry (**31**), compiled under the direction of Taira Kazuhiko of the National Diet Library, who, along with Professor Ichiko Chūzō, ranks as one of Japan's foremost experts in the field of modern Chinese bibliography. This bibliography has been updated in the 1960, 1962 and 1964 editions of *Chūgoku seiji keizai sōran* (see **33** and **34** below).

Coverage of Japanese periodical literature on China for the years 1946–1957 (September), inclusive, is provided by the two lists (**35** and **36**) prepared under the direction of Professor Ishikawa Tadao of Keio University, an authority on the early years of Chinese Communism. Current Japanese books and periodical literature can be located easily through the yearly compilations of Kyoto University (**30**), and non-periodical literature in the general Japanese bibliographies, *Zen Nihon shuppambutsu sōmokuroku—Japanese National Bibliography* and *Shuppan nenkan* (Publications Yearbook). The index to Japanese periodicals prepared by the National Diet Library (*Zasshi kiji sakuin—Japanese Periodicals Index*) is yet another guide to current periodical literature. (The bibliography compiled by the Association for the Study of Contemporary China (**37**) provides references also to articles in periodicals not covered by the National Diet Library index.)

It should be noted that Japanese learned journals in the China field, as well as some of the basic reference works, are described in the Fairbank-Banno bibliographical guide (**41**), and, additionally, in the Kyoto University bibliography (**30**) and the English-language bibliography published by the Institute of Oriental Culture (Tōhō Gakkai, **38**).

30 **Kyōto Daigaku, Jimbun Kagaku Kenkyūjo** 京都大學人文科學研究所 (Kyoto University, Research Institute for Humanistic Studies). *Tōyōshi kenkyū bunken ruimoku,* 1934— 東洋史研究文獻類目
Annual Bibliography of Oriental Studies, 1934—. Kyōto, 1935—.

An extensive bibliography of books and articles in the Asian field published in Japan, China (Mainland and Taiwan), Korea, and the West covering the acquisitions of the Institute library, Kyoto University Libraries, the Institute for Oriental Culture of Tokyo University, the Department of Chinese Literature and Philosophy of Tokyo University, the Tōyō Bunko (東洋文庫 Oriental Library), the National Diet Library, and the library of the China Research Institute (Chūgoku Kenkyūjo). In effect, this represents a comprehensive annual bibliography for the preceding year, with a typical volume containing over 4,000 Chinese and Japanese and over 2,000 Western (including Russian) books and articles. (From 1938 to 1956, with the exception of the 1946–1950 volume, it has appeared every two years.)

Reflecting the research interests of the Institute (the most distinguished Japanese center of ancient and medieval Chinese studies), over half of the volume is devoted to China, but only a small part concerns the contemporary period.

The bibliography is divided in two language parts: Japanese-Chinese, and Western languages (including Russian). Each language part is divided into books and articles which, in turn, are further divided into eighteen categories (with sub-categories): history, geography, social history, economic history, political history, legal history, history of religion, philosophy, thought and education, history of science, literature, history of art, archeology, inscriptions and paleography, ethnography, philology, bibliography, series, periodicals and miscellaneous, and the academic world. Entries provide full bibliographical data, including pagination and size, and occasionally, in the case of both books and articles, contain references to reviews.

Four author indexes: Japanese according to the Japanese syllabary; Chinese and Korean by stroke count, and Western and Russian (Cyrillic) in alphabetical order.

Beginning with the 1961 volume (published in 1964), the Japanese title was slightly amended, to indicate more precisely the scope of the bibliography, to *Tōyōgaku kenkyū bunken ruimoku—Annual Bibliography of Oriental Studies* (not *Tōyōshi*—Oriental history).

A comprehensive table of contents of Japanese journals and collections of articles in the Oriental field published since the Meiji era through 1962 is currently under preparation at the Department of Oriental History, Tokyo University. The first volume, covering the contents of seventy-four journals (out of a projected 1885) and listing by volume some 20,000 articles, appeared in March 1964 (Tōyōshi Kenkyū Rombun Mokuroku Henshū Iinkai 東洋史研究論文目錄編集委員會 Committee for the Compilation of the Catalog of Articles on Oriental History, comp., *Nihon ni okeru Tōyōshi rombun mokuroku* 日本における東洋史論文目錄 (Catalog of Japanese Articles on Oriental History), Tokyo: Nihon Gakujutsu Shinkōkai, 日本學術振興會, 402p.).

The most reliable and best organized current Japanese bibliography in the Asian field.

31 Kitagawa, Kazuhiko 北川和彦 **and Kamei, Keiko** 龜井慶子. *Sengo jūnen Chūgoku kankei tosho mokuroku* 戰後十年中國關係圖書目錄
(A Bibliography of Books on China Published from 1945 to 1955). Tokyo: Kyokutō Shoten 極東書店, 1955. 95p.

A bibliography of 1,373 books and pamphlets on China published in Japan from September 1945 through June 1955, largely in the fields of social science (about 400 entries), literature (300) and history (225). Based on the holdings of the National Diet Library, *Zen Nihon shuppambutsu sōmokuroku* 全日本出版物總目錄—*Japanese National Bibliography*, *Shuppan nenkan* 出版年鑑 (Publications Yearbook), *Tōyōshi kenkyū bunken ruimoku* 東洋史研究文獻類目—*Annual Bibliography of Oriental Studies*, and other general bibliographies, the volume was prepared under the direction of Taira Kazuhiko 平和彦, then acting head of the China Documentation Office of the National Diet Library.

Entries are arranged by the Nippon Decimal Classification System and alphabetically by author within each category, with data provided on the author, title, edition, imprint (except Tokyo) and collations. As a rule, only the latest edition is listed together with a note on previous editions. Author index arranged in alphabetical order, with Chinese authors listed according to the Japanese pronunciation of their names. Mimeographed.

This is the most comprehensive bibliography of postwar Japanese non-periodical literature on China. (See also **34**.)

32 Kokuritsu Kokkai Toshokan 國立國會圖書館 (National Diet Library). *Sengo gonen Chūgoku kankei tosho mokuroku* 戰後五年中國關係圖書目錄
(A Bibliography of Books on China Published from 1945 to 1950). Tokyo, 1950. 198p.

A bibliography compiled by Taira Kazuhiko, containing some 530 books and pamphlets on China, largely in the fields of history, social science and literature, published in Japan from September 1945 through August 1950. It includes some titles on Asia in general, as well as on Korea, Mongolia, Vietnam and other neighboring countries. The entries, both original Japanese works and translations from foreign languages, are arranged according to the Nippon Decimal Classification System and alphabetically by author within each category. A table of contents, and book review references are provided for the more important books. Alphabetical author index. Limited distribution. Mimeographed.

Largely superseded by the preceding entry.

33 Taira, Kazuhiko 平和彦. 'Hōbun gendai Chūgoku bunken mokuroku' 邦文現代中國文獻目錄

(Bibliography of Japanese-Language Materials on Contemporary China) in *Chūgoku seiji keizai sōran* 中國政治經濟綜覽 *Political and Economic Views on Present Day China*, 1954 edition, 1954, pp. 1032–1059.

A bibliography of 560 Japanese books and articles on China published from approximately 1950 to 1953. The articles are taken largely from the humanities and social sciences portion of the *Zasshi kiji sakuin* 雜誌記事索引—*Japanese Periodicals Index*, published by the National Diet Library. Some titles are accompanied by their tables of contents. Entries are arranged by subject (general; modern history; Communist China and its history; politics; political thought; election system; legal system; national minorities; Overseas Chinese; international relations; military affairs; biography; economics; public finance, taxation, customs; banking, currency; corporations, cooperatives; insurance; labor, women; mining and industry; cotton manufacture; agriculture; land reform; fishery, forestry; irrigation; trade; transportation), and are subdivided by date of publication. For continuations of this bibliography, see the successive editions of the *Chūgoku seiji keizai sōran* (next entry).

34 Taira, Kazuhiko 平和彦. 'Chūgoku kenkyū shiryō mokuroku' 中國研究資料目錄
(A Bibliography of Materials for the Study of China) in *Chūgoku seiji keizai sōran* 中國政治經濟綜覽 *Political and Economic Views on Present Day China*, 1960 edition (Tokyo: Hitotsubashi Shobō 一橋書房, 1960), pp. 1115–1203.

A bibliography of some 1,750 Japanese, Chinese, Western and Russian books on China published between 1953 and 1959, with an emphasis on politics, economics, social developments and contemporary history. Arranged first by language: Japanese (some 435 entries), Chinese (670), Western (500) and Russian (135); and then by subject matter (general; philosophy and religion; history and biography; geography and travel; politics, law, diplomatic and military affairs; finance, economics and statistics; social, education and customs; natural science; industry; agriculture, forestry and fishery; commerce, transportation and communications). Of the Japanese-language sections, the largest are politics, law, diplomatic and military affairs (125); finance, economics and statistics (60) and history and biography (50). The same holds true of the Chinese-language sections with the addition of natural science; industry; and agriculture, forestry and fishery (75 to 100 entries each). Entries give full bibliographical citation, including size.

The volume updates the preceding entry (33) and the bibliography of Japanese books by Kitagawa and Kamei (the latter covers Japanese publications from 1945 to 1955; see 31).

The 1962 edition of *Chūgoku seiji keizai sōran*, pp. 1396–1368 (reverse pagination) lists 175 additional Japanese and Chinese-language titles published in 1960 and 1961; the 1964 edition, pp. 1092–1072, provides 600 titles for the period October 1961–June 1963.

35 **Ishikawa, Tadao** 石川忠雄. *Sengo Nihon ni okeru gendai Chūgoku kankei shuyō zasshi rombun mokuroku* 戰後日本における現代中國關係主要雜誌論文目錄 (A List of Important Periodical Articles on Contemporary China Published in Japan After the War). Tokyo: Keiō Daigaku Hōgaku Kenkyūkai 慶應大學法學研究會, 1956. 100p.

A classified bibliography of some 3,300 articles on contemporary China published in Japan from January 1946 to July 1955. In six parts: politics (some 1,100 entries), economics (1350), law (140), social (180), culture (240) and miscellaneous (300). Within each category, entries are arranged chronologically by year of publication, and include title, periodical, volume number and author (no pagination). No author index. The bibliography originally appeared in six instalments in *Hōgaku kenkyū*, 法學研究 *Journal of Law, Politics and Sociology*, Vol. 29, Nos. 6–11 (June–November 1956).

Together with the other list compiled under the direction of Professor Ishikawa, bringing up the coverage to September 1957 (see next entry), the volume affords the most comprehensive coverage of Japanese periodical literature on contemporary China.

36 **Ishikawa, Tadao** 石川忠雄. *Saikin Nihon ni okeru gendai Chūgoku kankei shuyō zasshi rombun mokuroku* 最近日本における現代中國關係主要雜誌論文目錄 (A List of Recent Important Periodical Articles on Contemporary China Published in Japan). Tokyo: Keiō Daigaku Hōgaku Kenkyūkai 慶應大學法學研究會, 1958. 47p.

A continuation of the author's classified bibliography of articles on contemporary China published in Japan (see preceding entry). The present bibliography of over 1,500 items covers the period April 1955 to September 1957 (also providing additional titles for the period April–July 1955 covered in the preceding compilation). The arrangement follows that of the first bibliography: politics (about 400 entries), economics (650), law (50), social (50), culture (250), and miscellaneous (150). Entries are placed chronologically by year of publication within each category. No author index.

This bibliography originally appeared in two instalments in *Hōgaku kenkyū*, Vol. 31, Nos. 11 and 12 (November and December 1958).

37 **Gendai Chūgoku Gakkai, Aichi Daigaku Shibu** 現代中國學會愛知大學支部 (Association for the Study of Contemporary China, Aichi University Chapter). 'Gendai Chūgoku Gakkai kaiin 1960–1961 nendo chosaku mokuroku' 現代中國學會會員 1960–1961 年度著作目錄 (A Catalog of Writings by Members of the Association for the Study of Contemporary China in 1960–1961), *Kokusai Mondai Kenkyūjo kiyō* 國際問題研究所紀要 *The Memoirs of [the] Institute of International Affairs*, No. 33 (September 1962), pp. 107–114.

A list of over 230 books and articles (some in English), published from October 1960 to November 1961 by the members of the Association and reported to the Aichi University Chapter. It is divided into subject categories (political history; ideology; the Chinese Communist Party; diplomatic history and international affairs; Japanese-Chinese relations; economic theory; economic policy; the communes; literature and literary history; etc.). Full bibliographical citations are provided but no pagination. The list covering the period November 1961 to October 1962 appeared in *The Memoirs*, No. 35 (August 1963), pp. 105–111.

The list represents the first attempt to compile an accurate annual bibliography of the writings of the leading Japanese specialists on contemporary China. Based only on returned questionnaires, it obviously lacks comprehensiveness.

38 **Toho Gakkai** 東方學會 (Institute of Oriental Culture).
Books and Articles on Oriental Subjects Published in Japan During 1954—. Tokyo. Annual.

A yearly compilation which appears in one or two issues of *Tōhōgaku* (Eastern Studies) and is later published separately. From a forty-page pamphlet first published in 1954, it has grown to about 100 pages (1960). In two parts: books and articles. The books appear in alphabetical order by author. The articles are divided geographically: China, Korea, Manchuria, North Asia, Central Asia, Western Asia and Tibet, Southeast Asia, India and Nepal, and Asian relations with Japan. China is further subdivided into a number of categories, among them 'The Modern Period'. Each entry provides the author's name in romanization (with characters in parenthesis), the English translation of the title (with the Japanese title in parenthesis) and the usual bibliographical citation. An alphabetical index to authors is appended beginning with the 1958 volume. Starting with the 1960 issue, some entries are provided with English annotations.

The bibliography is especially noteworthy for its coverage of articles in academic journals.

39 **Chūgoku Kenkyūjo, Toshokan** 中國研究所圖書館 (China Research Institute, Library). *Chūgoku kankei zasshi rombun kiji sakuin oyobi shuyō tosho mokuroku, 1957 nen* 中國關係雜誌論文記事索引及主要圖書目錄 1957 年
(An Index to Periodical Articles and a List of Important Books on China, 1957). Tokyo, 1957. 38; 10p.

The index covers some 750 articles on China which appeared in Japanese journals published during January to June 1957, based on the holdings of the Institute library, the index to periodicals published by the National Diet Library, and other catalogs. Entries are arranged under broad categories: general (80 entries); thought and religion (40); history and geography (80); politics (60); international and foreign relations (80); economics and industry (220); social, cultural and education (80); language and literature (100). The list provides some 200 titles (books and pamphlets) on China published in Japan during the same period. Entries are arranged as above. Full bibliographical citations are given. Limited distribution. Mimeographed.

40   Teng, Ssu-yu, comp.

Japanese Studies on Japan and the Far East, A Short Biographical and Bibliographical Introduction. Hong Kong: Hong Kong University Press, 1961. 485p.

A bibliography of almost 5,000 books and articles written before 1958 on Japan, China, Korea, India and the Far East in general, in the fields of the humanities and social sciences (including the history of science and technology), by nearly 800 contemporary Japanese scholars. Its contents are arranged according to broad subject categories, within which authors are listed in alphabetical order. Each author's works follow a brief biographical sketch, with books preceding the articles, each in chronological order of publication (Chinese characters for author, title and publisher). General index to authors, book titles and subject matter.

Although a number of Japanese scholars in the contemporary China field appear in the chapter on Chinese history (in the section dealing with the nineteenth and twentieth centuries) and in a section on modern Chinese literature in the chapter on Chinese literature, the rest are scattered through other chapters and are difficult to locate. This bibliography is only an incomplete list of scholars with but a fraction of their works. Poorly edited.

See also Marius P. Jansen's review in *The Journal of Asian Studies*, Vol. 21, No. 4 (August 1962), pp. 553–554.

41   Fairbank, John K. and Banno, Masataka, comps.

Japanese Studies of Modern China: A Bibliographical Guide to Historical and Social-Science Research on the 19th and 20th Centuries. Rutland, Vt. and Tokyo: Charles E. Tuttle, 1955. 331p.

A bibliography of over 1,000 Japanese books and articles on modern China with critical annotations. Although works on post-1949 China are few in number (the cut-off date is mid-1953), the volume nevertheless provides annotations for many basic reference works and current learned journals which are useful for the study of the post-1949 period (Chapter 9). Alphabetical general index and character index of authors' names arranged by stroke count.

4. BIBLIOGRAPHIES OF WORKS IN RUSSIAN

The most important single bibliography covering Soviet works on China is the second edition of the massive work by the distinguished Soviet bibliographer, Skachkov, which lists publications through 1957 (**42**). Books on China published in 1958–1959, and articles for 1958, are listed in the bibliographies in the Soviet journal, Problems of Oriental Studies (see **49** and **50**). Also recommended are the selected and annotated bibliography of books published through 1960 compiled by Egorov (**46**), and that of Solov'eva (**45**) which, in addition to books, covers periodical and newspaper literature through 1959.

For more recent Soviet books and articles concerning China, the Soviet national bibliography *(Knizhnaia letopis')*, the indexes to periodical articles *(Letopis' zhurnal'nykh statei)*, newspaper articles *(Letopis' gazetnykh statei)*, and book reviews *(Letopis' retsenzii)* are useful guides. The reader should also consult the bibliographical references in the Russian works on Sino-Soviet relations included in Chapter XVI.

Because Soviet bibliographies tend to omit politically 'outdated' publications and works by purged leaders, two American compilations, one by T. L. Yuan (**43**), and the other by Peter Berton (**44**), also should be consulted.

42 Skachkov, P. E. comp. *Bibliografiia Kitaia*
(Bibliography of China). Moscow: Izdatel'stvo vostochnoi literatury, 1960. 691p.

An updated and revised edition of the author's work published in 1932 (and reprinted in the United States by the American Council of Learned Societies in 1948). The present edition, prepared under the auspices of the Institute of the Peoples of Asia of the Soviet Academy of Sciences, lists close to 20,000 books and parts thereof, pamphlets, abstracts, articles in periodicals dealing with the Far East, articles in compendia and book reviews on China published in Russia and the Soviet Union from 1730 through 1957.

A few exclusions should be noted: (1) Russian fiction on China is limited to books, (2) ephemera and small notices have been omitted, and (3) anonymous writings listed are those which deal with topics not covered by other works. To these exclusions, listed in the author's preface, one must add the writings of persons purged by Stalin or his successors. A casual comparison of the author's indexes in the 1932 and 1960 editions reveals the omission of the writings on China by many such persons who were at one time intimately concerned with Chinese affairs.

In the current edition, the classification of the bibliography has been changed to a modified version of the system used currently for the Soviet national bibliography. The arrangement is topical with separate chapters devoted to the Chinese People's Republic. The bibliography is divided into twenty-five chapters (with numerous subdivisions): (1) the founders of Marxism-Leninism on China; (2) 'the Communist International and the Communist Party of the Soviet Union on China'; (3) the Chinese Communist Party (including the period after the establishment of the Chinese People's Republic, 1949–1955); (4) the Communist Youth League and the New Democratic Youth Corps; (5) general works on China; (6) philosophy, social and political studies; (7) history (including China's relations with Russia up to 1949); (8) The Chinese People's Republic, 1949–1957; (9) the Soviet Union and the Chinese People's Republic, 1949–1957; (10) geography—general (description and travel); (11) natural and geographical environment; (12) population; (13) economy (up to 1949); (14) state and law (up to 1949); (15) military forces (up to 1949); (16) public health and medicine (up to 1949); (17) science and education (up to 1949); (18) language and system of writing; (19) belles-lettres and literary criticism; (20) art; (21) religion; (22) the press;

(23) Chinese studies in Russia and the Soviet Union; (24) bibliographical guides, book reviews; (25) directories, weights and measures.

The chapter on the Chinese People's Republic is further divided into the following categories: general works; the establishment of the Chinese People's Republic; 'political and economic achievements from 1949 to 1957'; government; 'the struggle of the Chinese People's Republic for peace'; international relations; economic development; industrialization; agriculture; transportation and communications; finance; trade; industrial cooperatives; culture, education, public health; women's movement; youth movement; art; travel accounts.

It should be noted that although most of the material on the post-1949 period is grouped in the above-mentioned chapter, relations with the Soviet Union, 1949–1957, are listed in a separate chapter, and belles-lettres, the natural sciences and bibliographies are listed in other sections.

The longest chapter is on pre-1949 Chinese history (162 pages containing some 5,000 items, or a quarter of all entries in the bibliography). The chapters on the Chinese People's Republic and its relations with the Soviet Union, 1949–1957, occupy 73 pages and account for some 2,650 entries. Other substantial chapters are: pre-1949 economy—90 pages with over 3,500 entries; literature—60 pages with some 2,800 entries; and Chinese studies—45 pages with nearly 1,400 entries.

Within the chapters, books and pamphlets are listed first, followed by articles (except in the case of short chapters where there is no such division). An exception is the chapter on belles-lettres, where translations from Chinese authors are listed first (books preceding articles), followed by literary criticism and, finally, works on Chinese literature. Occasionally the entries contain a table of contents and brief annotations on the inclusion of bibliographical references, book reviews, etc.

An index to authors, editors, and titles (for which no author is given) is provided. The lack of a subject index makes the use of the bibliography difficult, particularly so since books on several topics receive only a single listing. Also, the lack of a geographical index and the classification system have both been criticized by the principal bibliographers of the Lenin Library (*Sovetskaia bibliografiia*, No. 3 (No. 67), 1961, pp. 79–81).

It has been reported in a Soviet Oriental journal that a second volume is under preparation. This compilation will contain (1) material covering the years 1958 through 1962; (2) omissions from the coverage of the previous period; (3) books and articles by Russian and Soviet Sinologists published in the Soviet Union and abroad in Western European and Chinese languages, as well as translations of their works into Western European, Chinese, Japanese and other languages.

This is the most comprehensive bibliography of Russian-language works on China for the period covered. Other bibliographies must be consulted, however, for works which may have been excluded for political reasons.

43 Yuan, Tung-li, comp.
Russian Works on China, 1918–1960, in American Libraries. New Haven, Conn.: Yale University, Far Eastern Publications, 1961. 162p.

A bibliography of over 1,300 Russian-language books and pamphlets on China published between 1918 and 1960 and located in American libraries. Arranged under six main chapter divisions according to specific areas of Russian interest: (1) China proper, (2) Northeastern Provinces, (3) Mongolia, (4) Sinkiang, (5) Tibet, (6) Taiwan. Under each division, entries are further arranged by subject (bibliographies and catalogs, general works, geography and travel, history, law and legislation, labor and social conditions, religion and folklore, foreign relations, economic conditions, etc.). Chapter 7 lists thirty periodicals which contain material on China. An 'addenda' and a 'supplementary addenda' appear on p. 145 and pp. 161–162.

All Russian titles are accompanied by English translations. Only the latest editions are listed, the dates of previous editions being noted in the annotation. Works on China in other European languages translated into Russian, and translations into European languages from Russian original works, have been included as separate items. Contains a comprehensive index of authors, translators, editors and compilers. A thorough listing of Russian works on China located in American libraries. This bibliography incorporates the author's 'Russian Works on China, 1918–1958—A Selected Bibliography', *Monumenta Serica*, Vol. 18 (1959), pp. 388–430.

44 Berton, Peter, comp.
Soviet Works on China: A Bibliography of Non-Periodical Literature, 1946–1955.
Los Angeles: University of Southern California Press, 1959. 158p. (University of Southern California, School of International Relations, Far Eastern and Russian Research Series, No. 2).

A bibliography of almost 400 books, pamphlets, abstracts of theses and dissertations, and other types of non-periodical literature published in the Soviet Union on China during the first postwar decade. Based on the national Soviet bibliography and other bibliographical sources and library holdings in the United States, it represents the entire Soviet non-periodical output on China for the period covered. The bibliography is arranged topically in six parts (with further subcategories): bibliographies—14 entries; general works—66; environment—74; history and government—119; economic and social conditions—33; and culture —84.

A glossary of Russian terms is provided, together with names of libraries and other institutions, series, and publishers. General alphabetical index. The bibliography is preceded by a forty-page essay on Soviet publications in the Asian field, with special reference to China, which provides statistical data on, and analysis of, original Soviet work on Asia, translations from Asian languages, and publications in Asian languages (including Chinese). One part of the introductory essay contains a list of general and special periodical publications which in turn contain material on China (including scholarly series of monographs), a list of the major Soviet bibliographies on China published from the 1920's to the present

(twelve items) and a list of general bibliographical tools for keeping up with the
Soviet output on China.

The fullest listing of Soviet non-periodical literature on China for the period
covered.

45 Solov'eva, N. N., ed. *Kitaiskaia Narodnaia Respublika—Rekomendatel'nyi*
ukazatel' literatury, 1949–1959
(Chinese People's Republic—A Guide to Recommended Literature for 1949–
1959). Moscow, 1959. 63p.

A bibliography of 187 books, and periodical and newspaper articles on Communist China prepared on the occasion of the tenth anniversary of the establishment of the Chinese People's Republic. The volume supersedes Kazakov's
bibliography published in 1955 (see **48**).

In eight parts: (1) 'The Inviolate Friendship between the Soviet Union and
the Chinese People's Republic'—23 items consisting of treaties, communiqués,
writings of Khrushchev, Mao Tse-tung, etc. (Molotov omitted); (2) China's
history—23 items by Marx, Lenin, Mao Tse-tung (Stalin omitted); (3) 'The
Communist Party—the Leading and Guiding Force of the Chinese People's
Republic'—10; (4) 'The Chinese People Build Socialism'—30; (5) 'Along Free
China' (geography and description and travel)—37; (6) belles-lettres and art—41;
(7) representational arts, the theatre, motion pictures and music—17; (8) reference
works—6. Roughly one-half of the entries are annotated. Index to authors and
titles.

46 Egorov, V. N., comp. *Mezhdunarodnye otnosheniia—Bibliograficheskii spravoch-*
nik, 1945–1960 gg.
(International Relations—A Bibliographical Guide, 1945–1960). Moscow:
Izdatel'stvo Instituta mezhdunarodnykh otnoshenii, 1961. 406p.

A substantial annotated bibliography of Soviet books published in the years
1945–1960, inclusive, on foreign policy, international relations, international
economics, the international Communist movement, international law and
international organization. Contains about 100 works on China (in two separate
sections), of which almost one-half are post-1957 publications, and therefore
not in Skachkov's bibliography (**42**).

Author index (includes editors when no author is given). No subject index,
although the volume is heavily cross-referenced.

47 Voiakina, S. M. *Strany Azii—Rekomendatel'nyi ukazatel' literatury*
(The Countries of Asia—A Guide to Recommended Literature). Moscow:
Biblioteka SSSR, 1960. 137p.

A popular annotated guide to Russian publications on Asia prepared by the staff of the Lenin Library in Moscow. Some fifty books and articles are listed in the section on the Chinese People's Republic, including travel accounts and translations from the Chinese. Almost all entries are annotated (up to over one-half a page), and summaries of contents are frequently provided. Author index, with title or titles listed after author's name.

48 **Kazakov, S. V.** *Uspekhi Kitaiskoi Narodnoi Respubliki, Rekomendatel'nyi ukazatel' literatury*
(The Achievements of the Chinese People's Republic; A Guide to Recommended Literature). Second revised edition. Moscow, 1955. 68p.

A bibliography of some 200 Russian-language books, and periodical and newspaper articles on China (including many translations into Russian) prepared at the Lenin Library for librarians, lecturers, etc. Classified under a number of topical categories ('The Significance of the People's Revolution in China for World History', 'The Inviolate Friendship Between the Soviet Union and the People's Republic of China', belles-lettres on the new China, etc.) An index is provided, classified according to type of material. The first edition appeared in 1952.

This bibliography has been largely superseded by Solov'eva's work prepared in 1959 (see **45**).

49 **'Knigi o Kitae na russkom iazyke, izdannye v SSSR v 1958–1959 godakh'**
(Russian-Language Books on China Published in the U.S.S.R. in 1958–1959), *Problemy vostokovedeniia* (Problems of Oriental Studies), Moscow, No. 5 (1959), pp. 265–271.

A bibliography of some 200 Russian-language books and pamphlets on China published in the Soviet Union in the years 1958–1959 inclusive, containing translation of Chinese literature and non-fiction, and abstracts of theses and processed publications. Entries are arranged under the following topical headings: Chinese People's Republic and the Chinese Communist Party; trade unions; economy; state and law; the Soviet Union and China; philosophy and ideology; history; geography; culture, science and the press; literature, art and folklore; linguistics; and travel accounts.

An important supplement to Skachkov's bibliography (see **42**).

50 **'Stat'i o Kitae, opublikovannye v SSSR v 1958 godu'**
(Periodical Articles on China Published in the U.S.S.R. in 1958), *Problemy vostokovedeniia* (Problems of Oriental Studies), Moscow, No. 5 (1959), pp. 271–283.

A bibliography of roughly 400 Russian-language articles on China published in 1958 in Soviet periodicals, scholarly transactions and books (newspaper articles are excluded). The list is arranged according to some twenty-five topical categories (ideology, economics, ancient and medieval history, modern and contemporary history, science and history of science, Chinese studies, bibliography, etc.).

The present list serves as an important updated supplement to Skachkov's bibliography (see **42**).

51 U.S. Library of Congress, Air Information Division.
List of Russian Monographs Dealing With China in the Fields of Economic Geography, Military Doctrine, and Science and Technology—SIR No. 2954. Washington, D.C., 1958. 10p.

An unannotated list of seventy-one Russian-language books and pamphlets on China grouped under the following seven headings: *(a)* bibliography (2 entries); *(b)* geography (35); *(c)* military science (3); *(d)* economic conditions (15); *(e)* technology (10); *(f)* history (4); *(g)* general (2). Mimeographed. Not very useful.

52 U.S.S.R., Vsesoiuznaia gosudarstvennaia biblioteka inostrannoi literatury (U.S.S.R., National State Library of Foreign Literature). *Kitaiskaia Narodnaia Respublika; Vyborochnaia bibliografiia po materialam sovetskoi pechati* (Chinese People's Republic; Selected Bibliography of Materials in Soviet Periodical Literature). Moscow, Nos. 1–3, 1950. Irregular.

Three lists (seventeen to twenty-three pages in length) containing references to China in the Soviet press during the period January 1949 to February 1950, the crucial period from the final stages of the Communist victory on the Mainland to the conclusion of the Soviet-Chinese Treaty of Friendship, Alliance and Mutual Assistance.

5. BIBLIOGRAPHIES OF WORKS IN OTHER LANGUAGES

Save for the Noack bibliography covering the output of East Germany (**54**), no comprehensive bibliography of French, German or Italian works on China is available. Current German publications can be traced through the bibliography in *Nachrichten der G.F.N.V.O.* (**55**). A retrospective bibliography of French postwar writings on China is under preparation. See also the bibliography section on French publications on China in *Les cahiers Franco-Chinois* (**1205**). The Italian bibliography (**54a**) unfortunately does not go beyond 1958.

That four out of six entries listed below are Soviet bloc products—East German, Hungarian, Czech and Polish—is, of course, hardly a matter of accident. Upon closer scrutiny, it will be seen that the bibliographies from the Eastern European countries are characterized by a relative paucity of original contributions and a high proportion of works translated from the Chinese, Russian, English and other languages, reflecting perhaps the state of research on China east of the Elbe.

53 Wendelin, Lidia Ferenczy, comp. *Kínai—Magyar Bibliográfia*
(Chinese-Hungarian Bibliography). Budapest, 1959. 334p.

Lists some 5,000 translations of Chinese belles-lettres into Hungarian, as well as Hungarian books, periodicals and newspaper articles relating to China published from the eighteenth century to October 1959. Book reviews of Hungarian writings on China published both in Hungary and abroad are included. The volume is limited to China proper; Tibet, Sinkiang, Inner Mongolia, Manchuria and Taiwan are to be dealt with in a subsequent volume. Emphasis has been placed on the social sciences and humanities.

In three main parts (titles of chapters are in Hungarian, Russian and English): (1) studies and bibliographies dealing with China in general, and works on Sinology and a bibliographical survey of Sinological literature; (2) scientific and educational works, and books and articles on geography, history, politics, culture, science, the arts, etc. (3) belles-lettres (listed in alphabetical order by Chinese author), including works on Chinese authors. Alphabetical author index.

Published in commemoration of the tenth anniversary of the Chinese People's Republic, the present volume is the most comprehensive bibliography of Hungarian writings on China.

54 Noack, Lutz. *Neues China—Eine empfehlende Bibliographie*
(New China—A Recommended Bibliography). Leipzig: VEB Verlag für Buch- und Bibliothekswesen, 1957. 71p.

Provides annotations for 482 books and articles on China published in East Germany since 1955, including translations into German from Western European and Russian sources as well as German-language publications of the Foreign Languages Press in Peking. Arranged in six broad groupings with further subdivisions: (1) general, travel accounts, geography, ethnography—76 entries; (2) history—39; (3) Chinese Communist Party—35; (4) the state, law, public organizations—82; (5) economy, transportation, social—140; (6) culture—110. Subject index.

See also W. Panzer, 'Neue deutsche Bücher über die Volksrepublik China' (New German Books on the People's Republic of China), *Geographische Rundschau*, 12 (1960), pp. 454–455.

54a Lanciotti, Lionello and Pinto, Olga, eds. *Contributo Italiano alla conoscenza dell'Oriente—Repertorio bibliografico dal 1935 al 1958*
(Italian Contributions to the Knowledge of the Orient—A Bibliographical List for the 1935–1958 Period). Florence: Casa Editrice le Monnier [for] Commissione Nazionale Italiana per l'UNESCO, 1962. 279p.

A bibliography of books and articles written by Italians in Italian on Asia and Africa (including translations) which serves as a continuation of similar bibliographies for the 1861–1911 and 1912–1934 periods (complete bibliographical citations will be found on p. 10). The bibliographical part is preceded by an introductory essay on Italian contributions to the exploration of Asia and Africa, Italian archeological expeditions and cultural missions to Asia and Africa, and a description of the major Italian institutions of Oriental and African studies (academic institutions, cultural institutes, libraries, museums and other organizations).

The section on China (pp. 237–254), compiled by Professor Lanciotti, co-editor of *East and West* and Keeper of the Library of the Italian Institute for the Middle and Far East contains some 250 entries, largely articles and mostly on pre-modern China. Author index.

For current Italian writings on China, see the bibliography section in *Cina* (**1206**).

55 'Deutschsprachige Ostasien-Publikationen'
(German-Language Publications on East Asia) in *Nachrichten der Gesellschaft für Natur- und Völkerkunde Ostasiens/Hamburg* (Transactions of the [German] Society for the Study of the Countries and Peoples of East Asia in Hamburg), (Wiesbaden, West Germany: Harrassowitz). Irregular.

A bibliography of German-language books and articles on East Asia published in West and East Germany, Austria and Switzerland, and by the Foreign Languages Press in Peking. Includes translations into German from English, French, Chinese and other languages. Arranged according to geographical areas (Asia general, China, Tibet, Japan, etc.), with a special section on art and archeology.

Originally, a bibliographical section appeared in almost every volume of the transactions: Vols. 71–81 (1951–1957), except Vol. 77 (1955). In recent years it has become a survey of German-language literature for a longer period: 1956–1958 in Vol. 84 (1958), pp. 61–72; 1958–1959 in Vol. 87 (1960), pp. 66–71; 1960–1961 in Vol. 92 (1962), pp. 53–57.

Although the bibliography is far from being exhaustive, it is the only current bibliography of German-language publications on contemporary China.

Publications dealing with history, archeology and linguistics also may be found in *Orientalische Literaturzeitung (Oriental Bibliographical News)*, a monthly, published by the German Academy of Sciences in East Berlin.

56 Kaftan, Miroslav. *Čína—Bibliografický seznam literatúry*
(China—A Bibliography). Prague: Universitní knihovna v Praze, 1955. 40p. (No. 2).

An annotated list of 193 books and pamphlets on China published in Czechoslovakia in the period 1946–1955, designed for librarians and general readers. Most of the items are translations from Russian, English, Chinese and Japanese

(Carl Crow, Stuart Gelder, Harrison Forman, Hewlett Johnson, Lin Yutang, etc.). The few Czech contributions included are mostly those of Jaroslav Prušek and Zdenek Hrdlička.

Classified by subject: (1) 'Birth of New China'—8 entries; (2) history—24; (3) geography, travel accounts, political, economic and cultural developments—48; (4) Chinese Communist Party—13; (5) New China and its development—16; (6) journalistic accounts and collections of articles—18; (7) belles-lettres—49; (8) 'China Through the Eyes of Friends'—8; and (9) miscellaneous—9. Name and author index.

57 Poland, Akademia Nauk, Komitet Orientalistyczny (Poland, Academy of Sciences, Oriental Committee). *Bibliografia polskich prac orientalistycznych* (Bibliography of Polish Oriental Works). Warsaw: Państwowe Wydawnictwo Naukowe, 1957. 91p.

A bibliography of 707 Polish works in the Oriental field covering the period 1945–1955. In nine parts: periodical literature, history and organization of Oriental studies, the ancient Orient, the Near East, the Far East (pp. 50–56), translations, etc. No index.

For a continuation of this work to 1959, see V. Zaionchkovskii, 'Bibliografiia pol'skikh vostokovedcheskikh rabot, 1955–1959' (Bibliography of Polish Oriental Works) in *Soobshcheniia pol'skikh orientalistov, Sbornik* (A Collection of Reports by Polish Orientalists) edited by A. S. Tveritinova, Vol. 2 (Moscow, 1961), pp. 105–119.

For current Polish writings on China, see the bibliography section in *Przegląd orientalistyczny* (**1209**).

D. CHINA—REGIONAL

The local press is without question the most important source—and occasionally the only source—of information on provincial China. This is particularly true of Communist China where little local news is reported in the central press in Peking. Unfortunately, local newspapers have been available only in limited numbers away from the Mainland, and even on the Mainland they do not circulate freely. (See the lists of newspapers and periodicals in Chapter II, the indexes to major Mainland newspapers and periodicals in Chapter III, and the Union Research Institute's catalog of newspapers and periodicals, **1751**.) A list of local and provincial newspapers in the Library of Congress is under preparation. In this connection, the reader should note that publications of the Hong Kong American Consulate General and the J.P.R.S. reports (Chapter XX) carry translations of local news items from time to time. The *Union Research Service* (**1065**) and the *China News Analysis* (**1034**) also provide translations of or commentary on significant local events.

For the period 1958 through 1960, the first two entries, compiled in Taiwan, serve as excellent guides to sources of local Mainland information, including newspaper and periodical literature. Concerning the periods preceding and following that covered

38 BIBLIOGRAPHIES

in the National War College bibliography, the general bibliographical sources must be consulted. Also deserving of mention is the index to literature on geography in newspapers and periodicals, largely in provincial publications listed in the economic and social section below (**115**).

The main sources for the coverage of local affairs in Taiwan are the Taiwan Provincial Government's Gazette (see **685**), and the local newspapers in Chapter XVIII. Translations of selected reports on local conditions are included in the *Press and Publications Summary* published by the U.S.I.S. in Taipei (see **1074**). The *Indicus Taiwanica* (see **195**) provides bibliographical coverage of current Taiwan newspaper and periodical literature on present-day Taiwan. Other bibliographies in this section cover Tibet, Sinkiang, Manchuria and Mongolia.

For guides to administrative divisions on the Mainland, see Chapter IX. See also provincial surveys and directories in Chapters IV and VI, respectively.

58 Kuo-fang yen-chiu yüan, T'u-shu kuan 國防研究院 圖書館 (National War College, Library). *Ti-ch'ü fei-ch'ing ts'an-k'ao tzu-liao so-yin* 地區匪情參考資料索引

(Index to Reference Materials on Regional Bandit Situation). Yangmingshan, 1961. 1 vol.

A 500-page index to Chinese Communist periodical and newspaper articles (also to *Fei-ch'ing yüeh-pao* 匪情月報 and *Fei-ch'ing yen-chiu* 匪情研究, published in Taipei) primarily concerned with regional developments on the Mainland, and secondarily with Communist China's external relations. Based on holdings of the National War College Library, the index covers materials published between January 1958 and December 1960 inclusive, and is arranged under 'Peking' and 'Shanghai', followed by provinces for the Mainland, and by continent in the case of other countries. Each entry is accompanied by full bibliographical information under title of article. Mimeographed. Limited distribution.

See also next entry for coverage of books and pamphlets on the subject.

59 Kuo-fang yen-chiu yüan, T'u-shu kuan 國防研究院 圖書館 (National War College, Library). *Ti-ch'ü fei-ch'ing ts'an-k'ao t'u-shu yao-mu* 地區匪情參考圖書要目

(Bibliography of Reference Materials on Regional Bandit Situation). Yangmingshan, 1961. 16; 27p.

A companion volume to the preceding entry, comprising monographs and pamphlets on Chinese regional developments and foreign relations. Based on holdings of the National War College Library, this bibliography is likewise arranged under 'Peking', 'Shanghai', followed by provinces for the Mainland, and by continent in the case of other countries. Each entry is accompanied by full bibliographical information under title of publication. Mimeographed. Limited distribution.

Together, this and the preceding volume provide the best available guide to materials on local developments on the Mainland for the period covered.

60 Hsü, Chin-chih 徐近之.
A Bibliography of the Tibetan Highland and Its Adjacent Districts. Peking: Science Press, 1958. 462p.

A bibliography of more than 5,000 titles in Western languages, including Russian, on the physical geography of the highlands of Asia (comprising Tibet, Tsinghai, Sikang, Pamirs, Kashmir, Kumaon and Garhwal, Nepal, and Sikkim and Bhutan) published to the end of 1957. In three parts: subject index, author index (each with an addendum), and a separate list of works in Russian. A full bibliographical citation is given for each entry and Chinese characters are supplied for Chinese authors' names.

A comprehensive compilation, useful not only for physical geography, but also for the history, languages, literature, fine arts and religion of the regions.

See also Yakushi, Yoshimi. *Selected Index of Reports on Himalaya, Tibet, and Central Asia to the Geographical Journal (The Royal Geographical Society), Vol. 1 (1893)—Vol. 125 (1959)* (Kyoto, 1960), 52p.

61 U.S. Department of State, External Research Staff.
Ethnic Minorities of Southern China. Washington, D.C., July 1963, 18p. (External Research Paper 140).

A list of references in European languages (one-third of which are in Russian) on the ethnic minorities of southern China and the adjoining borderlands. Arranged alphabetically by author under books (75 entries) and periodical articles (129 entries). Whereas only about one-half of the books have a post-1949 imprint, the articles are predominantly concerned with the postwar period. Mimeographed.

62 Yuan, T. L. 袁同禮 **and Watanabe, H.** 渡邊宏, **comps.** *Hsin-chiang yen-chiu wen-hsien mu-lu—Shinkyō kenkyū bunken mokuroku* 新疆研究文獻目錄
Classified Bibliography of Japanese Books and Articles Concerning Sinkiang, 1886–1962. Tokyo, 1962. 92p.

A classified bibliography of 1,166 Japanese-language books and articles on Sinkiang (including translations) by Japanese authors, published in Japan from 1886 to 1962. Works by Japanese published overseas, foreign-language works published in Japan, and newspaper articles are excluded. The compilation is based on the holdings of the National Diet Library, the Tōyō Bunko, Keio University Library, the library of Tōhō Gakkai in Tokyo, and the Library of Congress in Washington, as well as on standard Japanese bibliographical works.

Divided into nine parts (with subdivisions): general works, the social sciences, history, geography, art, religion, language, industry and transportation and communications, and science. Within each section, entries are listed by author with full bibliographical data (including pagination) but in no apparent order. Alphabetical author and subject indexes.

A comprehensive compilation of Japanese-language works on Sinkiang, about one-third of which were published in the postwar period. Of these only a small number deal with current developments.

63 **Bibliography of Recent Soviet Source Material on Soviet Central Asia and the Borderlands.** London: Central Asian Research Centre, No. 1—, 1957—. Semi-annual.

A supplement to the *Central Asian Review* (see **1089**), the bibliography covers Soviet books and articles in periodicals, provincial newspapers, and scholarly transactions concerned with Soviet Central Asia and the several countries and regions bordering on the Soviet Asian republics, including Sinkiang and Tibet. Each entry provides the number of pages in the case of books or the number of words in the case of articles, with a brief summary of contents.

64 **Berton, Peter A., comp.**
Manchuria: An Annotated Bibliography. Washington, D.C.: The Library of Congress, 1951. 187p.

A selected bibliography on Manchuria listing over 800 works in Japanese, Chinese, Russian and Western languages with descriptive annotations. While the emphasis is on prewar Japanese publications, the bibliography also contains a number of Chinese Communist items, most of which were published in Manchuria in the immediate postwar period.

The first section of this work was issued separately in July 1951 under the title *Manchuria: A Selected List of Bibliographies.*

See also U.S. Department of the Army, Office of Military History, *Guide to Japanese Monographs and Japanese Studies on Manchuria, 1945–1960* (Washington, D.C., 1962 [?]), 282p.

65 **Iwamura, Shinobu** 岩村忍 **and Fujieda, Akira** 藤枝晃. *Mōko kenkyū bunken mokuroku, 1900–1950 nen* 蒙古研究文献目録 1900–1950 年
Bibliography of Mongolia for 1900–1950. Kyoto:Kyōto Daigaku, Jimbun Kagaku Kenkyūjo 京都大學人文科學研究所 (Kyoto University, Research Institute for Humanistic Studies), 1953. 46p. (Annual Bibliography of Oriental Studies, Special Number 1).

A bibliography of some 1,500 Japanese-language books and articles on both Inner and Outer Mongolia published between 1900 and 1950. Entries are arranged alphabetically by author (works by the same author are listed in order of publication). An alphabetical list of over 200 periodicals under survey precedes the bibliography.

E. Bibliographies of the Writings of chinese Leaders

Modern Chinese political leaders have in most cases been energetic publicists. Regrettably, for political and other reasons, not all of their writings are readily available for examination. In the case of Mao Tse-tung, his earlier writings are only partially represented in his *Selected Works*, and of those which have been incorporated, a number have been extensively revised. Stuart R. Schram's book, *The Political Thought of Mao Tse-tung* (New York: Praeger, 1963), identifies a large number of the original versions of Mao's works. Karl A. Wittfogel is also engaged in similar research, but his findings have not yet been published.

Of the five Chinese bibliographies included in this section, only one was available for examination—and it is by no means a complete record of Mao's writings (for a description of Mao's *Selected Works* see **568**). The list prepared by the External Research Division of the State Department (**66**) is perhaps the most comprehensive of all those available. But, like the others, it is a poor source for Mao's writings of the 1920's and the early 1930's.

The Columbia list of the writings of members of the Central Committee of the C.C.P. (**74**), and Rhoda Weidenbaum's study of Liu Shao-ch'i (**75**) are the only available references to the writings of other Chinese Communist leaders. No comparable compilations exist for the works of Chinese Nationalist leaders, except for those of Chiang Kai-shek (**579–581**).

It hardly needs mention that a thorough check through the card catalogs of the major libraries will turn up additional titles by both Chinese Communist and Nationalist authors. The Tōyō Bunko compilation, listed in the next section (**77**), should also be consulted.

66 **U. S. Department of State, External Research Division.**
The Thought of Mao Tse-tung, A Selected List of References to the Published Works and Statements Attributed to Mao Tse-tung and to the Literature on the Chinese Communist Leader. Washington, D.C., 1962. 73p. (External Research Paper 138).

A bibliography listing books (all editions), articles and statements attributed to Mao Tse-tung, plus a number of commentaries, interviews and discussions which purport to reveal or clarify Mao's views, published in Chinese, Japanese, English, French, German, and Russian. In two parts: (1) Mao Tse-tung—published works; and (2) interpretations of Mao Tse-tung. Part 1 is divided into the following sections: (1) bibliography; (2) collections—Chinese; (3) collections—translations; (4) pamphlets and periodical articles—Chinese; and (5) pamphlets and periodical articles—translations. Part 2 is a straight alphabetical listing by author. Works in Part 1 are listed alphabetically by title within each section under the main heading 'Mao Tse-tung'. Full bibliographical citations are supplied for each item, including translations for Chinese and Japanese titles. No Chinese characters are given. A list of Mao's statements reported in the *New York Times* (September 23, 1945; January 2 and 3, 1948) and *The Times* (London) (January 20, 1950 to October 24, 1951) is appended.

The most comprehensive bibliography listed in this section, and the only bibliography in which articles in Mao's *Selected Works* are listed by title. Many typographical errors. Mimeographed.

67　Pei-ching t'u-shu kuan 北京圖書館 (National Library of Peking). *Hsüeh-hsi Mao chu-hsi chu-tso shu-mu* 學習毛主席著作書目 (A Bibliography of Mao Tse-tung). Peking: Pei-ching t'u-shu kuan, 1958. 75p.

A bibliography of the writings of, and works about, Mao Tse-tung. A total of 606 titles, including various editions and translations arranged chronologically by the date of writing, 1926–1957 inclusive. There are 323 Chinese titles (210 by Mao Tse-tung with annotations, 18 on his thought, and 25 biographies), and 283 translations into Russian, Western, and Asian languages, including those of the minority groups in China.

A useful semi-official guide, but the listing is far from complete (a number of the earlier editions of his works are not included).

For a translation of this book, see J.P.R.S. No. 10539, *Bibliography for the Study of Chairman Mao's Works*, October 17, 1961 (U.S.G.P.O. Monthly Catalog, 1962, No. 1111), 99p.

68　Pei-ching t'u-shu kuan, Shu-mu so-yin tsu 北京圖書館 書目索引組 (National Library of Peking, Bibliography and Index Section). 'Hsüeh-hsi Mao chu-hsi chu-tso tsui-hsin shu-mu', 學習毛主席著作最新書目 (The Most Recent Bibliography on Studying Chairman Mao's Works), *T'u-shu kuan hsüeh t'ung-hsün* 圖書館學通訊 (Library Science Bulletin), No. 3, 1960 (March 20, 1960), p.11.

A bibliography of nineteen bibliographies on the thought of Mao Tse-tung, including three now published and sixteen in preparation by various libraries in Communist China as of January 1960. The three published items are (1) *Mao Tse-tung chu-tso chu-t'i so-yin* 毛澤東著作主題索引 (see next entry); (2) *Mao Tse-tung chu-tso yen-lun wen-tien mu-lu* 毛澤東著作言論文電目錄 (see **70**); and (3) *Kao-chü Mao Tse-tung ssu-hsiang hung-ch'i hsien-ch'i ssu-hsiang chien-she kao-ch'ao—tzu-liao so-yin* 高舉毛澤東思想紅旗掀起思想建設高潮一資料索引 (see **71**).

69　Chung-kuo jen-min ta-hsüeh, T'u-shu kuan 中國人民大學 圖書館 (Chinese People's University, Library). *Mao Tse-tung chu-tso chu-t'i so-yin* 毛澤東著作主題索引 (A Subject Index to Mao Tse-tung's Works). Peking, 1960. 179p.

An index primarily to works published in the second edition of *Mao Tse-tung hsüan-chi* 毛澤東選集 (Selected Works of Mao Tse-tung), his writings after 1949, and others not included in the pre-1949 editions of his *Selected Works*. Indexed also are both pre and post-1949 directives and telegrams signed by Mao

Tse-tung, and his letters and speeches. Mimeographed. The volume was not available for examination.

70 Chung-kuo jen-min ta-hsüeh, T'u-shu kuan 中國人民大學 圖書館 (Chinese People's University, Library). *Mao Tse-tung chu-tso yen-lun wen-tien mu-lu* 毛澤東著作言論文電目錄 (A Bibilography of Mao Tse-tung's Works, Speeches, Statements and Telegrams). Peking, 1960. 40p.

Covers Mao's works in the period from July 1919 to December 1959, excluding those written between October 1949 and December 1958. A bibliography of the latter has been published by the Jen-min ch'u-pan she 人民出版社 (People's Publishing House). Mimeographed. Neither this item nor the bibliography published by the People's Publishing House was available for examination.

71 Kan-su sheng t'u-shu kuan 甘肅省圖書館 (Kansu Provincial Library). *Kao-chü Mao Tse-tung ssu-hsiang hung-ch'i hsien-ch'i ssu-hsiang chien-she kao-ch'ao— tzu-liao so-yin* 高舉毛澤東思想紅旗掀起思想建設高潮——資料索引 (Raise High the Red Flag of Mao Tse-tung's Thought and Generate a High Tide of Thought Construction—A Bibliography). [Lanchow], 1960. 14p.

A mimeographed bibliography of works on Mao Tse-tung's thought. This item was not available for examination.

72 Columbia University Libraries, East Asiatic Library.
Guide to the Writings of Mao Tse-tung in the East Asiatic Library. New York, 1951. 16p. Supplement 1, 1952: 8p.

A list of the writings of Mao Tse-tung, including translations, in the East Asiatic Library as of March 1952, among which are a number of articles not included in the bibliography compiled by the National Library of Peking (see **67**). Both main list and supplement are arranged chronologically by date of original writing. Entries carry full bibliographical citations and East Asiatic Library call numbers.

73 Committee for a Free Asia, Inc., Historical Research Branch.
List of the Writings of Mao Tse-tung Found in the Hoover Library at Stanford University. Stanford, Calif., 1951. 25p.

A list of Mao Tse-tung's writings, including translations, in the Hoover Institution as of 1950. Grouped by date of original publication, all titles carry full bibliographical data.

74 Columbia University Libraries, East Asiatic Library.
Writings of the Members of the Central Committee of the Chinese Communist Party. New York, 1952. 41p.

A bibliography of the writings, both in Chinese and in Western languages, of members of the Central Committee of the Chinese Communist Party holding office as of January 1, 1950. Included are periodical articles, titles in collected works and items published separately. All items in this bibliography are located in the East Asiatic Library. Entries are arranged alphabetically by author and, within each author group, chronologically insofar as date of writing is known. In the absence of such information, works are arranged by date of the publication in which they appear. A list of 'Works Consulted' comprises 116 titles in both Chinese and English. Subject index. Mimeographed.

A very useful guide to works published as of 1950.

75 Weidenbaum, Rhoda Sussman.
'The Career and Writings of Liu Shao-ch'i', *East Asian Institute Studies, Columbia University*, No. 3 (1957), pp. 53-78.

An abstract of the author's Master's thesis done at Columbia in 1953. In three parts: (1) introduction; (2) the career of Liu Shao-ch'i; (3) the writings of Liu Shao-ch'i, and a bibliography. Part 2 is an analysis of five of Liu's most important theoretical papers: 'On the Training of a Communist Party Member', 'On Inner Party Struggle', 'Liquidate the Menshevist Ideology in the Party', 'On the Party', and 'Internationalism and Nationalism'. The bibliography lists all of Liu's writings chronologically by date of publication with annotations given for all except the five works analyzed in Part 2, and in addition it contains a section on biographical sources in Chinese and Japanese, as well as a section on English language sources.

One of the very few studies on Liu, a noted Communist theoretician, and currently the President of the People's Republic of China.

F. Bibliographies of Biographies

The following section comprises the two available bibliographies of biographies, the first of which is annotated. The second contains more entries on currently active Chinese leaders. The reader also is referred to the biographical materials listed in Chapter VII.

76 Wu, Eugene, comp.
Leaders of Twentieth-Century China: An Annotated Bibliography of Selected Chinese Biographical Works in the Hoover Library. Stanford, Calif.: Stanford University Press, 1956. 106p.

Contains some 500 biographies, autobiographies, memoirs, diaries, etc., of modern and contemporary Chinese leaders, arranged under eight sections: (1) general collective biographies; (2) biographies of political figures; (3) biographies of military figures; (4) biographies of intellectuals; (5) biographies of industrialists and businessmen; (6) biographies of Overseas Chinese; (7) directories and school yearbooks; (8) serials. A full bibliographical citation is given for each entry, including romanization, characters, and translation, as well as the Hoover Library call number in parenthesis. There is an alphabetical index to names of biographees, authors, individual editors and compilers, and titles of books appearing in the bibliography.

The only available annotated reference work of its kind. A supplementary volume is under preparation.

77 Ichiko, Chūzō 市古宙三 **and Kunioka, Taeko** 國岡妙子. 'Tōyō Bunko shozō kin hyaku nenrai Chūgoku meijin kankei tosho mokuroku' 東洋文庫所藏近百年來中國名人關係圖書目錄
(A List of Books in the Tōyō Bunko By and On Important Chinese of the Past One Hundred Years), *Kindai Chūgoku kenkyū* 近代中國研究 *Studies on Modern China*, Tokyo, Vol. 4 (1960), pp. 1-136.

Contains some 2,000 works by and about approximately 600 Chinese who lived after 1840, including a few persons active in the post-1949 period. Most of the works are in Chinese, although a number of English and Japanese items have been included. Arrangement is by Japanese syllabary according to the Japanese reading of the Chinese name. As a rule, works are listed under the subject's name (with date of birth and death in parenthesis) in the following order: collected works, letters, diaries and monographs and single volume works by the subject, followed by biographies, chronologies, studies and criticisms. Japanese and English works are usually listed last. The list is preceded by a table of contents which gives the authors' names, followed by page references.

G. Subject Bibliographies

The present section, a collection of some ninety subject bibliographies, is arranged in the following order:

There are countless subjects for which no special bibliographies are available. Nor are the available subject bibliographies the last, or for that matter, the most reliable, word on any given subject. It is therefore imperative to consult the relevant sections in the general bibliographies, the indexes to periodical literature listed in Chapter III, the documentary materials in Part Three, and the pertinent periodicals in Part Four. The more important general sources are also given in the introductory note at the beginning of this Part (pp. 1–3).

Finally, because the various general bibliographies are anything but uniform in their topical classifications, it is difficult, if not impossible, to evaluate the entire body of literature on any given subject. Moreover, as we have suggested, the unequal development of the subject bibliographies does little to ease the situation. For this reason, the introductory notes preceding each of the following subsections are directed only to a consideration of the matter at hand. No attempt has been made to compare the coverage of the subject bibliographies with the literature on the same subjects in the general bibliographies, or to consider them jointly in a broad-gauge assessment of any particular field.

I. HISTORY

The reinterpretation and plain rewriting of history is practiced to some extent by most totalitarian governments, and Communist regimes have proved particularly adept in this respect. Since 1949, Communist China has put considerable effort into formulating and expounding an orthodox version of Chinese history and of the Chinese Communist movement.

The production of historical literature on the Mainland since 1949 is given adequate coverage in the first two entries in this section, together with such journals as *Li-shih yen-chiu* 歷史研究 (Historical Studies) and *Li-shih chiao-hsüeh* 歷史教學 (Teaching of History), and the general bibliographies described above in this chapter. The handbook for secondary school teachers (the first entry) lists some 600 books on all periods of Chinese history and carries a substantial index to periodical and newspaper articles on historical subjects published from 1949 to 1957. The bibliography by Professor Feuerwerker and Miss Cheng (**79**) provides critical annotations for approximately 500 books and pamphlets on modern Chinese history. The compilations on the history of the Chinese Communist movement by Professors Wilbur and Shirato (**80** and **81** respectively) are of a different nature. Listing both Communist and non-Communist sources in Chinese and Japanese, these companion volumes provide access to materials on the movement to 1952, with an emphasis on the pre-1949 period. Mention might also be made of the more general *Bibliography on Chinese Social History* by E-tu Zen Sun and John De Francis (Yale University, Far Eastern Publications, 1952, 150p.), not described below.

There are no bibliographies dealing specifically with post-1949 history of Taiwan. The reader should consult the National Bibliography of the Republic of China (**10**) and other general bibliographical sources, including the periodical indexes (**192**ff).

78 **Wang, Chih-chiu** 王芝九 **and Sung, Kuo-chu** 宋國柱. *Chung-hsüeh li-shih chiao-shih shou-ts'e* 中學歷史教師手冊
(A Handbook for Secondary School History Teachers). Shanghai: Chiao-yü ch'u-pan she 教育出版社, 1958. 408p.

A volume combining the functions of a teaching guide and reference work. Part 1 (the first eight chapters, 82p.) is, in essence, an introduction to the teaching of history in the secondary schools from a dialectical materialistic point of view. Part 2 is a reference section, incorporating a chronology of Chinese and world events (3500 B.C.–1957 A.D.), by year until October 1949, by month thereafter, pp. 83–236; a period chart of Chinese and world history, pp. 237–274; a select bibliography of some 600 Chinese historical works published on the Mainland between October 1949 and December 1957 (arranged by title under topic; e.g., Chinese history, general; Chinese history, modern), pp. 275–301; and an index to periodical and newspaper articles on historical subjects which appeared in the period October 1949–July 1957 inclusive, pp. 302–408.

The periodicals indexed include *Li-shih yen-chiu* 歷史研究, *Li-shih chiao-hsüeh* 歷史教學, *Hsin shih-hsüeh t'ung-hsün* 新史學通訊, *Chung-hsüeh li-shih chiao-hsüeh* 中學歷史教學, *Chin-tai shih tzu-liao* 近代史資料, *Wen shih che* 文史哲, *Shih-hsüeh yüeh-k'an* 史學月刊, *Shih-hsüeh i-ts'ung* 史學譯叢 and others. Newspaper articles are taken mainly from *Jen-min jih-pao* 人民日報, *Kuang-ming jih-pao* 光明日報, *Wen-hui pao* 文滙報, *Ta-kung pao* 大公報, *Kung-jen jih-pao* 工人日報, *Chung-kuo ch'ing-nien pao* 中國青年報 and a few provincial papers.

The only available handbook of its kind on Chinese history published by the Chinese Communists.

79 Feuerwerker, Albert and Cheng, S.

Chinese Communist Studies of Modern Chinese History. Cambridge, Mass.: Harvard University, East Asian Research Center, 1961. 25; 287p.

A bibliography of nearly 500 books on modern Chinese history published in Communist China between 1949 and 1959 with critical annotations, arranged under the following sections: (1) general works; (2) the Ming and Ch'ing dynasties; (3) the Republic; (4) economic history; (5) intellectual and cultural history; and (6) reference works. The introduction is a good essay on Chinese Communist historiography, and additional introductory remarks precede each section. A list of frequently cited publishers is provided, as is a comprehensive author, title, and subject index. Many of the titles appear in the bibliography section of the preceding entry.

The only source for evaluating Chinese Communist historical writings and, as such, extremely important. For a review of this work by S. Y. Teng, see *The Journal of Asian Studies*, Vol. 16, No. 3 (May 1962), pp. 378–379.

80 Wilbur, C. Martin, ed.

Chinese Sources on the History of the Chinese Communist Movement: An Annotated Bibliography of Materials in the East Asiatic Library of Columbia University. New York: Columbia University, East Asian Institute, 1950. 56p. (Columbia University, East Asian Institute Studies, No. 1).

Lists most of the materials in Chinese in the East Asiatic Library as of March 1950 (over 200 items) on the Chinese Communist movement to October 1949, including books, parts thereof, periodicals, and articles in periodicals. It does not list items in Chinese newspapers, nor does it cover analyses of Chinese society and history written from a Marxist point of view or influenced by Marxist interpretation. Arranged in seven chronological parts (with subsections), including 'Post War Years—"Truce" and Civil War: August 1945–October 1949'. Alphabetical author, title, and subject index. Private distribution.

Useful for locating periodical articles on the earlier period of the movement. Somewhat weak for the post-1945 period. See also next entry.

81 Shirato, Ichiro, comp.
Japanese Sources on the History of the Chinese Communist Movement. New York: Columbia University, East Asian Institute, 1953. 69p. (Columbia University, East Asian Institute Studies, No. 2).

An annotated bibliography of 441 Japanese-language books, parts thereof, monographs, pamphlets and significant periodical articles on the history of the Chinese Communist movement in the East Asiatic Library of Columbia University and the Division of Orientalia, Library of Congress, as of 1952. The bibliography is a companion volume to *Chinese Sources on the History of the Chinese Communist Movement* (see preceding entry).

Arranged in nine parts: reference works, general histories, and specific periods of the Chinese Communist movement, including 'China under the People's Republic: October 1949–1952'. The reference works are further subdivided into bibliography (bibliographies on Communism and general reference works) and biography (collected biographies and separate biographies—Mao Tse-tung, Chu Te, Chou En-lai, and others). The other parts are divided into topical subcategories. Items are entered under the periods with which they deal rather than by date of publication. More general and substantial scholarly works are listed first, followed by specialized and less important items.

The appendix provides a chronological list of the official documents of the Chinese Communist Party from 1922 to 1950 which have appeared in Japanese translation. Index to authors, principal persons listed in the bibliography, and titles for which no author is given.

Good descriptive annotations for the limited number of items on the 1949 to 1952 period.

82 Etō, Shinkichi 衛藤瀋吉. 'Chūkyō shi kenkyū nōto' 中共史研究ノート
'Brief Guide to the Studies on the History of Chinese Communists,' *Tōyō gakuhō* 東洋學報 *Reports of the Oriental Society*, Tokyo, Vol. 43, No. 2 (September 1960), pp. 63–87.

Chapter 1 is a general introduction to the study of the history of Chinese Communism, discussing the principal general works, bibliographies, dictionaries, yearbooks, chronologies, biographical dictionaries, document collections, periodical literature, and principal source materials divided by period, and biographies and memoirs in Japanese and Western languages (Chinese and Russian-language sources are to be covered in a separate report).

Chapter 2 surveys prewar Japanese studies of the Chinese Communist movement and provides several pertinent suggestions for the future development of the field. A survey of Japanese studies in the postwar period, as well as a survey of Western studies on the subject, are scheduled to be published at a later date. This brief but useful survey is the work of Professor Etō of Tokyo University, one of the leading younger scholars of Chinese Communism.

83 **Yoshida, Tora** 吉田寅 **and Tanada, Naohiko** 棚田直彦, **comps.** *Chūgoku rekishi chiri kenkyū rombun mokuroku* 中國歷史地理研究論文目錄 (A Bibliography of Articles on Chinese Historical Geography). Tokyo: Tōkyō Kyōiku Daigaku 東京教育大學, 1960. 162p.

A classified bibliography of over 2,000 Japanese and Chinese books and articles on the historical geography of China published from 1868 to 1957 (with a few more recent items supplied), prepared under the auspices of the Society for the Study of Asian History of the Tokyo University of Education. Based largely on the bibliographies of Oriental history published by the Ōtsuka Historical Society (*Tōyōshi rombun yōmoku* 東洋史論文要目) and Kyoto University (*Tōyōshi kenkyū bunken ruimoku* 東洋史研究文獻類目), the volume is given over mainly to entries on the pre-1949 period, and provides full bibliographical citations, including pagination. Mimeographed. No index.

84 **Perevertailo, A. S., et al., eds.** *Ocherki istorii Kitaia v noveishee vremia.* (Collection of Articles on the History of China in Recent Times). Moscow: Izdatel'stvo vostochnoi literatury, 1959. 696p. 17 maps.

Scholarly articles on the recent history of China, prepared at the Institute of Chinese Studies, Moscow. The volume includes a chronology of some 700 entries for the period 1917–1957. A classified bibliography has been provided, containing over 500 items, including pronouncements on China by Lenin and other Soviet leaders (about 100 items), writings by Chinese Communist leaders, source materials, memoirs, monographs, etc., in Russian, Chinese and Western European languages. Personal name and geographical indexes.

2. LANGUAGE AND LITERATURE

Apart from China itself, the country most thoroughly immersed in the study of Chinese language and literature is Japan. This interest carries over to the kindred subjects of language reform under the Communists and contemporary Chinese literature. It is hardly surprising, then, that over half of the entries in the present section are Japanese compilations, covering not only Japanese-language works, but Chinese and Western-language sources as well.

No comprehensive bibliographies are available that afford coverage to sources in all languages on the various aspects of the Chinese language. For Mainland Chinese publications of the years 1950–1960, see the first entry (**85**). The Mainland national bibliography (**8, 9**) and the index to major newspapers and periodicals (**184**), as well as the philological journals (*Chung-kuo yü-wen* [Chinese language], *Wen-tzu kai-ko* [Language Reform], etc.) provide additional sources.

For Japanese sources on the Chinese language, comprehensive bibliographies are available for the period 1945–1961 (**88, 89**). Subsequent years are adequately covered in the annual bibliography of Kyoto University (**30**).

Chinese literature is more thoroughly covered than Chinese language. The semi-annual *Journal of Chinese Literature*, published by Kyoto University (**90**), provides current bibliography on the subject in all languages. A Russian bibliography on Chinese literature (**94**) is likewise available and listed in this section. The relevant portions of Skachkov's general bibliography (**42**) should be consulted for materials through 1957, as should the other Soviet general bibliographies for current sources.

The reader is reminded that the principal sources on Chinese literature are the Mainland and Taiwan literary journals such as *Jen-min wen-hsüeh* (People's Literature), *Chinese Literature; Wen-hsüeh tsa-chih* (Literary Review), *Wen-tan* (Literary Forum), etc., described in Part Four. Mention might also be made of *Wen-hsieh shih-nien* (see **749**), which provides a list of works published by members of the China Association of Literature and Arts in Taiwan during the 1950's.

For Japanese books, and for periodical and newspaper articles of pre-Second World War vintage on Chinese literature, there is the *Gendai Chūgoku bungaku kenkyū bunken mokuroku, 1919–1945* 現代中國文學研究文獻目錄 (Bibliography of Materials on Contemporary Chinese Literature, 1919–1945), compiled by Iida Yoshirō (Tokyo: Chūgoku Bunka Kenkyūkai 中國文化研究會 [Society for the Study of Chinese Culture], 1959, 87 p.). For a supplement to this bibliography, see the additional 117 entries published by Iida under the title 'Gendai Chūgoku bungaku kenkyū bunken mokuroku hoi' (An Addendum to the Bibliography of Materials on Contemporary Chinese Literature) in *Daian*, Vol. 7, Nos. 4–5 (April and May 1961), pp. 23–26 and 27–29, respectively.

85 Tseng, Maurice H., comp.
Recent Chinese Publications on the Chinese Language, An Annotated Bibliography. New Haven, Conn.: Yale University, The Institute of Far Eastern Languages, 1961. 45p.

Lists 110 books, published mostly in Communist China between 1950 and 1960 under the following subject headings: (1) linguistics, (2) Chinese language, (3) phonology, (4) grammar, (5) vocabulary, (6) characters and language reform, (7) dialects, and (8) minority languages. Chapter 4, on grammar, constitutes the bulk of the bibliography, having a total of fifty titles. All entries are provided with full bibliographical information, including Chinese characters for the names of authors and titles, as well as English translations of the titles. Annotations are mainly descriptive, with some critical evaluations. No index.

A comprehensive, though not exhaustive, compilation.

86 Tenri Daigaku, Jimbun Gakkai 天理大學人文學會 (Tenri University, Humanities Association). *Chūgoku kan shimbun zasshi shokei Chūgoku gogaku, bungaku rombun mokuroku (1957 nemban . . .)* 中國刊新聞雜誌所揭中國語學文學論文目錄 (List of Articles on Chinese Language and Literature Which Appeared in Newspapers and Periodicals Published in China [1957—]). Tenri, Nara Prefecture, 1960—.

A classified list of articles on Chinese language and literature in Chinese Communist newspapers and periodicals listed in *Ch'üan-kuo chu-yao pao-k'an tzu-liao so-yin* 全國主要報刊資料索引 (Index to Major Newspapers and Periodicals of China). The volume covering the 1957 issues of the Index (actually February 1957–January 1958 inclusive) contains over 600 entries on Chinese language and over 2,800 in the field of Chinese literature. The volume for 1958 (published in 1961) lists some 950 and 4,300 entries on language and literature, respectively, covering the February through December 1958 issues of the Index.

The articles are arranged in roughly ten categories under language, and in over twenty categories under literature. Entries provide title, author, name of periodical, date of publication, volume number and page.

87 Wang, William S. Y., comp.
Synchronic Studies in Mandarin Grammar. Columbus, Ohio: Ohio State University, Research Foundation, 1962. 15p. (RF Project 1303, Report 2).

A bibliography of 164 (largely postwar) books, pamphlets, and periodical articles on Chinese grammar, mostly in Chinese with some English, Japanese and Russian titles. Entries are arranged alphabetically by author. Names of Chinese authors and of works written in Chinese are romanized according to the Yale system. Full bibliographical citations are given, and include translation of titles and characters for Chinese and Japanese authors, titles, and some publishers. There are no annotations.

88 Chūgoku Gogaku Kenkyūkai 中國語學研究會 (Society for the Study of the Chinese Language). *Chūgoku gogaku bunken mokuroku—1945 nen 8 gatsu—1957 nen 7 gatsu* 中國語學文獻目錄 1945 年 8 月–1957 年 7 月 (Bibliography of Works on Chinese Linguistics—August 1945 to July 1957). Tokyo, 1957. 61p.

A classified list of some 1,400 Japanese-language books, pamphlets and articles (including translations into Japanese) on Chinese linguistics published in Japan from August 1945 to July 1957. The volume is based largely on the bibliography of Kyoto University (*Tōyōshi kenkyū bunken ruimoku*, **30**), the bibliography on Oriental languages and literatures published by the Japan Science Council (*Bungaku, tetsugaku, shigaku bunken—Tōyō bungaku, gogaku hen*, **92**), and the bibliography in the *Journal of Chinese Literature* (*Chūgoku bungakuhō*, **90**). Arranged according to twelve topical categories (grammar, phonetics, dialects, history of linguistics, education, dictionaries, indexes, etc.), entries provide full bibliographical citations and, in the case of some books, a short table of contents. Lists of publishers, research institutes and academic associations are appended. See also next entry.

89 Chūgoku Gogaku Kenkyūkai 中國語學研究會 (Society for the Study of the Chinese Language). *Chūgoku gogaku bunken mokuroku—II* 中國語學文獻目錄 (Bibliography of Works on Chinese Linguistics—II). Tokyo, 1963. 70p.

A continuation of the preceding entry, covering the period August 1957–December 1961, with additional materials on Tibetan and other minority languages. The bibliography is an almost exhaustive compilation of scholarly works. (See also Gotō Kimpei 後藤均平, 'Postwar Japanese Studies on the Chinese Language', *Monumenta Serica*, Vol. 20 [1961], pp. 368–393, listing 154 most important works on the subject with descriptive annotations.)

90 'Saikin bunken mokuroku—Chūgoku bungaku' 最近文獻錄目——中國文學 (A Bibliography of Books and Articles on Chinese Literature Published in Japan, China and the West) in *Chūgoku bungakuhō* 中國文學報 *Journal of Chinese Literature* (Kyoto: Kyōto Daigaku, Bungakubu, Chūgoku Gogaku Chūgoku Bungaku Kenkyūshitsu 京都大學文學部中國語學中國文學研究室), Vol. 1—, 1954—. Semi-annual.

A semi-annual bibliography appearing regularly in the *Journal of Chinese Literature* published by the Department of Chinese Language and Literature at Kyoto University. Each instalment, ranging from twenty to thirty-five pages, covers pertinent literature for the preceding six months period (the October issue covers the period January through June, while the April issue covers the period July through December of the preceding year). The bibliography lists from 500 to 1,000 books, pamphlets, newspaper and periodical articles and reviews, and is divided into three parts: Japanese, Chinese (both Mainland and Taiwan), and Western publications (including Russian). The Japanese and Chinese parts are further subdivided into a number of categories, including one entitled 'Contemporary Literature'. The Western-language part is divided into books, translations, articles, reviews and 'Bibliography and Conference', and is organized alphabetically by author within each category. A full bibliographical citation is provided for each entry.

In the early issues of the bibliography, the coverage was extended to works on the Chinese language and for this reason the Chinese and Japanese parts in these issues are first subdivided into language and literature sub-categories. The first issue covers the period from November 1953 to August 1954, and has no Western-language entries. For Japanese-language sources for the period prior to November 1953, see Nihon Gakujutsu Kaigi (Japan Science Council), *Bungaku, tetsugaku, shigaku bunken mokuroku, III, Tōyō bungaku, gogaku hen* (Bibliography of Materials on Literature, Philosophy and History, III—Oriental Literature and Languages, 92). No index.

The most comprehensive current coverage of books and articles on Chinese literature in all languages; weaker in Western-language sources. The Western-language part also contains many typographical errors.

91   Hsia, C. T.
A History of Modern Chinese Fiction, 1917–1957, with an Appendix on Taiwan. New Haven, Conn.: Yale University Press, 1961. 12; 662p.

The bibliography (pp. 531–571) is in five parts: surveys and histories, anthologies and bibliographies; influential magazines; and works by Chinese critics, novelists and story writers. Works (and translations) by and on twenty modern Chinese authors—including Mao Tun, Lao She, Pa Chin, Ting Ling, Chao Shu-li, Eileen Chang, Chiang Kuei and others active in the postwar period on the Mainland, Taiwan and Hong Kong—are listed in the last part.

92   Nihon Gakujutsu Kaigi 日本學術會議 (Japan Science Council). *Bungaku, tetsugaku, shigaku bunken mokuroku,* III—*Tōyō bungaku, gogaku hen* 文學, 哲學, 史學文獻目錄, III 東洋文學語學篇 (Bibliography of Materials on Literature, Philosophy, and History, III—Oriental Literature and Languages). Tokyo, 1954. 138p.

A bibliography of Japanese original works, translations and compilations on Oriental languages and literature, published from August 15, 1945 through October 1953. Two-thirds of the volume is devoted to Chinese language and literature (over 400 and 2,000 entries respectively). The subsection on contemporary Chinese literature contains roughly 1,000 entries which are further subdivided by Chinese writers. Entries are arranged in broad categories (Oriental linguistics—general; Oriental literature—general; Altaic languages and literature; Chinese linguistics; Chinese literature; etc.), with many subheadings. Within each section the arrangement is from the general to the specific and from original contributions to translations and compilations. Full bibliographical citations are provided for all entries. Contains an index to journals with their publishers and an author index, both arranged according to the Japanese syllabary.

For a continuation, see next entry.

93   Nihon Gakujutsu Kaigi 日本學術會議 (Japan Science Council). *Bungaku, tetsugaku, shigaku bunken mokuroku,* III—*Tōyō bungaku, gogaku hen hoi* 文學, 哲學, 史學文獻目錄 III — 東洋文學語學篇補遺

(Bibliography of Materials on Literature, Philosophy, and History, III—Oriental Literature and Languages, Supplement). Tokyo, 1958. 127p.

A supplement to the previous compilation covering materials published in the period November 1953 to December 1956 and containing some 600 entries on contemporary Chinese literature (p. 73–93). The two entries taken together provide good coverage of postwar Japanese works on Chinese literature, especially prior to the publication of the *Journal of Chinese Literature* (**90**).

For Japanese works on Chinese language, consult the special bibliography (**88** and **89**) listed above.

94   Skachkov, P. E. and Glagoleva, I. K., comps. *Kitaiskaia khudozhestvennaia literatura—Bibliografiia russkikh perevodov i kriticheskoi literatury na russkom iazyke*
(Chinese Belles-Lettres—A Bibliography of Russian Translations and of Literary Criticism in Russian). Moscow: Vsesoiuznaia knizhnaia palata, 1957. 164p.

A bibliography prepared at the State Library of Foreign Literature, containing a total of 1,823 books, parts thereof, and articles in periodicals, newspapers and compendia comprising Russian translations of, and literary criticism on, Chinese belles-lettres published in Russia and the Soviet Union from 1775 to 1955. (Articles in newspapers are generally limited to those which appeared in the central press during the period 1945–1955.) Also included are translations of literary criticism by Chinese authors. Most of the translations are from Chinese-language originals, but in some cases the Russian translations were made from European-language translations of Chinese literature, a fact which goes unnoted.

The bibliography is arranged in five parts: general works on Chinese literature —180 entries; collections and anthologies—67; works by individual authors and literary criticism on their works—1,415; works by unknown authors and anonymous literature—52; folklore—105. The largest part—that on individual authors —is arranged alphabetically under two subsections, one dealing with pre-twentieth century period literature, the other with contemporary literature. In each, works by Chinese authors are listed first, followed by those about them. Two indexes: Chinese authors and translators, and authors of critical literature.

Covering the works of more than 500 Chinese novelists, poets, playwrights, etc. and almost an equal number of Russian translators and literary critics, this bibliography comes close to being exhaustive.

95   Kunin, V. V., comp. *Mao Dun'—bio-bibliograficheskii ukazatel'*
(Mao Tun—A Bio-bibliographical Guide). Moscow: Izdatel'stvo vsesoiuznoi knizhnoi palaty, 1958. 45p.

A bibliography in the series on foreign writers prepared at the State Library of Foreign Literature.

96 **Tōkyō Toritsu Daigaku, Jimbun Gakubu, Chūgoku Bungaku Kenkyūshi-tsu** 東京都立大學人文學部中國文學研究室 (Tokyo Metropolitan University, Faculty of Humanities, Department of Chinese Literature). *Ma-jun hyōron mokuroku, miteikō* 茅盾評論目錄未定稿
(Bibliography of Mao Tun's Essays—Draft). Tokyo, 1957. 38p.

A list of Mao Tun's essays, published in the period 1919–1957, issued as a supplement to *Ma-jun hyōronshū* (Collection of Essays on Mao Tun), No. 1. No. 2 (1958) contains a list of Mao Tun's translations (pp. 169–188). No. 3 (1958) contains a list of Japanese translations of Mao Tun's works (pp. 171–176). Mimeographed.

3. RELIGION AND THOUGHT

For Chinese-language works on religion and thought, the reader is referred to the national bibliographies, the indexes to periodical literature and other general reference tools described at the beginning of this Part, as well as to Chinese-language journals in the field, such as *Che-hsüeh yen-chiu* (Philosophical Studies), *Hsien-tai fo-hsüeh* (Modern Buddhism), etc., described in Part Four. Some of this material is also available in English translation through the publications of the American Consulate General in Hong Kong and in the J.P.R.S. translation series, *Sociological-Educational-Cultural Information on Communist China* (**1063**).

The standard bibliography of Chinese philosophy by Professor Wing-tsit Chan, *An Outline and Annotated Bibliography of Chinese Philosophy* (revised and expanded edition, Yale University, Far Eastern Publications, 1961, 133p.), is not described here because of its almost exclusive coverage of works published before 1949. An annotated bibliography of Mainland publications on Chinese philosophy for the years 1949–1963 prepared by Professor Chan is to be published by the East-West Center in Honolulu.

For works on Christianity in China—especially in recent years—consult the bibliography of Frank Price (**98**) listed below.

Japanese concern for Chinese culture, religion and thought has endured for over a thousand years, and has thrived even in the face of mounting Western influence—a fact well illustrated by the bibliography of Japanese writings on the subject for the last ninety years containing some ten thousand articles (see **97**). The bulk of this material was, however, produced before 1949 and is oriented to pre-modern China. More recent writings, too, are more concerned with traditional than with contemporary China.

See also the bibliography of Japanese-language materials on education and Christianity (**101**) in the section on education and indoctrination below.

97 **Chūgoku Shisō Shūkyōshi Kenkyūkai** 中國思想宗教史研究會 (Society for the Study of the History of Chinese Thought and Religion). *Chūgoku shisō, shūkyō bunka kankei rombun mokuroku—wabun* 中國思想, 宗教文化關係論文目錄 (和文)
(A Bibliography of Japanese-Language Articles on Chinese Thought, Religion and Culture). Tokyo, 1960. 383p.

A classified bibliography containing some 10,000 articles on Chinese thought, religion and culture, published in Japan from 1868 to 1957. Based largely on the bibliographies of Oriental history published by the Ōtsuka Historical Society (*Tōyōshi rombun yōmoku* 東洋史論文要目) and Kyoto University (*Tōyōshi kenkyū bunken ruimoku* 東洋史研究文獻類目) and on index card catalogs of the Department of Oriental History of Tokyo University of Education, the volume was prepared under the direction of Professor Yamazaki Hiroshi (山崎宏) of the Tokyo University of Education. Most of the entries are for the pre-1949 period, and all contain full bibliographical data. A list of journals surveyed is appended. Author index arranged according to the Japanese syllabary. Mimeographed.

98   Price, Frank W., comp.
'Selected Bibliography of Books, Pamphlets and Articles on Communist China and the Christian Church in China', *Occasional Bulletin from the Missionary Research Library*, New York, Vol. 9, No. 8 (September 30, 1958), 21p.

A selected bibliography of more than 400 books, pamphlets and articles published since 1948, mostly in the English language, including a few translations from the Chinese. Organized as follows: (1) books and pamphlets—general; (2) magazine articles—general; (3) the church in China—books and pamphlets; (4) the church in China—magazine articles; (5) missionary experiences under the Communist regime; (6) 'Lessons from the China Crisis'; (7) periodicals and other sources *re* Communist China and the church in China; and (8) organizations doing research on Communist China.

A very useful bibliography on the subject and valuable for references to first-hand reports of experiences and impressions of former residents and visitors to Communist China.

4. EDUCATION AND INDOCTRINATION

Education as an instrument for the fulfilment of national goals has been used by both the Chinese Nationalist and Communist governments.

Considering the effectiveness of Chinese Communist programs in this field, it can only be disappointing that so little exists in the way of special bibliographical references on the subject. The present section lists one entry (**100**), a 1951 index to Mainland newspaper and periodical literature. For other sources on the Chinese Communist educational system and policies, consult the general bibliographies listed at the beginning of this Part, as well as the indexes to *Kuang-ming jih-pao* (**837**) and the Shanghai *Wen-hui pao* (**846**) in Chapter XVII. See also **1490**.

For materials in English translation, see the J.P.R.S. series, *Sociological-Educational-Cultural Information on Communist China* (**1063**) and Hong Kong American Consulate General series (**1038** ff.).

Education in Taiwan is covered by the first entry (**99**) listed below. Taiwan educational statistics and directories of schools and universities are listed in Chapters V and VI, respectively. Selected Taiwan and Mainland periodicals on education, such as *Chiao-yü yü wen-hua* 教育與文化 (Education and Culture), *T'ai-wan chiao-yü* 臺灣教育 (Taiwan Education Review), *Chiao-hsüeh yü yen-chiu* 教學與研究 (Teaching and Research), and *Jen-min chiao-yü* 人民教育 (People's Education), as well as university publications, are described in Part Four. For compilations of laws on education and related documentary material, see Chapters XII and XV (Laws and Regulations; Education and Culture). Particular reference might be made to Volume Eight of the Reference Materials on Culture and Education published in Peking (**741**).

In totalitarian countries the division between education and indoctrination is exceedingly thin. With the advent of the Korean War much attention in the West has been focused on 'brain-washing'. A substantial bibliography on the subject, with particular emphasis on Chinese techniques, is to be found at the end of this section (**102**).

99 Ssu, Ch'i 司琦, **comp.** *Chin shih-nien chiao-yü lun-wen so-yin* 近十年教育論文索引 (An Index to Periodical Literature on Education, 1946–56). Taipei: Chung-hua wen-hua ch'u-pan shih-yeh wei-yüan hui 中華文化出版事業委員會, 1957. 347p.

An index to literature on education in sixteen educational and four general periodicals published in Taiwan from 1946 to 1956, with the exception of one, *Chiao-yü t'ung-hsün* 教育通訊 (Education Bulletin), which was published in 1946 in Nanking. The 4,086 entries are arranged under special topics such as 'Higher Education', 'Mass Education', 'Comparative Education', etc., and under each topic by subject. Each entry is given in the following order: title, author or translator, name of periodical, volume number, and date. Appended is an author index arranged by stroke count.

A comprehensive index for the period covered.

For a continuation of this index, see Taiwan Provincial Normal University Library, comp. 臺灣省立師範大學圖書館 *Chin wu-nien chiao-yü lun-wen so-yin* 近五年教育論文索引 (An Index to Periodical Literature on Education, 1957–1961), 1963, 86p., containing 3,800 articles which appeared in journals (a list of indexed journals is appended); and *Chiao-yü lun-wen so-yin, 1962* (150p.) also published in 1963.

100 Tung-pei jen-min cheng-fu, Chiao-yü pu, Tzu-liao shih 東北人民政府教育部資料室 (Northeast People's Government, Department of Education, Reference Materials Section). *I-chiu-wu-i nien wu-yüeh chih pa-yüeh pao-chih chi-k'an chiao-yü tzu-liao so-yin* 一九五一年五月至八月報紙期刊教育資料索引 (Education Index, May–August, 1951). Mukden: Tung-pei chiao-yü she 東北教育社, 1951. 59p.

An index to articles on education in Communist China which appeared in fifteen daily newspapers and fifty-one periodicals between May and August 1951. Arranged by subject, the period covered is short; but the index is extremely useful in the study of the initial stage of Chinese Communist educational policy.

101 Taga, Akigorō 多賀秋五郎 **and Yazawa, Toshihiko** 矢澤利彦. *Chūgoku bunka shi Nihongo bunken mokuroku—kyōiku, kirisutokyō* 中國文化史日本語文獻目錄——教育キリスト教
(Bibliography of Japanese-Language Materials on Chinese Cultural History—Education, Christianity). Tokyo: Kindai Chūgoku Kenkyū Iinkai 近代中國研究委員會, 1955. 84p.

Contains two bibliographies of books and articles on education and Christianity in China published in Japan from the 1890's to 1955. Translations into Japanese are included. The first part, on education, contains some 1,000 items classified into thirty-eight categories (history of education, intellectual history, educational system, textbooks, student movement, etc.). The second part contains 270 items arranged in six topical and chronological categories: bibliographies, general histories, the period from 1844 to 1948, the contemporary period, etc. Mimeographed.

Contains very few references to post-1949 developments.

102 Shapiro, Seymour, comp.
Brainwashing: A Partial Bibliography. Washington, D.C.: The American University, Special Operations Research Office, 1958. 18p. (The Library, Bibliographical Section, Special Bibliography No. 1).

Lists forty-five books and pamphlets and 264 periodical articles on 'brainwashing' in general, and the indoctrination of prisoners of war during the Korean War in particular. In the books and pamphlets section are listed such basic works on the subject as Pavlov's *Conditioned Reflexes and Psychiatry* and R. A. Bauer's *The New Man in Soviet Psychology.* Articles are taken from academic and popular journals (as well as government documents), such as the *American Journal of Psychiatry, Journal of Social Issues, Journal of Experimental Psychology, Canadian Journal of Psychology, Life, Time, U.S. News and World Report,* and the *Department of State Bulletin.* Works listed are all in English except for two which are in French. Full bibliographical information is provided but without annotations.

For additional sources on the subject, consult the bibliographies given in Robert J. Lifton's *Thought Reform and the Psychology of Totalism* (New York, 1960) and Edgar H. Schein's *Coercive Persuasion* (New York, 1961).

5. LAW

While comprehensive bibliographies of books and articles on Nationalist law are described below (see **106a** and **106b**), there are no available bibliographies of Chinese-language sources on Chinese Communist law. All four bibliographies concerned with Mainland law in this section deal with translations and non-Chinese materials.

Indexes to laws are listed in Chapter III. Compendia of laws, statutes, etc., are covered in Chapter XII. The reader should consult also the legal periodicals such as *Cheng-fa yen-chiu* 政法研究 (Studies in Government and Law; see **854**); *Fa-lü* *p'ing-lun* 法律評論 (The Law Review; see **961**); etc., described in Part Four, as well as the German periodical *Osteuropa-Recht* (East European Law), which sometimes carries bibliographies on Chinese Communist law (e.g., Vol. 6, No. 4, and Vol. 4, No. 2).

103 Rickett, W. Allyn, comp.
'Selected Bibliography of Legal Thought and Institutions of Modern China' in *Legal Thought and Institutions of the People's Republic of China: Selected Documents (Preliminary Draft)*, (Philadelphia, Pa., 1963), pp. 352–362.

Contains more than 125 English articles on, and translations of, Chinese Nationalist and Communist law (mostly the latter). In three parts: (1) the Republican period, 1912–1949; (2) People's China, 1949–1962; and (3) a selected list of Joint Publications Research Service reports dealing with Chinese Communist law. In the first two parts, bibliographies are generally listed first, followed by translations of documents and articles. The third part lists J.P.R.S. translations in the following order: laws and regulations, official reports, and general articles. Mimeographed.
The most comprehensive compilation of its kind.

104 Bodde, Derk and Clark, Anne B.
Chinese Law: A Selected Bibliography, with a Bibliography of the Communist Period. Cambridge, Mass.: Harvard University, East Asian Research Center, 1961. 8p.

Part 1 consists of two sections: (1) bibliography—general; (2) monographs and periodical articles (containing thirty-four titles in English, French, and German, covering the period from ancient times to 1949). Part 2 is given over to the Communist period from 1949 to the present, and is arranged under (1) documents, (2) monographs, and (3) periodical literature. All titles listed in this part are in English, with annotations. The documents section lists the 'Constitution', 'Organic Laws', 'Marriage Law', etc. The section on periodical literature provides citations to translations in J.P.R.S. and articles on the Chinese Communist legal system which appeared in the *China News Analysis*.

105 'Japanisches Schrifttum zum Recht der Volksdemokratien Asiens'
(Japanese Literature on the Law of Asian People's Democracies), *Osteuropa-Recht* (East European Law), Vol. 6, No. 4 (December 1960), pp. 303–305.

Fifty Japanese-language books and articles on Chinese Communist law published from 1946 through 1957 are listed in topical categories (philosophy of law, history of law, civil law, criminal law, etc.). Each entry provides a full bibliographical citation including the title in English translation, but not in the original Japanese. This compilation is based on the bibliography of Japanese literature on law in *Japan Science Review*, No. 2, 1951 to No. 10, 1959. For a continuation see next entry.

106   Uchida, Hisashi. 'Japanisches Schrifttum zum Recht der Ostblockstaaten' (Japanese Literature on the Law of the Communist Bloc), *Osteuropa-Recht* (East European Law), Vol. 9, No. 3 (September 1963), pp. 239–264.

A continuation of the preceding entry covering the period 1958–1962. Contains some sixty books and articles on Chinese Communist law (translations, book reviews, and non-academic essays have been omitted). The arrangement follows that of the preceding entry. The entries provide full bibliographical citations which include Chinese characters for the author and titles of books and periodicals, romanization and translation.

See also Hirano, Katsuaki 平野克明, 'Sengo ni okeru Chūgoku hō kankei bunken mokuroku' 戰後における中國法關係文獻目錄 (A Bibliography of Postwar Publications on Chinese Law), *Hōgaku shirin* 法學志林 ([Hosei University] Review of Law and Political Science), Vol. 58, No. 3/4 (February 1961), pp. 178–199.

106a   Wang, Tse-yen 王澤延, **comp.** 'T'ai-wan hsin-yin fa-lü shu-mu' 台灣新印 法律書目
'A Catalog of Law Books Printed in Taiwan', *The Monthly List of Chinese Books*, Vol. 3, No. 7 (July 1962), pp. 1–28.

Contains some 500 books in the field of law, largely in Chinese, published in Taiwan from 1949 to 1961. Arranged by title under broad categories: jurisprudence, constitution, civil code, criminal procedure, etc. (English-language books are listed by author). *Supplement I*, covering 1962–1963, as well as additions for the previous period, appeared in the same *Monthly List*,Vol. 4, No. 7/8 (July–August 1963), pp. 13–19.

For periodical literature on Nationalist law, see next entry.

106b   Yüan, K'un-hsiang 袁坤祥, **comp.** *Fa-lü lun-wen fen-lei so-yin* 法律論文分類 索引
Classified Index to Legal Literature From Current Chinese Periodicals. Taipei: Soochow University, 1963. 504p.

Covers more than 6,300 articles on law selected from eighty-three Taiwan and six Hong Kong periodicals published between January 1947 and December 1962. The *Index* is arranged under ninety-four topical headings with subsections. Under each section the title of the article is followed by the name of the author or translator, name of the periodical in which the article appears, volume number, page number, date of publication, and remarks. There is an author index arranged by stroke count.

None of the articles deals with the legal system of Communist China, but for coverage of writings on Chinese Nationalist law, this is a most useful and comprehensive bibliography and the only one available for the period covered. A second volume is reportedly under preparation.

6. ECONOMIC AND SOCIAL DEVELOPMENTS

The forced pace of Communist China's economic growth that has absorbed so much of the energy of its people, and the social change attendant upon 'socialist reconstruction', has perhaps been subjected to more intensive study in the West and in Japan than any other Mainland internal development. That there is an abundance of source material on the subject is clear from the two bibliographies (the first two entries) compiled respectively by the National Library of Peking and by Dr. Nai-ruenn Chen of the University of California at Berkeley. The first contains over 30,000 books and articles, and the second lists approximately 14,000 books and articles. Although many of the items listed in the Peking bibliography (including the bibliography itself) are unavailable outside the Mainland, Dr. Chen's work does go a long way toward filling this gap and also provides the most recent information.

In addition, there are a number of other works, notably Professor Ichiko's bibliography (**109**), the compilations of Chao Kuo-chün (**110–112**), and the two prepared in Taiwan in connection with the 'Three Red Flags' movement (**113** and **114**), which also provide access to a substantial body of available literature. Of these, Professor Ichiko's bibliography, containing descriptive annotations, is at once the most recent and the most comprehensive. Reference should also be made to the Index to Literature on Geography, published by the Chinese Academy of Sciences in Peking (**115**), which covers newspaper and periodical literature on economic geography for the period 1953–1956, inclusive. A number of bibliographies dealing with the land problem, population, and economic statistics round out the Mainland portion of this section. For bibliographical data on the communes, see the next section in this chapter.

In many ways, Taiwan's economic progress—especially in the area of land reform— has been remarkable, though it has not attracted the attention it merits. The most comprehensive guide to economic literature on Taiwan is the quarterly index published by the Bank of Taiwan (**123**).

The contents of this section, in conjunction with the general bibliographical guides discussed at the beginning of the chapter, are essential to a command of the literature. Reference should also be made to Chapters IV and V, dealing with yearbooks and statistics respectively, and to Chapter X, in which dictionaries (economic, foreign trade, finance) are described. Chapter XIV, containing economic and social documentation, is also of relevance here.

The reader should consult the pertinent newspapers and periodicals in Part Four, such as *Ta-kung pao*, *Ching-chi yen-chiu* (Economic Studies), *Chi-hua yü t'ung-chi* (Planning and Statistics), *Ts'ai-cheng* (Finance), *Chung-kuo kung-yeh* (Chinese Industry) for the Mainland; and *Cheng-hsin hsin-wen pao* (Financial and Economic News), *Chung-kuo ching-chi—The China Economist*, *T'ai-wan yin-hang chi-k'an* (Bank of Taiwan Quarterly), *Kung-shang yüeh-k'an* (The Industry and Commerce Monthly), and *Industry of Free China* for Taiwan.

Materials available in English translation are listed in Chapter XX, notably the publications of the Hong Kong American Consulate General, the Taipei U.S.I.S., (**1074**), the Union Research Service (**1065**), and the reports of the J.P.R.S., among them *Translations from Ta-kung pao* (**841**), and *Economic Information on Communist China* (**1059**).

107 Pei-ching t'u-shu kuan 北京圖書館 (National Library of Peking). *Shih-nien lai wo-kuo she-hui chu-i ching-chi chien-she ch'eng-chiu tzu-liao mu-lu (ch'u-kao)* 十年來我國社會主義經濟建設成就資料目錄 (初稿)
(A Draft Bibliography of Publications on the Achievements of Socialist Economic Construction of Our Country During the Last Ten Years). Peking, 1959. 3 vols. 2,361p.

Contains more than 31,700 items covering books published to June 1959 and periodical and newspaper articles published to December 1958. Divided into five major categories: (1) general, (2) finance and trade, (3) communications and transportation, (4) industrial development, and (5) agricultural development. Mimeographed. The volumes were not available for examination.

108 Chen, Nai-ruenn, comp.
The Economy of Mainland China, 1949–1963: A Bibliography of Materials in English. Berkeley, Calif.: Social Science Research Council, Committee on the Economy of China, 1963. 27;297p.

Contains approximately 14,000 entries of translations of Chinese Communist publications in the Chinese language (mostly articles), as well as books and articles on the Chinese Communist economy published in English both in and outside Mainland China, covering the period from 1949 through July 1963. In two parts. Part 1 lists the primary sources originating in Communist China. These are classified into three categories: (1) official documents, including laws and regulations, government and party decisions and resolutions, and communiqués; (2) reports, speeches, and other statements made by government and party officials; and (3) semi-official and non-official publications, including editorials, articles, and news reports. Part 2 is restricted to secondary sources published outside the Chinese Mainland, including scholarly works, analyses, and reports. Both parts are minutely subdivided under topical headings shown in the table of contents, the latter serving also as the index to the bibliography. Full bibliographical information is given for each item, but without annotation. Part 1 accounts for about 85 per cent (256 pages) of the volume; Part 2 takes up the balance (41 pages). The major sources of the translations are the translation series published by the American Consulate General in Hong Kong, Joint Publications Research Service reports, *Union Research Service, People's China, Peking Review, China Reconstructs*, etc.

This is the most comprehensive bibliography on the Chinese Communist economy available in any language.

109 Ichiko, Chūzō 市古宙三, **ed.** *Gendai Chūgoku no keizai* 現代中國の經濟
(The Economy of Contemporary China). Tokyo: Ajia Keizai Kenkyūjo アジア 經濟研究所, 1962. 310p. (Bibliographical Series 3).

An annotated bibliography of 364 Chinese-language books largely on the economy of Communist China, limited to Chinese Communist publications issued on the Mainland and in Hong Kong. The bibliography is compiled from the holdings of the Tōyō Bunko with some titles drawn from other research libraries in Tokyo.

Of the thirteen chapters, the first is devoted to the period between the Opium War and 1949 (78 items), while the remaining twelve deal with the post-1949 period under the following headings: (1) general, (2) economic theory, (3) economic conditions, (4) economic policy, (5) five-year plans, (6) agriculture and fishery, (7) people's communes, (8) industry, (9) commerce, (10) money, banking and prices, (11) public finance, and (12) labor and social problems. Each chapter contains a short introductory note, followed by bibliographical entries arranged according to date of publication (each entry includes a full citation together with the Tōyō Bunko shelf list number, if the book is available in that library). Annotations are descriptive and vary in length. The length of the annotation, however, does not necessarily indicate the relative importance of the entry in question. In the case of symposia, the annotations list the individual titles contained in the volumes.

The volume contains a title index, two author indexes (one for individual authors, the other for corporate authors), all arranged according to the Japanese syllabary.

Professor Ichiko, one of the organizers of the Seminar on Modern China at the Tōyō Bunko, is one of Japan's foremost experts on modern Chinese bibliography. This bibliography was prepared for the government-sponsored Institute of Asian Economic Affairs.

An indispensable reference.

110 **Chao, Kuo-chün** 趙國鈞, **comp.**
Source Materials from Communist China. Cambridge, Mass.: Harvard University, Russian Research Center, 1952. 3 vols. 41; 64; 96p.

A three-volume bibliography of Chinese Communist documents on *Agrarian Policy* (Vol. 1—193 items), *Aspects of Economic Planning* (Vol. 2—177 items), and *Fiscal, Monetary and International Economic Policies* (Vol. 3—147 items). The entries are mostly taken from newspapers and periodicals. In each volume the arrangement is by subject, with excerpts, summaries and critical notes for the more important items, followed by a list of items of secondary importance with annotations of varying length. Mimeographed.

The most comprehensive guide to available Chinese Communist publications on the subject to 1952. See also the expanded versions listed below.

111 **Chao, Kuo-chün, comp.**
Agrarian Policies of Mainland China: A Documentary Study (1949-1956). Cambridge, Mass.: Harvard University Press, 1957. 13; 276p.

A collection of translated articles and excerpts from post-1949 Chinese Communist publications on Communist China's agrarian policies arranged by subject. An expanded version of the compiler's *Agrarian Policy* (see above), the present volume includes introductory notes to each section, and a glossary and index to documents (see also next entry).

112   Chao, Kuo-chün 趙國鈞, **comp.**
Economic Planning and Organization in Mainland China: A Documentary Study (1949–1957). Cambridge, Mass.: Harvard University Press, 1959–1960. 2 vols.

A continuation of the preceding entry with a similar format, and an expanded version of *Aspects of Economic Planning* and *Fiscal, Monetary and International Policies of the Chinese Communist Government* (see **110**). Together the two form a series of indispensable guides to documentary sources for the study of Communist China's agrarian policies and economic planning to 1957.

113   Kuo-fang yen-chiu yüan, T'u-shu kuan 國防研究院 圖書館 (National War College, Library). *Kung-fei 'san-mien hung-ch'i' ts'an-k'ao tzu-liao so-yin* 共匪 [三面紅旗] 參考資料索引
(A Bibliography of Reference Materials on Communist Bandits' 'Three Red Flags' Program). Yangmingshan, 1960. [90p.]

A bibliography in three parts on Communist China's 'Three Red Flags' program of 'Socialist Reconstruction', 'The Great Leap Forward', and the 'People's Communes'. The volume contains an appendix on the people's militia compiled from both Chinese Communist and non-Communist books, pamphlets, periodical and newspaper articles published from June 1957 to August 1960, in the library of the National War College in Taiwan. Within each part, books and pamphlets are listed first, followed by periodical and newspaper articles.
An important reference work on the subject for the period covered. For more current listings of similar materials, see the *Chinese Periodicals Index*, also published by the National War College Library (**193**). Mimeographed. Limited distribution.

114   Kuo-chi kuan-hsi yen-chiu hui 國際關係研究會 (Institute of International Relations of the Republic of China). *Ti-ch'ing yen-chiu ts'an-k'ao tzu-liao so-yin* 敵情研究參考資料索引
(Index to Materials for the Study of Bandit Information). Taipei, 1960. 102p.

An index to important articles and news reports on the 'Three Red Flags' movement which appeared in the *Ta-kung pao* and *Kuang-ming jih-pao* between January 1958 and October 1959. In four parts: 'General Line,' 'The Great Leap Forward', 'People's Commune', and 'Militia'. Grouped under the following headings: general economy, industry, agriculture, communications and transportation, and commerce. Each entry supplies title, author, name of newspaper, and date. Most of the articles indexed are those on the 'Great Leap Forward'. Limited distribution.

115 Chung-kuo k'o-hsüeh yüan, Ti-li yen-chiu so 中國科學院地理研究所 (Chinese Academy of Sciences, Institute of Geography). *Kuo-nei pao-k'an yu-kuan ti-li tzu-liao so-yin, 1953–1956* 國內報刊有關地理資料索引, 1953–1956 (Index to Literature on Geography in Chinese Newspapers and Periodicals, 1953–1956). Peking: K'o-hsüeh ch'u-pan she 科學出版社, 1954–1958. 4 vols.

An index to newspaper and periodical articles on the economic geography of China and related fields (e.g., commerce, industry, agriculture, irrigation, forestry, transportation, communications, etc.). Especially useful for information on economic development at the provincial level. An average of fifty periodicals and thirty newspapers (mostly provincial publications) are indexed each year for the four-year period 1953–1956.

An important index containing more articles on the subject than the Index to Major Newspapers and Periodicals (**184**).

116 Langdon, Arthur H., comp.
Bibliography—Economic Development of Communist China. [New York, n.d.] 80p.

A bibliography on the economic development of Communist China containing fifteen English-language books and over 500 articles, largely from the *Far Eastern Economic Review* (Vol. 6, 1949 through Vol. 14, No. 26, 1953) and *People's China* (Vol. 1, 1950 to December 1954). All of the books and some of the more important articles are annotated. In five parts: general, agriculture, industry and mining, trade and finance, and transportation. The first part contains all of the books and a periodicals section which is further subdivided into (1) miscellaneous periodicals, (2) *Far Eastern Economic Review*, and (3) *People's China*. The remaining four parts contain only periodical articles, arranged as in Part 1. Within each category the articles are listed alphabetically by year of publication. Typewritten.

The bibliography was prepared in Professor Franklin L. Ho's seminar at the East Asian Institute, Columbia University.

117 Kanamaru, Kazuo 金丸一夫. 'Chūgoku keizai gakkai ni okeru keizai hōsoku ni kansuru rombun chosaku mokuroku—ji 1949 nen itaru 1958 nen 8 gatsu' 中國經濟學界における經濟法則に關する論文, 著作目錄——自 1949 年至 1958 年 8 月
'The Catalogue of Theses and Books Concerning the Law of Economy of New China's Political Economists—1949–August 1958', *Aichi Daigaku Kokusai Mondai Kenkyūjo kiyō* 愛知大學國際問題研究所紀要 *The Memoirs of [the] Institute of International Affairs, Aichi University*, No. 26 (1958), pp. 113–123.

A list of 244 books and articles by Chinese authors on economic theory, arranged by year of publication and further subdivided by topic, with full bibliographical information but no annotation. The bibliography is preceded by descriptions of the six Mainland journals in which most of the articles appeared.

118 **Chūgoku Tochi Seido Shi Kenkyūkai** 中國土地制度史研究會 (Society for the Study of the Chinese Land System). *Tochi mondai o chūshin to seru Chūgoku keizai shi kenkyū bunken mokuroku* 土地問題を中心とせる中國經濟史研究文獻目錄 (Bibliography of Materials on Chinese Economic History With Special Reference to the Land Problem). Tokyo, 1954. 116p.

A bibliography of Chinese, Japanese, and Western-language materials on modern Chinese economic history (from the end of the nineteenth century to 1954). Mimeographed.

119 **U.S. Department of Commerce, Bureau of Census.** *The Population and Manpower of China: An Annotated Bibliography.* Washington, D.C.: U.S. Government Printing Office, 1958. 132p.

Contains more than 600 books, articles, official reports, etc., pertaining mainly to the population and manpower of present-day China, and compiled primarily from holdings of the Library of Congress. About two-fifths of all entries are in English; another third are in Chinese; about one-fifth are in Japanese, and the remainder are in Russian, French, German, Dutch, and Hungarian. Arranged topically under the following headings: (1) general works, (2) population size and dynamics, (3) population distribution, (4) population characteristics, (5) labor force, (6) community studies and (7) reference works. Glossary and index of authors. As a rule, the Library of Congress call number is provided when available. The Chinese characters are given for titles of works in Chinese in addition to their romanization and English translation. The Chinese characters are also given in the 'Index of Authors' for names of Chinese authors who have published in Chinese.

An important bibliography.

120 **Aird, John S.**
The Size, Composition, and Growth of the Population of Mainland China. Washington, D.C.: U. S. Government Printing Office, 1961. 100p. (International Population Statistics Reports, Series P-90, No. 15).

A summary of data available as of January 1961. The volume contains a comprehensive bibliography of some 150 Chinese Communist newspaper and periodical articles, a number of which are annotated in the preceding entry.

121 **Li, Choh-ming.**
The Statistical System of Communist China. Berkeley and Los Angeles, Calif.: University of California Press, 1962. 174p.

Contains a comprehensive bibliography on the subject (pp. 151–161), including some 150 Chinese Communist policy statements published in newspapers and periodicals. Arranged under the following categories: books; communiqués; editorials; signed articles, statements and directives; and unsigned articles, statements, and dispatches.

122 Yuan, Tung-li, comp.
Economic and Social Development of Modern China: A Bibliographical Guide.
New Haven, Conn.: Human Relations Area Files, 1956. 130; 87p.

Lists monographs and pamphlets published in English, French and German on the economic and social development of modern China from 1900 through 1955, including a number of Portuguese works on Macao. Periodical articles are excluded. In two parts: (1) economic development, and (2) social development. Each part carries a separate alphabetical index to individual authors. Titles published since 1921 have been incorporated in the author's *China in Western Literature* (see **16**).

* * *

123 T'ai-wan yin-hang, Ching-chi yen-chiu shih 臺灣銀行 經濟研究室 (Bank of Taiwan, Office of Economic Research). *'T'ai-wan ching-chi wen-hsien fen-lei so-yin'* 臺灣經濟文獻分類索引
(A Topical Index to Economic Literature Concerning Taiwan) in *T'ai-wan yin-hang chi-k'an* 臺灣銀行季刊 (Bank of Taiwan Quarterly), Taipei, Vol. 2—, September 1948—.

A regular feature published in the *T'ai-wan yin-hang chi-k'an* since September 1948. Indexes economic literature concerning Taiwan published in Taiwan newspapers and periodicals under the following topical headings: general, finance, economy, prices, industry and mining, agriculture and forestry, transportation and communications, electric power, commerce, sugar industry, foodstuffs, cooperatives, land, statistics, and miscellaneous. Entries are accompanied by a full bibliographical citation.

An indispensable reference work, the most comprehensive on the subject.

124 Ch'en, Cheng-hsiang 陳正祥, **comp.** *T'ai-wan ching-chi ti-li wen-hsien so-yin* 臺灣經濟地理文獻索引
(Index to Literature on the Economic Geography of Taiwan). Taipei: T'ai-wan yin-hang 臺灣銀行, 1954. 113p.

Contains titles of works in Chinese, Japanese and Western languages published from 1931 to June 1952. The material is arranged chronologically by date of of publication under the following categories: (1) geography, (2) meteorology, (3) geology, (4) soil and plants, (5) population and demography, (6) water conservation and land utilization, (7) agriculture, (8) sugar industry, (9) forest and forestry, (10) cattle industry and marine products, (11) industry and mineral resources, (12) communications and commerce, (13) general statistics and reports, (14) local statistics, and (15) miscellaneous.

Comprehensive coverage, useful especially for Japanese-language publications.

7. COMMUNES

The radical departure in the economic development of Communist China marked
by the inauguration of the people's communes has given rise to a flood of books,
pamphlets, reports, and newspaper and periodical articles published on the Mainland
and abroad. Among the many observers, the Japanese have shown a particular interest
and have, as a result, compiled the most comprehensive guides for the control of the
mass of information on the subject. Of these, the most complete coverage of books
and pamphlets in Chinese, Japanese and English is provided by the catalog prepared
by Professor Noma (**125**). Chinese-language articles on the initial phase of the
development of this institution are listed in **126**. The best available source for Japanese-
language materials on the subject is the bibliography in *Ajia keizai jumpō* (**128**).

Reference should be made to the general bibliographies on the contemporary Chinese
economy by Professor Ichiko (**109**) and Dr. Chen (**108**), the Mainland national bibliographies (**8** and **9**), the index to major Mainland newspapers and periodicals (**184**),
the indexes to Mainland newspapers (Chapter XVII), the indexes to materials on the
'Three Red Flags' compiled by the National War College Library and by the Institute
of International Relations in Taipei (**113** and **114**), and finally the section on communes
in the documentary chapter on economic and social developments (Chapter XIV).

125 **Noma, Kiyoshi** 野間清. 'Chūgoku jimmin kōsha kankei no tosho shōsasshi
mokuroku' 中國人民公社關係の圖書小冊子目錄
'The Catalogue of the Books and Pamphlets on Chinese People's Communes',
Kokusai Mondai Kenkyūjo kiyō 國際問題研究所紀要 *The Memoirs of* [*the*]
Institute of International Affairs, Aichi University, Tōyōhashi, Aichi Prefecture,
No. 32 (February 1962), pp. 95–115.

A bibliography of some 140 books and pamphlets on the people's communes
published on the Mainland, and in Hong Kong, Taiwan, India and the West.
Of the entries, 109 are Chinese-language publications, 24 are in Japanese and
10 in English. Most entries contain a contents note (but no annotation) and
include location symbols for the major Japanese libraries and private collections.

A continuation of this bibliography covering periodical literature as well as
additional books is to be published in the same periodical at a later date and
should provide the most comprehensive coverage of literature on the communes
in all languages. The compiler, Professor Noma of Aichi University, was a
long-time resident in prewar China.

126 **Chūgoku Kenkyūjo** 中國研究所 (China Research Institute). 'Jimmin kōsha ni
kansuru shiryō mokuroku' 人民公社にかんする資料目錄
(A Bibliography of Materials on the People's Communes) in *Chūgoku shakaishugi no kenkyū* 中國社會主義の研究 (Studies in Chinese Socialism), (Tokyo:
Gōdō Shuppansha 合同出版社), 1959, pp. 1–8.

A list of some 150 newspaper and periodical articles on the people's communes,
largely selected from *Kuan-yü wo-kuo jen-min kung-she ti t'u-shu pao-k'an*

tzu-liao so-yin 關於我國人民公社的圖書報刊資料索引 (Index to Books, and Newspaper and Periodical Articles on the People's Communes, No. 1, Library of the Economic Research Institute of the Chinese Academy of Sciences), covering materials from August 1, 1958 to November 14, 1958. Arranged under twelve categories (some with sub-categories), including resolutions and directives, the process of 'communization', organziation and management, industry and transportation, urban communes, etc. Entries provide the title (in Japanese translation), author, source and date or volume number.

See also next entry.

127 **Chūgoku Kenkyūjo** 中國研究所 (China Research Institute). 'Jimmin kōsha ni kansuru tosho mokuroku' 人民公社にかんする圖書目錄 (A Bibliography of Books on the People's Communes) in *Chūgoku shakaishugi no kenkyū* 中國社會主義の研究 (Studies in Chinese Socialism), (Tokyo: Gōdō Shuppansha 合同出版社), 1959, pp. 8–15.

A list of some ninety Chinese-language books and pamphlets on the people's communes, largely selected from the same source used in the preceding entry. Entries provide the title, author, publisher, date of publication and pagination. Pages 13 and 14 contain a list of some twenty-five European and American references on the subject (mostly articles in English plus a few in French, Russian and Polish), arranged by country of publication. Eight Japanese-language books and pamphlets (including translations from the Chinese) on the people's communes are listed on pp. 14–15.

These two lists will be superseded by Professor Noma's compilations cited above (**125**).

128 **'Jimmin kōsha shiryō sakuin'** 人民公社資料索引 (Index to Materials on the People's Communes), *Ajia keizai jumpō* アジア經濟旬報 (Ten-Day Report on Asian Economy), Tokyo, No. 500 (April 1962), pp. 51–63.

A bibliography of 230 articles published in Japan on the people's communes, based on *Zasshi kiji sakuin* 雜誌記事索引 (*Japanese Periodicals Index*, Humanities and Social Science Division) Vol. 11, No. 4 to Vol. 14, No. 1 (September 1958—March 1961) published by the National Diet Library. Arranged under twenty-two categories: general—57 entries; the process of 'communization'; leadership of the Chinese Communist Party; system of ownership; agriculture—35 entries; industry; labor force; management; commerce; living conditions; transition to Communism; comparison with the Soviet Union; ideology; education; women; literature; resolutions; urban communes; personal accounts—35 entries; etc. Within each category, arrangement is generally chronological, following the appearance of the article in the *Japanese Periodicals Index*. Author, title, name of periodical, volume and number are provided. Pagination is omitted.

The most comprehensive listing of Japanese-language articles on the subject available.

129 'Jimmin kōsha kankei shiryō' 人民公社關係資料
(Materials on the People's Communes), *Daian* 大安, Tokyo, Vol. 8, No. 6
(July 1962), pp. 13–16.

A list of roughly 100 articles on the people's communes which appeared in
the Japanese-language journal *Jimmin Chūgoku* 人民中國 (People's China)
published in Peking, from the July issue of 1958 through the May issue of 1962.
Arranged according to eleven categories: historical background; communes—
general; agriculture; natural calamities; etc. Title, author, issue number and
pagination are given.

8. MILITARY

Sources on the history and development of the 'People's Liberation Army' are scarce,
scattered, and not easily located. The best sources of current information, *Chieh-fang
chün-pao* 解放軍報 (Liberation Army News; see **861**), *Chieh-fang chün chan-shih*
解放軍戰士 (The Liberation Army Warriors), *Chieh-fang chün hua-pao* 解放軍畫報
(Liberation Army Pictorial, **860**), *Kung-tso t'ung-hsün* 工作通訊 (Bulletin of Activities,
895), and *Chün-hsün tsa-chih* 軍訓雜誌 (Military Training Magazine), are mostly not
available outside the Mainland.

The meager offerings in this section are supplemented to some extent by materials
on the armed forces found in Chapters VI and VII, and the translated documentation
in Chapter XX.

The Chinese military as a subject, for one reason or another, has not received much
attention from bibliographers, although an annotated bibliography to be entitled *The
Chinese Red Army, 1927–1963* is under preparation at the East Asian Research Center
of Harvard University by Edward J. M. Rhoads. The compilation on the Peoples'
Liberation Army (first entry) is the only comprehensive subject bibliography available,
but unhappily, considering the temporal scope of the present volume, its emphasis
is on the period 1937–1949.

The last entry (**134**), is a catalog of general works on military science published in
Taiwan, including a number of titles on the strategy and tactics of the Communist
army on the Mainland. There is no bibliography on the Nationalist army comparable
to the first entry above. It should be noted, however, that some current information
on Taiwan military affairs can be obtained from the Chinese and English editions of
the *China Yearbook* (**239, 240**) and to a lesser degree from such journals as *Chung-kuo
ti k'ung-chün* 中國的空軍 *Chinese Air Force* (**958**), and *Chung-kuo hai-chün* 中國海軍
Chinese Navy (**953**), listed in Chapter XVIII.

Although not entirely relevant, mention might be made of the dictionaries of
military terms in Chapter X below.

130 Pei-ching t'u-shu kuan 北京圖書館 (National Library of Peking). *Kuan-ts'ang
yu-kuan Chung-kuo jen-min chieh-fang chün shu-mu* 館藏有關中國人民解放軍書目
(A Bibliography of the People's Liberation Army: Books in the National Library
of Peking). Peking: Pei-ching t'u-shu kuan, 1958. 2 vols. 58; 95p.

A bibliography of more than 1,500 books (excluding periodical articles) in the National Library of Peking, published on the People's Liberation Army from 1938 to 1958. Vol. 1 classifies books under the following seven topics: (1) 'Development, Strategy, Tactics'; (2) 'Political Work in the Army', (3) 'History of the Liberation Army and Campaigns'; (4) 'Essays on Current Campaigns'; (5) 'Heroic Deeds'; (6) 'Personal Narratives'; and (7) 'People's Militia'. Vol. 2 is devoted to the listing of literary works on the People's Liberation Army. Mimeographed.

The only available bibliography of Chinese-language materials on the subject. The emphasis is on the period 1937 to 1949. Primary sources on the pre-1937 period are entirely lacking, although some secondary sources are listed.

131 Hanrahan, Gene Z.
An Exploratory Critical Bibliography on the Chinese Red Army (1927–1945), A Tentative Report on Source Material in the English and Chinese Languages. New York, 1952. 22p.

An annotated bibliography of 148 books and periodical articles on the organization, development, strategy, and tactics of the Chinese Red Army, 1927–1945, arranged by language (48 English and 100 Chinese). Under each language division, works are listed alphabetically by author. The compilation is not exhaustive, but it does contain non-Communist sources and some Chinese titles not included in the preceding entry.

132 Hanrahan, Gene Z., comp.
The Chinese Communist Guerrilla Movement—An Annotated Bibliography of Selected Chinese, Japanese and English Source Material Available at the Hoover Library, Stanford University. [n.p.], 1952. 13p.

Twenty-nine books, arranged under (1) general historical material, (2) campaigns and operations, (3) guerrilla strategy and tactical techniques, (4) guerrilla training and education, (5) the militia, (6) Manchuria guerrillas, (7) South China guerrillas, and (8) postwar guerrillas. Some titles are also included in the preceding entry. Mimeographed.

The bibliography is incomplete, and it also excludes periodical articles which are an important source.

133 Martynov, A. A. 'Literatura o narodno-osvoboditel'noi armii Kitaia' (Bibliography on the National Liberation Army of China) in *Slavnaia narodno-osvoboditel'naia armiia Kitaia* (The Glorious National Liberation Army of China), (Moscow: Voennoe izdatel'stvo Ministerstva Oborony Soiuza SSR, 1957), pp. 152–157.

A bibliography of over 100 Russian-language books and articles on the Chinese Communist army, some translations from the Chinese, others original Russian contributions. In two parts: political and military works, and belles-lettres. A translation of the bibliography appears as Appendix C in Department of the Army, *Communist China: Ruthless Enemy or Paper Tiger—A Bibliographic Survey*, pp. 117–121 (see **18**).

134 Kuo-fang yen-chiu yüan, T'u-shu kuan 國防研究院圖書館 (National War College, Library). *Chung-hua min-kuo ko chün-shih chi-kou hsüeh-hsiao tsai T'ai ch'u-pan chih chün-shih t'u-shu lien-ho mu-lu —ti-i chi* 中華民國各軍事機構學校在臺出版之軍事圖書聯合目錄——第一輯
Union Catalogue of Books on Military Field Published in Taiwan—First Series.
Yangmingshan, 1960. 50p.

Contains about 1,200 Chinese works on military science published in Taiwan prior to January 1960, incorporating some pre-1949 titles published on the Mainland. Chinese translations from Western-language works are included except for those made from American publications by the headquarters of the Chinese army, which have been published in a separate catalog. The arrangement of this list is by topic (military systems, tactics, weapons, etc.). A number of titles are on the strategy and tactics of the Chinese Communist army. The listing is by title with full bibliographical citations including location in Taipei government libraries.

A general catalog, not very useful for the study of the Nationalist Army.

9. OVERSEAS CHINESE

From the time they were organized by Sun Yat-sen in support of his anti-Manchu revolutionary movement toward the end of the nineteenth century, the Overseas Chinese have played a significant role in Chinese politics. Since 1949, their allegiance has been courted by both the Nationalists and the Communists, with both Taipei and Peking maintaining governmental and semi-governmental commissions and organizations concerned with Overseas Chinese affairs.

No Mainland bibliographies concerned specifically with the Overseas Chinese are available. Of the three titles in this section, the first two are indexes to both pre- and post-1949 Nationalist publications, while the third, compiled by Professor Uchida, contains a comprehensive list of works in all languages on the Overseas Chinese, based on the holdings of the Hoover Institution as of 1959. See also a bibliography on the subject in *Ch'iao-wu erh-shih-wu nien* 僑務二十五年 (Twenty-Five Years of Overseas Chinese Affairs, **707**).

For current information on Nationalist and Communist policies, statements, etc., on the subject, the reader is directed to two periodicals: *Chiao-wu yüeh-pao* 僑務月報 (Overseas Chinese Affairs Monthly, **946**), and *Chiao-wu pao* 僑務報 (Bulletin of Overseas Chinese Affairs, **859**), published in Taipei and Peking, respectively. Also of interest is the Overseas Chinese Economic Yearbook (**246**), as well as other yearbooks in Chapter IV.

135 **Chung-kuo ch'iao-cheng hsüeh-hui** 中國僑政學會 (Chinese Association of Overseas Chinese Affairs). *Hua-ch'iao wen-t'i tzu-liao mu-lu so-yin* 華僑問題資料目錄索引
(Index to Materials on the Overseas Chinese). Taipei: Hai-wai ch'u-pan she 海外出版社, 1956–57. 2 vols.

An index to books and newspaper and periodical articles on the Overseas Chinese, published mainly in Taiwan and Hong Kong since 1952, including some titles published on the Mainland during the late 1930's and the 1940's. Arranged by country of residence, followed by a 'General' section which is subdivided into several categories (political affairs, economic affairs, cultural affairs, social affairs, history and geography, Communist activities, and miscellaneous). Full bibliographical information is given for each entry, including location in Taipei libraries. An annotated bibliography of Taiwan publications on the subject is included in the second volume.

A comprehensive guide to non-Communist publications on the subject for the period covered.

136 **Kuo-fang yen-chiu yüan, T'u-shu kuan** 國防研究院圖書館 (National War College, Library). *Ch'iao-ch'ing tzu-liao so-yin* 僑情資料索引
(Index to Materials on the Overseas Chinese). Taipei, 1961. 118p.

Based on the Library's collection, the index is in two parts, the first part being devoted to books, the second to periodical and newspaper articles. Arranged under six broad catagories: general, policies governing Overseas Chinese affairs, education, economy, political parties, and history. Each entry gives title, author, publisher, and date. Parts 1 and 2 contain approximately 500 entries each. Appended is a catalog of similar materials in the library of the Overseas Chinese Affairs Commission. Mimeographed. Limited distribution.

137 **Uchida, Naosaku.**
The Overseas Chinese: A Bibliographical Essay Based on the Resources of the Hoover Institution. Stanford, Calif.: Hoover Institution on War, Revolution, and Peace, 1959. 134p.

In two parts: Part 1 is an essay on the structure and function of Overseas Chinese communities, including comments on the utilization of certain selected sources for further study of this question. Part 2 is a supplementary bibliography of 679 works on the Overseas Chinese in all languages (principally Chinese) available in the Hoover Institution, compiled by Eugene Wu in collaboration with Chün-tu Hsüeh. It includes most of the books and pamphlets listed in the preceding two entries. Chapters 1 and 5 ('Reference Works' and 'Communist China and the Overseas Chinese') are of particular interest.

Professor Uchida spent a number of years in teaching and research in China before and during the Second World War and is one of Japan's leading authorities on Overseas Chinese.

10. FOREIGN RELATIONS

Bibliographies on the foreign relations of Communist China are few in number, and on Chinese Nationalist foreign relations non-existent, although a great amount of primary source material—especially on or about the Mainland—is available for study (see Chapter XVI on foreign relations documentation). The bibliographies listed here are the few available, and are largely directed to such topics as Peking's relations with the Soviet Union, Japan, India, and the United States, the Korean War, etc.

See also **1487**.

138 U.S. Department of State, External Research Division.
Sino-Soviet Economic Relations, 1954–1959, A Selective Bibliography. Washington, D.C., 1960. 15p.

The bibliography lists 170 items in English and Russian on Sino-Soviet economic relations from 1954 to 1959. Alphabetically arranged by author (or title when no author is indicated) in two parts: books (42 entries) and periodical articles (128). A good compilation, though not exhaustive. Mimeographed.

139 Kapitsa, M. S. 'Spisok ispol'zovannoi literatury'
(A Bibliography of Consulted Works) in *Sovetsko-kitaiskie otnosheniia* (Soviet-Chinese Relations), (Moscow: Gosudarstvennoe izdatel'stvo politicheskoi literatury, 1958), pp. 413–421.

A bibliography of some 300 books, articles, periodicals and archival materials on Sino-Soviet relations in Russian, Chinese and English, including 70 items by leading Communist authorities (23 by Lenin, 18 by Mao Tse-tung, 10 by Stalin, etc.) which are of only general interest.

A bibliographical guide to books and articles on 'Chinese-Soviet Friendship' for the period October 1, 1949 through the end of 1957 was compiled jointly by the National Library of Peking and the State Library of Foreign Literature in Moscow. The manuscript was completed in October 1958 and was to have been published by the Jen-min ch'u-pan she in both Chinese and Russian (in four parts: general, economic aid and cooperation, scientific cooperation, and cultural ties). The deterioration of relations between the two countries may have prevented the publication of the guide.

140 Mayer, Peter.
'Bibliography' in *Sino-Soviet Relations Since the Death of Stalin* (Hong Kong: Union Research Institute, 1962), pp. B-1 to B-89. (Communist China Problem Research Series EC No. 27).

Lists some 1,750 English-language books, documents, pamphlets, and periodical and newspaper articles on the subject (including translations from Chinese and Russian). Arranged under primary and secondary sources, with further sub-categories.

141 **'Nihonjin no shin Chūgoku ryokōki'** 日本人の新中國旅行記
(Japanese Travel Accounts of New China), *Kindai Chūgoku Kenkyū Sentā ihō*
近代中國研究センター彙報 (Bulletin of the Center for the Study of Modern
China), No. 4 (April 1964), pp. 17–27.

An annotated bibliography of some sixty Japanese-language book-length
travel accounts by Japanese visitors to Communist China from 1952 to 1962.
The entries, with full bibliographical citations, are arranged by the date of visit
to the Mainland irrespective of the date of publication. The annotations provide
the date of the trip, meetings attended and places visited, the names of other
persons in the party, and the purpose of the visit.

Inasmuch as innumerable travel accounts appear in Japanese periodicals
(excluded from the present listing), this bibliography represents only a fraction
of the available documentation on an important subject.

142 **Tewari, B. C. and Phadnis, Urmila, comps.**
'India-China Border Areas' Dispute: A Selected Bibliography,' *India Quarterly*,
New Delhi, Vol. 16, No. 2, (April–June 1960), pp. 155–169.

A bibliography of some 250 English-language publications, the majority of
which are individual documents and articles.

In two parts: Part 1 comprises three sections: maps, collected documents,
and individual documents arranged by year (1958, 1959 and 1960). Part 2 lists
periodical articles according to year of publication, and, under year, alphabetically by author or by title if no author is indicated. Except for a few items from
the *Peking Review*, the bibliography is limited to Indian Government documents
and Indian and Western periodical articles.

See also S. Ansari, 'Chinese Aggression on India: Select Bibliography',
*International Studies, Quarterly Journal of the Indian School of International
Studies*, Vol. 5, Nos. 1–2 (July-October 1963), pp. 201–211, and the bibliography
section regularly appearing in *India Quarterly*.

143 **Kuo-chi wen-t'i i-ts'ung pien-chi pu** 國際問題譯叢編輯部 (Translation
Digest of International Affairs, Editorial Department). 'Kuan-yü Mei ti-kuo
chu-i ch'in-lüeh wo-kuo T'ai-wan wen-t'i wen-chien ho Jen-min jih-pao
she-lun so-yin' 關於美帝國主義侵略我國臺灣問題文件和人民日報社論索引
(Index to Documents and *Jen-min jih-pao* Editorials Concerning the Question
of American Imperialist Aggression Against Taiwan), *Kuo-chi wen-t'i i-ts'ung*,
No. 6 (September 22, 1958), pp. 46–49.

A bibliography consisting for the most part of Chinese Communist, American,
British and Russian official documents (proclamations, statements, speeches, etc.)
concerning the 'Formosa Question' published between December 1, 1943
(Cairo Declaration), and September 12, 1958. In two parts: documents and
editorials. The documents are arranged chronologically (without indication of
sources). The list of *Jen-min jih-pao* editorials is likewise arranged by date of

publication and covers all editorials on the subject published between March 16,
1949 and September 15, 1958. The editorials are also indexed in the *Jen-min
jih-pao she-lun so-yin* (**833**).

A conveniently arranged guide, especially useful for Chinese Communist
statements. Consult the section on the 'Taiwan Question' in Chapter XVI for
texts for these and other more current statements by both the Chinese Communist and Nationalist governments.

144 China (People's Republic of China, 1949—), Wen-hua pu, Wen-wu chü
中華人民共和國 文化部 文物局 (China [People's Republic of China, 1949—],
Ministry of Culture, Bureau of Cultural Relics). *K'ang-Mei yüan-Ch'ao tzu-liao
mu-lu* 抗美援朝資料目錄
(Reference Materials on the Resist-America Aid-Korea Campaign). Peking,
December 1950. 358p.

Compiled by the National Library of Peking for the Ministry of Culture, this
bibliography, published as a supplement to the *Wen-wu ts'an-k'ao tzu-liao*
文物參考資料 (Reference Materials on Cultural Relics), No. 11, lists 253 books,
together with articles from 54 periodicals and 30 newspapers published between
June 26 and December 10, 1950, on the Resist-America Aid-Korea campaign.
The bibliography is divided into three parts: books, periodical articles, and
newspaper articles. Each part contains the following five main topics: (1)
general, (2) American imperialist invasion and plot, (3) people's resistance,
(4) American imperialists are paper-tigers, (5) people's strength for defending
peace.

This is the most comprehensive bibliography of Chinese Communist publications on the first six months of the Korean War.

145 U.S. Department of the Army, Headquarters.
'Korean War, 1950–1953: A Bibliography' in *Communist China: Ruthless Enemy
or Paper Tiger? A Bibliographic Survey* (Washington, D.C., 1962), Appendix C,
pp. 125–135.

Based on the holdings of the Army Library, the bibliography consists of two
sections (1) a list of 110 English-language books and pamphlets (including
one in German); and (2) 211 periodical articles (including one each in German
and French). In each category the entries are arranged alphabetically by author,
or by title if no author is available. The periodical section is especially good for
articles on the Korean War published in the journals of the U.S. Armed Forces.
No annotations. See also the section on Korea in Part 2.

146 London, Imperial War Museum Library.
The War in Korea, 1950–1953, A List of Selected References. London,
[1961?]. 11p.

In two sections: books and pamphlets (122 titles), and periodical articles (143 titles). Each section is further divided into British Commonwealth publications and foreign publications, the majority of the latter being American works. Useful for locating periodical literature on the Korean War, particularly publications of the American and British armed forces. Mimeographed.

11. LIBRARY SCIENCE

It has already been said that impressive progress has been made on the Mainland since 1949 in library development and bibliographical work. The bibliography of over 2,000 bibliographies, catalogs and related reference works compiled by libraries in Communist China in the years 1949–1957 (**148**) is perhaps the best illustration of the enormous range of the work thus far undertaken. (In this connection, see also the two issues of the *Union Research Service* [Vol. 19, Nos. 8 and 10, April and May, 1960] devoted to the development of library work on the Mainland.)

Of the three subject bibliographies on library science given here, the first two are complementary and together provide the most comprehensive coverage of literature in the field for the period 1910–1957 inclusive. The last item (**149**) covers 1959, but bibliographies for the intervening period are not available. No similar bibliographies are available for Taiwan, although the *Journal of Library Science* published by Tunghai University Library, No. 4 (July 1962), contains a union list of library science serials in Taiwan.

A few additional references are in order. Mainland library classification schemes (**1757** and **1758**) are listed in Appendix A. Chapter X lists an encyclopedia of library science (**480**). Current information on library development and bibliographical work is to be found in the journals described in Part Four: *T'u-shu kuan* 圖書館 (Libraries, **911**, formerly published under the title *T'u-shu kuan hsüeh t'ung-hsün* 圖書館學通訊 [Library Science Bulletin, **912**]) and *T'u-shu kuan kung-tso* 圖書館工作 (Library Work, **913**) for the Mainland; and for Taiwan, *Chung-kuo t'u-shu kuan hsüeh-hui hui-k'an* 中國圖書館學會會刊 (Bulletin of the Chinese Library Association, **959**).

147 **Li, Chung-li** 李鍾履, **ed.** *T'u-shu kuan hsüeh shu-chi lien-ho mu-lu* 圖書館學書籍聯合目錄
(A Union List of Library Literature). Peking: Chung-hua shu-chü 中華書局, 1958. 72p.

A union list of 1,026 Chinese monographic publications (including translations) on library science and bibliography published from 1910 through the first half of 1957. The entries are arranged by the number of strokes and numbered consecutively. Separate indexes by subject, and author or translator; arranged likewise by stroke count. See also next entry.

148 **Nan-ching t'u-shu kuan** 南京圖書館 (Library of Nanking). *T'u-shu kuan hsüeh lun-wen so-yin, ti erh chi* 圖書館學論文索引 (第二輯)
(Index to Library Literature, Vol. 2). Peking: Shang-wu yin-shu kuan 商務印書館, 1959. 140p.

An index to 2,037 Chinese periodical and newspaper articles on library science
published between October 1949 and December 1957, arranged by subject
(library education, administration, bibliography, publishing, etc.). Within each
subject-group entries are listed by title with full bibliographical data. There is a
classification table which serves as a brief subject index to the body of the work,
and also an author index arranged by stroke count. Volume 1 lists articles
published from the early 1900's to September 1949. See also next entry.

149 Ting, Tien 丁典, **comp.** '*T'u-shu kuan hsüeh mu-lu hsüeh hsin t'u-shu tzu-liao
hsüan-mu*' 圖書館學目錄學新圖書資料選目
(A Selected Bibliography of Recent Publications on Library Science and
Bibliography), *T'u-shu kuan hsüeh t'ung-hsün* 圖書館學通訊 (Library Science
Bulletin), No. 2, 1960 (February 20, 1960), pp. 43–48; No. 4, 1960 (April 20,
1960), pp. 43–46.

Lists books and periodical articles published in 1959 in Chinese (51 items),
Russian (44), German (30), English (50), and Japanese (31). Provides full
bibliographical citations including Chinese translation of titles.

12. AGRICULTURE AND FORESTRY

The first entry, a U.S. Department of Agriculture bibliography, is a good introduction to Mainland publications, although limited, unfortunately, to monographs
available in the United States. For other kinds of publication, the general bibliographical sources should be consulted.

Concerning Taiwan agriculture and forestry, fairly comprehensive bibliographies
are available. As in the case of the Mainland, further sources are to be found in the
general bibliographies.

Bibliographical coverage of agricultural policy and related non-technical aspects of
agriculture is discussed above in the economic and social section (see in particular
the works of Chao Kuo-chün [**110–112**] and the Japanese bibliography on the land
problem [**118**]). Parenthetically, documentary sources on agriculture are listed in
Chapter XIV, and English translations in Chapter XX (see also the pertinent periodical
entries in Part Four).

150 Kuo, Leslie T. C. and Schroeder, Peter B., comps.
Communist Chinese Monographs in the USDA Library. Washington, D.C.:
United States Department of Agriculture Library, 1961. 87p. (Library List
No. 71).

An annotated bibliography of Communist Chinese monographs on agriculture
and related fields in the USDA Library (The National Agricultural Library),
classified under the following subjects: agriculture (general); plant science;
agricultural methods; forestry and forest products; animal science; fisheries;
apiculture; sericulture; food and nutrition; processing of agricultural products;
biology and chemistry; nation's economy; geology, geography, meteorology,

and pedology; glossaries, dictionaries, abstracts, and handbooks; maps and wall charts. Within each subject group, items are arranged alphabetically by author. Each item is accompanied by full bibliographical information, including titles in translation. An author index and a list of publishers, in English and in Chinese, are included.

An important bibliography, and the only one available.

See also *Communist Chinese Periodicals in the Agricultural Sciences* (**1771**) in Appendix A. For a similar compilation on Taiwan, see William J. C. Logan, comp., *Chinese Agricultural Publications from the Republic of China since 1947* (Washington, D.C., 1964), 55p. (Library List No. 81).

151 T'ai-wan nung-yeh wen-hsien so-yin 臺灣農業文獻索引
(Index to Literature on Taiwan's Agriculture, 1945–56). Taipei, 1956. 11; 273p.

A comprehensive index to periodical and newspaper articles, books, reports, and pamphlets on agriculture in Taiwan. Entries are classified under fifteen broad categories: general, crops, horticulture, forestry, marine products, animal husbandry and veterinary science, sericulture, insects, plant pathology, agricultural chemistry, soil and fertilizer, agricultural economics, agricultural extension, agricultural engineering, and food (with further classification by minor subject headings). Entries are arranged chronologically by date of publication with full bibliographical information, including pagination.

Compiled by an editorial board composed of representatives from such organizations as the Agricultural Association of China, Forestry Association of China, Horticultural Society of China, and the Taiwan Society of Fisheries. A good index and the only one available for the period covered.

152 Wang, Tzu-ting 王子定, **comp.** *T'ai-wan lin-yeh wen-hsien so-yin* 臺灣林業文獻索引
(Index to Literature on Forestry of Taiwan). Taipei: T'ai-wan yin-hang 臺灣銀行, 1953. 245p.

Contains periodical and newspaper articles published between 1888 and 1951, inclusive. Divided by languages—Chinese, Japanese, and English—into three parts, and within each part the materials are arranged chronologically by date of publication under subject (e.g., afforestation, utilization, etc.). A comprehensive compilation, especially useful for Japanese publications, which constitute the bulk of this index.

13. SCIENCE, TECHNOLOGY AND MEDICINE

The Chinese Communists have placed heavy emphasis on scientific and technological development in an effort to come abreast of the industrial West. While there is a general awareness of the great progress made since 1949, and of the Soviet assistance rendered during the initial stages which provided impetus to Chinese economic development, any accurate assessment—either qualitative or quantitative—of Mainland scientific and technological achievements or potential is handicapped by the lack of available information. Nonetheless, a general picture emerges from the symposium sponsored by the American Association for the Advancement of Science (**155**) and the article in the *Science News Letter* (**156**) reproducing some of the Communists' own claims in this area.

The first two bibliographies (**153** and **154**) listed in this section provide a good entrée to published sources in the broad area of science and technology. The *KWIC Index to the Science Abstracts of China* (see **933**) performs the same service with respect to scientific and technical materials available in the United States. Also listed here are topical bibliographies in the fields of nuclear research and technology, medicine, mathematics, meteorology, etc.

No reference works of similar character are available for Taiwan. The best source of information on the level and extent of scientific research now in progress is the *Handbook of Current Research Projects on the Republic of China* (**1735**). Learned societies and research institutes are listed in the *Directory of Cultural Organizations of the Republic of China* (**341**).

Bibliographies on the scientific and technical aspects of agriculture and forestry are described in the preceding section. Lists of Chinese Communist scientific journals are provided in the next chapter, and descriptions of a select number of the journals themselves appear in Chapter XVII (e.g., *K'o-hsüeh t'ung-pao* [**894**], *Science Abstracts of China* [**932**], *Science Record* [**934**], *Scientia Sinica* [**935**], etc.). Scientific and technical dictionaries and glossaries are listed in Chapter X.

153 **Chao, Chi-sheng** 趙繼生, **comp.** *K'o-hsüeh chi-shu ts'an-k'ao shu t'i-yao* 科學 技術參考書提要

(A Guide to Scientific and Technical Reference Works). Peking: Shang-wu yin-shu kuan 商務印書館, 1958. 12; 539p.

A bibliography of 1,554 scientific and technical reference works, most of which were published between 1950 and October 1957. The work is divided into (1) general references (95 titles); (2) mathematics and chemistry (165); (3) geology and geography (154); (4) biology (193); (5) medical science (261); (6) agriculture (133); (7) applied science (553). Within each group, titles are listed in the following order: (1) bibliographies, indexes, digests; (2) glossaries, dictionaries; (3) cyclopedias, handbooks; (4) diagrams, charts; (5) tables; (6) laws and regulations; (7) history and biography; (8) general works; and (9) essays and miscellany. Entries are numbered consecutively and provide a full bibliographical citation and a concise annotation. Separate title and author indexes arranged by the stroke count of the abbreviated characters. (Cross references are given from the regular to the abbreviated form.) There is also a separate index for Russian authors and one for Western authors.

A most basic compilation of Chinese Communist scientific and technical reference works, and the only one available.

154 K'o-hsüeh ch'u-pan she 科學出版社 (Science Publishing House). *Chung-kuo k'o-hsüeh yüan k'o-hsüeh ch'u-pan she t'u-shu mu-lu* 中國科學院科學出版社圖書目錄 (Catalog of Books Published by the Science Publishing House of the Chinese Academy of Sciences). Peking, 1959. 154p.

A catalog of 1,894 books published by the Science Publishing House (one of the largest Mainland publishers of scientific books as well as scholarly works in other fields) from the time of its establishment in 1950 through September 1959. Original Chinese works and translations in the social sciences, natural sciences and technology are included, as are all published Chinese, Russian, English, German, and Latin bilingual scientific and technical glossaries. Seventy-eight scholarly journals published by the Science Publishing House as of September 1959 are listed in the appendix. Entries are classified by subject (philosophy, sociology, history, archeology, economics, culture and education, linguistics, literature and literary criticism, and many scientific and technical categories). Except for pagination, full bibliographical information is provided.

The volume was not available for examination. The information given above was obtained from the Soviet bibliographical journal, *Sovetskaia bibliografiia*, No. 2, 1960 (No. 60), p. 119, and *Problemy vostokovedeniia* (Problems of Oriental Studies), No. 4, 1960, p. 238.

155 Gould, Sidney H., ed.
Sciences in Communist China. Washington, D.C.: American Association for the Advancement of Science, 1961. 782p.

A symposium presented at the New York meeting of the American Association for the Advancement of Science, December 26–27, 1960. The first article, 'Organization and Development of Science', by John M. H. Lindbeck, is a particularly good reference for the organization and development of the Chinese Academy of Sciences. Other parts are 'Biological and Medical Sciences', 'Atmosphere and Earth Sciences', 'Mathematics and the Physical Sciences', 'Engineering Sciences and Electronics'. Nearly all of the papers are accompanied by extensive reference sections (some also with bibliographies). Some of the more substantial bibliographies are botany (pp. 187–195); agriculture (pp. 286–296); geography (pp. 469–472); geology (pp. 516–519); hydrology (pp. 541–549), (see **165**); oceanography (pp. 553–554); meteorology (pp. 558–601), (see **164**). Three indexes: author, geographical and subject.

An objective assessment of scientific development in Communist China. The bibliographies are quite comprehensive in coverage (two of the more detailed ones are separately listed in this section).

156 'Communist Chinese Claims Regarding Scientific Progress in the Last Decade, With Appended Bibliographic Notes,' *Science News Letter*, Vol. 78, No. 24 (December 10, 1960), pp. 377–392.

Contains a reprint of an article by Du Ruen-sheng (Tu Jun-sheng), Deputy Secretary of the Chinese Academy of Sciences in Peking, originally published in English and Chinese in the November 1959 issue of *Scientia Sinica*, Vol. 8, No. 11, pp. 1196–1217, entitled 'Great Progress Made in the Natural Sciences in China During the Last Decade' (in commemoration of the tenth anniversary of the establishment of the Chinese Communist government on the Mainland). A most comprehensive document for the study of Chinese Communist scientific philosophy, their claims to progress and achievement, and the shortcomings which they have frankly acknowledged. Appended bibliographical notes refer to 113 available English translations of Chinese review or summary articles occasioned by the tenth anniversary celebration. The notes are listed by romanized title of the article, followed by its English translation, author(s), and source, including the name of the government agency in Washington from which the translation may be purchased (Office of Technical Services of the U.S. Department of Commerce, the Library of Congress, and the National Library of Medicine); included also in most cases, is the price.

One of the very few available bibliographies of its kind.

157   U.S. Library of Congress, Air Information Division.
Survey of Scientific and Technical Monographs Published in China—SIR No. 2975. Washington, D.C., November, 1958. 13:102p.

A guide to selected monographs based on the examination of 250 catalogs, preceded by a survey article. The volume contains eight statistical charts of Chinese scientific and technical monographs published in China from 1950 to 1958, broken down by discipline, etc. A list of some 500 selected Chinese scientific and technical monographs is appended. The list is arranged under fifteen categories (science and technology—general, astronomy, chemistry, biology, etc.), and provides full bibliographical information including romanized title with the English translation and pagination.

158   U.S. Department of Commerce, Office of Technical Services.
Chinese Mainland Science and Technology (OTS Selective Bibliography). Washington, D.C., 1960. 18p.

A bibliography of reports and translations of articles drawn from Chinese Communist and Russian scientific and technical journals listed in the two OTS monthly abstract journals, U.S. *Government Research Reports* and *Technical Translations*. Entries are grouped under the following subject headings: agriculture, biological and behavioral sciences, chemistry, earth sciences, engineering, materials, metallurgy, physics and mathematics, research techniques, and bibliography. Within each subject group, translations are listed by translated title followed by name of author, number of pages of original article, and other bibliographical information.

159 **U.S. Department of State, Bureau of Intelligence and Research, External Research Staff.**
Nuclear Research and Technology in Communist China—A List of Monographs and Periodical and Newspaper Articles in the English Language on Atomic Energy Research and Technology in Communist China. Washington, D.C., 1963. 7p. (External Research Paper 139).

An alphabetical list containing seventy-one English-language periodical articles, translations, and monographs on nuclear research and technology in Communist China. The articles were taken from publications such as *China Quarterly*, *Current History* and *U.S. News and World Report*, while the translations were selected from the Hong Kong American Consulate General translation series and J.P.R.S. reports (largely New China News Agency releases). Except for Alice L. Hsieh's *Communist China's Strategy in the Nuclear Era*, the two or three other listed monographs deal only indirectly with the subject. Annotations are provided for some selected items. Mimeographed.

See also External Research Paper No. 148—a bibliography on scientific and technical manpower in Communist China (**1488**).

160 **China (People's Republic of China, 1949—), Wen-hua pu, K'o-hsüeh p'u-chi chü** 中華人民共和國文化部科學普及局 (China [People's Republic of China, 1949—], Ministry of Culture, Science Extention Bureau). *T"ung-su k'o-hsüeh ch'i-k'an p'ien-mu so-yin (1)* 通俗科學期刊篇目索引 (1) (Index to Popular Science Periodicals, No. 1). Peking: Hsin-hua shu-tien 新華書店, 1951. 81p.

The first issue of a projected semi-annual subject index to sixty-three popular and semi-technical periodicals in the natural sciences, and engineering and technology, published in Communist China between January and June 1950. Not indexed are editor's notes, and reports on local activities and articles 'falling under the category of economics'. A list of the sixty-three periodicals under survey is included.

161 **Nan-ching i-hsüeh yüan, T'u-shu kuan** 南京醫學院圖書館 (Nanking Medical College, Library). *Chung-wen i-hsüeh wen-hsien fen-lei so-yin* 中文醫學文獻分類索引 (Index to Chinese Medical Literature). Peking: Jen-min wei-sheng ch'u-pan she 人民衛生出版社, 1958. 12; 674p.

An index to approximately 24,600 articles in more than eighty Chinese medical journals published primarily between 1949 and 1956 (a few items were published before 1949), arranged by subject (a table of subject classification scheme is provided). Undoubtedly the most exhaustive index to Chinese medical literature published to 1956.

See also Joint Publications Research Service translation No. 14,460, July 13, 1962, 395p. (U.S.G.P.O. Monthly Catalog 1962, No. 17,763), entitled *Collection of Theses on Achievements in Medical Sciences in Commemoration of the Tenth National Foundation Day of China.*

162   **Chung-hua i-hsüeh hui** 中華醫學會 (Chinese Medical Association). *Chung-hua i-hsüeh hui tsung-hui tsa-chih tsung so-yin, 1954, 1955, 1956, 1957* 中華醫學會總會雜誌總索引 1954, 1955, 1956, 1957
(Index to Journals Published by the Chinese Medical Association, 1954, 1955, 1956, 1957). Peking: Jen-min wei-sheng ch'u-pan she 人民衛生出版社, 1958. 4 vols.

An index to about fifteen Chinese medical journals published by the Chinese Medical Association for the years 1954 through 1957. In two parts: author and subject, both by stroke count. Supplements the preceding entry.

163   **Tsao, Chia Kuei.**
Bibliography of Mathematics Published in Communist China During the Period 1949–1960. Providence, R. I.: American Mathematical Society, 1961. 83p. (Contemporary Chinese Research Mathematics, Vol. 1).

Compiled by Dr. Tsao of Wayne State University, the volume is divided as follows: introduction; a list of Chinese periodicals containing articles on mathematics (70 titles); and bibliography (pp. 7–83). The latter contains English titles of 1,335 articles by some 370 Chinese authors and some fifty non-Chinese authors, arranged alphabetically by author, with indications as to the original language of the article and the existence of summaries in other languages. Chinese characters are also supplied for the names of Chinese authors.

A most comprehensive and the only available work of its kind.

See also the *Bibliography of Chinese Mathematics, 1918–1960*, compiled by Yuan Tung-li (Washington, D.C., 1960).

164   **Rice, Mary L., comp.**
'Bibliography on Meteorological Articles (1949–1960)' in Sidney H. Gould, ed., *Sciences in Communist China* (Washington, D.C.: American Association for the Advancement of Science, 1961), pp. 558–601.

A list of some 650 items arranged by subject under broad categories (general geophysics and meteorology, dynamic meteorology, weather modification, etc.), then alphabetically by author, or by title if no author is available. Most entries are Chinese-language items with the title and name of periodical given only in English translation. This is also true of Russian and other non-English language entries.

165   **Rice, Mary L., comp.**
'Bibliography on Hydrology' in Sidney H. Gould, ed., *Sciences in Communist China* (Washington, D.C.: American Association for the Advancement of Science, 1961), pp. 541–549.

A list of 106 books and articles (mostly in Chinese) on hydrology, arranged under twelve subject headings. Chinese-language materials are cited with the title in English translation only, the name of the journal in romanization followed by the English translation in parenthesis, although some journals are listed only by the English translated title. Russian-language entries list titles in both romanization and translation, but the name of the journal is given in romanization without translation.

166 Hsiang, Wang-nien 相望年, **comp.** *Chung-kuo chen-chün-hsüeh yü chih-wu ping-li-hsüeh wen-hsien* 中國眞菌學與植物病理學文獻 (A Bibliography of Chinese Works on Mycology and Phytopathology). Peking: K'o-hsüeh ch'u-pan she 科學出版社, 1957. 323p.

An annotated bibliography, containing 2,600 articles published in China from 1914 to 1955 inclusive, and 670 articles published abroad before 1949, arranged by subject. Includes lists of (1) pre-1949 Chinese-language journals, (2) pre-1949 Western-language journals published in China, (3) post-1949 Chinese-language journals, and (4) foreign journals.

H. Bibliographies of Translations

Translations from Chinese

Standard general bibliographies of Western-language translations from the Chinese, such as Martha Davidson's *A List of Published Translations from Chinese into English, French, and German* (New Haven, Conn.: Yale University, Far Eastern Publications, 1951–1952, 2 vols.) are excluded here, as they are almost entirely devoted to pre-modern China.

With the establishment of the Communist regime on the Mainland, a substantial body of material—political, economic and social in content—emanating from the Mainland has been translated into English. The largest collections of post-1949 translations are as follows: the publications of the American Consulate General in Hong Kong (**1038** ff.), the reports of the Joint Publications Research Service (**1047** ff.), the *Union Research Service* (**1065**), the *Foreign Broadcast Information Service* (**1071**), the New China News Agency releases (**849** and **850**), and the translations of the Foreign Languages Press in Peking.

A sizeable quantity of material is being translated into English in Taiwan—the *China Yearbook* (**240**), for example. The U.S.I.S. in Taipei, in its *Press and Publications Summary* (**1074**), regularly provides translations from the Taiwan press and periodicals. All of the above, together with bibliographies and indexes to these sources, are described in some detail in Chapter XX. Documentary sources in English translation are listed in Part Three. Mainland, Taiwan and Hong Kong English-language newspapers and periodicals are described in Part Four.

Reflecting the great Japanese interest in Chinese culture, the number of Japanese-language translations from the Chinese is enormous. A fairly comprehensive coverage of this material can be found in the series of two bibliographies listed below (**168** and **169**).

Russian translations from the Chinese up to 1958 are carried in Skachkov's bibliographies (see **42** and **94**). Translations of the period 1958 and after are dealt with in the Russian bibliographies listed after Skachkov's. For statistical information and analysis of translations from Chinese into Russian, see Chapter II, 'Soviet Publications in the Chinese Field', in *Soviet Works on China* (**44**).

Translations into Chinese

One measure of the Western impact on China is the number and type of Western works translated into Chinese during the past one hundred years or so. The first entry is a list of such translations.

The relative dependence of the Chinese Communists on Soviet technical and other publications is well known. However, no separate bibliography of post-1949 Mainland translations is available. The necessary information can be derived by a careful scanning of Peking's national bibliography.

167 **Chung-yang t'u-shu kuan** 中央圖書館 (National Central Library). *Chin pai-nien lai Chung-i hsi-shu mu-lu* 近百年來中譯西書目錄
A Catalog of Chinese Translations of Western Language Publications During the Last Hundred Years. Taipei: Chung-hua wen-hua ch'u-pan shih-yeh wei-yüan hui 中華文化出版事業委員會, 1958. 328p.

A classified catalog of more than 5,000 Western-language works translated into Chinese from 1867 to October 1956 (post-1949 publications limited to those published in Taiwan only) arranged under the following headings: general, philosophy, religion, natural sciences, applied sciences, the social sciences, history and geography, language and literature, and fine arts. There is a further division into sub-categories, in which works are entered, without any apparent order, under the translated title followed by name of translator, date and place of publication, and name of publisher (this information is not always complete). The name of author and title in the original language are given when available.

The usefulness of this important publication is reduced by the absence of an index.

168 **Sanetō, Keishū** 實藤惠秀 **and Ogawa, Hiroshi** 小川博. *Nihon'yaku Chūgokusho mokuroku* 日本譯中國書目錄
(Bibliography of Japanese Translations of Chinese Works). Tokyo: Nihon Gakusei Hōsō Kyōkai 日本學生放送協會, 1956. 58p.

A bibliography of over 1,300 Japanese translations of Chinese works published from 1868 until March 1956 (material covering the period June 1954 to March 1956 appears in an appendix).

In three parts: (1) works by a single author—arranged by the Japanese reading of the Chinese author's name according to the Japanese syllabary; (2) works for which authorship is not indicated, arranged by topic (classics, folklore, politics-economics, law, etc.); (3) works by joint authors—arranged by the year of publication. Entries provide the author (if any), title, translator, publisher, date of publication and remarks.

For the continuation of this bibliography to January 1960, see the next entry.

169 **Sanetō, Keishū** 實藤惠秀 **and Ogawa, Hiroshi** 小川博. 'Nihon'yaku Chūgoku-sho mokuroku' 日本譯中國書目錄
(Bibliography of Japanese Translations of Chinese Works), *Daian* 大安, Vol. 6, No. 3 (March 1960), pp. 25–29; No. 4 (April 1960), pp. 36–40; No. 5 (May 1960), pp. 24–30; No. 6 (June 1960), pp. 29–30.

A continuation of the authors' work published in 1956 (see preceding entry), covering the period June 1954 to January 1960 and containing about 300 items. Entries are arranged in three parts: literature, classics, and social science, and are listed within these categories by the Japanese syllabary according to the Japanese reading of the Chinese author's name. Author, title, translator, publisher and date are provided.

Together, the two entries constitute the most comprehensive listing of Japanese translations of Chinese works.

CHAPTER II

LISTS OF NEWSPAPERS AND PERIODICALS

A. General   170–179
B. Scientific 180–183

For the study of contemporary China, the Chinese press and periodical literature emerge as singularly important sources. That such is the case is due in part to the fact that the mass media (including broadcasting), particularly on the Mainland, alone provide much information normally obtained in other countries from a variety of other sources. Fortunately for scholarship, there is no dearth of such publications (although since 1959 access to Mainland newspapers and periodicals has been severely restricted). Over 1,000 newspapers and some 1,300 periodicals are reported to be published on the Mainland, over 500 newspapers and periodicals on Taiwan, and roughly 100 in Hong Kong. The Mainland, Taiwan and Hong Kong press is discussed in somewhat greater detail in the introductions to the appropriate chapters in Part Four, which also provides annotations for the more significant or representative newspapers and periodicals. Library holdings of these publications are for the most part listed in Appendix A, although a few of the more comprehensive catalogs, constituting for all practical purposes bibliographies of the subject, are incorporated in the present chapter.

The lists described in this chapter are divided into two categories: general and scientific. Except for the three bibliographies of social science periodicals and monograph series for the Mainland, Taiwan and Hong Kong, prepared by the Bureau of the Census of the U.S. Department of Commerce (174–176), they are largely unannotated. For Mainland coverage, several good lists of newspapers and periodicals exist and are included here. Parenthetically, reference should be made to the *Ch'üan-kuo tsung shu-mu* 全國總書目 (Cumulative National Bibliography; see 9) which provides the most complete listing of newspapers and periodicals published between 1949 and 1958, and to the Index to Major Newspapers and Periodicals (184), which carries in each issue an extensive list of the newspapers and periodicals indexed. In addition, available Mainland periodicals are listed in *Chinese Periodicals, International Holdings, 1949–1960* and in *International Union List of Communist Chinese Serials* (1709 and 1708).

The most up-to-date lists of Mainland newspapers and periodicals are the Hong Kong American Consulate compilations, which are the first two entries in this chapter. Another comprehensive list covering Chinese periodicals published in the years 1949–1956 is provided by the catalog of the Shanghai Library (172).

For comprehensive treatment of Taiwan newspapers and periodicals, the reader should consult the appropriate Chinese-language reference works: the Journalism Yearbook, published in 1961 (247), which provides a list of newspapers and periodicals; the 1954 Chinese Periodicals Yearbook (248), giving one to two-page descriptions of 148 periodicals published in Taiwan since 1945; the *Classified Index to Chinese Periodicals*, Series III, published by the National Taiwan University Library in 1963

(**192**), which includes a list of more than 450 Chinese-language periodicals published from 1946 through 1961; the Chinese edition of the *China Yearbook* (**239**); the *Directory of the Cultural Organizations of the Republic of China* (**341**), which, in its coverage of publications, also serves as a guide to the scholarly journals and proceedings of learned societies; and the 1961 Directory of Mass Communication Agencies (**346**).

No complete list of newspapers and periodicals published in Hong Kong seems to be available (the publication of the U.S. Department of Commerce [**176**] is far from complete), although a partial listing is provided in the 1962 edition of the *Hong Kong Yearbook* (see **256**).

For Japanese-language periodicals dealing with China, the two lists (**177** and **178**) should be consulted. The bibliography of Western-language periodicals compiled by Professor Walker (**179**) has not been kept current, a situation which is remedied by reference to such sources as the appendix listing some 500 periodicals (particularly the more current periodical literature) in T. L. Yuan's *China in Western Literature* (**16**), and the section entitled 'Periodicals and Serials' in the part on China in the annual 'Bibliography of Asian Studies' (**15**).

A good selected list of over 300 newspapers and periodicals concerned with contemporary China in Chinese, English, Japanese, Russian and other languages is provided in Part Four of the present work.

Reference is also made to *Mainland China Organizations of Higher Learning in Science and Technology and Their Publications: A Selected Guide*, prepared at the Library of Congress (**330**).

A. General

170 American Consulate General, Hong Kong.
Chinese Communist Newspapers Believed Published as of January 1, 1960. Hong Kong, 1960. 87p.

An alphabetical list of some 1,055 newspapers. For similar listings for previous years, see *Current Background*, No. 478, (October 28, 1957), and two other lists entitled *Chinese Communist Newspapers* issued by the Consulate General on September 6, 1955, and September 26, 1956, respectively.

171 American Consulate General, Hong Kong.
Chinese Communist Periodicals Believed to Have Been Published as of January 1, 1960. Hong Kong, 1960. 121p.

An alphabetical list of some 1,334 Mainland Chinese periodicals. Forty-three periodicals published in Hong Kong are listed separately at the end. See also *Current Background*, Nos. 283 (March 30, 1954), 387 (June 1, 1956), 436 (January 30, 1957), and two other Consulate General publications (*Chinese Communist Periodicals*, December 29, 1955, and *Chinese Communist Periodicals Available on Subscription*, January 1, 1956) for similar listings for previous years.

172 Shang-hai shih pao-k'an t'u-shu kuan 上海市報刊圖書館 (Shanghai Municipal Newspaper and Periodical Library). *Shang-hai shih pao-k'an t'u-shu kuan Chung-wen ch'i-k'an mu-lu* 上海市報刊圖書館中文期刊目錄
(A Catalog of Chinese Periodicals in the Shanghai Municipal Newspaper and Periodical Library). Shanghai: Shang-hai shih pao-k'an t'u-shu kuan, 1956–1957. 2 vols.

Volume 1 contains a list of 8,037 periodicals published between 1881 and 1949. Volume 2 lists more than 1,500 titles published between 1949 and 1956. Both are arranged by the number of strokes of the first word in the title and provide holdings and bibliographical information. Volume 2 also has a subject index.

Since the Shanghai Municipal Library holds the leading newspaper and periodical collection on the Mainland, this catalog represents the most complete list of Chinese Communist periodicals published to 1956.

173 Guozi Shudian 國際書店 (International Book Company). *Chung-kuo pao-k'an mu-lu* 中國報刊目錄
Newspapers and Periodicals in Chinese. Peking, 1957. 64p.

A bilingual (Chinese-English) pamphlet issued in 1957 by the Guozi Shudian in Peking, listing more than 300 periodicals and eight newspapers available for subscription for 1958. Provides brief annotations for a limited number of titles. The Guozi Shudian is the official agency for the sale of Chinese Communist publications abroad.

174 U.S. Department of Commerce, Bureau of the Census, Foreign Manpower Research Office.
Bibliography of Social Science Periodicals and Monograph Series: Mainland China, 1949–1960. Washington, D.C.: U.S. Government Printing Office, 1961. 32p. (Foreign Social Science Bibliographies, Series P-92, No. 3).

Includes all periodicals and monograph series devoted primarily to the social sciences published in Mainland China since 1949 and available in the Library of Congress. Of the 142 publications listed, 107 are periodicals and 35 are serial monographs. Essentially technical publications—especially in the fields of public health, economics, and statistics—are excluded, as are newspapers and publications of a popular or semi-popular nature. Entries are arranged by subject, and under each subject titles are arranged alphabetically by issuing agency, or by title if no agency is listed. A full bibliographical citation is provided for each title, including Chinese characters for titles and their translations, a brief abstract of the contents, and, in the case of periodicals, titles of five representative articles appearing in the most recent issues. Library of Congress holdings are also included. Indexes: subject, title, author (of individual monographs), and issuing agencies.

For similar compilations of Taiwan and Hong Kong publications, see next entries.

175 **U.S. Department of Commerce, Bureau of the Census, Foreign Manpower Research Office.**
Bibliography of Social Science Periodicals and Monograph Series: Republic of China, 1949–1961. Washington, D.C.: U.S. Government Printing Office, 1961. 24p. (Foreign Social Science Bibliographies, Series P-92, No. 4).

Covers social science periodicals and monograph series published in Taiwan since 1949 and available in the Library of Congress. Of the 84 publications listed, 57 are periodicals and 27 are serial monographs. The arrangement and the information provided in the annotations are the same as in the preceding entry. For a similar work on Hong Kong publications, see next entry.

176 **U.S. Department of Commerce, Bureau of the Census, Foreign Manpower Research Office.**
Bibliography of Social Science Periodicals and Monograph Series: Hong Kong, 1950–1961. Washington, D.C.: U.S. Government Printing Office, 1962. 13p. (Foreign Social Science Bibliographies, Series P-92, No. 7).

Covers all periodicals and monograph series devoted primarily to the social sciences published in Hong Kong since 1950 and available in the Library of Congress. Of the 49 publications listed, 27 are periodicals and 22 are serial monographs. The arrangement and the information provided in the annotations are the same as in the two preceding entries. In their coverage of Library of Congress holdings, the three lists seem to be quite selective in the fields under survey. The annotations for some of the more important titles are rather brief and do not provide sufficient information.

177 **Torii, Hisayasu** 鳥居久靖. 'Kokunai kan tōhōshi mokuroku—sengo no bu' 國內刊東方誌目錄——戰後の部
(A List of Periodicals in the Oriental Field Published in Japan—Postwar), *Tenri Daigaku gakuhō* 天理大學學報 (Journal of Tenri University), Tenri, Nara Prefecture, No. 26 (September 1958), pp. 99–122.

A list of 208 Japanese-language periodicals in the Oriental field, largely dealing with China and excluding South and Southwest Asia, published in Japan from August 1945 to March 1958.

Classified under the following categories: (1) general—56 periodicals (subdivided into general, 29; China study group journals, 23; journals issued by bookdealers, 4); (2) humanities—77 (philosophy, ethics, religion, thought and history, 45; language and literature, 32); (3) social sciences—46; and (4) special journals—29 (journals on Korea, 16; and Chinese-language journals published by Chinese residents in Japan, 13). Within each category entries are arranged according to the Japanese syllabary. Entries provide the date of the first issue, date of temporary suspension (if any), date of last issue (in the case of current journals, the volume and number as of March 1958), sponsoring organization, publisher and place of publication, frequency, size, price and remarks. No index.

A comprehensive list. See also next entry.

178 Torii, Hisayasu 鳥居久靖. 'Sengo kokunai kan tōhōshi tembō, No. 1–15'
戰後國內刊東方誌展望
(A Survey of Postwar Japanese Journals in the Oriental Field) in *Shohō* 書報
(Book News), Tokyo, September, November, December 1958; January–June,
August–October, December 1959; February–March 1960 (15 instalments).

Contains descriptions of 129 journals in the Chinese field (almost all of them
in the humanities) published in Japan after the war. Arranged by broad category:
general—27 journals; China study group journals—18; publishers' and bibliographical journals—5; philosophy, thought and history—45; and language and
literature—34. Within the categories the journals are arranged according to the
first publication date. The annotations range from a few lines to almost a page
(some include photographs of the title page) and provide information on the
beginning date, frequency, sponsoring organization, number of pages, size,
publisher and place of publication; the history of the journal including changes
of titles, dates of suspension and date of final issue (if relevant); and description
of the contents including characteristic features.

Proved extremely useful in the preparation of the present Guide, especially
Part Four.

179 Walker, Richard L.
Western Language Periodicals on China (A Selective List). New Haven, Conn.:
Yale University, Institute of Far Eastern Languages, 1949. 30p.

A list of 189 Western-language periodicals (with one in Russian) arranged in
three sections: (1) 54 periodicals which constitute major sources for reliable,
scholarly material on China; (2) 72 periodicals of lesser importance on China
and East Asia and specialized journals on China and Asia which contain important articles in their fields; (3) 63 Western-language journals in specialized fields
containing occasional important articles on China. Titles are arranged alphabetically in each section with a full bibliographical citation accompanied by notes
on the emphasis of the periodical. (Section 1 in addition provides critical
evaluation of the contents and the names of outstanding contributors.)

A good general bibliography of pre-1949 periodical publications.

B. Scientific

**180 U.S. Library of Congress, Air Information Division, Library Services
Section.**
List of Communist Chinese Scientific and Technical Periodicals. Washington,
D.C., 1961. 63p. (AID Report 61–21).

An annotated bibliography of 247 Chinese Communist scientific and technical
periodicals, excluding those in the life sciences (with Air Information Division
holdings). Titles are arranged alphabetically and are in each instance followed
by Chinese characters and a translation of the title. The annotation lists frequency,

place of publication, and publisher, together with a description of the journal and a brief analysis of its contents. Other notes provide additional pertinent data (e.g., title changes). A subject index to the periodical titles is provided.

181 U.S. Library of Congress, Science and Technology Division. *Journals in Science and Technology Published in Japan and Mainland China.* Washington, D.C., 1961. 47p.

A selected bibliography of 119 current Mainland Chinese and 212 Japanese serials in science and technology, arranged under the following topics: science, general; pure science (physical science, earth science, biological science); technology, general; technology (civil engineering, railroad engineering, mechanical engineering, electrical engineering, nuclear engineering, aeronautical engineering, chemical and industrial engineering, mining engineering and metallurgy, shipbuilding and navigation); medicine; and agriculture. Journals of primary interest to farmers and practicing physicians are excluded.

Under each topic Mainland Chinese journals are listed first (none listed under nuclear engineering and aeronautical engineering), followed by journals from Japan. The following information is given for each journal: romanized title; Latin title, if any; title in characters; translated title; name and address of editor and publisher, if available; and brief annotations which include frequency, languages used in table of contents, kinds of articles and features selected, languages used in summaries, and a sentence on the extent of documentation in the articles. There is an alphabetical title index, including Latin titles.

A useful list containing fewer titles with briefer annotations than in the preceding entry.

182 Chinese Communist Scientific and Technical Periodicals. [n.p., n.d.]. 19p.

Presents 'information on scientific and technical periodical publications in Communist China, based on a survey of these publications for the years 1955–1958.' The list includes 202 periodicals and is preceded by an introduction on the coverage, scope, frequency, and circulation of the publications. Arranged alphabetically with place of publication and frequency given when known. Each title also carries an annotation, indicating the type of material usually found in that periodical. Mimeographed. Informative but outdated.

183 Jen-min wei-sheng ch'u-pan she 人民衛生出版社 (People's Hygiene Press). *Catalogue of Chinese Medical Publications.* Peking, 1957. 40p.

A bilingual annotated catalog of 117 Chinese medical publications (including facsimile editions of pre-1949 works) published by the People's Hygiene Press from the time of its establishment in 1953 to the end of 1956. Arranged by subject. Title index in Chinese and English. Apart from the listings in the national bibliography, the only available catalog.

CHAPTER III

INDEXES

A. INDEXES TO PERIODICALS AND NEWSPAPERS

Periodical literature published during the last decade or so in both the Mainland and Taiwan has been brought under far closer bibliographical control than heretofore. Although a general comprehensive index to all periodicals or newspapers for either the Mainland or Taiwan is still wanting, there do exist three good indexes to a selected number of the major publications: the Index to Major Newspapers and Periodicals, compiled on the Mainland (**184**); and for Taiwan the *Classified Index to Chinese Periodicals* compiled by the National Taiwan University Library (**192**); and the *Chinese Periodicals Index* prepared by the National War College Library (**193**). The Mainland compilations are broader in scope than those of Taiwan and, unlike the latter, include newspaper articles in their coverage.

A large number of Mainland newspapers and periodicals provide their own indexes, whereas Taiwan publications in general do not. All such separate indexes are listed in Part Four next to their respective parent publications (e.g., the index to the People's Daily follows the main entry for the publication itself in Part Four). It should be noted in passing that the annotations for Mainland, Taiwan and Hong Kong periodicals in Part Four indicate whether the periodical in question is indexed in the periodical indexes listed in this chapter.

Finally, mention must be made of the fact that a number of indexes on specific subject matters were excluded from the present chapter and listed together with the subject bibliographies. Standard periodical indexes covering pre-1949 publications or limited to listing articles concerning traditional Sinology, such as *Chung-kuo shih-hsüeh lun-wen so-yin* 中國史學論文索引 (Index to Periodical Articles on Chinese History), (Peking, 1957), or *Chung-kuo shih-hsüeh lun-wen yin-te* 中國史學論文引得 *1902–1962—Chinese History: Index to Learned Articles, 1902–1962* by Yü Ping-ch'üan (Ping-Kuen Yu) 余秉權 (Hong Kong, 1963), are likewise excluded.

1. INDEXES TO MAINLAND MATERIALS

The first entry in this section supplies the most comprehensive coverage of Mainland newspapers and periodicals, although, unfortunately, no issues have been available for the period since July 1960. The three indexes prepared in Taiwan and the five of Japanese origin serve as useful supplements to the Mainland index. The two-volume index compiled by the National War College Library in Taiwan (**185**) is valuable additionally as a guide to non-Communist periodical literature on the Mainland.

Mention should also be made of the index to selected newspapers and periodicals available in the *Hsin-hua pan-yüeh k'an* (New China Semi-monthly) starting with Vol. 3, No. 4 (February 25, 1951), (see **882**).

184   Ch'üan-kuo chu-yao pao-k'an tzu-liao so-yin 全國主要報刊資料索引
(Index to Major Newspapers and Periodicals of China). Shanghai: Shang-hai shih pao-k'an t'u-shu kuan 上海市報刊圖書館, No. 1—, March 1955—. Monthly.

The most important periodical and newspaper index of Communist China, the first five issues of which appeared between March and November 1955 as a periodical index under the title *Ch'üan-kuo chu-yao ch'i-k'an tzu-liao so-yin* 全國主要期刊資料索引 (Index to Major Periodicals of China). Beginning with No. 6 (also designated No. 1, 1956) in February 1956, the present title was adopted and coverage was expanded to include newspaper articles. Beginning with No. 1, 1959 (consecutive No. 39), the Index has been published in two parts—one on the humanities and social sciences and the other on natural sciences and technology. Published as a bi-monthly between March 1955 and June 1956 (consecutive Nos. 1–8) and as a monthly since July 1956 (consecutive No. 9).

Each issue indexes articles from newspapers and periodicals published during the preceding month and received by the Shanghai Municipal Newspaper and Periodical Library. The average number of newspapers and periodicals indexed per issue from Nos. 1–49 (March 1955 to May 1959) are 40 and 262 respectively, with an average number of 6,044 items listed in each issue. (From Nos. 1–5 the average number of periodicals indexed per issue is 190, and the average number of items, 5,860; from Nos. 6–38 the averages are 38 newspapers, 272 periodicals, and 6,736 items; from Nos. 39–43, 43 newspapers, 263 periodicals, and 5,537 items.) It should be noted that none of the publications are indexed in full. Only the more substantial items are indexed, and certain kinds of publications receive no attention whatsoever (e.g., juvenile, popular, and religious literature). A 'List of Titles Indexed' appears in every issue.

The Index is arranged topically according to the classification scheme (third edition) of the Chinese People's University Library in Peking (see **1757**). Under each topic, items are listed by title, author or translator, name of newspaper or periodical, volume number, consecutive number if any, and page number. Newspaper articles appear first, followed by periodical articles. Consecutive Nos. 33 to 36, July to October 1958, also carry an author index.

A microfilm of this Index covering Nos. 1–38 and Nos. 39–57 (for the humanities and social sciences section, January 1959–July 1960) and Nos. 39–50 (for the natural sciences and technology, January–December 1959) is available for purchase from the Photoduplication Service, The Library of Congress.

An indispensable reference guide to Mainland newspaper and periodical articles.

185 Kuo-fang yen-chiu yüan, T'u-shu kuan 國防研究院圖書館 (National War College, Library). *Fei-k'an lun-wen chi fei-ch'ing yen-p'an tzu-liao so-yin* 匪刊論文及匪情研判資料索引

(An Index to Bandit Periodicals and Reference Materials on Bandit Information). Yangmingshan, [1960–1961]. 2 vols.

The first two issues of a projected semi-annual index to selected periodical articles on Communism in general and on Communist China in particular from both Chinese Communist and non-Communist periodicals in the Library of the National War College in Taiwan.

Periodicals indexed are those published during 1960, including *Hung-ch'i* 紅旗, *Hsin kuan-ch'a* 新觀察, *Hsin chien-she* 新建設, *Chung-kuo ch'ing-nien* 中國青年, *Shih-chieh chih-shih* 世界知識, *Lü-hsing chia* 旅行家, *Kuo-chi wen-t'i i-ts'ung* 國際問題譯叢 , *Ching-chi i-ts'ung* 經濟譯叢, *Ching-chi tao-pao* 經濟導報, *Ho-p'ing ho she-hui chu-i wen-t'i* 和平和社會主義問題, *Shih-chieh kung-hui yün-tung* 世界工會運動, and a number of leading non-Communist publications on Communist China and the Communist bloc, such as *Fei-ch'ing yüeh-pao* 匪情月報, *Fei-ch'ing yen-chiu* 匪情研究, *Wen-t'i yü yen-chiu* 問題與研究, *Chin-jih ta-lu* 今日大陸, *Chung-kuo i-chou* 中國一週, *Min-chu p'ing-lun* 民主評論, *Fan kung* 反攻 and others.

The index is arranged according to the *Chung-kuo t'u-shu fen-lei fa* 中國圖書分類法 (Classification Scheme for Chinese Books), based on a decimal system. Limited distribution.

A useful index, especially for Taiwan publications, despite its selectivity.

186 Ko-ming shih-chien yen-chiu yüan, T'u-shu kuan 革命實踐研究院圖書館 (National War College, Library). *Fei-pao chung-yao nei-jung so-yin* 匪報重要內容索引

(Index to Important Articles in Bandit Newspapers). Taipei, 1952–1955. Irregular.

An index to selected articles in *Jen-min jih-pao* 人民日報, *Chieh-fang jih-pao* 解放日報, *Ch'ang-chiang jih-pao* 長江日報, *Ching-pu jih-pao* 進步日報, and *Nan-fang jih-pao* 南方日報. Arranged under the following sections (with subheadings): party, politics, foreign affairs, economy, society, education, science and culture, military affairs, and history. Each entry provides title, author, name of the newspaper, and date of publication.

The index first appeared in November 1952 as a monthly; irregular thereafter (at two to six-month intervals). The last issue covers the period July to December 1955. Limited distribution.

An important source, though the newspapers are not fully indexed.

187 Kuo-chi kuan-hsi yen-chiu hui 國際關係研究會 (Institute of International Relations of the Republic of China). *Fei-ch'ing tsa-chih lun-wen so-yin* 匪情雜誌論文索引

(Index to Periodical Literature on Bandit Information). Taipei, 1960—. Semiannual.

An index to selected editorials, articles, and translations as they appeared in *Chung-kuo ch'ing-nien*, *Yü-wen chih-shih*, 語文知識, *Kuo-chi wen-t'i i-ts'ung*, *Shih-chieh chih-shih*, *Ching-chi tao-pao*, *Ching-chi i-ts'ung*, *Kuo-chi wen-t'i yen-chiu* 國際問題研究, *Ti-li chih-shih* 地理知識, *Hsin chien-she*, etc. Emphasis is on current international affairs.

Arranged by subject, the entries provide title, author, name of journal, volume, number, page, and date. Two issues have been published: No. 1 (26p.) covers the period from January to June 1960; No. 2 (34p.), July to December 1960.

188 Kaji shimbun kiji sakuin 華字新聞記事索引
(An Index to Articles in Chinese Newspapers). Tokyo: Gendai Chūgoku Kenkyū Iinkai 現代中國研究委員會, 1950–1953. Monthly.

An index to the principal Chinese Mainland and Hong Kong newspapers (*Jen-min jih-pao*, *Tung-pei jih-pao* 東北日報, *Nan-fang jih-pao*, the Shanghai *Ta-kung pao*, the Hong Kong *Ta-kung pao*, etc.). Entries are arranged under several categories (social and cultural, politics, economics, etc.) and supply title, author, newspaper, date and page. Mimeographed.

The index was prepared by the Seminar on Contemporary China at the Institute for Oriental Culture, Tokyo University.

See also next entry.

189 'Chūgoku shimbun zasshi rombun mokuroku' 中國新聞雜誌論文目錄
(An Index to Articles in Chinese Newspapers and Periodicals) in *Nitchū bunka* 日中文化 (Japanese-Chinese Cultural Relations). Tokyo: Nitchū Hon'yaku Shuppan Konwakai 日中翻譯出版懇話會, No. [?]–41, 1953[?]–1956.

An index to important articles in Communist Chinese newspapers and magazines, particularly those in *Jen-min jih-pao* and *Kuang-ming jih-pao*, arranged according to broad categories (politics-social, finance-economics, culture-education, etc.). Until December 1955, the index was published under the title 'Shimbun zasshi jūyō kiji mokuroku' (An Index to Important Articles in Newspapers and Magazines) in the journal *Nitchū hon'yaku shiryō tsūshin* 日中翻譯資料通信 (Bulletin of Chinese-Japanese Translated Materials), the predecessor to *Nitchū bunka*.

See also next entry.

190 'Chūgoku shuyōshi no shuyō rombun sakuin' 中國主要紙の主要論文索引
(Index to Important Articles in Principal Chinese Newspapers and Periodicals), *Ajia keizai jumpō* アジア經濟旬報 (Ten-Day Report on Asian Economy), Tokyo, No. 292–336 (July 1956–September 1957).

An index to several principal Chinese newspapers (*Jen-min jih-pao*, *Ta-kung pao*, *Kung-jen jih-pao*, *Kuang-ming jih-pao*, and periodicals *Hsüeh-hsi* 學習, *Hsin chien-she* 新建設, *Che-hsüeh yen-chiu* 哲學研究, etc.) for a period of about six weeks prior to publication of index. The entries from each newspaper are grouped separately, and are further subdivided into editorials and major articles. Data on title, author, if any, and the date are supplied. Periodical articles are simply listed under the issue of the periodical being indexed.

In the first issues, the index was entitled 'Chūgoku shuyōshi no shuyō ronsetsu' 中國主要紙の主要論說 (Important Articles in Principal Chinese Newspapers and Periodicals). Together with the preceding two entries, the index provides rough coverage of important articles in the Mainland press from 1950 to 1957.

See also the 'Index to Important Articles in the People's Daily' (**834**).

191 **'Chūgoku shuyō gakuhō, zasshi keisai bunken sakuin'** 中國主要學報, 雜誌揭載文獻索引
(Index to Articles in Important Chinese Academic Journals and Periodicals) in *Daian* 大安, Tokyo, Vol. 4, No. 11–Vol. 5, No. 10 (November 1958–October 1959).

A twelve-instalment series, each issue listing from 100 to 500 articles arranged according to broad categories (politics, economics, philosophy and thought, language, literature, history and archeology). Entries provide title, author, date, name of periodical and volume and number. The last three instalments have a slightly different title—'Chūgoku shuyō gakuhō zasshi keisai bunken mokuroku' (Bibliography of Articles in Important Chinese Academic Journals and Periodicals).

2. INDEXES TO TAIWAN AND HONG KONG MATERIALS

None of the Taiwan newspapers and few of the periodicals provide the reader with indexes. For this reason, the five indexes listed in the present section loom particularly important. The newspaper index (see **194a**) began coverage only from 1962. Among periodical indexes, there is, unavoidably, some duplication of material, but in general they complement one another. The classified index prepared at the National Taiwan University (first entry) covers the more scholarly periodicals and is more comprehensive than the others. The last index (**195**) is noteworthy because it deals exclusively with Taiwan periodical articles concerned with Taiwan.

192 **T'ai-wan ta-hsüeh, T'u-shu kuan** 臺灣大學圖書館 (National Taiwan University, Library). *Chung-wen ch'i-k'an lun-wen fen-lei so-yin* 中文期刊論文分類索引
Classified Index to Chinese Periodicals. Taipei, 1960, 1962, 1963. Vol. 1—13; 516p.; Vol. 2—20; 552p.; Vol. 3—17; 450; 47p.

Volume 1 is an index to some 8,500 articles in twenty-five Taiwan and five Hong Kong Chinese periodicals (mostly academic journals) published from 1947 to the end of 1957. Education periodicals indexed in *Chin shih-nien lai chiao-yü lun-wen so-yin* 近十年來教育論文索引 (An Index to Periodical Literature on Education, 1946–1956) compiled by Ssu Ch'i 司琦 (see **99**), are excluded, as are editorials, news, commentaries, book reviews, and creative writing. Arranged under the following subject headings: bibliography and general, philosophy, religion, natural science, applied science, the social sciences, history and geography, language and literature, and fine arts.

Entries in the index are arranged in the order of title giving also the author or translator, name of journal, place of publication, volume number and date. A list of the thirty journals indexed is provided at the beginning, and an English translation of the same list is appended.

Volume 2 (some 8,000 entries), published in the same format as Volume 1, brings the coverage up to the end of 1960 and covers forty more Taiwan, Hong Kong and Macao periodicals for the period 1947–1960, making a total of some seventy periodicals indexed in this volume.

Volume 3, containing more than 6,700 entries selected from seventy-five periodicals (thirty-two of which are indexed for the first time in this volume), provides coverage to the end of 1961 and brings to slightly more than 100 the number of periodicals indexed in all three volumes. The format is the same as that adopted for the first two volumes except for the addition of a list of more than 450 Chinese-language periodicals published in Taiwan since 1946 arranged by subject. Information provided in this list includes title, first date of publication, publisher, address, and a 'remarks' column which indicates frequency, and whether or not publication has ceased. There is also a title index to this list arranged by stroke count.

Future volumes are under preparation. The most important periodical index covering Taiwan (and Hong Kong) publications, especially academic journals. An indispensable reference work.

193 **Kuo-fang yen-chiu yüan, T'u-shu kuan** 國防研究院圖書館 (National War College, Library). *Ch'i-k'an lun-wen so-yin* 期刊論文索引 *Chinese Periodicals Index.* Yangmingshan, No. 1—, 1960—. Monthly.

A monthly index to 155 current Chinese periodicals published in Taiwan, Hong Kong and Macao since 1960, arranged under the following subject headings: bibliography and general, philosophy, religion, natural science, applied science, the social sciences, history and geography, language and literature, and fine arts. Only the more substantive articles are indexed.

An index to articles on Communist China from the same journals is appended to each issue under the title *Yu-kuan yen-chiu ti-ch'ing lun-wen so-yin* 有關研究 敵情論文索引 (Index to Articles Concerning the Study of Enemy Situation). Arranged by subject according to the *Chung-kuo t'u-shu fen-lei fa* (Classification Scheme for Chinese Books) based on a decimal system.

While there is some duplication, most of the periodicals covered are new titles not indexed in the preceding entry. Quite useful.

194 **'Hui-yüan tsa-chih lun-wen so-yin'** 會員雜誌論文索引 (Index to Periodicals Published by the Members of the Taiwan Association of

Periodical Publishers) in *Chung-hua min-kuo tsa-chih nien-chien* 中華民國雜誌年鑑 (Chinese Periodicals Yearbook), (Taipei, 1954), 5th section, pp. 1–141.

An index to selected articles in 148 periodicals published in Taiwan from roughly 1950 to 1954, arranged by subject (military, politics, international relations, social conditions, Overseas Chinese, science, literature, etc.). Within each subject division, articles from the same periodical dealing on the same subject are listed together chronologically (while the periodicals themselves are listed randomly). The last subject division is 'Bandit Information', containing some 335 articles. The index is a good supplement to the two preceding entries for articles published to 1954, in that it covers a number of periodicals not indexed in either of them, and it is especially useful for locating literary publications.

194a Kuo-li cheng-chih ta-hsüeh, She-hui k'o-hsüeh tzu-liao chung-hsin 國立政治大學社會科學資料中心 (National Chengchi University, Social Science Materials Center). *Chung-wen pao-chih lun-wen fen-lei so-yin* 中文報紙論文分類索引 *Classified Index to Chinese Newspapers, 1962.* Taipei, 1963. 411p.

An index to scholarly articles in the fields of the social sciences and humanities published in the following sixteen Taiwan and Hong Kong Chinese newspapers in 1962: *Chung-yang jih-pao* 中央日報, *Chung-hua jih-pao* 中華日報, *T'ai-wan hsin-sheng pao* 臺灣新生報, *Lien-ho pao* 聯合報, *Cheng-hsin hsin-wen pao* 徵信新聞報, *Kung-lun pao* 公論報, *Ch'ing-nien chan-shih pao* 青年戰士報, *Ta-hua wan-pao* 大華晚報, *Min-tsu wan-pao* 民族晚報, *Tzu-li wan-pao* 自立晚報, *Kung-shang jih-pao* 工商日報, *Hua-ch'iao jih-pao* 華僑日報, *Hsiang-kang shih-pao* 香港時報, *Hsing-tao jih-pao* 星島日報, *T'ien-wen t'ai* 天文臺, and *Tzu-yu pao* 自由報. (The last six are Hong Kong publications.)

Articles are arranged by subject, and under the title of each article the following bibliographical information is given: name of author (unsigned articles selected from a special supplement are attributed to that supplement; editorials are so indicated), name of newspaper, date of publication, page number, and remarks. Projected as an annual publication. The 1963 volume is now available.

195 T'ai-wan sheng wen-hsien wei-yüan hui 臺灣省文獻委員會 (Taiwan Historical Research Commission). *T'ai-wan wen-hsien fen-lei so-yin* 臺灣文獻分類索引 *Indicus Taiwanica.* Taipei, 1961—. Annual.

A classified index to newspaper and periodical literature concerned with Taiwan. Vol. 1 (472p.) surveys some 190 Taiwan newspapers and periodicals, for the year 1959, and the articles selected for inclusion are entered under 142 headings (conforming to the subject divisions of the Preliminary Draft of the General History of Taiwan). News items, short articles and book reviews are excluded. Author, title, periodical, volume and number of issue, and date of publication are given for each of the more than 700 entries. Vol. 2 (307p.)

covers 215 newspapers and periodicals published in 1960 and more than 10,000 articles are divided under 155 headings. Volume 1 is mimeographed.

The *Indicus Taiwanica* is a comprehensive rather than critical survey, and is most useful for locating articles published in lesser known local Taiwan newspapers and periodicals.

B. INDEXES TO LAWS, AND TREATIES AND AGREEMENTS

The chapters on laws and regulations (XII) and foreign relations (XVI) contain two documentary sources for which there are indexes listed in the present section. It is well to note, however, that some of the compendia described in Chapters XII and XVI are equipped with their own indexes and receive no further attention in the Guide.

Laws and Regulations

To the authors' knowledge, no index to laws and regulations has appeared to date in Communist China. The present section contains several Japanese compilations which contribute to the filling of this gap. Together the first three entries cover the most important laws promulgated on the Mainland from 1949 to 1963, and constitute the best guide available in any language. See also the index available at the Union Research Institute (**1750**). Nothing comparable to these exists for Nationalist China.

Treaties and Agreements

No special indexes to treaties and agreements exist that bracket the entire range of Peking's or Taipei's post-1949 foreign relations, except for the 1962 and 1964 editions of *Chūgoku seiji keizai sōran* (**198**) and the list of agreements between Communist China and foreign countries prepared by the American Consulate General in Hong Kong (**200**). The *Calendar of Soviet Treaties, 1917–1957* (**201**) provides coverage through 1957 on the mutually important relations between the Chinese People's Republic and the Soviet Union.

196 Taira, Kazuhiko 平和彦. *Chūka Jimmin Kyōwakoku hōrei sakuin, 1949 nen 10 gatsu–1953 nen 12 gatsu* 中華人民共和國法令索引 1949 年 10 月–1953 年 12月

(Index to Laws and Regulations of the People's Republic of China—October 1949–December 1953). Tokyo: Kokuritsu Kokkai Toshokan 國立國會圖書館, 1954. 145p.

Classified and chronological indexes to 2,000 laws and regulations (largely political, economic and social) promulgated in Communist China from October 1949 to December 1953 (including a few issued prior to October 1949), based on official Chinese Communist sources.

The first index is arranged by subject under seventeen major categories (fundamental laws, administrative law, civil service law, domestic affairs, foreign affairs, military affairs, public finance, taxation, banking, foreign trade, industry, agriculture and irrigation, land, labor, transportation and postal and telecommunication services, culture and education, and the judicial system). It is further arranged by date of promulgation. The second is arranged by date of promulgation. Both indexes give the name of the law in question, the promulgating agency and source. Also included are lists of sources and of promulgating agencies.

For classified indexes to laws and regulations after December 1953, see following entries.

197 **'Chūka Jimmin Kyōwakoku hōrei sakuin'** 中華人民共和國法令索引 (Index to Laws and Regulations of the People's Republic of China) in *Chūgoku seiji keizai sōran* 中國政治經濟綜覽 *Political and Economic Views on Present Day China*, 1960 edition (Tokyo: Hitotsubashi Shobō 一橋書房, 1960), pp. 1069–1114.

Updates the preceding entry to December 1959. The index lists about 1,000 laws and regulations in force largely in the political, economic and cultural spheres. In ten categories (with further subdivisions): basic laws, administrative law (some 100 items), internal affairs (90), judiciary and public peace, foreign affairs, military affairs, economics (over 300), industry (over 200), transportation and communications, and culture and education (175). Each entry provides the title of the law, promulgating agency, date and source. No chronological index.

See also next entry.

198 **'Chūka Jimmin Kyōwakoku hōrei, jōyaku, kyōtei sakuin'** 中華人民共和國 法令, 條約, 協定索引 (Indexes to Laws and Regulations, and Treaties and Agreements of the People's Republic of China) in *Chūgoku seiji keizai sōran* 中國政治經濟綜覽 *Political and Economic Views on Present Day China*, 1962 edition (Tokyo: Nikkan Rōdō Tsūshinsha 日刊勞働通信社, 1962), pp. 1410–1397 (reverse pagination).

Updates the preceding index to laws and regulations to June 1961 and provides an index to treaties and agreements for the period January 1960 to June 1961. The two indexes list about 100 laws and regulations and about 120 treaties and agreements. The laws are arranged in eight categories (with further subdivisions). The treaties and agreements are arranged in five categories: treaties and border agreements (16), trade agreements and protocols (46), cultural agreements (27), scientific agreements (23), and miscellaneous. The treaty index provides the name of the treaty or agreement, date of signing (also including in some instances the dates of ratification and exchange of ratified copies), place of signing (or exchange of ratifications), and source. The 1964 edition provides an index to some 70 additional laws and 130 treaties and agreements for the period July 1961–June 1963, pp. 1114–1101 (reverse pagination).

These compilations taken together represent the most comprehensive index to Mainland laws and regulations in any language.

199 Aichi Daigaku, Kokusai Mondai Kenkyūjo 愛知大學國際問題研究所 (Aichi University, Institute of International Affairs). *Chūka Jimmin Kyōwakoku hōrei mokuroku, 1949 nen–1954 nen 6 gatsu* 中華人民共和國法令目錄 1949年— 1954 年 6 月

(List of Laws and Regulations of the Chinese People's Republic, 1949–June 1954). Toyohashi, 1954. 80p.

A classified list of some 500 important laws, treaties, statements, declarations, etc., originating in the period from the founding of the Chinese People's Republic in 1949 to the adoption of the 1954 constitution. The volume was prepared as a by-product of the Institute's Project on Chinese Communist Laws. In four broad categories: political-social, finance-economics, education-culture, and treaties, with further subdivisions. Entries provide the name of the law, date of promulgation, issuing agency or authority, and source.

Except for the period January-June 1954, this list has been superseded by *Chūka Jimmin Kyōwakoku hōrei sakuin* (see **196**).

200 American Consulate General, Hong Kong.

'Agreements Between Communist China and Foreign Countries, October 1949– December 1957,' *Current Background*, No. 545 (January 20, 1959), 25p.

A list of treaties, agreements, and protocols concluded between the Chinese Communist government and other countries with which it maintains diplomatic relations, for the period October 1949 through December 1957, arranged under three parts: (1) bi-lateral, (2) plural-lateral, and (3) multi-lateral agreements and conventions. Part 1 is further grouped by country, with the Communist countries listed first. No index. Supersedes *Current Background*, No. 438 (March 6, 1957).

References to the text of each document as it is available in the *Survey of China Mainland Press* and other issues of *Current Background* are given in each case. See also No. 651 (April 19, 1961), 14p., for the period January 1958 to December 1960.

201 Slusser, Robert M., and Triska, Jan F.

A Calendar of Soviet Treaties, 1917–1957. Stanford, Calif.: Stanford University Press, 1959. 530p.

Catalogs all verified international agreements entered into by Soviet Russia, regardless of their form, in the period 1917–1957, inclusive. The individual agreement is the basic unit of the *Calendar*, and is listed together with the following information: (1) a serial number, serving to identify the agreement; (2) a title or subject; (3) the main body of the entry, consisting of a précis of data concerning the agreement, followed by a list of (4) sources; and/or (5) references. The following sections are provided in the appendix: (1) unratified treaties, (2) secret Soviet-German military agreements, 1921–1933, (3) nongovernmental agreements, (4) unverified treaties, (5) addenda (agreements and data identified after completion of the main text). The index is arranged by country and is accompanied by a 'Table of Index Headings' (entries for China appear under 'China' [38 entries] and 'Chinese People's Republic' [97]). The first supplement covering the period January-December 1958 was published in *Osteuropa-Recht*, No. 1/2 (June 1961), pp. 100–131. A basic reference volume.

See also 'A Bibliographical List of Treaties and Agreements Concluded Between Communist China and the Soviet Union, 1949–1957', in *Communist China's Relations with the Soviet Union, 1949–1957* by Chin Szu-k'ai (Hong Kong: Union Research Institute, Communist China Problem Research Series EC 26, 1961), pp. i-ix.

PART TWO

GENERAL REFERENCE WORKS

Part One of this Guide is essentially bibliographical in nature. The focus of Part Two is on reference works which themselves provide substantive material on contemporary China.

Of the seven chapters making up Part Two, the largest is devoted to dictionaries and glossaries (over 140 entries), followed by encyclopedias and yearbooks (63), directories (55), biographical materials (37), and statistical compilations (30). In considering the contents of Part Two, it cannot be overstated that the reader in pursuing his subject must frequently consult more than one, and occasionally several, chapters to draw full advantage from the present Guide. Chronologies, biographies, directories and statistical compilations are, for example, all listed in separate chapters, but they also appear as sections of encyclopedias, yearbooks and handbooks. The chapters on directories and biographies contain related data and must be consulted together.

It might be mentioned also that some of the documentary collections described in Part Three contain chronologies, name lists and other reference data.

CHAPTER IV

ENCYCLOPEDIAS, YEARBOOKS AND HANDBOOKS

A. GENERAL

While yearbooks, handbooks and the like concerning either the Mainland or Taiwan exist in fairly large numbers, those dealing with them jointly are mainly of Japanese origin. Ten publications covering both Taiwan and the Mainland appear in this section.

The most comprehensive of these is the handbook published by the Japanese Society for Asian Political and Economic Studies, over 1,000 pages in length (first entry). Also listed here are the H.R.A.F. China volume (**203**), the *Far Eastern Economic Review Yearbook* (**205**), several Japanese yearbooks and dictionaries of Asian history, the World Knowledge Yearbook published in Peking (**204**), and two Russian-language encyclopedic works on China (**210** and **211**).

The works contained herein should be consulted together with those which appear in the following separate sections on the Mainland and Taiwan.

202 **Ajia Seikei Gakkai** アジア政經學會 (Society for Asian Political and Economic Studies). *Chūgoku seiji keizai sōran* 中國政治經濟綜覽
Political and Economic Views on Present Day China. Tokyo: Nikkan Rōdō Tsūshinsha 日刊勞働通信社, 1954, 1960, 1962 1964. 4 vols.

A detailed handbook (of roughly 1,000–1,500 pages) on Communist China, Taiwan and the Overseas Chinese, compiled under the auspices of the Society for Asian Political and Economic Studies, with contributions by fifty specialists from the Foreign Ministry, Minisrty of Education, the National Diet Library, Economic Planning Board, Cabinet Research Office, the Asahi and Mainichi newspapers, the Kyodo Press, and professors from Tokyo, Kyoto, Hitotsubashi, Aichi, Seijō, Keio and other universities. The volume emphasizes political and economic conditions in the postwar period. (The most recent volumes have also included sections on both North and South Korea and Outer Mongolia.) The body of the material is divided by topic with numerous subdivisions (geography; modern history; politics; military affairs; foreign relations; economics; production—agriculture, mining and industry, commerce, transportation and communications; foreign trade and economic aid; society and culture; Nationalist China, Overseas Chinese).

The appendices, which occupy roughly a third of each volume, contain a documentary section (over 100 pages of texts of laws, treaties and other important documents); a chronology (see **391**); indexes to Chinese Communist laws and regulations, and treaties and agreements (see **196–198**); a bibliography of books and articles on China (see **33, 34**); a biographical section (in the first edition only), and other useful data. Title and table of contents are given in English. Index arranged according to the Japanese syllabary.

This compilation is more factual and objective than the analogous publications of the Chūgoku Kenkyūjo (China Research Institute; see next section).

203 Hu, Chang-tu, ed.
China: Its People, Its Society, Its Culture. New Haven, Conn.: Human Relations Area Files Press, 1960. 611p.

A handbook based in part on a number of background studies prepared for the Human Relations Area Files by the two China projects at the University of Washington and Stanford University. Contains useful tables and a good, selected bibliography with very brief annotations of more than 500 books and articles in English, arranged to parallel the twenty-four chapters of the book (e.g., 'The Culture and the Society', 'Dynamics of Political Behavior', 'Industry', 'National Attitudes', etc.). Indexed.

A concise, informative volume, conveniently arranged.

204 Shih-chieh chih-shih nien-chien 世界知識年鑑
(World Knowledge Yearbook). Peking: Shih-chieh chih-shih ch'u-pan she 世界知識出版社, 1953—.

Published under title *Shih-chieh chih-shih shou-ts'e* 世界知識手冊 (World Knowledge Handbook) from 1953 to 1957, the volume was given its present title with the 1958 edition. The earlier volumes devoted one complete section and a number of scattered entries to the coverage of Communist China. (The section on China did not appear in the 1961 edition.) No volumes seem to have been published in either 1956 or 1960.

Although a general reference work, the Yearbook is useful in the study of Chinese Communist attitudes towards other countries.

205 Far Eastern Economic Review Yearbook. Hong Kong: Far Eastern Economic Review, 1960—. Annual.

Supersedes the Special Christmas Issue of the *Far Eastern Economic Review*. The bulk of the *Yearbook* comprises separate economic surveys of each country or territory, arranged in alphabetical order (including sections on the Mainland and Taiwan). All except a few minor surveys are divided into seven standard sections: politics, economy, finance, trade, agriculture, industry, and power and transport. In each edition there is also a general review of the whole region, presenting major developments and principal trends in the economic sphere. A special textile survey of Asia was appended to the 1961 issue.

Comprehensive and up-to-date.

206 Japan, Gaimushō, Ajiakyoku 日本外務省アジア局 (Japan, Ministry of Foreign Affairs, Bureau of Asian Affairs). *Ajia nenkan* アジア年鑑
(Asian Yearbook). Tokyo: Tōa Jijō Chōsakai 東亞事情調査會, 1953. 783p.

The first comprehensive handbook on Asia published under the supervision of a Japanese government agency. The data, largely political and economic in emphasis, is given as of March 1953. The first half of the volume is devoted to a description of Asia by country (Japan is excluded), with 100 pages given over to Communist China, twenty pages to Nationalist China, and ten pages to Hong Kong and Macao. The second half consists of government documents, economic and trade statistics, etc. No chronology is provided, and the volume is not indexed. No further volumes published.

207 Kokusai Nihon Kyōkai 國際日本協會 (Japan International Association). *Ajia seiji keizai nenkan* アジア政治經濟年鑑 (Yearbook of Asian Politics and Economics). Tokyo: Kokusai Nihon Kyōkai, 1956. 960; 191p.

Contains a substantial section (over 200 p.) devoted to Asia, including the Asian policies of the major powers, and separate sections on each Asian country. The section on Mainland China is over 150 pages in length; Taiwan, 20 pages; Hong Kong and Macao, 15 pages. Each section is further subdivided into a number of topics, with an emphasis on politics, economics and trade. Some eighty specialists contributed to the volume and most articles are documented and signed.

Appendices include a chronology of contemporary Asian history, 1945–1955 (68p.); the texts of constitutions of various countries; a list of treaties concluded by each country classified by treaty subject and by treaty partner; a bibliography of Japanese and Western works on Asia and Asian countries published between 1945 and 1955 (including over 400 Japanese-language works and some 100 Western-language [including Russian] works on China); and a statistical section. Subject and personal name indexes.

208 Heibonsha 平凡社 (Heibonsha Company). *Ajia rekishi jiten* アジア歴史事典 (Dictionary of Asian History). Tokyo, 1959–1962. 10 vols.

The first eight volumes (each averaging 450 pages) comprise a dictionary of Asian and African history arranged according to the Japanese syllabary. Over half of the material is devoted to China and includes current developments. Each subject entry supplies the Japanese syllabary, Chinese characters and romanization, and a signed article accompanied by references.

Volume 9 contains a number of appendices, among them a list of the most important Japanese journals in the Oriental field, providing information on the date of publication of each volume and issue. Volume 10 is given over to three indexes: Chinese character, Japanese syllabary (both arranged in Japanese syllabic order), and alphabetical (Latin). The last two indexes refer to foreign names and expressions.

209 Kyōto Daigaku, Bungakubu, Tōyōshi Kenkyūshitsu 京都大學文學部東洋史研究室 (Department of Oriental History of the Faculty of Letters of Kyoto University). *Tōyōshi jiten* 東洋史辭典 (Dictionary of Oriental History). Tokyo: Sōgensha 創元社, 1961. 994p.

A dictionary of Oriental history, which in Japan signifies primarily Chinese history. The volume includes a number of articles on contemporary Chinese leaders, contemporary institutions, journals, etc. Articles are arranged according to the Japanese syllabary and contain bibliographical references. Index arranged according to Japanese syllabary.

210 Bol'shaia Sovetskaia Entsiklopediia
(The Large Soviet Encyclopedia). *Kitai* (China). Moscow, 1954. 464p.

A re-publication of an article on China which occupied a quarter of Volume 21 of the Large Soviet Encyclopedia (second edition). This richly illustrated work is divided into twenty-four topical chapters, most of them containing substantial bibliographies of sources in Russian, Chinese and Western languages. The last chapter consists of a chronology of Chinese history from prehistoric times to February 1953. General alphabetical index.

For current data, see the articles on China in the yearly supplements to the encyclopedia (*Ezhegodnik Bol'shoi Sovetskoi Entsiklopedii*, 1957—).

211 Shkarenkova, G., ed. *Nash drug Kitai; Slovar'—Spravochnik*
(Our Friend China; Encyclopedic Handbook). Moscow: Gosudarstvennoe izdatel'stvo politicheskoi literatury, 1959. 630p.

A small encyclopedic handbook, divided into five parts: (1) geography, (2) social organization (includes politics and government), (3) economy, (4) culture, and (5) history. Within each part the entries are arranged in alphabetical order. Subject index.

B. MAINLAND

In addition to the few yearbooks and handbooks published on the Mainland, reference works of a similar nature from Hong Kong, Taiwan, Japan and the Soviet Union are also included in this section.

The only current and authoritative compilation is the semi-official *Jen-min shou-ts'e* (People's Handbook, first entry). It differs, however, from ordinary yearbooks in its extensive reproduction of official documents, which is for all practical purposes its *raison d'être*. The usual components of a yearbook (chronologies, biographies, etc.) are relegated to a position of secondary importance or omitted altogether. The English-language *Handbook on People's China* (213) is likewise not a full-fledged yearbook. For that matter, at the present time the only English-language yearbook dealing with Communist China is *Communist China Yearbook 1962*, published by the China Research Associates in Hong Kong (225).

This is not the case with the prolific Japanese output in this field, which is mainly the contribution of the Japanese government and a number of private organizations of varied political outlook. Perhaps most useful are the various yearbooks issued by the leftist China Research Institute. Systematic compilations of Mainland data were begun by the Institute with an annual for 1949 published in 1950 *(Shin Chūgoku nempō)*, followed by three editions of a handbook on contemporary China *(Gendai*

Chūgoku jiten) for 1950, 1952 and 1954, which was in turn superseded by the China Yearbook *(Chūgoku nenkan)* in 1955. (Beginning with the 1962 volume, the title changed to New China Yearbook—*Shin Chūgoku nenkan*, (see **215–218**). In addition, in 1954 the Institute published a popular encyclopedic pocketbook on China (**220**), followed in 1959 by a comprehensive encyclopedic dictionary of contemporary China (**219**). Although the China Research Institute does not evaluate Mainland data and tends to follow the party line, its various compilations are very useful collections of scattered Mainland data.

The Japanese Foreign Office produced a handbook on Communist China in 1949 and 1950, and the latter, in a different format, has appeared as an annual since 1955 (**221, 222**). The publication of the Office of Asian Documentation of the International Friendship Club (Tokyo), Communist China—Developments with Critical Commentary (annual since 1956), provides an element of balance to the official Mainland data compiled by the China Research Institute (see **223**).

Reference should also be made to the various available surveys: the ten-year survey published on the Mainland, and the annual and ten-year surveys published in Hong Kong and Taiwan. From Taiwan there are also three useful local surveys of present day Kwangtung, Inner Mongolia and the Kwangsi Chuang autonomous region.

Topical yearbooks and handbooks, such as those listed for Taiwan (see below), are not available for the Mainland.

212 Jen-min shou-ts'e 人民手冊
(People's Handbook). Shanghai, Tientsin, Peking: Ta-kung pao 大公報, 1950—

Issued annually since 1950 (none appeared for 1954), the semi-official People's Handbook was published in Shanghai 1950–1952, in Tientsin 1953–1956, and in Peking since 1957. The last volume available is for 1964.

The Handbook, the only available general yearbook published on the Mainland, is largely given over to the reproduction of documents on domestic developments and foreign relations (the documents are topically arranged and are accompanied by bibliographical citations). Especially noteworthy is the inclusion of documents which have not appeared in other collections, such as foreign policy statements and the proceedings and resolutions of various conferences and meetings. In the 1956 edition, a good select bibliography was appended to each section.

The Handbook lacks many of the features customarily found in publications of this type. A chronology was included in the years 1950–1955, but was dropped thereafter. Biographies are entirely omitted, and such statistics as are included are few and generally meaningless. The Handbook does contain current government directories, administrative divisions, etc. For a sample table of contents, see the J.P.R.S. Report, No. 3991, September 26, 1960 (U.S.G.P.O. Monthly Catalog, 1960, No. 17,340), 'Table of Contents of the 1959 People's Handbook'. See also the translations of seventeen important articles from the 1962 Handbook in the political and sociological fields in J.P.R.S. No. 18,454, March 31, 1963 (1963, No. 8,813), *Translations of Political and Sociological Information*, No. 72, 232p.

The major usefulness of the People's Handbook is in its documentary material on both domestic and foreign affairs.

213 Handbook on People's China. Peking: Foreign Languages Press, 1957. 236p.

An expanded version of *A Guide to New China* (Peking: Foreign Languages Press, 1952). An official publication containing brief descriptions of government organs, political parties, mass organizations, etc. Included also is a chronology of events in Communist China, September 1949 to March 1957 (46p.). The only English-language handbook of its kind published on the Mainland.

214 Chou, Fang 周方. *Wo-kuo kuo-chia chi-kou* 我國國家機構 (Structure of Our Government). Peking: Chung-kuo ch'ing-nien ch'u-pan she 中國青年出版社, 1955. 144p.

A useful primer on the organization and structure of the government of Communist China.

215 Chūgoku Kenkyūjo 中國研究所 (China Research Institute). *Chūgoku nenkan* 中國年鑑 (China Yearbook). Tokyo: Ishizaki Shoten 石崎書店, 1955–1961. Annual.

An annual yearbook on Communist China superseding the *Gendai Chūgoku jiten* 現代中國辭典 (Handbook on Contemporary China) published by the Institute in 1950 (revised in 1952 and 1954). The 500-page-plus yearbook, based on the People's Handbook and other Chinese Communist publications, is divided into the following chapters (with many subdivisions): general review of the preceding year; land, people and history; China in world affairs; politics; economics (over one-third of the volume); social and cultural; and resolutions of major conferences, etc., and other documentary materials. The yearbooks are laden with statistics and cover Chinese-Japanese political, cultural and trade relations in detail.

The appendices carry a chronology for the preceding year and, from time to time, texts of important laws and regulations; classified lists of important laws and regulations for the preceding year; classified lists of important Chinese-language periodicals published on the Mainland; rosters of government, party, and people's cultural, educational and religious organizations; lists of the above organizations with addresses, names of officers and publications; lists of important state enterprises, government trade corporations, and research institutions; lists of Japanese delegations to China including names of chairmen and dates; geographical administrative divisions; lists of over 1,000 important persons arranged by Japanese syllabary in accordance with the Japanese pronunciation; and miscellaneous data (e.g., lists of simplified characters, weights and measures, etc.).

Subject and personal name indexes. Folded map of China. Superseded by *Shin Chūgoku nenkan* 新中國年鑑 (New China Yearbook; see next entry).

216 Chūgoku Kenkyūjo 中國研究所 (China Research Institute). *Shin Chūgoku nenkan, 1962——* 新中國年鑑
(New China Yearbook, 1962—). Tokyo: Kyokutō Shoten 極東書店, 1962—. Annual.

A continuation of *Chūgoku nenkan* 中國年鑑 (China Yearbook; see preceding entry). While the emphasis continues to be on economic developments, the cultural and educational sections have been expanded, and the documentary part doubled in size.

The new yearbook is different in format: a large-size volume of some 400 pages arranged in three columns. In addition to the material contained in the China Yearbook, the new publication carries biographies of some 100 prominent Chinese leaders, a chronology of modern Chinese history from 1839 to date (including a detailed separate chronology for the preceding year), and a glossary of new words and expressions. There is also a list of important articles in the Japanese-language periodical *Jimmin Chūgoku* 人民中國 (People's China) published in Peking during the preceding year.

Probably the most useful yearbook on Communist China in any language.

217 Chūgoku Kenkyūjo 中國研究所 (China Research Institute). *Gendai Chūgoku jiten* 現代中國辭典
(Dictionary on Contemporary China). Tokyo, 1950, 1952, 1954. 3 vols.

A detailed handbook mainly concerned with Communist China's foreign relations, politics and economic policy, based on Chinese Communist sources, prepared by some fifty contributors, many of them staff members of the China Research Institute. (Taiwan is not covered.)

The volumes, ranging in length from 800 to 900 large-size pages, are arranged (with subdivisions) as follows: physical environment, international relations, politics, economics, society and culture, literature and the arts, and history. Each section is accompanied by bibliographical references. The appendices contain a biographical section (over 500 biographical sketches arranged according to the Japanese reading of the subject's name in Japanese syllabic order, with an alphabetical index according to Wade-Giles romanization); some 40 pages of texts of important laws; a 30–40 page chronology of China from 1839 to the present; and a list of China research centers in various countries. General index arranged according to the Japanese syllabary.

Superseded by China Yearbook (see **215**). The handbook is a useful summary of Chinese Communist data, but uncritically presented.

218 Chūgoku Kenkyūjo 中國研究所 (China Research Institute). *Shin Chūgoku nempō, 1949* 新中國年報
(New China Annual, 1949). Tokyo: Getsuyō Shobō 月曜書房, 1950. 264p.

A handbook on Communist China for the year 1949, containing a description of the establishment of the Communist government in Peking, economic conditions on the Mainland and foreign relations. Texts of documents, a chronology for 1949, and statistics are appended.

Superseded by *Gendai Chūgoku jiten* 現代中國辭典 (Dictionary on Contemporary China; see preceding entry).

219   Chūgoku Kenkyūjo 中國研究所 (China Research Institute). *Gendai Chūgoku jiten* 現代中國事典
(Encyclopedic Dictionary of Contemporary China). Tokyo: Iwasaki Shoten 岩崎書店, 1959. 742; 118; 26p.

The first 742 pages comprise signed articles, with illustrations, on various aspects of modern China, contributed by members of the Institute as well as by some forty specialists from other institutions. Arrangement is by Japanese syllabary. The appendices (118p.) contain texts of important documents, statistics, rosters of government and party organizations, lists of Japanese organizations concerned with China and a 48-page chronology of modern Chinese history, 1839–1959, arranged in three columns (politics-economics, culture, and international relations). The subject index is arranged under broad categories with subdivisions (e.g., economics—general, finance, agriculture, industry, etc.) A name and subject index is provided, arranged according to the Japanese syllabary.

The only available encyclopedic dictionary on Communist China in any language.

220   Chūgoku Kenkyūjo 中國研究所 (China Research Institute). *Shin Chūgoku jiten* 新中國事典
(Encyclopedic Dictionary of New China). Tokyo: Aoki Shoten 青木書店, 1954. 280; 18p.

A popular pocket-size volume almost entirely devoted to China's post-1949 political, economic and cultural developments and foreign relations. Articles are arranged according to the Japanese syllabary. Brief chronology, 1949–1953 (pp. 271–277). Subject and name indexes.

221   Japan, Gaimushō, Ajiakyoku 日本外務省アジア局 (Japan, Ministry of Foreign Affairs, Bureau of Asian Affairs). *Chūkyō benran* 中共便覽
(Handbook on Communist China). Tokyo: Nihon Kokusai Mondai Kenkyūjo 日本國際問題研究所, 1955—. Annual.

A part of *Ajia shokoku benran sōsho* アジア諸國便覽叢書 (Series of Handbooks on Asian Countries), revised annually by the Ministry, the handbook covers geography, history, foreign relations, and political, economic (particularly long-range economic plans), military and cultural affairs on the Mainland. A short list of the most important officials is provided, together with information on Japanese residents on the Mainland and Chinese residents in Japan. No bibliography. Not indexed. 80–120 pages.

There are also shorter handbooks on Nationalist China and Hong Kong (see **241** and **257**).

222 Yoshikawa, Shigezō 吉川重藏. *Chūkyō sōran* 中共總覽 (Handbook on Communist China). Tokyo: Jiji Tsūshin Sha 時事通信社, 1950. 381p.

The trade edition, expanded and updated, of *Chūkyō gairon* 中共概論 (An Outline of Communist China) prepared in March 1949 by the staff of the China Section of the Ministry of Foreign Affairs under the supervision of the Chief of Section, who is listed as the author. The first postwar handbook on China prepared by an agency of the Japanese government, the volume covers the history of the Communist movement in China, the organization of the Communist party, political, economic and cultural developments, as well as the foreign relations of the Chinese Communist regime. The appendix contains a few key documents and organizational charts, and a chronology of the Communist movement in China, 1917–March 1950 (pp. 326–350), emphasizing the period after 1945. A name index and a subject index are provided, both arranged according to the Japanese syllabary.

223 Kokusai Zenrin Kurabu, Ajia Shiryōshitsu 國際善隣俱樂部アジア資料室 (International Friendship Club, Office of Asian Documentation). *Chūkyō— kensetsu to hihan (1955-nen no . . .)* 中共—建設と批判 (一九五五年 . . .) (Communist China—Developments with Critical Commentary [in 1955 . . .]). Tokyo, 1956—. Annual.

A yearly 300 to 500-page survey of Communist China emphasizing politics, ideology and economic policy, based on Mainland, Hong Kong, Taiwan and Japanese newspapers, periodicals, and other sources. Documents and statistics constitute about a third of the volume. Appended to the volumes for 1957, 1958 and 1959 are chronological lists of titles of editorials from *Jen-min jih-pao* and *Ta-kung pao*, accompanied by a description of the contents when the title is not explicit.

In contrast to the yearbooks published by the China Research Institute, these volumes provide a critical evaluation of Chinese Communist data.

224 Union Research Institute.
Communist China, 1955—. Hong Kong, 1956—. Annual. (Communist China Problem Research Series).

An annual survey of Communist China comprised of signed articles, based on Mainland sources, on such topics as the Chinese Communist Party, finance and trade, industry, natural calamities, agriculture, trade unions, cultural activities, and scientific work. Originally issued in one volume, the survey has expanded to two volumes with the 1960 edition (published in 1962). In 1959 it appeared in three volumes, covering the first decade (1949–1959) of the Communist regime on the Mainland. Also published in Chinese; see **227**). The most recent volume is for the year 1961 (published in 1963).

The articles are prepared by staff members of the Union Research Institute, a private anti-Communist research organization in Hong Kong. Informative and well documented.

225 **Communist China Yearbook 1962.** Hong Kong: China Research Associates, 1963. 588p.

Coverage extends from the beginning of 1961 through the first quarter of 1962. In seven parts (with subsections): (1) major meetings and statements; (2) political; (3) military; (4) people's communes; (5) economics; (6) culture and education; and (7) foreign relations. Emphasis is placed on political matters (286p.), the economy (120p.), and foreign relations (146p.).

The *Yearbook*, the only English-language publication of its kind thus far available, resembles the People's Handbook in format, and like the latter, provides texts of original documents (but in translation) with an indication of source. There is roughly a twenty per cent overlap in the contents of the two publications, but in other respects they differ significantly. In general, in terms of the selection of documents, the People's Handbook betrays a bias, whereas the *Yearbook* tends to be more analytical and objective. The *Yearbook* contains more detailed information on the political and administrative divisions of China. Changes are reported chronologically by month (January–December 1962). On the other hand, the directory section of the *Yearbook* is based on the 1961 edition of the People's Handbook, and as such is not as up-to-date as the latter's 1962 edition. The *Yearbook's* section on foreign relations lacks the very useful list of treaties concluded between Communist China and other countries during the year under review which is usually included in the People's Handbook.

The two volumes complement each other, and are useful source books on Communist China for their respective periods of coverage. (The 1962 People's Handbook covers the last half of 1961 and the first half of 1962.)

226 **Hui-huang ti shih-nien** 輝煌的十年
(Glorious Ten Years). Peking: Jen-min jih-pao ch'u-pan she 人民日報出版社, 1959. 2 vols. 792p.

A collection of articles by high government officials reviewing the accomplishments of Communist China during the decade 1949–1959. Comprehensive coverage and informative. For official statistics covering the same period, see *Wei-ta ti shih-nien—Chung-hua jen-min kung-ho kuo ching-chi ho wen-hua chien-she ch'eng-chiu ti t'ung-chi* 偉大的十年——中華人民共和國經濟和文化建設成就的統計 (**264**).

227 **Tsu-kuo chou-k'an she** 祖國週刊社 (China Weekly Publishing House). *Chung-kung shih-nien* 中共十年

(Communist China, 1949–1959). Hong Kong: Yu·lien ch'u-pan she 友聯出版社, 1960. 520p.

A symposium of sixteen articles on Communist China, 1949–1959. Topics covered: (1) C.C.P. party work, (2) political and legal affairs, (3) agriculture, (4) petroleum and electrical power industries, (5) economy, (6) socialist reconstruction of agriculture, (7) foreign trade, (8) industry, (9) literature and art, (10) labor movement, (11) foreign affairs, (12) military affairs, (13) propaganda, (14) requisition and distribution of grains, (15) education, (16) youth movement. Material for the articles is taken from Chinese Communist publications. Useful charts, statistics and footnotes. For a translation of this work, see *Communist China, 1949–1959*, 3 vols. (**224**).

228 Kung-fei pao-cheng shih-nien pien-chi wei-yüan hui 共匪暴政十年編輯委員會 (Editorial Committee of 'Ten Years of Communist Bandit Despotism'). *Kung-fei pao-cheng shih-nien* 共匪暴政十年
(Ten Years of Communist Bandit Despotism). Taipei: Chung-yang wen-wu kung-ying she 中央文物供應社, 1959. 432p.

A survey of Chinese Communist policies, programs and objectives from 1949 to 1959. The materials, which appear in twenty-one subsections, are organized around five main headings: politics and government, finance and economy, culture and education, military affairs, and social conditions. Appended is a chronology of the ten-year period.

229 Chung-kuo kuo-min tang, Chung-yang wei-yüan hui, Ti liu tsu 中國國民黨中央委員會第六組 (Kuomintang, Central Committee, Sixth Section). *Kung-fei pao-cheng chi yao* 共匪暴政紀要
(A Brief Record of Communist Bandit Despotism). Taipei: Chung-yang wen-wu kung-ying she 中央文物供應社, 1961. 2 vols. 820p.

A companion volume to *Kung-fei pao-cheng shih-nien* (see preceding entry), listing in chronological order the principal events of the Chinese Communist rule of the Mainland from October 1949 to October 1961. Six subject headings: party affairs, government, military affairs, economics and finance, culture and education, and social conditions. Under each heading are a number of sections and subsections. While the *Kung-fei pao-cheng shih-nien* is analytical in treatment, this volume is purely descriptive.

230 Shen, Sung-fang 沈頌芳, ed. *I-chiu-wu-ling jen-min nien-chien* 一九五〇人民年鑑 (People's Yearbook, 1950). Hong Kong: Ta-kung shu-chü 大公書局, 1950. 1 vol.

A one-volume yearbook, divided topically under the following major section headings: (1) China's internal situation, (2) political parties and people's groups, (3) the international situation, (4) documents, and (5) 'important persons of the new epoch'. Section 4 (64 pages) contains several documents on the organization of the new Communist government and speeches by important leaders. Section 5 (76 pages) contains over 200 one-paragraph biographies of government and party leaders of Communist China in 1949. This is the only volume published.

231 **Ch'ang-chiang jih-pao** 長江日報 (Yangtze Daily). *Tu-pao shou-ts'e* 讀報手冊 (Newspaper Handbook). Hankow: Ch'ang-chiang jih-pao, 1950. 1 vol. (pagination varies).

A general yearbook in two parts. Part 1, comprising the major portion of the volume, is concerned with Communist China between October 1949 and April 1950, and includes official documents on political, economic, social, cultural, military and international affairs. Part 2 is devoted to other countries.

232 **China, Kuo-fang pu, Ch'ing-pao chü** 中華民國國防部情報局 (China, Ministry of National Defense, Bureau of Intelligence). *Wei Kuang-tung sheng ti-ch'ü ch'ing-k'uang tiao-ch'a chuan-chi* 偽廣東省地區情況調查專集 (A Special Survey of Local Conditions in Puppet Kwangtung Province). Taipei, 1962. 393p.

The survey, based on Chinese Communist published and other verified sources and presented in tabular form, covers the period to June 1962. Divided into the following chapters: (1) physical geography, (2) political conditions, (3) military establishments, (4) agricultural conditions, (5) industrial conditions, (6) communications and transportation, and (7) cultural, educational and sanitary conditions. Each topical chapter is further divided into subsections. For instance, under 'Agricultural Conditions' detailed information is provided under the following four subsections: (1) state farms, (2) people's communes, (3) water works, and (4) natural disasters. Limited distribution.

The most complete and informative survey of any Mainland province available. An extremely valuable source.

233 **China, Kuo-fang pu, Ch'ing-pao chü** 中華民國國防部情報局 (China, Ministry of National Defense, Bureau of Intelligence). *Wei Nei Meng-ku tzu-chih ch'ü kai-k'uang* 偽內蒙古自治區概況 (Survey of the Puppet Inner Mongolia Autonomous Region). Taipei, 1962. 308p.

Divided into nine chapters: (1) the history of Inner Mongolia; (2) national characteristics and religious beliefs; (3) political conditions under Communist rule; (4) agriculture, livestock, forestry, water works, sand control, and meteorology; (5) industry; (6) 'socialist construction' and communes; (7) culture, education, and hygiene; (8) training of cadres in minority groups; and (9) transportation. Charts and maps are provided. It appears that information contained in this volume is based on published Chinese Communist sources, although specific references are rarely given. Limited distribution.

An informative compilation.

234   **China, Kuo-fang pu, Ch'ing-pao chü** 中華民國國防部情報局 (China, Ministry of National Defense, Bureau of Intelligence). *Wei Kuang-hsi Chuang tsu tzu-chih ch'ü kai-k'uang* 僞廣西僮族自治區概況
(A Survey of the Puppet Kwangsi Chuang Autonomous Region). Taipei, 1962. 124p.

Like the preceding entry, this survey is based on Chinese Communist published and other verified sources including monitored local broadcasts covering the period to 1962. Divided into eight chapters: (1) physical geography, (2) history of the Chuang people, (3) other minority groups in Kwangsi, (4) the history and administrative division of the Autonomous Region, (5) Chinese Communist rule and programs, (6) economic exploitation, (7) cultural, educational and sanitary conditions, and (8) communications and transportation. Again, as in the case of the preceding entry, each chapter is further divided into sections. Limited distribution.

The most comprehensive survey of the Chuang Autonomous Region available.

235   **Pei-ching ch'u-pan she** 北京出版社 (Peking Publishing House). *Pei-ching yu-lan shou-ts'e* 北京遊覽手冊
(Guide-Book to Peking). Peking: Pei-ching ch'u-pan she, 1959. 215p.

A traveler's guide to Peking, covering its historical and geographical setting, important monuments, cultural and business centers, and leading stores. Includes a detailed map of the city, a map of the transportation system, and photographs. This is a revised edition of the 1957 edition published under the same title.

J.P.R.S. No. 16,111, November 9, 1962, 921p. (U.S.G.P.O. Monthly Catalog 1963, No. 657) is a full translation of *Pei-ching shih chieh-hsiang ming-ch'eng lu* 北京市街巷名稱錄 (Complete Guide to Peking Streets and Alleys), compiled by the Peking Public Security Bureau (Peking, 1958), 497p.

See also *Peking, A Tourist Guide* (Peking, 1960), 192p., containing descriptions of museums, libraries, parks, recreation and amusement centers, stores and restaurants; and *Peking, An Album* (Peking, 1959), 291p.

236   **Ta-kung pao ch'u-pan wei-yüan hui** 大公報出版委員會 (Ta-kung pao, Publication Committee). *Hsin Shang-hai pien-lan* 新上海便覽
(New Shanghai Guide-Book). Shanghai: Ta-kung pao, 1951. 608p.

Describes Shanghai under Communist rule since 1949, under the following chapter divisions: (1) people's government, (2) industry and trade unions, (3) banking and commerce, (4) culture and education, (5) social work, (6) public transportation, (7) parks and landmarks, (8) restaurants, hotels and amusement centers, and (9) chronology (since the Communist take-over in May 1949 to May 1950).

237 U.S.S.R., Akademiia nauk, Institut mirovoi ekonomiki i mezhdunarodnykh otnoshenii (U.S.S.R., Academy of Sciences, Institute of World Economy and International Relations). *Mezhdunarodnyi politiko-ekonomicheskii ezhegodnik*
(International Political-Economic Yearbook). Moscow: Gosudarstvennoe izdatel'stvo politicheskoi literatury, 1958—. Annual.

A reference volume (450 to 750 pages) containing a number of articles on Soviet foreign policy and international problems; a section on international developments during the preceding year and a statistical section (some 100 pages), both classified by country; a chronology for the preceding year; and a bibliography (not in every issue).

The 1959 volume contains a bibliography (pp. 526–580) of Soviet works on Soviet foreign policy, international relations and international economics published from 1954 to 1958. The 1960 volume contains a similarly arranged bibliography (pp. 465–503) for 1959. Each bibliography contains a small number of works on Communist China. No index.

238 Nauchno-issledovatel'skii kon'iunkturnyi institut MVT SSSR (Institute of Economic Research of the U.S.S.R. Ministry of Foreign Trade). *Razvitie ekonomiki stran narodnoi demokratii—Obzor za 1952—*
(Economic Development of the People's Democracies—Survey for 1952—). Moscow: Izdatel'stvo sotsial'no-ekonomicheskoi literatury, 1953—. Annual.

An annual survey, ranging from 150 to 600 pages, of the economic development of the eleven countries of the Communist bloc (excluding the U.S.S.R.). Coverage is extended to such topics as industry, agriculture, transportation, domestic commerce, foreign trade, budget and 'the upsurge in the material welfare and cultural level of the toilers.' The section on Communist China in some volumes exceeds 200 pages in length. A statistical supplement available in more recent volumes is useful for comparative purposes.

The volumes for 1952 and 1953 (published in 1953 and 1954 respectively) were issued under the title *Khoziaistvennoe razvitie stran narodnoi demokratii* (Economic Development of the People's Democracies). The 1955 and 1956 surveys were issued separately for the European and Asian countries: *Razvitie ekonomiki evropeiskikh stran narodnoi demokratii* and *Razvitie ekonomiki stran narodnoi demokratii Azii*.

C. Taiwan

1. General

No official yearbooks were issued regularly by the Nationalist government until 1951, at which time a systematic publishing program was undertaken. Since the launching of the program, the Chinese-language and English-language editions of the *China Yearbook* (the first two entries) have become the two most important general reference works on Taiwan. The contents of the publications are approximately the same; however, the Chinese edition gives more emphasis to domestic affairs, while foreign relations receive more attention in the English-language edition. The latter also provides a 'who's who' section lacking in the Chinese edition.

Mention also should be made of the Taiwan Yearbook and of the official survey of Taiwan (243 and 243a), although no volumes of the Yearbook have appeared since 1954.

A number of yearbooks devoted to specific areas of activity on Taiwan are dealt with separately below.

239 **Chung-hua min-kuo nien-chien** 中華民國年鑑
(Republic of China Yearbook). Taipei: Chung-hua min-kuo nien-chien she 中華民國年鑑社, 1951—. Annual.

A yearbook on Taiwan, published annually at Taipei since 1951. The contents of each volume are divided into four major sections in twenty-three chapters: (1) general, (2) political parties, (3) the presidency, (4) administration, (5) legislation, (6) judiciary, (7) examination, (8) control, (9) domestic affairs, (10) foreign affairs, (11) military, (12) finance, (13) economy, (14) transportation and communications, (15) education, (16) administration of justice, (17) Overseas Chinese affairs, (18) Mongolian and Tibetan affairs, (19) information service, (20) Sino-American economic cooperation, (21) Taiwan, (22) the offshore islands, (23) Communist activities on the Mainland. A chronology of events of the preceding year appears in an appendix. (The 1961 issue contains a chronology of major events, 1911–1961, pp. 697–712.) Beginning with the 1959 volume, a chapter entitled 'Social and Mass Activities' has been added.

Officially sponsored, this yearbook is a basic reference work on Taiwan. For an English edition of the yearbook, see next entry.

240 **China Yearbook, 1951—.** Taipei: China Publishing Company, 1951—. Annual.

An English annual published in Taiwan since 1951 consisting of approximately 1,000 pages. Published under the title *China Handbook* from 1951 to 1957, the current title has been used since the 1958–1959 edition. (There is also a 1950 edition entitled *China Handbook* published by the Rockport Press, New York.)

Arranged topically, the contents are usually divided as follows: (1) general information, (2) the government and its functions, (3) national defense, (4) international affairs, (5) national economy, (6) cultural and social affairs, (7) the Chinese Communist regime, (8) a chronology, and (9) a who's who. The appendix includes translations of laws enacted during the year under review as well as selected diplomatic documents. Alphabetical index.

Like the preceding entry, this is an official publication providing essential information on the Republic of China on Taiwan.

241 **Japan, Gaimushō, Ajiakyoku** 日本外務省アジア局 (Japan, Ministry of Foreign Affairs, Bureau of Asian Affairs). *Chūka minkoku benran* 中華民國便覽 (Handbook on the Republic of China). Tokyo: Nihon Kokusai Mondai Kenkyūjo 日本國際問題研究所, 1955—. Annual.

A part of the *Ajia shokoku benran sōsho* アジア諸國便覽叢書 (Series of Hand-books on Asian Countries) revised annually by the Ministry, the handbook covers geography; history; foreign relations; and political, economic, military and cultural affairs on Taiwan. A short list of the most important officials is provided, together with information on Chinese and Taiwanese residents in Japan, and Japanese residents on Taiwan. No bibliography. Not indexed. 30–40 pages.

242 **Chung-hua nien-pao, 1953—** 中華年報 (民國四十二年—)
(China Annual, 1953—). Taipei: Chung-kuo hsin-wen ch'u-pan she 中國新聞 出版社, 1954–1958 [?].

A yearbook published since 1954, superseding and incorporating the following four titles published in 1952–1953: *Chung-kuo nien-pao* 中國年報 (China Annual), *Shih-chieh nien-pao* 世界年報 (World Annual), *T'ai-wan ching-chi nien-pao* 臺灣經濟年報 (Taiwan Economic Annual), and *Ta-lu fei-ch'ing nien-pao* 大陸匪情年報 (Mainland Bandit Information Annual). The four parts of the yearbook are equivalent to the subject matter of the four absorbed publications. Publication is believed to have ceased in 1958.

Especially informative on the economic reconstruction program in Taiwan.

243 **T'ai-wan nien-chien** 臺灣年鑑
(Taiwan Yearbook). Taipei, 2 vols. (1947, 1954).

A yearbook of the Province of Taiwan. The 1947 edition, published by the *Hsin-sheng pao* 新生報, contains information through the end of 1946; the 1952 edition, published by the *Kung-lun pao* 公論報, contains information as of the end of 1951. Both were compiled under the direction of Li Wan-chü 李萬居. Arranged by topic (politics and government, economy, culture and education, military affairs, public welfare, etc.), the volumes include information and statistics on the pre-1945 period of Japanese occupation. No further volumes have been published.

See also *Tseng-ting T'ai-wan t'ung-lan* 增訂臺灣通覽 (Taiwan Handbook, revised edition, 1963) published by the Ta-hua Evening Post (大華晚報) 616p. (First edition appeared in 1960.)

243a **Taiwan, Hsin-wen ch'u** 臺灣省政府 新聞處 (Taiwan, Department of Infor-mation). *T'ai-wan ti chien-she: Chung-hua min-kuo san-shih ssu nien chih wu-shih i nien* 臺灣的建設: 中華民國三十四年至五十一年
(Taiwan's Reconstruction: 1945–1962). Taichung, 1962. 1 vol. 1,023p.

An official survey of Taiwan's political, economic, cultural, and social achieve-ments under the Nationalist Government during the seventeen-year period 1945–1962. The book is arranged in twenty chapters: (1) general; (2) people's representative governments; (3) governmental system; (4) administration; (5) finance; (6) land reform and utilization; (7) agriculture; (8) food supply; (9)

water conservation and hydro-electricity; (10) industry; (11) mining; (12) commerce; (13) communications; (14) education; (15) culture and mass communication media; (16) public health; (17) social security; (18) social problems and police work; (19) city and rural rehabilitation; and (20) social conditions (civic organizations, tourism, etc.). An appendix contains a chronology of major events covering the period from October 25, 1945 to December 31, 1961.

A most comprehensive compilation.

244 Fan-jung chin-pu ti T'ai-wan pien-chi wei-yüan hui 繁榮進步的臺灣編輯 委員會 (Compilation Committee of 'A Prosperous and Progressive Taiwan'). *Fan-jung chin-pu ti T'ai-wan* 繁榮進步的臺灣 (A Prosperous and Progressive Taiwan). Taipei: Shih-chieh hua-k'an she 世界 畫刊社, 1959. 512p.

A popular general handbook on Taiwan since 1945, in fifteen chapters: (1) history of Taiwan, (2) geography of Taiwan, (3) political developments, (4) economic developments, (5) military developments, (6) cultural developments, (7) social developments, (8) Overseas Chinese, (9) women's work, (10) youth movement, (11) 'Achievements of the Asian People's Anti-Communist League', (12) veterans' rehabilitation, (13) refugee and relief work, (14) achievements of local governments, and (15) 'The World Anti-Communist Movement from the Point of Taiwan's Prosperity'.

245 Taiwan, Hsin-wen ch'u 臺灣省政府 新聞處 (Taiwan, Department of Information). *Taiwan, Ten Years of Progress*. Taipei, 1956. 106p.

An illustrated pamphlet issued in commemoration of the tenth anniversary of Taiwan's retrocession to China.

See also a 1,000-page, Chinese-language publication by the same agency entitled *T'ai-wan ti chien-she* 臺灣的建設 (The Development of Taiwan), Taichung, 1962.

246 China, Ch'iao-wu wei-yüan hui 中華民國 僑務委員會 (China, Overseas Chinese Affairs Commission). *Hua-ch'iao ching-chi nien-chien* 華僑經濟年鑑 (Overseas Chinese Economic Yearbook). Taipei, 1957—. Annual.

A yearbook intended to provide the Overseas Chinese with current information on the general economic situation, economic policies and trade of the Republic of China, together with data on Communist economic infiltration in different countries. The yearbook provides brief summaries of world economic developments, and the economic condition of the Chinese populations in Asia. First published in 1957 as an annual under the title *Hua-ch'iao ching-chi nien-pao* 華僑經濟年報; changed to the present title in 1958.

2. TOPICAL

Special yearbooks are available on the following subjects: journalism and other mass communication media, periodical publishing, education, finance, cooperatives, agriculture, fisheries, and water conservation and control.

247 **T'ai-pei shih hsin-wen chi-che kung-hui** 臺北市新聞記者公會 (Taipei News Reporters' Association). *Chung-hua min-kuo hsin-wen nien-chien* 中華民國新聞年鑑 (Journalism Yearbook of the Republic of China). Taipei, 1961. 1 vol. (pagination varies).

A guide to Chinese mass communication media, with particular emphasis on journalism, both in Taiwan and in Chinese communities overseas. In seven parts. Part 1 takes up the historical development of Chinese journalism, press and news agencies (both Taiwan and overseas), and the broadcasting industry. Party 2 contains current data on the various news agencies, local and overseas newspapers, broadcasting stations and newsreel producers. Part 3 covers the membership, organization and activities of the Chinese Broadcasting Association and the various press associations in Taiwan. Part 4 provides an overview of journalism education in China and presents brief accounts of the various schools of journalism in Taiwan. Part 5 contains laws, regulations, outstanding editorials, convention resolutions, and other documents on the subject. Chronology of major events in Chinese journalism comprises Part 6. Part 7 consists of two appendices: a selected bibliography of books on journalism in Chinese and Japanese, and a brief history of periodical publishing in China.

See also a directory of mass communication agencies of Taiwan (**346**).

248 **T'ai-wan sheng tsa-chih shih-yeh hsieh-hui tsa-chih nien-chien pien-chi wei-yüan hui** 臺灣省雜誌事業協會雜誌年鑑編輯委員會 (Taiwan Association of Periodical Publishers, Committee for the Compilation of the Chinese Periodicals Yearbook). *Chung-hua min-kuo tsa-chih nien-chien* 中華民國雜誌年鑑 (Chinese Periodicals Yearbook). Taipei, 1954. [397p.]

In four parts: (1) general essays on magazine publishing; (2) the publishing of periodicals in China and the history of the Taiwan Association of Periodical Publishers; (3) publications of members of the Taiwan Association of Periodical Publishers (a one to two-page description of each of the 148 periodicals published since 1945); and (4) appendix (laws and regulations). At the end of the volume is a topical index, arranged by title, to about 9,500 selected articles from the 148 periodicals described above, including the topic 'Bandit Information' (Communist China; see **194**).

249 **China, Chiao-yü pu, Chiao-yü nien-chien pien-tsuan wei-yüan hui** 中華民國 教育部 教育年鑑編纂委員會 (China, Ministry of Education, Committee for the Compilation of the China Education Yearbook). *Chung-kuo chiao-yü nien-chien, ti-san tz'u* 中國教育年鑑, 第三次 (China Education Yearbook, Third Edition). Taipei: Cheng-chung shu-chü 正中書局, 1957. 2 vols. 1,237p.

A continuation of the first two editions (1934, 1948) of the *China Education Yearbook*. In fourteen major chapters: (1) general, (2) educational administration, (3) mass education, (4) secondary education, (5) normal education, (6) vocational education, (7) higher education, (8) cultural and research organizations, (9) international exchange, (10) social education, (11) education for minority groups, (12) education for Overseas Chinese, (13) physical education, hygiene, military training and scouting, and (14) youth guidance and counseling. The appendix includes statistics and other miscellaneous data.

The Yearbook provides useful information on education on the Mainland before 1949 and in Taiwan since 1945.

250 **T'ai-wan yin-hang, Ching-chi yen-chiu shih** 臺灣銀行經濟研究室 (Bank of Taiwan, Office of Economic Research). *T'ai-wan chin-jung nien-pao* 臺灣金融年報 (Taiwan Finance Yearbook). Taipei, 1947—. Annual.

A yearly summary, first published in 1947, of the financial developments of the previous year. In three chapters: (1) 'Financial Statistics', concerning the issuing of the New Taiwan Dollar, rates of interest, exchange of bills and notes, remittance and exchange; (2) 'Banking Activity', containing reports on banks and banking and the Public Treasury; (3) 'Other Financial Organizations', incorporating information on such organizations as post offices (money-order departments), savings banks, farmers' cooperatives, and insurance companies.

See also the periodical reports of the Bank of Taiwan (*T'ai-wan yin-hang pao-kao* 臺灣銀行報告) which present (with an abridged English section) a general summary of economic developments in Taiwan.

251 **Chung-kuo ho-tso shih-yeh hsieh-hui, T'ai-wan sheng fen-hui** 中國合作 事業協會臺灣省分會 (Chinese Cooperatives Association, Taiwan Provincial Branch). *Chung-hua min-kuo T'ai-wan sheng ho-tso nien-chien* 中華民國臺灣省 合作年鑑 (Cooperatives Yearbook of the Taiwan Province of the Republic of China). Taipei, 1962. 454p.

The second edition of the Cooperatives Yearbook published by the Taiwan Provincial Branch of the Chinese Cooperatives Association (the first edition was published in 1957). Divided into two sections—national and Taiwan, the latter being the major section. Each section covers the following subject matter: (1) administration; (2) organization; (3) functions; (4) education; (5) finance; and (6) societies. The appendix includes a chronology of the history of the development of cooperatives in Taiwan; selected government regulations; and an index to periodical literature on cooperatives published in Taiwan from 1956 to 1961 (pp. 345–362).

252 **Taiwan, Nung-lin t'ing** 臺灣省政府農林廳 (Taiwan, Department of Agriculture and Forestry). *T'ai-wan nung-yeh nien-pao* 臺灣農業年報 (Taiwan Agriculture Yearbook). Taipei, Taichung, 1946—. Annual.

An annual compilation of statistics first published in 1946 (covering 1946) on the land and arable land, ownership and management of arable land, farm population and farm families, agricultural production, weather and agricultural disasters, fertilizer, and marine products. Prepared bilingually in Chinese and English since 1949.

253 **Taiwan, Nung-lin t'ing, Yü-yeh kuan-li ch'u** 臺灣省政府農林廳漁業管理處 (Taiwan, Department of Agriculture and Forestry, Bureau of Fisheries). *T'ai-wan yü-yeh nien-pao* 臺灣漁業年報 (Taiwan Fishery Yearbook). Taipei, 1954—. Annual.

An annual bilingual (Chinese and English) compilation of statistics, first published in 1954 (covering 1953), on the fishing industry of Taiwan. Usually contains a general review of Taiwan fisheries, with charts and tables showing the number of persons engaged in fishing; the number of vessels, with data on those damaged or lost; fishery production classified by year, month, species, and geographical location; and such related information as ice manufacture, cold storage industry, etc.

254 **Taiwan, Shui-li chü** 臺灣省水利局 (Taiwan, Bureau of Water Conservancy). *T'ai-wan sheng shui-li chü nien-pao* 臺灣省水利局年報 (Taiwan Provincial Bureau of Water Conservancy Yearbook). Taipei, 1949—. Irregular.

A yearbook, first published in 1949 (covering 1948), devoted to water conservancy in Taiwan. Arranged in eight parts: general; flood control; irrigation; reservoirs; surveys; administration; materials; and budgets, accounts and statistics. Since 1958, the Bureau has also published an annual report emphasizing its work as an organization, complementing the yearbook which tends to focus on the engineering and technical aspects of water conservation.

D. HONG KONG AND MACAO

Six of the nine entries in this section concern Hong Kong. An officially published English-language annual report and a detailed Chinese-language Hong Kong yearbook are the first and second entries, respectively. The other yearbooks and directories of Hong Kong are largely concerned with economic affairs.

The remainder are publications originating in the Portuguese colony of Macao. Two are Portuguese-language yearbooks published by the Macao Provincial Government; the last is a Chinese-language annual on commerce and industry.

255 **Hong Kong; Report for the Year 1946—.** Hong Kong: Government Press, 1946—. Annual.

An official yearbook of some 400–450 pages. The 1961 issue, published in 1962, follows the general arrangement of previous volumes. In three parts: (1) a review article on an important problem (e.g., the water supply, census, etc.); (2) some twenty topical chapters on population, employment, industry and trade, education, health, etc.; (3) several chapters on geography, natural history, history, constitution and administration, bibliography, etc. The bibliography in the 1961 issue (pp. 359–388) is an unannotated list of over 700 books on Hong Kong from the 1840's to the present. The appendices contain, in addition to many statistics, a list of official publications of the Hong Kong government for the preceding year and a list of leading English and Chinese-language newspapers and magazines. Index.

Also useful are the *Annual Departmental Reports* by the various branches of the Hong Kong government, pamphlets (some 50 pages in length) issued by the Commissioner of Police, the Commissioner for Resettlement, etc.

256 Hsiang-kang nien-chien (Ti-i hui—) 香港年鑑 (第一回—)
Hong Kong Year Book. Hong Kong: Wah Kiu Yat Po 華僑日報, 1948—. Annual (pagination varies).

A massive yearbook containing a general review for the preceding year; laws and regulations; a gazetteer; a biographical section (of roughly 1,000 entries); lists of medical and educational institutions, and social organizations; and a classified directory of over 300 pages listing some 20,000–25,000 firms. The fifteenth edition was published in 1962.

257 Japan, Gaimushō, Ajiakyoku 日本外務省アジア局 (Japan, Ministry of Foreign Affairs, Bureau of Asian Affairs). *Honkon benran* 香港便覽
(Handbook on Hong Kong). Tokyo: Nihon Kokusai Mondai Kenkyūjo 日本國際問題研究所, 1955—. Annual.

A part of the *Ajia shokoku benran sōsho* アジア諸國便覽叢書 (Series of Handbooks on Asian Countries) revised annually by the Ministry, the handbook covers geography, history, the political structure, foreign, economic, and social affairs in Hong Kong. A short list of the most important officials is provided. No bibliography. Not indexed. 30–40 pages.

258 Hsiang-kang ching-chi nien-chien 香港經濟年鑑
(Hong Kong Economic Yearbook). Hong Kong: Ching-chi tao-pao she 經濟導報社, 1955—. Annual.

Published by the Hong Kong *Ta-kung pao*, 1955–1960. Beginning with the 1961 edition, this yearbook has been issued by the Ching-chi tao-pao she which also publishes the *Ching-chi tao-pao—Economic Bulletin* (see **1023**). The latest volume examined was the 1963 edition.

In four parts: (1) economic conditions in Hong Kong; (2) economic conditions of countries trading in Hong Kong; (3) statistics; and (4) commercial directory of Hong Kong. In addition to describing the various sectors of Hong Kong's economy during the year under review (the year preceding publication), Part 1 also provides a section describing the major economic events which have taken place in Hong Kong for that year, together with selections of important economic and financial regulations, and other pertinent documents. The emphasis of Part 2 is on the economic conditions in the countries of South and Southeast Asia now trading in Hong Kong. The once substantial section on Communist China included in this part has been omitted since 1961. The statistics given in Part 3 are equally divided among those for Hong Kong and other areas of the world. The commercial directory in Part 4 is quite comprehensive and useful.

A pro-Communist publication, although the once pronounced pro-Communist stand has appeared less obvious in recent editions.

259 Hong Kong, Department of Commerce and Industry.
Directory of Commerce Industry Finance. Hong Kong, 1953—. Annual.

A richly illustrated, 200-page official guide and directory. Sixteen chapters cover the fields of history, geography, population, economic developments and commerce (presented with statistical tables and charts). A classified section of Hong Kong-produced commodities, brand names and firms is appended. Index.

260 The Hong Kong Dollar Directory. Hong Kong, 1961.

A directory containing a 'Hongs' section (808 pages), a classified section (150p.) on governmental agencies, hospitals, educational institutions, etc., and a who's who listing some 20,000 names (providing the name, title, office, but lacking addresses and telephone numbers).

See also *Business Directory, 1964,* published by the O.K. Printing Press, Hong Kong, in 1963, which contains a list of organizations and a who's who section.

261 Macao, Repartição Provincial dos Serviços de Economia e Estatística Geral.
Anuário de Macau. Macao, 1932—. Irregular.

A 400-page handbook, with a 25-page English section (primarily of interest to tourists). First published in 1932 under the title *Directório de Macau*, the handbook assumed its present title in 1938. The thirteenth—latest issue to date —was published in 1958 for 1956–1957.

262 Macao, Repartição Provincial dos Serviços de Economia e Estatística Geral, Secção de Estatística.
Anuário Estatístico de Macau ano de 19—. Macao, 1953—.

An official 200-page statistical yearbook published by the Macao provincial government.

263   Ao-men kung-shang nien-chien 澳門工商年鑑
Anuário Comercial e Industrial de Macau. Macao: Tai Chung Pou, 1951—.

A commercially published yearbook of commerce and industry. The latest edition examined contained a thirteen-page who's who section listing some 300 persons. First entitled *Directório de Macau*. The fifth edition for 1960–1961 was published in 1961.

CHAPTER V

STATISTICAL COMPILATIONS

The available statistics for Communist China do not compare in volume, variety or quality with those for Taiwan. This imbalance is reflected in the contents of the present chapter, less than a third of which relate to the Mainland.

In general, the statistical compilations included in this chapter are selected. Others—especially those which are rooted in special subject-areas—are available and should be traced through the national bibliographies of both the Mainland and Taiwan. In this connection, it should be noted that yearbooks (see Chapter IV) also contain statistical information.

A. People's Republic of China

The problems encountered with Mainland statistics are in many ways similar to those which have frustrated generations of economists and others dealing with the Soviet Union. The available information, insufficient to begin with, is quite commonly manipulated so as better to serve the needs of propaganda for domestic and foreign consumption. With the mid-air collapse of China's 'Great Leap Forward', Mainland statistics are even more difficult to come by.

Of what we have, the most comprehensive compilation of official Chinese Communist statistics—in this case embracing the economic, educational and cultural sectors—is the first entry.

On economic, and particularly industrial, growth there are the Harvard compilation and that of the Japanese Economic Planning Board (**265** and **266,** respectively). These are, however, less comprehensive and cover a relatively shorter time span than the first entry. Other works in this section deal with specific sectors of Mainland industry (iron and steel, electric power, coal, capital goods production, textiles, etc.).

Apart from the People's Handbook (see **212**) there are no annual or other periodically issued statistical compilations available from the Mainland, and the figures presented in the Handbook lack detail and are too inadequate and too insufficient to support any serious study. The reader can augment this meager Mainland fare with the materials on Mainland statistical work in Chapter XIV (**711, 712**), and with the various periodicals listed in Part Four.

Reference should be made to Mainland statistics—rather uncritically compiled—in the various handbooks and yearbooks published in Japan (**215** ff.), as well as those to be found in some of the Japanese periodicals, such as the *Ajia keizai jumpō* (Ten-Day Report on Asian Economy) and other publications of the China Research Institute (Chūgoku Kenkyūjo) in Tokyo (see Chapter XXI B).

For general background information on Mainland statistical work, the authoritative study of Professor Li Choh-ming, *The Statistical System of Communist China* (**121**), should be consulted.

For critically evaluated statistics on national income, see the work by Professor Ta-chung Liu and Kung-chia Yeh, *The Economy of the Chinese Mainland: National*

Income and Economic Development, 1933–1959 (see **1397**), and Professor Alexander Eckstein's *The National Income of Communist China* (New York: Free Press of Glencoe, 1962). Professor Y. L. Wu's *Economic Development and the Use of Energy Resources in Communist China* (New York: Frederick A. Praeger, 1963), published for the Hoover Institution, provides statistics on fuel and power. Statistics on steel and iron are included in Professor Wu's study, *The Steel Industry in Communist China* (New York: Frederick A. Praeger, 1965). See also Professor William Hollister's *China's Gross National Product and Social Accounts, 1950–1957* (New York: Free Press of Glencoe, 1958), and Cheng Chu-yuan's *Communist China's Economy, 1949–1957; Structural Changes and Crisis* (South Orange, N.J.: Seton Hall University Press, 1963).

264 China (People's Republic of China, 1949—), Kuo-chia t'ung-chi chü
中華人民共和國 國家統計局　(China [People's Republic of China, 1949—], State Statistics Bureau). *Wei-ta ti shih-nien—Chung-hua jen-min kung-ho kuo ching-chi ho wen-hua chien-she ch'eng-chiu ti t'ung-chi* 偉大的十年——中華人民共和國經濟和文化建設成就的統計
(Ten Great Years: Statistics of the Economic and Cultural Achievements of the People's Republic of China). Peking, 1959. 10; 198p.

A collection of official statistical compilations (some 135 tables) bearing on Communist Chinese economic and cultural developments, 1949–1959, arranged under the following topical headings: (1) 'The Growth and Development of the People's Republic of China', (2) 'The Great Victory of the Socialist Revolution and the People's Commune Movement', (3) 'The Expansion of Capital Construction', (4) 'The High Rate of Growth of Industrial Output', (5) 'The Tremendous Growth of Socialist Agriculture', (6) 'The Rapid Development of Transport and Post and Telecommunications', (7) 'The Expansion of Domestic and Foreign Trade', (8) 'The Unprecedented Increase in the Number of Workers and Other Employees', (9) 'The Tremendous Progress in Culture and Education', and (10) 'The Great Improvement in the Living Standard of the People'.

Two English translations are available: *Ten Great Years: Statistics of the Economic and Cultural Achievements of the People's Republic of China* (Peking: Foreign Languages Press, 1960), and *Economic and Cultural Statistics on Communist China* (Washington, D.C.: Central Intelligence Agency, 1960).

Conveniently arranged.

265 Yin, Helen and Yin, Yi-chang, comps.
Economic Statistics of Mainland China (1949–1957). Cambridge, Mass.: Harvard University, Center for East Asian Studies, 1960. 106p.

A collection of some one hundred statistical tables bringing together official Chinese Communist statistics from a large number of scattered sources and covering the period from 1949 through 1957. Arranged in eight chapters: population, national income, agriculture, industry, trade, labor, public finance and banking, and communications, transport, posts and telecommunications. Fully documented, with sources also listed in a bibliography.

A conveniently arranged compilation of official Chinese Communist statistics for the first eight years of the regime.

266 **Japan, Keizai Kikakuchō, Chōsakyoku, Kaigai Chōsaka** 日本經濟企畫廳 調查局海外調查課 (Japan, Economic Planning Board, Research Bureau, Overseas Research Section). *Chūgoku shuyō kōgyō tōkeishū* 中國主要工業統計集 (Important Industrial Statistics of China). Tokyo, 1959. 128p.

A collection of 189 statistical tables based on Chinese Communist sources, covering, for the most part, the period 1949–1957. The tables are arranged under six chapters (iron and steel, machinery, coal, electric power, paper and textiles) with many subdivisions. Each chapter is preceded by introductory comments, and the statistical tables are accompanied by notes. Mimeographed.

267 **China (People's Republic of China, 1949—), Kuo-chia t'ung-chi chü, Kung-yeh t'ung-chi ssu** 中華人民共和國 國家統計局 工業統計司 (China [People's Republic of China, 1949—], State Statistics Bureau, Industrial Statistics Section). *Wo-kuo kang-t'ieh tien-li mei-t'an chi-hsieh fang-chih tsao-chih kung-yeh ti chin-hsi* 我國鋼鐵電力煤炭機械紡織造紙工業的今昔
(The Past and Present of the Steel and Iron, Electric Power, Coal, Machine Manufacturing, Textile, and Paper-Making Industries of China). Peking: T'ung-chi ch'u-pan she 統計出版社, 1958. 225p.

A comprehensive compilation of comparative statistics (with analysis) on Chinese industrial growth. Figures include those for the pre-1949 years and extend to 1957 under the six industrial categories given in the title. The volume paints a favorable picture of China's industrial development under Communism since 1949.

268 **Chung-kuo k'o-hsüeh yüan, Ching-chi yen-chiu so, Shou kung-yeh tsu** 中國科學院經濟研究所手工業組 (Chinese Academy of Sciences, Institute of Economic Research, Handicraft Industry Section). *I-chiu wu-ssu nien ch'üan-kuo ko-t'i shou kung-yeh tiao-ch'a tzu-liao* 一九五四年全國個體手工業調查資料 (National Survey of Independent Handicraft Industry—1954). Peking: Sheng-huo, Tu-shu, Hsin-chih San-lien shu-tien 生活讀書新知三聯書店, 1957. 252p.

A compendium of surveys of the status and characteristics of independent handicraft and cottage industries (excluding cooperatives) in fifteen municipalities, nineteen provinces, and the Inner Mongolia Autonomous Region. Statistical tables on employment, number of households, production volume, output value, marketing data, etc.
Generally regarded as one of the more meaningful compilations for the period covered.

269 China (People's Republic of China, 1949—), Nung-yeh pu, Chi-hua chü
中華人民共和國 農業部 計劃局 (China [People's Republic of China, 1949—],
Ministry of Agriculture, Bureau of Planning). *Chung-kuo yü shih-chieh chu-yao
kuo-chia nung-yeh sheng-ch'an t'ung-chi tzu-liao hui-pien* 中國與世界主要國家
農業生產統計資料彙編
(Collected Agricultural Statistics of China and Other Major Countries of the
World). Peking: Nung-yeh ch'u-pan she 農業出版社, 1958. 79p.

Statistics for foreign countries drawn mainly from United Nations sources.
The items listed for Communist China were compiled in accordance with
government-planned targets, including the planted areas and output of food
grains, tea and fruits, economic crops, and number of cattle. The period covered
is the peak year of output prior to 1949, the years 1949 and 1952, and 1953
through 1957.

270 Chung-kuo k'o-hsüeh yüan, Shang-hai ching-chi yen-chiu so 中國科學院
上海經濟研究所 (Chinese Academy of Sciences, Shanghai Economic Research
Institute). *Shang-hai chieh-fang ch'ien-hou wu-chia tzu-liao hui-pien, 1921–1957*
上海解放前後物價資料彙編, 1921–1957
(Reference Materials on Prices in Shanghai Before and After the Liberation,
1921–1957). Shanghai: Jen-min ch'u-pan she 人民出版社, 1958. 600p.

Edited jointly by the Shanghai Economic Research Institute of the Chinese
Academy of Sciences and the Economic Research Institute of the Shanghai
Academy of Social Sciences (上海社會科學院經濟研究所), this volume is
primarily a price index for Shanghai for the period 1921 to 1957. Appended are
sixteen documents on price control issued mostly by the State Council between
May 28, 1949 and August 9, 1957. A useful reference work.

271 Chandrasekhar, Sripati.
China's Population, Census and Vital Statistics. Second edition, revised and
enlarged. Hong Kong: Hong Kong University Press, 1960. 73p.

Two lectures given at Hong Kong University in 1959 by Professor S. Chandrasekhar, Director of the Indian Institute for Population Studies, Madras.
Data were drawn from both published and unpublished sources given to him by
Chinese Communist officials. A very valuable study of Communist China's
population problems, even though 'the statistics are fragmentary and occasionally
contradictory.' There is a good bibliography comprising mostly periodical
articles in Chinese and English.

B. REPUBLIC OF CHINA

Statistics for Taiwan are available in quantity, variety and sophistication approaching
Western standards. However, innumerable changes in titles and frequency of issue,

and the inaccessibility of certain publications, make the compilation of anything near an exhaustive list of statistical works difficult in the extreme.

The materials contained in the present chapter are arranged in three sections: (1) central government, (2) Taiwan provincial, and (3) Taipei municipal. To assure the fullest coverage of the available statistical literature, the reader should also consult the yearbooks and handbooks published on Taiwan (listed in the previous chapter) and the Economic Reference Materials (734) included in Chapter XIV.

1. CENTRAL GOVERNMENT

The most comprehensive source for statistics on Taiwan and other areas under the effective jurisdiction of the Nationalist government is the annual bilingual *Statistical Abstract of the Republic of China* listed directly below. An additional source of significant statistical data is the detailed report on the General Census conducted in the autumn of 1956 (273). The last two entries (274, 275) concern various aspects of domestic affairs (elections, land reform, police, labor, health, education, etc.). The present section should be consulted together with the following two sections on Taiwan provincial and Taipei municipal data.

272 **China, Hsing-cheng yüan, Chu-chi ch'u** 中華民國行政院主計處 (China, Executive Yüan, Directorate-General of Budgets, Accounts and Statistics). *Chung-hua min-kuo t'ung-chi t'i-yao* 中華民國統計提要 *Statistical Abstract of the Republic of China.* Taipei, 1955—. Annual.

A confidential statistical summary of the political, social, industrial and economic organization of the Republic of China. The volume serves both as a primary source for statistical data, and as a reference guide to other statistical sources (citations are provided for all tabular material). The statistical data are divided into four categories: primary statistics for the Republic of China prior to the government's withdrawal from the Mainland; current statistics on the administration and operation of the Central Government, its subsidiary organs, and public enterprises on Taiwan; basic statistics concerning Taiwan; and statistical results of special surveys and censuses undertaken by government agencies in recent years on Taiwan.

The plan of the first Taipei annual edition (1955) has in general been followed in subsequent editions: area and population; agriculture, forestry, fishery, and animal husbandry; mining and industry; foreign trade; public finance; money and prices; transportation and communications; education and culture; social affairs and public health; general administration; and comparative statistics on selected foreign countries. With the exception of the short prefatory note at the head of each chapter, the volume is bilingual. Limited distribution.

The first edition of the *Abstract* appeared in 1935 in Nanking. The 1955 volume was the first one published since 1949.

The most comprehensive collection of statistical data on Taiwan.

273 Taiwan, Hu-k'ou p'u-ch'a ch'u 臺灣省 戶口普查處 (Taiwan, Bureau of Census). *Chung-hua min-kuo hu-k'ou p'u-ch'a pao-kao shu* 中華民國戶口普查報告書
(General Census Report of the Republic of China). Taichung, 1959. 10 vols. 8,317p.

A comprehensive census planned and executed by the Census Bureau of the Provincial Government of Taiwan. The census was conducted as of September 16, 1956, and coverage was extended to include Taiwan, the Pescadores, Quemoy, Matsu and other off-shore islands. In three parts. Part 1 is devoted to methodology. Part 2, concerned with Taiwan Province, consists of eight volumes: Vol. 1, general tables; Vol. 2, age and marriage; Vols. 3 and 4, education; Vol. 5, trades; Vol. 6, professions; Vols. 7 and 8, trades and professions. Part 3, 'Fukien Province' (Quemoy, Matsu and other off-shore islands), is composed of general tables and statistics. A single-volume abstract is available.

274 China, Nei-cheng pu, T'ung-chi ch'u 中華民國內政部統計處 (China, Ministry of Interior, Bureau of Statistics). *Chung-hua min-kuo nei-cheng t'ung-chi t'i-yao* 中華民國內政統計提要
(Statistical Abstract of Interior Affairs). Taipei, 1957—. Annual.

An annual compilation of statistics on domestic administration. Some 150 tables are arranged in seven parts: area and population, legislators at national level and local elections, land reform, police, society, labor and health.

275 China, Chiao-yü pu 中華民國教育部 (China, Ministry of Education). *Chunghua min-kuo chiao-yü t'ung-chi—Min-kuo wu-shih nien* 中華民國教育統計—民國五十年
Educational Statistics of the Republic of China, 1961. [Taipei, 1962]. 73p.

A bilingual statistical abstract covering the years 1954 through 1961. The data are arranged as follows: (1) pre-school children; (2) primary education; (3) secondary education; (4) teacher training; (5) higher education; (6) special education; (7) adult education; (8) international cultural relations; and (9) public expenditure on education.
Contains the most up-to-date information on education in Taiwan. The 1959 and 1960 volumes cover the years 1952 through 1959, and 1953 through 1960, respectively.

2. PROVINCIAL GOVERNMENT

Apart from the first two entries, which are general compilations, the present section contains a wide range of specialized collections of statistics (on education, transportation and communications, industry and commerce, government-owned enterprises, commodity prices, sugar, etc.) available for Taiwan. It should be noted that the section is by no means exhaustive, and that additional information can be obtained by consulting the national bibliography as well as the entries in the preceding section.

276 Taiwan, Chu-ch'i chu 臺灣省政府主計處 (Taiwan, Bureau of Accounting and Statistics). *T'ai-wan sheng t'ung-chi yao-lan* 臺灣省統計要覽
Taiwan Statistical Abstract. Taipei, Taichung. No. 1—, October 1946—. Irregular.

Nos. 1 to 3 were issued by the Bureau of Statistics of the Office of the Governor of Taiwan, October 1946–March 1947. Since No. 4/5 (September 1947), the *Abstract* has been issued by the Bureau of Accounting and Statistics of the Taiwan Provincial Government. Bilingual edition since No. 14 (?).

Contents vary slightly from issue to issue. No. 16 (the last issue examined, reporting figures for 1954 and 1955 with no date of publication given) is arranged as follows: (1) land; (2) population; (3) political organization; (4) agriculture; (5) forestry; (6) fishery; (7) livestock; (8) mining and manufacturing; (9) commerce; (10) irrigation and water power; (11) finance; (12) banking; (13) railway; (14) highway; (15) navigation; (16) post and telegram; (17) education; (18) health and medical care; (19) social affairs; (20) police administration; and (21) information.

Contains more detailed data than the Taiwan section in the *Statistical Abstract of the Republic of China* (**272**). See also next entry for more current data.

277 China, Hsing-cheng yüan, Mei-yüan yün-yung wei-yüan hui, Ching-chi yen-chiu shih 中華民國行政院美援運用委員會經濟研究室 (China, Executive Yuan, Council for U.S. Aid, Economic Research Center).
Taiwan Statistical Data Book. Taipei, 1962–1963. 2 vols. 179; 181p.

Two volumes have been published—one for 1962 and one for 1963—covering the years 1949–1961 and 1952–1962, respectively. Both are arranged in fifteen parts: (1) indicators; (2) area and population; (3) national income; (4) agriculture; (5) industry; (6) transportation and communications; (7) money and banking; (8) public finance; (9) prices and wages; (10) balance of payments, foreign exchange and trade; (11) U.S. aid; (12) education; (13) health and medical care; (14) social affairs; and (15) international statistics. The tables are compiled from materials collected from the appropriate agencies (source of data is given for each index). The year 1949 or 1952 is used as the base period for the 1962 volume, and 1952 for the 1963 volume.

Less detailed than the preceding compilations. Conveniently arranged for quick reference.

278 Taiwan, Chiao-yü t'ing, Chu-chi shih 臺灣省教育廳主計室 (Taiwan, Department of Education, Bureau of Budgets, Accounts and Statistics).
T'ai-wan sheng chiao-yü t'ung-chi 臺灣省教育統計
(Taiwan Education Statistics). Taichung, 1949—. Annual.

Published from 1949 to 1952 under the title *T'ai-wan sheng chih chiao-yü t'ung-chi* (Educational Statistics of the Province of Taiwan), the survey acquired its present title in 1953. While the volumes are not always uniform in the kinds of data presented, they usually include statistical information on higher education, secondary education, primary education, social education, funds and budgets, organization and personnel, etc. The data, both accurate and current, are based on the provincial and local government budgets and the periodic reports of the different educational institutions and offices. As a rule, each issue contains approximately 150 pages and includes, for purposes of comparison, certain statistics for previous years. An organization chart of the Chinese educational system is appended.

279 Taiwan, Chiao-t'ung ch'u 臺灣省交通處 (Taiwan, Department of Communications). *T'ai-wan sheng chiao-t'ung t'ung-chi hui-pao* 臺灣省交通統計彙報 *Annual Statistical Report of Taiwan Communications and Transportation*. Taipei, Taichung, 1947—. Annual.

Published annually since 1947, each issue usually runs to more than 200 pages. The English title, *Annual Statistical Data of Taiwan Communications and Transportation*, was added in 1956, and was replaced by its present English title a year later. The volumes provide statistical data on the communication and transportation systems of Taiwan, arranged according to the following subjects: administration of communications and transportation, railways, highways, harbor affairs, shipping, tourism, post and telecommunications, aviation. Descriptive material accompanies statistical data, and in each volume emphasis has been placed on comparison and analysis. Metric system is used except in the case of ship tonnage.

280 Taiwan, Chien-she t'ing 臺灣省政府建設廳 (Taiwan, Department of Reconstruction). *T'ai-wan sheng lao-kung t'ung-chi pao-kao* 臺灣省勞工統計報告 *Taiwan Labor Statistics*. Taipei, Taichung, 1954—. Annual.

An annual bilingual statistical compilation on employment, hours of work, wages and labor income, cost-of-living index and retail prices, labor insurance, industrial injuries, labor turnover, and family status of workers. First published in 1954 (covering the years 1946–53). The report is patterned after the *Yearbook of Labor Statistics* published by the International Labor Office. The International Standard Industrial Classification of All Economic Activities adopted by the Economic and Social Council of the U.N. is used as the basis for arrangement of industries.

Up to its fifth issue (covering 1957, published 1958), the report contained thirty-five tables distributed through some 350 pages. Since its sixth issue (covering 1958, published 1959), the report has been reduced to roughly 100 pages containing some thirty tables. Except for a change of format, outlines of the general compilation remain the same.

281 **Taiwan, She-hui ch'u** 臺灣省政府社會處 (Taiwan, Department of Social Affairs). *T'ai-wan sheng lao-kung sheng-huo k'ai-k'uang tiao-ch'a t'ung-chi pao-kao* 臺灣省勞工生活概況調查統計報告
Taiwan Labor Conditions. Taipei, 1957. 106p.

A bilingual report of a sample survey on the living condition of workers in the textile, machine, soda, sugar, ship-building, steel, petroleum, power, chemical fertilizer, coal mining, communications and transportation industries, with emphasis on housing, education (including the education of childrent, health and medical care. Preceded by brief descriptions, the twenty-eigh) statistical tables are divided into general, education, housing, health and medical care sections.
Not so comprehensive as the preceding entry.

282 **The Executive Group of Industry and Commerce Census of Taiwan.**
T'ai-wan sheng kung-shang p'u-ch'a tsung pao-kao 臺灣省工商普查總報告
General Report on Industry and Commerce Census of Taiwan. Taipei, 1956. 741p.

A bilingual report based on data obtained from the Census of Industry and Commerce in Taiwan (1954). The static data are given as of December 31, 1954, while the cumulative figures (salaries, wages, business income, man-hours, sales, brokerage, etc.) are those for the year January–December, 1954. Introductory notes and a general summary precede the body of the report, which comprises seventy-seven tables grouped under the following headings: summary, mining, manufacturing, construction industries, electricity supply, water supply, general merchandise stores, and other industries and commerce. No index.
An important and comprehensive statistical survey of the economic organization of Taiwan.

283 **China, Hsing-cheng yüan, Chu-chi ch'u** 中華民國行政院主計處 (China, Executive Yuan, Directorate-General of Budgets, Accounts and Statistics). *T'ai-wan kung-ying shih-yeh chin-k'uang t'ung-chi* 臺灣公營事業近況統計
Statistical Abstract of Government-Owned Enterprises of Taiwan. Taipei, 1954. 297p.

Issued for the three-year period 1951 to 1953, inclusive. Statistics are provided for forty-nine enterprises arranged under the following categories: (1) organization; (2) employees and wages; (3) gross product and types of products; (4) gross income; (5) capital expenditure and capital formation; (6) final account. A useful compilation.

284 **Taiwan, Chu-chi ch'u** 臺灣省政府主計處 (Taiwan, Bureau of Accounting and Statistics). *T'ai-wan wu-chia t'ung-chi yüeh-pao* 臺灣物價統計月報
Taiwan Monthly of Commodity-Price Statistics. Taipei, Taichung, 1946—.

A monthly report on wholesale and retail prices in major Taiwan cities. Since July 1961, the publication has consisted of four sections: explanatory notes, wholesale prices, retail prices, and an appendix. First published in 1946 to provide price indices for Taipei, the report was expanded to cover other Taiwan cities in January 1957, at which time certain other changes were effected (among them an alteration in the base period and in the equations used for computations). The monthly was given its present format in January 1959, when it absorbed *T'ai-pei shih wu-chia pien-tung fen-hsi pao-kao* 臺北市物價變動分析報告 (Analytical Report on Price Fluctuation in Taipei) also published by the Bureau, and was re-numbered No. 1. The publication varies in length (usually around 55 pages), and as a rule contains six tables and two charts.

285 **China, Ts'ai-cheng pu, T'ung-chi ch'u** 中華民國財政部統計處 (China, Ministry of Finance, Department of Statistics). *Chung-hua min-kuo T'ai-wan chin-ch'u-kou mao-i chih-shu* 中華民國臺灣進出口貿易指數
Index Numbers of the Import and Export Trade of China (Taiwan Only). Taipei, 1955—. Semi-monthly.

A bilingual compilation of indices to the import-export trade. First published in April 1955 as a monthly (actual appearance was irregular), the report, after January 1959, was issued on a semi-monthly basis. The indices, based on data available at the Inspectorate General of Customs, are classified under a general index and a group index consisting of five tables. Lists of representative import and export items and a summary of the net value of imports and exports are appended.

286 **Taiwan, Nung-lin t'ing, Chien-yen chü** 臺灣省農林廳檢驗局 (Taiwan, Department of Agriculture and Forestry, Bureau of Inspections and Quarantine). *Chien-yen t'ung-chi yao-lan* 檢驗統計要覽
Summary of Inspection and Quarantine Statistics. Taipei, Vol. 1—, 1952—. Annual.

A bilingual publication appearing annually since May 1952, summarizing inspection and quarantine statistics on tea, canned foods, cereals, livestock, feathers, fertilizers, brown sugar, essential oils, vegetables and plants, and other agricultural products. (Volume 1 presents a statistical summary covering the years 1946–1951.) Also provides information on the inspection of such goods for both the foreign and domestic markets, the supervision of manufacturers and factories, etc. A table of international weights and measures is appended.

287 **Taiwan, Liang-shih chü, T'ung-chi shih** 臺灣省糧食局統計室 (Taiwan, Food Bureau, Office of Statistics). *T'ai-wan liang-shih t'ung-chi yao-lan* 臺灣糧食統計要覽
Taiwan Food Statistics Book. Taichung, 1959. 210p.

A bilingual abstract of Taiwan's food supply statistics from 1905 to 1958. More detailed statistical coverage for the post-1945 period than for the previous years. A useful compilation.

288 Taiwan, Yen chiu kung-mai chü, Chu-chi shih 臺灣省菸酒公賣局主計室 (Taiwan, Tobacco and Wine Monopoly Bureau, Section of Budgets, Accounts, and Statistics). *T'ai-wan sheng yen-chiu shih-yeh t'ung-chi nien-pao* 臺灣省菸酒 事業統計年報 (Taiwan Tobacco and Wine Statistical Yearbook). Taipei, 1947—.

First published in 1947 under the title *T'ai-wan sheng yen-chiu shih-yeh k'ai-k'uang—A General Report on the Tobacco and Wine Industry*, the yearbook acquired its present title in 1948. The volumes, containing descriptive articles and statistical tables on various aspects of the wine and tobacco industries, have over the years been expanded in size and in extent of coverage.

In view of the importance of wine and tobacco revenues to the Taiwan economy, the volumes are of considerable importance.

289 Taiwan, Nung-lin t'ing 臺灣省政府農林廳 (Taiwan, Department of Agriculture and Forestry). *T'ai-wan t'ang-yeh t'ung-chi* 臺灣糖業統計 (Taiwan Sugar Statistics). Taipei, Taichung, 1946—. Annual.

An annual compilation of statistics, first published in October 1946, covering various aspects of the production and distribution of sugar on Taiwan (capitalization, plant capacity and production costs, subsidies, loans, taxes and duties, alcohol production and utilization of sugar cane dregs). Information on weather conditions, acreage under cultivation, irrigation, farm population, etc., is frequently appended.

An important compilation on Taiwan's major agricultural industry.

290 Taiwan, Lin-yeh kuan-li chü, Chu-chi shih 臺灣省林業管理局主計室 (Taiwan, Bureau of Forestry, Department of Accounting and Statistics). *T'ai-wan lin-yeh t'ung-chi nien-pao* 臺灣林業統計年報 *Forestry Statistics of Taiwan*. Taipei, 1959—. Annual.

An annual bilingual compilation of forestry statistics showing acreage, reserves, seedling, marketing, disasters, organization and personnel. Fifteen charts and seven tables appear in its pages. First published as an annual in 1959 (covering the years 1957–58). An earlier issue was published in 1950 covering the years 1948–49.

291 T'ai-wan sheng mei-yeh tiao-chieh wei-yüan hui, Chu-chi shih 臺灣省 煤業調節委員會主計室 (Taiwan Coal Commission, Bureau of Accounting and Statistics). *T'ai-wan sheng mei-yeh tiao-chieh wei-yüan hui t'ung-chi nien-pao* 臺灣省煤業調節委員會統計年報 (Annual Statistical Abstract of the Taiwan Coal Commission). Taipei, 1951—.

Provides statistics on organization, personnel, production, marketing, subsidies and loans, and equipment of the coal industry in Taiwan, together with other related information. Publication commenced in March 1951 (covering the years 1946–1950) under the title *T'ai-wan sheng shih-t'an t'iao-cheng wei-yüan hui t'ung-chi yao-lan* 臺灣省石炭調整委員會統計要覽. The title was changed to *T'ai-wan sheng mei-yeh tiao-chieh wei-yüan hui t'ung-chi yao-lan* 臺灣省煤業調節委員會統計要覽 in 1955. The annual has been published under its present title since 1957.

3. TAIPEI MUNICIPAL GOVERNMENT

The first entry is the most comprehensive source of statistical data on the City of Taipei. The second entry, containing demographic information, is badly outdated. For more up-to-date information see *General Census Report of the Republic of China* (**273**) listed above.

292   **Taipei, Chu-chi chü** 臺北市政府主計局 (Taipei, Bureau of Accounting and Statistics). *T'ai-pei shih t'ung-chi yao-lan* 臺北市統計要覽
The Statistical Abstract of Taipei Municipality. Taipei, 1947—. Annual.

A compilation of statistical data covering the political, economic and social organization of Taipei. Some 180 tables are arranged under sixteen categories: land, population, political organization, agriculture, industry and mining, commerce, finance, prices, public finance, public works, post and telecommunication, public utilities, education, society, cooperatives, and police. The abstract first appeared in 1947 (covering 1946) and has been published as a bilingual publication (Chinese and English) since its ninth issue (1957, covering the year 1956).

293   **Taipei, Chu-chi chü** 臺北市政府主計局 (Taipei, Bureau of Accounting and Statistics). *T'ai-pei shih jen-k'ou t'ung-chi* 臺北市人口統計
(Taipei Population Statistics). Taipei, August 1950. 1 vol.

A compilation of statistics on the population of Taipei (household, resident aliens, birth, death, density and fluctuation of population). Fifty-eight tables provide population statistics before and after Taiwan was restored to China. Though intended as a periodic publication, only one issue has been published thus far.

CHAPTER VI

DIRECTORIES

Assembled in this chapter are directories for institutions and organizations on both the Mainland and Taiwan. Roughly four-fifths of the entries are devoted to the Mainland. In this context it is worth noting that if either Peking or Taipei publishes directories of its government and party organs, they are not available to the general public. Three other governments issue political directories for the Mainland, but apparently no government or other organization does so for the Republic of China.

The reader is encouraged to use the present chapter in conjunction with those concerned with biographical materials (Chapter VII) and handbooks and yearbooks (Chapter IV), the contents of which in many instances serve to update the directories. It is also worth noting that a number of documentary collections listed in Part Three, especially the records of congresses and other meetings, include name lists of the participants. Other name lists, directories, diplomatic lists, etc., are to be found in the translations of Mainland data described in Chapter XX.

A. Mainland

The numerous directories available for the Mainland have been grouped, for convenience, into three categories: political (twenty-seven entries), economic and trade (nine entries), and educational (eight entries).

It should be pointed out, however, that certain of the directories primarily concerned with the governmental and party structure of Communist China listed in the first section include data on organizations which are essentially economic, cultural or educational in character.

I. POLITICAL

The largest number of Mainland-oriented directories deal with governmental and party structure and are the compilations of the three governments most concerned with happenings in Communist China—namely, the United States, Japan and Nationalist China. (Information on Soviet compilations is not available.) Such compilations are invariably based on the Mainland press. For directories issuing from the Mainland itself, see the listings included in the People's Handbook.

The first entry in the present section, compiled by the U.S. Department of State, provides the most detailed data as of April 1963. The directory compiled by the Japanese Cabinet Research Office (**298**) is the most comprehensive in coverage insofar as the number of listed government agencies and organizations is concerned, but it suffers from a lack of detail. For the most current and detailed information, consult the 'Bandit and Puppet Personnel Changes' (**301** and **303**), which appear regularly in *Fei-ch'ing yüeh-pao* (Bandit Intelligence Monthly) and *Fei-ch'ing yen-chiu* (Bandit Intelligence Studies).

The Reference Materials on the Purge of Communist Bandit and Puppet Personnel (**308**) merits special attention in that it supplies the names of both Communist and non-Communist leaders purged in the aftermath of the Hundred Flowers Movement. The directory of Fukien (**309**) is the only provincial directory available for the Mainland.

In addition to general directories, some of the rather more specialized directories, such as those of the People's Consultative Conference, the State Council, and the various sessions of the National People's Congress, as well as those concerned with the military establishment, the C.C.P. Central Committee, official and private delegations to and from Communist China, and diplomatic lists, have been included in this section.

294   U.S. Department of State, Bureau of Intelligence and Research
Directory of Chinese Communist Officials—Biographic Reference Aid. Washington, D.C., May 1963. 2 vols. (BA 63–7).

A loose-leaf directory of Chinese Communist institutions, organizations and personalities (political, governmental and socio-cultural) as of April 1963. Data are drawn entirely from published sources, primarily the dispatches of the New China News Agency. Volume 1, the directory proper, gives the names of the incumbent office holders, and is arranged under the following headings: political party, central government, legislative and consultative bodies, international representation, military establishment, autonomous region governments, provincial governments, selected municipal governments, mass organizations, academies, and institutions of higher learning. Volume 2 is an alphabetical index to the names of individuals listed in the first volume.

This directory was originally published in 1960 under the title *Directory of Party and Government Officials of Communist China.*

The most comprehensive English-language directory of Communist China. See also the following entries.

295   American Consulate General, Hong Kong.
Biographic Information, Report No. 1—Directory of Chinese Communist Leadership. Hong Kong, November 1960. 97p.

The first issue of a series prepared by the Biographic Information Section of the Press and Publications Unit, American Consulate General, Hong Kong, bringing up to date *Current Background*, No. 513 (July 16, 1958), 'Directory of Top National Positions in Chinese Communist Party, Government and Armed Forces' (see **310**). The data are drawn from Chinese Mainland sources available as of November 1960. This publication, less comprehensive in coverage than the preceding entry but with similar arrangement, is divided into the following sections: Chinese Communist Party (Eighth Central Committee), government, armed forces, and other national organizations. Chinese characters are given for all names. Alphabetical index.

See also the following entries.

296 American Consulate General, Hong Kong.
*Biographic Information, Report No. 1-a—Supplementary Report to the Directory
of Chinese Communist Leadership.* Hong Kong, May 1961. 6p.

A supplement in three parts to the preceding entry, incorporating information
available through May 1, 1961. Part 1 contains a brief explanation of the more
important changes that have taken place since the publication of *Report No. 1*.
Part 2 is a list of single-entry changes that should be entered on the pages of
B.I.R., No. 1. Part 3 consists of insert pages to replace the corresponding ones
in B.I.R., No. 1. Alphabetical index.
See also next entry.

297 American Consulate General, Hong Kong.
*Biographic Information, Report No. 2—Directory of Chinese Communist Leader-
ship.* Hong Kong, May 1962. 109p.

Updates and augments the two preceding entries. The organization of the
directory remains unchanged. Chinese characters are given for all names.
Alphabetical index. Reports 3 and 4 (May 1963) provide the latest information
on party and government personnel in Kwangtung Province and the Canton
Municipality, respectively. The first three Hong Kong lists provide position
data to April 1962.

For more current data, see the Nationalist Chinese compilations listed below
(**301** and **302**).

298 Japan, Naikaku Kambō, Naikaku Chōsashitsu 日本 內閣 官房 內閣調查室
(Japan, Cabinet Secretariat, Cabinet Research Office). *Chūka Jimmin Kyōwakoku
soshikibetsu jimmeihyō* 中華人民共和國 組織別人名表
(Directory of Organizational Personnel in the People's Republic of China).
Tokyo, 1957—. Irregular.

A compilation based on *Jen-min jih-pao* and other official Chinese Communist
sources, containing lists of leading governmental, party, military and mass
organization personnel arranged according to position or positions held for the
previous several years. The first volume, published in 1957, listed information
up to October 1957; the second, published in 1959, to April 1959; and the third,
published in 1962, to December 1961. The fourth volume, bringing the information up to December 1963, was published for the Cabinet Research Office by
the Institute for the Study of Democracy (Minshushugi Kenkyūkai 民主主義
研究會) in January 1964.

The directory is arranged according to broad categories: Chinese Communist
Party and other 'democratic' parties, government organization, the military,
the People's Political Consultative Conference, the Academy of Sciences and
other educational institutions, and over 100 people's organizations. In most cases
the names of appointee, position, date of appointment, location of organization,

and source are supplied. Party functionaries are listed down to and including the rank of *hsien* secretary; government officials down to section head; military officers include some of field grade; school administrators include assistant deans; and, in case of organizations, the directors, officers and committee members are listed. The 1959 and 1962 volumes each contain a name index to some 1,700 persons, arranged by Japanese syllabary in accordance with the Japanese reading of the Chinese name. (The 1957 volume contains no index.) Limited distribution. Mimeographed.

This is the most detailed Japanese compilation, and on the whole compares favorably with similar U.S. and Taiwan compilations which tend to be more detailed, but less comprehensive.

See also next entry.

299 Ajia Kenkyūjo アジア研究所 (Research Institute on Asia). *1963 nemban Chūka Jimmin Kyōwakoku chihōbetsu soshiki jimmeihyō* 一九六三年版中華人民共和國地方別組織人名表

(1963 Edition of a Regional Directory of the Chinese People's Republic). Tokyo, 1963. 195; 71p.

A rearrangement of the preceding directory with some additional information. Chinese Communist Party, government, military and mass organization personnel are listed by region (Peking, Shanghai, the provinces, and the autonomous districts) for the period January 1958 to October 1962. Source of information is indicated. Index of persons arranged according to the Japanese reading of the Chinese name in Japanese syllabic order.

300 Japan, Naikaku Kambō, Naikaku Chōsashitsu 日本 内閣 官房 内閣調査室 (Japan, Cabinet Secretariat, Cabinet Research Office). *Chūkyō jimmin dantai shiryō* 中共人民團體資料

(Materials on Chinese Communist Mass Organizations). Tokyo, 1959. 172p.

A directory of seventeen important Communist Chinese organizations active in the international Communist movement (e.g., China Peace Committee, Asian and African Solidarity Committee of China, All-China Federation of Trade Unions, China Committee for the Promotion of International Trade, All-China Students' Federation, the Chinese People's Institute of Foreign Affairs, Red Cross Society of China).

Based on official Chinese Communist sources, the information supplied concerning each organization is as follows (in two to twenty pages): date of establishment and brief history; objectives; organization (with a list of officers, directors, etc., as of the end of 1958); international affiliations and activities with particular emphasis on those related to Japan (e.g., list of statements on Japan, telegrams and invitations sent to Japan, list of members of Communist Chinese delegations to Japan, etc.). Limited distribution. No index. Mimeographed.

An informative directory of some of the most influential Chinese Communist mass organizations, especially with respect to their ties with Japan.

301 'I-yüeh lai fei-wei chung-yao jen-shih tung-t'ai' 一月來匪僞重要人事動態 (Important Bandit and Puppet Personnel Changes During the Preceding Month) in *Fei-ch'ing yüeh pao* 匪情月報 (Bandit Intelligence Monthly). Vol. 1, No. 1—, February 1958—.

Published regularly in the *Fei-ch'ing yüeh-pao* (see **991**), this entry lists important personnel changes on both the national and local levels during the month previous to publication, including names of newly elected officers of various academic and mass organizations, and personnel who died during the period covered. See also next entry.

302 'Fei-wei tsu-chih jen-shih tung-t'ai' 匪僞組織人事動態 (Bandit and Puppet Personnel Changes) in *Fei-ch'ing yen-chiu* 匪情研究 (Bandit Intelligence Studies), Vol. 1, No. 1—, March 1958—.

Published regularly in the *Fei-ch'ing yen-chiu* (see **990**), this compilation provides information on personnel changes in Communist China during the month preceding publication. The information provided includes appointments, dismissals, and deaths. This and the preceding entry are the best sources for current position data published on a regular basis.

303 **China, Kuo-fang pu, Ch'ing-pao chü** 中華民國 國防部 情報局 (China, Ministry of National Defense, Bureau of Intelligence). *Wei cheng-ch'üan chung-yang chung-yao tsu-chih jen-shih tiao-ch'a hui-pien* 僞政權中央重要組織人事調查彙編 (A Comprehensive Directory of Important Organizations and Personnel of the Puppet Central Regime). Taipei, 1962. 236p.

Based on published and other verified sources, the directory provides position data as well as all organizational and personnel changes (complete with dates)— for the years 1959 through 1962 for each of the organs listed. Limited distribution.

This is the most comprehensive directory of the central organs of the Peking government (excluding the Chinese Communist Party) for the period covered.

304 **China, Kuo-fang pu, Ch'ing-pao chü** 中華民國 國防部 情報局 (China, Ministry of National Defense, Bureau of Intelligence). *San-nien lai fei-wei chung-yao tsu-chih jen-shih hui-pien* 三年來匪僞重要組織人事彙編 (Select Bandit and Puppet Biographical and Organizational Information, 1958–1960). Taipei, 1961. 10; 224p.

Position data concerning Chinese Communist political, governmental and socio-cultural leaders as of the end of 1960. The directory is divided into three major sections: government reorganization, personnel, and position data. The last section constitutes the body of the work and is further divided into four subsections: (1) government; (2) political parties and mass organizations; (3) a

'Rightists' roster (including those relieved of duties, those cleared of charges, and an amnesty list of 'war criminals'); and (4) an obituary for prominent leaders who died between January 1958 and October 1960. Not indexed. Limited distribution.

An important source.

305 China, Ssu-fa hsing-cheng pu, Tiao-ch'a chü 中華民國司法行政部調查局 (China, Ministry of Justice, Bureau of Investigation). *Fei-wei chung-yao jen-shih ming-ts'e* 匪偽重要人事名冊
(Directory of Important Bandit and Puppet Personnel). Taipei, 1959. 190p.

A directory of political, governmental and military leaders of Communist China, compiled from Communist sources available as of October 1959. Published in three parts: The Chinese Communist Party, central and provincial governments, and military organization. Biographical information is given in most cases in tabular form, and includes date of birth, native place, education and position data. Informative but partially out-dated. Limited distribution.

306 China, Nei-cheng pu, Tiao-ch'a chü 中華民國內政部調查局 (China, Ministry of Interior, Bureau of Investigation). *Fei-wei chung-yao jen-shih tiao-ch'a* 匪偽重要人事調查
(Directory of Important Bandit and Puppet Personnel). Taipei, 1954. 209p.

A directory of the political, governmental, and social and cultural organizations and institutions of Communist China (with names of incumbent officials) compiled from Communist sources available as of June 1954. The volume, which contains no biographical information, is divided into four parts: political parties, First National People's Congress, central government, and mass organizations. Out-dated; for a more current edition, see preceding entry. Limited distribution.

307 Fei-wei jen-shih tzu-liao tiao-ch'a yen-chiu hui 匪偽人事資料調查研究會 (Committee for the Compilation of Biographical Information on Bandit-Puppet Personnel). *Wei cheng-hsieh chi she-t'uan tsu-chih jen-shih tiao-ch'a* 偽政協及社團組織人事調查
(Directory of the Puppet People's Political Consultative Conference and Mass Organizations). Taipei, 1957–1959. 3 vols.

A guide to the People's Political Consultative Conference on both the national and local levels, political parties other than the Communist Party, and mass organizations (including professional, labor, religious, welfare, and others). Names of officers are provided. Accurate information. Limited distribution.

308 China, Ssu-fa hsing-cheng pu, Tiao-ch'a chü 中華民國司法行政部調查局 (China, Ministry of Justice, Bureau of Investigation). *Kung-fei cheng-su fei-wei fen-tzu tzu-liao hui-pien* 共匪整肅匪偽份子資料彙編

(Reference Materials on the Purge of Communist Bandit and Puppet Personnel). Taipei, July 1958. 186p.

A list of 267 Communist and non-Communist political, governmental, and cultural leaders purged in the aftermath of the Hundred Flowers Movement, including in each case political affiliation, native place, position(s) held prior to purge, position(s) relieved of, date and brief account of the purge, and source of information.

A very important compilation. A supplement was issued in November 1958 (106p.) listing twenty-one additional persons and supplying further information on ninety-four of those included in the first volume. Limited distribution in the case of both publications.

309 China, Kuo-fang pu, Ch'ing-pao chü 中華民國國防部情報局 (China, Ministry of National Defense, Bureau of Intelligence). *Fei Fu-chien sheng tang cheng chün chung-yao tsu-chih jen-shih tiao-ch'a* 匪福建省黨政軍重要組織人事調查 (An Organizational and Personnel Directory of the Party, Government and Military of the Bandit Fukien Province). Taipei, 1962. 36p.

A directory of the Chinese Communist Party, the government, military, educational institutions and mass organizations in Fukien as of 1962. The most complete directory of any Mainland province available. Limited distribution.

310 American Consulate General, Hong Kong.
'Directory of Top National Positions in Chinese Communist Party, Government and Armed Forces,' *Current Background*, No. 513 (July 16, 1958), 42p.

A revised edition, with an alphabetical index, of the following three lists: (1) 'Directory of Top National Positions in the Government and Armed Forces of Communist China,' *Current Background*, No. 404 (July 26, 1956); (2) 'Directory of Top National Positions in Chinese Communist Party, Government, and Armed Forces,' *Current Background*, No. 316 (March 7, 1955); and (3) 'Government Directory of Top National Positions, People's Republic of China (October 1, 1953),' *Current Background*, No. 263 (October 1, 1953). With supplement. Largely outdated.

311 American Consulate General, Hong Kong.
'Leading Personnel of the Chinese Communist Regime,' *Current Background*, No. 578 (May 15, 1959), 11p.

A list of the leaders of Communist China before and after the First Session of the Second National People's Congress, April 1959.

312 American Consulate General, Hong Kong.
'Leading Personnel of the State Council in Communist China,' *Current Background*, No. 597 (October 8, 1959), 24p.

Includes a directory of the ministries and commissions under the jurisdiction of the State Council.

313 American Consulate General, Hong Kong.
'Chinese Communist Military Leaders,' *Current Background*, No. 111 (August 29, 1951), 9p.

A list of the personnel of the People's Revolutionary Military Council; the high command of the Chinese People's Liberation Army, and of the field armies comprising the People's Liberation Army; and the commanders and political commissars of the major military districts as of August 1951. Appended are brief biographical sketches of nine top Chinese Communist generals.

314 American Consulate General, Hong Kong.
'Biographic List of the 8th Central Committee of the Communist Party of China,' *Current Background*, No. 431 (December 11, 1956), 25p.

Provides the following information concerning each member of the Eighth Central Committee: (1) rank on Eighth Central Committee, (2) rank on Seventh Central Committee, (3) current post(s) in the government (only the most important listed), (4) post in the party on the eve of the Eighth Congress, and (5) post in the Party Center after the First Plenum of the Eighth Central Committee. The arrangement of the list is by 'group,' on the assumption that people listed in the same group have received the same number of votes and, as such, should have the same ranking. No index.

315 American Consulate General, Hong Kong.
'Composition of the 1st National People's Congress,' *Current Background*, No. 290 (September 5, 1954), 31p.

A study of the composition of the First National People's Congress held on September 15, 1954. Included is a list of 1,226 deputies elected to the congress.

316 American Consulate General, Hong Kong.
'Namelist of Second National People's Congress,' *Current Background*, No. 551 (March 23, 1959), 24p.

A roster of 1,222 deputies elected to the Second National People's Congress held in April 1959.

317 'I-yüeh lai fei-wei p'ai-ch'u yü yao-chin ko-chung tai-piao t'uan tiao-cha'
一月來匪僞派出與邀進各種代表團調查
(Directory of Official and Private Visiting Delegations To and From Communist China During the Preceding Month) in *Fei-ch'ing yüeh-pao* 匪情月報 (Bandit Intelligence Monthly), Vol. 1, No. 1—, February 1958—.

Published regularly in the *Fei-ch'ing yüeh-pao* (see **991**). The directory provides information on the various delegations to and from the Mainland, their activities, etc. Delegations sent abroad are listed first, followed by visiting delegations. For a comprehensive listing of these delegations for the years 1958 to 1960, see next entry.

318 **China, Kuo-fang pu, Ch'ing-pao chü** 中華民國國防部情報局 (China, Ministry of National Defense, Bureau of Intelligence). *San-nien lai kung-fei p'ai-ch'u yü yao-chin ko-chung tai-piao t'uan tiao-ch'a* 三年來共匪派出與邀進各種代表團調查 (Directory of Official and Private Visiting Delegations To and From Communist China, 1958–1960). Taipei, 1961. 582p.

Contains information, based on Chinese Communist sources and arranged by year, on 2,088 official and private Chinese and foreign delegations, visiting in and traveling from Communist China (1,565 and 523 respectively) for the period January 1958 through December 1960. Under each year the arrangement is by in-bound and out-bound delegations which are further grouped into five categories: political, economic, military, cultural, and mass organizations. Under each of the five categories, the following information is provided: (1) name of country (to and from); (2) name of delegation; (3) composition of delegation (names and position data); (4) place and date of arrival; and (5) primary mission and activities.

This is the most comprehensive compilation of its kind for the period covered. Limited distribution.

319 **China (People's Republic of China, 1949—), Wai-chiao pu** 中華人民共和國外交部 (China [People's Republic of China, 1949—], Ministry of Foreign Affairs). *Wai-chiao kuan hsien-ming lu* 外交官衝名錄 (Diplomatic List). Peking, 1961. 130p.

Foreign diplomatic representatives stationed in Peking as of September 1961. In Chinese-Russian-English, the list includes names, addresses, and telephone numbers of embassies, legations, offices of chargés d'affaires, economic missions and their staff. The latest original diplomatic list is not available. For later lists in translation, see next entry.

320 **American Consulate General, Hong Kong.**
'Foreign Diplomatic Representatives in Communist China and Communist Chinese Diplomatic Missions in Foreign Countries,' *Current Background*, No. 687 (August 2, 1962), 6p.

The diplomatic list of Communist China as of July 1962, superseding that of September 1960, *Current Background*, No. 635 (October 7, 1960); 'Listing of Diplomatic Representatives To and From Communist China,' *Current Background*, No. 266 (October 25, 1953); and 'Peking's Foreign Relations,'

Current Background, No. 121 (October 1951). Arranged as follows: (1) foreign diplomatic representatives in Peking; (2) Communist Chinese diplomatic missions abroad; and (3) foreign consulates in Communist China. Alphabetical listing by country with only the title and name of the representative given in each case.

2. ECONOMIC AND TRADE

It is a regrettable fact that Mainland compilations in the economic sphere are not to be had (some directories may be found in the appropriate sections of People's Handbook). Of the compilations prepared in other countries, those of Japanese origin, dealing with Communist China's trade in general and, understandably, the latter's trade with Japan in particular, are greatest in number. The most recent of these is the industrial and trade handbook (**322**). The Japanese trade directories contain similar types of information and are suitably arranged for reference purposes. The latest English-language compilation is a 1957 Hong Kong guide (the first entry) which, like most of the other entries in this section, is outdated.

For more current data, see the relevant sections of the various yearbooks and handbooks on Communist China published in Japan (Chapter IV).

321 Ta Kung Pao.
Trade with China, A Practical Guide. Hong Kong, 1957. 147p.

A guide to trade with Communist China. In three parts: Part 1 contains general information on Communist China's foreign trade, including customs regulations, etc.; Part 2 provides (a) a list of sixteen leading Chinese Communist national import and export corporations, (b) the three Hong Kong agencies for the Chinese national import and export corporations, and (c) information on the banking operations of the Bank of China; Part 3 deals with commodity inspection and testing in Communist China, the Foreign Trade Arbitration Committee, and specifications of major import and export commodities. The appendix contains a series of related procedural regulations, tables of exchange rates for conversion of Jen-min pi (People's Currency) into other currencies, and the text of the Second Five-Year Plan, 1958–1962. The contents of the book are not indexed, but there is an index to advertisers. Somewhat outdated. No other editions published.

For current information, see *Chung-hua jen-min kung-ho kuo tui-wai mao-i* 中華人民共和國對外貿易 *Foreign Trade of the People's Republic of China*, a quarterly catalog of commercial products published in Chinese and English since 1958. A 'List of Chinese National Organizations of Foreign Trade and Their Branches' is included in every issue.

See also *Chung-hua jen-min kung-ho kuo hai-kuan chin-ch'u k'ou shui-tse* 中華人民共和國海關進出口稅則 (Handbook of Export-Import Customs Duties in the Chinese People's Republic), (Peking: Fa-lü ch'u-pan she 法律出版社, 1961), 118p.

322 Ajia Tsūshinsha 亞細亞通信社 (Asia Press Agency). *Chūgoku sangyō bōeki sōran* 中國產業貿易總覽 (Industrial and Trade Handbook of China). Tokyo, 1963. 356p.

The handbook is arranged by branch of industry (metallurgical, chemical, textile, paper, etc.), with a separate section on Mainland China's foreign trade. Contains 140 illustrations and 400 statistical tables.

323 Miyashita, Tadao 宮下忠雄. *Chūgoku no bōeki soshiki* 中國の貿易組織 (The Organization of China's Trade). Tokyo: Tokyo Daigaku Shuppankai 東京大學出版會, 1961. 190p.

Monograph No. 17 in the Asian Economic Research Series of the Japanese Government's Institute of Asian Economic Affairs (Ajia Keizai Kenkyūjo アジア經濟研究所). The volume describes the development of the administrative structure of Communist China's foreign trade apparatus and its present-day policies, activity and organization, including such specific matters as customs, foreign exchange and trade agreement practices. Appended are a number of important pertinent laws and regulations and a bibliography. Professor Miyashita of Kobe University was a long-time resident in prewar China.

See also the author's *Shin Chūgoku no keizai seido* 新中國の經濟制度 (The Economic System of New China), (Tokyo: Yūhikaku 有斐閣, 1964).

324 Nihon Kōekisha, Chōsabu 日本交易社調査部 (Japan Trade Company, Research Department). *Chūgoku saishin shōkō meikan—1958* 中國最新商工名鑑 (Most Recent Directory of Commerce and Industry of [Communist] China—1958). Tokyo: Nihon Kōekisha, 1958. 157p.

A directory of some 1,400 business enterprises and organizations, 150 research institutes, 150 universities and several hundred publications, based on data from Chinese Communist newspapers and other sources. Business enterprises are classified by type (e.g., foreign trade, iron and steel, metals, etc.) and are listed together with information on addresses, type of ownership (state, public or private) and commodities handled, etc. Research organizations are classified by field of specialization (machinery, electricity, agriculture, medicine, etc.). The universities are listed with their addresses and departments. The publications section covers newspapers and magazines. Periodical entries are classified by subject and provide the title, frequency, and place of publication. Mimeographed. No further volumes published.

325 Nitchū Yushutsunyū Kumiai 日中輸出入組合 (Japan-China Exporters and Importers Association). *Nitchū bōeki yōran—1957 nen* 日中貿易要覽一九五七年 *Nicchu* [sic] *Trade Handbook—1957*. Tokyo, 1957. 436p.

Contains a list of Communist Chinese government agencies concerned with trade (including addresses, names of important officials and commodities handled), trade agreements, trade statistics, procedures, laws and regulations, etc. Included also are lists of Japanese agencies and associations concerned with trade with Communist China; a chronology of Japanese-Chinese trade (pp. 367–372); and a Japanese-Chinese-English glossary of trade terms. No further volumes published.

The Japan-China Exporters and Importers Association consists of Japanese firms with China trade interests and conducts activities designed to promote trade between Japan and Communist China.

For more up-to-date information see Tanishiki Hiroshi 谷敷寬 *Nitchū bōeki annai* 日中貿易案内 (Guide to Japanese-Chinese Trade), (Tokyo: Nihon Keizai Shimbun Sha 日本經濟新聞社, 1964), 380p.

326 **Chū-Nichi Kōshō Fukumusha** 中日工商服務社 (Chinese-Japanese Industry and Commerce Promotion Company). *Chūgoku bōeki shōkō sōran* 中國貿易商工總覽 (Handbook of Chinese Foreign Trade, Commerce and Industry). Tokyo, 1955. 393p.

Compiled by a Chinese company in Japan, the handbook covers Communist China's foreign trade and industry. Part 1 contains a description of trade and industry on the Mainland. Part 2 provides information on thirty-five government enterprises (including some 250 branch offices) engaged in foreign trade and 715 firms arranged by location; over 1,000 government and private enterprises arranged by the types of commodities handled; a list of foreign firms on the Mainland arranged by country; and a list of firms in Hong Kong and Macao engaged in trade with Communist China. Part 3 contains pertinent laws and regulations, while Part 4 lists treaties, agreements and other documentary material.

327 **Chūgoku Kenkyūjo** 中國研究所 (China Research Institute). *Nitchū bōeki handobukku* 日中貿易ハンドブック (Handbook of Japanese-Chinese Trade). Tokyo: Yūhikaku 有斐閣, 1955. 304; 19p.

Contains a survey of Japanese trade with Communist China, trade statistics, trade restrictions, transportation and payment arrangements, and trade agreements; a list of Japanese firms which engaged in trade with Communist China in 1954; an overview of Communist China's trade, trade policy, trade regulations and organizations; a survey of Communist China's trade with the Soviet Union and the Communist bloc and its trade with 'capitalist' countries; a list of Communist China's export and import commodities; a chronology of Japanese-Chinese trade; and a Japanese-Chinese-English list of trade terms. Index arranged according to the Japanese syllabary.

328 **Nitchū Gyogyō Kyōgikai** 日中漁業協議會 (Japan-[Communist] China Fishery Conference). *Nitchū gyogyō sōran* 日中漁業總覽 (Handbook on Japan-[Communist] China Fisheries). Tokyo, 1957. 234p.

Contains texts of fishery agreements between Japan and Communist China; Japanese and Chinese domestic regulations pertaining thereto; a survey of the negotiations leading to the conclusion of the agreement; and such related materials as statistics, rosters, etc. A chronology of Japanese-Chinese Communist relations with respect to fishing from 1949 to 1957 appears on pages 190–202.

329 **Nitchū Bōeki Jitsumu Kenkyūkai** 日中貿易實務研究會 (Society for Practical Study of Trade Between Japan and [Communist] China). *Chūgoku shōhin jiten* 中國商品事典
(Dictionary of Chinese Merchandise). Tokyo: Kyokutō Shoten 極東書店, 1960. 608p.

Contains a list of over 100 commodities important in Japan's trade with Communist China, compiled by sixteen persons actually engaged in trade with that country. Items are arranged by category (mineral products—32 commodities; agricultural and marine products—49; chemicals, etc.). On the average, some five pages are devoted to each commodity, providing the name, place of origin or manufacture, production method, types, uses, grades, specifications, production and export figures, transaction conditions and other useful data. Indexes (subject and geographical) are arranged according to the Japanese syllabary. Appended are a bibliography of some seventy entries, trade statistics, etc.

3. EDUCATIONAL

Brought together in this section are, for the most part, lists compiled on the Mainland of institutions of higher learning. It is unfortunate in view of the importance of the educational sector that the most recent available Mainland imprint is 1957. The most comprehensive and, at the same time, the most recent guide to Mainland educational institutions is of American origin—that prepared by the Library of Congress in 1961 (the first entry in this section).

330 **Wang, Chi, comp.**
Mainland China Organizations of Higher Learning in Science and Technology and Their Publications: A Selected Guide. Washington, D.C.: Library of Congress, Reference Department, Science and Technology Division, 1961. 104p.

The guide identifies and describes scientific organizations and publications of Mainland China. Included are (1) learned societies; (2) universities and colleges; (3) Chinese Academy of Sciences and affiliated research institutes; (4) Chinese Academy of Medical Sciences, and branch institutes; (5) Chinese Academy of Agricultural Sciences, and branch institutes; (6) governmental research organizations; and (7) libraries.

Information supplied for each entry, when available, is given in the following order: (1) official name in romanization; (2) official name in Chinese characters; (3) official name in English translation as it appears on publications (in parentheses when supplied by compiler); (4) location or address; (5) founding date;

(6) officials; (7) research activities and facilities, and (8) principal publications. Other information given: for learned societies, membership totals and number of local branches; for universities and colleges, names of scientific departments; for libraries and botanical gardens, approximate size and type of collections.

Publications listed fall into the following categories: (1) serial publications; (2) abstracting and indexing services; (3) bibliographies; and (4) dictionaries. Citations are given in the following order: (1) romanized titles in Wade-Giles, in the Chinese Communist *P'in-yin* romanization when provided in the original publication; (2) frequency; (3) languages used in table of contents; (4) availability of English or Russian summaries; and (5) availability of extensive references. The date of publication is supplied for bibliographies and dictionaries. An asterisk preceding the title denotes its availability in the Library of Congress. Six indexes. In addition to the English and romanized indexes to institutions, four separate romanized indexes are also provided for serial publications, indexing and abstracting services, bibliographies, and dictionaries. A list of sources is also included.

Carefully compiled. The most comprehensive guide of its kind.

331 **Orleans, Leo A.**
Professional Manpower and Education in Communist China. Washington, D.C.: National Science Foundation, 1961. 12; 260p.

The study 'examines the characteristics and training of Chinese professional manpower and their relationship to Communist China's technological development.' Includes a number of very useful statistical tables and appendices. The latter comprise the following: (1) tables on education; (2) sample curricula; (3) institutions of higher education; (4) institutions offering post-graduate courses and courses offered; (5) list of specializations in higher technological institutions; (6) regulations governing the enrolment of new students by institutions of higher education; (7) outlines of selected examinations for matriculation to institutions of higher education; (8) constitution of the All-China Students' Federation; and (9) scientific research institutes in China. The last is a list of institutes of the Academy of Sciences compiled by Mr. Wang Chi. See preceding entry.

332 **American Consulate General, Hong Kong.**
'Some Institutions of Higher Learning in Communist China,' *Current Background*, No. 585 (July 30, 1959), 21p.

A collection of translated articles which appeared in *Wen-hui pao* 文滙報 and *Kuang-ming jih-pao* 光明日報 in June 1959, describing eleven institutions of higher learning, largely in the fields of technology and medicine.

333 **China (People's Republic of China, 1949—), Kao-teng chiao-yü pu** 中華 人民共和國高等教育部 (China [People's Republic of China, 1949—], Ministry

of Higher Education). *I-chiu-wu-liu nien shu-ch'i kao-teng hsüeh-hsiao chao-sheng sheng-hsüeh chih-tao* 一九五六年暑期高等學校招生升學指導
(Guide to Institutions of Higher Learning, Summer, 1956). Peking: Kao-teng chiao-yü ch'u-pan she 高等教育出版社, 1956. 3 vols.

A three-volume guide designed for middle school graduates seeking to enter colleges and universities in Communist China. Volume 1, science and engineering; Volume 2, medicine, agriculture and physical education; Volume 3, the humanities and social sciences. Each volume is divided into two parts. Part 1: a general description of course content by specialization; Part 2: a comprehensive listing of universities and colleges offering these courses, and the duration of their programs. See also next entry.

334 **China (People's Republic of China, 1949—), Kao-teng chiao-yü pu** 中華人民共和國高等教育部 (China [People's Republic of China, 1949—], Ministry of Higher Education). *Kao-teng hsüeh-hsiao chao-sheng sheng-hsüeh chih-tao* 高等學校招生升學指導
(Guide to Institutions of Higher Learning). Shanghai: Kao-teng chiao-yü ch'u-pan she 高等教育出版社, 1957. 35p.

A listing similar to the preceding entry, but lacking Part 1. For a translation of this brochure, see *Current Background*, No. 462 (July 1, 1957), under the title 'Institutions of Higher Learning in Communist China' (54p.).

335 **Hsiang-kang hsüeh-sheng shu-tien** 香港學生書店 (Hong Kong Student Book Store). *I-chiu-wu-ssu nien t'ou-k'ao ta-hsüeh chih-tao* 一九五四年投考大學指導
(Guide to Institutions of Higher Learning, 1954). Hong Kong: Hsiang-kang hsüeh-sheng shu-tien, 1954. 130p.

A list of 190 universities and colleges in Communist China as of 1954. Institutions are listed according to geographical region. The guide includes courses offered, and indicates the duration of different college programs. Appended are examination questions given at the National Joint College Entrance Examinations in Communist China in 1953.

336 **Wen-hui pao** 文滙報 (Wen-hui Daily). *T'ou-k'ao ta-hsüeh shou-ts'e* 投考大學手冊
(Handbook of Colleges and Universities). Shanghai, 1951. 177p.

A directory of universities and colleges on Mainland China as of 1951.

337 **China (People's Republic of China, 1949—), Kao-teng chiao-yü pu** 中華人民共和國高等教育部 (China [People's Republic of China, 1949—], Ministry of Higher Education). *I-chiu-wu-liu nien chung-teng chuan-yeh hsüeh-hsiao chao-sheng sheng-hsüeh chih-tao* 一九五六年中等專業學校招生升學指導

(Guide to Vocational Schools, 1956). Peking: Kao-teng chiao-yü ch'u-pan she 高等教育出版社, 1956. 110p.

In two parts: (1) brief descriptions of the course content of the curriculum arranged by vocation; and (2) a listing of vocational schools by province, including courses offered at each school.

B. TAIWAN

This section is given over to general directories and directories to educational and cultural institutions, mass media, civic organizations and business enterprises.

The most comprehensive directory of cultural organizations, under which are included institutions of higher learning, is that compiled by the National Central Library (341). The directories to institutions of higher education contained in the present section largely speak for themselves. The Directory of Mass Communication Agencies, the Fifty Years of Civic Organizations and the *Taiwan Buyer's Guide* (346–348) also deserve special mention as the most comprehensive compilations in their respective fields.

For further and more up-to-date information, consult the general and topical yearbooks and handbooks, as well as the Bulletin of the Office of the President (676) and other government gazettes listed in Chapter XIII.

338   Li, Chen-yang 李振揚, **ed.** *Tzu-yu Chung-kuo yao-lan* 自由中國要覽
(Free China Directory). Taipei: Hsing-wen-tsai Book Co., 1953. 164p.

A single-volume directory containing descriptive and statistical data on the political, economic and educational organization of the Republic of China. The material is drawn from official reports and scholarly journals and is arranged by major areas of government activity (i.e., civil affairs, finance, food and agriculture, etc.). The statistics are those of 1952. Because 1952 was the year in which the Four Year Plan Towards Economic Self-Sufficiency and the Land-to-Tillers Program were launched, the directory gives considerable attention to the economic sector. A bibliography of books, reports and statistical compilations is appended. Largely outdated.

339   Shu, T'ao, 舒桃 **ed.** *Chin-jih Chung-kuo yao-lan* 今日中國要覽
(China Today). Taipei: Tzu-yu Press, 1957. 387p.

A guide to industry and commerce on Taiwan. In four parts: Part 1 provides a brief description of the communications and transportation industries in Taiwan, together with such other industries as cement, sugar and textiles. Part 2 contains data on various governmental agencies and public enterprises, including banking, finance and insurance. Part 3 comprises lists of flour mills, trucking companies and coal mines, arranged geographically. Part 4 is given over to an alphabetical directory of importers and exporters. A list of the various business associations, accompanied by data on their histories, activities and directors, appears at the end of the volume.

340 **Directory of Taiwan.** Taipei: The China News and Publication Service, Ltd., 1951—. Annual.

An annual tourist guide book on Taiwan, including useful information on government organizations, universities and colleges, etc.

341 **Chung-yang t'u-shu kuan** 中央圖書館 (National Central Library). *Chung-hua min-kuo hsüeh-shu chi-kou lu* 中華民國學術機構錄 *Directory of the Cultural Organizations of the Republic of China.* Revised edition. Taipei, 1963. 142p.

Originally published in 1961, this is a guide to (1) learned societies, (2) research institutes, (3) libraries, museums, social education centers, (4) universities and colleges, and (5) research departments in public and private organizations in Taiwan. The institutions are arranged in alphabetical order within the five broad categories listed above. Concerning each, the following data are provided: name, address, telephone number, date of founding, purposes and objectives, functions, membership, staff or faculty, names of principal officers together with brief biographical sketches, major activities and publications. In English, with names and addresses in Chinese.

While the amount of information provided varies, this organizational who's who is by far the most comprehensive and up-to-date compilation of its kind and is both reliable and conveniently organized. Since publications of the organizations are listed in detail, the volume also serves as a directory to scholarly journals and proceedings of the learned societies.

342 **Hai-wai ch'u-pan she** 海外出版社 (Overseas Publishing Company). *Tzu-yu Chung-kuo ta chuan hsüeh-hsiao kai-lan* 自由中國大專學校概覽 (Directory of Universities and Colleges in Free China). Taipei: Hai-wai ch'u-pan she, 1956. 448p.

Contains descriptions of seventeen universities and colleges in Taiwan, including courses offered at each institution and examination questions given at the 1955 Joint College Entrance Examinations by five institutions of higher learning, including the National Taiwan University. See next entry.

343 **Hai-wai ch'u-pan she** 海外出版社 (Overseas Publishing Company). *Tzu-yu Chung-kuo ta chung hsüeh-hsiao chien-chieh* 自由中國大中學校簡介 (Directory of Universities, Colleges, and Middle Schools in Free China). Taipei: Hai-wai ch'u-pan she, 1957. 385p.

A revised edition of the preceding entry. Added to the directory are descriptions of sixteen middle schools (including vocational schools).

344 **Chang, Ch'i-yün** 張其昀, **et al.** *Chung-hua min-kuo ta-hsüeh chih* 中華民國大學誌 (Chinese Universities). Taipei: Chinese Culture Publication Foundation, 1954. 2 vols. 480p.

Two volumes providing descriptions of some fifty Chinese universities, written by their presidents, former presidents or professors. While most of the universities in question are located on the Mainland, some of them have been reconstituted on Taiwan in the form of research institutes and, as such, play an important role in the island's system of higher education.

345 Chung-hua nung-hsüeh hui 中華農學會 (Agricultural Association of China). *Manual of Agricultural Institutions in Taiwan.* Taipei, 1961. 14; 84p.

Lists seventy-four agricultural organizations in Taiwan, grouped in seven parts: (1) experimental and research organizations; (2) administrative organizations; (3) educational organizations; (4) enterprises; (5) financial organizations; (6) farmers' organizations; and (7) agricultural academic societies. Information given for each institution includes its organization, history, major work in progress, activities, significant achievements, and publications, if any.

Dependable information and well edited.

346 Taiwan, Hsin-wen ch'u 臺灣省 新聞處 (Taiwan, Department of Information). *Hsin-wen shih-yeh chi-kou i-lan* 新聞事業機構一覽 (Directory of Mass Communication Agencies). Taichung, 1961. 22; 151p.

An annual listing of all officially registered newspapers, news agencies, periodicals, publishing houses, disc manufacturers, broadcasting stations, and pro-Nationalist Overseas Chinese newspapers and periodicals. The amount of information provided varies from section to section. In the case of newspapers and news agencies, address, publisher, and officers are given; for journals, publishing houses, phonograph record manufacturers, and broadcasting stations, additional information is provided where appropriate. Index is arranged according to the number of strokes of the first character, and is classified by city and country, and under that, by media.

The directory is less reliable when dealing with minor publishing houses and periodicals whose officers and addresses are subject to frequent change.

For a more comprehensive listing, see *Chung-hua min-kuo hsin-wen nien-chien* (**247**).

See also *Ch'u-pan shih-yeh teng-chi i-lan* 出版事業登記一覽 (Directory of Publishers in the Republic of China) published by the Department of Publication of the Ministry of Interior in 1963 (214p.)

347 Chung-hua min-kuo min-chung t'uan-t'i huo-tung chung-hsin 中華民國 民眾團體活動中心 (Chinese Civic Organization Activity Center). *Chung-hua min-kuo wu-shih nien lai ti min-chung t'uan-t'i* 中華民國五十年來的民眾團體 (Fifty Years of Civic Organizations in the Republic of China). Taipei, 1961. 1,125p.

A directory to such organizations as labor unions, professional associations, trade guilds, learned societies, alumni clubs, clan associations, chambers of commerce, social clubs, and provincial benevolent associations. In three parts. Part 1, 'Historical Review of Civic Organizations in China' comprises three chapters: (1) the history of civic organizations and the role they played in the early Republican period; (2) the evolution of these organizations from the time of the Northern Expedition to the end of the Second World War; and (3) their restoration and reorganization after the transfer of the government to Taiwan. Part 2, 'Descriptive Directory of the Civic Organizations at Various Levels,' consists of five chapters: (1) organizations at the national level; (2) regional organizations (mostly business); (3) civic organizations at the provincial level; (4) civic organizations in the Quemoy and Matsu areas; and (5) organizations in the city of Taipei. Part 3 reviews the formation of the Chinese communities abroad and the recent activities of their various civic organizations. Related laws and regulations and a list of all the organizations in Taiwan (by geographical division) are appended. No index.

The most informative directory to civic organizations ever published in China. Not only is it a good directory, but it is also an indispensable source for the study of social organization and control in China.

348 **China Productivity and Trade Center.**
Taiwan Buyer's Guide, 1962 Edition. Taipei, 1962. 652p.

A directory of some 7,000 manufacturers and 1,900 importers in Taiwan, compiled by the China Productivity and Trade Center (a companion volume has been issued in Chinese under the title *T'ai-wan kung-sheng ming-lu* 臺灣工商名錄). The data concerning each firm includes address, telephone numbers and cable addresses, types of products or services, capital assets, etc. In three parts. Part 1 contains a classified list of products and a list of manufacturers; Part 2, classified lists of export, import and import-export firms; Part 3 is concerned with tourism and includes lists of tourist promotion organizations, guide services, hotels, restaurants, travel and shipping agencies, and airlines. The appendices incorporate such information as diplomatic and consular establishments in China, Chinese diplomatic and commercial representatives abroad, industrial and commercial consultants, banks, stock exchanges, insurance agencies, Overseas Chinese commercial organizations, etc.

The index in the *Guide* serves both the English and Chinese editions. The present volume is an enlarged edition of the two bilingual editions revised in 1958 and 1960.

CHAPTER VII

BIOGRAPHICAL MATERIALS

The biographical compilations contained in the present chapter fall most conveniently into four categories: (1) general, (2) Mainland, (3) Taiwan, and (4) Hong Kong. The general section, as its name implies, covers personalities on both the Mainland and Taiwan and, frequently, elsewhere. The other sections require no further comment.

Additional biographical information can be obtained by referring to the directories and related materials in the preceding chapter, and by consulting the biographical sections in the various handbooks and yearbooks described in Chapter IV.

It hardly needs mention that the reader can locate additional references in the two bibliographies of biographies (see **76** and **77**).

A. GENERAL

Of the biographies which concern themselves with both Nationalist and Communist Chinese, the most comprehensive and probably the most accurate are the compilations of the China Section of the Japanese Foreign Ministry. The last (1962) edition lists some 8,000 persons, the largest number of Chinese biographies assembled in a single source in any language. All four editions of this compilation are included in the present section, owing to the fact that deceased persons and historical personages of lesser importance have been removed from the later editions.

Of the several English-language compilations, the *Who's Who in China* (sixth edition, **355**), though outdated, provides fairly dependable data for non-Communist Chinese as of 1950; however, the sketches for the Communists are for the most part based on unevaluated newspaper accounts. Perleberg's *Who's Who in Modern China* (**353**) contains the most entries (over 2,000), but the biographical data are usually derivative and often inaccurate. The *Asia Who's Who* (**354**) lists over 1,000 Chinese, but adds very little factual data to what is contained in other sources.

349 **Japan, Gaimushō, Chōsakyoku** 日本外務省調査局 (Japan, Ministry of Foreign Affairs, Research Bureau). *Gendai Tōa jimmei kan—Shōwa 25 nemban* 現代東亞人名鑑昭和二十五年版
(Who's Who in Present-Day East Asia—1950 Edition). Tokyo: Tōhō Kenkyūkai 東邦研究會, 1950. 197p.

The first comprehensive postwar Japanese biographical compilation on Asia prepared by government specialists. While the Who's Who also covers Korea and Southeast Asia, some 500 biographical sketches—more than half of the volume's contents—concern Chinese personalities (29 pages are devoted to Nationalist Chinese, 55 to the Communists). The division into Nationalists and Communists, however, is not always up to date. The subjects are, for the most part, leaders in politics and government, and the sketches emphasize their postwar careers.

The sketches are grouped by country in Japanese syllabic order according to the Japanese reading of the subject's name. A number of lists on governmental organization, etc., are appended. Japanese syllabic index according to the Japanese pronunciation and an alphabetical index arranged under each letter by country.

For successive biographical compilations of the Foreign Ministry, see the next entries.

350 **Japan, Gaimushō, Ajiakyoku** 日本外務省アジア局 (Japan, Ministry of Foreign Affairs, Bureau of Asian Affairs). *Gendai Chūgoku Chōsen jimmei kan* 現代中國朝鮮人名鑑
(Who's Who in Present-Day China and Korea). Tokyo, 1953. [397p.]

A revision of the China and Korea sections of the preceding entry, covering persons in Nationalist and Communist China and North and South Korea. Emphasis is given to persons active during 1952, as well as a number of important historical personages. The compilation provides biographical information on roughly 2,000 Chinese. In the Chinese section the arrangement is by the Japanese pronunciation of the subject's name. Lists of persons in Nationalist and Communist Chinese government and political organizations are appended. Two indexes—one by Japanese syllabary according to Japanese pronunciation, the other alphabetical (Wade-Giles) according to the Chinese pronunciation.
See also next entry.

351 **Kasumigasekikai** 霞關會 (Kasumigaseki Society). *Gendai Chūgoku jimmei jiten* 現代中國人名辭典
(Biographical Dictionary of Contemporary China). Tokyo: Kōnan Shoin 江南書院, 1957. 718; 73; 129p.

A biographical dictionary based on official Chinese Communist sources, prepared by the staff of the China Section of the Ministry of Foreign Affairs. The volume is a revision and development of the biographical compilations (see the preceding entries) published in 1950 and 1953. The sketches vary in length from one line to a page, and are provided for some 7,000 prominent Chinese (particularly in political and economic circles) on the Mainland, Taiwan and overseas. With a few exceptions, non-contemporary personages are not included. The sketches, arranged by the Japanese syllabary in accordance with the Japanese reading of the Chinese name, provide the subject's name in characters and in romanization, courtesy name, date and place of birth, personal history, occupation, present position and publications. The personal history emphasizes the postwar period.

The two indexes are arranged as in the preceding entry. For a revised edition, see next entry.

352 **Kasumigasekikai** 霞關會 (Kasumigaseki Society). *Gendai Chūgoku jimmei jiten, 1962 nemban* 現代中國人名辭典一九六二年版

(Biographical Dictionary of Contemporary China, 1962 Edition). Tokyo: Gaikō Jihō Sha 外交時報社, 1962. 116; 789p.

A revision of the 1957 biographical dictionary (see preceding entry). In addition to revisions and corrections, some 1,000 subjects have been added to the 7,000 contained in the earlier edition. A number of persons whose importance has declined in the past several years, as well as deceased persons below the rank of minister, have been omitted in the new edition. The dictionary is particularly helpful for identifying lesser-known officials. Three indexes: (1) alphabetical according to the Wade-Giles romanization; (2) by Japanese syllabary in accordance with the Japanese reading of the name; (3) by stroke count.

Without question, this is the most comprehensive biographical dictionary on contemporary China available in any language. Although a number of factual errors have not yet been corrected, it still remains the most useful compilation of contemporary Chinese biographies.

353 Perleberg, Max, ed.
Who's Who in Modern China. Hong Kong: Ye Olde Printerie, 1954. 428p.

Contains more than 2,000 biographical sketches covering the period from the beginning of the Chinese Republic to the end of 1953. The biographies range from one line to a full page, and include Chinese characters for personal and geographical names, organizations, titles of books, etc. A number of directories for both the Nationalist and Communist governments, and for the Chinese Communist Party, the Kuomintang and other minor parties, mass organizations, etc., are provided, as is a glossary of new terms used in contemporary Chinese. Two indexes: English-Chinese (alphabetical—Wade-Giles) and Chinese (according to the number of strokes).

The *Who's Who*, while based on published sources, is often inaccurate and unedited.

354 Asia Who's Who. Third edition. Hong Kong: Pan-Asia Newspaper Alliance, 1960. 939p.

Over 3,000 biographical sketches of prominent persons in Asian countries east of Afghanistan. The sketches, ranging in length from a few lines to over a page, are arranged by country listed in alphabetical order, except for the Communist countries which are included in the appendix. Biographical coverage is extended to some 600 Chinese on the Mainland (pp. 711–867), 270 on Taiwan (pp. 67–135), 50 in Hong Kong (pp. 137–158), and 70 Overseas Chinese in Malaya and Singapore. A list of the most important government officials precedes the body of sketches for each country. Indexed alphabetically.

The 1957 edition includes over 2,000 biographical sketches in straight alphabetical order, except in the case of biographees in Communist-dominated countries who are listed alphabetically in the appendix. The volume provides data on over 300 Chinese on the Mainland, 200 on Taiwan, and 80 in Hong Kong and overseas.

Adds little information that is not contained in other sources.

355 Who's Who in China. Sixth edition. Shanghai: The China Weekly Review [Preface date June 1950]. 263p.

Contains biographical sketches (mostly with portraits) of more than 1,000 Chinese, including many lesser government functionaries. A number of leading members of the Chinese Communist Party and of the Chinese Communist government are included. Their biographies were added in late 1948 and early 1949 (the volume was begun in 1946), and with few exceptions were compiled from newspaper accounts published after the end of the Second World War. Information for the others is supplied by the individuals themselves and revised in light of the rapid march of events. Chinese characters are provided for names appearing in the text and in the alphabetical index.

356 Boorman, Howard L., ed.
Men and Politics in Modern China. New York: Columbia University, 1960. 173p.

Fifty preliminary biographical sketches of prominent men of Republican China, including sixteen sketches of Communist leaders. This is the first part of a planned biographical dictionary of leading figures of twentieth-century China from the time of the 1911 Revolution to the establishment of the Central People's Government in Peking in 1949. The individuals, in order to be included, must have achieved influence or prominence prior to 1949. Information on the post-1949 activities of living persons is limited to summary rather than detailed treatment. The dictionary, when completed, will include men in a number of fields; e.g., politics, business and banking, diplomacy, literature, etc. The biographical sketches are presented chronologically in narrative form, and include when feasible a brief critical estimate of the man's significance or influence in his particular sphere or spheres of activity. Each entry includes the subject's name(s) and native place in Chinese characters.

Chinese characters and references are to be included in the finished version which is scheduled for publication by the Columbia University Press under the title *Men and Politics in Republican China: A Biographical Dictionary.* A full listing of the 560 entries was issued by the research project on Men and Politics in Modern China, Columbia University, in February 1964.

B. MAINLAND

Not a single Mainland biographical publication is available. The blackout on such data extends even to the official People's Handbook.

The most extensive biographical work on the Mainland Chinese has been carried on in Japan, Taiwan and the United States, mostly under official auspices. As has already been indicated, the most comprehensive compilations are those of the Japanese

Foreign Ministry, which has at its command up-to-date biographical files. Less detailed, though more up-to-date, is the biographical dictionary compiled by the Asia Research Institute (**359**). Taiwan compilations include the twenty-two-volume biography (**363**) issued between the years 1957 and 1959, providing information on some 4,000 biographies. The biographical directory prepared by the Central Committee of the Kuomintang (**365**) supplies fairly detailed data on the regular and alternate members of the Eighth Central Committee of the Chinese Communist Party. Another work of some importance is the collection of biographies of ten Communist marshals (**366**), published at Taipei in 1962. For detailed information—both background and current —on the more important Chinese Communists, consult the biographical sections in the *Fei-ch'ing yen-chiu* (Bandit Intelligence Studies) and the *Fei-ch'ing yüeh-pao* (Bandit Intelligence Monthly), (**360** and **361,** respectively). Finally, it should be noted that American governmental biographical files have not been processed for publication since 1950, except in the case of a few directories containing position data (see the preceding chapter).

English-language information on over 830 Mainland Chinese is available through the *Biographical Service* of the Union Research Institute in Hong Kong, supplemented by the three volumes compiled by Donald Klein (first and second entries, respectively). Further, biographical data for the period April 1960–January 1963 is supplied by the *Activities of Prominent Chinese Communist Personalities*, published by the U.S. Joint Publications Research Service (**362**).

See also an article by William Ayers entitled 'Current Biography in Communist China', *Journal of Asian Studies*, Vol. 21, No. 4 (August 1962), pp. 477–485.

357 Biographical Service. Hong Kong: Union Research Institute, No. 1—, July 3, 1956—.

Published as a supplement to the Union Research Service (see **1065**). As a rule, each issue consists of one short biography (some issues contain two biographies) of some leading party or government official of Communist China. A total of 839 biographies had been published to December 31, 1963. An alphabetical index covering Nos. 1 to 734 was issued in 1963, incorporating three earlier ones covering Nos. 1–158, Nos. 159–389, and Nos. 1–600, respectively. (An index to Nos. 390–600 was also compiled by the East Asian Collection of the Hoover Institution in January 1962.) Mimeographed. Information is presented in more detail for the post-1949 period than for the earlier years. Especially useful for biographical information on the lesser known personalities of Communist China. A comprehensive who's who in book form is under preparation.

For supplementary information on some of the biographies included here, see next entry.

358 Klein, Donald W.
Who's Who of Communist China. New York, 1959. 3 vols.

Biographical sketches of approximately 540 leaders of Communist China— mostly members of the Chinese Communist Party— incorporating information in the *Biographical Service* published by the Union Research Institute since 1956 with data obtained from other sources. The biographies are on the average one to two legal-size pages long. As in the case of the *Biographical Service*, sketches in this volume are more detailed for the post-1949 period than for the earlier years. Also a good source for biographies of lesser known officials. Mimeographed.

359 **Ajia Kenkyūjo** アジア研究所 **(Asia Research Institute), comp.** *1964 nemban Chūka Jimmin Kyōwakoku genshoku jimmei jiten* 一九六四年版中華人民共和國現職人名辭典 (Biographical Dictionary of Persons on Active Service in the Chinese People's Republic, 1964 Edition). Tokyo, November 1963. 658p.

Contains biographical information on 8,450 persons prominent in Communist China as of October 1963, based on published Mainland sources and the files of Japanese companies trading with the Mainland. Charts of the central government, the Chinese Communist Party, and the import-export organization are appended.

The biographical sketches, arranged in Japanese syllabic order, are less detailed than those in the compilations of the Japanese Foreign Ministry (see **349-352**). Mimeographed.

360 **'Fei-wei jen-wu chih'** 匪偽人物誌 (Who's Who of the Bandit and Puppet Personnel) in *Fei-ch'ing yen-chiu* 匪情研究 (Bandit Intelligence Studies), Vol. 1, No. 1—, March 1958—.

Published under the title 'Fei-wei tung-t'ai jen-wu chih' 匪偽動態人物誌 (Who's Who of the Bandit and Puppet Personnel and Their Activities) in *Fei-ch'ing yen-chiu* (see **990**), Vol. 1, No. 1–Vol. 5, No. 2 (March 1958–February 1962), this who's who section usually contains biographical sketches of two high-ranking party or government officials in Communist China. Includes the most recent activities of the subjects. Particularly useful for data for the 1920's and 1930's, usually poorly covered in other biographical sources.

361 **'Chung-yao fei-chiu yen-hsing chi-yao'** 重要匪酋言行紀要 (Important Speeches and Activities of Bandit Leaders) in *Fei-ch'ing yüeh-pao* 匪情月報 (Bandit Intelligence Monthly), Vol. 1, No. 1—, February 1958—.

Published regularly in the *Fei-ch'ing yüeh-pao* (see **991**), the present entry is essentially a chronology of the activities of the leaders of Communist China, occasionally incorporating digests of important speeches. The entries are arranged chronologically under the individual concerned (e.g., Mao Tse-tung, Liu Shao-ch'i, etc.). The most current publication of its kind. See also the next entry for a similar compilation in English.

362 U.S. Joint Publications Research Service.
Activities of Prominent Chinese Communist Personalities. Washington, D.C., 12
issues, and Nos. 1–62 (November 29, 1960—February 26, 1963). Irregular.

A record of activities of prominent Chinese Communist leaders for the period
from April 1960 to January 1963, compiled mainly from *Jen-min jih-pao* (People's
Daily). Straight alphabetical listing through November 1960. Arranged alphabetically under two sections thereafter. One covers 'high echelon leaders'; the
other, all other personalities. Mimeographed.

The following numbers of the J.P.R.S. reports are special issues of this title:

PUBLICATION NO.	J.P.R.S. NO.	PERIOD COVERED	U.S.G.P.O. MONTHLY CATALOG NO.
	6311	Apr. 1960	1961– 1058
	6482	May 1960	2297
	6580	Jun. 1960	4496
	6674	Jun.-Jul. 1960	4549
	6731	Aug. 1960	7753
	8001	Sep. 1960	12981
	6975	Oct. 1960	9365
	8449	Nov. 1960	13317
	8474	Dec. 1960	13333
	8475	Jan. 1961	13334
	8465	Feb. 1961	13328
	8531	Mar. 1961	15098
1	8560	Apr. 1961	15104
2	8708	May 1961	15188
3	8842	Jun. 1961	17490
4	10540	Jul. 1961	1962– 1112
5	11089	Aug. 1961	1471
6	11515	Sep. 1961	3074
7	12013	Oct. 1961	5942
8	12085	Nov. 1961	6000
9	12248	Dec. 1961	6124
10	12326	Jan. 1962	6161
11	12438	Jan. 1962	8042
12	12554	Jan. 1962	8129
13	12642	Jan.-Feb. 1962	8185
14	12847	Feb. 1962	1962– 8282
15	12906	Feb. 1962	9988
16	13077	Feb. 1962	10140
17	13174	Feb.-Mar. 1962	10217
18	13255	Mar. 1962	10267
19	13382	Mar. 1962	10343
20	13440	Mar. 1962	12087
21	13518	Mar. 1962	12151
22	13603	Apr. 1962	12223
23	13684	Apr. 1962	12274
24	13732	Apr. 1962	12304
25	13776	Apr. 1962	14041
26	13951	Apr.-May 1962	14204
27	14037	May 1962	14284
28	14146	Jun. 1962	14346
29	14193	May 1962	15783
30	14407	Jun. 1962	17724
31	14451	Jun. 1962	17758
32	14481	Jun. 1962	15952
33	14488	Jun. 1962	15956
34	14617	Jun. 1962	17888
35	14723	Jul. 1962	17980

PUBLICATION NO.	J.P.R.S. NO.	PERIOD COVERED	U.S.G.P.O. MONTHLY CATALOG NO.
36	14822	Jul. 1962	18047
37	14910	Jul. 1962	19673
38	15011	Jul. 1962	19769
39	15054	Jul.-Aug. 1962	19809
40	15121	Aug. 1962	19868
41	15237	Aug. 1962	19981
42	15347	Aug. 1962	20024
43	15446	Aug.-Sep. 1962	22082
44	15570	Sep. 1962	22201
45	15635	Sep. 1962	22264
46	15773	Sep. 1962	22395
47	15928	Sep. 1962	23762
48	16012	Sep.-Oct. 1962	23841
49	16108	Oct. 1962	23926
50	16194	Oct. 1962	1963– 729
51	16225	Oct. 1962	759
52	16308	Oct. 1962	841
53	16708	Oct.-Nov. 1962	1153
54	16812	Nov. 1962	2624
55	16916	Nov.-Dec. 1962	2724
56	16997	Dec. 1962	2804
57	17173	Dec. 1962	2970
58	17285	Dec.1962–Jan.1963	not listed
59	17409	Jan. 1963	5291
60	17522	Jan. 1963	5395
61	17662	Jan. 1963	6745
62	17800	Jan. 1963	6873

The most comprehensive English-language compilation for the period covered.

363 **Fei-wei jen-shih tzu-liao tiao-ch'a yen-chiu hui** 匪僞人事資料調查研究會 (Committee for the Compilation of Biographical Information on Bandit-Puppet Personnel). *Fei-wei jen-shih tzu-liao hui-pien—jen-wu chih tsu-chih piao* 匪僞人事資料彙編——人物誌組織表 (Collection of Biographical Information on Bandit-Puppet Personnel—Biographies and Organizational Charts). Taipei, 1957–1959. 22 vols.

Eighteen volumes issued between 1957 and 1959 (including three supplements in five volumes and a separate pamphlet containing portraits), providing biographical data on 4,169 leading personalities of Communist China. Entries include information on age of subject, native place, education, political affiliation, incumbent position, and experience, and are arranged by the number of strokes of the last name. An additional four volumes contain some 249 organizational charts showing names of office holders, arranged under (1) the Chinese Communist Party; (2) government (national and local); and (3) military. The last volume summarizes and up-dates information contained in the first three.

Taken together, the twenty-two volumes provide the most comprehensive biographical coverage in Chinese to October 1959. Limited distribution.

364   **Fei-wei jen-shih tzu-liao tiao-ch'a yen-chiu hui** 匪偽人事資料調查研究會
(Committee for the Compilation of Biographical Information on Bandit-Puppet
Personnel). *Fei-wei chung-yao jen-shih tiao-ch'a* 匪偽重要人事調查
(Biographical Directory of Important Bandit-Puppet Personnel). Taipei, 1959.
376p.

A condensed edition of the preceding entry, containing biographical information on 821 persons, accompanied by thirty-three charts. Persons selected
for inclusion are (1) C.C.P. officials down to the level of the first secretaries of
the provincial committees; (2) government officials down to the chairmen and
vice-chairmen of the Provincial People's Committees; and (3) military personnel
down to the rank of regional commanders and regional political commissars.
The biographical section is arranged according to the number of strokes of the
last name. The charts are given under the same three categories: C.C.P.,
government, and military establishment. Limited distribution.

365   **Chung-kuo kuo-min tang, Chung-yang wei-yüan hui, Ti 6 tsu** 中國國民黨
中央委員會第六組 (Kuomintang, Central Committee, Sixth Section). *Fei-tang
chung-yang jen-shih tzu-liao* 匪黨中央人事資料
(Biographical Information of Members of the Central Committee of the Bandit
Party). Taipei, 1960. 522p.

A biographical directory of the Eighth Central Committee of the C.C.P., covering its 95 regular members and 96 alternates. Names are arranged in the order of
their official listing as released by the Chinese Communist Party. The entries, most
of which are accompanied by a portrait of the subject, provide the following information: name; pseudonyms, if any; year of birth; place of birth; education; incumbent position(s); a chronological listing of positions held in the party and in the
Chinese Communist movement; and other biographical information, including
family background, personal idiosyncrasies, and current alignment in the party.

This compilation provides access to little known facts and anecdotes about
the people under study, and is especially useful for information not available
elsewhere on the earlier period of their lives. Limited distribution.

366   **China, Kuo-fang pu, Ch'ing-pao chü** 中華民國 國防部 情報局 (China,
Ministry of National Defense, Bureau of Intelligence). *Kung-fei shih-ko yüan-
shuai chien-li tiao-ch'a* 共匪十個元帥簡歷調查
(Biographies of Ten Communist Bandit Marshals). Taipei, 1961. 60p.

Biographies of Chu Teh 朱德, P'eng Te-huai 彭德懷, Lin Piao 林彪, Liu Po-
ch'eng 劉伯承, Ho Lung 賀龍, Ch'en Yi 陳毅, Lo Jung-huan 羅榮桓, Hsü
Hsiang-ch'ien 徐向前, Nien Jung-chen 聶榮臻, and Yeh Chien-ying 葉劍英.
Especially informative with respect to the earlier years of their association
with the Chinese Communist Party.

For nineteen biographies of second echelon military personnel, see Anne B.
Clark's *Selected Biographies of Chinese Communist Military Leaders* (Cambridge,
Mass.: Harvard University, 1964), 60p.

367 **Chang, Ta-chün** 張大軍, **ed.** *Chung-kung jen-ming tien* 中共人名典
(Who's Who of Communist China). Kowloon: Tzu-yu ch'u-pan she 自由出版社,
1956. 224p.

Contains biographical data on roughly 2,200 prominent officials of Communist China as of 1956. Biographical sketches are reserved for only the most
important personalities, and most entries merely contain position data (one to
five lines). Arranged by the number of strokes. Useful for the identification of
lesser known officials. The editor is the chief archivist of the Kuomintang Party
Archives at Taichung.

368 **Chou-mo pao-she** 週末報社. *Hsin Chung-kuo jen-wu chih* 新中國人物誌
(Who's Who in New China). Hong Kong: Chou-mo pao-she, 1950. 278; 268p.

Biographical sketches of 208 leaders of Communist China, based on the
Chinese Communist press and information available to the compilers. While
most of the biographees are members of the C.C.P., some are members of
other political parties serving in the Chinese Communist Government as of
1950. Provides some biographical information concerning the Chinese Communist leaders not available elsewhere.

369 **Chung-kung jen-wu** 中共人物
(Chinese Communist Personalities). Shanghai: She-hui ch'u-pan she 社會出版社,
1949. 60p.

A collection of forty-two short but informative biographical sketches of
Chinese Communist leaders.

370 **Cheng, Yü-te** 鄭餘德, **ed.** *Chung-kung jen-wu ch'ün-hsiang* 中共人物群像
(Profiles of Chinese Communist Leaders). Shanghai: Ta-chung ch'u-pan she
大眾出版社, 1949. 50p.

Short biographical sketches of thirty-two Communist leaders. The appendix
contains brief notes on forty-seven others.

371 **Chao, Kuan-i** 趙貫一 **and Wei, Tan-po** 韋丹柏. *Chung-kung jen-wu su-miao*
中共人物素描
(Biographical Sketches of Chinese Communist Leaders). Kowloon: Tzu-yu
ch'u-pan she 自由出版社, 1951. 106p.

Contains short biographical sketches of twenty-two Chinese Communist
leaders emphasizing the personal characteristics of each.
An anti-Communist publication.

372 **U.S. Department of State, Office of Libraries and Intelligence Acquisition, Division of Biographic Information.**
Leaders of Communist China. Washington, D.C., 1950. 280p.

A who's who of Communist China containing brief biographical sketches of the country's most important persons, the majority of whom are Communist Party members. Emphasis has been placed on the subject's connections with important party events and his association with other persons in the party. For non-party members, the sketches indicate briefly the role each person has played in the development of his own political party. Alphabetically arranged by name with Chinese characters. There is also a directory of important positions in the Chinese Communist Party and the Central People's Government (with an addendum as of August 1950). The directory section is outdated.

373 **Wales, Nym (pseud.).**
Red Dust: Autobiographies of Chinese Communists as Told to Nym Wales. Stanford, Calif.: Stanford University Press, 1952. 238p.

Twenty-four autobiographies of prominent Chinese Communist personalities, excepting the top leadership (Mao Tse-tung, Chu Teh, Chou En-lai, et al.), as told to Nym Wales (Helen Foster Snow) in the Communist regions of China in 1937. Each sketch contains a brief account of Nym Wales' own impression of the person whose autobiography follows. The sketches vary in length. They all provide, however, some information on the family and educational background of the subjects themselves as well as their role and activity within the party. Most sketches are accompanied by a portrait of the biographee.

Robert C. North has contributed an introduction, 'Communists of the Chinese Revolution' (pp. 3–22) and two appendices: (A) brief sketches (4 to 14 lines) of twenty-seven contemporary Chinese Communist leaders; and (B) a suggested bibliography of thirty-four easily obtainable English-language titles representing different points of view. Notes and index.

374 **Elegant, Robert S.**
China's Red Masters: Political Biographies of the Chinese Communist Leaders. New York: Twayne Publishers, 1951. 264p.

Biographies of Chinese Communist political and military leaders, written by a journalist. For a review by Benjamin Schwartz, see the *Far Eastern Quarterly*, Vol. 11, No. 2 (February 1952), pp. 248–249.

375 **Rowe, David Nelson, and Kendall, Willmore, eds.**
China: An Area Manual. Washington, D.C.: Operations Research Office, 1955. 2 vols.

Contains brief biographical sketches of 100 top Chinese Communist leaders with information current as of April 1953.

C. TAIWAN

In addition to the general compilations listed in the first section above, there are a number of biographical sources devoted exclusively to residents of Taiwan. Of these, the most comprehensive, although partially outdated, is the 1953 Who's Who, listing some 5,000 Mainlanders and Taiwanese (first entry). The English-language *China Yearbook* published in Taiwan (**240**) provides later information on some of the more prominent personalities. In addition, specialized biographical compilations are available, supplying data on Nationalist legislators, scholars and researchers, persons engaged in industry, etc. (For a who's who of some 3,800 persons prominent in industry and commerce, see **381**.)

For a more comprehensive listing of biographies of Kuomintang members, especially those published on the Mainland before 1949, see Eugene Wu, *Leaders of Twentieth-Century China* (**76**).

376 **Chung-hua min-kuo jen-shih lu** 中華民國人事錄
(Who's Who in the Republic of China). Taipei: Chung-hua min-kuo jen-shih lu pien-tsuan wei-yüan hui 中華民國人事錄編纂委員會, 1953. 470p.

A collection of brief biographical sketches of more than 5,600 prominent Chinese (including Taiwanese) of Nationalist China as of October 1953. Entries are arranged by stroke count, and provide information on the biographee's age (*sui*), native place, educational background, publications, if any, and positions held up to October 1953. There is also an index by stroke count. A comprehensive and dependable source, though partially outdated.

377 **Shih-chieh wen-hua fu-wu she pien-tsuan wei-yüan hui** 世界文化服務社 編纂委員會 (World Culture Service Company, Editorial Committee). *Tzu-yu Chung-kuo ming-jen chuan* 自由中國名人傳
(Who's Who in Free China). Taipei, 1952. 313p.

A revised edition of the *Chung-kuo tang-tai ming-jen chuan* 中國當代名人傳 (Who's Who in Present-Day China) published in Shanghai in 1948. Contains biographical sketches of 170 high government officials, providing highlights of their educational backgrounds and careers in government service.

378 **China, Li-fa yüan** 中華民國立法院 (China, Legislative Yuan). *Ti-i chieh li-fa wei-yüan ming-chien* 第一屆立法委員名鑑
(A Directory of Members of the Legislative Yuan, First Session). Taipei: Li-fa yüan li-fa wei-yüan ming-chien pien-chi wei-yüan hui 立法院立法委員名鑑編 輯委員會, 1953. 288p.

The directory, arranged by stroke count, contains biographical information (with portraits) on 551 members of the First Session of the Legislative Yuan of the Republic of China, all except seventeen of whom were in office on Taiwan as of August 1953. Provides name, courtesy name (if any), sex, age, native place, district represented, education, and other positions held. Appended are lists of members who were no longer in office through death, resignation, and other reasons. Name index by stroke count.

379 **Ch'üan-min jih-pao she** 全民日報社 (Ch'üan-min Daily). *T'ai-wan sheng shou-chieh ts'an-i yüan ming-chien* 臺灣省首屆參議員名鑑 (A Directory of Taiwan Provincial Councilors, First Session). Taipei: Ch'üan-min jih-pao she, 1951. 338p.

A roster of provincial, municipal, and *hsien* councilors of Taiwan as of March 1951, including reviews of the various sessions and brief histories of each council. Names and biographical information on members (age, native place, education, and qualifications) accompany the data on the councils.

380 **Chang, Tzu-hui** 章子惠, **ed.** *T'ai-wan shih-jen chih, Ti 1 chi* 臺灣時人誌, 第一集 (Who's Who in Taiwan, Vol. 1). Taipei: Kuo-kuang ch'u-pan she 國光出版社, 1947. 227p.

Biographical sketches (with portraits) of more than 1,000 Taiwanese. Also a name index arranged by stroke count. One of the very few biographical sources on native Taiwanese.

381 **Chung-hua min-kuo kung-shang hsieh-ching hui** 中華民國工商協進會 (Chinese Industry and Commerce Association). *Tzu-yu Chung-kuo kung-shang jen-wu chih* 自由中國工商人物誌 (Who's Who in Industry and Commerce in Free China). Taipei, 1955. 372p.

Contains abbreviated biographical information on more than 3,800 persons prominent in industry and commerce (directors, managers, agents, and responsible officers of important firms and corporations; and members of the Legislative Yuan and the National Assembly elected by industry and commerce, etc.). Arranged by the number of strokes and by the radical of the person's surname. Information includes name, courtesy name(s), age, place of birth, education, experience, and present position. Also a stroke index.

Appended to the volume are directories of various manufacturers' associations, chambers of commerce, Chinese-foreign cultural-economic associations, and such governmental agencies as the Ministries of Economic Affairs and Finance, Foreign Exchange Commission, customs, tax collecting bureaus, bureaus of inspection of export goods, etc.

Informative and, for reference purposes, well organized.

382 **Chung-kuo shih-yeh ch'u-pan she** 中國實業出版社 (China Industry Publishing House). *Tzu-yu Chung-kuo shih-yeh ming-jen chuan* 自由中國實業名人傳 (Free China's Who's Who in Industry). Taipei, 1954. 108p.

Contains biographies of ninety-seven Chinese industrial leaders. Except for coverage given to persons not actively engaged in industry and those who are leaders in industrial education, the present volume has been superseded by the preceding entry. Index arranged by stroke count.

383 China, Chiao-yü pu, K'o-hsüeh chiao-yü wei-yüan hui 中華民國教育部 科學教育委員會 (China, Ministry of Education, Committee on Scientific Education). *Chung-kuo k'o-hsüeh jen-ts'ai yen-chiu kung-tso tiao-ch'a lu, kuo-nei pu-fen* 中國科學人才研究工作調查錄, 國內部分

(A Directory of Chinese Research Personnel, Taiwan Section). Taipei [preface date 1955]. 2 vols. 502p.

A directory of Chinese research personnel in Taiwan. Grouped under three broad subject areas: natural science, applied science, and the social sciences. All names arranged by stroke count and accompanied by the following information: age, native place, education, qualifications, present position, address, publications, and current research. Name index arranged by stroke count.

The information on research is outdated. For up-to-date data, see *Handbook of Current Research Projects in the Republic of China* (**1735**).

384 China, Chiao-yü pu, K'o-hsüeh chiao-yü wei-yüan hui 中華民國教育部 科學教育委員會 (China, Ministry of Education, Committee on Scientific Education). *Chung-kuo k'o-hsüeh jen-ts'ai yen-chiu kung-tso tiao-ch'a lu, kuo-wai pu-fen* 中國科學人才研究工作調查錄, 國外部分

(A Directory of Chinese Research Personnel, Overseas Section). Taipei [preface date 1955]. 282p.

A directory of Overseas Chinese research personnel now residing in the United States. The format is the same as that of the preceding entry. Name index by stroke count. The listing is incomplete.

D. Hong Kong

In addition to the *Hong Kong Who's Who* listed below, biographical information on Chinese residents of Hong Kong can be obtained from some of the general biographical compilations listed in the first section of this chapter, as well as from the biographical sections in the various yearbooks published in Hong Kong (see Chapter IV).

385 Luzzatto, Rola, ed.
Hong Kong Who's Who—An Almanac of Personalities and Their History. Hong Kong, 1958–1960. 288; 18p.

Brief biographical sketches, ranging from one paragraph to over a page, on 800 leading residents of Hong Kong. Two indexes: an alphabetical name index and an index classified by profession, listed in alphabetical order (art, business, etc.).

CHAPTER VIII

CHRONOLOGIES

No substantial general chronologies are available covering both the Mainland and Taiwan. The chronologies of the two areas are treated in separate sections, that on the Mainland being divided into two: general, and relations with other countries.

Reference should be made to yearbooks, handbooks and similar compilations, which in many cases carry chronologies for a given period.

A. MAINLAND

I. GENERAL

The most comprehensive Mainland chronologies are the first three publications listed in this section prepared by the American Consulate General in Hong Kong, the Chinese Nationalist Government in Taiwan, and the Japanese Cabinet Research Office, respectively. Both the Nationalist and Japanese compilations are monthlies and are excellent for tracing local events. The Hong Kong American Consulate publication appears three times a year and is largely concerned with national developments. The American compilation has been published since 1953; the Taiwan and Japanese compilations have been issued only since 1958 and 1960, respectively. The Cabinet Research Office also published a detailed chronology on Communist China covering the period from 1946 through April 1953 (see **390** below).

The only available general chronology of events in Communist China produced on the Mainland—that prepared at Nankai University (**389**)—compares rather poorly with the three entries discussed above. It does not cover developments after September 1956. The chronology appended to the People's Handbook also ceased publication in 1956. Mention might be made of a special chronology of events in Tibet for the ten-year period 1949–1959, published in Peking (**397**).

For fairly detailed coverage of Chinese political and economic developments (for successive ten-day periods), the chronology in *Ajia keizai jumpō* (Ten-Day Report on Asian Economy, **394**) is to be recommended.

Finally, chronology sections are to be found in *Hsin-hua pan-yüeh-k'an* (New China Semi-Monthly, **882**), *Contemporary China* (**14**), the *China Quarterly* (**1093**), the *Documentary History of Chinese Communism* by Brandt, Schwartz and Fairbank (**578**), and the documentary volumes compiled by Robert Carin on agricultural developments on the Mainland (**720** and **721**).

386 American Consulate General, Hong Kong.
'Chronology of Events in Communist China' in *Current Background*, Nos. (see below), March 15, 1955—.

Based exclusively on published Chinese Communist sources, the Chronology has been issued in the *Current Background* series since March 15, 1955. The emphasis is more on national than local events.

The following is a list of *Current Background* numbers containing the chronologies covering the period from January 1953 through August 1961:

C. B. NO. AND DATE		PERIOD COVERED	
321	3–15–55	Jan.-Apr.	1953
322	3–20–55	May-Aug.	1953
323	3–25–55	Sep.-Dec.	1953
329	5–15–55	Jan.-Apr.	1954
330	5–20–55	May-Aug.	1954
331	5–25–55	Sep.-Dec.	1954
340	7–29–55	Jan.-Apr.	1955
361	10– 5–55	May-Aug.	1955
378	2–17–56	Sep.-Dec.	1955
396	7– 6–56	Jan.-Apr.	1956
432	12–18–56	May-Aug.	1956
457	6–17–57	Sep.-Dec.	1956
472	8– 1–57	Jan.-Apr.	1957
481	12– 3–57	May-Aug.	1957
489	1–29–58	Sep.-Dec.	1957
506	5–14–58	Jan.-Apr.	1958
519	9–19–58	May-Aug.	1958
546	1–23–59	Sep.-Dec.	1958
572	5–12–59	Jan.-Apr.	1959
591	9–14–59	May-Aug.	1959
611	2– 1–60	Sep.-Dec.	1959
619	5–23–60	Jan.-Apr.	1960
631	9–21–60	May-Aug.	1960
650	4–12–61	Sep.-Dec.	1960
653	5–31–61	Jan.-Apr.	1961
668	11– 7–61	May-Aug.	1961
679	3– 7–62	Sep.-Dec.	1961
684	6–20–62	Jan.-Apr.	1962
695	10–31–62	May-Aug.	1962
705	2–20–63	Sep.-Dec.	1962
708	7–11–63	Jan.-Apr.	1963
721	11– 4–63	May-Aug.	1963
735	6–19–64	Sep.-Dec.	1963

387 Chūkyō gesshi 中共月誌
(Monthly Chronology of Communist China). [Tokyo: Naikaku Kambō, Naikaku Chōsashitsu 內閣官房內閣調查室], April 1960—. Monthly.

A 40 to 80-page mimeographed chronology of Communist China based largely on Chinese Communist sources, but also on Russian and other sources including broadcasts, prepared by the Cabinet Research Office. The chronology is arranged by day in four columns: domestic developments, foreign relations, Japanese-Chinese relations, and important world events. A convenient summary of the most important developments during the month under review precedes the chronology. Limited distribution.

A useful guide to current affairs on the Mainland with particularly detailed coverage of the relations between Japan and Communist China and local developments on the Mainland.

388 **'I-yüeh lai fei-ch'ing chi-yao'** 一月來匪情紀要
(A Chronology of Important Bandit Events During the Preceding Month) and
'I-yüeh lai fei-wei chung-yao hui-i'—月來匪偽重要會議 (Important Bandit and
Puppet Meetings During the Preceding Month) in *Fei-ch'ing yüeh-pao* 匪情月報
(Bandit Intelligence Monthly), Vol. 1, No. 1—, February 1958—.

Published regularly in the *Fei-ch'ing yüeh-pao* (see **991**), the chronology is
arranged under (1) party affairs, (2) mass movements, (3) political affairs, (4)
economic affairs, and (5) military affairs. The list of meetings provides information on the name of the meeting, date(s), place, participants, nature of
the meeting, business transacted, and remarks (name of official sponsor).
Information taken from published sources, Mainland news releases, and monitored radio broadcasts.

Comprehensive coverage; especially important for local events. The best
compilation of its kind since publication began in 1958.

389 **Nan-k'ai ta-hsüeh, Li-shih hsi** 南開大學歷史系 (Nankai University, Department of History). *Chung-hua jen-min kung-ho kuo ta-shih chi* 中華人民共和國
大事記
(Chronology of Events in People's Republic of China). Pao-ting 保定: Ho-pei
jen-min ch'u-pan she 河北人民出版社, 1958. 2 vols. 136; 142p.

Volume 1 covers the period October 1, 1949 through December 1952; Volume
2, January 1, 1953 to September 14, 1956. An average of thirty entries to a
month. A handy reference volume.

See also a translation of the chronology published in *Hsin-hua pan-yüeh-k'an*,
Nos. 15–24 (August 12–December 27, 1960) in *Chronology of Domestic and
Foreign Events—Communist China*. J.P.R.S. No. 14,470, July 13, 1962, 117p.
(U.S.G.P.O. Monthly Catalog, 1962, No. 17,771) and a chronology (1949–1959)
which appeared in the *Peking Review* on the occasion of the tenth anniversary
of the Chinese People's Republic in 1959 (No. 38, pp. 22–25; No. 39, pp. 24–26;
No. 40, pp. 31–34).

390 **Japan, Naikaku Kambō, Naikaku Chōsashitsu** 日本內閣官房內閣調查室
(Japan, Cabinet Secretariat, Cabinet Research Office). *Sengo no Chūkyō nenshi*
戰後の中共年誌
(Postwar Yearly Chronology of Events in Communist China). Tokyo, 1954 [?]
277p.

A detailed chronology of the Chinese Communist movement from January
1946 through April 1953. The chronology (90 pages in length) is arranged in
three columns: China, world events (including Japan), and explanatory remarks.
A chronology of the Korean war, June 1950 to June 1953, follows on pages
91–96. The chronology is supplemented by an outline of the development of
Chinese Communist administrative, political and military organizations; the

civil war, 1945–1949; and a brief sketch of the Communist movement in Manchuria. The appendices incorporate party and government laws and regulations, as well as a number of maps, charts, tables and lists. Limited distribution.

391 **Seki, Hiroharu** 關寬治. 'Chūkyō nempyō' 中共年表
(Chronology of Events in Communist China) in *Chūgoku seiji keizai sōran* 中國政治經濟綜覽 *Political and Economic Views on Present Day China* (Tokyo: Hitotsubashi Shobō 一橋書房, 1960), pp. 994–1068.

A detailed 75-page chronology of the period December 1949 through the year 1959, emphasizing political, economic and diplomatic developments, including Sino-Japanese relations.

See also a continuation of this chronology to June 1961 in the 1962 edition, pp. 1119–1288, and from July 1961 to June 1963 in the 1964 edition, pp. 992–1008.

392 **Mezhdunarodnaia zhizn' KNR v datakh i faktakh—Khronika sobytii**
(International Relations of the People's Republic of China in Dates and Facts—A Chronology of Events). Moscow: Izdatel'stvo sotsial'no-ekonomicheskoi literatury, 1959. 203p.

A chronology of the first decade of Communist China (October 1949 to October 1959) preceded by an introductory article. Emphasis has been placed on the international position and foreign relations of Communist China. For popular consumption.

393 **Tang, Peter S. H.**
Communist China Today, Volume II: Chronological and Documentary Supplement. New York: Praeger, 1958. 137p.

The chronology, with an emphasis on the post-1949 period (pp. 2–68), covers the years 1918 to 1956. Documents included are: (1) the Constitution of the Chinese Communist Party, 1945; (2) the Constitution of the People's Republic of China, 1954; (3) the Constitution of the Chinese Communist Party, 1956; and (4) a list of members of the Central Committee and other central organs of the Chinese Communist Party.

394 **'Ajia seikei nisshi'** アジア政經日誌
(Chronology of Asian Politics and Economics) in *Ajia keizai jumpō* アジア經濟旬報 (Ten-Day Report on Asian Economy). October 1949—. Three times a month.

A one-page chronology of economic and political developments in Asia for the corresponding ten-day period of the preceding month, with heavy emphasis on the economy of Communist China. The chronology, which appears regularly in the journal, was originally entitled 'Ajia keizai nisshi'' アジア經濟日誌 (Asian Economic Chronology).

395 Saitō, Akio 齋藤秋男 **and Niijima, Atsuyoshi** 新島淳良. 'Chūgoku gendai kyōiku shi nempyō' 中國現代教育史年表
(A Chronology of the History of Education in Contemporary China) in *Chūgoku gendai kyōiku shi* (History of Education in Contemporary China), (Tokyo: Kokudosha 國土社, 1962), pp. 261–278.

Covers educational developments in China from 1838 to September 1958, including the founding of organizations and journals, promulgation of laws relevant to education, etc. Post-1949 entries are restricted to Mainland events.

396 Andō, Hikotarō 安藤彦太郎, **et al.** 'Gendai Chūgoku kyōiku bunka shi nempyō' 現代中國教育文化史年表
'Chronology of Contemporary China in the Field of Education and Culture', *Chūgoku kenkyū* 中國研究 *The China Research*, Tokyo, No. 16 (September 1952), pp. 94–128.

A chronology of cultural and educational developments on the Mainland from October 1949 to the end of 1951, including literature, the arts, etc. Notes the beginning date of periodicals and newspapers. Political and world events are listed in a parallel column.

397 Kuo, Tsu-wen 郭茲文, **ed.** *Hsi-tsang ta-shih chi, 1949–1959* 西藏大事記, *1949–1959*
(Chronology of Events in Tibet, 1949–1959). Peking: Min-tsu ch'u-pan she 民族出版社, 1959. 72p.

In two parts: (1) a chronology of events in Tibet from July 8, 1949 to April 28, 1959 (about a month and a half after the Tibetan Revolt); and (2) a collection of official Chinese Communist documents and selected *Jen-min jih-pao* editorials on Tibet for the period May 23, 1951 to September 20, 1956, inclusive. A convenient guide for the study of Chinese Communist attitudes and policies toward Tibet since 1949.

For a translation, see J.P.R.S. No. 831, August 28, 1959, 22p. (U.S.G.P.O. Monthly Catalog, 1959, No. 14,799).

2. RELATIONS WITH OTHER COUNTRIES

The chronologies listed in the present section pertain to Communist China's foreign relations. Half of them, Japanese in origin, concern Sino-Japanese relations, reflecting a deeply rooted interest in things Chinese. Their coverage ranges from Chinese foreign relations in general to such specific subjects as Sino-Soviet and Sino-Indian relations, Sino-Japanese trade, the Korean question, etc. One—the second item and the best available—logs the comings and goings between the Mainland and Japan of Japanese businessmen, socialist politicians, leftist labor leaders and intellectuals.

Reference should be made to the chronologies to be found in the collections of documents on foreign affairs published in Peking. The Great Resist-America Aid-Korea Campaign (**761**), and Economic Relations of the U.S.S.R. with China (**776**), all of which are listed in Chapter XVI.

398 **Ajia Seikei Gakkai** アジア政經學會 (Society for Asian Political and Economic Studies). 'Gaikō nempyō' 外交年表
(Diplomatic Chronology) in *Chūka Jimmin Kyōwakoku gaikō shiryō sōran* 中華人民共和國外交資料總覽 (Collection of Diplomatic Documents of the People's Republic of China), (Tokyo: Hitotsubashi Shobō 一橋書房, 1960), pp. 1061–1085

A chronology of Communist China's foreign relations, with particular emphasis on Sino-Japanese relations from October 1, 1949 to the end of 1958. An average of six entries per month. More important events are set in bold-face type.

399 **[Japan, Naikaku Kambō, Naikaku Chōsashitsu** 日本內閣官房內閣調查室] (Japan, Cabinet Secretariat, Cabinet Research Office). *Nihon, Chūkyō kōryū nenshi,* 1949–1957; 1958— 日本中共交流年誌
(Chronology of Interchange Between Japan and Communist China), 1949–1957; 1958—. Tokyo, [n.d.]. Annual.

A 200–300 page chronology, providing a very detailed, thorough and systematic coverage of all aspects of the relations between Japan and Communist China. A survey of the highlights of Japanese-Chinese relations during the year under review precedes a 150–page day-by-day chronology arranged in three columns: Japan, Japanese-Chinese relations, and Communist China (including world events). A documentary section provides the texts of resolutions, editorials, joint declarations, Radio Peking statements, etc., arranged by date. A number of charts on the exchange of persons, Japanese repatriates from China, agreements, seizures of and attacks upon Japanese fishing vessels are appended. Five indexes: (1) a name index divided into Japanese and Chinese; (2) an index to organizations divided into Japanese and Chinese; (3) a chronological index to exchange of persons; (4) a chronological index to important events; and (5) a list of editorials, radio statements and news releases. The first volume (1949–1957) carries no index.

400 **Nitchū Bōeki Sokushin Giin Remmei** 日中貿易促進議員連盟 (Diet Members' League for the Promotion of Trade Between Japan and [Communist] China). 'Nempyō' 年表
(Chronology) in *Nitchū kankei shiryō shū* 日中關係資料集 (Collection of Documents on Relations Between Japan and [Communist] China), (Tokyo, 1961), pp. 247–330

A chronology of Japan's relations with Communist China, with an emphasis on the years 1949–1961, inclusive. Some 700 entries are arranged in two columns: China and world events. Limited distribution.

401 **Nitchū Yushutsunyū Kumiai** 日中輸出入組合 (Japan-China Exporters and Importers Association). 'Nitchū bōeki nempyō' 日中貿易年表

(Chronology of Japanese-Chinese Trade) in *Nitchū bōeki yōran—1957 nen* 日中貿易要覽——一九五七年 *Nicchu* [sic] *Trade Handbook—1957* (Tokyo, 1957), pp. 367–372.

A chronology of postwar trade between Japan and Communist China.

402 **Kurdiukov, I. F., Nikiforov, V. N. and Perevertailo, A. S., eds.** 'Khronika Sovetsko-kitaiskikh otnoshenii, 1917–1957 gg.'
(Chronology of Soviet-Chinese Relations, 1917–1957) in *Sovetsko-kitaiskie otnosheniia, 1917–1957* (Soviet-Chinese Relations, 1917–1957), (Moscow: Izdatel'stvo vostochnoi literatury, 1959), pp. 433–448.

A chronology of Soviet-Chinese relations (including items on cultural relations) from November 1917 to October 1958. Particularly detailed for the years 1920, 1924, 1929 and after 1949.

403 **Berton, Peter, comp.**
'Chronology' in *The Chinese-Russian Dialogue of 1963* (Los Angeles: University of Southern California, 1963), pp. 1–16.

A chronology of Sino-Soviet relations and related events covering the period from 1949 to November 1963. Two-thirds of the approximately 600 entries are on the 1961–1963 period. Mimeographed.

For more detailed coverage of the August 1952–December 1953 period, see Howard L. Boorman, 'Chronology of Sino-Soviet Relations,' *Problems of Communism*, Vol. 3, No. 3 (May–June 1954), pp. 14–21.

404 **Ahmed, S. H.**
'Chronology of the Sino-Indian Border Dispute,' *International Studies: Quarterly Journal of the Indian School of International Studies*, Vol. 5, Nos. 1–2 (July–October 1963), pp. 212–220.

Covers the period 1954 to the end of 1962.

405 **Shih-chieh chih-shih** 世界知識 (World Culture).
A Chronicle of Principal Events Relating to the Korean Question, 1945–1954. Peking: Shih-chieh chih-shih, 1954. 93 p.

Translated from a special supplement to the April 20, 1954 issue (No. 8) of *Shih-chieh chih-shih*—a Chinese fortnightly published in Peking—the chronology covers the period August 15, 1945 to February 18, 1954 when the Neutral Nations Repatriation Commission was dissolved.

B. TAIWAN

The contents of the present section, limited to three entries, provide adequate chronological coverage of happenings on Taiwan. The first entry is a substantial chronology of events on Taiwan through 1956, which is supplemented and updated by the *China Yearbook* (both the Chinese and English-language editions; see **239** and **240**). The Bank of Taiwan Quarterly, the second item (**407**), provides continuous coverage of important events with economic implications and is an indispensable source for the study of Taiwan's economic development. The chronology contained in Economic Reference Materials, described in Chapter XIV (**734**), also should be consulted.

406 Kao, Yin-tsu 高蔭祖, **ed.** *Chung-hua min-kuo ta-shih chi* 中華民國大事記 (Chronology of Events in the Republic of China). Taipei: Shih-chieh she 世界社, 1957. 704p.

Spans the period from January 1, 1912 to December 31, 1956, inclusive. The 1920's are treated in greater detail (averaging thirty entries per month) than the other years (averaging eighteen entries). Events on the Mainland after 1949 are not included.

407 T'ai-wan yin-hang, Ching-chi yen-chiu shih 臺灣銀行經濟研究室 (Bank of Taiwan, Office of Economic Research). 'T'ai-wan ching-chi jih-chih' 臺灣經濟日誌 (Chronology of Economic Events in Taiwan) in *T'ai-wan yin-hang chi-k'an* 臺灣銀行季刊 (Bank of Taiwan Quarterly), Taipei, Vol. 1—, June 1947—.

A regular feature of the Bank of Taiwan Quarterly since June 1947, covering economic and financial developments. The Bank of Taiwan maintains a reference library and research staff, and provides good coverage of economic developments in Taiwan.

The following chart indicates the periods covered in each volume:

VOLUME NUMBER	PERIOD COVERED
Vol. 1, Nos. 1–4 (Jun. 1947–Mar. 1948)	Aug. 15, 1945–Dec. 31, 1947
Vol. 2, Nos. 1–4 (Sep. 1948–Jun. 1949)	Jan. 1, 1948–Mar. 31, 1949
Vol. 3, Nos. 1–4 (Dec. 1949–Oct. 1950)	Apr. 1, 1949–Jun. 30, 1950
Vol. 4, Nos. 1–4 (Mar.–Dec. 1951)	Jul. 1, 1950–Sep. 30, 1951
Vol. 5, Nos. 1–4 (Jun. 1952–Mar. 1953)	Oct. 1, 1951–Dec. 31, 1952
Vol. 6, Nos. 1–4 (Sep. 1953–Jun. 1954)	Jan. 1, 1953–Mar. 31, 1954
Vol. 7, Nos. 1–4 (Dec. 1954–Sep. 1955)	Apr. 1, 1954–Jun. 30, 1955
Vol. 8, Nos. 1–4 (Mar.–Dec. 1956)	Jul. 1, 1955–Sep. 30, 1956
Vol. 9, Nos. 1–4 (Jun. 1957–Mar. 1958)	Oct. 1, 1956–Dec. 31, 1957
Vol. 10, Nos. 1–4 (Sep. 1958–Jun. 1959)	Jan. 1, 1958–Mar. 31, 1959
Vol. 11, Nos. 1–4 (May–Dec. 1960)	Apr. 1959–Sep. 30, 1960
Vol. 12, Nos. 1–4 (Mar.–Dec. 1961)	Oct. 1, 1960–Sep. 30, 1961
Vol. 13, Nos. 1–4 (Mar.–Dec. 1962)	Oct. 1, 1961–Sep. 30, 1962
Vol. 14, Nos. 1–4 (Mar.–Dec. 1963)	Oct. 1, 1962–Sep. 30, 1963

408 Fujii, Shōzō 藤井昇三. 'Chūka minkoku nempyō' 中華民國年表 (Chronology of Events in the Republic of China) in *Chūgoku seiji keizai sōran* 中國政治經濟綜覽 *Political and Economic Views on Present Day China* (Tokyo: Nikkan Rōdō Tsūshinsha 日刊勞働通信社, 1964), pp. 1046–1062.

Covers the period October 1911 to June 1963.

CHAPTER IX

ATLASES, DICTIONARIES OF PLACE NAMES, AND GUIDES TO ADMINISTRATIVE DIVISIONS

This chapter is at best an extremely selective listing of available Chinese atlases, dictionaries of place names, and guides to administrative divisions, each treated in its respective section below. Unfortunately, very few items are recent Mainland publications; however, for bibliographical information concerning what does exist, consult the appropriate sections in Peking's national bibliography.

A. ATLASES

The five entries listed in this section are the most recent atlas (1956), three maps of Mainland China (1960 and 1962), and the 1959 Taiwan atlas generally considered to be the best in use. Unfortunately, none of the latest atlases or provincial maps prepared on the Mainland are available.

Commercially published maps of China have not been included here, nor have the maps issued by the U.S. Army Map Service or the standard world atlases, such as the London *Times* atlas and the Soviet world atlas, which is reputedly one of the best available.

409 **U.S. Central Intelligence Agency.**
China: Provisional Atlas of Communist Administrative Units. Washington, D.C.: U.S. Department of Commerce, Office of Technical Services, 1959. 29 plates: 14p.

Twenty-five provincial maps reproduced on larger scales from *Chung-kuo fen-sheng ti-t'u* 中國分省地圖 (The Provincial Atlas of China), Shanghai, Ti-t'u ch'u-pan she 地圖出版社, 1956, together with maps and lists of administrative units based on information from *Chung-hua jen-min kung-ho kuo hsing-cheng ch'ü-hua chien-ts'e* (Peking, 1957), (see **419**). Information up to November 1958 from other sources also has been incorporated. There is an alphabetical index of approximately 5,000 entries including the names of all administrative units at and above the *hsien* level.

The most recent atlas of Communist China available. Reviewed by Norton Ginsburg in *The Journal of Asian Studies*, Vol. 22, No. 3 (May 1963), pp. 327–328. For more recent maps, see the next three entries.

410 **Ti-t'u ch'u-pan she** 地圖出版社 (Map Publishing House). *Chung-hua jen-min kung-ho kuo ti-t'u* 中華人民共和國地圖
(Map of the People's Republic of China). Peking: Ti-t'u ch'u-pan she, July 1962. 1 sheet (3′ 6″ × 2′ 6″), color. Scale: 1:5,600,000.

Originally issued in October 1956, the present map (the second edition, revised) appeared in July 1962. (It may be noted that the second edition went through twelve printings in the same month it was issued.) Useful for tracing transportation lines, administrative divisions (as of the end of 1961), and rough population figures of cities and *hsien* (indicated as over one million, thirty thousand to one million, ten to thirty thousand, and under ten thousand).

411 **Ti-t'u ch'u-pan she** 地圖出版社 (Map Publishing House). *Chung-kuo chiao-t'ung t'u* 中國交通圖
(Transportation Map of China). Peking: Hsin-hua shu-tien 新華書店, November 1962. 1 sheet (3′ 5″ × 2′ 5″), color. Scale: 1:4,000,000.

This is perhaps the most recent map of China published on the Mainland and available in the United States. Originally issued in March 1956 for middle school use, the present map (sixth printing of the second edition) appeared in November 1962.

Extremely useful for tracing major railways, highways (both those completed and under construction), airways, waterways, and ocean navigation lines. Unlike the preceding entry this map does not show administrative divisions. It differs also from the next entry in that only cities located along the various transportation routes are shown, but not the *hsien* or towns. Also shown are rough population figures of cities (indicated as three hundred thousand to one million, one hundred thousand to three hundred thousand, and under one hundred thousand).

412 **Ti-t'u ch'u-pan she** 地圖出版社 (Map Publishing House). *Chung-kuo chiao-t'ung lü-hsing t'u* 中國交通旅行圖
(Transportation Map of China). Peking: Ti-t'u ch'u-pan she, 1960. 1 sheet (3′ 3″ × 2′ 4″), color. Scale: 1:8,000.000.

Showing Communist China's transportation lines (railways, highways, and inland navigation routes) as of the beginning of 1960. Four inserts: (1) air transportation lines, (2) detailed map of the Peking-Tientsin area, (3) detailed map of the Shanghai-Nanking-Hanchow area, and (4) South China Sea islands. The map shows cities, *hsien*, and towns located along the various routes.

413 **Chang, Ch'i-yün** 張其昀, **ed.** *Chung-hua min-kuo ti-t'u chi* 中華民國地圖集
Atlas of the Republic of China. Taipei: Kuo-fang yen-chiu yüan 國防研究院 and Chung-kuo ti-hsüeh yen-chiu so 中國地學研究所, 1959–1962. 5 vols.

A five-volume bilingual (Chinese-English) atlas of China published by the National War College and the Chinese Geographical Institute. Each volume contains some 20–35 large-size color maps. Volume 1 is an atlas of Taiwan; Volume 2, of Tibet, Sinkiang and Mongolia (Outer); Volume 3, North China (including Manchuria); Volume 4, Central, South and Southwest China; Volume 5, general maps of China (including meteorological, rainfall and other specialized maps).

Volumes 2, 3 and 4 carry stroke and alphabetical indexes. Volume 1 is the most recent atlas of Taiwan, and the only useful map of the series. The others no longer depict actual conditions on the Mainland.

B. Dictionaries of Place Names

This section contains three American gazetteers prepared under official auspices, similar recent Japanese and Hong Kong publications, and a Mainland index to place names dated 1955. Provincial gazetteers are unavailable, except for occasional translations in the J.P.R.S. reports, such as the *Hunan Province Gazetteer*, J.P.R.S. No. 16, 387, November 27, 1962, 238p. (U.S.G.P.O. Monthly Catalog, 1963, No. 916).

414   U.S. Department of Interior, Office of Geography.
Mainland China, Administrative Divisions and Their Seats, Official Standard Names Approved by Board on Geographic Names. Washington, D.C.: U.S. Government Printing Office, January 1963. 253p. (Gazetteer No. 70).

Contains the names of administrative divisions of Mainland China under the Chinese Communist regime at the province, sub-province and *hsien* levels, and the seats of all such administrative divisions both as established by the government of the Republic of China before 1947 and as of 1960 according to official Communist sources.

In three parts. Part 1—general list: an alphabetical list of about 11,900 entries containing the names of all Communist administrative divisions at the province, sub-province and *hsien* levels and the names of Communist and Nationalist seats with Nationalist names, conventional names and unapproved variant names cross-referenced to Communist names. Part 2—administrative seats: parallel lists of about 2,560 names of present and former Communist and Nationalist administrative seats alphabetically arranged by Communist name. Part 3—administrative divisions: names of the 2,156 provincial, sub-provincial and *hsien*-level administrative areas of Mainland (Communist) China in separate listings for the 28 first-order divisions (21 provinces, 5 autonomous regions and 2 municipalities). Includes Sinkiang and Tibet. Excludes Taiwan, Quemoy and other islands under Nationalist control. Each entry provides the name, designation (administrative division, populated place, etc.), coordinates and the province in which the entry is located. Limited distribution.

This gazetteer, based on pre-1948 Nationalist sources and on the 1960 edition of *Chung-hua jen-min kung-ho kuo hsing-cheng ch'ü-hua chien-ts'e* (A Simplified Handbook of the Administrative Areas of the People's Republic of China), is the latest one available.

415   Chūgoku Sōgō Kenkyūjo 中國總合研究所 **(Combined Research Institute on China), comp.** *Chūgoku chimei jiten* 中國地名辭典
China Gazetteer 1963. Tokyo, October 1962.

Over 2,300 entries (cities, provinces, etc.) alphabetically arranged according to the Wade-Giles system. Provides Chinese characters, province in which the entry is located, and coordinates. Information as of July 1, 1962.

See also H. C. Tien, et al., *Gazetteer of China* (Hong Kong: Oriental Book Company, 1961).

416 U.S. Department of Interior, Office of Geography.
China: Official Standard Names Approved by the U.S. Board on Geographic Names. Washington, D.C.: U.S. Government Printing Office, 1956. 2 vols. 979p.

Contains about 37,600 entries comprising names of places and geographical features in China, exclusive of Hong Kong, Macao, Sinkiang, Taiwan, and Tibet (see next entry).

417 U.S. Department of Interior, Office of Geography.
Hong Kong, Macao, Sinkiang, Taiwan, and Tibet: Official Standard Names Approved by the U.S. Board on Geographic Names. Washington, D.C.: U.S. Government Printing Office, 1955. 390p.

Contains more than 27,000 entries: 1,225 for Hong Kong, 70 for Macao, 5,900 for Sinkiang, 17,800 for Taiwan, and 2,300 for Tibet. Both the approved standard names and unapproved variant names are included, the latter cross referenced to the standard names. Names in this gazetteer supersede those in all previous Board of Geographic Names lists for these areas. Each entry provides the name, designation (populated place, area, railroad station, island, etc.), coordinates, code number assigned to the area in which the place is located, and a reference number to a map or chart.

See also *A Gazetteer of Place Names in Hong Kong, Kowloon and the New Territories* (Hong Kong: Government Press, 1960), 248p.

418 Lai, Ho-ch'u 來荷初, **ed.** *Chung-kuo ti-ming so-yin* 中國地名索引 (Index to Chinese Place Names). Shanghai: Hsin chih-shih ch'u-pan she 新知識出版社, 1955. 142p.

Arranged by the number of strokes, each entry is followed by coordinates, the name of the province in which the place is located, and remarks concerning administrative changes since 1949. Includes also a list of provinces in which autonomous regions have been created, and the names of the *hsien* under the jurisdiction of each of these autonomous regions. Data as of the end of June 1955. A one-page addendum brings the information up to July 1955 when Jehol and Sikang were reorganized into autonomous regions.

C. Guides to Administrative Divisions

As the Chinese Communists extended the territory under their control during the final stages of the civil war, they frequently created new administrative divisions, a practice that continued even after their consolidation of power on the Mainland. The most comprehensive reference work on the background of this development and the various changes in the administrative divisions is the Taiwan compilation listed below (**423**). The best current guides to the administrative area divisions are the several editions of the handbook published by the Legal Publishing House in Peking (**419** through **422**, including one Hong Kong American Consulate General translation).

For recent changes in the administrative areas, see the late editions of the People's Handbook. Mainland data in translation is available in the *Current Background* series published by the Hong Kong American Consulate, as well as in the J.P.R.S. reports.

No comparable handbooks or analyses seem to be available for Taiwan, although some basic information is given in the pertinent sections of the Taiwan Yearbook (**243**) and the *China Yearbook* (**240**).

419 China (People's Republic of China, 1949—), Nei-wu pu 中華人民共和國 內務部 (China [People's Republic of China, 1949—], Ministry of Internal Affairs). *Chung-hua jen-min kung-ho kuo hsing-cheng ch'ü-hua chien-ts'e, 1958* 中華人民共和國行政區劃簡冊, 1958
(A Simplified Handbook of the Administrative Areas of the People's Republic of China, 1958). Peking: Fa-lü ch'u-pan she 法律出版社, 1958. 151p.

A guide to the political and administrative divisions of Communist China as they existed at the end of 1957. The volume contains a complete list of the divisions above the *hsien* 縣 and *shih* 市 levels, with pertinent statistical data. Information is brought up to April 1958 in an appendix. Place name index arranged by stroke count. The standard reference work for the period covered. This handbook has been translated and published as *Current Background*, No. 529, with added information (see next entry).

420 American Consulate General, Hong Kong.
'Administrative Areas of Communist China', *Current Background*, No. 529 (October 29, 1958), 102p.

A good translation of the preceding entry, supplemented by lists of changes in administrative areas published in the *Jen-min jih-pao* (People's Daily), up to October 25, 1958. Includes all government administrative areas down to the *hsien* and *shih* levels, omitting the smaller *hsiang* 鄉, *ch'ü* 區, *chen* 鎮, and *shih-ch'ü* 市區. A list of the number of the various types of administrative districts in each province (as of January 1, 1958), excepting the *shih* and the autonomous minority areas, is appended. Alphabetical index.

421 China (People's Republic of China, 1949—), Nei-wu pu 中華人民共和國 內務部 (China [People's Republic of China, 1949—], Ministry of Internal Affairs). *Chung-hua jen-min kung-ho kuo hsing-cheng ch'ü-hua chien-ts'e* 中華人民 共和國行政區劃簡冊
(A Simplified Handbook of the Administrative Areas of the People's Republic of China). Peking: Ti-t'u ch'u-pan she 地圖出版社, 1960. 145p.

A continuation of the 1958 edition (**419**) bringing the information up to January 1960. Includes locations of people's congresses and statistical data of administrative areas of various levels (data on the people's communes are based on statistics of the Statistical Bureau through December 1959). For a translation of this book, including the stroke place name index, see J.P.R.S. No. 10,342, *Handbook on Administrative Divisions of the People's Republic of China*, October 11, 1961, 290p. (U.S.G.P.O. Monthly Catalog, 1961, No. 21,033).

422   **China (People's Republic of China, 1949—), Nei-wu pu** 中華人民共和國 內務部 (China [People's Republic of China, 1949—], Ministry of Internal Affairs). *Chung-hua jen-min kung-ho kuo hsing-cheng ch'ü-hua shou-ts'e* 中華人民共和國 行政區劃手冊 (Handbook of Administrative Divisions of the People's Republic of China). Peking: Ti-t'u ch'u-pan she 地圖出版社, 1962. 180p.

Updating the preceding entry with the same format and organization, and incorporating data available up to December 31, 1961. The original work was not available for examination, but a translation was published as J.P.R.S. No. 15,444 under the title *Handbook of Administrative Divisions of the People's Republic of China*, September 26, 1962, 322p. (U.S.G.P.O. Monthly Catalog, 1962, No. 22,080).

For changes in administrative demarcation for the period July 1 to October 31, 1963, see *Survey of China Mainland Press*, No. 3113 (December 5, 1963), pp. 3–4.

423   **Kuan, Wei-lan** 官蔚藍. *Kung-fei hsing-cheng ch'ü-hua hsien-chuang chi ch'i yen-pien* 共匪行政區劃現狀及其演變 (Current Status and Development of Communist Bandit Administrative Areas). Taipei: Hsing-cheng yüan ti-ch'ing yen-chiu shih 行政院敵情研究室, [preface date 1961]. 290p.

Current information as of September 1960. In three parts: (1) current status; (2) history and development; and (3) analysis. While the preceding entries give mostly raw data, this volume provides a running narrative and a good analysis of the changes made since 1949.

424   **U.S. Joint Publications Research Service.** *Delineation of Administrative Regions of the People's Republic of China.* J.P.R.S. Report No. 650D (April 14, 1959), 30p.

A translation of *Chung-hua jen-min kung-ho kuo hsing-cheng chü-yü ti hua-fen* 中華人民共和國行政區域的劃分 by Hsüeh I-yüan 薛貽源, *Ti-li hsüeh-pao* 地理 學報 *Acta Geographica Sinica*, Vol. 24, No. 1 (February 1958), pp. 84–97. An informative study of the history and development of the demarcation of administrative areas in Communist China up to 1958.

425   **American Consulate General, Hong Kong.** 'Revisions in Administrative Areas of Communist China, up to March 31, 1959,' *Current Background*, No. 581 (June 1, 1959), 9p.

A translation of the New China News Agency dispatch of April 16, 1959, announcing changes made by the Ministry of Internal Affairs in the administrative divisions in Communist China during the months of January, February and March 1959. This supplements *Current Background*, Nos. 554 and 529 (see **420**).

See also similar compilations previously published in *Current Background* as follows: No. 245 (May 25, 1953); No. 170 (April 8, 1952); No. 37 (December 7, 1950), and No. 27 (November 20, 1950).

CHAPTER X

DICTIONARIES AND GLOSSARIES

Confronted by the compelling need for rapid industrialization, the Chinese Communists sought to provide the prerequisites for such a program, one of which was the creation of a trained labor force. An initial move in this direction has been the steps taken towards the elimination of illiteracy and the establishment of an elaborate school system. Another has been the preparation of numerous dictionaries and glossaries to enable the Chinese to absorb the enormous flow of scientific and technical data coming largely from the Soviet Union and Eastern Europe. This interest by no means has been restricted exclusively to the technical area. A number of subject dictionaries in the social sciences have appeared, and because of the linguistic demands accompanying Communist China's increasing activity in world affairs, the publication of language dictionaries (Vietnamese-Chinese, Indonesian-Chinese, Spanish-Chinese, Japanese-Chinese, etc.) has inevitably followed.

Conversely, the awareness of Mainland China's role in international affairs has stimulated an increased interest in the Chinese language in the United States, the Soviet Union and Japan, an interest which has been reflected in the training of Chinese language students and the production of various Chinese-language dictionaries and glossaries. In Taiwan, dictionary publishing has kept up with the increased tempo of general publishing activities on the island during the last few years. A number of standard dictionaries have been reprinted, and the new compilation of the *Chung-wen ta tz'u-tien* (Encyclopedic Dictionary of the Chinese Language, see the first entry below), when completed, will be the most comprehensive Chinese dictionary ever published in China in modern times. New scientific glossaries also have been published by the National Institute of Compilation and Translation, and a new revised edition of the seven-volume Collections of Scientific and Technical Terms (see **482**) also is reportedly under way.

The present chapter is divided into three main sections: language dictionaries, subject dictionaries, and scientific and technical glossaries. The latter should not be regarded as exhaustive, but rather as an illustrative listing of available titles. Additional Mainland dictionaries can be located through the national bibliography and the catalog of the Science Publishing House (see **154**). A list of over 150 Chinese dictionaries and glossaries published on the Mainland between 1949 and 1959 was published in the September 1959 issue of *Shohō-Chūgoku tosho no zasshi* (Book News—Journal of Chinese Publications), pp. 24–27.

A. LANGUAGE DICTIONARIES

The following section is divided into Chinese-language dictionaries, Chinese-foreign language dictionaries and foreign language-Chinese dictionaries.

I. CHINESE LANGUAGE

Standard works such as *Tz'u hai* 辭海, *Tz'u yüan* 辭源, etc., are not listed here, and the reader is referred to the dictionary section in Ssu-yü Teng and Knight Biggerstaff, *An Annotated Bibliography of Selected Chinese Reference Works* (revised edition; Cambridge, Mass.: Harvard University Press, 1950). An exception is made, however, in the case of the first two entries. The first entry, *Chung-wen ta tz'u-tien* (Encyclopedic Dictionary of the Chinese Language), a Taiwan publication, will consist of thirty volumes when completed. The second entry, *Han-yü tz'u-tien*, the abridged edition of the standard *Kuo-yü tz'u-tien*, has been found to be extremely useful for both intermediate and advanced students of Chinese.

For Japanese compilations of Chinese-language dictionaries, see the dictionary section in *Nihon no sankō tosho* 日本の参考圖書 (Japanese Reference Works), (Tokyo, 1962). Special mention must be made of the monumental dictionary of Chinese characters compiled by Morohashi Tetsuji, Professor Emeritus at the Tokyo University of Education, entitled *Dai Kanwa jiten* 大漢和辭典 (The Great Chinese-Japanese Dictionary), (Tokyo: Daishūkan, 1955–1960; twelve volumes plus an index volume). Containing almost 50,000 characters and over half a million compounds (including present-day Chinese words in use), it is the most comprehensive dictionary of the Chinese language now available.

Although standard dictionaries have been omitted, this section does include a number of less commonly known but very useful compilations—especially for the handling of contemporary writings—such as dictionaries of new terms and phrases that have come into common use on the Mainland since 1949, as well as dictionaries of the Peking and Taiwan dialects. (Chinese-English glossaries of current terms are listed in the next section.)

The inauguration of mass literacy campaigns on the Mainland has been accompanied by systematic efforts to simplify the written language and the experimental use of a new romanization system. Hundreds of characters have been simplified, a number of them beyond recognition. The new romanization, though a long way from replacing Chinese characters, is nonetheless gradually coming into wider use. Included in this section are guides to the new romanization system and lists of simplified characters. (See also Hsia and Penn, *Dictionary of Simplified Chinese* (**442**) listed in the next section.)

a. General

426 Chang, Ch'i-yün 張其昀, **Lin, Yin** 林尹, **and Kao, Ming** 高明, **eds.** *Chung-wen ta tz'u-tien* 中文大辭典
(Encyclopedic Dictionary of the Chinese Language). Taipei: Chung-kuo wen-hua yen-chiu so 中國文化研究所, 1962—.

The first eleven volumes of a projected thirty-volume set had appeared by 1965. Published by the Institute for Advanced Chinese Studies in co-operation with the National War College in Taipei, the dictionary will contain 50,000 characters. Each character is accompanied by detailed explanations as to its etymology, morphological structure and pronunciation, as well as numerous compounds. Sources and meanings of each compound are also provided, as are illustrations. Arranged by the radical system, each volume also carries a stroke and a four-corner index.

This monumental compilation is based on all available Chinese lexicographic works from *Shuo wen* 說文 to *Kuo-yü tz'u-tien* 國語辭典 and will be the most comprehensive Chinese dictionary published in China in modern times.

427 Chung-kuo ta tz'u-tien pien-tsuan ch'u 中國大辭典編纂處 (Compilation Committee of the Large Chinese Dictionary). *Han-yü tz'u-tien, chien-pen* 漢語辭典 簡本
(Chinese Dictionary, Abridged Edition). Shanghai: Shang-wu yin-shu kuan 商務印書館, 1957. 18; 1,254; 27p.

An abridged edition of the eight-volume *Kuo-yü tz'u-tien* (Mandarin Dictionary), (Changsha: Shang-wu yin-shu kuan, 1947). Little revision has been attempted. Terms and phrases peculiar to the Peking dialect which are characteristic of the original edition and some standard literary expressions have been retained. The abridged edition does not contain any expressions which have come into general use since 1949 on the Mainland. The pronunciation, as in the original edition, is given in the National Phonetic Alphabet (國音字母).

This abridged dictionary was also reprinted in Taiwan under the title *Kuo-yü ta tz'u-tien* (Taipei: Hai-yen ch'u-pan she 海燕出版社, 1961).

428 Chūgoku Gogaku Kenkyūkai 中國語學研究會 (Society for the Study of Chinese Language). *Chūgoku gogaku jiten* 中國語學事典
(Encyclopedia of the Chinese Language). Tokyo: Kōnan Shoin 江南書院, 1958. 23; 1,129p.

Contributions by seventy-five Japanese and two foreign scholars on all aspects of the Chinese language arranged under eleven topical chapters.

429 Chung-kuo wen-tzu kai-ko wei-yüan hui, Tz'u-hui hsiao-tsu 中國文字改革委員會 詞彙小組 (Chinese Language Reform Committee, Terminology Section). *Han-yü p'in-yin tz'u-hui (ch'u-kao)* 漢語拼音詞滙（初稿）
(Dictionary of P'in-yin Chinese, Preliminary Edition). Peking: Hsin-hua shu-tien 新華書店, 1958. 394p.

Contains some 20,000 words arranged alphabetically by the new Chinese romanization system followed by Chinese characters. A useful reference.

430 Tien, H. C., Hsia, Ronald and Penn, Peter, comps. *Han-yü p'in-yin piao* 漢語拼音表
A Guide to the New Latin Spelling of Chinese. Hong Kong: Oriental Book Company, 1963. 64p.

An alphabetical listing of the 411 basic sounds of the new Chinese Communist romanization (P'in-yin) system with their equivalents according to the national Chinese romanization of 1926, the Wade-Giles system, and the Yale romanization. Each entry is also followed by tonal designations. Two indexes: Wade-Giles and Yale. A conveniently arranged list.

431　**Wen-tzu kai-ko ch'u-pan she** 文字改革出版社 (Language Reform Publishing House). *San-p'i i t'ui-hsing ti chien-hua han-tzu piao* 三批已推行的簡化漢字表 (Three Approved Lists of Simplified Characters in Use). Peking: Wen-tzu kai-ko ch'u-pan she, 1958. 22p.

A compilation of three official lists totaling 425 currently used simplified characters approved by the State Council between February 1, 1956 and May 15, 1958. There is also a P'in-yin index and a stroke index arranged according to the simplified characters. The original characters are given in brackets after their simplified form throughout the publication.

For the fourth list (92 characters) approved by the State Council for general use on July 15, 1959, see *Wen-tzu kai-ko* 文字改革, 1959 No. 13, p. 21.

432　**Fei 'wen-tzu kai-ko' yu-kuan tzu-liao hui-pien** 匪匚文字改革冂有關資料彙編 (Compendium of Reference Materials on the Bandit 'Language Reform'). Taipei: Yang-ming shan-chuang 陽明山莊, 1955. 142p.

A collection of Chinese Communist documents on language reform with special emphasis on the simplification of Chinese characters. Included are articles by members of the Committee for Reforming the Chinese Written Language and a 'Draft Resolution on the Simplification of Chinese Characters' issued jointly by the Committee and the Ministry of Education in 1955. The draft resolution comprises three tables: (1) proposed simplified forms for 798 characters, (2) proposed list of 400 variants or doubles of other characters to be abolished, and (3) proposed simplified forms for 54 'side elements'. There is also a list of 1,500 'Most Commonly Used Characters' issued by the Ministry of Education in 1955. A useful collection.

See also Harriet C. Mills, 'Language Reform in China; Some Recent Developments', *Far Eastern Quarterly*, Vol. 15, No. 4 (August 1956), pp. 517–540; Tao-tai Hsia, *China's Language Reforms*, Mirror Series A, No. 21 (New Haven, Conn.: Yale University, Institute of Far Eastern Languages, 1956), 200p.; and *Reform of the Chinese Written Language* (Peking, 1958), 52p.

433　**Chin, Shou-shen** 金受申, ed. *Pei-ching hua yü-hui* 北京話語滙 (Glossary of Peking Colloquial Expressions). Peking: Shang-wu yin-shu kuan 商務印書館, 1961. 214p.

Contains more than one thousand Peking colloquial expressions arranged alphabetically by Chinese Communist romanization (which is also provided for the reading of the terms). Definitions are accompanied by examples. Expressions not included fall under the following categories: (1) 'terms derived from and exhorting the virtues of feudalism'; (2) 'terms tinted with superstitious thoughts and fatalism'; (3) derogatory and vulgar expressions; (4) 'terms that tend to confuse, submerge, or destroy the idea of struggle and class struggle'; (5) obsolete expressions; and (6) witty and humorous terms. Despite these omissions, the work remains the most useful dictionary of its kind. The short preface by the editor provides an informative introduction to the study of Peking colloquial expressions.

434   **Wang, Yü-te** 王育德. *Taiwango jōyō goi* 臺灣語常用語彙
The Basic Vocabulaly [sic] of the Formosan Dialect. Tokyo: Eiwa Gogakusha 永和語學社, 1957. 475p.

Some 5,000 words arranged alphabetically in romanized form, followed by Chinese characters and Japanese explanations. The Formosan dialect is discussed in an introductory article (pp. 1–54). Appendix contains a chart on dialect differences. Index arranged according to the Japanese syllabary. Mimeographed.

435   **Lien, Heng** 連橫. *T'ai-wan yü-tien* 臺灣語典
(A Dictionary of Taiwanese). Taipei: Chung-hua ts'ung-shu wei-yüan hui 中華叢書委員會, 1957. 152p.

Contains 1,100 common words or expressions of Taiwanese—a dialect spoken in the southern part of Fukien Province and in Taiwan. Each entry provides definition, pronunciation and origin.

b. Special Terms and Phrases

436   **Hsin ming-tz'u tz'u-tien** 新名詞辭典
(Dictionary of New Terms and Phrases). Revised edition. Shanghai: Ch'un-ming ch'u-pan she 春明出版社, 1952. 60; 9,134; 28p.

A popular dictionary that has gone through twenty-six printings since its first publication in 1949. Arranged under the following sections: (1) international affairs; (2) politics; (3) economics; (4) history; (5) geography; (6) social affairs; (7) philosophy; (8) science; (9) literature and art; and (10) biography. Stroke index. The appendix contains texts of the General Program, the land reform law, the trade union law, regulations for the punishment of anti-revolutionary activities, the marriage law, and the anti-corruption law. Included also are the name lists of the Political Consultative Council and of the leading personnel of the Central People's Government.

437   **Hsin tz'u-shu pien-i she** 新辭書編譯社 (New Dictionary Publishing Company).
Chung-kuo jen-min shu-yü tz'u-tien 中國人民術語辭典

(A Dictionary of Chinese Terms). Shanghai: T'ai-p'ing yang ch'u-pan she 太平洋出版社, 1950. 452p.

Covers approximately 1,200 political, economic, and military terms in popular use.

438 **Yale University, The Institute of Far Eastern Languages.**
Chinese Newspaper Manual. New Haven, Conn.: Far Eastern Publications, 1952. 24; 262p.

A guide to the reading of Chinese newspapers based on a preliminary draft compiled by the Foreign Service Institute's Chinese Language School in pre-1949 Peiping. In five chapters: (1) news agencies, press services, newspapers and periodicals frequently quoted in the Chinese press; (2) Chinese geographical aids; (3) foreign geographical aids; (4) governmental organizations; (5) Chinese and foreign who's who. Useful except Chapter 4, which is out of date.

A revised edition was published in 1963 (270p.) edited by Professor Tien-yi Li. Included in the new edition is a list of all Chinese terms appearing in the book arranged according to the number of strokes.

439 **Chiang, Pi-k'un** 蔣碧崑. *Chung-hua jen-min kung-ho kuo hsien-fa ming-tz'u chien-shuo* 中華人民共和國憲法名詞簡說
(Brief Commentaries on Terms Found in the Constitution of the People's Republic of China). Wuhan: Hu-pei jen-min ch'u-pan she 湖北人民出版社, 1957. 55p.

A short, popular dictionary of fifty-eight major terms and legal concepts found in the constitution of Communist China adopted in September 1954.

2. FROM CHINESE TO OTHER LANGUAGES

a. Chinese-English

The standard Chinese-English dictionaries such as Giles and Mathews are virtually devoid of definitions of contemporary expressions. The five publications which appear below go at least part way toward meeting this need. See also *Modern Chinese-English Technical and General Dictionary* listed below (**481**).

440 **U.S. Joint Publications Research Service.**
Chinese-English Dictionary of Modern Communist Chinese Usage. September 1963. 831p. (J.P.R.S. 20,904; U.S.G.P.O. Monthly Catalog, 1963, No. 17,846).

A translation into English of the second edition of the Chinese-German dictionary compiled by the German Department of the Peking Foreign Languages Institute (see **455**). Some 35,000 words are arranged by character in alphabetical order according to the P'in-yin system.

441 Dien, Albert E., comp.
Dictionary of Chinese Current Terminology. Honolulu: University of Hawaii, Center for Cultural and Technical Interchange Between East and West, Institute of Advanced Projects, Research Translations, 1962. 331p.

The volume is a re-compilation of existing works, including **443** and **444** listed below, the volumes issued in the *Studies in Chinese Communist Terminology* published by the Center for Chinese Studies of the University of California (Berkeley) and several other sources. Arranged by the radical system, the entries are given in Chinese characters, followed by Wade-Giles romanization, and English definition(s). The original works are listed in a table at the beginning of the volume with each title represented by an abbreviated symbol (A, B, C, D, etc.). The symbols are used after each item in the text to indicate source. There is a list of radicals, and a list of simplified characters (with regular forms) arranged by stroke count. Mimeographed.

Coverage is comprehensive and useful.

442 Hsia, Ronald and Penn, Peter, comps.
Dictionary of Simplified Chinese. Hong Kong: Oriental Book Company, 1959. 122p.

A dictionary of the 425 simplified Chinese characters approved by the Chinese Communist government, arranged by stroke count according to the simplified form and by the P'in-yin system. All entries are accompanied by their regular forms, Wade-Giles romanizations, and English definitions. The appendices include, among other useful features, a list of the 116 simplified characters still in trial circulation, and a list of the 54 simplified 'side elements.' There is a radical index and an index by the Wade-Giles romanization.

See also entries in the first section of this chapter and Anna Chennault, comp., *Dictionary of New Simplified Chinese Characters* (Washington, D.C.: Georgetown University, Machine Translation, Chinese Section, 1962), 88p.

443 U.S. Department of State, Foreign Service Institute.
A Chinese-English Glossary of Current Reading Texts. Taichung, Taiwan, 1961. 146p.

A glossary comprising some 4,500 entries, produced at the Chinese Language and Area Training Center of the Foreign Service Institute of the Department of State at Taichung, Taiwan. The vocabulary for the glossary was drawn from the following texts: (1) *Newspaper Primer*, (2) *Selections of Chinese Communist Literature*, (3) *Dictatorship of the People's Democracy*, (4) *Newspaper Selections* (4 vols.), (5) *Newspaper Selections of the Mainland Press*, (6) *Agricultural Economics*, (7) *Mao Tse-tung's Speech on Contradictions* (annotated), and (8) *Lectures on Economics by Professor Chang Yen-t'ien* (given at Taichung). (The first three titles are Yale University publications, while the last five are texts prepared by the F.S.I. staff at Taichung.)

Entries are arranged by radical and number of strokes of the Chinese characters; about 200 simplified characters are given in parenthesis in the traditional form, followed by the Yale romanization, English definition, and reference to the relevant page numbers in the various publications listed above. A radical index is supplied.

Accurate definitions, carefully compiled.

See also *Readings in Chinese Communist Documents* compiled by Wen-shun Chi (University of California Press, 1963), which contains two glossaries and a table of conversions of the Wade-Giles, Yale and P'in-yin romanization systems.

444 U.S. Joint Publications Research Service.
J.P.R.S. Handbook: Standard Translations of Chinese Communist Terms. October 1963. 133p. (J.P.R.S. No. 21,387; U.S.G.P.O. Monthly Catalog, 1963, No. 19,689).

A compilation of approximately 1,850 selected Chinese Communist political, economic, military, and sociological terms with recommended translations or equivalents. The terms are grouped under the following subject categories: government and political terminology, scientific and educational organizations, and economic terminology. Under each category the terms are given 'organizationally or functionally as feasible'. In three columns: Wade-Giles romanization, Chinese characters, and standardized translation. Mimeographed.

A Chinese-English Dictionary of Communist Chinese Terminology of approximately 30,000 terms is in the process of being compiled by Dr. Dennis J. Doolin of the Hoover Institution, Stanford University.

b. Chinese-Russian

The first entry listed below is the standard Chinese-Russian dictionary arranged by character, now in its third edition.

Soviet Sinologists are now working on a monumental four-volume dictionary of the Chinese language.

445 Oshanin, Il'ia Mikhailovich, ed. *Kitaisko-russkii slovar'*
(Chinese-Russian Dictionary). Third edition. Moscow: Gosudarstvennoe izdatel'stvo inostrannykh i natsional'nykh slovarei, 1959. 1,100p.

A dictionary containing over 70,000 words and expressions, prepared by the staff of the Institute of Oriental Studies. The volume provides Chinese characters with compounds under each character, accompanied by examples of usage. A table of 798 simplified characters and 400 variant characters slated for abolition is included (pp. 891–893). The appendix lists the geographical place names in Chinese, Korean and Japanese that do not appear in the body of the dictionary (pp. 901–920), and contains chronological tables. Three indexes: an index to characters according to the 214 radicals; an index arranged according to the four-corner system; and a phonetic index arranged according to the Russian alphabet. Earlier editions appeared in 1952 and 1955.

The present work is the most comprehensive Chinese dictionary prepared in the Soviet Union.

446 **Hu, Shu-wei** 胡叔煒, **et al., eds.** *Hua-O tz'u-tien* 華俄辭典 (Chinese-Russian Dictionary). Peking and Shanghai: Wu-shih nien-tai she 五十年代社, 1955. 26; 485p.

Covers more than 25,000 words. In addition to words of everyday usage, the emphasis is on political and economic expressions. Arranged by character (by the number of strokes), in each case accompanied by compounds and examples. A list of characters with page references precedes the main part of the dictionary.

447 **Grigor'ev, G. M., comp.; Oshanin, I. M., ed.** *Kratkii kitaisko-russkii slovar'* (Concise Chinese-Russian Dictionary). Second edition. Moscow: Gosudarstvennoe izdatel'stvo inostrannykh i natsional'nykh slovarei, 1962. 480p.

Contains 2,871 characters, including the 2,000 basic characters adopted by the Ministry of Education in Peking in 1953, and 19,000 words. Arranged by character, with compounds accompanied by examples. The characters included in the dictionary are listed separately together with the page on which each appears. Radical and phonetic indexes. The first edition appeared in 1956.

448 **Isaenko, B., comp.** *Opyt kitaisko-russkogo foneticheskogo slovaria* (Experimental Chinese-Russian Phonetic Dictionary). Moscow: Gosudarstvennoe izdatel'stvo inostrannykh i natsional'nykh slovarei, 1957. 319p.

Contains about 5,500 words arranged in alphabetical order in accordance with Chinese Communist romanization (characters in parenthesis), followed by the Russian translation with examples. A long article on Chinese grammar is appended (pp. 239–318).

Of interest also is the Chinese-Russian-German-English-French-Spanish Dictionary of Terms Used in International Conferences compiled by Jean Herbert (漢, 俄, 德, 英, 法, 西語對照國際會議術語滙編 *Han-O-Te-Ying-Fa-Hsi yü tui-chao kuo-chi hui-i shu-yü hui-pien*), (Peking: Shang-wu yin-shu kuan 商務印書館, 1962), 284p.

c. Chinese-Japanese

The two dictionaries listed at the beginning of the present section are most widely used in Japan. The first is currently the more comprehensive; the second has for many years enjoyed the reputation of being the standard Chinese-Japanese dictionary. A most ambitious project now under way (described in the last entry) will produce a Chinese-Japanese dictionary more comprehensive than any now in existence.

A number of other Chinese-Japanese dictionaries are listed in *Nihon no sankō tosho* (Japanese Reference Works), (Tokyo, 1962), pp. 67–68.

In addition, a Chinese-Japanese dictionary (漢日辭典, 商務印書館) is being compiled on the Mainland.

449　Kanegae, Nobumitsu 鐘ヶ江信光. *Chūgokugo jiten* 中國語辭典 (Dictionary of the Chinese language). Tokyo: Daigaku Shorin 大學書林, 1960. 1,157p.

Contains 10,408 characters and 68,536 compounds arranged alphabetically by character in accordance with the Chinese pronunciation. Provides 14,108 examples and 15,125 synonyms, antonyms, etc. Radical index, stroke indexes and index according to Japanese pronunciation.

The most comprehensive Chinese-Japanese dictionary available, although the selection could have been more discriminating.

450　Inoue, Midori 井上翠. *Inoue Chūgokugo shinjiten* 井上中國語新辭典 (Inoue's New Chinese-Japanese Dictionary). New revised and enlarged edition. Tokyo: Kōnan Shoin 江南書院, 1954. 1,111; 63p.

The standard Chinese-language dictionary in Japan for many years. Arranged according to the Wade-Giles romanization.

451　Kuraishi, Takeshirō 倉石武四郎. *Ratenka shimmoji ni yoru Chūgokugo jiten* ラテン化新文字による中國語辭典 (Chinese Dictionary Arranged According to the New Latinization). Tokyo: Wahei Shuppansha 和平出版社, 1954–1958. 7 vols.

Some 10,000 words arranged alphabetically according to the P'in-yin system of romanization. Each entry supplies the Chinese word in romanization, followed by Chinese character(s) and the Japanese definition. An alphabetical index is provided in Volume 6; Volume 7 is entirely given over to a stroke index. Mimeographed.

This dictionary was published under the title *Iwanami Chūgokugo jiten* 岩波中國語辭典 (The Iwanami Chinese Dictionary) in September 1963, 942p.

452　Suzuki, Takurō 鈴木擇郎, **ed.** *Chū-Nichi dai jiten* 中日大辭典 (Great Chinese-Japanese Dictionary).

What will be the most comprehensive modern Chinese-Japanese dictionary is now in preparation at Aichi University under the direction of Professor Suzuki Takurō. Begun before the war at Tōa Dōbun Shoin 東亞同文書院, a Japanese-sponsored college in Shanghai, the dictionary project was revived in 1955. The dictionary will contain some 10,000 characters and 120,000 compounds, and will probably be some 1,000 pages in length. It will be arranged in alphabetical order in accordance with the new Communist system of romanization.

d. Chinese-Other Languages

Included in this section are Chinese-French, Chinese-German and Chinese-Mongolian dictionaries published on the Mainland, and two Chinese-German dictionaries arranged alphabetically by character—one published in West Germany, the other in East Germany.

453 **Pei-ching ta-hsüeh, Hsi-yü hsi, Fa-yü chuan-yeh** 北京大學 西語系 法語 專業 (Peking University, Department of Foreign Languages, French Section). *Han-Fa tz'u-tien* 漢法辭典 *Dictionnaire Chinois-Français* (Chinese-French Dictionary). Peking: Shang-wu yin-shu kuan 商務印書館, 1959. 646; 27p.

Contains more than 6,000 single character entries and about 30,000 compounds, emphasizing the more commonly used terms and phrases. Arranged by the Chinese Communist P'in-yin system. Single character entries are in the traditional form (those having officially approved simplified forms are so indicated in parenthesis). Simplified characters are used throughout for compounds. A radical index is provided to both traditional and simplified characters.

See also Hussenet, René, *Essai de Dictionnaire Chinois-Français* (Seoul: Dong-A, 1960), 310p., a Chinese-French dictionary of words and expressions used in the press, with an estimate of their frequency of appearance.

454 **Rüdenberg, Werner.** *Chinesisch-Deutsches Wörterbuch* (Chinese-German Dictionary). Third, completely revised edition by Hans O. H. Stange. Hamburg: Cram, de Gruyter & Co., 1963. 821p.

A thorough revision of the famous Rüdenberg dictionary originally published in 1924. Arranged alphabetically by Chinese character with German explanations and compounds.

455 **Pei-ching wai-kuo yü hsüeh-yüan, Te-yü hsi** 北京外國語學院 德語系 (Peking Foreign Languages Institute, Department of German). *Han-Te tz'u-tien* 漢德辭典 *Chinesisch-Deutsches Wörterbuch* (Chinese-German Dictionary). Peking: Shang-wu yin-shu kuan 商務印書館, 1959. 789; 14; 27p.

Includes about 35,000 entries with an emphasis on commonly used words and phrases—especially those terms which have come into general use in China since 1949. Arranged by character in alphabetical order according to the P'in-yin system. Officially approved simplified characters are used in the entries, accompanied by their traditional form in parenthesis. There is a radical index to both traditional and simplified characters.

The second edition of this dictionary, which appeared in 1960, was converted into English (see **440**).

456 Piasek, Martin. *Chinesisch-Deutsches Wörterbuch*
(Chinese-German Dictionary). Leipzig: Verlag Enzyklopädie, 1960. 360p.

Based on Chinese, Russian and English dictionaries, this dictionary, containing 12,000 words, is arranged by Chinese character and is very similar in format to the Rose-Innes dictionary. The author is research associate at the East Asian Institute, Karl Marx University at Leipzig in East Germany.

457 Nei Meng-ku Meng-ku yü-wen yen-chiu hui 內蒙古蒙古語文研究會
(Mongolian Language Association of Inner Mongolia). *Han-Meng chien-lüeh tz'u-tien* 漢蒙簡略辭典
(Concise Chinese-Mongolian Dictionary). Hu-ho-hao-t'e 呼和浩特: Nei Meng-ku hsin-hua shu-tien 內蒙古新華書店, 1955. 672p.

Contains about 3,000 characters. Two indexes: Mongolian and Chinese. The first is arranged according to the Mongolian alphabet (in Cyrillic script). The latter is arranged phonetically (A, An, etc.). The appendix includes lists of technical terms, geographical names, and names of prominent persons, all arranged by stroke count.

3. FROM OTHER LANGUAGES TO CHINESE

The foreign language-Chinese dictionaries listed below include English, Russian, Japanese, Spanish, Vietnamese, Malay, and Indonesian.

In addition, even a partial list of dictionaries published or under compilation on the Mainland should include the following: German-Chinese, Czech-Chinese, Hindi-Chinese, Esperanto-Chinese, Arabic-Chinese, Burmese-Chinese, Thai-Chinese, Hungarian-Chinese and Rumanian-Chinese.

Reference should also be made to the *English-Hakka Dictionary* compiled by Man Ssu-ch'ien (Hong Kong: Ch'i Kuang ch'u-pan she, 1958), 620p.

458 Kuo-chi Ying-Han shuang-chieh ta tz'u-tien 國際英漢雙解大辭典
International Dictionary, English through English, English-Chinese. Taipei: Ch'i-ming shu-chü 啟明書局, 1960. 1,852p.

Based on *Webster's New International Dictionary*, second edition, this is the most comprehensive English-Chinese dictionary ever published. The original three-column page format is retained. Only portions of the appendix lack Chinese translation. The present volume is a Taiwan reprint of the edition published by the Commercial Press in Shanghai.

459 Cheng, I-li 鄭易里, ed. *Ying-Hua ta tz'u-tien* 英華大辭典
A New English-Chinese Dictionary. Revised edition. Peking: Shih-tai ch'u-pan she 時代出版社, 1961. 1,542p.

Reportedly the most popular English-Chinese dictionary in use in Mainland China to-day, the dictionary contains a large number of American slang expressions and current terms. Vernacular Chinese is used in the definitions and explanation of examples given. The Chinese index in the original (1950) edition is left out of the 1957 revised edition, of which this is the sixth printing.

A New English-Chinese Dictionary with Index in Chinese (*Tsui-hsin hsiang-chieh Ying-Hua ta tz'u-tien* 最新詳解英華大辭典) compiled by the author appeared in March 1963.

460 **Wang, Tzu-yün** 王子雲, **comp.; Liu, Tse-jung** 劉澤榮, **ed.** *Bol'shoi russko-kitaiskii slovar'—O-Han ta tz'u-tien* 俄漢大辭典
(Large Russian-Chinese Dictionary). Peking: Shang-wu yin-shu kuan 商務印書館, 1962. 1,384p.

An expanded version of the two-volume edition published in 1956–1958. Contains about 105,000 words.

461 **Ch'en, Ch'ang-hao, Dubrovskii, A. G. and Kotov, A., comps.; Ch'en, Ch'ang-hao and Isaenko, B. S., eds.** *Russko-kitaiskii slovar'*
(Russian-Chinese Dictionary). Third revised and enlarged edition. Moscow: Gosudarstvennoe izdatel'stvo inostrannykh i natsional'nykh slovarei, 1953. 16; 975p.

Countains 26,000 words with an emphasis on expressions used in everyday life as well as in the political, social and economic fields rather than in the natural sciences or belles-lettres. The first Russian-Chinese dictionary to be compiled in the Soviet Union, the present volume has also been revised and published by Shih-tai ch'u-pan she 時代出版社 in Peking in 1953 (736p.).

462 **Palei, Ia. B. and Iustov, V. K., comps.** *Kratkii russko-kitaiskii slovar'*
(Concise Russian-Chinese Dictionary). Fourth revised edition. Moscow: Gosudarstvennoe izdatel'stvo inostrannykh i natsional'nykh slovarei, 1963. 590p.

Contains 16,000 words. First edition appeared in 1957.

463 **Ch'en, T'ao** 陳濤, **et al., eds.** *Jih-Han tz'u-tien* 日漢辭典
(Japanese-Chinese Dictionary). Peking: Shang-wu yin-shu kuan 商務印書館, 1959. 2,587p.

Includes more than 60,000 entries, arranged according to the Japanese syllabary and accompanied by Chinese characters and Chinese definition. A reprint was issued by the Daian Company in Tokyo in 1959.

464 **The Japan Times, ed.**
The Japan Times' 6-Language Dictionary. Tokyo: Hara Shobō, 1958. 678p.

Japanese-English-German-French-Russian-Chinese dictionary in table form. Contains 10,000 'living' words. Appendix 1 (pp. 517–596) consists of brief sections on English, German, French, Russian and Chinese grammars. Appendix 2 (pp. 597–619) lists place names, personal names, weights and measures, etc. Appendix 3 (pp. 621–629) provides useful conversational phrases. There is also an index to the English section. The German, French, Russian and Chinese sections are not indexed.

465 Pei-ching wai-kuo yü hsüeh-yüan, Hsi-pan-ya yü hsi 北京外國語學院 西班牙語系 (Peking Foreign Language Institute, Department of Spanish). *Hsi-Han tz'u-tien* 西漢辭典 *Diccionario español-chino* (Spanish-Chinese Dictionary). Peking: Shang-wu yin-shu kuan 商務印書館, 1959. 888p.

Contains about 50,000 words. No index.

466 Ho, Ch'eng 何成, **et al., eds.** *Yüeh-Han tz'u-tien* 越漢辭典 (Vietnamese-Chinese Dictionary). Peking: Shang-wu yin-shu kuan 商務印書館, 1960. 1,372p.

Contains about 50,000 words arranged alphabetically by romanized Vietnamese.

467 Lin, Huan-wen 林煥文, **ed.** *Kamus Mĕlayu-Tionghoa* (Chien-ming Ma-Hua tz'u-tien) 簡明馬華辭典 (Malay-Chinese Dictionary). Singapore: Shang-hai shu-chü 上海書局, 1959. 661p.

Arranged by romanized Malay. Based largely on R. O. Winstedt, ed., *An Unabridged Malay-English Dictionary*.

468 Li, Juk Kuy 李毓愷 **(Li, Yü-k'ai), ed.** *Kamus Baharu Bahasa Indonesia-Tionghoa* (Yin-ni Chung-hua ta tz'u-tien) 印尼中華大辭典 (Indonesian-Chinese Dictionary). Djakarta: Kuo Min Book Company, 1953. 661p.

Arranged by romanized Indonesian.

An Indonesian-Chinese dictionary was published by the Shang-wu yin-shu kuan 商務印書館 in Peking in June 1963.

B. Subject Dictionaries

The present section comprises a sample of those subject dictionaries available in the United States, Japan and Taiwan, in the fields of general economics, finance and foreign trade, military and library science. Most are Chinese-language dictionaries, although a few are Chinese-Russian and Russian-Chinese.

1. ECONOMICS, FINANCE AND FOREIGN TRADE

469 Su, Yüan-lei 蘇淵雷, **ed.** *Kuo-min ching-chi shih-yung tz'u-tien* 國民經濟實用
辭典
(People's Practical Dictionary of Economics). Shanghai: Ch'un-ming ch'u-pan
she 春明出版社, 1953. 980p.

Arranged according to a Russian classification system under the following
nine categories: (1) general, (2) industry, (3) agriculture, (4) commerce, (5)
cooperatives, (6) communications, (7) finance, (8) money and banking, and
(9) labor. Includes not only ordinary economic terms, but also special terms and
phrases adopted and popularized by the Chinese Communists.

470 Pisarev, I. Iu. *She-hui ching-chi t'ung-chi tz'u-tien* 社會經濟統計辭典
(Dictionary of Socio-Economic Statistics). [n.p.]: Tung-pei ts'ai-ching ch'u-pan
she 東北財經出版社, 1951. 528p.

A translation of the 1948 edition of I. Iu. Pisarev's *Slovar'-spravochnik po
sotsial'no-ekonomicheskoi statistike* published in Moscow. Arranged under broad
categories, such as industrial statistics, agricultural statistics, commercial
statistics, etc. The index provides a complete listing of the 1,000-odd terms
contained in the dictionary arranged under the same categories. No general
alphabetical index. A very useful reference tool.

471 T'ung-su tu-wu ch'u-pan she 通俗讀物出版社 (Popular Publications Press).
Nung-yeh ho-tso hua ming-tz'u chieh-shih 農業合作化名詞解釋
(Glossary of Terms on Cooperative Agriculture). Peking: T'ung-su tu-wu
ch'u-pan she, 1956. 28p.

A brief list for general readers.

472 Chien-ming tui-wai mao-i tz'u-tien 簡明對外貿易辭典
(A Concise Dictionary of Foreign Trade). Peking: Ts'ai-cheng ching-chi
ch'u-pan she 財政經濟出版社, 1959. 241p.

Translation of the *Kratkii vneshnetorgovyi slovar'* published in Moscow in
1954. Arranged by number of strokes. Long descriptive articles.

473 Zorin, I. N., comp. *Kitaisko-russkii obshcheekonomicheskii i vneshnetorgovyi
slovar'*
(Chinese-Russian Dictionary of Economics and Foreign Trade). Moscow:
Vneshtorgizdat, 1962. 699p.

Some 20,000 terms in the fields of economics and foreign trade, as well as
widely used words pertaining to politics, diplomacy, law and banking.

474 Shelekasov, P. V., comp.; Kolokolov, V. S., ed. *Kratkii russko-kitaiskii i kitaisko-russkii vneshnetorgovyi slovar'*
(A Concise Russian-Chinese and Chinese-Russian Dictionary of Foreign Trade).
Moscow: Vneshtorgizdat, 1952. 303p.

About 4,000 words. The Russian-Chinese part (pp. 5–158) gives the Russian word and the Chinese translation in characters and Russian transliteration. The Chinese-Russian part (pp. 167–301) supplies Chinese characters with Russian transliteration followed by Russian translation.

475 Senin, V. P., comp. *Kitaisko-russkii i russko-kitaiskii slovar' eksportno-importnykh tovarov*
(Chinese-Russian and Russian-Chinese Dictionary of Export-Import Commodities). Moscow: Vneshtorgizdat, 1961. 980p.

Contains some 15,000 terms commonly used in connection with trade between the Soviet Union and Communist China. Arranged according to topical category (machinery and plants, fuels, metals, mining resources, foodstuffs, etc.). Alphabetical index of commodities.

476 Chung-kuo jen-min yin-hang tsung-hang, Chuan-chia kung-tso shih
中國人民銀行總行 專家工作室 (People's Bank of China, Head Office, Office of Specialists). *O-Hua chin-jung hsiao tz'u-tien* 俄華金融小辭典
(Concise Russian-Chinese Dictionary of Financial Terms). Peking: Chin-jung ch'u-pan she 金融出版社, 1959. 379p.

Includes more than 8,000 terms employed in banking and finance.

2. MILITARY TERMS

477 China, Kuo-fang pu, Kuo-chün chün-yü tz'u-tien pien-tsuan wei-yüan hui
國民政府 國防部 國軍軍語辭典編纂委員會 (China, Ministry of National Defense, Editorial Committee of the Dictionary of Military Terms of the Chinese Armed Forces). *Kuo-chün chün-yü tz'u-tien* 國軍軍語辭典
(Dictionary of Military Terms of the Chinese Armed Forces). Taipei: Wu-hsüeh shu-chü ku-fen yu-hsien kung-ssu 武學書局股份有限公司, 1956. 1,326p.

A collection of more than 22,000 military terms currently used by the Nationalist Chinese armed forces, arranged in twenty-five categories. English translations are provided for terms of English origin. An index arranged according to the number of strokes occupies the first 307 pages. The most comprehensive compilation available.
See also the *Modern Chinese-English Technical and General Dictionary* (**481**).

478 Li, Pao-king.
A Text of Chinese Military Terms. New Haven, Conn.: The Institute of Far Eastern Languages, 1959. 390p.

An introduction to Chinese military terminology. Divided into twenty-four lessons, this book has a 'vocabulary index' alphabetically arranged by the Yale romanization system (pp. 283–373). There are six appendices in ten parts arranged to facilitate quick reference.

479 Hanrahan, Gene Z., comp.
A Guide to Chinese Communist Military and Political Terminology. Revised edition. Stanford, Calif.: Hoover Institute and Library, 1952. 13p.

A glossary of 312 terms frequently encountered in Chinese Communist military and political writings up to 1952, a number of them not usually available in Chinese-English glossaries of military terms. Mimeographed. Limited distribution.

3. LIBRARY SCIENCE

480 Lu, Chen-ching 盧震京, **ed.** *T'u-shu kuan hsüeh tz'u-tien* 圖書館學辭典 (Encyclopedia of Library Science). Peking: Shang-wu yin-shu kuan 商務印書館, 1958. 26; 898p.

A revised edition of the author's *T'u-shu hsüeh ta tz'u-tien* 圖書學大辭典 (Changsha: Shang-wu yin-shu kuan, 1940, 2 vols.) to which a number of entries on Russian and Chinese Communist terms and practices (including the various Chinese Communist classification schemes) have been added. Two useful lists of library terms are provided: (1) Russian-Chinese-English-German-French-Latin; and (2) English-Chinese-Russian.

Entries are arranged by the number of strokes, as is the table of contents, and both use simplified Chinese characters. The appendix includes two annotated bibliographies covering publications in Chinese, and Chinese translations of works on library science appearing in the pre- and post-1949 periods, respectively. However, a number of useful lists of catalogs, bibliographies and indexes provided in the appendix to the 1940 edition have been omitted from the present volume.

The author, accused of having taken a 'petty-bourgeois' approach to the study of library science, has been the subject of bitter denunciation by his colleagues because of the contents of the 1958 edition. (See *T'u-shu kuan hsüeh t'ung-hsün* 圖書館學通訊 [Library Science Bulletin], 1959 No. 1 [January 31, 1959], pp. 25–33.)

C. SCIENTIFIC AND TECHNICAL GLOSSARIES

Until recently, persons working with Chinese scientific and technical publications have had to refer to a number of separately published glossaries. This tedious consultation process has been greatly simplified, if not eliminated, with the appearance of the *Modern Chinese-English Technical and General Dictionary* (**481**), with its more more than 200,000 entries, eighty per cent of which are common scientific and technical terms (the remainder are general terms—political, economic, military, etc.).

This excellent compilation is supplemented by a number of separately published glossaries originating in Mainland China and Taiwan which also are listed in this chapter. The listing of the glossaries is far from exhaustive, the titles provided below being but an illustrative sample of those available in the United States, Japan and Taiwan.

The second entry (482) is a comprehensive collection of scientific and technical glossaries originally published on the Mainland before 1949 (and subsequently on Taiwan), the majority of which are English-Chinese. There exists no similar collection of post-1949 Mainland compilations, a good many of which are Russian-Chinese, but the catalog of the Science Publishing House of the Chinese Academy of Sciences (154) is believed to contain a complete list of such glossaries published as of September 1959. Wang Chi's *Mainland China Organizations of Higher Learning in Science and Technology and Their Publications: A Selected Guide* (330) is another excellent source for locating publications of this type.

In addition to the general scientific and technical glossaries, the present section (in subsequent subsections) lists specialized glossaries in the fields of mathematics, physics, chemistry, geography, geology, meteorology, biology, botany, zoology, agriculture and forestry, medicine, pharmacology and public health, and many branches of engineering such as mechanical, electrical, aeronautical, mining, civil, as well as surveying, architecture, etc. The reader is warned, however, that inasmuch as these glossaries are published primarily for the use of Chinese working with Western and Russian scientific publications, they are as a rule oriented from English, Russian, etc., to Chinese. Their value to the scholar translating Chinese scientific publications into English is, therefore, somewhat limited unless the glossary is accompanied by a Chinese index.

I. GENERAL

481 Modern Chinese-English Technical and General Dictionary. New York, Toronto, London: McGraw-Hill Book Company, 1963. 3 vols. 3,864p.

> Contains 212,000 entries, of which more than eighty per cent are common scientific and technical terms. Terms used in mathematics, chemistry, medicine, atomic physics, geology, mineralogy, and military affairs are particularly well represented. Included also are general terms used in political and economic materials published on Mainland China, as well as important Chinese place names and names of prominent Chinese personalities. Volumes 2 and 3, containing the same material but arranged differently, constitute the body of this dictionary. Volume 2 is arranged by standard Chinese Communist telegraphic code in numerical sequence, and Volume 3 by the P'in-yin romanization in alphabetical order. Each entry is accompanied by an English definition. Chinese characters are not provided in the body of the text, except that the P'in-yin romanization for a given term in both Volume 2 and 3 is followed by digits indicating tones of characters contained in that particular term. Volume 1 is a volume of tables which serves as the key to the use of the two other volumes. Included in Volume 1 are such aids as a Wade-Giles—P'in-yin conversion table,

a radical-stroke index to characters, and an alphabetic P'in-yin index to characters (Chinese characters are supplied for the last two indexes.)

The dictionary is undoubtedly the most recent and the most comprehensive compilation of its kind.

482 Kuo-li pien-i kuan 國立編譯館 (The National Institute of Compilation and Translation). *K'o-hsüeh ming-tz'u hui-pien* 科學名詞彙編
(Collections of Scientific and Technical Terms). Taipei: Cheng-chung shu-chü 正中書局, 1958. 7 vols.

A collection of thirty-two glossaries (mostly reprints) of scientific and technical terms compiled by The National Institute of Compilation and Translation from 1932 to 1957, and approved by the Ministry of Education. Twenty-five of these were published on the Mainland before 1949 and seven in Taiwan thereafter until 1957. The majority of the glossaries are English-Chinese (a few are Latin-English-Chinese or Latin-English-German-Chinese). Only a few carry a Chinese index.

The contents of the seven volumes are as follows: Vol. 1—mathematics, physics, chemical nomenclature and equipment (with Chinese index), and atomic energy; Vol. 2—astronomy (with Chinese index), meteorology (with Chinese index), and forestry; Vol. 3—embryology (with Chinese index), human anatomy, comparative anatomy, and bacterio-immunology; Vol. 4—pathology, psychopathology (with Chinese index) and pharmacology (with Chinese index); Vol. 5—mineralogy, pedology, and fertilizers; Vol. 6—mechanical engineering, electrical engineering, chemical engineering, and hydraulic engineering; Vol. 7—sociology, economics, statistics, psychology (with Chinese index), education, physical education, and Appendix (standard Chinese translations for 8,504 foreign geographical names).

A revised edition reportedly is forthcoming.

483 K'o-hsüeh chi-shu tz'u-tien 科學技術辭典
(Dictionary of Science and Technology). Peking: Hsin-hua shu-tien 新華書店, 1960. 1,207p.

Covers some 15,000 terms arranged by the number of strokes. Each entry provides the Russian translation together with explanations in Chinese.

484 Chung-kuo k'o-hsüeh yüan, Tui-wai lien-lo chü, Fan-i shih 中國科學院對外連絡局翻譯室 (Chinese Academy of Sciences, Bureau of Foreign Liaison, Translation Office). *Han-Ying k'o-chi ch'ang-yung tz'u-hui* 漢英科技常用辭滙
(Chinese-English Dictionary of Commonly Used Scientific and Technical Terms). Peking: Shang-wu yin-shu kuan 商務印書館, 1961. 404p.

Contains an English index.

485 **Chien-ming k'o-chi tz'u-tien pien-chi wei-yüan hui** 簡明科技辭典編輯
委員會 (Editorial Committee of the Concise Scientific and Technological
Dictionary). *Chien-ming k'o-chi tz'u-tien* 簡明科技辭典
(Concise Scientific and Technological Dictionary). Shanghai: K'o-hsüeh chi-shu
ch'u-pan she 科學技術出版社, 1958. 2,050; 57p.

Approximately 10,000 entries, arranged by branch of science or industry
(physics, mathematics, mining, chemical engineering, etc.). Emphasis is placed
on terms relating primarily to industrial and agricultural production. Highly
specialized terms and those in common use are excluded. Stroke index.

486 **Zozulia, V. N. et al., comps.; Kolokolov, V. S., ed.** *Kitaisko-russkii slovar'
nauchnykh i tekhnicheskikh terminov*
(Chinese-Russian Dictionary of Scientific and Technical Terms). Moscow:
Institut nauchnoi informatsii Akademii Nauk SSSR, 1959. 568p.

Contains 32,000 terms in the fields of mathematics, physics, astronomy,
chemistry, geology, biology, meteorology, agriculture, etc., compiled at the
Institute of Scientific Information of the U.S.S.R. Academy of Sciences. Table
of abbreviated characters.

A critical review of this dictionary appeared in *Narody Azii i Afriki* (The
Peoples of Asia and Africa), 1961 No. 2, pp. 216–218.

487 **Evsiukov, Iu. M.** *O-Han tsung-ho k'o-chi tz'u-hui* 俄漢綜合科技辭滙
(A Comprehensive Russian-Chinese Dictionary of Science and Technology).
Peking: K'o-hsüeh ch'u-pan she 科學出版社, 1960. 1,303p.

Contains more than 70,000 scientific and technical terms with emphasis on
machine building, metallurgy, electrical engineering, chemistry, chemical
engineering, automobile industry, radio, agriculture, and mathematics.

488 **Chung-kuo k'o-hsüeh yüan, Tui-wai lien-lo chü, Fan-i shih** 中國科學院
對外連絡局翻譯室 (Chinese Academy of Sciences, Bureau of Foreign Liaison,
Translation Office). *Han-O k'o-chi ch'ang-yung tz'u-hui* 漢俄科技常用辭滙
(Chinese-Russian Dictionary of Commonly Used Scientific and Technical
Terms). Peking: Shang-wu yin-shu kuan 商務印書館, 1962. 538p.

Contains 14,000 words. A Russian index is appended.

489 **Pei-ching O-wen chuan-hsiu hsüeh-hsiao** 北京俄文專修學校 (Peking
Russian Language Institute). *O-Hua chi-shu tz'u-tien* 俄華技術辭典
(Russian-Chinese Technological Dictionary). Peking: Ch'ün-chung shu-tien
群衆書店, 1954. 1,074; 25p.

Covers approximately 30,000 terms, mostly in the fields of mathematics,
physics, chemistry, mechanical engineering, electrical engineering, and architecture.

490 **China (People's Republic of China, 1949—), Tien-li kung-yeh pu, Shang-hai chi-pen chien-she chü** 中華人民共和國 電力工業部 上海基本建設局 (China [People's Republic of China, 1949—], Ministry of Electric Power, Shanghai Basic Construction Bureau). *Chieh-Hua chi-shu tz'u-tien* 捷華技術辭典

(Czechoslovak-Chinese Dictionary of Technical Terms). Shanghai: K'o-hsüeh chi-shu ch'u-pan she 科學技術出版社, 1957. 506p.

A general dictionary of scientific and technical terms. Contains approximately 45,000 entries with emphasis on electrical and mechanical engineering, physics, chemistry, radio and mining.

2. PHYSICAL SCIENCES

a. Mathematics

491 **Chung-kuo k'o-hsüeh yüan, Pien-i ch'u-pan wei-yüan hui, Ming-tz'u shih** 中國科學院 編譯出版委員會 名詞室 (Chinese Academy of Sciences, Translation and Publication Committee, Terminology Office). *Shu-hsüeh ming-tz'u* 數學名詞 (Glossary of Mathematics). Peking: K'o-hsüeh ch'u-pan she 科學出版社, 1958. 26p.

Contains more than 9,000 terms. English-Chinese.

492 **Chung-kuo k'o-hsüeh yüan, Pien-i ch'u-pan wei-yüan hui, Ming-tz'u shih** 中國科學院 編譯出版委員會 名詞室 (Chinese Academy of Sciences, Translation and Publication Committee, Terminology Office). *O-Chung shu-hsüeh ming-tz'u* 俄中數學名詞 (Russian-Chinese Glossary of Mathematics). Peking: K'o-hsüeh ch'u-pan she 科學出版社, 1959. 58p.

Covers more than 3,000 terms. A new edition was published in July 1963.

b. Physics

493 **Chung-kuo k'o-hsüeh yüan, Pien-i chü** 中國科學院 編譯局 (Chinese Academy of Sciences, Compilation and Translation Bureau). *Wu-li hsüeh ming-tz'u* 物理學名詞 (Glossary of Physics). Shanghai: Shang-wu yin-shu kuan 商務印書館, 1953. 358p.

Includes more than 9,500 terms. Chinese-English and English-Chinese.

494 **Chung-kuo k'o-hsüeh yüan, Pien-i ch'u-pan wei-yüan hui, Ming-tz'u shih** 中國科學院 編譯出版委員會 名詞室 (Chinese Academy of Sciences, Translation and Publication Committee, Terminology Office). *O-Han wu-li hsüeh tz'u-hui* 俄漢物理學辭彙

(Russian-Chinese Glossary of Physics). Peking: K'o-hsüeh ch'u-pan she 科學出版社, 1959. 178p.

Contains 14,000 terms.

495 **Chung-kuo k'o-hsüeh yüan** 中國科學院 (Chinese Academy of Sciences). *Ying-Han yüan-tzu ho tz'u-tien* 英漢原子核辭典 (English-Chinese Nuclear Dictionary). Peking: Chung-kuo kung-yeh ch'u-pan she 中國工業出版社, 1963[?].

Based on the *English-Russian Nuclear Dictionary* compiled by David I. Voskoboinik (Moscow, 1960). Contains over 20,000 terms relating to nuclear science and engineering.

c. Chemistry

496 **Kao, Hsien** 高銛, **ed. and tr.** *Hua-hsüeh yao-p'in tz'u-tien* 化學藥品辭典 (Chemical Dictionary). Shanghai: K'o-hsüeh chi-shu ch'u-pan she 科學技術出版社, 1957. 2 vols. 843; 456p.

Volume 1 is a translation of *The Condensed Chemical Dictionary*, second edition, edited by Thomas C. Gregory (New York, 1930); Vol. 2 is translated from the fourth edition, edited by Arthur and Elizabeth Rose (New York, 1950). The arrangement is by the number of strokes, with an English alphabetical index. In the entry, English terms are given in parenthesis following the Chinese characters.

497 **Ch'en, Meng-hsien** 陳孟閑, **ed.** *Chi-pen hua-hsüeh shu-yü tz'u-tien* 基本化學術語辭典 *Dictionary of Basic Chemical Terms*. Shanghai: Ssu-lien ch'u-pan she 四聯出版社, 1954. 137p.

An English-Chinese dictionary of chemical terms containing approximately 840 items. Stroke index.

498 **Chu, Chi-hsüan** 朱積煊, **ed.** *Ying-yung hua-hsüeh tz'u-tien* 應用化學辭典 (Dictionary of Applied Chemistry). Hong Kong: Shang-wu yin-shu kuan 商務印書館, 1960. 972; 139p.

Contains approximately 6,800 terms, alphabetically arranged from English to Chinese, with a Chinese stroke index. A reprint of the 1954 Commercial Press edition published in Shanghai.

499 **Huang, Su-feng** 黃素封, **comp.** *O-Hua hua-hsüeh tz'u-hui* 俄華化學辭彙 (Russian-Chinese Glossary of Chemistry). Shanghai: Chung-wai shu-chü 中外書局, 1955. 1,211p.

Originally compiled by Kuo Ming-ta 郭明達, this revised edition contains roughly 28,000 chemical terms.

500 **Chung-kuo k'o-hsüeh yüan, Pien-i chü** 中國科學院 編譯局 (Chinese Academy of Sciences, Compilation and Translation Bureau). *O-Chung-Ying hua-hsüeh hua-kung shu-yü* 俄中英化學化工術語 (Russian-Chinese-English Chemical and Chemical Engineering Dictionary). Peking: Chung-kuo k'o-hsüeh yüan, 1955. 768p.

Contains 16,000 entries alphabetically arranged in Russian.
See also Yang, Pao-shang, et al., *English-Chinese Dictionary of Chemistry and Chemical Engineering* (Hong Kong: Practical Science Press, 1961), 1,458p.

501 **Wang, Ch'eng-ming** 王承明, **comp.** *O-Hua Ying hua-kung shu-yü hui-pien* 俄華英化工術語彙編 (Russian-Chinese-English Glossary of Chemical Engineering). Shanghai: Chung-kuo k'o-hsüeh t'u-shu i-ch'i kung-ssu 中國科學圖書儀器公司, 1954. 279p.

More than 8,600 entries, including many general chemical terms.

502 **Chung-kuo k'o-hsüeh yüan, Pien-i ch'u-pan wei-yüan hui, Ming-tz'u shih** 中國科學院 編譯出版委員會 名詞室 (Chinese Academy of Sciences, Translation and Publication Committee, Terminology Office). *O-Chung-Ying wu-chi hua-ho-wu ming-tz'u* 俄中英無機化合物名詞 (Russian-Chinese-English Glossary of Inorganic Compounds). Peking: K'o-hsüeh ch'u-pan she 科學出版社, 1957. 120p.

Contains almost 2,000 terms in inorganic chemistry. Index to Chinese and English terms.

503 **Chung-kuo k'o-hsüeh yüan, Pien-i ch'u-pan wei-yüan hui, Ming-tz'u shih** 中國科學院 編譯出版委員會 名詞室 (Chinese Academy of Sciences, Translation and Publication Committee, Terminology Office). *O-Chung-Ying yu-chi jan-liao ming-tz'u* 俄中英有機染料名詞 (Russian-Chinese-English Glossary of Dyestuffs). Peking: K'o-hsüeh ch'u-pan she 科學出版社, 1956. 233p.

Includes 510 terms (each accompanied by a chemical formula) and Russian-Chinese and English-Chinese indexes.

3. EARTH SCIENCES

a. Geography

504 **Chung-kuo k'o-hsüeh yüan, Pien-i ch'u-pan wei-yüan hui, Ming-tz'u shih** 中國科學院 編譯出版委員會 名詞室 (Chinese Academy of Sciences, Translation and Publication Committee, Terminology Office). *Tzu-jan ti-li ming-tz'u: ti-hsing chih pu* 自然地理名詞: 地形之部

(Glossary of Natural Geography: Part on Topography). Peking: K'o-hsüeh ch'u-pan she 科學出版社, 1958. 61p.

Contains more than 2,000 terms. Chinese-English and English-Chinese. A handbook of common foreign geographical names in Chinese, Russian and English (漢俄英對照常用外國地名參考資料 *Han-O-Ying tui-chao ch'ang-yung wai-kuo ti-ming ts'an-k'ao tzu-liao*) was published by Ti-t'u ch'u-pan she 地圖出版社 in 1959 (167p.)

b. Geology

505 Chung-kuo k'o-hsüeh yüan, Pien-i ch'u-pan wei-yüan hui, Ming-tz'u shih
中國科學院 編譯出版委員會 名詞室 (Chinese Academy of Sciences, Translation and Publication Committee, Terminology Office). *Tsung-ho ti-chih ming-tz'u* 綜合地質名詞
(Comprehensive Glossary of Geology). Peking: K'o-hsüeh ch'u-pan she 科學出版社, 1957. 244p.

Includes more than 16,000 terms. English-Chinese and Chinese-English.

506 Chung-kuo k'o-hsüeh yüan, Pien-i ch'u-pan wei-yüan hui, Ming-tz'u shih
中國科學院 編譯出版委員會 名詞室 (Chinese Academy of Sciences, Translation and Publication Committee, Terminology Office). *Shui-wen ti-chih hsüeh chi kung-ch'eng ti-chih hsüeh ming-tz'u* 水文地質學及工程地質學名詞
(Glossary of Hydro-Geology and Engineering Geology). Peking: K'o-hsüeh ch'u-pan she 科學出版社, 1957. 57p.

A preliminary Russian-Chinese and Chinese-Russian edition containing more than 3,500 terms.

507 Bradley, J. E. S. and Barnes, A. C., comps.
Chinese-English Glossary of Mineral Names. New York: Consultants Bureau, 1963. 132p.

Contains approximately 2,000 Chinese mineral names and the word elements of which they are composed with their English equivalents. The English index makes it also an English-Chinese glossary of mineral names.

508 Chung-kuo k'o-hsüeh yüan, Pien-i ch'u-pan wei-yüan hui, Ming-tz'u shih
中國科學院 編譯出版委員會 名詞室 (Chinese Academy of Sciences, Translation and Publication Committee, Terminology Office). *K'uang-wu hsüeh ming-tz'u* 礦物學名詞
(Glossary of Mineralogy). Peking: K'o-hsüeh ch'u-pan she 科學出版社, 1957. 279p.

A preliminary Russian-English-Chinese edition containing more than 8,800 terms.

509 **Chung-kuo k'o-hsüeh yüan, Pien-i ch'u-pan wei-yüan hui, Ming-tz'u shih**
中國科學院 編譯出版委員會 名詞室 (Chinese Academy of Sciences, Translation
and Publication Committee, Terminology Office). *Yen-shih hsüeh ming-tz'u*
岩石學名詞
(Glossary of Petrology). Peking: K'o-hsüeh ch'u-pan she 科學出版社, 1956.
352p.

A Chinese-Russian and Russian-Chinese edition containing more than 4,500
terms with an index from German, English and French to Chinese and Russian.

510 **Shih-yu kung-yeh ch'u-pan she** 石油工業出版社 (Petroleum Industry
Publishing House). *O-Han shih-yu tz'u-tien* 俄漢石油辭典
(Russian-Chinese Dictionary of Petroleum Engineering). Peking: Shih-yu
kung-yeh ch'u-pan she, 1958. 436p.

Covers approximately 30,000 terms.

511 **Chung-kuo k'o-hsüeh yüan, Pien-i ch'u-pan wei-yüan hui, Ming-tz'u shih**
中國科學院 編譯出版委員會 名詞室 (Chinese Academy of Sciences, Translation
and Publication Committee, Terminology Office). *T'u-jang hsüeh ming-tz'u*
土壤學名詞
(Glossary of Pedology). Revised edition. Peking: K'o-hsüeh ch'u-pan she
科學出版社, 1957. 66p.

A preliminary Russian-Chinese edition, covering more than 4,000 terms.
A revised edition of the 1955 imprint.

512 **Chung-kuo k'o-hsüeh yüan, Pien-i ch'u-pan wei-yüan hui, Ming-tz'u shih**
中國科學院 編譯出版委員會 名詞室 (Chinese Academy of Sciences, Translation
and Publication Committee, Terminology Office). *T'u-chih hsüeh chi t'u-li hsüeh
ming-tz'u* 土質學及土力學名詞
(Glossary of Soil Classification and Soil Mechanics). Peking: K'o-hsüeh ch'u-
pan she 科學出版社, 1957. 26p.

A preliminary edition of some 1,000 terms. Chinese-Russian and Russian-
Chinese.

513 **Chung-kuo k'o-hsüeh yüan, Pien-i ch'u-pan wei-yüan hui, Ming-tz'u shih**
中國科學院 編譯出版委員會 名詞室 (Chinese Academy of Sciences, Translation
and Publication Committee, Terminology Office). *Ying-O-Chung ku sheng-wu
hsüeh ming-tz'u* 英俄中古生物學名詞
(English-Russian-Chinese Glossary of Paleontology). Peking: K'o-hsüeh ch'u-
pan she 科學出版社, 1956. 200p.

Covers more than 2,100 terms. Also in Chinese-English-Russian.

c. Meteorology

514 **Chung-kuo k'o-hsüeh yüan, Pien-i ch'u-pan wei-yüan hui, Ming-tz'u shih**
中國科學院 編譯出版委員會 名詞室 (Chinese Academy of Sciences, Translation
and Publication Committee, Terminology Office). *Ch'i-hsiang hsüeh ming-tz'u*
氣象學名詞
(Glossary of Meteorology). Peking: K'o-hsüeh ch'u-pan she 科學出版社,
1958. 408p.

Covers more than 8,300 terms. A preliminary Russian-English-Chinese
edition.

4. BIOLOGICAL SCIENCES

a. Biology

515 **Shih, Hu** 施溚, **ed.** *O-Hua sheng-wu tz'u-tien* 俄華生物辭典
(Russian-Chinese Dictionary of Biology). Peking: Ch'ün-chung shu-tien
群衆書店, 1954. 656p.

Contains about 20,000 terms.

516 **Chung-kuo k'o-hsüeh yüan, Pien-i chü** 中國科學院 編譯局 (Chinese
Academy of Sciences, Compilation and Translation Bureau). *Hsi-pao hsüeh
ming-tz'u* 細胞學名詞
(Glossary of Cytology). Shanghai: Shang-wu yin-shu kuan 商務印書館, 1953.
43p.

Contains more than 600 terms. Chinese-English and English-Chinese.

517 **Nishi, Takeo** 西武男. *Suisan dōshokubutsu mei Kan-Wa jiten* 水產動植物名
漢和辭典
(Chinese-Japanese Dictionary of Marine Fauna and Flora). Tokyo: Nōrin
Kyōkai 農林協會, 1958. 492p.

Published by the Agriculture and Forestry Association, a semi-governmental
organization affiliated with the Japanese Ministry of Agriculture and Forestry.

b. Botany

518 **Ting, Kuang-ch'i** 丁廣奇. *Chih-wu chung-ming shih* 植物種名釋
(A Glossary of Botanical Terms). Peking: K'o-hsüeh ch'u-pan she 科學出版社,
1957. 114p.

Covers more than 9,000 terms. Based primarily on G. F. Zimmer's *A Popular
Dictionary of Botanical Names and Terms* and L. H. Bailey's *How Plants Get
Their Names*. Latin-Chinese.

519 **Chung-kuo k'o-hsüeh yüan, Pien-i ch'u-pan wei-yüan hui, Ming-tz'u shih**
中國科學院 編譯出版委員會 名詞室 (Chinese Academy of Sciences, Translation and Publication Committee, Terminology Office). *Ying-Chung chih-wu hsüeh ming-tz'u hui-pien* 英中植物學名詞彙編
(English-Chinese Glossary of Botanical Terms). Peking: K'o-hsüeh ch'u-pan she 科學出版社, 1958. 152p.

    A glossary covering more than 10,000 terms, including a list of the principal diseases affecting Chinese economic plant life.

    A Russian-Chinese dictionary of botanical terms (俄漢植物學詞滙 *O-Han chih-wu hsüeh tz'u-hui*) was published by the Chinese Academy of Sciences in 1960 (317p.).

520 **Chung-kuo k'o-hsüeh yüan, Pien-i ch'u-pan wei-yüan hui, Ming-tz'u shih**
中國科學院 編譯出版委員會 名詞室 (Chinese Academy of Sciences, Translation and Publication Committee, Terminology Office). *O-Ying-Chung chih-wu ti-li hsüeh, chih-wu sheng-t'ai hsüeh, ti chih-wu hsüeh ming-tz'u* 俄英中植物地理學, 植物生態學, 地植物學名詞
(Russian-English-Chinese Glossary of Plant Geography, Plant Ecology, and Geobotany). Peking: K'o-hsüeh ch'u-pan she 科學出版社, 1956. 258p.

    Includes more than 2,200 terms and a Chinese-English-Russian index.

521 **Chung-kuo k'o-hsüeh yüan, Chih-wu yen-chiu so, Pei-ching chih-wu yüan** 中國科學院 植物研究所 北京植物園 (Chinese Academy of Sciences, Institute of Botany, Peking Botanical Garden). *Tsai-p'ei chih-wu ming-lu* 栽培植物名錄
(List of Cultivated Plants). Peking: Hsin-hua shu-tien 新華書店, 1959. 560p.

    Includes about 3,000 plants cultivated at the Peking Botanical Garden. Indexes in Chinese and Latin. Chinese index by stroke count.

522 **Hou, K'uan-chao** 侯寬昭, **ed.** *Chung-kuo chung-tzu chih-wu k'o-shu tz'u-tien* 中國種子植物科屬辭典
(A Dictionary of Chinese Seed-Plant Species). Peking: K'o-hsüeh ch'u-pan she 科學出社版, 1958, 553p.

    A Latin-Chinese dictionary covering approximately 23,042 species of 2,614 genera of 260 families. Includes a Chinese-Latin list of names.

523 **Chung-kuo k'o-hsüeh yüan, Pien-i ch'u-pan wei-yüan hui, Ming-tz'u shih**
中國科學院 編譯出版委員會 名詞室 (Chinese Academy of Sciences, Translation and Publication Committee, Terminology Office). *Chung-tzu chih-wu ming-ch'eng* 種子植物名稱
(Glossary of Seed-Plant Names). Peking: Chung-kuo k'o-hsüeh yüan, 1954. 160p.

    Covers more than 2,300 terms. Chinese-Latin and Latin-Chinese.

524 **Chung-kuo k'o-hsüeh yüan, Pien-i chü** 中國科學院 編譯局 (Chinese Academy of Sciences, Compilation and Translation Bureau). *Chung-tzu chih-wu hsing-t'ai hsüeh ming-tz'u* 種子植物形態學名詞
(Glossary of Seed-Plant Morphology), Shanghai: Shang-wu yin-shu kuan 商務印書館, 1953. 126p.

Contains more than 2,200 terms. Chinese-English-Latin and English-Latin-Chinese.

525 **Chung-kuo k'o-hsüeh yüan, Pien-i ch'u-pan wei-yüan hui, Ming-tz'u shih** 中國科學院 編譯出版委員會 名詞室 (Chinese Academy of Sciences, Translation and Publication Committee, Terminology Office). *O-Ying-Chung chung-tzu chih-wu wai-pu hsing-t'ai hsüeh ming-tz'u* 俄英中種子植物外部形態學名詞
(Russian-English-Chinese Glossary of Seed-Plant Morphology). Peking: K'o-hsüeh ch'u-pan she 科學出版社, 1957. 113p.

Includes about 2,800 terms.

526 **Chung-kuo k'o-hsüeh yüan, Pien-i chü** 中國科學院 編譯局 (Chinese Academy of Sciences, Compilation and Translation Bureau). *Pao-tzu chih-wu ming-ch'eng* 孢子植物名稱
(Glossary of Spore-Plant Names). Peking: Chung-kuo k'o-hsüeh yüan, 1955. 163p.

Covers more than 1,600 terms in Chinese-Latin and Latin-Chinese. (For a supplement to this glossary, see next entry.)

527 **Chung-kuo k'o-hsüeh yüan, Pien-i ch'u-pan wei-yüan hui, Ming-tz'u shih** 中國科學院 編譯出版委員會 名詞室 (Chinese Academy of Sciences, Translation and Publication Committee, Terminology Office). *La-Han pao-tzu chih-wu ming-ch'eng (pu pien)* 拉漢孢子植物名稱 (補編)
(Latin-Chinese Glossary of Spore-Plant Names [Supplement]). Peking: K'o-hsüeh ch'u-pan she 科學出版社, 1959. 165p.

Contains approximately 6,600 terms.

528 **P'ei, Chien** 裴鑑 **and Chou, T'ai-yen** 周太炎 *Chung-kuo yao-yung chih-wu chih* 中國藥用植物誌
(Icons of Chinese Medicinal Plants). Peking: K'o-hsüeh ch'u-pan she 科學出版社, 1951–1957. 5 vols.

Edited by the Institute of Botany of the Chinese Academy of Sciences, this publication contains illustrations and detailed biological, economic and chemical studies of 250 plants (fifty plants in each volume). Volume 2 has a two-page summary in English giving the Latin name, romanized Chinese name, and the uses of each plant described in the volume. The other volumes do not have English summaries.

529 **Chung-kuo k'o-hsüeh yüan, Pien-i ch'u-pan wei-yüan hui, Ming-tz'u shih** 中國科學院 編譯出版委員會 名詞室 (Chinese Academy of Sciences, Translation and Publication Committee, Terminology Office). *Ying-Chung chih-wu ping-li hsüeh ming-tz'u* 英中植物病理學名詞 (English-Chinese Glossary of Plant Pathology). Revised edition. Peking: K'o-hsüeh ch'u-pan she 科學出版社, 1959. 101p.

Covers more than 3,000 terms and includes a list of names of pathogens and plant diseases.

530 **Chung-kuo k'o-hsüeh yüan, Pien-i ch'u-pan wei-yüan hui, Ming-tz'u shih** 中國科學院 編譯出版委員會 名詞室 (Chinese Academy of Sciences, Translation and Publication Committee, Terminology Office). *Ying-Han yüan-i hsüeh ming-tz'u* 英漢園藝學名詞 (English-Chinese Glossary of Horticulture). Peking: K'o-hsüeh ch'u-pan she 科學出版社, 1959. 47p.

Covers more than 3,000 terms.

531 **Chung-kuo k'o-hsüeh yüan, Pien-i ch'u-pan wei-yüan hui, Ming-tz'u shih** 中國科學院 編譯出版委員會 名詞室 (Chinese Academy of Sciences, Translation and Publication Committee, Terminology Office). *Yüan-i hsüeh ming-tz'u* 園藝學名詞 (Glossary of Horticulture). Peking: K'o-hsüeh ch'u-pan she 科學出版社, 1958. 47p.

A preliminary Russian-Chinese edition covering more than 2,000 terms and including a Latin-Russian-Chinese list of common plants, principal diseases and insect pests.

532 **Chung-kuo k'o-hsüeh yüan, Pien-i chü** 中國科學院 編譯局 (Chinese Academy of Sciences, Compilation and Translation Bureau). *Chih-wu chieh-p'ou hsüeh ming-tz'u* 植物解剖學名詞 (Glossary of Plant Anatomy). Shanghai: Shang-wu yin-shu kuan 商務印書館, 1953. 42p.

Contains more than 500 terms. Chinese-English and English-Chinese.

533 **Chung-kuo k'o-hsüeh yüan, Pien-i chü** 中國科學院 編譯局 (Chinese Academy of Sciences, Compilation and Translation Bureau). *Chih-wu sheng-t'ai hsüeh ming-tz'u* 植物生態學名詞

(Glossary of Plant Ecology). Shanghai: Shang-wu yin-shu kuan 商務印書館, 1953. 36p.

Covers roughly a thousand terms. Chinese-English and English-Chinese.

c. Zoology

534 **Chung-kuo k'o-hsüeh yüan, Pien-i chü** 中國科學院 編譯局 (Chinese Academy of Sciences, Compilation and Translation Bureau). *Chi-ch'ui tung-wu chieh-p'ou hsüeh ming-tz'u* 脊椎動物解剖學名詞 (Glossary of Vertebrate Anatomy). Peking: Chung-kuo k'o-hsüeh yüan, 1954. 156p.

Contains more than 5,000 terms. Chinese-Latin and Latin-Chinese.

An English-Chinese dictionary of zoological terms (英漢動物學詞滙 *Ying-Han tung-wu hsüeh tz'u-hui*) was published by the Chinese Academy of Sciences in 1962 (477p.).

535 **Chung-kuo k'o-hsüeh yüan, Pien-i ch'u-pan wei-yüan hui, Ming-tz'u shih** 中國科學院 編譯出版委員會 名詞室 (Chinese Academy of Sciences, Translation and Publication Committee, Terminology Office). *O-La-Chung chia-hsü chieh-p'ou hsüeh ming-tz'u* 俄拉中家畜解剖學名詞 (Russian-Latin-Chinese Glossary of Anatomical Terms for Domestic Animals). Peking: K'o-hsüeh ch'u-pan she 科學出版社, 1957. 216p.

Contains more than 4,700 terms.

536 **Chung-kuo k'o-hsüeh yüan, Pien-i chü** 中國科學院 編譯局 (Chinese Academy of Sciences, Compilation and Translation Bureau). *Tung-wu tsu-chih hsüeh ming-tz'u* 動物組織學名詞 (Glossary of Animal Histology). Peking: Chung-kuo k'o-hsüeh yüan, 1955. 74p.

Contains more than 2,800 terms. Chinese-English and English-Chinese.

537 **Chung-kuo k'o-hsüeh yüan, Pien-i ch'u-pan wei-yüan hui, Ming-tz'u shih** 中國科學院 編譯出版委員會 名詞室 (Chinese Academy of Sciences, Translation and Publication Committee, Terminology Office). *O-Chung tung-wu tsu-chih hsüeh ming-tz'u* 俄中動物組織學名詞 (Russian-Chinese Glossary of Animal Histology). Peking: K'o-hsüeh ch'u-pan she 科學出版社, 1957. 49p.

Covers more than 3,600 terms.

5. AGRICULTURE AND FORESTRY

538 **Chung-kuo k'o-hsüeh yüan, Pien-i ch'u-pan wei-yüan hui, Ming-tz'u shih** 中國科學院 編譯出版委員會 名詞室 (Chinese Academy of Sciences,

Translation and Publication Committee, Terminology Office). *Ying-Han nung-hsüeh ming-tz'u* 英漢農學名詞
(English-Chinese Glossary of Agriculture). Peking: K'o-hsüeh ch'u-pan she 科學出版社, 1959. 21p.

Contains more than 1,300 terms, mostly non-technical.

539 **Tung-pei nung-hsüeh yüan** 東北農學院 (Northeast Agricultural College). *O-Hua nung-yeh tz'u-tien* 俄華農業辭典
(Russian-Chinese Dictionary of Agriculture). Peking: Nung-yeh ch'u-pan she 農業出版社, 1958. 563p.

Contains about 40,000 entries.
A Russian-Chinese dictionary of mechanized and electrified agriculture (俄漢農業機械化電氣化辭典 *O-Han nung-yeh chi-hsieh hua tien-ch'i hua tz'u-tien*) compiled by the Peking Institute of Mechanized Agriculture (北京農業機械化學院) was published in March 1963.

540 **China (People's Republic of China, 1949—), Lin-yeh pu, Wai-shih ch'u** 中華人民共和國 林業部 外事處 (China [People's Republic of China, 1949—], Ministry of Forestry, Foreign Affairs Department). *O-Hua lin-yeh tz'u-tien* 俄華林業辭典
(Russian-Chinese Dictionary of Forestry). Peking: Chung-kuo lin-yeh ch'u-pan she 中國林業出版社, 1959. 727p.

Covers more than 35,000 terms, including all those contained in the *Lin-yeh ming-tz'u* 林業名詞 (Glossary of Forestry) published by the Chinese Academy of Sciences in 1954. Appended is a list of names of shrubs and trees in Chinese-Russian-Latin.

6. MEDICINE, PHARMACOLOGY AND PUBLIC HEALTH

541 **Jen-min wei-sheng ch'u-pan she** 人民衛生出版社 (People's Hygiene Press). *I-hsüeh ming-tz'u hui-pien* 醫學名詞彙編
(A Dictionary of Medical Terms). Peking: Jen-min wei-sheng ch'u-pan she, 1958. 761p.

An English-Chinese medical dictionary, incorporating all glossaries published since 1949, and encompassing more than 35,000 terms. A new edition was published in June 1963.

542 **Ho, Huai-te** 何懷德, **and T'ien, Li-chih** 田立志, **eds.** *O-Ying-Chung i-hsüeh tz'u-hui* 俄英中醫學辭彙
(Russian-English-Chinese Glossary of Medical Terms). Peking: Jen-min wei-sheng ch'u-pan she 人民衛生出版社, 1954. 714p.

Contains about 15,000 terms.

543 **China (People's Republic of China, 1949—), Wei-sheng pu, Wei-sheng chiao-ts'ai pien-shen wei-yüan hui** 中華人民共和國 衛生部 衛生教材編審委員會 (China [People's Republic of China, 1949—], Ministry of Health, Committee on Public Health Education Material). *Kung-kung wei-sheng hsüeh ming-tz'u* 公共衛生學名詞
(Glossary of Public Health). Peking: Jen-min wei-sheng ch'u-pan she 人民衛生出版社, 1956. 95p.

Consists of two sections: Russian-Chinese-English and English-Chinese. The first covers more than 3,000 terms; the second about 1,800.

544 **Chung-kuo k'o-hsüeh yüan, Pien-i ch'u-pan wei-yüan hui, Ming-tz'u shih** 中國科學院 編譯出版委員會 名詞室 (Chinese Academy of Sciences, Translation and Publication Committee, Terminology Office). *Ying-Han wei-sheng-wu ming-tz'u* 英漢微生物名詞
(English-Chinese Glossary of Microbiology). Peking: K'o-hsüeh ch'u-pan she 科學出版社, 1959. 92p.

Contains more than 5,000 terms.

545 **Lu, Te-hsing** 魯德馨, **ed.** *Ying-Chung i-hsüeh tz'u-hui* 英中醫學辭彙
An English-Chinese Medical Lexicon. Peking: Jen-min wei-sheng ch'u-pan she 人民衛生出版社, 1955. 610p.

Contains approximately 50,000 medical terms.

546 **Chung-kuo k'o-hsüeh yüan, Pien-i ch'u-pan wei-yüan hui, Ming-tz'u shih** 中國科學院 編譯出版委員會 名詞室 (Chinese Academy of Sciences, Translation and Publication Committee, Terminology Office). *Wei-sheng-wu ming-ch'eng* 微生物名稱
(A Glossary of Microbiology). Peking: K'o-hsüeh ch'u-pan she 科學出版社, 1958. 170p.

A Latin-Chinese list of more than 4,000 terms.

547 **Chung-kuo k'o-hsüeh yüan, Pien-i chü** 中國科學院 編譯局 (Chinese Academy of Sciences, Compilation and Translation Bureau). *P'ei-t'ai hsüeh ming-tz'u* 胚胎學名詞
(Glossary of Embryological Terms). Peking: Chung-kuo k'o-hsüeh yüan, 1954. 62p.

Covers about 2,100 terms. Chinese-English and English-Chinese.

548 **Shih-chieh shu-chü** 世界書局 (World Book Company). *Chung-kuo yao-hsüeh ta tz'u-tien* 中國藥學大辭典
(A Chinese Pharmacopoeia). Peking: Jen-min wei-sheng ch'u-pan she 人民衛生出版社, 1956. 2 vols., 1,986p.

An illustrated encyclopedia. English, Latin, and Japanese names of medicinal plants and herbs are given when available. Arranged by the number of strokes.

The Encyclopedia of Chinese Medicine (中國醫學大辭典 Chung-kuo i-hsüeh ta tz'u-tien) by Hsieh Kuan 謝觀 (first edition in July 1921) was republished by Shang-wu ch'u-pan she 商務出版社 in April, 1963; 4 vols.

7. TECHNOLOGY

Some of the glossaries listed in the preceding sections also contain technological terms such as those used in petroleum engineering (in the geology section), the chemical industry (in the chemistry section), etc.

549 T'ang, Hsin-yü 湯心豫, ed. *Chi-kung tz'u-tien* 機工詞典
(Dictionary of Mechanical Engineering). Shanghai: K'o-chi wei-sheng ch'u-pan she 科技衛生出版社, 1958. 268; 49p.

A general dictionary of some 3,000 mechanical engineering terms in Chinese for the use of mechanics. Includes a Chinese index arranged by stroke count and alphabetical indexes in English and Russian.

550 Liu, Ting-yüeh 劉鼎嶽 ed. *Chi-hsieh yung-yü hsin tzu-tien* 機械用語新字典
(New Technical Dictionary of Mechanical Terms). Taipei: Tung-fang ch'u-pan she 東方出版社, 1960. 250p.

Contains more than 4,500 terms. English-Chinese-Japanese. Japanese index only.

551 Chiang, Ts'ung-chi 蔣聰吉, ed. *O-Hua-Ying tien-kung tz'u-hui* 俄華英電工辭滙
(Russian-Chinese-English Dictionary of Electrical Engineering). Shanghai: K'o-hsüeh chi-shu ch'u-pan she 科學技術出版社, 1957. 437p.

Contains approximately 12,000 terms.

A new English-Chinese dictionary of electrical engineering (最新英華電工辭典 *Tsui-hsin Ying-Hua tien-kung tz'u-tien*) edited by Chang Hsüeh-kung 張學工 was published in April 1962.

The Chinese Academy of Sciences is engaged in the compilation of a polyglot dictionary of electrical engineering (國際電工辭典 *Kuo-chi tien-kung tz'u-tien*) in Chinese, Russian, English, French, German, Spanish, Italian, Dutch, Polish and Swedish. The dictionary is published serially, and the sixteenth instalment containing 187 terms appeared in May 1963.

552 China (People's Republic of China, 1949—), Yu-tien pu, Tien-hsin chi-shu yen-chiu so 中華人民共和國郵電部電信技術研究所 (China [People's Republic of China, 1949—], Ministry of Posts and Tele-Communications, Institute of Telecommunications). *O-Hua-Ying wu-hsien-tien tz'u-tien* 俄華英無線電辭典 (Russian-Chinese-English Dictionary of Radio Communication). Peking: Hsin-hua shu-tien 新華書店, 1954. 598p.

Covers approximately 13,000 terms, including a list of technical abbreviations.

553 China (People's Republic of China, 1949—), Yu-tien pu, Pien-i shih 中華人民共和國 郵電部 編譯室 (China [People's Republic of China, 1949—], Ministry of Posts and Telecommunications, Bureau of Translation and Compilation). *O-Hua tien-hsin tz'u-tien* 俄華電信辭典 (Russian-Chinese Dictionary of Telecommunications). Peking: Hsin-hua shu-tien 新華書店, 1955. 522p.

Contains some 32,000 terms and a list of technical abbreviations.
An English-Chinese Telecommunications Dictionary (英漢電信辭典 *Ying-Han tien-hsin tz'u-tien*) was published in 1962 (721 p.).

554 O-Han hang-k'ung kung-ch'eng tz'u-tien pien-chi wei-yüan hui 俄漢航空工程辭典編輯委員會 (Compilation Committee of a Russian-Chinese Dictionary of Aeronautical Engineering). *O-Han hang-k'ung kung-ch'eng tz'u-tien* 俄漢航空工程辭典 (Russian-Chinese Dictionary of Aeronautical Engineering). Peking: Kuo-fang kung-yeh ch'u-pan she 國防工業出版社, 1957. 728p.

Approximately 40,000 terms.
A Russian-Chinese dictionary of aeronautical terms (俄漢航空綜合辭典 *O-Han hang-k'ung tsung-ho tz'u-tien*) was published in 1962.

555 Shanghai, Shih-cheng kung-ch'eng chü, O-wen hsüeh-hsi wei-yüan hui 上海市 市政工程局 俄文學習委員會 (Shanghai, Office of the City Engineer, Russian Study Committee). *O-Hua tu-mu kung-ch'eng tz'u-tien* 俄華土木工程辭典 (Russian-Chinese Dictionary of Civil Engineering). Shanghai: Lung-men lien-ho shu-chü 龍門聯合書局, 1957. 420p.

Contains about 33,000 terms.

556 Chung-kuo k'o-hsüeh yüan, Pien-i ch'u-pan wei-yüan hui, Ming-tz'u shih 中國科學院 編譯出版委員會 名詞室 (Chinese Academy of Sciences, Translation and Publication Committee, Terminology Office). *Ying-Han chien-chu kung-ch'eng ming-tz'u* 英漢建築工程名詞 (English-Chinese Glossary of Architectural Engineering). Peking: K'o-hsüeh ch'u-pan she 科學出版社, 1959. 251p.

Covers approximately 17,000 terms.

557 **Chien-chu kung-ch'eng ch'u-pan she** 建築工程出版社 (Architectural Engineering Publishing House). *O-Han chien-chu kung-ch'eng tz'u-tien* 俄漢建築工程辭典 (Russian-Chinese Dictionary of Architectural Engineering). Peking: Hsin-hua shu-tien 新華書店, 1959. 753p.

Contains about 45,000 terms.

558 **Chung-kuo k'o-hsüeh yüan, Pien-i ch'u-pan wei-yüan hui, Ming-tz'u shih** 中國科學院 編譯出版委員會 名詞室 (Chinese Academy of Sciences, Translation and Publication Committee, Office of Terminology). *Chi-shui p'ai-shui kung-nuan t'ung-feng kung-ch'eng ming-tz'u* 給水排水供暖通風工程名詞 (Glossary of Plumbing, Heating and Ventilation). Peking: K'o-hsüeh ch'u-pan she 科學出版社, 1957. 154p.

About 3,700 terms. Russian-English-Chinese. Basic terms in the fields of physics and chemistry are generally omitted.

559 **Hu, Ming-ch'eng** 胡明城, **et al., eds.** *O-Hua chien-ming ts'e-hui tz'u-tien* 俄華簡明測繪辭典 (Russian-Chinese Concise Dictionary of Surveying). Peking: Hsin-hua shu-tien 新華店書, 1954. 467p.

Covers about 10,000 terms. The appendix provides a list of abbreviations and symbols.

560 **Chung-kuo k'o-hsüeh yüan, Pien-i ch'u-pan wei-yüan hui, Ming-tz'u shih** 中國科學院 編譯出版委員會 名詞室 (Chinese Academy of Sciences, Translation and Publication Committee, Terminology Office). *Ts'e-liang hsüeh ming-tz'u* 測量學名詞 (Glossary of Surveying). Peking: K'o-hsüeh ch'u-pan she 科學出版社, 1956. 206p.

Includes more than 4,200 terms. Chinese-English-German and English-German-Chinese.

561 **Chung-kuo k'o-hsüeh yüan, Pien-i ch'u-pan wei-yüan hui, Ming-tz'u shih** 中國科學院 編譯出版委員會 名詞室 (Chinese Academy of Sciences, Translation and Publication Committee, Terminology Office). *T'ieh-tao yü kung-lu ming-tz'u* 鐵道與公路名詞 (Glossary of Railway and Road Engineering). Peking: K'o-hsüeh ch'u-pan she 科學出版社, 1956. 11; 218p.

Contains more than 8,700 terms. In two parts: Chinese-English and English-Chinese.

A Russian-Chinese dictionary of road engineering (俄華公路工程辭典 *O-Hua kung-lu kung-ch'eng tz'u-tien*) was published in 1959 (534p.).

562 **China (People's Republic of China, 1949—), T'ieh-tao pu, Kuo-chi lien-yün chü, Fan-i ch'u** 中華人民共和國 鐵道部 國際聯運局 翻譯處 (China [People's Republic of China, 1949—], Ministry of Railways, Bureau of International Freight, Translation Section). *O-Hua t'ieh-lu tz'u-tien* 俄華鐵路辭典 (Russian-Chinese Dictionary of Railroad Terms). Peking: Hsin-hua shu-tien 新華書店, 1959. 885p.

Contains more than 57,000 terms.

563 **China (People's Republic of China, 1949—), T'ieh-tao pu, Chuan-chia kung-tso shih** 中華人民共和國 鐵道部 專家工作室 (China [People's Republic of China, 1949—], Ministry of Railways, Office of Specialists). *O-Hua t'ieh-lu chuan-yeh ch'ang-yung tz'u-hui* 俄華鐵路專業常用辭彙 (Russian-Chinese Dictionary of Railroad Terms). Peking: Wu-shih nien-tai ch'u-pan she 五十年代出版社, 1955. 322p.

Covers approximately 9,000 terms.

564 **O-Han k'uang-yeh chi-shu tz'u-tien pien-shen wei-yüan hui** 俄漢鑛業技術辭典編審委員會 (Compilation Committee of a Russian-Chinese Dictionary of Mining Engineering). *O-Han k'uang-yeh chi-shu tz'u-tien* 俄漢礦業技術辭典 (Russian-Chinese Dictionary of Mining Engineering). Peking: Mei-t'an kung-yeh ch'u-pan she 煤炭工業出版社, 1958. 556p.

Roughly 34,500 terms.

565 **Chung-kuo k'o-hsüeh yüan, Pien-i chü** 中國科學院 編譯局 (Chinese Academy of Sciences, Compilation and Translation Bureau). *Yeh-chin hsüeh ming-tz'u* 冶金學名詞 (Glossary of Metallurgy). Peking: Chung-kuo k'o-hsüeh yüan, 1955. 524p.

About 8,000 terms. Chinese-English-Russian.

566 **China (People's Republic of China, 1949—), Chung kung-yeh pu, Hei-se yeh-chin she-chi yüan** 中華人民共和國 重工業部 黑色冶金設計院 (China [People's Republic of China, 1949—], Ministry of Heavy Industry, Ferrous Metal Institute). *O-Hua hei-se yeh-chin kung-yeh tz'u-tien* 俄華黑色冶金工業辭典 (Russian-Chinese Dictionary of Ferrous Metallurgy). Peking: Hsin-hua shu-tien 新華書店, 1955. 1,030p.

About 40,000 terms, mostly concerning production, construction and design. A list of abbreviations of technical terms.

567 **China (People's Republic of China, 1949—), Fang-chih kung-yeh pu, Yen-chiu shih, Fan-i k'o** 中華人民共和國 紡織工業部 研究室 翻譯科 (China [People's Republic of China, 1949—], Ministry of Textile Industry, Office of Research, Translation Section). *O-Hua fang-chih tz'u-tien* 俄華紡織辭典 (Russian-Chinese Dictionary of Textile Terms). Peking: Chung-hua t'u-shu fa-hsing kung-ssu 中華圖書發行公司, 1953. 381p.

Contains about 7,500 terms.

PART THREE

SELECTED DOCUMENTARY MATERIALS

It is impossible to bring within the confines of a single part such as this all of the available documentary sources encompassing the political, economic and social life of post-1949 Mainland China and Taiwan. As the title of this Part indicates, the contents of the six chapters that follow are to be taken only as a sample of the most important or more representative documentation on Mainland China and Taiwan. In part, the selection is a matter of deliberate choice, but in part it is due to the non-availability of materials. Even a cursory look into Peking's national bibliography reveals mountains of documentary material—most of it, unfortunately, unavailable outside of the Mainland. Hence, the selection of Mainland materials is of necessity almost entirely limited to those available in the United States, Japan, Hong Kong and Taiwan.

There are few formal restrictions on the circulation of the published documents of the Nationalist government, but they are difficult to locate and acquire. Even the National Central Library at Taipei does not have a complete collection. In the case of certain publications, details concerning such matters as the first date of publication, changes of title, frequency and the like, remain bibliographical nightmares.

The present Part comprises five topical chapters in addition to a general chapter: laws and regulations; government, political parties and mass organizations; economic and social developments; education and culture; and foreign relations. Each chapter, in turn, is divided into documentation for the Mainland and Taiwan respectively (without regard to place of publication), arranged under topical sections. The assignment of documentary compilations to the various chapters is, like any such distribution, rather arbitrary but, it is hoped, not at the expense of clarity. By way of illustration, materials on the women's and youth organizations, both Mainland and Taiwan, have been placed in Chapter XIII (Government, Political Parties and Mass Organizations), while documentation on a number of mass organizations is located in other topical chapters: trade unions in Chapter XIV (Economic and Social Developments); literary associations in Chapter XV (Education and Culture). Statistical materials, including those of an official character, are dealt with in Part Two (Chapter V). Newspapers and periodicals appear in Part Four, including, for example, the organs of the Communist Party, the Kuomintang and mass organizations. Official gazettes, on the other hand, are located in the appropriate chapters of this Part—Chapter XIII (Government, Political Parties, and Mass Organizations), Chapter XII (Laws and Regulations), Chapter XVI (Foreign Relations), etc.

It hardly can be overemphasized that the reader should consult this Part in conjunction with the appropriate sections of chapters in Parts One and Two (e.g., the economic and social section in the bibliography chapter, the chronology of foreign relations, name lists of delegates to the National People's Congresses, biographies of members of the C.C.P. Central Committee, and so on). Part Four, in this connection, should not be overlooked.

Most of the documentary sources in this Part are in Chinese. Reference should be made to the various compilations of translated documents listed in Chapter XX.

CHAPTER XI

GENERAL

A. Mainland

A substantial quantity of documentary source material is sufficiently general in character to defy assignment in the present volume to the specific areas of law, government, political parties, foreign relations, or the like. Statements by Chinese Communist leaders appearing in the official press and elsewhere embrace the entire domestic and external sphere, ranging freely over such diverse subject matter as ideological development, Communist bloc relations, military thought, and the communes in theory and practice, to mention only a few. Mao Tse-tung has commented at length on all phases of human conduct, and his pronouncements constitute the basic source on Chinese Communism. In addition to the pre-1949 editions of his selected works, a new series has been published since 1951. As of 1963, four volumes had appeared, covering his literary output to 1949. (For bibliographies of Mao's writings, consult **66–73** in Chapter I.) Unfortunately, not all of his writings for that period are included in these volumes.

Beyond the kinds of material already mentioned, the present section includes such general sources as the collection of selected editorials from *Jen-min jih-pao* (People's Daily), the organ of the Chinese Communist Party (**570**). (The newspaper itself and its indexes are described in Chapter XVII, **831** ff.) Of the several English-language collections of documents, the Harvard compilation devoted to internal developments on the Mainland from 1955 to 1959 is noteworthy.

The reader is advised to refer to the People's Handbook (**212**) and other yearbooks in Chapter IV, to the major newspapers and periodicals listed in Part Four, such as the People's Daily and Red Flag, and to the official publications of the various ministries and the organs of mass organizations (Chapter XVII). Reference also should be made to the translations issued by the American Consulate General in Hong Kong (**1038** ff.), the Joint Publications Research Service reports (*Communist China Digest* [**1052**], etc.), the *Union Research Service* (**1065**), and the transcripts of monitored radio broadcasts (**1071**), as well as to the Taiwan compilations of Chinese Communist documents (**990** ff. in Chapter XVIII).

568 **Mao, Tse-tung.** *Mao Tse-tung hsüan-chi* 毛澤東選集
(Selected Works of Mao Tse-tung). Peking: Jen-min ch'u-pan she 人民出版社, 1951, 1952, 1953, 1960. 4 vols.

Volume 1 contains Mao's writings for the period 1926 to 1936; Volume 2, 1937–1941; Volume 3, 1941–1945; Volume 4, 1945–1949. Works selected are arranged chronologically by date of publication or by date of original writing. Volume 4 contains seventy-two items hitherto unpublished. Volumes 1 to 4 have been translated into English in five volumes under the title *Selected Works* (New York: International Publishers, 1954–1962 [Volume 1, 1926–1936;

Volume 2, 1937–1938; Volume 3, 1939–1941; Volume, 4, 1941–1945; Volume 5, 1945–1949]). Volume 4 of the Chinese edition was originally translated and published by the Peking Foreign Languages Press in 1961 under the title *Selected Works, Volume 4;* Volume 5 of the International Publishers edition is a reprint of this Peking translation.

It should be noted that a number of Mao's earlier writings are not included here. Many of those which are included in these volumes are revised versions which no longer resemble the originals. Professor Stuart R. Schram's book, *The Political Thought of Mao Tse-tung* (New York: Praeger, 1963), identifies a large number of the earlier versions.

569 **China, Kuo-fang pu, Ch'ing-pao ts'an-mou tz'u-chang shih** 中華民國 國防部 情報參謀次長室 (China, Ministry of National Defense, Office of the Deputy Chief of General Staff For Intelligence). *Fei chün 'hsüeh-hsi Mao chu-hsi chün-shih chu-tso'* 匪軍 ﹝學習毛主席軍事著作﹞ ('Study Chairman Mao's Military Writings': Articles by Members of the Bandit Armed Forces). Taipei, 1961. 150p.

A collection of twenty-three articles on Mao Tse-tung's military writings which originally appeared in two of Communist China's 'internal publications': *Pa-i tsa-chih* 八一雜誌 (August 1st Magazine) and *Chün-hsün tsa-chih* 軍訓雜誌 (Journal of Military Education). An excellent reference for the study of Mao's military thought and Communist China's military system, strategy and tactics. Limited distribution.

For a collection of Mao's military writings in English translation, see *Selected Military Writings of Mao Tse-tung* (Peking: Foreign Languages Press, 1963).

570 **Jen-min jih-pao** 人民日報 (People's Daily). *Jen-min jih-pao she-lun hsüan-chi* 人民日報社論選輯 (Selected Editorials of the People's Daily). Peking: Jen-min jih-pao ch'u-pan she 人民日報出版社, 1957(?)—.

Selected editorials of the *Jen-min jih-pao* published in book form (approximately 130 p.) several volumes to a year. Arrangement is by subject matter. The volumes are not indexed. For a complete index to all editorials published between 1949 and 1958, see *Jen-min jih-pao she-lun so-yin* (Index to Editorials of the People's Daily, **833**).

571 **Communist China 1955–1959: Policy Documents and Analysis.** Cambridge, Mass.: Harvard University Press, 1962. 611p.

A selection of forty-eight basic policy documents, in English translation, on the internal developments of Communist China, 1955–1959, with a foreword by Robert R. Bowie and John K. Fairbank.

In eleven chapters: (1) 'The First Five-Year Plan'; (2) 'The Speed-Up of Agricultural Cooperativization, 1955–1956'; (3) 'Flowers and Schools'; (4) 'The

Eighth Party Congress'; (5) 'China and the Socialist Camp, 1956–57'; (6) 'Contradictions and Rectification'; (7) 'The Great Leap Forward'; (8) 'The People's Communes: The Phase of Enthusiasm'; (9) 'The People's Communes: Disillusion and Consolidation'; (10) 'Anti-Rightist Campaign'; (11) 'The Celebration of the Tenth Anniversary'. There is a general introduction entitled 'Domestic Policy Trends in Communist China, 1955–1959' (pp. 1–41), as well as introductory notes to each chapter and to each document (including reference material for further reading). Selective index to important themes, events, ideas, and persons discussed in the commentaries and documents.

A good selection of documents with helpful commentaries and references. (Reviewed by Peter S. H. Tang in *The Journal of Asian Studies*, Vol. 22, No. 2 [February 1963], p. 210.)

572 Chen, Theodore Hsi-en.
The Chinese Communist Regime: A Documentary Study. [Los Angeles]: University of Southern California, 1956. 2 vols. 380p.

A collection of fifty-six laws, government and party directives, speeches and writings of prominent Chinese Communist leaders, constitutions of various mass organizations and the like, for the period 1949–1955, prepared in connection with a course on Chinese Communism at the University of Southern California. Mimeographed.

A revised edition extends coverage of the documentation to 1963 (1965).

573 Irie, Keishirō 入江啓四郎, **ed.** *Shin Chūgoku shiryō shūsei* 新中國資料集成 (New China Documentary Collection). Tokyo: Nihon Kokusai Mondai Kenkyūjo 日本國際問題研究所, Vol. 1—, 1963—.

A multi-volume collection of documents on postwar China covering the period from 1945 to 1958 under compilation at the Japan Institute for the Study of International Problems, an auxiliary organization of the Japanese Foreign Ministry. The first volume, containing 130 documents for the period April 1945–December 1947, was published in December 1963 (704p.). Volumes for the periods 1948–September 1949, October 1949–1952, 1953–1955 and 1956–1958 are scheduled for publication during the next few years. A detailed chronology for the fourteen-year period is also contemplated.

A monumental documentary history of the Chinese Communist movement *Shiryō shūsei Chūgoku kyōsantō shi* 資料集成中國共產黨史 (The History of the Chinese Communist Party: A Documentary Collection) was compiled in the prewar period by the veteran China expert Hatano Ken'ichi 波多野乾一 and was republished by Jiji Tsūshinsha in June 1961 in seven volumes (covering the years 1920–1937).

574 Jacobs, Dan N. and Baerwald, Hans, eds.
Chinese Communism; Selected Documents. New York: Harper Torchbooks, July 1963. 242p.

A paper-bound collection of some twenty documents (with commentaries) on domestic and foreign policy. All documents except four are for the period 1957–1962.

575 Steiner, H. Arthur.
Chinese Communism in Action. Los Angeles: University of California at Los Angeles, 1953. 3 vols. 313p.

Three volumes comprising eighteen chapters of translated source materials on political and economic developments in Communist China, with an emphasis on the Chinese Communists' own estimates of themselves and their programs, policies, objectives, intentions, and operating methods. Materials are drawn from the Chinese Communist press, and are mostly translations of full articles as compared with the short quotations contained in the following entry (although the coverage of this entry extends only to 1953). Each chapter has an introductory note. A checklist of personalities is also appended. Mimeographed.

576 Steiner, H. Arthur.
Maoism: A Sourcebook; Selections From the Writings of Mao Tse-tung. Los Angeles: University of California at Los Angeles, 1952. 142p.

Contains translations of twenty articles by Mao Tse-tung written between January 1934 and October 1951. Carefully selected with good, concise introductory notes. Mimeographed.

577 U.S. Department of State, Bureau of Intelligence and Research.
Chinese Communist World Outlook—A Handbook of Chinese Communist Statements, the Public Record of a Militant Ideology. Washington, D.C.: U.S. Government Printing Office, 1962. 139p. (Department of State Publication 7379, Far Eastern Series 112).

A collection of short quotations from statements by Chinese Communist leaders designed to show in their own words the principal motivating ideas and theories of Chinese Communism. Arranged in three main parts: (1) ideology and ideological problems, (2) domestic problems and policies, and (3) foreign policy. Under each part the quotations are given in chronological order under various sections and subsections with indication of source. The period covered is from 1921 to late 1961, with major emphasis on the post-1949 period. There is an alphabetical list of the thirty-eight principal individuals quoted, and the ten major sources cited (Mao Tse-tung's *Selected Works*, People's Daily, Red Flag, New China News Agency releases, etc.). Subject index.

Very weak for the years 1921 to 1949, the volume is quite useful for the period since 1949. Statements by such important leaders of the early stage of the Chinese Communist Movement as Ch'en Tu-hsiu, Chang Kuo-t'ao and Li Li-san are not included at all.

578 Brandt, Conrad, Schwartz, Benjamin, and Fairbank, John K.
A Documentary History of Chinese Communism. Cambridge, Mass.: Harvard University Press, 1952. 552p.

A documentary study of the Chinese Communist Party line from 1921 to 1950, containing translations of forty selected documents, with critical commentaries, which mark significant stages or aspects of the ideological development of the Chinese Communist movement during the period covered. Divided into seven main chronological sections (with twenty-four subsections) including the post-war period, 1945–1950.

There is a useful 'Chronology of the Communist Movement in China, 1918–1950' at the beginning of the volume (pp. 29–47), including events that have had an important bearing on the Chinese Communist movement, especially those that are not commonly known (such as pertinent meetings of the Executive Committee of the Communist International and reference citations for data not listed in general reference works such as yearbooks).

In addition to the reference notes, two bibliographies and a glossary of Chinese names and terms are appended. Bibliography A is a list of documents translated; Bibliography B is a list of works cited. Both are alphabetically arranged with full citations.

The glossary section contains approximately 700 abbreviations, names of Chinese persons, names of organizations or organizational units, and a selection of vocabulary phrases and special terms commonly used in Chinese works covering Communism, drawn by the compilers from texts cited in this volume, all arranged in alphabetical order followed by Chinese characters and English translations.

The Chinese texts of some of the documents translated from non-Communist sources have since become available, and additional key documents may also be found in the Chen Cheng Collection as well as in the library of the Bureau of Investigation of the Ministry of Justice in Taipei.

B. TAIWAN

There seem to be no general collections of recent Nationalist documentary material in translation, although several items lying within certain specific subject areas do exist and are included in subsequent chapters. In the Chinese language, no such complaint can be registered. The writings of Chiang Kai-shek, which are included in this section, appear in selected form in two volumes, and in the collected works of some twenty volumes (accompanied by a topical dictionary). Also deserving of mention is the last entry in the section—a collection of basic Nationalist statements on policy.

Additional source material is to be encountered in the various official gazettes listed in subsequent chapters of this Part, as well as in the documents section of the *China Yearbook* (see **239** and **240**), and other official and semi-official newspapers and periodicals listed in Chapter XVIII.

579 Chiang, Kai-shek. *Chiang tsung-t'ung yen-lun hui-pien* 蔣總統言論彙編 (Collected Works of President Chiang). Taipei: Cheng-chung shu-chü 正中書局, 1956. 24 vols.

The selected works of Chiang Kai-shek, 1921 to 1956, chronologically arranged under the following headings: monographs, speeches, proclamations, statements, and miscellaneous writings. Vol. 1 contains a table of contents, a subject index (arranged under the following categories: Three People's Principles, philosophy, science, military science, party affairs, political affairs, military affairs, education, economy and finance, society, international relations, and miscellany), and a chronology of Chiang Kai-shek's writings, 1912–1955. A supplement in three volumes was published in 1959.

For English-language translations of some of the more important statements, see *Selected Speeches and Messages of President Chiang Kai-shek*, published annually by the Government Information Office in Taipei. The period 1949–1952 is covered in one volume published in 1952 (104p.).

580 Wu, Huan-chi 吳環吉, ed. *Chiang tsung-t'ung yen-lun ta tz'u-tien* 蔣總統言論大辭典 (A Dictionary of the Writings of President Chiang). Taipei, 1960. 2 vols. 1,066p.

A comprehensive topical directory (with quotations) to the writings of Chiang Kai-shek as published in the preceding entry and its supplement, arranged by the number of strokes.

581 Chiang, Kai-shek. *Chiang tsung-t'ung chi* 蔣統總集 (Collected Works of President Chiang). Taipei: Kuo-fang yen-chiu yüan 國防研究院, 1960. 2 vols. 2,486p.

Contains selected writings of Chiang Kai-shek for the period 1912 to June 1960. In five parts: (1) essays, (2) speeches, (3) declarations and communiqués, (4) interviews, and (5) miscellaneous writings. Three useful appendices: (1) a chronological table of his writings; (2) a title index; and (3) a subject index. The last two are arranged by the number of strokes. Contents and arrangement are practically the same as in the preceding collection, except for the addition of Chiang's *Su-O tsai Chung-kuo* 蘇俄在中國 (Soviet Russia in China) and the updating of all parts to 1960.

582 China, Hsing-cheng yüan, Hsin-wen chü 中華民國 行政院 新聞局 (China, Executive Yüan, Government Information Office). *Yu-kuan tang-ch'ien chung-yao wen-t'i chih chi-pen ts'an-k'ao tz'u-liao* 有關當前重要問題之基本參考資料 (Basic Reference Materials Concerning the Important Questions of Today). Taipei, 1961. 112p.

An official publication comprising quotations from statements made by Chiang Kai-shek, Chen Cheng and other high government officials on Nationalist China's policies, programs, and objectives. The quotations are arranged under the three major sections of military affairs, foreign relations, and government. Each section is further divided into subsections as follows: 1—military affairs *(a)* organization and development, *(b)* 'Mainland Recovery', *(c)* Quemoy and Matsu; 2—foreign relations *(a)* basic policy, *(b)* international relations, *(c)* 'Global Plot of Russia and Communist China'; 3—government *(a)* general political measures, *(b)* analysis of the Chinese Communist situation, *(c)* Taiwan development, *(d)* Overseas Chinese. A nineteen-item general description of Taiwan is appended.

A convenient collection of policy statements.

CHAPTER XII

LAWS AND REGULATIONS

Both the Republic of China and the People's Republic of China have evolved elaborate legal systems, the study of which provides insights into the interplay of Western influence and traditional Chinese concepts of law and justice. This interplay between the traditional and the modern makes the comparative study of Soviet and Chinese Communist law particularly relevant. Nationalist law has been a subject of investigation in the West for years. The study of Chinese Communist law, still in its infancy, has been impeded by a lack of necessary source materials—especially cases, interpretations and precedents.

The collection of laws, statutes, decrees, regulations, etc., contained in the present chapter are arranged in two subsections (general and topical) under both the Mainland and Taiwan. Texts of single laws are not listed separately because they are included in the general collections.

Reference should be made to the bibliographies on Chinese law in Chapter I (**103**ff).

A. People's Republic of China

1. General

The first two entries below together constitute the basic compendium of Chinese Communist laws, statutes, decrees and regulations promulgated since 1949. The third entry (**585**), intended for the use of the judiciary, is a concise selection of the more important laws, regulations, etc.

A number of the fundamental laws, accompanied by background information, are available in English translation in the compilations by Professors Rickett, Cohen and Blaustein (**587-589**). Others are available in the Joint Publications Research Service translations (Chapter XX).

For further study of the Mainland legal system, the indexes to Mainland laws and regulations compiled in Japan (**196**ff.) are of utmost importance, as are the *Cheng-fa yen-chiu* (Studies in Government and Law, **854**), *Jen-min jih-pao* (People's Daily, **831**) and *Kuang-ming jih-pao* (**836**) described in Chapter XVII, the Gazette of the State Council (**634**) covered in Chapter XIII, and entries listed in the next section.

583 **China (People's Republic of China, 1949—), Fa-chih wei-yüan hui** 中央人民政府 法制委員會 (China [People's Republic of China, 1949—], Commission on Legislative Affairs). *Chung-yang jen-min cheng-fu fa-ling hui-pien* 中央人民政府法令彙編 (Compendium of Laws and Decrees of the Central People's Government). Peking: Jen-min ch'u-pan she 人民出版社, 1952–1954; Fa-lü ch'u-pan she 法律出版社, 1955. 5 vols.

A comprehensive compendium of laws, decrees, directives, resolutions and other measures having the force of law issued by the Central People's Government, the State Council, the Supreme People's Court, and the People's Procurator-General's Office from 1949 to September 1954. Included also are certain decrees issued by the five committees under the State Council and by the various ministries, commissions, and administrative units above the provincial level on national policy and its implementation and enforcement.

The materials in each volume are arranged in chronological order under the following six subject headings: (1) general (organic law of the Central People's Government, the organic law of the People's Political Consultative Conference, etc.); (2) political and legal affairs; (3) financial and economic affairs; (4) cultural and educational affairs; (5) control; (6) personnel and organization (omitted with the publication of the 1952 volume).

The compendium has been continued under a slightly different title, *Chung-hua jen-min kung-ho kuo fa-kuei hui-pien* 中華人民共和國法規彙編 (Compendium of Laws and Regulations of the People's Republic of China) since the adoption of the new state constitution in September 1954 (see next entry).

The following is a summary of period coverage of the five volumes published:

VOLUME NO. AND PERIOD COVERED		DATE OF PUBLICATION
Vol. 1	1949–1950	1952
Vol. 2	1951	1953
Vol. 3	1952	1954
Vol. 4	1953	1955
Vol. 5	Jan.-Sep. 1954	1955

584 China (People's Republic of China, 1949—), Kuo-wu yüan, Fa-chih chü 中華人民共和國 國務院 法制局 (China [People's Republic of China, 1949—], State Council, Bureau of Legislative Affairs). *Chung-hua jen-min kung-ho kuo fa-kuei hui-pien* 中華人民共和國法規彙編 (Compendium of Laws and Regulations of the People's Republic of China). Peking: Fa-lü ch'u-pan she 法律出版社, 1956—.

A continuation of the *Chung-yang jen-min cheng-fu fa-ling hui-pien* (see preceding entry) covering the period from the adoption of the new state constitution (September 1954) to the present. The scope is similar to that of the earlier publication, but the arrangement of materials differs and is less uniform. The major subject groupings are state administration, economic plans, basic construction, foreign affairs, domestic affairs, military affairs, public security, financial and economic affairs, food grains, commerce, industry, agriculture, culture and education, transportation and communications, Overseas Chinese and minority groups.

The following is a summary of period coverage of volumes published to date:

VOLUME NO. AND PERIOD COVERED		DATE OF PUBLICATION
Vol. 1	Sep. 1954–Jun. 1955	1956
Vol. 2	Jul.–Dec. 1956	1956
Vol. 3	Jan.–Jun. 1956	1956
Vol. 4	Jul.–Dec. 1956	1957
Vol. 5	Jan.–Jun. 1957	1957
Vol. 6	Jul.–Dec. 1957	1958
Vol. 7	Jan.–Jun. 1958	1958
Vol. 8	Jul.–Dec. 1958	1959
Vol. 9	Jan.–Jun. 1959	1959
Vol. 10	Jul.–Dec. 1959	1960
Vol. 11	Jan.–Jun. 1960	1960
Vol. 12	Jul. 1960–Dec. 1961	1962

This and the preceding entry form the basic collection of laws, statutes, decrees and other regulations in force promulgated by the government of Communist China since 1949.

For English translations of these compendia, see the following J.R.P.S. reports:

VOLUME NO.	J.P.R.S. NO. AND DATE	U.S.G.P.O. MONTHLY CATALOG NO.
3	14,673 7–31–62	1962—19,624
5	337 10–21–58	1958—16,148
8	14,335 7– 2–62	1962—15,906
9	14,346 7– 2–62	1962—15,912

585 China (People's Republic of China, 1949—), Ssu-fa pu 中華人民共和國司法部 (China [People's Republic of China, 1949—], Ministry of Justice). *Chung-hua jen-min kung-ho kuo fa-kuei hsüan-chi* 中華人民共和國法規選輯 (Selections from Compendium of Laws and Regulations of the People's Republic of China). Peking: Fa-lü ch'u-pan she 法律出版社, 1957. 853p.

Laws, decrees, regulations, etc., promulgated from 1949 to 1957, selected for the use of the judiciary in the administration of justice. Documents are arranged by subject matter and under each subject by date. The subject divisions are (1) general (the Constitution, etc.), (2) state structure, (3) elections, (4) land reform, (5) 'Socialist Construction', (6) 'Capital Construction', (7) administration of justice and public security, (8) military affairs, (9) finance and money and banking, (10) food grains, (11) commerce, (12) industrial management, (13) transportation and communications, (14) agriculture and forestry, (15) labor, (16) culture, (17) hygiene, (18) minorities affairs, (19) Overseas Chinese, and (20) government service regulations. Amendments to and revisions of existing laws are inserted.

586 Chung-yang cheng-fa kan-pu hsüeh-hsiao, Kuo-chia fa chiao-yen shih 中央政法幹部學校 國家法教研室 (Central School for Political and Judici l

Cadres, Institute of Domestic Law). *Chung-hua jen-min kung-ho kuo hsien-fa hsüeh-hsi ts'an-kao tzu-liao* 中華人民共和國憲法學習參考資料 (Study and Reference Materials on the Constitution of the People's Republic of China). Peking: Fa-lü ch'u-pan she 法律出版社, 1957. 541p.

A comprehensive collection of documents on the constitution of Communist China adopted in September 1954, including a number of background papers such as Mao Tse-tung's pre-1949 writings on government and law, and the bills of rights adopted by Communist governments in the various border areas before 1949. The materials are arranged parallel to the organization of the constitution in the following order: general, preamble, general principles, the state structure, fundamental rights and duties of citizens, and the national flag, national emblem, and national capital. The text does not include all documents listed in the table of contents. Those not included are considered to be 'easily obtainable', and they are marked in the table of contents with full bibliographical citation.

587 Rickett, W. Allyn, ed.
Legal Thought and Institutions of the People's Republic of China: Selected Documents (Preliminary Draft). Philadelphia, Pa., 1963. 362p.

A collection of English translations of Communist China's laws, statutes, and other legal documents prepared for the course on Chinese legal thought at the University of Pennsylvania. Some of the translations were done by the editor; others were taken from such sources as the Hong Kong American Consulate General series and the Joint Publications Research Service reports. In eight chapters: (1) theory of state and law; (2) state structure and legal organs; (3) suppression of counter-revolutionaries; (4) the *San-fan wu-fan* (Three-Anti and Five-Anti) movement; (5) aspects of civil law; (6) selected cases; (7) the Chinese system of administrative justice; and (8) bibliographies. An extensive bibliography of English writings on and translations of Chinese Nationalist and Communist law (mostly the latter) and a selected list of J.P.R.S. reports dealing with Chinese Communist law is provided (see **103**). Mimeographed.

More comprehensive in coverage than the two following entries.

588 Cohen, Jerome A., ed.
Preliminary Materials on the Law of Communist China. Berkeley, Calif.: A.S.U.C. Store, 1961. 242p.

A collection of primary and secondary sources on Chinese law and jurisprudence prepared as background reading for a seminar at the University of California (Berkeley) in 'Political Institutions and Law in the Communist World'. Articles by Franz Michael, Benjamin Schwartz, and H. F. Schurmann are included in the volume which consists essentially of translations of laws, regulations, decrees, etc. Six chapters: (1) the Chinese legal tradition; (2) Chinese Communist theory: party, state and law; (3) the basic structure of government; (4) judicial and administrative organs of control; (5) criminal law and procedure; and (6) private law aspects.

A convenient compilation of scattered sources.

589 Blaustein, Albert P., ed.
Fundamental Legal Documents of Communist China.
South Hackensack, N.J.: Fred B. Rothman & Co., 1962. 1 vol.

A collection of English translations of Communist China's fundamental laws. In three parts. Part 1 contains the constitution and its predecessor, the Common Program, as well as the constitution of the Chinese Communist Party. Part 2 gives the organic laws which provide for the organization, powers and procedures of the basic organs of government. Part 3 is a collection of the nationalities and election laws; penal laws; marriage law; property laws and regulations; and labor laws and regulations. The various property laws contain documents from the land reform period immediately after 1949, through the cooperative agriculture movement to the commune movement. The regulations of the Weihsing (Sputnik) People's Commune are included among the more recent documents. An introduction on Chinese Communist law has been contributed by the editor.

Reviewed by H. Arthur Steiner in *The Journal of Asian Studies*, Vol. 22, No. 2 (February 1963), pp. 210–211.

590 Hirano, Yoshitarō 平野義太郎, **comp. and tr.** *Gendai Chūgoku hōrei shū* 現代中國法令集 (A Collection of Laws and Decrees of Contemporary China). Tokyo: Nihon Hyōron Shinsha 日本評論新社, 1955. 293p.

A Japanese compilation and translation of selected Chinese Communist laws and decrees from October 1949 to October 1954, with commentaries by the compiler and other members of the China Research Institute (Chūgoku Kenkyūjo 中國研究所). In four parts: basic laws, economic and labor, etc. A 27-page chronology of laws and regulations promulgated during the period is appended.

2. TOPICAL

The collections of laws and regulations contained in the present section are arranged according to the following categories of legal subject matter: land reform, agriculture and forestry, finance, money and banking, industry and commerce, taxation, labor and trade unions, marriage, minorities affairs, education, elections, public security.

The above occupy but a small segment of the spectrum of special laws and regulations. For other subject areas, consult the appropriate parts in the general collections discussed in the previous section.

591 Pei-ching cheng-fa hsüeh-yüan, Min-fa chiao-yen shih 北京政法學院 民法教研室 (Peking College of Political Science and Law, Institute of Civil

Law). *Chung-hua jen-min kung-ho kuo t'u-ti fa ts'an-k'ao tzu-liao hui-pien* 中華人民共和國土地法參考資料彙編 (Collection of Reference Materials on the Land Law of the People's Republic of China). Peking: Fa-lü ch'u-pan she 法律出版社, 1957. 407p.

A compendium of 107 laws, regulations, and related documents (including *Jen-min jih-pao* editorials) issued from October 1949 up to the first part of 1957, arranged under the following sections: (1) agricultural land, (2) forestry and forestry land, (3) irrigation and water conservation, (4) city land, (5) land for special use, (6) condemned land, (7) land laws and regulations of the old revolutionary bases (including the Kiangsi Soviet land laws, the Ching-kang shan land laws, and land laws of the various border areas).

See also the *Agrarian Reform Law of the People's Republic of China (1950) and Other Relevant Documents*, fourth edition (Peking: Foreign Languages Press, 1959), 88p.

592 Tung-pei jen-min cheng-fu, Nung-lin pu 東北人民政府 農林部 (Northeast People's Government, Ministry of Agriculture and Forestry). *T'u-ti cheng-ts'e fa-ling hui-pien* 土地政策法令彙編 (Compendium of Land Laws). Revised edition. Mukden, 1950. 241p.

A compilation of fifty-seven laws, regulations, decrees, directives, etc., concerning agricultural land reform (including urban real estate) in Manchuria, emanating from both the Central Committee of the Chinese Communist Party and its Northeast Bureau in Manchuria between 1947 and 1950. The contents are arranged by subject (land reform, real estate, etc.), and, under each subject heading, chronologically by date of issuance.

593 Fa-lü ch'u-pan she 法律出版社 (Legal Publishing House). *Nung-ts'un shih-yung fa-kuei shou-ts'e* 農村適用法規手冊 (Handbook of Laws and Regulations Concerning Rural Areas). Peking: Fa-lü ch'u-pan she, 1958. 420p.

A handbook designed primarily for the use of cadres working in rural areas and agricultural cooperatives, containing a selection of laws, regulations, and related documents issued by the Chinese Communist Party and the Chinese government. The following topics are documented: (1) agricultural production; (2) agricultural land and irrigation; (3) afforestation and forest protection; (4) agricultural tax and loans; (5) unified requisition and distribution; (6) land; (7) culture, education and hygiene; (8) marriage, military service, and public safety. A selection of reports on the progress of economic and cultural activities in various rural communities is provided in the appendix.

594 China (People's Republic of China, 1949—), Kuo-wu yüan, Fa-chih chü, Ts'ai-cheng ching-chi tsu 中華人民共和國 國務院 法制局 財政經濟組

(China [People's Republic of China, 1949—], State Council, Legislative Bureau, Financial and Economic Section), and Ts'ai-cheng pu, Shui-wu tsung-chü, Nung-yeh shui ch'u 財政部 稅務總局 農業稅處 (Ministry of Finance, Bureau of Taxation, Agricultural Tax Section). *Chung-hua jen-min kung-ho kuo nung-yeh shui tiao-li wen-ta* 中華人民共和國 農業稅條例問答 (Questions and Answers Concerning the Agricultural Tax Regulations of the People's Republic of China). Peking: Fa-lü ch'u-pan she 法律出版社, 1958. 71p.

Forty-four questions and answers concerning the agricultural tax regulations promulgated on June 3, 1958 (text provided). Regulations issued between 1950 and 1956, now defunct, are listed in the appendix.

595 China (People's Republic of China, 1949—), Lin-yeh pu 中華人民共和國 林業部 (China [People's Republic of China, 1949—], Ministry of Forestry). *Lin-yeh fa-ling hui-pien* 林業法令彙編 (Compendium of Forestry Laws and Decrees). Peking: Chung-kuo lin-yeh pien-chi wei-yüan hui 中國林業編輯委員會, 1952. 289p.

Texts of laws, decrees, orders, directives, regulations, etc., concerning forestry. The materials are arranged by region (North, Northeast, Northwest, East, Central South, Southwest, and Inner Mongolia). This is the third series covering the years 1951 and 1952 (information on the first two series is not available). Whether publication continued beyond 1952 also is not known.

596 Chung-kuo jen-min yin-hang tsung-hang 中國人民銀行總行 (People's Bank of China, Head Office). *Chin-jung fa-kuei hui-pien* 金融法規彙編 (Compendium of Fiscal Laws and Regulations). Peking: Ts'ai-cheng ching-chi ch'u-pan she 財政經濟出版社, 1956—.

Contains mostly directives, circulars, regulations, and decisions on matters concerning money and banking issued by the People's Bank of China. Included also are related laws and decrees promulgated by the State Council and other agencies of the government, *Jen-min jih-pao* editorials, and statements by high government officials on financial matters. The arrangement of the materials, which varies in each volume, adheres to the following basic outline: (1) loans and credits, (2) savings, (3) bonds, (4) cash control, (5) private enterprises, (6) overseas enterprises, (7) final account, (8) auditing, (9) agricultural economics, (10) budget, (11) statistics, and (12) personnel training. The 1953 and 1954 volumes were published under the title 金融法令彙編.

The following is a summary of period coverage of volumes published to date:

VOLUME NO. AND PERIOD COVERED		DATE OF PUBLICATION
Vol. 1	1949–1952	1956
Vol. 2	1953	1955
Vol. 3	1954	1955
Vol. 4	1955	1956
Vol. 5	1956	1957
Vol. 6	1957	1958
Vol. 7	1958–1960	1962

For a translation of Volume 7, see *Collection of Fiscal Laws and Regulations, 1958–1960, Communist China*, J.P.R.S. No. 19,499, May 31, 1963, 306p. (U.S.G.P.O. Monthly Catalog, 1963, No. 12,589).

597 China (People's Republic of China, 1949—), Ts'ai-cheng pu 中華人民共和國 財政部 (China [People's Republic of China, 1949—], Ministry of Finance). *Chung-yang ts'ai-cheng fa-kuei hui-pien* 中央財政法規彙編 (Compendium of Financial Laws and Regulations of the People's Republic of China). Peking: Ts'ai-cheng ch'u-pan she 財政出版社, 1957—.

Contains financial laws and regulations promulgated by the National People's Congress, the State Council, and the Ministry of Finance. Arrangement is by subject matter under the following main headings: (1) budget, (2) 'Economic Construction,' (3) culture and education, (4) taxation, (5) financial administration of government agencies, (6) business accounting, and (7) insurance. Special subject headings are also used as required (for example, 'Financial Administration of People's Communes').

Summary of period coverage of volumes published to 1959:

VOLUME NO. AND PERIOD COVERED		DATE OF PUBLICATION
Vol. 1	1955	1957
Vol. 2	1956	None published (?)
Vol. 3	Jan.–Jun. 1957	Information unavailable
Vol. 4	Jul.–Dec. 1957	1958
Vol. 5	Jan.–Jun. 1958	1958
Vol. 6	Jul.–Dec. 1958	Information unavailable
Vol. 7	Jan.–Jun. 1959	1959
Vol. 8	Jul.–Dec. 1959	1960

598 China (People's Republic of China, 1949—), Cheng-wu yüan, Ts'ai-cheng ching-chi wei-yüan hui 中華人民共和國 政務院 財政經濟委員會 (China [People's Republic of China, 1949—], State Council, Committee on Financial and Economic Affairs). *Chung-yang ts'ai-ching cheng-ts'e fa-ling hui-pien* 中央財經政策法令彙編 (Compendium of Financial and Economic Laws and Decrees of the People's Republic of China). Peking: Hsin-hua shu-tien 新華書店, 1950–1952. 4 vols.

A comprehensive collection of financial and economic laws, decrees, regulations, directives, official reports and *Jen-min jih-pao* editorials on financial and economic matters issued from 1949 to about July 1951, in three parts (four volumes). Part 1, published in August 1950 in two volumes, comprises the following sections: general, finance, money and banking, communications, commerce, industry, agriculture, labor, and an appendix. Part 2, published in June 1951, has one section added for cooperatives. Part 3, published in March 1952, has another section added on maritime customs.

599 Hua-tung ch'ü chün-cheng wei-yüan hui, Ts'ai-cheng ching-chi wei-yüan hui 華東區軍政委員會 財政經濟委員會 (East China Military and Administrative Committee, Committee on Financial and Economic Affairs). *Hua-tung ch'ü ts'ai-cheng ching-chi fa-ling hui-pien* 華東區財政經濟法令彙編 (Compendium of Financial and Economic Laws and Decrees of the East China Area). Shanghai: Hua-tung jen-min ch'u-pan she 華東人民出版社, 1951. 2 vols. 2,033p.

Contains laws, decrees, regulations, directives, etc., issued by both the Central People's Government and the East China Military and Administrative Committee from 1949 to May 1951. Arranged under eleven sections: general, finance, money and banking, commerce, industry, agriculture and water conservation, communications, labor, cooperatives, land, and miscellaneous. The East China Military and Administrative Committee had jurisdiction over Kiangsu, Chekiang, Anhwei, Fukien and Shantung provinces, and the two municipalities of Shanghai and Nanking.

600 Fa-lü ch'u-pan she 法律出版社 (Legal Publishing House). *Ch'ang-k'uang ch'i-yeh shih-yung fa-kuei shou-ts'e* 廠鑛企業適用法規手冊 (Handbook of Industrial Laws and Regulations). Peking: Fa-lü ch'u-pan she, 1958. 469p.

A handbook designed primarily for the use of cadres and industrial workers, containing pertinent industrial laws, regulations, etc., in force as of 1958. Arranged under the following topical headings: general, labor safety, wages, welfare, marriage, public safety, and literacy program.

601 Fa-lü ch'u-pan she 法律出版社 (Legal Publishing House). *Shang-yeh shih-yung fa-kuei shou ts'e* 商業適用法規手冊 (Handbook of Commercial Laws and Regulations). Peking: Fa-lü ch'u-pan she, 1958. 524p.

Contains regulations, directives, official reports, and related documents on the domestic commerce of Communist China issued between March 1957 and August 1958. In nine parts: (1) management; (2) commodities; (3) production; (4) agricultural implements; (5) requisition of agricultural products; (6) hygiene; (7) produce; (8) tea, mulberry, and fruits; and (9) restaurants, hotels, etc.

602 China (People's Republic of China, 1949—), Kuo-wu yüan, Chung-yang kung-shang hsing-cheng kuan-li chü, Mi-shu ch'u 中華人民共和國 國務院 中央工商行政管理局 秘書處 (China [People's Republic of China, 1949—], State Council, Central Administration of Industry and Commerce, Secretariat). *Ssu-ying kung-shang yeh ti she-hui chu-i kai-tsao cheng-ts'e fa-ling hsüan-pien* 私營工商業的社會主義改造政策法令選編

(Selections of Laws and Decrees Concerning the Socialist Reconstruction of Private Business Enterprises). Peking: Ts'ai-cheng ching-chi ch'u-pan she 財政經濟出版社, 1957. 356p.

Volume I of a two-volume compilation comprising policy statements, selected official directives, orders, decisions, regulations, and *Jen-min jih-pao* editorials concerning the 'socialist reconstruction of private business enterprises' in Communist China during 'the restoration period of the people's economy, 1949-1952'. The documents are arranged under the following five sections: (1) general, (2) industry and commerce, (3) finance and money, (4) labor, and (5) 'The Five-Anti Movement'. Appended is a comprehensive index to periodical literature (mainly the *Hsin-hua yüeh-pao*) and documents in the *Chung-yang ts'ai-ching cheng-ts'e fa-ling hui-pien* (see **598**) and the *Chin-jung fa-kuei hui-pien* (see **596**) concerning Chinese Communist industrial and commercial policies during the 1949-1952 period.

Volume 2 of this series, covering the period of the First Five-Year Plan, 1953-1957, is not available.

603 **Chung-yang shui-wu kung-pao, Pien-chi pu** 中央稅務公報 編輯部 (Central Tax Gazette, Editorial Department). *Chung-yang shui-wu fa-ling hui-chi* 中央稅務法令彙集 (Compendium of Tax Laws of the Central Government). Peking: Chung-yang shui-wu kung-pao, Fa-hsing pu 中央稅務公報發行部, 1952. 346p.

A collection of tax laws issued by the Chinese Communist government from October 1949 through August 1952, arranged under the following categories: (1) general, (2) commodity tax, (3) tax on industry and commerce, (4) interest income tax, (5) stamp tax, (6) abattoir tax, (7) urban real estate tax, (8) special consumption tax, (9) vehicle and vessel license tax, (10) tax investigation and auditing, and (11) miscellany. Each entry contains the text of the law or regulation in question, together with the name of the issuing agency and the date of issuance. No index.

604 **China (People's Republic of China, 1949—), Lao-tung pu, Lao-tung cheng-ts'e yen-chiu shih** 中華人民共和國 勞動部 勞動政策研究室 (China [People's Republic of China, 1949—], Ministry of Labor, Labor Policy Research Office). *Chung-yang lao-tung fa-ling hui-pien* 中央勞動法令彙編 (Compendium of Labor Laws of the People's Republic of China). Peking: Jen-min ch'u-pan she 人民出版社, 1953. 12; 433p.

Contains laws, decrees, regulations, directives, etc., issued from 1949 through March 1953, arranged under eight sections: (1) general, (2) labor relations, (3) industrial safety, (4) labor insurance, (5) wages and working hours, (6) unemployment relief and rehabilitation, (7) adult education, and (8) 'Labor Heroes and Inventions'.

See also *Important Labour Laws and Regulations of the People's Republic of China* (enlarged edition), published by the Foreign Languages Press in Peking (1961). 82p.

605 China (People's Republic of China, 1949—), Lao-tung pu, Lao-tung cheng-ts'e yen-chiu shih 中華人民共和國 勞動部 勞動政策研究室 (China [People's Republic of China, 1949—], Ministry of Labor, Labor Policy Research Office). *Kung-hui fa chi ch'i yu-kuan wen-chien* 工會法及其有關文件 (Trade Union Law and Related Documents). Peking: Jen-min ch'u-pan she 人民出版社, 1953. 50p.

Includes the Trade Union Law of 1950 and subsequent government directives and regulations on the enforcement of the law. Laws concerning labor safety, labor insurance, industrial management, labor-management relations, and labor education are excluded from this volume, but may be found in the *Chung-yang lao-tung fa-ling hui-pien* (see preceding entry).

For an English translation of the original law, see *The Trade Union Law of the People's Republic of China* (Peking: Foreign Languages Press, 1951), 38p.

606 China (People's Republic of China, 1949—), Fa-chih wei-yüan hui 中央人民政府 法制委員會 (China [People's Republic of China, 1949—], Commission of Legislative Affairs). *Hun-yin wen-t'i ts'an-k'ao tzu-liao hui-pien* 婚姻問題參考資料彙編 (Collection of Reference Materials on Marriage Problems). Shanghai: Hsin-hua shu-tien 新華書店, 1950. 154p.

The first and only volume published in the series. Contains case histories, court decisions, the Marriage Law of 1950, and a bibliography of twelve items. The case histories and court decisions shed some light on the marriage problem in China during the initial stage of Communist rule of the country.

See also *The Marriage Law of the People's Republic of China*, with explanatory materials by Teng Ying-chao, fifth printing (Peking: Foreign Languages Press, 1959). 44p.

607 Jen-min ch'u-pan she 人民出版社 (People's Publishing House). *Min-tsu cheng-ts'e wen-chien hui-pien* 民族政策文件彙編 (Collections of Policy Documents on National Minorities Affairs). Peking: Jen-min ch'u-pan she, 1953, 1958, 1960. 3 vols.

Contains documents on minorities affairs of Communist China, including laws, decrees, directives, resolutions, speeches by Mao Tse-tung, etc. The documents are arranged in chronological order by subject matter (e.g., culture and education, autonomous regions). See also next entry.

For a translation of some of the important documents in Vol. 1 (1953), see *Policy Towards Nationalities of the People's Republic of China* (Peking: Foreign Languages Press, 1953), 70p.

608 **Jen-min ch'u-pan she** 人民出版社 (People's Publishing House). *Min-tsu cheng-ts'e wen-hsien hui-pien* 民族政策文獻彙編 (Collections of Policy Documents on National Minorities Affairs). Peking: Jen-min ch'u-pan she, 1953, Min-tsu ch'u-pan she 民族出版社, 1958; 2 vols.

A companion publication supplementing the *Min-tsu cheng-ts'e wen-chien hui-pien* (see preceding entry). Consists mostly of official reports, speeches, etc., on Communist China's minorities affairs. Contents are arranged in chronological order by subject.

609 **Fa-lü ch'u-pan she** 法律出版社 (Legal Publishing House). *Min-tsu kung-tso shih-yung fa-kuei shou-ts'e* 民族工作適用法規手冊 (Handbook of Laws and Regulations Concerning Work with National Minorities). Peking: Fa-lü ch'u-pan she, 1958. 570p.

Texts of laws, regulations, etc., pertaining to minorities affairs, arranged in four groups: general (government organization); minorities affairs (general); production; culture, education, public hygiene, and marriage. The appendix includes a number of speeches and official reports on work with minorities. Comprehensive coverage as of 1958.

610 **China (People's Republic of China, 1949—), Kao-teng chiao-yü pu** 中華人民共和國 高等教育部 (China [People's Republic of China, 1949—], Ministry of Higher Education). *Chung-teng chuan-yeh chiao-yü fa-ling hui-pien* 中等專業教育法令彙編 (Compendium of Laws and Decrees Concerning Secondary Vocational Education). Peking: Kao-teng chiao-yü ch'u-pan she 高等教育出版社, 1957. 316p.

Contains laws, decrees, and regulations governing vocational education at the secondary school level for the period roughly from 1951 to 1956. The materials are arranged under the following nine sections: (1) school administration and organization, (2) teaching, (3) teacher training, (4) personnel and organization, (5) wages, (6) scholarship, (7) training abroad (including foreign students in China), (8) student health, and (9) miscellaneous. An appendix contains a translation of the 1955-1956 Russian curriculum of vocational training at the secondary school level.

611 **China (People's Republic of China, 1949—), Chung-yang hsüan-chü wei-yüan hui** 中華人民共和國 中央選舉委員會 (China [People's Republic of China, 1949—], Central Election Committee). *Hsüan-chü kung-tso shou-ts'e* 選舉工作手冊 (Handbook on Elections). Peking (?), [1953]. 110p.

Contains laws and directives on census-taking and elections (registration, balloting, etc.) issued between January and April 1953 (prior to the election of the National People's Congress in 1954). Commentaries by government officials on the electoral law are included.

See also *The Electoral Law of the People's Republic of China* (Peking: Foreign Languages Press, 1953), 48p., containing an explanation on the electoral law by Teng Hsiao-ping.

612 Chung-hua jen-min kung-ho kuo yu-kuan kung-an kung-tso fa-kuei hui-pien 中華人民共和國有關公安工作法規彙編

(Compendium of Laws and Regulations Concerning Public Security of the People's Republic of China). Peking: Ch'ün-chung ch'u-pan she 羣衆出版社, 1958. 150p.

A list of laws, decrees, regulations and other documents concerning public security, promulgated by the Central People's Government from October 1949 to June 1957. Arranged chronologically under the following sections: (1) 'Suppression of Counter-Revolutionary Activities', (2) public security administration, (3) public security organization, (4) foreign nationals, (5) public security checks in border areas, and (6) miscellaneous. The appendix contains the 'Provisional Regulations on Safeguarding Matters Concerning National Security' issued by the State Council on June 8, 1951.

B. REPUBLIC OF CHINA

I. GENERAL

While the framework of the legal system in Taiwan remains essentially as it existed on the Mainland before 1949, special problems peculiar to the local setting have given rise to new laws and regulations. Included in this section are general collections of those laws, statutes, and regulations currently in force in the Republic of China. Standard collections such as the Six Laws (六法全書) are omitted. The first two entries provide coverage as of 1960. The third entry (**615**) is a special collection of judicial laws, decrees and regulations.

It should be noted that the 'Bulletin of the Office of the President' (**676**) provides the most recently enacted laws and regulations, as do the other government gazettes. Both the Chinese and the English-language editions of the *China Yearbook* (**239** and **240**) also carry in each issue a selection of the most important laws enacted during the year under review. Reference also should be made to the excellent index to economic laws which appears regularly in the Bank of Taiwan Quarterly (**626**). *Fa-ling yüeh-k'an* (The Law Monthly, **960**), *Fa-lü p'ing-lun* (The Law Review, **961**) and similar periodicals described in Chapter XVIII supplement this section and contain much of value for the study of the legal system of the Republic of China.

A compilation of texts of the fundamental laws in translation, prepared by the Council for United States Aid, appears as the fourth entry (**616**).

613 Chung-hua min-kuo hsien-hsing fa-kuei ta-ch'üan pien-chi wei-yüan hui
中華民國現行法規大全編輯委員會 (Committee for the Compilation of a

Compendium of Laws and Decrees of the Republic of China). *Chung-hua min-kuo hsien-hsing fa-kuei ta-ch'üan* 中華民國現行法規大全 (Compendium of Laws and Regulations of the Republic of China). Taipei, 1954. 3 vols.

A collection of laws and regulations of the Republic of China in force as of May 1954. Each law is accompanied by the name of the promulgating agency and the date (or dates in the case of multiple revisions) on which the law or decree went into effect. In eight parts (paralleling closely the structure of the state) as follows: (1) constitution; (2) National Assembly; (3) Office of the President; (4) administration; (5) legislation; (6) judiciary; (7) examination; (8) control. The addendum provides new and revised laws and decrees promulgated while the present volume was in press. Appendix 1 gives a table of laws and regulations pending in the Legislative Yuan at the time the book went to press. Appendix 2 lists laws and regulations which became defunct during the time the volume was in press. A collection of laws and statutes of the Province of Taiwan is provided in Appendix 3. Index by title of the law, arranged by stroke count.

A supplementary volume was published in 1960, with the same arrangement, under the title *Chung-hua min-kuo hsien-hsing fa-kuei ta-ch'üan hsü-pien* . . . 續編 (Supplement to the Compendium of Laws and Regulations of the Republic of China). Includes a similar addendum and two appendices (defunct law and regulations, and laws and statutes of the Province of Taiwan). No index.

614 **China, Li-fa yüan (Ti-i chieh)** 中華民國立法院 (第一屆) (China, Legislative Yuan [First Session]). *Chung-hua min-kuo fa-lü hui-pien* 中華民國法律彙編 (Collections of Laws and Statutes of the Republic of China). Taipei, 1958. 3 vols. 3,370p.

A compendium of laws and statutes of the Republic of China to 1958, compiled and published by the Legislative Yuan. Containing 550 laws and eleven decrees in force as of January 21, 1958, the collection is divided into the following ten categories: constitution, National Assembly, Office of the President, administration, legislation, judiciary, examination, control, local administration, and miscellany.

615 **China, Ssu-fa hsing-cheng pu** 中華民國 司法行政部 (China, Ministry of Justice). *Chung-hua min-kuo ssu-fa fa-ling hui-pien* 中華民國 司法法令彙編 (Compendium of Judicial Laws and Decrees of the Republic of China). Taipei, 1955. 4 vols. 4,030p.

Contains 283 judicial and other related laws and 537 decrees and regulations in force in the Republic of China as of 1955. Arranged under nine topical headings: (1) the constitution and related laws, (2) organic laws of the central government and related laws, (3) civil laws, (4) criminal laws, (5) prison laws, (6) personnel laws, (7) accounting and auditing laws, (8) laws concerning the administration of justice, and (9) other laws. Each category is further classified under subsections. The appendix provides a list of defunct laws arranged chronologically by date of annulment, as well as the texts of fifteen laws no longer in force, mostly concerning subversion, martial laws, and narcotics. There is also a stroke index.

616 China, Ssu-fa hsing-cheng pu 中華民國 司法行政部 (China, Ministry of Justice). *Chung-hua min-kuo ssu-fa fa-ling hui-pien hsü-pien* 中華民國司法法令彙編續編
(Compendium of Judicial Laws and Decrees of the Republic of China—Supplement). Taipei, 1957—. Annual.

An annual compilation of judicial and other related laws and decrees in force in the Republic of China supplementing the preceding entry. The arrangement of the supplementary series follows that of the four-volume compendium, although not all of the nine categories are covered in each volume. Provisions of annulled laws and statutes that have some value for reference purposes are included in the appendix. The appendix also contains a list of laws and statutes no longer in force. Since 1959, each volume has also contained a list of laws published in all the preceding volumes and currently in force.

617 Council for United States Aid, Law Revision Planning Group.
Laws of the Republic of China: First Series—Major Laws. Taipei, 1961–1962. 2 vols. 1,479; 985p.

Compiled for the purpose of acquainting foreigners with the Chinese legal system and as a legal reference volume for prospective foreign investors, the first volume presents in translation some sixty-eight basic laws in force on Taiwan. Divided into sections: constitutional law, the civil code and related laws, the code of civil procedure and related laws, the criminal code and related laws, the code of criminal procedure and related laws, and administrative laws. The second volume contains sixty-three laws and regulations relating to investment, land, internal revenue and customs, and labor matters. Neither volume is indexed.

The two volumes constitute the first official translation of Chinese Nationalist laws.

2. TOPICAL

The compilations of laws and regulations contained in the present section are arranged according to the following categories of legal subject matter: administration of justice, military law, police law, law of general mobilization, criminal law and procedure, economic and financial laws, transportation and communications, and personnel regulations.

Special mention should be given to the three translations in the Sino-American Legal Series (in bilingual editions; see **623–625**), and to the translation of the income tax law (**631**).

In the field of economics, the two outstanding current compilations are those published in the Bank of Taiwan Quarterly (975) and Economic Reference Materials (734).

Concerning other subject areas, consult the appropriate parts in the general compilations discussed in the previous section.

618 Ch'en, P'u-sheng 陳樸生, **ed.** *Ssu-fa fa-ling p'an-chieh hui-pien* 司法法令判解彙編

(Collected Judicial Laws, Decrees, Precedents, and Interpretations). Taipei, 1959. 14; 2,369p.

A single-volume reference work containing judicial laws, decrees, and interpretations, as well as decisions and precedents. Arranged in four parts: general, civil, criminal, and administrative. Contains a detailed table of contents. No index. Carefully edited.

619 China, Kuo-fang pu, Chün-fa chü 中華民國 國防部軍法局 (China, Ministry of National Defense, Bureau of Military Law). *Tsui-hsin chün-fa hui-pien* 最新軍法彙編

(A Collection of Military Laws). Taipei, 1952. 2 vols. 1,632p.

A comprehensive compilation of military laws and regulations, each accompanied by the relevant interpretations, decisions and precedents (with sources provided). A number of laws and regulations no longer in force are included in the appendix. The volume is divided into the following sections: the constitution and basic laws; the criminal code for the armed forces; court martial laws; and miscellaneous related laws and regulations. A detailed table of contents is provided, but no index.

Supersedes *Hsien-hsing chün-fa lei-pien* (現行軍法類編 1940, revised edition 1944) and the *Chün-fa shou-ts'e* 軍法手冊 1947), both prepared by the Judge Advocate General's Department. Selected laws, regulations, interpretations, decisions, etc., issued since 1952 are published in the *Chün-fa chuan-k'an* 軍法專刊 *The Military Law Journal;* see 950).

620 Shih, Yü-sung 石毓嵩, **comp.** *Chün-fa fa-ling p'an-chieh hui-pien* 軍法法令判解彙編

(Collected Precedents and Interpretations of Military Laws and Regulations). Taipei, 1960. 810p.

A compilation of legal precedents, judicial decisions and interpretations with respect to military laws and regulations, both substantive and procedural, arranged chronologically under the appropriate article of law or regulation.

Emphasis has been placed on the criminal law of the armed forces, martial law, military trial law and the criminal code. Complete texts of the pertinent laws and regulations are provided. Interpretations are usually given in the form of direct quotations, and sources are supplied. No index.

621 Taiwan, Ching-wu ch'u, Chuan-yüan shih 臺灣省警務處 專員室 (Taiwan, Police Commission, Office of Specialists). *Ching-ch'a fa-ling hui-pien* 警察法令彙編
(Collected Police Laws and Regulations). Taipei, 1952. 31; 1,198p.

A compendium of police laws and regulations effective as of June 1952. Arranged in twelve sections: basic laws and regulations, organization, personnel, service, administration, 'Peace Precaution', judicial police, economic police, alien affairs, mountain area police affairs, administrative remedies, and miscellaneous. The material is also classified by legal subject matter, and is accompanied by data concerning dates and agencies of promulgation and subsequent amendments. A few laws not currently in force have been included for reference purposes, as are summaries of other laws relating to police matters. Selected legal interpretations are appended to the laws and regulations.

See also Cheng Tse-kuang 鄭澤光, comp., *Wen-hua shih-yeh kuan-hsi fa-ling chih shih-yung* 文化事業關係法令之實用 (Laws Governing Cultural Enterprises), (Taipei, 1960), 317p.

622 Pao, Ta-chang 包達璋, **comp.** *T'ai-wan ti-ch'ü ju-ching ch'u-ching fa-kuei shou-hsü hsiang-chieh* 臺灣地區入境出境法規手續詳解
(Entry and Exit Regulations of Taiwan). Taipei, 1957. 112p.

A comprehensive collection of regulations as of 1957, including a question and answer section and sample application forms. Largely outdated.

623 Fuller, Lawrence J. and Fisher, Henry A., Jr., trs.
The Law for the Punishment of Police Offenses of the Republic of China. Bilingual edition. Taipei, 1960. 37; 37p. (Sino-American Legal Series).

A translation of the law promulgated by the Nationalist Government on September 3, 1943, and put into effect on October 1, 1943 (including four minor subsequent amendments). In this entry (as in the two which follow), the English translation and the Chinese text appear on facing pages.

624 Fuller, Lawrence J. and Fisher, Henry A., Jr., trs.
The Code of Criminal Procedure of the Republic of China. Bilingual edition. Taipei, 1960. 25; 141; 141p. (Sino-American Legal Series).

A translation of the Code of Criminal Procedure promulgated on January 1, 1935 (put into effect on July 1 of the same year) including the amendments made on December 26, 1945 to forty-seven of the 516 articles. The introduction by Colonel Fuller contains an historical sketch of procedural developments in Chinese law as well as a detailed summary of criminal procedure in the courts of the Republic.

625 Fuller, Lawrence J. and Fisher, Henry A., Jr., trs.
The Criminal Code of the Republic of China. Bilingual edition. Taipei, 1960. 15; 128; 128p. (Sino-American Legal Series).

A translation of the code promulgated on January 1, 1935 and put into effect on July 1 of the same year. It also includes translation of the three amendments made in 1948 and 1954.

The translations of this and the preceding two entries are recommended by Mr. Cha Liang-chien, Vice Minister of Justice of the Republic of China, as the best and only current English versions of the Chinese texts, and have been incorporated in *Laws of the Republic of China* (see **616**).

626 T'ai-wan yin-hang, Ching-chi yen-chiu shih 臺灣銀行 經濟研究室 (Bank of Taiwan, Office of Economic Research). 'T'ai-wan ching-chi fa-kuei' 臺灣 經濟法規
(Economic Laws and Regulations of Taiwan) in *T'ai-wan yin-hang chi-k'an* 臺灣銀行季刊 (Bank of Taiwan Quarterly), Taipei, Vol. 1—, June 1947—.

A collection of documents which has been a regular feature of the Bank of Taiwan Quarterly since June 1947. The following chart indicates the periods covered in each volume.

VOLUME NUMBER	PERIOD COVERED
V. 1, No. 1–4 (Jun. 1947–Mar. 1948)	Sep. 1, 1945–Dec. 31, 1947
V. 2, No. 1–4 (Sep. 1948–Jun. 1949)	Jan. 1, 1948–Mar. 31, 1949
V. 3, No. 1–4 (Dec. 1949–Oct. 1950)	Apr. 1, 1949–Jun. 30, 1950
V. 4, No. 1–4 (Mar.–Dec. 1951)	Jul. 1, 1950–Sep. 30, 1951
V. 5, No. 1–4 (Jun. 1952–Mar. 1953)	Oct. 1, 1951–Dec. 31, 1952
V. 6, No. 1–4 (Sep. 1953–Jun. 1954)	Jan. 1, 1953–Mar. 31, 1954
V. 7, No. 1–4 (Dec. 1954–Sep. 1955)	Apr. 1, 1954–Jun. 30, 1955
V. 8, No. 1–4 (Mar.–Dec. 1956)	Jul. 1, 1955–Sep. 30, 1956
V. 9, No. 1–4 (Jun. 1957–Mar. 1958)	Oct. 1, 1956–Dec. 31, 1957
V. 10, No. 1–4 (Sep. 1958–Jun. 1959)	Jan. 1, 1958–Mar. 31, 1959
V. 11, No. 1–4 (Mar.–Dec. 1960)	Apr. 1959–Sep. 1960
V. 12, No. 1–4 (Mar.–Dec. 1961)	Oct. 1960–Sep. 1961
V. 13, No. 1–4 (Mar.–Dec. 1962)	Oct. 1961–Sep. 1962
V. 14, No. 1–4 (Mar.–Dec. 1963)	Oct. 1962–Sep. 1963

627 Chung-yang hsin-t'o-chü, T'ai-wan fen-chü 中央信託局 臺灣分局 (Central Trust of China, Taiwan Branch). *T'ai-wan sheng hsien-hsing chin-jung mao-i fa-kuei hui-pien* 臺灣省現行金融貿易法規彙編
(Current Laws and Regulations Governing Finance and Trade in Taiwan). Taipei, 1950. 220p.

A collection of laws and regulations governing finance and trade in Taiwan to October 1950. Brief annotations precede some of the laws and regulations. Appended is a classified list of import and export commodities promulgated in September 1949.

628 Taiwan, Min-cheng t'ing, Ti-cheng chü 臺灣省民政廳 地政局 (Taiwan, Department of Civil Affairs, Bureau of Land Administration). *T'ai-wan sheng ti-cheng fa-ling chi-yao* 臺灣省地政法令輯要
(Important Laws and Regulations Governing Land Administration in Taiwan Province). Revised edition. Taipei, 1952. 2 vols.

The compendium, which first appeared in 1951, is a collection of important laws and regulations governing land administration, with particular emphasis on those presently in force in Taiwan. Laws and regulations are grouped under such broad categories as general, title, price and assessment, right of property, administration of state-owned land, land utility, and miscellaneous. In two parts: laws and regulations promulgated before the end of September 1948 are included in Part 1, while those promulgated after October 1, 1948 make up Part 2.

629 Tai-wan, Kung-ch'an kuan-li ch'u 臺灣省公產管理處 (Taiwan Administration of Public Properties). *T'ai-wan sheng kung-ch'an kuan-li fa-ling hui-pien* 臺灣省公產管理法令彙編
(Collected Laws and Regulations Governing the Administration of Public Properties in Taiwan). Taipei, 1951. 16; 282p.

A collection of more than 160 laws, regulations, and administrative orders governing the administration of properties that formerly belonged to Japanese nationals or to the Japanese government before the retrocession of Taiwan to China in 1945. Arranged by broad categories covering organization, transfer, real estate; bank accounts, bonds, and bills; sales and liquidation; title and change of titles; management of public properties, etc.

630 Chang, I-fu 章逸夫, **comp.** *Tsung tung-yüan fa-kuei hui-tsuan* 總動員法規彙纂 (Compendium of Laws and Regulations Pertaining to General Mobilization). Taipei: Kuo-min ch'u-pan she 國民出版社, 1956. 711p.

In three parts: general, special, and addendum. The general section comprises largely laws and regulations of a general nature pertaining to mobilization (including the Martial Law) which were promulgated before 1949 with interpretations and court decisions. The special section, the main body of this compilation, contains specific laws and regulations promulgated prior to August 1956, and is divided into the following sections: resources control, price control, economic control, manpower control, social control, cultural control, and penalties. The addendum contains a few laws promulgated or amended in September 1956.

See also *Labour Laws and Regulations of the Republic of China* (110p.) published by the Ministry of Interior in 1961.

631 Lee, James M.
The Income Tax Law of the Republic of China (1956). Taipei, 1956. 40p.

An unofficial translation of the income tax law (120 articles) promulgated on December 23, 1955 and put into effect on January 1, 1956. The translation also includes the Statute on Income Tax Rates for 1956. Mr. Lee is a legal adviser to the Ministry of Justice of the Republic of China.

632 Chiao-tung fa-ling hui-k'an 交通法令彙刊
(Collected Laws and Regulations on Transportation and Communications). Taipei: Chiao-tung pu 交通部, Vol. 1, No. 1—, September 15, 1960—. Monthly.

A monthly listing of laws, decrees and regulations governing transportation and communications in Taiwan, published by the Ministry of Communication. Included also are cases and court decisions involving transportation and communications matters.

633 Ch'en, Ch'eng-chou 陳澄洲, **comp.** *T'ai-wan sheng hsien-hsing jen-shih fa-ling hui-pien* 臺灣省現行人事法令彙編
(Compendium of Personnel Regulations of Taiwan). Taipei: Ho-tso ching-chi yüeh-k'an she 合作經濟月刊社, 1960. 2 vols.

A comprehensive collection of civil service laws and regulations of Taiwan. The materials are taken from the *Gazette of Taiwan Provincial Government* (see **685**) and arranged under fifteen sections (examination, organization, personnel management, appointments, etc.). Each section is preceded by a table of contents which includes references to the *Gazette*.

CHAPTER XIII

GOVERNMENT, POLITICAL PARTIES, AND MASS ORGANIZATIONS

It is difficult to separate the works on government, political parties and mass organizations in countries that are ruled by essentially one party with the support of mobilized mass organizations. This is true of the Chinese Communists and Nationalists who, having been influenced by the Soviet model, came to adopt similar organizational structures.

Included in the present chapter are documentary materials on both the Chinese Communist and Nationalist governments, the Chinese Communist Party and the Kuomintang, as well as their respective affiliated women's and youth organizations. (Documentary materials on educational and cultural organizations, labor unions and other organizations are listed in Chapters XV and XIV on education and culture, and on economic and social developments, respectively.)

Rosters of personnel in both Communist and Nationalist governmental, party and mass organizations are listed in Chapters VI, VII, and VIII on directories, biographies and chronologies in Part Two.

A. PEOPLE'S REPUBLIC OF CHINA

Two sections—one on government, the other on the Communist Party and mass organizations—make up the Mainland portion of the present chapter. The section on government is further divided into a general subsection and two separate subsections dealing with the People's Political Consultative Conference and the National People's Congress. The second section, on party and mass organizations, is divided into (a) Communist Party (with a subsection on the Hundred Flowers Movement), (b) youth organizations, and (c) women's organizations.

The materials presented in these sections are mostly of Mainland origin, although some are derived from Hong Kong and Taiwan sources. Parenthetically, reference should be made to the translations of the American Consulate General in Hong Kong, the Joint Publications Research Service reports, and other translation series which appear in Chapter XX.

Attention is also drawn to a forthcoming publication of the East Asian Institute, Columbia University: Richard Sorich, *Party and Government Regulations of Communist China: Bibliography and Location of Chinese Compendia.*

I. GOVERNMENT

a. General

The People's Political Consultative Conference, convened in Peking in September of 1949, proclaimed the founding of the People's Republic of China, elected the Central People's Government Council, and adopted the Common Program which served as a provisional constitution until 1954 when succeeded by the instrument that is today the highest law of the land. With the adoption of this constitution in 1954, the National People's Congress became the supreme organ of the government, taking over the legislative functions of the Conference, which thereafter existed only in a nominal consultative capacity. A standing committee was created to act on behalf of the Congress when the latter was not in session.

Prior to the adoption of the new constitution, the government published a number of official gazettes under the auspices of various ministries. They were classified as 'internal publications' and hence were not available to the outside world. These separate gazettes suspended publication with the first issue of the gazette of the State Council in March 1955. The latter (listed directly below), together with the gazette of the Standing Committee of the National People's Congress (643) constitutes the basic source of primary documentation on the work of the Chinese Communist government.

The history and organization of the Central People's Government (including the activities of the People's Political Consultative Conference and the National People's Congress) are well documented. Such documentation is described in the appropriate sections below. Sources on government activity at the local level are not available, and for this deficiency the only remedy is the local press. (The reader should consult the catalog of local newspapers from the Mainland available at the Union Research Institute in Hong Kong, 1751), as well as the list of Mainland local newspapers available at the Library of Congress.

Convenient lists of meetings of the National People's Congress, the State Council, etc., are published yearly in *Current Background*:

VOLUME NO.	PERIOD COVERED
No. 637 (10–20–60)	July 1959 to June 1960
No. 658 (8–3–61)	July 1960 to June 1961
No. 686 (8–1–62)	July 1961 to June 1962
No. 711 (9–4–63)	July 1962 to June 1963
No. 746 (11–29–64)	July 1963 to June 1964

See also the relevant sections of the People's Handbook (212), the directories of the State Council, the People's Political Consultative Conference, and the National People's Congress in Chapter VI, and pertinent biographies in Chapter VII. Guides to administrative divisions are listed in Chapter IX.

634 Chung-hua jen-min kung-ho kuo kuo-wu yüan kung-pao 中華人民共和國國務院公報
(Official Gazette of the State Council of the People's Republic of China). Peking, 1954 No. 1— (No. 1—), March 1955—. Irregular.

One of the two most important official gazettes published by the government of the People's Republic of China (the other is the official gazette of the Standing Committee of the National People's Congress; see 643). The gazette of the State Council publishes laws and decrees proclaimed by the Chairman of the central government of the People's Republic of China; treaties and agreements signed and notes exchanged with other countries; resolutions, orders and directives issued by the State Council, together with important orders and directives issued by the various ministries and other agencies directly subordinate to the State Council. Resolutions, orders and directives emanating from the provincial, autonomous regional, and municipal governments which have national significance are also included.

Publication of the gazettes of the various ministries ceased with the appearance of the gazette of the State Council in March 1955. Annual subject index.

635 Jen-min ch'u-pan she 人民出版社 (People's Publishing House). *Cheng-fu kung-tso pao-kao, 1950* 政府工作報告 1950
(Reports on Government Work, 1950). Peking: Jen-min ch'u-pan she, 1951, 1,117p.

A comprehensive collection of official reports on the affairs of the state from October 1,1949 through 1950 by agencies of the central government and by local governments above the municipal level. Reports of the central government are given first, followed by local reports arranged by region. All reports are taken from newspapers, and those which were originally published in government gazettes have been checked, with discrepancies indicated in footnotes.

No reports of this scope are available in single volumes for later years; however, selections of the most important reports were published regularly in the *Hsin-hua yüeh-pao* (New China Monthly, **882**) and the People's Handbook (**212**).

b. People's Political Consultative Conference

Included in this section are the available documents on the various sessions of the P.P.C.C. Reference is made in the annotations to the People's Handbook for selections of important documents emerging from sessions not covered in single volumes. The extent of documentary coverage is indicated (single-volume collections by an asterisk, People's Handbook by the symbol '△', and People's Daily by a double asterisk) in the calendar of the National Committee meetings of the P.P.C.C. directly below.

*	First plenary session of the P.P.C.C.			Sep. 21–30, 1949
△	First National Committee, First Session			Oct. 9, 1949
△	,,	,,	,, Second Session	Jun. 14–23, 1950
*	,,	,,	,, Third Session	Oct. 23–Nov. 1, 1951
*	,,	,,	,, Fourth Session	Feb. 4–7, 1953
△	Second National Committee, First Session			Dec. 21–25, 1954
*	,,	,,	,, Second Session	Jan. 30–Feb. 7, 1956
*	,,	,,	,, Third Session	Mar. 5–20, 1957
△	Third National Committee, First Session			Apr. 17–29, 1959
**	,,	,,	,, Second Session	Mar. 29–Apr. 11, 1960
△	,,	,,	,, Third Session	Mar. 23–Apr. 18, 1962
**	,,	,,	,, Fourth Session	Nov. 17–Dec. 4, 1963

636Hsin min-chu ch'u-panshe 新民主出版社(New Democracy Publishing House). *Chung-hua jen-min kung-ho kuo k'ai-kuo wen-hsien* 中華人民共和國開國文獻 (Collection of Documents on the Founding of the People's Republic of China). Hong Kong: Hsin min-chu ch'u-pan she, 1949. 311p.

A collection of documents on the People's Political Consultative Conference held in Peking in September 1949. In four parts: (1) proceedings, (2) speeches by delegates (the major portion of the book), (3) basic documents on the Conference (including resolutions), and (4) an appendix containing editorials of the *Jen-min jih-pao* and *Pravda*, etc. A basic source on the founding of the Chinese Communist Government.

637 **Chung-kuo jen-min cheng-chih hsieh-shang hui-i ti-i chieh ch'üan-t'i hui-i chung-yao wen-hsien** 中國人民政治協商會議第一屆全體會議重要文獻 (Important Documents of the First Plenary Session of the Chinese People's Political Consultative Conference). Peking: Hsin-hua shu-tien 新華書店, 1949. 80p.

Incorporated in the present volume are the Organic Laws of the People's Consultative Conference and the Central People's Government, the 'Common Program', and the Declaration of the First Plenary Session. Addresses by Mao Tse-tung and Chu Teh are included. The volume also contains a conference name list. For a translation of the first four documents, see *The Important Documents of the First Plenary Session of the Chinese People's Political Consultative Conference* (Peking: Foreign Languages Press, 1949). The First Plenary Session was held in Peking, September 21–30, 1949.

638 **Hsin-hua shu-tien** 新華書店 (New China Book Company). *Chung-kuo jen-min cheng-chih hsieh-shang hui-i ti-i chieh ch'üan-t'i hui-i chiang-hua pao-kao fa-yen* 中國人民政治協商會議第一屆全體會議講話報告發言 (Messages, Reports and Speeches of the First Plenary Session of the People's Political Consultative Conference). Peking: Hsin-hua shu-tien, 1949. 250p.

A companion volume to the preceding entry. Together they duplicate the first entry.

639 **Chung-kuo jen-min cheng-chih hsieh-shang hui-i ti-i chieh ch'üan-kuo wei-yüan hui ti-san tz'u hui-i wen-chien** 中國人民政治協商會議第一屆全國委員會第三次會議文件 (Documents of the Third Session of the First National Committee of the People's Political Consultative Conference). Peking: Jen-min ch'u-pan she 人民出版社, 1951. 130p.

Contains Mao Tse-tung's opening and closing addresses, reports by Chou En-Lai (on the work of the government), P'eng Chen (on the Resist-America Aid-Korea Campaign), Ch'en Yün (on financial and economic affairs), Kuo

Mo-jo (on the cultural and educational programs), and Ch'en Shu-t'ung (on the work of the Standing Committee of the National Committee of the People's Political Consultative Conference). Resolutions are included. An appendix provides the texts of eight speeches delivered at the Third Session (October 23–November 1, 1951).

For highlights of the resolutions adopted by the First and Second Sessions of the First National Committee of the P.P.C.C., October 9, 1949 and June 14–23, 1950, see People's Handbook, 1952, pp. 160–161.

640 Chung-kuo jen-min cheng-chih hsieh-shang hui-i ti-i chieh ch'üan-kuo wei-yüan hui ti-ssu tz'u hui-i wen-chien 中國人民政治協商會議第一屆全國委員會第四次會議文件

(Documents of the Fourth Session of the First National Committee of the People's Political Consultative Conference). Peking: Jen-min ch'u-pan she 人民出版社, 1953. 65p.

Includes addresses by Mao Tse-tung, Chou En-lai (on the work of the government), Ch'en Shu-t'ung (on the work of the Standing Committee of the National Committee), Kuo Mo-jo (on the World Peace Congress) and An Tzu-wen (on anti-bureaucratism). Additionally, it carries texts of resolutions and name lists. The Fourth Session was held in Peking, February 4–7, 1953.

641 Chung-kuo jen-min cheng-chih hsieh-shang hui-i ti-erh chieh ch'üan-kuo wei-yüan hui ti-erh tz'u hui-i wen-chien 中國人民政治協商會議第二屆全國委員會第二次會議文件

(Documents of the Second Session of the Second National Committee of the People's Political Consultative Council). Peking: Jen-min ch'u-pan she 人民出版社, 1957. 117p.

Includes reports by Chou En-lai (on the work of the government), Li Chi-sheng (on the work of the Standing Committee of the National Committee), Kuo Mo-jo (on intellectuals), Ch'en Shu-t'ung (on the 'socialist construction' of industry and commerce), Tung Pi-wu (on the anti-revolutionaries), and Ch'en Po-ta (on agriculture). Appended is a *Jen-min jih-pao* editorial on the 'peaceful liberation' of Taiwan, and a name list of the Second Session, January 30–February 7, 1956. For a résumé of the resolutions adopted, see *Jen-min shou-ts'e, 1958*, p. 317.

For an English translation of Chou En-lai's report at the Second Session, see Chou En-lai, *Political Report* (Peking: Foreign Languages Press, 1956), 47p.

For selected documents of the First Session of the Second National Committee of the P.P.C.C., see *Hsin-hua yüeh-pao*, 1955 No. 1, pp. 1–58.

642 Chung-kuo jen-min cheng-chih hsieh-shang hui-i ti-erh chieh ch'üan-kuo wei-yüan hui ti-san tz'u hui-i wen-chien 中國人民政治協商會議第二屆全國委員會第三次會議文件

(Documents of the Third Session of the Second National Committee of the People's Political Consultative Conference). Peking: Jen-min ch'u-pan she 人民出版社, 1957. 99p.

Consists of reports by Chou En-lai (on his European visit, 1956–1957), Ch'en Shu-t'ung (on the work of the Standing Committee of the National Committee), Ch'en Yün (on increased production and austerity), Tung Pi-wu (on political and legal work), Ch'en Cheng-jen (on cooperative agriculture and agricultural production), resolutions passed during the session and an editorial from *Jen-min jih-pao*. The Third Session was held in Peking, March 5–20, 1957.

For selected documents of the First and Third Sessions of the Third National Committee of the People's Political Consultative Conference, April 17–29, 1959, and March 23–April 18, 1962, see People's Handbook, 1959, pp. 120–129, and the 1962 edition, pp. 9–12, respectively.

Documentation on the Second and Fourth Sessions of the Third National Committee is available in the People's Daily, March 29–April 11, 1960 and November 17–December 4, 1963.

c. National People's Congress

The available documentary coverage of the National People's Congress is indicated (single-volume collections by an asterisk, *Hsin-hua pan-yüeh-k'an* by the symbol '×', the People's Handbook by a '△', and the People's Daily by a double asterisk) in the calendar of sessions provided directly below.

*	First Congress, First Session	September 15–28, 1954
*	First Congress, Second Session	July 5–30, 1955
*	First Congress, Third Session	June 15–30, 1956
*	First Congress, Fourth Session	June 26–July 15, 1957
×	First Congress, Fifth Session	February 1–11, 1958
△	Second Congress, First Session	April 19–28, 1959
*	Second Congress, Second Session	March 30–April 10, 1960
**	Second Congress, Third Session	March 27–April 16, 1962
**	Second Congress, Fourth Session	November 17–December 3, 1963

A Taiwan compilation (**649**) contains in a single volume documents selected from sessions of the two congresses between September 1954 and April 1960. Reference should be made, of course, to the first entry in this section—the gazette of the Standing Committee (see also the gazette of the State Council, **634**, listed in the first section above).

643 **Chung-hua jen-min kung-ho kuo ch'üan-kuo jen-min tai-piao ta-hui ch'ang-wu wei-yüan hui kung-pao** 中華人民共和國全國人民代表大會常務委員會公報
(Official Gazette of the Standing Committee of the National People's Congress, People's Republic of China). Peking, No. 1—, April 1, 1957—. Irregular.

The Gazette publishes legislation and resolutions passed by the National People's Congress and various reports received by the Congress from government officials at its regular sessions. Included also are lists of appointments, dismissals and transfers. An index is available for Nos. 1–35, April 1, 1957–November 29, 1958, arranged under the following headings: general, state structure, politics and law, finance and economic affairs, culture and education, minorities affairs, Overseas Chinese affairs, foreign relations, committee personnel of the National People's Congress, delegates to the National People's Congress, appointments, transfers and dismissals.

An extremely important source for reference on Chinese Communist legislation.

644 Chung-hua jen-min kung-ho kuo ti-i chieh ch'üan-kuo jen-min tai-piao ta-hui ti-i tz'u hui-i wen-chien 中華人民共和國第一屆全國人民代表大會第一次會議文件

(Documents of the First Session of the First National People's Congress of the People's Republic of China). Peking: Jen-min ch'u-pan she 人民出版社, 1955. 189p.

Contains an opening address by Mao Tse-tung, a report by Liu Shao-ch'i on the draft constitution (together with the text of the constitution adopted in September 1954), and a report on the work of the government by Chou En-lai. Organic laws of the National People's Congress, the State Council, the People's Courts, the People's Procuratorates, the local people's congresses and councils are also incorporated in the volume, as are name lists of the Central People's Government, the State Council, the National Defense Commission, and the various committees of the National People's Congress, and the names of delegates to the general sessions of the Congress. The proceedings of the First Session of the Congress, September 15–28, 1954, are appended.

For an English translation, see *Documents of the First Session of the First National People's Congress of the People's Republic of China* (Peking: Foreign Languages Press, 1955), 231p., and *Report on the Draft Constitution of the People's Republic of China* by Liu Shao-ch'i, second edition (Peking: Foreign Languages Press, 1962), 94p.

645 Chung-hua jen-min kung-ho kuo ti-i chieh ch'üan-kuo jen-min tai-piao ta-hui ti-erh tz'u hui-i wen-chien 中華人民共和國第一屆全國人民代表大會第二次會議文件

(Documents of the Second Session of the First National People's Congress of the People's Republic of China). Peking: Jen-min ch'u-pan she 人民出版社, 1956. 341p.

Contains documents on the following subjects: the First Five-Year Plan, the final accounts of 1954 and the budget for 1955, reclamation of the Yellow River, the Military Draft Law, the work of the Standing Committee of the National

People's Congress, the abolition of the provinces of Jehol and Sikang, the abolition of the Ministry of Fuel Industry and the establishment of the Ministries of Coal Industry, Electrical Power Industry and Petroleum Industry.

For a selection of other important documents (including speeches) of this session, July 5–30, 1955, see the People's Handbook, 1956, pp. 159–248.

646 **Chung-hua jen-min kung-ho kuo ti-i chieh ch'üan-kuo jen-min tai-piao ta-hui ti-san tz'u hui-i wen-chien** 中華人民共和國第一屆全國人民代表大會第三次會議文件
(Documents of the Third Session of the First National People's Congress of the People's Republic of China). Peking: Jen-min ch'u-pan she 人民出版社, 1956. 364p.

Contains documents on the following subjects: final accounts of 1955 and the budget for 1956, model regulations for advanced agricultural producers' cooperatives, and the work of the Standing Committee of the National People's Congress. Selected speeches are included. For a complete collection of the latter, see *Chung-hua jen-min kung-ho kuo ti-i chieh ch'üan-kuo jen-min tai-piao ta-hui ti-san tz'u hui-i hui-k'an* 中華人民共和國第一屆全國人民代表大會第三次會議彙刊 (Compendium of Documents of the Third Session of the First National People's Congress of the People's Republic of China), (Peking: Jen-min ch'u-pan she, 1957), pp. 103–816. The Third Session was held in Peking June 15–30, 1956.

See also *New China Advances to Socialism*, containing reports by Chou En-lai and other leaders at the third session (Peking: Foreign Languages Press, 1956), 200p.

647 **Chung-hua jen-min kung-ho kuo ti-i chieh ch'üan-kuo jen-min tai-piao ta-hui ti-ssu tz'u hui-i hui-k'an** 中華人民共和國第一屆全國人民代表大會第四次會議彙刊
(Compendium of Documents of the Fourth Session of the First National People's Congress). Peking: Jen-min ch'u-pan she 人民出版社, 1957. 1,686p.

Contains documents on the following subjects: the agenda, final accounts of 1956 and the budget for 1957, the work of the Standing Committee of the National People's Congress, the work of the judiciary, the establishment of the Kwangsi Chuang and Ninghsia Hui Autonomous Regions, and the Sino-Burmese boundary question. Namelists, greetings, and speeches are included, the latter item forming the bulk of this compilation (1,327 pages). The Fourth Session was held in Peking, June 26–July 15, 1957.

For a collection of documents of the Fifth Session, February 1–11, 1958, see *Hsin-hua pan-yüeh k'an*, 1958 No. 5 (March 10, 1958), pp. 3–105.

648 **Second Session of the Second National People's Congress of the People's Republic of China (Documents).** Peking: Foreign Languages Press, 1960. 188p.

An English translation of some of the more important reports, resolutions and speeches of the Second Session of the Second National People's Congress held in Peking from March 30 to April 10, 1960, together with the full text of the National Program for Agricultural Development (1956–1967). *Chung-hua jen-min kung-ho kuo ti-erh chieh ch'üan-kuo jen-min tai-piao ta-hui ti-erh tz'u hui-i wen-chien* 中華人民共和國第二屆全國人民代表大會第二次會議文件 (Documents of the Second Session of the Second National People's Congress of the People's Republic of China), (Peking: Jen-min ch'u-pan she, 1960), 140p., was not available for examination.

See also *Speeches Given at Second Session of Second National People's Congress, Communist China*, translated in the Joint Publications Research Service reports:

J.P.R.S. NO.	DATE	PAGINATION	U.S.G.P.O. MONTHLY CATALOG NO.
3771	8–31–60	162p.	1960–17217
3877	9–13–60	72p.	17260
5373	8–29–60	15p.	17471
6027	9–20–60	106p.	17649
5307	9–15–60	519p.	18749
5635	10–21–60	217p.	1961– 856
6165	11–11–60	219p.	1007
6389	12–12–60	199p.	1112
6397	12–16–60	154p.	2259
6491	12–29–60	264p.	2301
6526	1– 9–61	65p.	2311
6493	1– 3–61	51p.	4458
6623	1–20–61	54p.	4523
6483	12–28–60	85p.	7699
6755	2–20–61	200p.	7765
6825	3– 1–61	122p.	7820

For a selection of documents of the First Session of the Second National People's Congress, April 19–28, 1959, see the People's Handbook 1959, pp. 86–119, and the next entry in this Guide. See also the *Report on the Work of the Government* delivered by Chou En-lai at the First Session (Peking: Foreign Languages Press, 1959), 72p.

Documentation on the Third and Fourth Sessions of the Second National People's Congress is available in the People's Daily, March 27–April 16, 1962 and November 17–December 3, 1963, respectively.

649 China, Kuo-fang pu, Ch'ing-pao chü 中華民國 國防部 情報局 (China, Ministry of National Defense, Bureau of Intelligence). *Wei jen-tai hui li-chieh ko-tz'u hui-i chung-yao tzu-liao hui-pien* 偽人代會歷屆各次會議重要資料彙編 (A Collection of Important Documents of the Puppet National People's Congresses). Taipei, 1962. 856p.

A Collection of documents covering the five sessions of the First Congress and the first two sessions of the Second Congress held between September 1954 and April 1960, selected so as to reflect the major themes and tasks up for discussion and action at each session. A brief historical note accompanies the documents. The first part of the volume is given over to a number of basic documents respecting the Congress, among them its organic law, the election laws and the constitution. The material has been carefully selected and is conveniently arranged. Limited distribution.

For a more complete collection of the documents (and English translations), see the preceding entries.

2. THE CHINESE COMMUNIST PARTY AND MASS ORGANIZATIONS

Although the Chinese Communist Party is the sole repository of power on the Mainland, the C.C.P. permits the existence of several minor parties, of which the China Democratic League and the Revolutionary Committee of the Kuomintang are fairly representative. There are, unfortunately, no major documentary collections dealing with the activities of these groups, although the *Kuang-ming jih-pao* (see **836**) presumably is published by the minor parties.

The political importance of the mass organizations to the Communist Party has resulted in the proliferation of such organizations as the All-China Federation of Trade Unions, the All-China Federation of Democratic Youth, the New China Democratic Youth League, the All-China Students Federation, the All-China Women's Democratic Federation, the All-China Journalists' Association, the All-China Federation of Scientific Societies, the All-China Federation of Literary and Art Circles, the Red Cross Society of China, and many others, including religious bodies and friendship associations with other countries. While all of these organizations, irrespective of their membership or stated concerns, have a definite political function, only materials on the women's and youth associations are included in the present section. Other mass organizations are dealt with elsewhere. For example, documents on the All-China Federation of Trade Unions (**732** and **733**) and the All-China Federation of Industry and Commerce (**728** and **729**) are located in chapter XIV. Various newspapers and periodicals, organs of the party and mass organizations are listed in Chapter XVII.

For a detailed description of some of the more important Mainland mass organizations, the reader is advised to consult the compilation of the Japanese Cabinet Research Office (**300**) and similar Taiwan compilations listed in Chapter VI on directories.

a. The Chinese Communist Party

The Eighth National Congress of the C.C.P., the first meeting of the Congress since the establishment on the Central People's Government in 1949, was convened in Peking in September of 1956. Prior to the meeting of the Eighth National Congress and the election on that occasion of the Eighth Central Committee, party affairs were administered by the Seventh Central Committee (elected in 1945) which between the years 1949 and 1956 met in eight plenary sessions. No published collections of documents are available concerning these sessions, but some of the more important resolutions and resumés of the meetings are included in the People's Handbook and in the People's Daily.

Included in the present section are only those collections of documents beginning with the Eighth National Congress and the Eighth Central Committee. The Congress as such is well documented by the first entry in this section. For the Eighth Central Committee, which held ten plenary sessions in the years 1956–September 1962 (three of them—the fourth, fifth and sixth—in 1958, an eventful year which saw the beginning of the 'Great Leap Forward' campaign and the inauguration of the communes), documentation is available for only three of the ten plenary sessions (the sixth, eighth and ninth), as well as for the second session of the Eighth National Congress. Similar documents on the other sessions can, however, be found in the People's Daily and the People's Handbook for the periods in question.

A good list of all Central Committee and Politburo meetings held between 1949 and 1959, complete with dates, location, and major resolutions of each session, is available in *Communist China, 1949–1959*, Vol. 1, pp. 11–15, published by the Union Research Institute in Hong Kong. (Two plenary sessions have been held since 1959: the Ninth Plenary Session, from January 14 to 18, 1961, and the Tenth Plenary Session, from September 24 to 27, 1962.)

The last three entries (**656–658**) in the present section concern indoctrination of cadres, useful sources for the study of party discipline and cadre education.

For the organization of the C.C.P., and for position and personal data of party personnel, see the directory and biography chapters in Part Two. Documentary material on the Hundred Flowers Movement is treated in a separate section directly below.

650   Chung-kuo kung-ch'an tang, Chung-yang pan-kung t'ing 中國共產黨中央辦公廳 (Chinese Communist Party, Central Committee, Secretariat). *Chung-kuo kung-ch'an tang ti-pa tz'u ch'üan-kuo tai-piao ta-hui wen-hsien* 中國共產黨第八次全國代表大會文獻
(Collected Documents of the Eighth National Congress of the Communist Party of China). Peking: Jen-min ch'u-pan she 人民出版社, 1957. 1,101p.

A comprehensive collection of documents emerging from the Eighth National Congress of the C.C.P. held in Peking in September 1956. Comprises the organization and proceedings of the Congress (including reports by Mao Tsetung, Liu Shao-ch'i, Chou En-lai, Teng Hsiao-p'ing, Tung Pi-wu, speeches by delegates, and greetings from Communist parties abroad), as well as the text of the constitution of the C.C.P.

A translation was published by the Peking Foreign Languages Press in 1956 under the title *Eighth National Congress of the Communist Party of China*, in three volumes (documents, speeches, and greetings from fraternal parties). Omitted from the latter were the report by Tung Pi-wu on the work of the Credentials Committee, the greater portion of speeches by delegates (only 24 of the 113 speeches were translated) and the part devoted to the organization of the Congress.

Another English compilation is also available in three parts under the title *8th C.C.P. Congress Proceedings and Related Materials*, containing more than the Peking Foreign Languages Press edition but less than the Chinese-language edition.

651 Second Session of the Eighth National Congress of the Communist Party of China. Peking: Foreign Languages Press, 1958. 95p.

Contains the following five documents: (1) report on the work of the Central Committee by Liu Shao-ch'i; (2) a resolution on the above report; (3) a resolution on the Moscow meetings of representatives of Communist and workers' parties; (4) explanations on the second revised draft of the national program for agricultural development (1956–1967) by Tan Chen-lin; and (5) a resolution on the program for agricultural development. The session was held from May 5 to 23, 1958.

Chung-kuo kung-ch'an tang ti-pa chieh ch'üan-kuo tai-piao ta-hui ti-erh tz'u hui-i wen-chien chi 中國共產黨第八屆全國代表大會第二次會議文件集 (Collected Documents of the Second Session of the Eighth National Congress of the Communist Party of China) was not available for examination.

652 Chung-kuo kung-ch'an tang ti-pa chieh chung-yang wei-yüan hui ti-liu tz'u ch'üan-t'i hui-i wen-chien 中國共產黨第八屆中央委員會第六次全體會議文件
(Documents of the Sixth Plenary Session of the Eighth Central Committee of the Chinese Communist Party). Peking: Jen-min ch'u-pan she 人民出版社, 1958. 32p.

Contains the following three documents: (1) the communiqué of the session; (2) resolutions on questions concerning the people's communes; and (3) the 'decision approving Comrade Mao Tse-tung's proposal that he will not stand as candidate for chairman of the People's Republic of China for the next term of office'. The session was held in Wuchang November 28–December 10, 1958.

For a translation of this work, see *Sixth Plenary Session of the Eighth Central Committee of the Communist Party of China* (Peking: Foreign Languages Press, 1958), 51p.

653 Chung-kuo kung-ch'an tang ti-pa chieh chung-yang wei-yüan hui ti-pa tz'u ch'üan-t'i hui-i wen-chien 中國共產黨第八屆中央委員會第八次全體會議文件
(Documents of the Eighth Plenary Session of the Eighth Central Committee of the Chinese Communist Party). Peking: Jen-min ch'u-pan she 人民出版社, 1959. 13p.

Contains the communiqué of the session and its resolution on 'developing the campaign for increasing production and practicing economy'. (The session was held at Lushan August 2–16, 1959.)

For a translation of this pamphlet see *Eighth Plenary Session of the Eighth Central Committee of the Communist Party of China (Documents)* (Peking: Foreign Languages Press, 1959), 27p.

654 Chung-kuo kung-ch'an tang ti-pa chieh chung-yang wei-yüan hui ti-chiu t'zu ch'üan-t'i hui-i kung-pao 中國共產黨第八屆中央委員會第九次全體會議公報

(Communiqué of the Ninth Plenary Session of the Eighth Central Committee of the Chinese Communist Party). Hong Kong: Sheng-huo tu-shu hsin-chih san-lien shu-tien 生活讀書新知三聯書店, 1961. 28p.

In addition to the final communiqué, the pamphlet contains a resolution approved at the session and a *Jen-min jih-pao* editorial of January 22, 1961, both on the 1960 Moscow Conference of the Communist and Workers' Parties.

For the text of the communiqué of the Tenth Plenary Session see People's Handbook, 1963, pp. 1–3, reprinted from the People's Daily, September 29, 1962.

655 Jen-min ch'u-pan she 人民出版社 (People's Publishing House). *Chung-kuo kung-ch'an tang ch'üan-kuo tai-piao hui-i wen-chien* 中國共產黨全國代表會議文件 (Documents of the National Conference of the Chinese Communist Party). Peking: Jen-min ch'u-pan she, 1955. 36p.

Contains four documents which emerged from the National Conference of the C.C.P. (Peking, March 21–31, 1955): (1) the communiqué of the conference issued by the Central Committee of the C.C.P. on April 4, 1955; (2) the resolution on the draft first five-year plan for the economic development of the country; (3) the resolution on the anti-party bloc of Kao Kang and Jao Shu-shih; and (4) the resolution on the establishment of central and local control committees of the party. The appendix carries four *Jen-min jih-pao* editorials on the resolutions.

For a translation of this work, see *Documents of the National Conference of the Communist Party of China (March 1955)* (Peking: Foreign Languages Press, 1955), 64p.

656 'Hsüeh-hsi' tsa-chih pien-chi pu '學習' 雜誌 編輯部 (Editorial Department of 'Study' Magazine). *She-hui chu-i chiao-yü k'o-ch'eng ti yüeh-tu wen-chien hui-pien* 社會主義教育課程的閱讀文件彙編

(Collected Readings and Documents for the Curriculum in Socialist Education). Peking: Jen-min ch'u-pan she 人民出版社, 1957–1958. 3 vols. 1,129; 1,112; 430p.

A collection of documents, speeches, etc., which emerged in connection with Mao Tse-tung's address 'On the Direct Handling of Contradictions Among the People', designed for use in the program of 'socialist education'. In two volumes:

Volume 1 (in two parts)—a 'minimum reading list' comprising 93 readings and documents (64 Chinese and 29 non-Chinese), published in December 1957; Volume 2—a 'maximum reading list' comprising 52 titles (38 Chinese and 14 non-Chinese), published in April 1958. Volume 3, a supplement to Volume 1 published in September 1958, consists of 38 items (34 Chinese and 4 non-Chinese).

Providing basic documentary materials bearing on Chinese Communist attitudes, methods and policies, the three volumes have considerable value.

A complete list in English translation of the titles of Chinese materials in Volume 1, including bibliographical data (among them citations to selected English-language translations available in the United States) was prepared by Professor H. Arthur Steiner and published in his article 'The Curriculum in Chinese Socialist Education: An Official Bibliography of "Maoism"', in *Pacific Affairs*, Vol. 31, No. 3 (September 1958).

657 **Chung-kuo kung-ch'an tang, Chung-yang Hua-nan fen-chü, Hsüan-chuan pu** 中國共產黨 中央華南分局 宣傳部 (Chinese Communist Party, South China Bureau, Propaganda Department). *Kan-pu hsüeh-hsi tzu-liao* 幹部學習資料 (Study Materials for Cadres). Canton: Hsin-hua shu-tien 新華書店 and Hua-nan jen-min ch'u-pan she 華南人民出版社, 1950–1953. 59 vols.

A pamphlet study series designed for the indoctrination of cadres. Each volume consists of a number of official documents (statements, speeches, proclamations, newspaper editorials, articles, etc.) on a special topic or topics such as Sino-Soviet relations (Vol. 1), the People's Political Consultative Conference (Vol. 3), the Korean War (Vol. 14), the Anti-Rightist campaign (Vol. 27), labor insurance (Vol. 32), religion (Vol. 33), the thirtieth anniversary of the founding of the Chinese Communist Party (Vols. 34–36), 'Studying Mao Tse-tung's Works' (Vol. 39), and the Three-Anti Movement (Vols. 42–44).

658 **China, Nei-cheng pu, Tiao-ch'a chü** 中華民國 內政部 調查局 (China, Ministry of Interior, Bureau of Investigation). *Kung-fei san-shih-chiu nien 'cheng-tang' tzu-liao hui-chi* 共匪三十九年 ⌊整黨⌉ 資料彙輯 (Compendium of Documents Concerning the 1950 'Party Rectification' Movement of the Communist Bandits). Taipei, 1950. 82p.

A collection of documents selected from Chinese Communist newspapers on the C.C.P. rectification movement in 1950, arranged in four sections. Section 1 contains documents and progress reports on the movement issued by C.C.P. regional bureaus. Section 2 contains reports by the New Democratic Youth Corps, the armed forces, trade unions and other organizations. Section 3 consists of three speeches on the movement by Mao Tse-tung, Liu Shao-ch'i and Hsiao Hsiang-jung. Section 4 is a collection of *Jen-min jih-pao* editorials. Two newspaper reports on the participation of other political parties in the movement appear in an appendix.

(1) *The Hundred Flowers Movement*

The Hundred Flowers Movement, initiated by the C.C.P. in 1956, rose and fell spectacularly within roughly a year's time. The constructive criticism that the regime had hoped to elicit from various segments of Chinese society, including its own membership, soon swelled out of control in both volume and variety, and came ultimately to challenge the very leadership of the party.

Except for the first entry listed below, no other similar collections of the criticisms aired in the years 1957–1958 are available from the Mainland, although much is to be found in newspapers such as the *Kuang-ming jih-pao* (**836**), for the period in question. A monthly periodical, *Cheng-ming* 爭鳴 (Contending), published by the Democratic League in response to the Hundred Flowers Movement, served as the forum for intellectuals for a brief period in 1957, and its first five issues (February–June 1957) carried open and frank criticisms of the C.C.P. and the government. In July 1957 the publication was converted by the party into an organ directed against the 'rightists'. A number of self-criticisms by high officials of the Democratic League appeared thereafter. The periodical was suspended in January 1959. The *Hsin-hua pan-yüeh k'an* (New China Semi-Monthly, **882**), 1957–1958, also contains a great deal on the anti-rightist campaign, as does the 1958 People's Handbook, pp. 28–182.

The other three compilations included in this section are of Hong Kong origin, and they provide the bulk of the criticism published in the Mainland press. The most substantial is the second entry. The last entry (**662**) is given over entirely to criticisms voiced by members of the party.

For translations of representative types of criticisms (together with a study of the movement), see Roderick MacFarquhar, *The Hundred Flowers Campaign and the Chinese Intellectuals* (New York: Frederick A. Praeger, 1960), and the translation series issued by the American Consulate General in Hong Kong for the period 1957–1958 (especially the 1957 issues of *Current Background*). Theodore H. E. Chen's *Thought Reform of the Chinese Intellectuals* (Hong Kong: Hong Kong University Press, 1959) is a good study of the role and treatment of intellectuals in Communist China, including the history of the early phase of the Hundred Flowers Movement. The book contains excerpts of some of the major criticisms aired against the party and the government. See also Mu Fu-sheng, *The Wilting of the Hundred Flowers: The Chinese Intelligentsia Under Mao* (New York: Praeger, 1963), 324p.

The *Kung-fei cheng-su fei-wei fen-tzu tzu-liao hui-pien* 共匪整肅匪偽份子資料彙編 (Reference Materials on the Purge of Communist Bandit and Puppet Personnel) provides a substantial list of more than 250 Communist and non-Communist political, governmental and cultural leaders purged in the aftermath of the Hundred Flowers Movement, complete with personal and position data, including the date and a brief account of the purge, accompanied by the source of information (see **308**).

659   Pei-ching shih hsüeh-sheng lien-ho hui 北京市學生聯合會 (Peking Student Union). *K'an! Che shih shih-mo yen-lun?* 看！這是什麽言論？ (Look! What Kind of Talk Is This?). Peking, 1957. 42p.

Smuggled into Hong Kong in 1962 by a refugee student, this is a collection of criticisms made by students from four Peking universities during the height of the Hundred Flowers campaign in May and June, 1957. Of the twelve items composing the original pamphlet, two are missing and four others are incomplete. Thirty of the original forty-two pages have been preserved. The statements range from reasoned arguments (items 1 and 2) to a scathing denunciation of Mao Tse-tung by a party member (item 11). Nearly all of the protestants are critical of the party's handling of the Hu Feng case, several selections treating this question at some length.

For an English translation, see Dennis J. Doolin, *Communist China, the Politics of Student Opposition* (Stanford: The Hoover Institution, 1964), 70p.

660 Ch'en, Ch'üan 陳權**, ed.** '*Ming Fang*' *hsüan-ts'ui* └ 鳴放 ┐ 選萃 (Selections of the Minutes of the 'Blooming and Contending' Campaign in Communist China). Hong Kong: Tzu-yu ch'u-pan she 自由出版社, 1958. 2 vols. 357p.

A comprehensive collection of criticisms aired during the Hundred Flowers Movement in 1957 based on Chinese Communist sources and compiled by an anti-Communist organization in Hong Kong. The material—criticisms attributed to 429 individuals—is arranged in eleven chapters. Chapter 1 is a collection of statements by leaders of various political parties and constitutes the most important part of this collection. The volume contains anti-party statements emanating from other sources: from cadres of various political parties working in local areas (Chapter 2), from officials in the central government (Chapter 3), from officials in local government (Chapter 4), from the intelligentsia (Chapter 5), from C.C.P. members (Chapter 6), from cadres in trade unions (Chapter 7), and from the judiciary (Chapter 8). Chapter 9 concerns the handling of minorities affairs; Chapter 10, the question of the role of women; and Chapter 11, criticisms on financial and economic affairs.

661 Ming-fang fan-kung ko-ming shih-lu shih 鳴放反共革命實錄史 (Hundred Flowers Movement—History of Anti-Communist Revolution). Hong Kong: Chung-kuo jen-min erh erh-ch'i ming-fang fan-kung ko-ming lien-ho hui ch'u-pan she 中國人民二二七鳴放反共革命聯合會出版社, 1958. 125p.

A collection similar to the preceding entry. The first two parts are arranged by region. Part 3 is a collection of criticisms by cadres of the party. While the present volume does not approach the comprehensiveness of the preceding entry, it is nonetheless a good supplementary source.

662 I, Ch'ung-kuang 易重光**, ed.** *Tang t'ien-hsia yü tang kuo-chia* 黨天下與黨國家 *Criticism on the Chinese Communist Party State.* Kowloon: Tzu-yu ch'u-pan she 自由出版社, 1958. 2 vols. 239p.

Another collection of criticisms directed at the C.C.P. and the Chinese Communist government. Included are excerpts of speeches by members of the C.C.P. and other political parties, arranged chronologically by date of publication of the speeches in the Chinese Communist press. A number of interesting cartoons have been incorporated.

b. Youth Organizations

Totalitarian parties, the Communist parties in particular, have traditionally stressed the importance of working with the young—in part for the purpose of building a broad base of support for policies and programs initiated by the regime, and in part as a means of infusing new blood into the ranks of the party. To this end the C.C.P. maintains, in addition to the Chinese Communist Youth League and its affiliated children's organization, a country-wide federation of youth organizations, the All-China Federation of Democratic Youth, which includes not only the Communist organizations but others as well (e.g., the All-China Students Federation).

The documents contained in this section emanate largely from various national congresses. Documentation is available for the three national congresses of the All-China Federation of Democratic Youth (1949, 1953, and 1958). The Chinese Communist Youth League (New Democratic Youth League until May 1947), modeled closely after the Russian Komsomol, held three national congresses (1949, 1953, and 1957). The next congress, designated the ninth, was held in June 1964. For the first congress separate documentation is available (**666** and **667**). The second congress receives brief attention in the People's Handbook, 1955 (p. 380), and the third congress is fairly well documented in the volume for 1957 (pp. 265–281). The report by Hu Yao-pang on the work of the league delivered at the ninth congress was published by Foreign Languages Press in 1964 under the title *Revolutionize Our Youth* (51p.). For detailed coverage, however, it is necessary to consult the *Chung-kuo ch'ing-nien pao* (China Youth Daily, **847**) and *Chung-kuo ch'ing-nien* (China Youth, **868**), both official organs of the league, and both of which serve also as sources for documentary coverage on the two national congresses (1955 and 1958) of the Young Activists for Socialist Construction (as do the last two entries—**671** and **672**), as well as on the Youth and Children's Corps (the Chinese Young Pioneers). For league personnel and position data, see the chapter on directories in Part One. *The Young Communist League: 1959–1960*, published in the Research Backgrounder series, provides a short summary of the history and development of the league, together with thirty documents, issued in 1959–1960, on the league and related subjects.

663 **Chung-kuo ch'ing-nien she** 中國青年社 (China Youth Publishing House). *Ch'üan-kuo ch'ing-nien t'uan-chieh ch'i-lai tsai Mao Tse-tung ch'i-chih hsia ch'ien-chin (Chung-hua ch'üan-kuo ch'ing-nien ti-i tz'u tai-piao ta-hui wen-hsien)* 全國青年團結起來在毛澤東旗幟下前進（中華全國青年第一次代表大會文獻） (Youth of China Unite, March Onward Under the Banner of Mao Tse-tung—Documents of the First All-China Youth Congress). Peking: Chung-kuo ch'ing-nien she, 1949. 68p.

Contains greetings, speeches, reports, and resolutions of the First All-China Youth Congress held in Peking May 4–11, 1949. The constitution of the National Committee of the All-China Federation of Democratic Youth is included, together with a namelist of the committee.

664   Chung-kuo ch'ing-nien ch'u-pan she 中國青年出版社 (China Youth Publishing House). *Wei pao-wei tsu-kuo ho chien-she tsu-kuo erh fen-tou (Chung-hua ch'üan-kuo ch'ing-nien ti-erh tz'u tai-piao ta-hui wen-hsien)* 爲保衞祖國和建設祖國而奮鬥（中華全國青年第二次代表大會文獻） (Struggle for the Defense and Construction of our Motherland—Documents of the Second All-China Youth Congress). Peking: Chung-kuo ch'ing-nien ch'u-pan she, 1953. 84p.

Contains documents similar to those found in the preceding entry. Appended are the proceedings of the congress and two newspaper editorials reproduced from the *Jen-min jih-pao* and the *Chung-kuo ch'ing-nien pao*. The second Congress was held in Peking, June 10–15, 1953.

665   Chung-kuo ch'ing-nien ch'u-pan she 中國青年出版社 (China Youth Publishing House). *Chung-hua ch'üan-kuo ch'ing-nien ti-san tz'u tai-piao ta-hui wen-hsien* 中華全國青年第三次代表大會文獻 (Documents of the Third All-China Youth Congress). Peking: Chung-kuo ch'ing-nien ch'u-pan she, 1958. 93p.

A compilation similar to the two preceding entries. The Third Congress was held in Peking, April 9–14, 1958.

666   Chung-kuo ch'ing-nien she 中國青年社 (China Youth Publishing House). *Wei t'uan-chieh chiao-yü ch'ing-nien i-tai erh tou-cheng (Chung-kuo hsin min-chu chu-i ch'ing-nien t'uan ti-i tz'u ch'üan-kuo tai-piao ta-hui wen-hsien)* 爲團結教育青年一代而鬥爭（中國新民主主義青年團第一次全國代表大會文獻） (Struggle for Uniting and Educating the Young Generation—Documents of the First National Congress of the New Democratic Youth League). Peking: Chung-kuo ch'ing-nien she, 1949. 104p.

Contains speeches and reports by Chu Teh, Jen Pi-shih 任弼時, Feng Wen-pin 馮文彬, Chiang Nan-hsiang 蔣南翔 and Hsiao Hua 蕭華, together with the program and constitution of the Youth League and the resolutions adopted by the congress, held in Peking April 11–18, 1949. There is also a namelist of the Central Committee (including the standing committee) and of the various departments of the Youth League. The appendix contains two New China News Agency releases, one on the work of the Youth League during the two and one-half years (from October 1946) of experimentation, and the other a brief description of Chinese Communist-led youth activities since 1921. The latter is an especially useful compilation of scattered information on the subject.

667 **Chung-kuo hsin min-chu chu-i ch'ing-nien t'uan ti-i tz'u ch'üan-kuo tai-piao ta-hui wen-hsien** 中國新民主主義青年團第一次全國代表大會文獻 (Documents of the First National Congress of the New Democratic Youth League). Hankow(?), 1949. 86p.

A compilation similar to the preceding entry with the following exceptions: (1) the resolution on establishing the New Democratic Youth League by the Central Committee of the C.C.P. (January 1, 1949) is added; (2) the two New China News Agency releases are omitted, and in their place are added three documents on (a) regional and local organization of the Youth League, (b) the establishment of the All-China Railroad Work Committee of the Youth League, and (c) the organization of the Youth League in the armed forces; (3) the speeches by Chu Teh and Hsiao Hua are not included in this edition.

668 **Chung-kuo hsin min-chu chu-i ch'ing-nien t'uan, Hua-nan kung-tso wei-yüan hui, Hsüan-ch'uan pu.** 中國新民主主義青年團 華南工作委員會 宣傳部 (Chinese New Democratic Youth League, South China Committee, Propaganda Department). *Ch'ing-nien t'uan wen-t'i chieh-ta* 青年團問題解答 (Questions and Answers on the Youth League). Canton: Ch'ing-nien ch'u-pan she, Hua-nan ying-yeh ch'u 青年出版社華南營業處, 1950. 10;72p.

An official pamphlet in question and answer form on the Chinese New Democratic Youth League issued primarily for the use of the Youth League members. A total of 108 questions are arranged in seven parts: (1) 'Do you Understand the Youth League?' (2) 'What is the Mission of the Youth League?' (3) 'Who is Eligible for Membership?' (4) 'How to Be a Good Member,' (5) 'How Is the League Organized?' (6) 'The Relationship Between the Youth League and Other Organizations,' (7) Miscellany. Useful and informative.

669 **Chung-kuo hsin min-chu chu-i ch'ing-nien t'uan, Hua-nan kung-tso wei-yüan hui, Shao-nien erh-t'ung pu** 中國新民主主義青年團 華南工作 委員會 少年兒童部 (Chinese New Democratic Youth League, South China Committee, Youth and Children's Department). *Chung-kuo shao-nien erh-t'ung tui kung-tso shou-ts'e* 中國少年兒童隊工作手冊 (China Youth and Children's Corps Manual). Canton: Ch'ing-nien ch'u-pan she, Hua-nan ying-yeh pu 青年出版社華南營業部, 1950. 42p.

A manual containing various documents for the use of party cadres, counselors, school teachers and others in their work with the Youth and Children's Corps. The name of the corps was changed to *Chung-kuo shao-nien hsien-feng tui* 中國少年先鋒隊 (Chinese Young Pioneers) at the Second National Congress of the New Democratic Youth League in June 1953.

670 **Chung-nan jen-min ch'u-pan she** 中南人民出版社 (South-Central China People's Publishing House). *Chung-kuo shao-nien erh-t'ung tui tui-yüan shou-ts'e* 中國少年兒童隊隊員手冊

(China Youth and Children's Corps Handbook). Canton: Hua-nan jen-min ch'u-pan she 華南人民出版社, 1951. 19p.

A handbook for the members of the China Youth and Children's Corps, including the constitution and other pertinent information.

671 Chung-kuo ch'ing-nien ch'u-pan she 中國青年出版社 (China Youth Publishing House). *Chung-kuo ch'ing-nien wei shih-hsien ti-i ko wu-nien chi-hua erh tou-cheng ti jen-wu (Ch'üan-kuo ch'ing-nien she-hui chu-i chien-she chi-chi fen-tzu ta-hui wen-hsien)* 中國青年爲實現第一個五年計劃而鬥爭的任務（全國青年社會主義建設積極份子大會文獻）
(The Mission of the Chinese Youth in Fulfilling the First Five-Year Plan— Documents of the National Congress of Young Activists for Socialist Construction). Peking: Chung-kuo ch'ing-nien ch'u-pan she, 1956. 234p.

Contains speeches on the First Five Year Plan by Teng Hsiao-p'ing (representing the C.C.P. Politburo), Hu Yao-pang 胡耀邦 (Secretary of the New Democratic Youth League) and government officials. Other documents included are 'guarantees', recommendations, and 'challenges' issued by delegates to the congress. The proceedings and name lists of the congress, as well as *Jen-min jih-pao*, and *Chung-kuo ch'ing-nien pao* editorials exhorting the delegates, are also included. The congress was held in Peking September 20–28, 1955. See also next entry.

672 Chung-kuo ch'ing-nien ch'u-pan she 中國青年出版社 (China Youth Publishing House). *Ti-erh tz'u ch'üan-kuo ch'ing-nien she-hui chu-i chien-she chi-chi fen-tzu ta-hui wen-chien* 第二次全國青年社會主義建設積極份子大會文件
(Documents of the Second National Congress of Young Activists for Socialist Construction). Peking: Chung-kuo ch'ing-nien ch'u-pan she, 1958. 34p.

Contains speeches by Chu Teh and Hu Yao-pang to the congress, and messages from the delegates to Mao Tse-tung, the armed forces stationed in Fukien Province, and the youth of China.

The Second Congress was held in Peking November 21–December 2, 1958.

c. Women's Organizations

Prior to the establishment of the Communist government at Peking, a national congress of Chinese women was held in that city in the spring of 1949. On this occasion, the All-China Democratic Women's Federation was founded with Madame Sun Yat-sen as one of its honorary chairmen (see the first entry).

The Federation has held three national congresses (March-April, 1949; April 1953; and September 1957, at which time the name of the organization was changed to the All-China Women's Federation), the documentation for which is contained in the present section.

It should be noted that the official organ of the Federation, *Chung-kuo fu-nü* 中國 婦女 (Women of China), and its English-language counterpart, *Women of China*, are described in Chapter XVII (**870** and **936**, respectively).

673　**Chung-hua ch'üan-kuo min-chu fu-nü lien-ho hui, Hsüan-ch'uan chiao-yü pu** 中華全國民主婦女聯合會 宣傳教育部 (All-China Democratic Women's Federation, Department of Propaganda and Education). *Chung-kuo fu-nü ti-i tz'u ch'üan-kuo tai-piao ta-hui chung-yao wen-hsien* 中國婦女第一次全國代表大 會重要文獻
(Collected Documents on the First National Congress of Chinese Women). Peking: Hsin-hua shu-tien 新華書店, 1949. 86p.

Contains speeches, reports, resolutions, and the proceedings of the congress held in Peking from March 24 to April 3, 1949. Two name lists are included, one of the presidium of the congress, the other of the executive committee of the All-China Democratic Women's Federation.

Documents emerging from the Second Congress (convened in Peking on April 15, 1953) seem not to have been published in a single volume. For a selection of the most important speeches and reports to the Second Congress, see *Hsin Chung-kuo fu-nü* 新中國婦女 (Women of New China), No. 5, 1953 (May 9, 1953). For documents on the Third Congress, see next entry.

674　**Chung-hua jen-min kung-ho kuo ch'üan-kuo fu-nü lien-ho hui** 中華人民 共和國 全國婦女聯合會 (All-China Women's Federation). *Chung-kuo fu-nü ti-san tz'u ch'üan-kuo tai-piao ta-hui chung-yao wen-hsien* 中國婦女第三次全國代 表大會重要文獻
(Collected Documents on the Third National Congress of Chinese Women). Peking: Chung-kuo fu-nü tsa-chih she 中國婦女雜誌社, 1958. 152p.

A collection of documents similar to those contained in the 1949 volume (see above). The Third National Congress of Chinese Women was held in Peking September 9–21, 1957.

675　**Chung-hua ch'üan-kuo min-chu fu-nü lien-ho hui, Hsüan-ch'uan chiao-yü-pu** 中華全國民主婦女聯合會 宣傳教育部 (All-China Democratic Women's Federation, Department of Propaganda and Education). *Chung-kuo fu-nü yün-tung ti chung-yao wen-chien* 中國婦女運動的重要文件
(Selected Documents on the Women's Movement in China). Peking: Jen-min ch'u-pan she 人民出版社, 1953. 76p.

Contains twelve selected Chinese Communist documents on the women's movement in China from February 1943 ('Resolution of the Central Committee of the C.C.P. on the Women's Movement in Anti-Japanese Areas') to February 1953 ('Directive by the All-China Democratic Women's Federation on Sup-porting and Implementing the Directive of the Central Committee of the C.C.P. and the Central People's Government on Carrying Out the Marriage Law').

B. Republic of China

The governing institutions of the Republic of China today consist of a national government and a provincial government for the actual administration of the province of Taiwan. Paralleling the formal structure of government in Taiwan, the present section has been subdivided into materials (all in Chinese and of Taiwan origin) dealing with (1) the central government and (2) the provincial government. A third subsection concerns the Kuomintang and mass organizations.

Reference should be made to the translations of the United States Information Service in Taipei—*Press and Publications Summary*, which appears in Chapter XX (**1074**).

1. CENTRAL GOVERNMENT

The apparatus of the central government was kept intact in the transfer from the Mainland to Taiwan. Of the five yuan, or branches of the Nationalist government, three (the Legislative, Judicial, and Control Yuan) regularly publish gazettes. The Executive and the Examination Yuan do not issue gazettes. Instead, the regulations, directives, etc., issued by the Executive Yuan can be found in the Bulletin of the Office of the President, the most important government gazette. The Examination Monthly published by the Examination Yuan can be regarded as its gazette. Of the various ministries, only the Ministry of Foreign Affairs and the Ministry of Finance issue gazettes at the present time. The former is included in Chapter XVI on foreign relations (**830**). The latter—as well as the gazettes of the various yuan mentioned above—is included in the present section. The Economic Reference Materials described in Chapter XIV (**734**) is an official publication of the Ministry of Economic Affairs.

Parenthetically, the National Assembly, which under the constitution is the supreme organ of the government, has not met in Taiwan, and no documentary materials are available concerning that body. For additional sources, the reader should refer to the statements, speeches, etc., of Chiang Kai-shek which are published annually and also in collections (see **579**ff.). Both the *Chung-yang jih-pao* (Central Daily News, **938**), the official organ of the Kuomintang, and the *China Yearbook* (**239** and **240**)—especially the Chinese edition—are equally important sources of official announcements and other documentation. The reader should consult the directory and biography chapters for data on government personnel.

Taiwan provincial administration is dealt with in the following section.

676 **Tsung-t'ung fu kung-pao** 總統府公報
(Bulletin of the Office of the President). Nanking, Taipei, No. 1—, May 1948—. Semi-weeekly (Tuesdays and Fridays).

Publication began in Nanking on May 20, 1948 as a daily, and resumed in Taipei in March 1950 when Chiang Kai-shek resumed the office of Presidency of the Republic of China. Contents are usually divided into three sections: presidential orders and mandates (including laws and statutes, treaties, appointments, transfers and dismissals, etc.); orders of the Executive Yuan; and public notices (made up primarily of decisions of the Administrative Court, reports of the Committee on the Discipline of Public Functionaries, etc.). Each issue ranges from ten to sixty pages.

Suceeds *Kuo-min cheng-fu kung-pao* 國民政府公報 (Gazette of the Central Government of the Republic of China), which ceased publication with No. 3,137 (May 19, 1948). The most important government gazette published in Taiwan.

677 Li-fa yüan kung-pao 立法院公報

(Gazette of the Legislative Yuan). (May 1948[?]—, First Session, No. 1—). Irregular.

The official record of the legislative branch of the government of the Republic of China. Included are bills, verbatim records of committee hearings, official reports and related documents. Frequency varies. Only the issues for the eighteenth through twenty-first sessions (December 1956–August 1958) are indexed.

678 Ssu-fa yüan kung-pao 司法院公報

(Gazette of the Judicial Yuan). Taipei, Vol. 1, No. 1—, January, 1959(?)—. Monthly.

Contains judicial interpretations or decisions by the three major organs of the Judicial Yuan: the Supreme Court, the Administrative Court, and the Committee on the Discipline of Public Functionaries. Texts of major laws and decrees frequently appear in its pages.

679 Ssu-fa chuan-k'an 司法專刊 (Journal of Judicial Law). Taipei: Ssu-fa hsing-cheng pu 司法行政部, No. 1—, April 1951—. Monthly.

Published by the Ministry of Justice of the Republic of China, the journal contains current judicial laws, regulations, decrees, and decisions. Annual topical index appears in the December issue.

680 K'ao-ch'üan yüeh-k'an 考銓月刊

(Examination Monthly). Taipei: K'ao-chüan yüeh-k'an she 考銓月刊社, Vol. 1, No. 1—, April 30, 1951—.

A semi-official publication on the civil service of the Republic of China. Includes laws and regulations, directives, appointments, dismissals, transfers and reports of the Examination Yuan.

681 Chien-ch'a yüan kung-pao 監察院公報
(Gazette of the Control Yuan). Taipei, January (?) 1951—. Monthly.

The official record of the work of the highest supervisory organ of the government of the Republic of China. Included are documents concerning consent, impeachment, censure and audit. Published bi-monthly from January (?) 1951 to May 1952 (Vol. 1, No. 1 –Vol. 2, No. 6); approximately three times a month thereafter through March 1957 (with a numbering system from August 18, 1952 with No. 1). A monthly since April 1957, the numbering remaining consecutive.

682 Ts'ai-cheng pu kung-pao 財政部公報
(Gazette of the Ministry of Finance). Taipei, Vol. 1, No. 1—, January 25, 1963—. Three times a month.

Publishes financial laws, regulations, directives, and public announcements mainly concerned with taxation, money and banking, and customs.

683 Kao, Ying-tu 高鷹篤, **et al.** *Chung-hua min-kuo nei-cheng chih* 中華民國內政誌 (Interior Administration of the Republic of China). Taipei: Chung-hua wen-hua ch'u-pan chih-yeh wei-yüan hui 中華文化出版事業委員會, 1957. 3 vols.

Three volumes dealing with various aspects of the internal administrative affairs of the Republic of China, consisting of articles by authors who are either leading authorities in their respective fields or directors of departments or divisions in the Ministry of the Interior. The following subjects receive attention: local self-government and elections, the code of conduct for civil servants, social customs, census, nationality, police, prohibition of opium smoking, social administration, cooperative administration, labor, land administration, public health, water conservancy and irrigation, and land reclamation.

An authoritative reference work.

2. PROVINCIAL GOVERNMENT

The official retrocession of the island of Taiwan to the Republic of China took place on October 25, 1945. From that time until May 15, 1947, the administration of the affairs of the island rested in the hands of the T"ai-wan sheng hsing-cheng chang-kuan kung-shu (the Provincial Administration). The name T'ai-wan sheng cheng-fu (Provincial Government) was adoped after May 16, 1947 when the administration was reorganized as a regular province of the Republic of China. For the two periods in question, the basic documentary sources are the official gazettes (the first two entries listed in the present section). Beyond the gazettes, there are also the semi-annual official reports reviewing the work of the various departments of the provincial government **(686)**.

From 1953 to June 1959, the legislative body of the government was the Provisional Provincial Assembly. The Assembly published a weekly gazette containing a complete record of the debates, bills, etc. **(687)**, which, together with the gazette of the Provincial Government, provides a rich fund of information on the administration of Taiwan. It should be pointed out that the proceedings of the Provisional Provincial

Assembly have been published separately, although some of the material contained therein is incorporated in the weekly record (see **688**). The Provisional Provincial Assembly was reconstituted the Provincial Assembly in June of 1959, and the title of the compilation changed accordingly, but the types of material carried remained essentially unchanged (see **689**).

Additional information can be found in the Taiwan Yearbook (**243**) and the *China Yearbook* (especially the Chinese edition, **239**), and in the biography and directory chapters in Part Two.

684   T'ai-wan sheng hsing-cheng chang-kuan kung-shu kung-pao 臺灣省行政長官公署公報
(Gazette of the Taiwan Provincial Administration). Taipei, Winter No. [1], 1945–Summer No. 39, 1947, December 1, 1945–May 15, 1947. Daily.

A complete and official record of the Taiwan Provincial Administration for the period December 1, 1945 to May 15, 1947, containing laws, regulations, directives, etc. Published every two days in the period December 1, 1945, through May 27, 1946 and daily thereafter (Sundays excluded). A total of 345 issues were published. It should be noted that only four issues were published from March 1–22, 1947 during the period of the anti-government riots. Concurrently with the establishment of the Taiwan Provincial Government on May 16, 1947, the title of the publication was changed to *T'ai-wan sheng cheng-fu kung-pao* (see next entry).

685   T'ai-wan sheng cheng-fu kung-pao 臺灣省政府公報
(Gazette of the Taiwan Provincial Government). Taipei and Taichung, Summer No. 1, 1947—, May 16, 1947—. Daily (except Sundays).

A complete and official record of the Taiwan Provincial Government, superseding the preceding entry. Quarterly index since Spring Quarter 1957.

686   Taiwan, Mi-shu ch'u 臺灣省政府 秘書處 (Taiwan, Secretariat). *T'ai-wan sheng cheng-fu shih-cheng pao-kao* 臺灣省政府施政報告
(Report of the Taiwan Provincial Government). Taipei, Taichung, 1946—. Semi-annual.

A semi-annual report, published every year in June and December, describing the work of the Departments of Civil Affairs; Finance; Education; Reconstruction; Agriculture and Forestry; Transportation and Communications; Social Affairs, Health, Police; Budgets, Accounts and Statistics; Information and Personnel; the Bureaus of Food and Supply; and the Taiwan Coal Commission. Reports on important lower level agencies are appended to those of their supervising departments.

The data are arranged by agency in two columns: work programs and their execution. Statistical tables are provided.

687 **T'ai-wan sheng lin-shih sheng i-hui kung-pao** 臺灣省臨時省議會公報
(Gazette of the Taiwan Provincial Provincial Assembly). Taipei: T'ai-wan
sheng lin-shih sheng i-hui, Mi-shu ch'u 臺灣省臨時省議會 秘書處, Vol. 1, No.
1 –Vol. 13, No. (?); January 12, 1953–June 1959. Weekly.

A weekly publication of Taiwan's legislative assembly for the period 1953–
1959, the gazette contains a complete record of minutes, bills, etc. Publication
ceased in June 1959.

688 **T'ai-wan sheng lin-shih i-hui, Mi-shu ch'u** 臺灣省臨時議會 秘書處 (Taiwan
Provincial Provincial Assembly, Secretariat). *T'ai-wan sheng lin-shih i-hui ta-
hui chuan-chi* 臺灣省臨時議會大會專輯
(Proceedings of Taiwan Provincial Provincial Assembly). Taipei, Taichung,
1952–1959.

Coverage extends from the first session of the First General Session through
the fourth session of the Third General Session, 1952–1959 (one or two volumes
for each session). The proceedings contain lists of bills and resolutions, minutes
of the various sessions, agenda and communications, records of ballots cast for the
election of the Speaker and the Vice-Speaker, and records of hearings into civic
affairs, public works, finance, education, food and agriculture, communications
and transportation, police, health, etc., in addition to the rosters of assemblymen
and resident members. Largely an accumulation of materials published in the preceding entry. The appendix comprises regulations governing the election and recall
of assemblymen, parliamentary procedure, organic laws of the screening committees, working procedures of the Secretariat and the various committees, a chronology of major events, a Secretariat staff directory, and an index to resolutions.

The Provisional Assembly was reconstituted the Provincial Assembly on June
24, 1959. See next entry.

689 **T'ai-wan sheng i-hui, Mi-shu ch'u** 臺灣省議會 秘書處 (Taiwan Provincial
Assembly, Secretariat). *T'ai-wan sheng i-hui ta-hui chuan-chi* 臺灣省議會大會專輯
(Proceedings of Taiwan Provincial Assembly). 1959—.

The contents of the proceedings are identical to those of the preceding entry.
While in session on June 24, 1959, the Taiwan Provisional Provincial Assembly
was reconstituted the Taiwan Provincial Assembly. (The first session of the
First General Session of the Provincial Assembly was in fact the fifth session
of the Third General Session of the Provisional Provincial Assembly.)

3. THE KUOMINTANG AND MASS ORGANIZATIONS

Following the removal of the Nationalist government to Taiwan in 1949, the Kuomintang entered a period of reorientation and reformation. A Central Reform Committee
was established in August 1949 to determine the most effective way to revitalize the
party. Among the tasks which the Committee undertook were the drafting of a new

party platform and the study of organizational changes. The recommendations of the Committee were subsequently adopted by the Seventh National Congress of the Kuomintang (October 10–20, 1952), when the former Central Executive Committee and the Central Supervisory Committee were replaced by a single Central Committee.

The first two entries in the present section document the history and work of the Central Reform Committee. Chiang Kai-shek's political report to the Seventh National Congress and the manifesto issuing from that Congress (**694** and **693**), as well as an official report made by the Central Reform Committee prior to the convocation of the Seventh National Congress (**692**), are important documents describing the Kuomintang's programs. No separately published materials seem to be available for the last two congresses of the Kuomintang, the Eighth National Congress, held October 10–23, 1957, and the Ninth National Congress, November 12–22, 1963, but selected reports and their manifestoes are available in the *Chung-yang jih-pao* (Central Daily News), October 11–24, 1957, and November 12–22, 1963, respectively.

Inasmuch as the territorial base of the Kuomintang has been confined to Taiwan, the official internal publication of the Taiwan Provincial Headquarters of the party, *T'ai-wan tang-wu* (Party Affairs in Taiwan, **695**), assumes particular importance for the study of the Kuomintang since 1949. *Chung-hua jih-pao* (China Daily News, **696**), also an official organ of the party's provincial headquarters, is on the other hand designed for the general public. Special note should also be made of the five entries (**697–701**) on the recruiting of members and the training of cadres, both high priority items on the party's agenda.

The intensification of training and indoctrination of cadres working with various mass organizations received heavy emphasis in the party's self-reformation movement. A large number of mass organizations established on the Mainland before 1949 continued to function in Taiwan side by side with those of recent origin. They include, for instance, the Chinese Federation of Labor 中華民國全國總工會, Chinese National Foreign Relations Association 中國國民外交協會, Chinese Women's Anti-Aggression League 中華婦女反共抗俄聯合會, National Association of Youth Organizations 中華民國青年團體聯合會, Chinese Moslem Association 中國回教協會, and others. For a history and directory of all mass organizations in the Republic of China, see *Chung-hua min-kuo wu-shih nien lai min-chung t'uan-t'i* 中華民國五十年來民衆團體 (Fifty Years of Civic Organizations in the Republic of China, **347**). Available documentation on party work in these organizations is uneven both in quantity and quality. Included in this section are seven entries to which scholars do have access, concerning work with youth, women's and Overseas Chinese groups. The *Min-yün kan-pu shou-ts'e* (Handbook for the Cadres in Mass Movement Work, **701**) is particularly noteworthy in that it contains brief descriptions of the nature, aim, and methods of work of the various mass organizations as well as pertinent texts of regulations. See also two Kuomintang reports (**737** and **738**) on agrarian problems in Chapter XIV.

It should be pointed out that current party publications issued for internal use are not available. To supplement those provided in this section, as well as to gain insight into the more current state of Kuomintang affairs, one should consult Chiang Kai-shek's writings, speeches, etc., as well as such sources as the *Chung-yang jih-pao* (Central Daily News, **938**), *T'ai-wan hsin-sheng pao* (Taiwan New Life Daily), organ of the

Taiwan provincial government (**939**), the Bulletin of the Office of the President (**676**), other government gazettes, collections of laws and statutes, the *China Yearbook* (**239, 240**), and other pertinent official and semi-official periodical literature described in Chapter XVIII. The *Press and Publications Summary* issued by the Taipei U.S.I.S. (**1074**) also contains translations of news items and editorials on Kuomintang affairs.

690 Yang-ming shan-chuang 陽明山莊 (Yangmingshan Institute). *Pen tang kai-tsao an* 本黨改造案
(The Proposal of Our Party's Reform). Taipei, 1951. 45p.

A collection of five basic documents concerning the Kuomintang Reform Program, instituted in 1950 to revitalize the party after the Communist take-over on the Mainland and the removal of the Nationalist government to Taiwan. The documents are (1) Chiang Kai-shek's speech introducing the program (an English translation is available in *China Handbook, 1952-53*, pp. 339-345); (2) an outline of the program; (3) measures and procedures adopted for the purpose of implementing the program; (4) organization of the Central Reform Committee; and (5) 'The Political Platform of Our Party at the Present Time', one of the very first Kuomintang proclamations issued from Taiwan (September 1, 1950). An important source.

691 Kai-tsao 改造
(Reform). Taipei: Chung-kuo kuo-min tang chung-yang kai-tsao wei-yüan hui 中國國民黨 中央改造委員會, No. 1—, September (?) 1950-1952 (?). Semi-monthly.

The official organ of the Kuomintang for the period 1950 to 1952 (?), edited and published by the Central Reform Committee. The *Kai-tsao* regularly published party directives, regulations, reports on party work, etc. Publication is believed to have been suspended in October 1952 when the Central Reform Committee was reconstituted as the Central Committee by the Seventh National Congress of the Kuomintang.

A basic source on the Kuomintang for the period covered.

692 Chung-kuo kuo-min tang, Chung-yang kai-tsao wei-yüan hui 中國國民黨 中央改造委員會 (Kuomintang, Central Reform Committee). *Chung-kuo kuo-min tang hsien-k'uang* 中國國民黨現況
(The Present State of the Kuomintang). Taipei, 1952. 134p.

A lengthy official statement, in twelve chapters, describing the Kuomintang's current and projected programs issued by the Central Reform Committee in 1952 prior to the convocation of the Seventh National Congress in August of the same year. A very important source on the Kuomintang since 1949.

693   Chung-kuo kuo-min tang ti-ch'i tz'u ch'üan-kuo tai-piao ta-hui hsüan-yen
中國國民黨第七次全國代表大會宣言
(Manifesto of the Seventh National Congress of the Kuomintang). Taipei:
Chung-yang wen-wu kung-ying she 中央文物供應社, 1953. 22p.

The Seventh National Congress of the Kuomintang was the party's first
national congress held in Taiwan (October 10–20, 1952). In addition to the
manifesto, the pamphlet also includes the opening speech by Chiang
Kai-shek.
See also *The Kuomintang Manifesto and Platform* (Taipei: China Cultural
Service, [1954]), 35p., in English and Chinese.

694   Chiang, Kai-shek, *Tsung-ts'ai tui ti-ch'i tz'u ch'üan-kuo tai-piao ta-hui cheng-
chih pao-kao* 總裁對第七次全國代表大會政治報告
(Political Report by the Director-General to the Seventh National Congress).
Taipei: Chung-yang wen-wu kung-ying she 中央文物供應社, 1954. 56p.

An analysis by Chiang Kai-shek of the causes of the Nationalist defeat on the
Mainland in which he proposes measures for revitalizing the party and establish-
ing a new revolutionary base. Included is a review by Chiang of the situation on
Taiwan and the Korean War. An 'internal' party publication not widely available.
Limited distribution.

695   T'ai-wan tang-wu 臺灣黨務
(Party Affairs in Taiwan). Taipei: Chung-kuo kuo-min tang, T'ai-wan sheng
tang-pu 中國國民黨臺灣省黨部, No. 1—, January 1951—. Semi-monthly.

The official organ of the Taiwan Provincial Headquarters of the Kuomintang,
T'ai-wan tang-wu is an 'internal' party publication which, in addition to providing party documents and Chiang Kai-shek's speeches, regularly carries articles
pertaining to matters on organization, discipline, mass movements, propaganda,
etc. The most basic source on Kuomintang's work in Taiwan. Limited distribution.
See also the next entry.

696   Chung-hua jih-pao 中華日報
(China Daily News). Taipei and Tainan, No. 1—, February 1946—.

An organ of the Taiwan Provincial Headquarters of the Kuomintang designed
for the general public. First published on February 20, 1946 in Tainan. A Taipei
edition was added two years later on February 20, 1948. The Tainan edition
enjoys the largest circulation of any newspaper in southern Taiwan. Both
editions run to four pages daily. Since 1962 indexed in the *Classified Index to
Chinese Newspapers* (see **194a**).
See also the preceding entry.

697 **Chung-kuo kuo-min tang, Chung-yang kai-tsao wei-yüan hui, Ti-san tsu**
中國國民黨 中央改造委員會 第三組 (Kuomintang, Central Reform Committee, Third Section). *Tsen-yang ch'ü cheng-ch'iu hsin tang-yüan* 怎樣去徵求新黨員 (How to Recruit New Members for the Party). Taipei, 1950. 15p.

A party directive concerning the recruitment of new members. Issued as an 'internal' party publication. Limited distribution.

698 **Chung-kuo kuo-min tang, Chung-yang wei-yüan hui, Ti-i tsu** 中國國民黨 中央委員會 第一組 (Kuomintang, Central Committee, First Section). *Ju-tang jen tu-pen—chia chung, i chung* 入黨人讀本──甲種, 乙種
(Readers for Party Candidates—Series A and B). Taipei: Chung-yang wen-wu kung-ying she 中央文物供應社, 1959. 2 vols. 410; 103p.

Series A is designed for civil service personnel and 'young intellectuals' (知識青年). Series B is for farmers, workers and those whose training is equivalent to education at the primary level. Both series cover the same ground (the Three People's Principles, the history of the Kuomintang, the KMT constitution and program, and the life and thought of Chiang Kai-shek) but differ in format (Series A is narrative in form and is more detailed; Series B is in question and answer form).

699 **Chung-kuo kuo-min tang, Chung-yang wei-yüan hui, Ti-i tsu** 中國國民黨 中央委員會 第一組 (Kuomintang, Central Committee, First Section). *Chien-li chi-ts'eng kan-pu chih-tu shou-ts'e* 建立基層幹部制度手冊
(Handbook on the Establishment of a Basic Cadres System). Taipei, 1954. 38p.

Contains five of the most important documents on the establishment of a system of 'basic party cadres' (基層幹部), a program devised for the purpose of revitalizing the party and insuring the thorough implementation of party policies and programs at the local level. Such matters as the training and indoctrination of cadres working closely with the masses receive treatment in the pamphlet. Among the documents included are an outline of the system; procedures for and regulations on implementation; quotations from Chiang Kai-shek's speeches on the necessity for such a system and the means by which it can be achieved.

An invaluable source for the study of the organization of the Kuomintang in recent years.

700 **Chung-kuo kuo-min tang, Chung-yang wei-yüan hui, Ti-i tsu** 中國國民黨 中央委員會 第一組 (Kuomintang, Central Committee, First Section). *Chi-ts'eng kan-pu shou-ts'e* 基層幹部手冊
(Basic Cadres Handbook). Taipei: Chung-yang wen-wu kung-ying she 中央文物供應社, 1956. 108p.

For the information and guidance of the Kuomintang cadres. In three parts: Part 1 deals with cadre responsibilities; Part 2 outlines their specific missions; and Part 3 centers on the techniques to be employed in carrying out such missions. Parts 1 and 2 are in question and answer form.

701   **Chung-kuo kuo-min tang, Chung-yang wei-yüan hui, Ti-wu tsu** 中國國民黨 中央委員會 第五組 (Kuomintang, Central Committee, Fifth Section). *Min-yün kan-pu shou-ts'e (ch'u-kao)* 民運幹部手冊 (初稿) (Handbook for the Cadres in Mass Movement Work—A Preliminary Edition). Taipei, 1954. 256p.

In two parts. The first part (pp. 1–93) provides brief descriptions of the nature, aim, and methods of work among various groups, such as youth, farmers, labor, etc. The second part (pp. 95–256) contains the texts of thirty-eight government and Kuomintang regulations concerning certain aspects of mass movements. A basic policy document.

702   **Chung-kuo kuo-min tang, Chung-yang kai-tsao wei-yüan hui** 中國國民黨 中央改造委員會 (Kuomintang, Central Reform Committee). *Chung-kuo kuo-min tang hsien chieh-tuan ch'ing-nien yün-tung chih-tao fang-an* 中國國民黨現階段 青年運動指導方案 (Proposal Concerning the Directing of the Kuomintang Youth Movement at the Present Time). Taipei, 1951. 5p.

An outline of a proposal approved by the Central Reform Committee on January 29, 1951 concerning the youth movement, arranged under the following section headings: (1) aims, (2) directing principles, (3) directing methods, (4) organization, (5) major activities, and (6) selection of cadres. An 'internal' party publication. A major primary source on the Kuomintang-led youth movement. Limited distribution.

703   **Chung-kuo ch'ing-nien fan-kung chiu-kuo t'uan** 中國青年反共救國團 (China Youth Anti-Communist and Salvation Corps). Taipei: Ch'ing-nien ch'u-pan she 青年出版社, [1952]. 46p.

Contains seven documents on the China Youth Anti-Communist and Salvation Corps, including Chiang Kai-shek's speech on the founding of the Corps. An appendix provides the text of the constitution of the organization.

704   **Chung-hua fu-nü fan-kung k'ang-O lien-ho hui** 中華婦女反共抗俄聯合會 (The Chinese Women's Anti-Aggression League). *Fu-lien ssu-nien* 婦聯四年 (Four Years of The Chinese Women's Anti-Aggression League). Taipei, 1954. 376p.

A collection of documents on the history of the Chinese Women's Anti-Aggression League. Included are official speeches, statements, proclamations, work progress reports, and a description of activities for the four-year period since the founding of the League (April 1950) by Madame Chiang Kai-shek.

Another volume commemorating the League's fifth anniversary was published in April 1955 under the title *Fu-lien wu chou-nien* 婦聯五週年 (The Fifth Anniversary of the Chinese Women's Anti-Aggression League).

705 Chung-kuo kuo-min tang, Chung-yang wei-yüan hui, Fu-nü kung-tso hui 中國國民黨 中央委員會 婦女工作會 (Kuomintang, Central Committee, Committee on Women's Activities). *Ssu-nien lai pen-tang ti fu-nü kung-tso* 四年來本黨的婦女工作
(Women's Activities of Our Party During the Last Four Years). Taipei, 1957. 24p.

A profusely illustrated pamphlet describing the work of the Committee on Women's Activities of the Central Committee of the Kuomintang for the period 1953 to 1957. Although issued primarily as a publicity volume, the pamphlet does contain some useful information on the work of the committee.

706 Chung-kuo kuo-min tang, Chung-yang kai-tsao wei-yuan hui, Ti-san tsu 中國國民黨 中央改造委員會 第三組 (Kuomintang, Central Reform Committee, Third Section). *Chung-kuo kuo-min tang hai-wai tang-wu kai-tsao fa-kuei chi-yao* 中國國民黨 海外黨務改造法規輯要
(Collection of Reform Regulations Concerning Overseas Party Affairs of the Kuomintang). Taipei, 1951. 119p.

The collection includes all regulations concerning overseas party work issued by the Central Reform Committee during the first year of the committee's existence (August 1950–August 1951). An important 'internal' party publication. Limited distribution.

707 Ch'iao-wu erh-shih wu nien pien-tsuan wei-yuan hui 僑務二十五年編纂委員會 (Compilation Committee of 'Twenty-Five Years of Overseas Chinese Affairs'). *Ch'iao-wu erh-shih wu nien* 僑務二十五年
(Twenty-Five Years of Overseas Chinese Affairs). Taipei: Hai-wai ch'u-pan she 海外出版社, 1957. 260p.

A special publication commemorating the twenty-fifth anniversary of the establishment of the Overseas Chinese Affairs Commission. The volume deals with the history, development and activities of the commission (Chapter 3 is a chronology of the commission's work). There are twenty-six statistical tables. The appendix (pp. 252–261) is a bibliography of works on the Overseas Chinese published between 1932 and 1957, listed by date of publication.

CHAPTER XIV

ECONOMIC AND SOCIAL DEVELOPMENTS

The economic and social transformation of the Mainland since 1949 has been a matter of central concern to students of contemporary China. Yet while research into certain aspects of the Chinese Communist economy—such as the rate of growth, national income, productivity and planning—is relatively advanced, a great deal still awaits scholarly attention. In general terms, little has been done on the economy of Taiwan, although the successful land reform program has commanded interest in many quarters.

Included in the present chapter are some of the major collections of documentary material in the economic and social fields. Because it is difficult to draw precise boundaries around that which may be designated 'economic and social', the reader is advised to consult the present chapter in conjunction with the other chapters in Part Three, in particular Chapter XII, Laws and Regulations, and Chapter XV, Education and Culture. Further specific references are given under each of the sections which follow directly below.

A. MAINLAND

The contents of the present section are grouped under the following subheadings: general, agriculture, communes, industry and commerce, and labor. The compilation should, of course, be taken as illustrative rather than exhaustive.

In this connection, reference should be made to the outstanding bibliography of Chinese Communist publications on the contemporary Mainland economy, *Gendai Chūgoku no keizai* (The Economy of Contemporary China) by Professor Ichiko, and to *The Economy of Mainland China, 1949–1963: A Bibliography of Materials in English* by Dr. Nai-ruenn Chen (**109** and **108**), as well as to the three-volume Mainland bibliography on 'economic construction' (**107**) and other bibliographies in the economic and social section in Chapter I. Also deserving of mention is the late Chao Kuo-chün's *Economic Planning and Organization in Mainland China: A Documentary Study (1949–1957)* (**112**). For alternate sources of documentary material, the reader should consult the yearbooks—in particular the People's Handbook (**212**) and directories in Chapter IV and VI, respectively.

Additional coverage of the economic and social sector can be obtained through a number of pertinent periodical publications, such as *Ching-chi yen-chiu* (Economic Studies, **863**), *Chi-hua ching-chi* (Planned Economy, **855**), and *Ts'ai-cheng* (Finance, **909**), all described in Chapter XVII.

For translations of economic and social material, see the various Joint Publications Research Service series, such as the *Economic Information on Communist China* (**1059**) and *Translations from Ta-kung pao* (**841**), as well as those of the American Consulate General (**1038** ff.) and the Union Research Service (**1065**) published in Hong Kong.

The present section comprises documentation on the 'General Line' and the two Five-Year Plans (1953–1957 and 1958–1962), as well as on Mainland statistical work. Concerning the latter, see also Chapter V on statistical compilations and Professor Li Choh-ming's *The Statistical System of Communist China* (**121**).

708 Kuo-tu shih-ch'i tsung lu-hsien hsüeh-hsi ts'an-k'ao tzu-liao 過渡時期 總路綫學習參考資料

(Study and Reference Materials on the General Line During the Transitional Period). Peking: Jen-min ch'u-pan she 人民出版社, 1954. 2 vols. 145; 111p.

A collection of *Jen-min jih-pao* editorials on the 'General Line' published during the three-month period of November 1953 to January 1954. Volume 1 contains editorials on agriculture and agricultural production. Those in Volume 2 concern industrial production.

709 Chung-hua jen-min kung-ho kuo fa-chan kuo-min ching-chi ti ti-i ko wu-nien chi-hua, 1953–1957 中華人民共和國發展國民經濟的第一個五年計劃, 1953–1957

(The First Five-Year Plan for the Development of the People's Economy of the People's Republic of China, 1953–1957). Peking: Jen-min ch'u-pan she 人民 出版社, 1955. 238p.

The text of the First Five-Year Plan and other documents: official communications between the C.C.P. National Congress and the State Council on the draft proposal of the Five-Year Plan and resolutions approving the draft proposal by the State Council and the National People's Congress. Includes also the full text of Li Fu-ch'un's report to the Second Session of the National People's Congress, July 5–6, 1955, on the progress of the Five-Year Plan. (Li was Vice Premier of the State Council and Director of the State Planning Commission.) For a translation of this publication, see the *First Five-Year Plan for the Development of the National Economy of the People's Republic of China in 1953–1957* (Peking: Foreign Languages Press, 1956), 231p.

See also *Report on National Economic Development and Fulfilment of the State Plan in 1954* and *Report on Fulfilment of the National Economic Plan of the People's Republic of China in 1955*, both issued by the State Statistical Bureau in 1956 (Peking: Foreign Languages Press), 48p. and 57p. respectively.

710 Chung-kuo kung-ch'an tang ti-pa tz'u ch'üan-kuo tai-piao ta-hui kuan-yü fa-chan kuo-min ching-chi ti ti-erh ko wu-nien chi-hua (1958 nien tao 1962 nien) ti chien-i 中國共產黨第八次全國代表大會關於發展國民經濟的 第二個五年計劃 (1958 年到 1962 年) 的建議

(Proposals of the Eighth National Congress of the Communist Party of China for the Second Five-Year Plan for Development of the National Economy [1958– 1962]. Peking: Jen-min ch'u-pan she 人民出版社, 1956. 72p.

The Second Five-Year Plan of Communist China. Issued with it is Chou En-lai's report on the proposed plan delivered at the Eighth National Congress of the Communist Party of China on September 16, 1956. For an official translation of these two documents, see *Proposals of the Eighth National Congress of the Communist Party of China for the Second Five-Year Plan for Development of the National Economy (1958–1962)* and *Report on the Proposals for the Second Five-Year Plan for Development of the National Economy* (Peking: Foreign Languages Press, 1956), 105p.

See also Chou En-lai, *Report on Adjusting the Major Targets of the 1959 National Economic Plan and Further Developing the Campaign for Increasing Production and Practising Economy* (Peking: Foreign Languages Press, 1959), 46p.; *Press Communiqué on the Growth of China's National Economy in 1959* (1960), 26p.; Li Fu-ch'un, *Raise High the Red Flag of the General Line and Continue to March Forward* (1960), 41p.; and Hsueh Mu-chiao, et al., *The Socialist Transformation of the National Economy in China* (1960), 287p.

711 **China (People's Republic of China, 1949—), Kuo-chia t'ung-chi chü** 中華人民共和國 國家統計局 (China [People's Republic of China, 1949—], State Statistical Bureau). *T'ung-chi kung-tso chung-yao wen-chien hui-pien* 統計工作重要文件彙編 (Compendium of Important Documents Concerning Statistical Work). Peking: T'ung-chi ch'u-pan she 統計出版社, Vol. 1—, 1955—.

An 'internal publication' containing regulations, directives, reports, and other pertinent documents on statistical work in Communist China. Documents on work at the provincial and municipal levels are excluded. The arrangement is by subject under which the documents are listed by date of issuance. The subject division in Volume 1 has been generally followed in the later volumes: (1) general, (2) industry, (3) capital construction, (4) agriculture and forestry, (5) communications and transportation, (6) trade and cooperatives, (7) logistics, and (8) culture, education, hygiene and civic affairs.

The following is a summary of the published volumes:

VOLUME NO.	PERIOD COVERED	DATE OF PUBLICATION
Vol. 1	January 1951–June 1955	1955
Vol. 2	July 1955–June 1957	1957
Vol. 3	July 1957–December 1958	1959

The most comprehensive available collection of documents on the subject.

712 **China (People's Republic of China, 1949—), Kuo-chia t'ung-chi chü, Kung-yeh t'ung-chi ssu** 中華人民共和國 國家統計局 工業統計司 (China [People's Republic of China, 1949—], State Statistical Bureau, Industrial

Statistics Section). *Wo-kuo kung-yeh t'ung-chi kung-tso ti ching-yen* 我國工業統計工作的經驗
(Experiences in Industrial Statistical Work). Peking: T'ung-chi ch'u-pan she 統計出版社, 1958. 94p.

An official review of Communist China's work in the field of industrial statistics, including analyses of the statistical system, data collection and processing. The appendix contains four sample reports by the local statistical bureaus of Liaoning, Shanghai, Kiangsu, and Szechwan. A basic reference volume.

2. AGRICULTURE

The agricultural system on the Mainland since 1949 has gone through several stages of development. The launching of the commune program was preceded by the initial drastic land reform drive, followed by the creation of mutual aid teams as the first step towards a larger system of cooperative agriculture. The collected documents bearing on this development contained in the present section are arranged within a chronological framework. The first two entries are examples of the type of documentation available for the initial land reform period. For land reform laws, see the compendium of laws and regulations and other compilations listed in the topical laws section of Chapter XII, such as *Chung-hua jen-min kung-ho kuo t'u-ti fa ts'an-kao tzu-liao hui-pien* (Collection of Reference Materials on the Land Law of the People's Republic of China, **591**). Documentation on the mutual aid teams and the cooperative agriculture movement is provided in the three entries (**715–717**) that follow. (The communes are dealt with in a separate section directly below.) The last two Chinese-language entries should be singled out for special mention. One is a rather typical report issued during the 'Great Leap Forward' campaign (**718**), and the other a somewhat more sober assessment of agricultural matters made in 1960 (**719**).

Chao Kuo-chün's *Agrarian Policies of Mainland China: A Documentary Survey (1949–1956)* (see **111**) is at once a bibliography and a compilation of Chinese Communist source materials. The reader should also consult the other agricultural and forestry bibliographies in the same chapter. Chapter V contains compilations of agricultural statistics.

Reference should be made to journals in Chapter XVII, such as *Chung-kuo nung-pao* (Chinese Agriculture Bulletin, **873**), and to the Joint Publications Research Service series, *Translations on Communist China's Agriculture, Animal Husbandry and Materials* (**1060**) in Chapter XX.

For a collection of materials on agriculture which appeared in the People's Daily, see *Jen-min jih-pao nung-yeh k'o-hsüeh wen-hsüan* 人民日報農業科學文選 (Selected Materials on Agricultural Science from the People's Daily). The first issue covering the period September 1962–March 1963 was published in July 1963; the second issue covering the period April to December 1963 was published in May 1964.

713 **Hsin-hua shu-tien** 新華書店 (New China Book Company). *T'u-ti kai-ko shou-ts'e* 土地改革手冊
(Handbook on Land Reform). Revised fourth edition. Shanghai: Hsin-hua shu-tien hua-tung tsung fen-tien 新華書店華東總分店, 1950. 164p.

A collection of official orders, directives, etc., issued by the Central People's Government and by the East China Military and Administrative Committee from July to October of 1950, on land reform procedures, the establishment of people's courts and peasants' associations.

714 **Fu-chien sheng nung-min hsieh-hui** 福建省農民協會 (The Peasants Association of Fukien). *Nung-yün kan-pu shou-ts'e* 農運幹部手冊 (Peasant Movement Cadre Handbook). Foochow (?), 1950. 101p.

A general handbook on the peasant movement for cadres working in Fukien province. Among the documents included are resolutions and directives issued by the East China Military and Administrative Committee, and selected editorials from the *Fu-chien jih-pao* and the *Jen-min jih-pao*, February to November 1950.

715 **Shih, Ching-t'ang** 史敬棠, **et al., eds.** *Chung-kuo nung-yeh ho-tso hua yün-tung shih-liao* 中國農業合作化運動史料 (Compendium of Source Materials Concerning Cooperative Agriculture Movement in China). Peking: Sheng-huo tu-shu hsin-chih san-lien shu-tien 生活讀書新知三聯書店, 1957, 1959. 2 vols. 1,088; 1,019p.

Volume 1 contains materials concerning the period 1925 to 1949, including a survey of traditional Chinese cooperative farming methods. Volume 2 provides sources on the post-1949 period preceding the establishment of the communes in 1958. Included are government orders, directives, regulations and detailed statistics. An excellent source.

See also the following English-language pamphlets published by the Foreign Languages Press in Peking: *Co-operative Farming in China* (1954), 34p.; *Decisions on Agricultural Co-operation* (1956), 55p.; *Draft Programme for Agricultural Development in the People's Republic of China (1956–1967)* (1956), 44p.; *Model Regulations for an Agricultural Producers' Co-operative* (March 1956), 52p.; *Model Regulations for Advanced Agricultural Producers' Co-operatives* (June 1956), 34p.; *National Programme for Agricultural Development, 1956–1967* (1960), 61p.; *Socialist Upsurge in China's Countryside (1956)* (1957), 505p.; Tung, Ta-lin, *Agricultural Cooperation in China* (1959), 179p.; Liao, Lu-yen, *The Whole Party and the Whole People Go In For Agriculture in a Big Way* (1960), 20p.; and Po, I-po and Liao, Lu-yen, *Socialist Industrialization and Agricultural Collectivization in China* (1964), 51p.

716 **Chung-kuo k'o-hsüeh yüan, Ching-chi yen-chiu so, Nung-yeh ching-chi tsu** 中國科學院 經濟研究所 農業經濟組 (Chinese Academy of Sciences, Institute of Economic Research, Agricultural Economics Section). *Kuo-min ching-chi hui-fu shih-ch'i nung-yeh sheng-ch'an ho-tso tzu-liao hui-pien* 國民經濟恢復時期農業生產合作資料彙編 (Compendium of Reference Materials on Cooperative Agriculture During the Restoration Period of the People's Economy, 1949–1952). Peking: K'o-hsüeh ch'u-pan she 科學出版社, 1957. 2 vols. 1,214p.

A collection of 138 documents on the cooperative agriculture movement in Communist China from 1949 to 1952, including government directives, policy statements, progress reports, model case studies, recommendations, etc. The documents, taken mostly from newspapers, are arranged by region and under each region by province. An extremely important source for the study of the Chinese Communist program of mutual aid teams and cooperative agriculture in the period covered.

717   **Fei 'nung-yeh ho-tso hua' yu-kuan tzu-liao hui-pien** 匪 ㄥ農業合作化ㄱ有關資料彙編
(Compendium of Reference Materials on Bandit 'Cooperative Agriculture'). Taipei: Yang-ming shan-chuang 陽明山莊, 1955. 2 vols. 150; 160p.

A collection of Chinese Communist documents on cooperative agriculture including Central Committee resolutions, official policy statements, speeches by C.C.P. leaders, and *Jen-min jih-pao* editorials covering the period from 1953 through 1955. Not exhaustive but convenient for reference purposes.

718   **China (People's Republic of China, 1949—), Nung-yeh pu, Liang-shih tso-wu sheng-ch'an chü** 中華人民共和國 農業部 糧食作物生產局 (China [People's Republic of China, 1949—], Ministry of Agriculture, Bureau of Food Stuffs). '*Ssu, wu, pa' liang-shih tseng-ch'an ching-yen hui-pien* '四、五、八' 糧食增產經驗彙編
(Collected Experiences in Boosting the Output of Food Stuffs Under the 'Four-Five-Eight' Program). Peking: K'o-hsüeh p'u-chi ch'u-pan she 科學普及出版社, 1958. 2 vols. 238; 149p.

A compilation of forty-one case reports from regions which were alleged to have fulfilled their agricultural production targets during the first year of the 'Four-Five-Eight Program.' The latter was a component part of the twelve-year agricultural development plan of Communist China (1956–1967 inclusive), under which food production was slated to increase from an average of 150 catties per acre per year to 400 catties, from 208 to 500 catties, and from 400 to 800 catties, depending on the area.

The publication is typical of those issued during the 'Great Leap Forward' campaign in 1958.

719   **China (People's Republic of China, 1949—), Kuo-chia t'ung-chi chü, Nung-yeh t'ung-chi ssu** 中華人民共和國 國家統計局 農業統計司 (China [People's Republic of China, 1949—], State Statistical Bureau, Agricultural Statistics Section). *Nung-tso wu ch'an-liang tiao-ch'a ching-yen hui-pien* 農作物產量調查經驗滙編
(Collected Experiences in Assessing Agricultural Output). Peking: T'ung-chi ch'u-pan she 統計出版社, 1960. 132p.

Eighteen reports given at the National Conference on Assessing Agricultural Output held in Chengtu, Szechwan, in 1960. The reports selected for inclusion in the volume are concerned with various kinds of agricultural products, regional problems, the organization of statistical work, etc., and are considered to be a representative sample of the 109 reports read before the conference.

720 **Carin, Robert.** *China's Land Problem Series.* Hong Kong, 1960–1962. 5 vols. (Research Backgrounder).

Volume 1 (144p.) is concerned with the land reform movement in Communist China; Volume 2 (642p.) deals with the cooperative agriculture movement; while Volumes 3, 4 and 5 are devoted to the rural communes (865p. on developments from September 1, 1958 to August 15, 1959; 853p. on the period August 1959 to March 1960; and 608p. on the period April to December 1960, respectively). The volumes are all characterized by extensive quotations from Chinese Communist sources with commentary, notes, and a chronology. Mimeographed.

721 **Carin, Robert.** *State Farms in Communist China (1947–1961).* Hong Kong, 1962. 323p. (Research Backgrounder).

An extensively documented study of the history and development of the state farms in Communist China, 1947–1961, relying exclusively on Chinese Communist sources, and divided into eleven chronologically arranged chapters. The volume is similar in form to the preceding entry and also includes a chronology of major events. Mimeographed.

3. COMMUNES

The establishment of the people's communes in the fall of 1958 was a radical measure at once designed to bring into being a strict regimentation of the population while achieving maximum utilization of available labor resources. It was also an attempt to jump ahead of the Soviet Union in the transition to 'Communism,' thereby strengthening Chinese claims to ideological superiority. While events have forced the Chinese Communists to amend or abandon some of their more radical programs, the warm debate their experiment stimulated continues both within and outside the Communist camp.

Documentary material on the communes emerging in the years since their inception is abundant. Included in the present section are mainly compilations of such documentation published on the Mainland, and in Hong Kong and Taiwan.

For other sources, in particular those not included in compilations, the reader should consult the *Hsin-hua pan-yüeh k'an* (**882**) since 1958, the 1959 People's Handbook, pp. 54–85, and the bibliographies on the communes in Chapter 1 (especially that prepared by Professor Noma of Aichi University in Japan, **125**). The Mainland Index to Major Newspapers and Periodicals (**184**) and the indexes to most of the major Mainland newspapers serve as excellent guides for the location of similar materials in the Communist press and periodical literature. Further information will be found in a comprehensive directory of some six thousand communes now under preparation by the Research Institute on Asia (Ajia Kenkyūjo アジア研究所) in Tokyo.

Documents in translation appear in *Communist China, 1955–1959: Policy Documents with Analysis* (see **571**), and in the various translation series listed in Chapter XX.

722 **Nung-yeh ch'u-pan she** 農業出版社 (Agricultural Publishing House). *Jen-min kung-she wan-sui* 人民公社萬歲
(Long Live the People's Communes). Peking: Nung-yeh ch'u-pan she, 1960. 397p.

Contains documents and articles on the background and development of the people's communes. In three parts: Part 1 includes important documents on cooperative agriculture in Communist China prior to 1958; Part 2 consists of the three basic documents on the establishment of the communes in 1958 (the C.C. of the C.C.P. resolution of August 29, 1958; the resolution of the Sixth Plenum of the Eighth Central Committee of the C.C.P., December 10, 1958; and a *Hung-ch'i* editorial reprinted from issue No. 1, 1959); Part 3 contains the documents concerning the people's communes issued by the Eighth Plenum of the Eighth Central Committee of the C.C.P., together with related articles and *Jen-min jih-pao* editorials.

A convenient reference volume.

723 **Nung-yeh ch'u-pan she** 農業出版社 (Agricultural Publishing House). *Jen-min kung-she wan-shou wu-chiang* 人民公社萬壽無疆 (Long Live the People's Communes). Peking: Nung-yeh ch'u-pan she, 1960(?) 308p.

Comprises surveys of forty-seven communes originally published in Mainland newspapers and periodicals. The communes are described under ten main categories (economy, industry, irrigation, electrification, etc.).

724 **Nung-yeh ch'u-pan she** 農業出版社 (Agricultural Publishing House). *Jen-min kung-she kuang-mang wan-chang—kung-she ching-chi tiao-ch'a* 人民公社光芒萬丈——公社經濟調查
(Brilliant Flashes Ten Thousand Feet High: the People's Communes—An Economic Survey of the Communes). Peking: Nung-yeh ch'u-pan she, 1960. 251p.

A collection of forty-four surveys and reports on the people's communes, selected from Chinese Communist newspapers and periodicals. Arranged in five parts: (1) general surveys and reports; (2) 'conquering nature and re-forming nature'; (3) multiple economic activities; (4) economic and cultural improvement of the communes; (5) management and organization of the communes.

725   Wen-hui pao 文滙報. *Jen-min kung-she wen-t'i tzu-liao* 人民公社問題資料 (Reference Materials on the People's Communes). Hong Kong, 1959. 247p.

A collection of Chinese Communist documents and reference materials on the people's communes, *Jen-min jih-pao* (People's Daily) editorials, and articles which appeared in *Hung-ch'i* (Red Flag) and other periodicals and newspapers.

726   People's Communes in China. Peking: Foreign Languages Press, 1958. 90p.

A translation of *Chung-kuo jen-min kung-she hua yün-tung* 中國人民公社化 運動, containing editorials and articles published in the *Jen-min jih-pao* and *Hung-ch'i* in September and October of 1958. It also includes the resolution of the Central Committee of the C.C.P. on the establishment of people's communes in rural areas (August 29, 1958) and the draft regulations of the Weihsing (Sputnik) People's Commune.

See also Robert Carin's three documentary volumes on the communes (**720**) listed in the preceding section.

727   China, Ssu-fa hsing-cheng pu, Tiao-ch'a chü 中華民國 司法行政部 調查局 (China, Ministry of Justice, Bureau of Investigation). *Kung-fei 'jen-min kung-she' pao-hsing t'u-piao hsüan-chi* 共匪 ⌐ 人民公社 ⌐ 暴行圖表選輯 (Charts Concerning the Tyranny of the 'People's Commune' of the Communist Bandits). Taipei, 1959. 70p.

Six groups of charts outlining the history and objective of the people's communes. Group 4 is a useful collection of charts on the organization of the communes.

For a more detailed graphic description of the commune system, see *Charts Concerning Chinese Communists on the Mainland* (sixth series) published by the Asian Peoples' Anti-Communist League, Republic of China, 1959.

4. INDUSTRY AND COMMERCE

'Socialist construction', the term applied to all economic activity on the Mainland, and particularly to industrial development, is the dominant theme of much of the documentation contained in general works. The four entries listed in the present section are rather representative collections of resolutions, official reports, etc. The last entry (**731**), on the handicraft industry, is perhaps the only such compilation available on a special sector of industry.

The reader is advised to consult the pertinent bibliographies and indexes in Chapters I and III, as well as such other sources as the People's Handbook and the various statistical compilations. Periodicals, such as *Chung-kuo kung-yeh* (Chinese Industry, **872**), *Chung kung-yeh t'ung-hsün* (Bulletin of Heavy Industry, **866**), etc., have obvious relevance.

Chapter XX contains various sources of translated documentation, such as *Translations on Communist China's Industry, Mining, Fuels and Power* (**1061**), and *Translations on Communist China's Trade, Finance, Transportation and Communications* (**1062**).

728 **Chung-hua ch'üan-kuo kung-shang yeh lien-ho hui** 中華全國工商業聯合會
(All-China Federation of Industry and Commerce). *Chung-hua ch'üan-kuo
kung-shang yeh lien-ho hui ti-erh chieh hui-yüan tai-piao ta-hui chu-yao wen-chien
hui-pien* 中華全國工商業聯合會第二屆會員代表大會主要文件彙編
(Collected Documents on the Second National Congress of the All-China
Federation of Industry and Commerce). Peking: Ts'ai-cheng ching-chi ch'u-
pan she 財政經濟出版社, 1957. 91p.

Contains speeches by government officials, reports on the work of the
federation and resolutions adopted at the congress held in Peking December
10-23, 1956. For a selection of speeches by delegates to the congress, see
next entry.

729 **Chung-hua ch'üan-kuo kung-shang yeh lien-ho hui** 中華全國工商業聯合會
(All-China Federation of Industry and Commerce). *Fa-yang ai-kuo chu-i ching-
shen, wei tsu-kuo kung-hsien li-liang (Chung-hua ch'üan-kuo kung-shang yeh lien-ho
hui ti-erh chieh hui-yüan tai-piao ta-hui tai-piao fa-yen hsüan-chi)* 發揚愛國主義
精神爲祖國貢獻力量(中華全國工商業聯合會第二屆會員代表大會代表發言選輯)
(Spreading the Spirit of Patriotism, Offering Help for the Motherland—Selected
Speeches by Delegates to the Second National Congress of the All-China
Federation of Industry and Commerce). Peking: Ts'ai-cheng ching-chi ch'u-
pan she 財政經濟出版社, 1957. 152p.

A supplementary publication to the preceding entry, containing the text of
sixty-six speeches.

730 **The National Conference of Outstanding Groups and Workers in
Socialist Construction in Industry, Commerce and Transport, Capital
Construction, Finance and Trade.** Peking: Foreign Languages Press,
1960. 143p.

Speeches by Chu Teh, Li Fu-ch'un, Lu Ting-yi and other prominent leaders
at the conference which was held from October 26 to November 8, 1959. The
first joint congress of the All-China Federation of Industry and Commerce
and the China Democratic National Construction Association was held from
February 19 to 21, 1960.

See also Kuan Ta-tung, *The Socialist Transformation of Capitalist Industry
and Commerce in China* (Peking: Foreign Languages Press, 1960), 133p.

731 **China, Kuo-fang pu, Ch'ing-pao chü** 中華民國 國防部 情報局 (China,
Ministry of National Defense, Bureau of Intelligence). *Fei-ch'ü shou kung-yeh
chung-yao tzu-liao hui-pien* 匪區手工業重要資料彙編
(Compendium of Important Materials on Handicraft Industry in Bandit Areas).
Taipei, 1962. 14; 10; 444p.

A collection of documents concerning the history and development of the handicraft industry in Communist China published in *Jen-min jih-pao* between 1950 and May 1962. The materials are arranged chronologically by date of publication under the following sections: (1) directives, (2) conferences, (3) editorials, (4) history of reconstruction and measures for increasing production, (5) undesirable tendencies, (6) work review and study, (7) appendix—industrial arts industry. An exhaustive compilation, conveniently arranged.

5. LABOR

The Seventh All-China Congress of Trade Unions held in 1953 was the first such meeting since the establishment of Communist rule on the Mainland. The Eighth Congress was held in 1957. The major documentation for these two meetings is provided in the present section. (For documentary material on other social movements, such as those concerning women and youth, see the section on mass organizations in the preceding chapter.)

Additional references to source materials can be found in the bibliographies and indexes contained in Chapters I and III, respectively. The reader should also consult the various yearbooks, statistical compilations, etc., listed in Part One.

The official publications of the Federation of Trade Unions, *Kung-jen jih-pao* (Worker's Daily, **842**) and *Chung-kuo kung-jen* (Chinese Worker, **871**) contain a wealth of useful data. Published documents in translation are covered in Chapter XX.

732   **Kung-jen ch'u-pan she** 工人出版社 (Workers' Publishing House). *Chung-kuo kung-hui ti-ch'i tz'u ch'üan-kuo tai-piao ta-hui chu-yao wen-chien* 中國工會第七次全國代表大會主要文件 (Principal Documents of the Seventh All-China Congress of Trade Unions). Peking: Kung-jen ch'u-pan she, 1953. 110p.

Contains greetings, reports, resolutions and two *Jen-min jih-pao* editorials. For a translation of selected documents, see *The Seventh All-China Congress of Trade Unions* (Peking: Foreign Languages Press, 1953), 141p. The Congress was held in Peking May 2–11, 1953.

733   **Kung-jen ch'u-pan she** 工人出版社 (Workers' Publishing House). *Chung-kuo kung-hui ti-pa tz'u ch'üan-kuo tai-piao ta-hui chu-yao wen-chien* 中國工會第八次全國代表大會主要文件 (Principal Documents of the Eighth All-China Congress of Trade Unions). Peking: Kung-jen ch'u-pan she, 1957. 154p.

Contains the constitution of the Congress of Trade Unions of the People's Republic of China, reports, resolutions and editorials from the *Jen-min jih-pao* and the *Kung-jen jih-pao* 工人日報 (Worker's Daily). For a translation of selected documents, see *Eighth All-China Congress of the Trade Unions* (Peking: Foreign Languages Press, 1958), 125p. The Congress was held in Peking, December 2–12, 1957.

B. TAIWAN

Primary sources on Taiwan's economic development in the post-1945 period are not scarce, but scattered. Collections of such materials have not been published.

The entries listed in the present section are five of perhaps the most important collections of Taiwan economic documentation available. Economic Reference Materials, published by the Ministry of Economic Affairs (first entry), provides a good overview of the island's economic regeneration. The J.C.R.R. general reports are indispensable for the study of rural developments, including the successful land reform program. The latter is also documented in somewhat greater detail in the last three entries. Documentation on the three successive Four-Year Plans (1953–1956, 1957–1960, 1960–1964) is not ample. Certain basic data can be obtained from both the Chinese and English-language editions of the *China Yearbook* (**239** and **240**), as well as such publications as *Highlights of the Second Four-Year Plan for the Economic Development in Taiwan* (Economic Stabilization Board, 1957), 30p., and *Taiwan's Third Four-Year Economic Development Plan, Abridged* (Ministry of Economic Affairs, 1961), 82p.

For texts of laws and regulations of the Republic of China relating to the present section, see Chapter XII. The section on mass organizations in the preceding chapter contains documentation on aspects of social conditions in Taiwan, including women's and youth movements. For additional references to economic and social documentation, the reader should consult the index to the Bank of Taiwan Quarterly (**123**) and the relevant bibliographies in Chapter I.

The reader should also refer to the following sources, which contain a variety of important materials: yearbooks (general as well as those concerned specifically with agriculture, agricultural cooperatives, fisheries, finance, etc.) in Chapter IV; statistical compilations (agriculture, industry, etc.) in Chapter V; directories (agriculture, trade) in Chapter VI; biographies of leaders in the field of industry and commerce (**381** and **382**) in Chapter VII; and the economic chronology in the Bank of Taiwan Quarterly (**407**).

Chapter XVIII contains a number of relevant periodicals including, in addition to the Bank of Taiwan Quarterly (**975**), the *Cheng-hsing hsin-wen pao* (Financial and Economic News, **941**), *T'u-ti kai-ko* (Land Reform, **978**), *Industry of Free China* (**987**), etc.

734 **China, Ching-chi pu** 中華民國 經濟部 (China, Ministry of Economic Affairs). *Ching-chi ts'an-k'ao tzu-liao* 經濟參考資料 (Economic Reference Materials). Taipei, No. 1—, July 7, 1951—.

Published three times a week from July 1951 to May 1952; continued on approximately a semi-monthly basis from June 1952 to the present. Each issue is devoted to the analysis of a particular aspect of Taiwan's economic program. Included also are economic statistics, a monthly chronology of economic activities, laws and regulations, and a monthly index to economic literature published in Taiwan.

This is one of the most important sources for the study of all sectors of Taiwan's economy. Limited distribution.

735 General Report of the Joint Commission on Rural Reconstruction. Taipei: Chinese-American Joint Commission on Rural Reconstruction, No. 1—, 1950—. Annual.

An annual report of the J.C.R.R. on its work in Taiwan, usually given under the following categories: (1) introduction, (2) farmers' organizations, (3) agricultural extension, (4) rural information, (5) economic research and statistics, (6) rural health, (7) land reform, (8) crops and fertilizers, (9) livestock production, (10) fisheries, (11) food and nutrition, (12) water use and control, (13) forestry and soil conservation, (14) agricultural credit. Fourteen reports have been issued through 1963, covering the period 1948 to 1963.

The reports provide an authoritative summary of the work of the J.C.R.R. (including its participation in the land reform program) that has contributed to the establishing of a sound agricultural base for Taiwan's economic development.

736 China, Nei-cheng pu 中華民國 內政部 (China, Ministry of Interior). *T'u-ti hsing-cheng kai-k'uang* 土地行政概況
(Survey of the Land Administration). Taipei, 1957. 214p.

An official survey of the land reform program in Taiwan with an emphasis on the 37·5% rental reduction and the 'land to the tillers' programs, and accompanied by descriptions of land reform activities in the urban areas. Statistics and regulations are also included.

For translations of relevant laws and regulations, see the appendix in Ch'en Ch'eng, *Land Reform in Taiwan* (Taipei: China Publishing Company, 1961). See also the next two entries.

737 Chung-kuo kuo-min tang, Chung-yang wei-yüan hui, Ti-wu tsu 中國國民黨 中央委員會 第五組 (Kuomintang, Central Committee, Fifth Section). *Chung-kuo kuo-min tang t'u-ti cheng-tse yü T'ai-wan sheng shih-shih keng-che yu ch'i tien* 中國國民黨土地政策與臺灣省實施耕者有其田
(Land Policy of the Kuomintang and the Land to the Tillers Program in Taiwan Province). Taipei, 1954. 120p.

An official report on Kuomintang's land policy with special emphasis on the party's role in Taiwan's successful land reform program. The appendix provides the texts of ten of the most important documents concerning the land reform program. See also next entry.

738 Chung-kuo kuo-min tang, Chung-yang wei-yüan hui, Ti-wu tsu 中國國民黨 中央委員會 第五組 (Kuomintang, Central Committee, Fifth Section). *Chung-kuo kuo-min tang nung-min yün-tung yü T'ai-wan sheng ko-chi nung-hui kai-chin* 中國國民黨 農民運動與臺灣省各級農會改進
(The Farmers' Movement Under the Kuomintang and the Reform of the Farmers' Association in Taiwan Province). Taipei, 1954. 140p.

An official report in seven sections on the Farmers' Movement under the Kuomintang, with special emphasis on the reform of the Farmers' Association in Taiwan. Appended are eight documents concerning the Farmers' Association, including its organic law, election regulations, directives on the work of the association, etc.

This and the two preceding entries constitute an extremely important source for the study of land reform and farmers' associations in Taiwan.

See also *A Study of Farmers' Associations in Taiwan*, a United Nations publication in its Community Development and Economic Development Series.

CHAPTER XV

EDUCATION AND CULTURE

Over the last decade, great strides have been made in the field of education on the Mainland as well as in Taiwan. Major efforts have been directed at eliminating illiteracy and at providing effective vocational and technical training.

General surveys of educational developments are available for both Mainland and Taiwan. They are included in the following sections (one for the Mainland; the other for Taiwan). Also described here are other more specialized documentary materials in the fields of education, religion, and culture.

A. MAINLAND

The entry appearing first in the present section provides an overview of developments in the field of education on the Mainland during the first decade of Communist rule. The remainder comprise collections of documents on religion, educational policy, teacher training and general cultural affairs, as well as documents emerging from congresses of scientists, writers, artists and musicians.

For further references, the reader is advised to consult the various subject bibliographies in Chapter I (on history, education and indoctrination, library science, science, technology and medicine, etc.); yearbooks (Chapter IV); directories to educational institutions (Chapter VI); and chronologies on education and culture in Chapter VIII. Relevant laws and regulations appear in Chapter XII.

The pertinent Mainland newspapers, notably the *Kuang-ming jih-pao* (**836**) and the *Wen-hui pao* (**845**), should not be neglected. The former usually carries articles on higher education, while the latter tends to concentrate on education at the primary and secondary levels. Periodicals such as *Jen-min chiao-yü* (People's Education, **889**), *Chiao-hsüeh yü yen-chiu* (Teaching and Research, **858**) and *Wen-tzu kai-ko* (Language Reform, **917**), are also important sources. For a compilation of translations on education, see Joint Publications Research Service series, *Sociological, Educational, Cultural Information on Communist China* (**1063**).

739 Jen-min chiao-yü ch'u-pan she 人民教育出版社 (People's Education Publishing House). *Chiao-yü shih-nien* 教育十年
(Ten Years of Education). Peking: Jen-min chiao-yü ch'u-pan she, 1960. 310p.

A collection of thirty-one newspaper and periodical articles on education in Communist China, 1949–1959, written in commemoration of the tenth anniversary of the founding of the People's Republic of China. The articles are official reports by local administrators in charge of education and are arranged by province and municipality under regions (North China, East China, Central China, etc.). The concluding four pieces concern the four autonomous regions of Sinkiang Uighur, Inner Mongolia, Kwangsi Chuang, and Ninghsia Hui. An article by Yang Hsiu-feng 楊秀峰, Minister of Education, appears at the beginning of the volume.

See also Part 2: Selected Documents, in Stewart Erskine Fraser, *Some Aspects of Higher Education in the People's Republic of China* (**2092**), and his compilation, *Chinese Communist Education: Records of the First Decade*, published by the Vanderbilt University Press, 1965 (542p.).

740 Merwin, Wallace C. and Jones, Francis P., comps.
Documents of the Three-Self Movement—Source Materials for the Study of the Protestant Church in Communist China. New York: National Council of the Churches of Christ in the U.S.A., Division of Foreign Missions, Far Eastern Office, 1963. 211p.

A collection of documents on the reorganization of the Protestant Church in China by the Communist authorities from 1948 to 1962. Contains fifty-two manifestoes, declarations, speeches, messages, reports, articles, pastoral letters and confessions by prominent Chinese Christians, as well as pertinent government edicts and regulations. Much of the source material has been translated from the Christian magazine *T'ien Feng* 天風 (Heavenly Wind), published in Shanghai. A biographical index of some one hundred prominent Chinese Christians, with brief identifications, precedes the documents.

741 China (People's Republic of China, 1949—), Cheng-wu yüan, Wen-hua chiao-yü wei-yüan hui 中華人民共和國 政務院 文化教育委員會 (China [People's Republic of China, 1949—], State Council, Committee on Culture and Education). *Wen-chiao ts'an-k'ao tzu-liao* 文教參考資料 (Reference Materials on Culture and Education). Peking, January 1950–February 1951. 10 vols.

A series designed to promote understanding of the cultural policies of Communist bloc countries and of the methods used for their implementation, and to provide and stimulate ideas among the cultural and educational workers in Communist China. The ten-volume set is primarily a collection of articles drawn from Russian and Chinese Communist newspapers and periodical publications. Volume 8 (November 1950) has a bibliography of Chinese Communist sources on propaganda activities. Volume 10 (February 1951) is a special issue on cultural and educational work in Communist China in 1950, including reports of achievements on both national and local levels.

742 The National Conference of Outstanding Groups and Individuals in Socialist Construction in Education, Culture, Health, Physical Culture and Journalism. Peking: Foreign Languages Press, 1960. 46p.

This conference was jointly convened by the Chinese Communist Party and the State Council on June 1, 1960. Contains the main address by Lu Ting-yi on behalf of the C.C.P. and the State Council, as well as other speeches and documents.

See also *Education Must Be Combined With Productive Labor*, by Lu Ting-yi (Peking: Foreign Languages Press, 1958), 33p. on the purpose of education in a socialist society.

743 Kwangtung, Wen-chiao t'ing 廣東省文教廳 (Kwangtung Provincial Government, Department of Culture and Education). *Chiao-yü kung-tso che hsüeh-hsi tzu-liao* 教育工作者學習資料
(Study Materials for Educational Workers). Canton: Hua-nan hsin-hua shu-tien 華南新華書店, 1950. 2 vols.

A collection of twenty-two articles by Mao Tse-tung, Liu Shao-ch'i and others on communism, Communist Party discipline, and Communist China's economic and educational policies, selected from newspapers and periodicals for the indoctrination of teachers. Helpful in gaining insights into policies in teacher training during the initial period of Communist rule on the Mainland.

744 Chung-hua ch'üan-kuo tzu-jan k'o-hsüeh kung-tso che tai-piao hui ch'ou-pei wei-yüan hui 中華全國自然科學工作者代表會籌備委員會 (Organization Committee for the All-China Scientific Workers' Congress). *Chung-hua chüan-kuo tzu-jan k'o-hsüeh kung-tso che tai-piao hui-i chi-nien chi* 中華全國自然科學工作者代表會議紀念集
(The All-China Scientific Workers' Congress). Peking: Jen-min ch'u-pan she 人民出版社, 1951. 175p.

A collection of documents on the All-China Scientific Workers' Congress held in Peking August 17–24, 1950. Included are speeches, reports, resolutions and proceedings of the Congress, and two name lists—one of the Presidium, the other of the delegates.

745 Chung-hua ch'üan-kuo wen-hsüeh i-shu kung-tso che tai-piao ta-hui, Hsüan-ch'uan ch'u 中華全國文學藝術工作者代表大會 宣傳處 (National Congress of Literary Workers and Artists, Department of Propaganda). *Chung-hua ch'üan-kuo wen-hsüeh i-shu kung-tso che tai-piao ta-hui chi-nien wen-chi* 中華全國文學藝術工作者代表大會紀念文集
(National Congress of Literary Workers and Artists). Peking: Hsin-hua shu-tien 新華書店, 1950. 601p.

Contains documents on the National Congress of Literary Workers and Artists held in Peking July 2–19, 1949. The materials are arranged in eight parts: (1) speeches, (2) reports, (3) proceedings, (4) greetings, (5) papers read at discussion sessions, (6) commemorative articles, (7) a name list of delegates to the congress (including the Presidium), and the constitution and name list of the All-China Federation of Literary and Art Circles, and (8) the entertainment program for the delegates to the congress. Parts 5 and 6 (372p.) constitute the major portion of this publication.

The second congress was held in 1953 and the third in 1960. For recent materials on culture and art, see a collection of thirty selections from the People's Daily published from August 1960 to the end of 1961 *(Jen-min jih-pao wen-i p'ing-lun hsüan-chi* 人民日報文藝評論選集). See also *The Path of Socialist Literature and Art in China*, a report delivered by Chou Yang to the third congress (Peking: Foreign Languages Press, 1960), 74p., his *A Great Debate on the Literary Front* (1958), 73p., and Lin Mo-han, *Raise Higher the Banner of Mao Tse-tung's Thought on Art and Literature* (1961), 41p.

746 **Chung-kuo yin-yüeh-chia hsieh-hui** 中國音樂家協會 (All-China Association of Musicians). *Wei kung nung ping fu-wu ti yin-yüeh i-shu* 爲工農兵服務的音樂藝術 (Music for the Workers, Peasants, and Soldiers). Peking: Yin-yüeh ch'u-pan she 音樂出版社, 1961. 154p.

Selected reports and speeches delivered at the Second National Congress of the All-China Association of Musicians held in Peking July 31 to August 5, 1960. The First National Congress was held in 1949.

747 **Jen-min t'i-yü ch'u-pan she** 人民體育出版社 (People's Athletics Publishing House). *Chung-hua jen-min kung-ho kuo t'i-yü yün-tung wen-chien hui-pien* 中華人民共和國體育運動文件彙編 (Collected Documents on Athletics in the People's Republic of China). Peking: Jen-min t'i-yü ch'u-pan she, 1955–1958. 3 vols.

Directives, regulations, resolutions, communiqués, etc., issued by the Chinese Communists concerning athletics. Volume 1 covers the period from July 1950 to September 1955; Volume 2, 1955 and 1956; Volume 3, 1957.

B. TAIWAN

While only two entries appear in the present section, the first provides comprehensive coverage on education in Taiwan for the years 1950–1961. For further material (or references to same), the reader is advised to consult the general and topical yearbooks (see Chapter IV), the statistical reports issued by the Ministry of Education (**275**) and the provincial Department of Education (**278**), respectively, and the various directories dealing with cultural organizations, universities and mass communication media (see Chapter VI). Biographies of scholars appear in Chapter VII (**383** and **384**).

Chapter XVIII lists a number of periodicals concerned with education in Taiwan, of which *T'ai-wan chiao-yü* (Taiwan Education, **973**) and *Chiao-yü yü wen-hua* (Education and Culture, **947**) are representative examples. Mention also might be made of a most useful index to educational literature, *Chin shih-nien chiao-yü lun-wen so-yin* (see **99**).

748 China, Chiao-yü pu 中華民國 教育部 (China, Ministry of Education). *Chiao-yü kai-k'uang—Chung-hua min-kuo san-shih chiu nien chih wu-shih nien* 教育概況 ——中華民國三十九年至五十年
(Report on Education—1950–1961). [Taipei, 1962.] 186p.

An official report on education in Taiwan from 1950 through 1961, emphasizing the achievements of the Nationalist Government. Divided into the following chapters: (1) primary education, (2) secondary education, (3) vocational education, (4) teacher training, (5) higher education, (6) international cultural relations, (7) adult education, (8) science education, (9) education of Overseas Chinese, (10) physical education, military training and the Boy Scouts, and (11) youth counseling.

749 Chung-kuo wen-i hsieh-hui 中國文藝協會 (China Association of Literature and Arts). *Wen-hsieh shih-nien* 文協十年
(Ten Years of the China Association of Literature and Arts). Taipei, 1960. 247p.

A special publication on the tenth anniversary of the founding of the China Association of Literature and Arts in Taiwan, surveying the history and activities of the association. Included in the appendix is a list of works published by members of the association during the ten-year period (pp. 225–247), which is useful as a checklist.

CHAPTER XVI

FOREIGN RELATIONS

A large body of documentation is available for the study of Communist China's foreign relations. Coverage for Taiwan, on the other hand, leaves much to be desired. Of the eighty or so entries listed in this chapter, all but three deal with the Mainland, comprising most of the major collections of Chinese Communist documents on their conduct of foreign relations.

A. People's Republic of China

Communist China's relations with the international community have ranged from an initial posture of strident belligerency following the establishment of the Central People's Government in 1949 to overt warfare during the Korean War; from the 'Five Principles of Peaceful Co-existence' advocated at Bandung in 1955 to the border clashes with India; from cooperation within the Soviet bloc to competition with the Soviet Union that has shaken the very structure of the bloc itself.

Included in the present section are some, but by no means all, of the basic documentary sources available for the study of Chinese foreign policy and its specific application to particular areas and problems. The section itself is divided into two subsections: (1) China's external relations in general, comprising collections of treaties, agreements, protocols, statements on policy, communiqués, speeches, declarations, etc.; and (2) Chinese relations with individual countries and special problems of Peking's diplomacy.

1. GENERAL

The first two entries appearing directly below—both Mainland compilations—are basic to the analysis of Communist Chinese foreign relations. The two series are complementary. The first comprises treaties and agreements concluded between China and other countries, while the second contains documents indicative of Peking's foreign policy: statements and speeches of Communist Chinese leaders and other persons only unofficially associated with the formulation or enunciation of policy (e.g., leaders of mass organizations). The third entry, a Japanese compilation based on the two official Peking publications mentioned above and other published Communist Chinese sources, is the only single-volume collection of diverse documentation, formal treaties, policy statements and the like emerging in the period 1949–1958 inclusive. The Gazette of the State Council (**634**) contains more current documents on foreign policy.

In conjunction with these and other entries listed in the present section, the reader should consult the bibliographies and indexes listed in Part One for additional references. Valuable material in Chinese can, in addition, be located in the section on foreign affairs in the People's Handbook (**212**) and also in the chronologies, directories, diplomatic lists, and similar materials listed in Part Two. Reference should also be made to the lists of treaties concluded by Communist China (**196** ff.), as well as the following German collections of treaties compiled by the Institute of Asian Studies in Hamburg: Schriften des Instituts für Asienkunde in Hamburg—Vol. 1, *Die Verträge der Volksrepublik China mit anderen Staaten* (The Treaties of the People's Repubic of China with Other States), 1957; Vol. 12, *Verträge der Volksrepublik China mit anderen Staaten*, Part 1, South and East Asia, 1962, and Part 2, The Countries of the Near East and Africa, 1963.

The major sources of English translations of Chinese documentation on foreign relations are, of course, the *Peking Review* (**930**), the Hong Kong American Consulate General series (**1038** ff.), the Joint Publications Research Service reports (**1047** ff.), the *Union Research Service* (**1065**), and the *Daily Report* of the Foreign Broadcast Information Service (**1071**).

750 China (People's Republic of China, 1949—), Wai-chiao pu 中華人民共和國外交部 (China [People's Republic of China, 1949—], Ministry of Foreign Affairs). *Chung-hua jen-min kung-ho kuo t'iao-yüeh chi* 中華人民共和國條約集 (Collected Treaties of the People's Republic of China). Peking: Fa-lü ch'u-pan she 法律出版社, 1957—.

Texts of bilateral treaties and agreements (including exchanges of notes, joint statements and communiqués) concluded between Communist China and foreign states since 1949, arranged by subject (e.g., political affairs, economic affairs, cultural affairs, postal and telecommunications, scientific and technical programs, etc.). Under each subject category, entries are arranged by country, and under country by date of signature. Commerical agreements with countries with which Communist China maintains no official relations (such as Japan and West Germany), and multilateral agreements to which China is a party are listed in an appendix. The index to each volume is arranged by date.

Summary of period coverage of volumes published to 1964 follows:

VOLUME NO. AND PERIOD COVERED		DATE OF PUBLICATION
Vol. 1	(1949–1951)	1957
Vol. 2	(1952–1953)	1957
Vol. 3	(1954)	1958
Vol. 4	(1955)	1958
Vol. 5	(1956)	1958
Vol. 6	(1957)	1958
Vol. 7	(1958)	1959
Vol. 8	(1959)	1960
Vol. 9	(1960)	1961
Vol. 10	(1961)	1962
Vol. 11	(1962)	1963
Vol. 12	(1963)	1964

For a translation of the table of contents of Volumes 6 and 7, see J.P.R.S. No. 1002D, November 6, 1959, 16p. (U.S.G.P.O. Monthly Catalog, 1960, No. 779). The official collection of treaties and agreements of Communist China.

751 **Shih-chieh chih-shih ch'u-pan she** 世界知識出版社 (World Knowledge Publishing Company). *Chung-hua jen-min kung-ho kuo tui-wai kuan-hsi wen-chien chi* 中華人民共和國對外關係文件集
(Documents on Foreign Affairs of the People's Republic of China). Peking: Shih-chieh chih-shih ch'u-pan she, 1957—.

A companion series to the *Chung-hua jen-min kung-ho kuo t'iao-yüeh chi* (see above), published since 1957. Each volume consists of two parts: (1) a collection of official government statements, memoranda, and speeches by government leaders on Communist China's foreign relations during the period under review, arranged by date; (2) an appendix containing statements on foreign affairs by representatives of mass organizations, a chronological list of titles of treaties and agreements signed between Communist China and foreign states, and a chronology of diplomatic events.

The following is a summary of contents:

VOLUME NO., PERIOD COVERED, AND APPENDIX	DATE OF PUBLICATION
Vol. 1 (1949–1950. List of titles of treaties, 1949–1950.)	1957
Vol. 2 (1951–1953. List of titles of treaties, 1951–1953. Chronology, Oct. 1, 1949–Dec. 31, 1953.)	1958
Vol. 3 (1954–1955. List of titles of treaties, 1954–1955. Chronology, 1954–1955.)	1958
Vol. 4 (1956–1957. List of titles of treaties, 1956–1957. Chronology, 1956–1957.)	1958
Vol. 5 (1958. List of titles of treaties, 1958. Chronology, 1958.)	1959
Vol. 6 (1959. Coverage *mutatis mutandis* as above.)	1961
Vol. 7 (1960)	1962
Vol. 8 (1961)	1962
Vol. 9 (1962)	1964
Vol. 10 (1963)	1965

For a translation of the tables of contents, the listing of treaties and agreements and the chronology of diplomatic events in Volumes 2 and 4, see J.P.R.S., No. 614D, March 26, 1959, 67p. (U.S.G.P.O. Monthly Catalog, 1959, No. 6,377).

While the preceding entry contains primarily formal treaties and agreements, this collection consists of documents on Communist China's foreign policy.

752 **Ajia Seikei Gakkai** アジア政経學會 (Society for Asian Political and Economic Studies). *Chūka Jimmin Kyōwakoku gaikō shiryō sōran* 中華人民共和國外交資料總覽
(Collection of Diplomatic Documents of the People's Republic of China). Tokyo: Hitotsubashi Shobō 一橋書房, 1960. 1,099p.

A collection of some 700 documents pertaining to the foreign relations of Communist China from October 1949 to the end of 1958, prepared by Professor Kawasaki Ichirō of Aichi University. The documents, drawn from a variety of Communist Chinese sources, are not restricted to formal treaties and agreements, but also include foreign policy statements, communiqués, speeches, reports, declarations, protocols, etc.

The volume is divided into twelve chapters, eight of which are topical (fundamentals of foreign policy, international peace and security, development of foreign trade, cultural and technical agreements, the problem of atomic energy, etc.) and the remainder geographical (Asia and the Pacific, Africa, Europe, the Americas). The chapters are further subdivided into sections, within which the documents are grouped chronologically. Source is indicated for each document. A detailed table of contents is to be found in the beginning of the volume (pp. 5–32). A chronology of Communist China's foreign relations from October 1949 through 1958 appears on pages 1061 to 1085. Subject and name indexes arranged according to the Japanese syllabary.

The best single-volume collection of treaties, agreements, and other foreign policy documents, conveniently arranged.

753 **Japan, Gaimushō, Ajiakyoku, Chūgokuka** 日本外務省アジア局中國課 (Japan, Ministry of Foreign Affairs, Bureau of Asian Affairs, China Section). *Chūkyō no gaikō shiryō* 中共の外交資料 (Diplomatic Documents of Communist China). Tokyo: Nihon Kokusai Mondai Kenkyūjo 日本國際問題研究所, Vol. 1—, 1961—.

A series of volumes of Chinese Communist diplomatic documents. Volume 2 deals with Japanese-Chinese relations (1962), 48p.

754 **Yonezawa, Hideo** 米澤秀夫 **and Satō, Masahiro** 佐藤剛弘, **comps. and trs.** 'Chūgoku taigai bōeki kyōtei shū' 中國對外貿易協定集 (Collection of Trade Agreements Between [Communist] China and Foreign Countries), *Chūgoku shiryō geppō*, 中國資料月報 (Monthly Report on Chinese Sources), No. 117 (1957), pp. 1–51.

A collection of full texts, in translation and with annotations, of some twenty-five trade and aid agreements, protocols, etc. The material is drawn from Chinese Communist documentary collections, official gazettes and *Jen-min jih-pao* and *Hsin-hua yüeh-pao*.

755 **Steiner, H. Arthur, comp.** *Major Chinese Communist Foreign Policy Positions and Attitudes, 1958.* Los Angeles: University of California at Los Angeles, 1959. 47p.

A selection of Chinese Communist documents compiled for a course in Far Eastern international relations at U.C.L.A. The materials, all official translations, reflect the principal policy positions and attitudes adopted by Communist China in terms of its basic objectives in the Far East and Asia generally. A supplement contains texts of Chinese trade and economic cooperation agreements.

A well selected compilation.

756 Dutt, Vidya Prakash, ed.
East Asia: China, Korea, Japan, 1947–1950. London: Oxford University Press, 1958. 747p.

A collection of texts of policy speeches by national leaders, together with texts of laws, treaties and international agreements and other published papers of the three East Asian countries for the period August 1957 to January 1950 (nearly half of the volume is given over to China). The documents are grouped by country within two sections: political and economic developments, and external relations. Introductory remarks precede each section. For China, sources are taken mainly from the U.S. White Paper, the *China Digest*, and the New China News Agency *Daily News Release*. The section on China's political, constitutional and economic developments lists documents for the period January 1, 1947 to October 1, 1949, and the section on China's external relations provides documents for the period January 7, 1947 to January 19, 1950.

A good selection of important official documents.

2. RELATIONS WITH INDIVIDUAL COUNTRIES AND SPECIAL PROBLEMS

In the sphere of international affairs, the question of recognition and representation in the United Nations has been a major preoccupation of the Chinese Communist leadership. Today, a decade and a half after the establishment of the Communist government on the Mainland, the regime has been successful in gaining recognition from less than one-half of the countries of the world, and the debate on the China representation question persists.

For the debates in the United Nations concerning the representation of China, the proceedings of the General Assembly (not dealt with in this Guide) contain abundant material. Apart from the documentation appearing in the present section under the heading 'Taiwan Question', there seem to be no separately published sources issuing from the Mainland on the subject.

Of the contacts—official and unofficial—which the Chinese Communists have had with other countries, those with the Soviet Union, India, Japan and, of course, with the United States have the greatest significance (the last particularly in view of the Taiwan and Korean questions and subsequent developments). These relations constitute much of the substance of the present section, although some entries are concerned with Peking's relations with Nepal, Vietnam, Laos, Cambodia, Burma, Turkey, the Arab states, Africa, and Cuba.

Although Peking's pronouncements on American foreign policy deal largely with the Taiwan question and the United States presence in East and Southeast Asia (described in the following section), mention might also be made of general critiques of U.S. foreign policy, such as *Drive U.S. Imperialism Out of Asia* (Peking: Foreign Languages Press, 1960), 48p.; *Two Tactics, One Aim—An Exposure of the Peace-Tricks of U.S. Imperialism* (1960), 146p.; *The Kennedy Administration Unmasked* (1962), 75p.; *Lun ti-kuo chu-i ti ch'in-lüeh pen-chih* 論帝國主義的侵略本質 (On the Aggressive Nature of Imperialism), (Hong Kong: San-lien shu-tien 三聯書店, 1960), 99p.; and *Lun fan-tui ti-kuo chu-i tou-cheng* 論反對帝國主義鬥爭 (On the Anti-Imperialist Struggle), (Hong Kong: San-lien shu-tien, 1960), 83p.

Because the selection of documents for inclusion in this section has been governed by availability, the supplementary references provided in the preceding section also have relevance here.

a. The 'Taiwan Question'

The present section comprises collections of the major Chinese Communist official statements on Taiwan issued through 1961. The statements, fairly crackling with hostility, convey a sustained concern for 'American aggression' and the 'two Chinas plot'. Portions of the second and third items (**758** and **759**) are given over to document-ation on the issue of Chinese representation in the United Nations.

For additional sources, the reader should consult the bibliography of documents and *Jen-min jih-pao* editorials 'Concerning the Question of American Imperialist Aggression against Taiwan' listed in Chapter I (**143**). Reference should also be made to the section on Taiwan in the People's Handbook, the indexes to Mainland newspapers listed in Chapter XVII, and the Index to Major Newspapers and Periodicals (**184**).

The 'Taiwan question,' of course, does not exist for the Nationalist government. On the U.N. representation issue, however, the *China Yearbook* (**240**) does provide a great deal of information.

Finally, mention should be made of the *Formosan Quarterly* (**1099**), *Ilha Formosa* (**1100**) and *Taiwan Chinglian* (**1180**) published in Japan and the United States by native Formosan nationalists, representing opposition to both Nationalist and Communist views of the 'Taiwan question'.

757 **Jen-min ch'u-pan she** 人民出版社 (People's Publishing House). *Tai-wan wen-t'i wen-chien* 臺灣問題文件
(Collected Documents on the Taiwan Question). Peking: Jen-min ch'u-pan she, 1955. 174p.

Thirty documents, mostly issued by the Chinese Communist government, dealing with the 'Taiwan question' in the period December 1943 (Cairo Declaration) through February 1955, inclusive. Lengthy documents have been abstracted, and are so indicated in the titles. Appended is a collection of *Jen-min jih-pao* editorials on Taiwan published between June 1950 and February 1955.

Seventeen of the thirty documents included here have been translated into English and published, together with two more statements by Chou En-lai dated April 23, 1955 and July 30, 1955, under the title *Important Documents Concerning the Question of Taiwan* (Peking: Foreign Languages Press, 1955), 184p.

758 Chung-kuo jen-min wai-chiao hsüeh-hui 中國人民外交學會 (The Chinese People's Institute of Foreign Affairs).
Oppose U.S. Occupation of Taiwan and 'Two Chinas' Plot. Peking: Foreign Languages Press, 1958. 161p.

A translation of *Fan-tui Mei-kuo pa-chan T'ai-wan, chih-tsao 'Liang-ko Chung-kuo' ti yin-mou* 反對美國霸佔臺灣, 製造「兩個中國」的陰謀, the volume comprises Chinese Communist documents on the 'Taiwan question' dated from the period June 1950 to August 1958, inclusive. In three parts. Part 1 contains some basic documents reflecting Communist China's opposition to American aid in Taiwan and its attitude toward the 'two Chinas' policy. Part 2 consists of seven documents relevant to Communist China's position on participation in the activities of international organizations. Part 3 is a collection of miscellaneous documents relating to Overseas Chinese affairs in Hong Kong, Great Britain, and France, and also two Chinese Communist documents on Sino-Japanese relations.
See also next entry.

759 Oppose the New U.S. Plots to Create 'Two Chinas'. Peking: Foreign Languages Press, 1962. 108p.

A translation of *Fan-tui Mei-kuo chih-tsao 'Liang-ko Chung-kuo' ti hsin yin-mou* 反對美國製造「兩個中國」的新陰謀, prepared as a supplement to the preceding entry. Contains Chinese Communist documents on the 'Taiwan question' which have appeared in the Mainland Chinese press since 1959, particularly those published in 1961. In three parts. Part 1 provides excerpts of speeches by Chou En-lai, Chen Yi, and P'eng Chen. Part 2 contains *Jen-min jih-pao* editorials together with the Chinese Communist Foreign Ministry's statement of December 21, 1961 on the question of China's representation at the United Nations and the Tibetan question. Part 3 reproduces two articles—one on the 'Taiwan question' and the other on 'A brief account of the U.S. "Two Chinas" plot (background material)'—from the *Jen-min jih-pao.*

760 Chung-kuo jen-min wai-chiao hsüeh-hui 中國人民外交學會 (The Chinese People's Institute of Foreign Affairs).
Oppose U.S. Military Provocations in the Taiwan Straits Area. Peking: Foreign Languages Press, 1958. 68p.

A translation of *Fan-tui Mei-kuo tsai T'ai-wan hai-hsia ti-ch'ü ti chün-shih t'iao-hsin* 反對美國在臺灣海峽地區的軍事挑釁. Contains statements on the 'Taiwan question' by leaders of Communist China in September 1958, including *Jen-min jih-pao* editorials.

b. Korea (Including the Korean War)

The documentation included in the present section is limited to that concerning Communist China's role in the Korean War and the domestic 'Resist-America Aid-Korea' campaign. All entries save one are of Mainland origin.

The first entry is a comprehensive collection of documents on the campaign itself, accompanied by personal narratives by members of the 'Chinese People's Volunteers' in Korea. The third entry (**763**) documents the cease-fire and the armistice negotiations.

In this connection, reference should also be made to a chronology of the Korean question (1945–1954, see **405**) and to a bibliography devoted specifically to the 'Resist-America Aid-Korea' campaign (**144**).

761 Chung-kuo jen-min k'ang-Mei yüan-Ch'ao tsung-hui, Hsüan-ch'uan pu 中華人民抗美援朝總會 宣傳部 (Chinese People's Resist-America Aid-Korea Campaign Committee, Propaganda Department). *Wei-ta ti k'ang-Mei yüan-Ch'ao yün-tung* 偉大的抗美援朝運動
(The Great Resist-America Aid-Korea Campaign). Peking: Jen-min ch'u-pan she 人民出版社, 1954. 29; 1,312p.

A collection of Chinese Communist documents on the Korean War, covering the period from June 1950 through July 1953. In three parts: official documents, campaign reports, and reports on national and local activities of the Resist-America Aid-Korea campaign (all given in chronological order). The second part, campaign reports, also includes biographies of 'war heroes' and personal narratives. At the end of the volume is a chronology of significant events from June 25, 1950 to July 31, 1953.

Apart from coverage of the truce talks (which are dealt with in detail elsewhere; see **763**), this is the most comprehensive collection of Chinese Communist sources on the Korean War published to date.

762 Jen-min ch'u-pan she 人民出版社 (People's Publishing House). *Ch'ao-hsien wen-t'i wen-chien hui-pien* 朝鮮問題文件彙編
(Collected Documents on the Korean Question). Peking: Jen-min ch'u-pan she, 1954. 502p.

More than 100 documents concerning the Korean question, ranging from the Cairo Declaration of 1943 to the Panmunjom Armistice in 1953, arranged chronologically. Whereas the preceding entry contains almost exclusively Chinese Communist documents, the present volume comprises essentially non-Chinese materials (a few statements and speeches by Mao Tse-tung and Chou En-lai have been included).

763 Chung-kuo jen-min pao-wei shih-chieh ho-p'ing fan-tui Mei-kuo ch'in-lüeh wei-yüan hui 中國人民保衛世界和平反對美國侵略委員會 (Chinese People's Committee for World Peace and Against American Aggression). *Ch'ao-hsien t'ing-chan t'an-p'an wen-t'i* 朝鮮停戰談判問題

(Cease-Fire and Armistice Negotiations in Korea). Peking: Shih-chieh chih-shih ch'u-pan she 世界知識出版社, 1951–1952. 4 vols. 344; 500; 391; 526p.

A collection of official documents on the Korean truce talks from June 1951 to November 1952. Included are exchanges of notes between the U.N. Command and the North Korean and Chinese Communist representatives, and special reports by the New China News Agency and *Jen-min jih-pao* editorials on the truce talks. The documents are arranged in chronological order. Volume 1 covers the period from June 23 to November 27, 1951; Volume 2, November 24, 1951 to March 21, 1952, and Volume 3, March 22 to May 31, 1952. Volume 4, published under the title *Ch'ao-hsien t'an-p'an chung ti chan-fu wen-t'i* 朝鮮談判中的戰俘問題 (The Question of Prisoners of War in the Korean Truce Talks), deals exclusively with the problem of war prisoners and their repatriation, and covers the period from June 1 to November 13, 1952.

For translations of selected documents from June 30 to September 9, 1951, see 'Documents on the Cease-Fire and Armistice Negotiations in Korea', *People's China*, Vol. 4, Nos. 3, 4, 6 and supplements (August–September 1951).

The most comprehensive coverage of the truce talks published in Chinese.

764 Support the Just and Patriotic Struggle of the South Korean People. Peking: Foreign Languages Press, 1960. 37p.

A translation of *Chih-ch'ih Nan Ch'ao-hsien jen-min ti ai-kuo cheng-i tou-cheng* 支持南朝鮮人民的愛國正義鬥爭, which reproduces two editorials, two speeches and a message from a mass rally in Peking concerning South Korea, following the fall of the Syngman Rhee government in 1960.

See also *Chih-ch'ih Ch'ao-hsien jen-min fan-Mei chiu-kuo tou-cheng* 支持朝鮮人民反美救國鬥爭 (Support the Patriotic Anti-American Struggle of the Korean People), published by Shih-chieh chih-shih ch'u-pan she 世界知識出版社 in November 1962.

765 U.S. Congress, Senate, Committee on Foreign Relations. *The United States and the Korean Problem.* Washington, D.C.: U.S. Government Printing Office, 1953. 168p.

A compilation of texts of important international agreements, United Nations resolutions and reports, and statements by United States officials concerning Korea, the Korean War, and the Korean armistice negotiations, covering the ten-year period from 1943 to 1953. In eight parts: (1) wartime agreements; (2) the United States-U.S.S.R. Joint Commission; (3) early U.N. efforts at unification; (4) U.S. assistance to Korea; (5) the outbreak of aggression; (6) early U.N. attempts at settlement of the Korean War; (7) the armistice negotiations; and (8) post-armistice developments. The appendix contains a brief chronology of events from December 1, 1943 to July 27, 1953, and summary charts on the contributions of United Nations members to operations in Korea.

c. Japan

Peking hammers constantly on the theme of Japanese remilitarization and its alliance with the United States. An authoritative source on the 'Japanese question' is the three-volume collection published on the Mainland (first entry, **766**). The China Section of the Japanese Ministry of Foreign Affairs likewise regularly publishes a collection of principal Chinese Communist pronouncements on Japan (**767**). The two collections supplement each other, differing in the following ways: (1) the Peking collection includes Soviet and other sources on the Japanese question, whereas the Japanese compilation does not; and (2) the Japanese Foreign Office tends to include all materials indicative of Peking's attitude toward Japan, while the Chinese include only what they consider to be authoritative. These differences reflect the divergent purposes of the two publications.

Although the Japanese government maintains diplomatic relations with the Nationalist government, it has endeavored to develop trade relations with the Mainland. A number of organizations in Japan have taken up the promotion of trade with Communist China, prominent among which are the Japan-China Friendship Association, the National Conference for the Restoration of Diplomatic Relations with Communist China, the Japan Association for the Promotion of International Trade, Japan-China Exporters and Importers Association, the Diet Members' League for the Promotion of Trade between Japan and Communist China, and the China Research Institute. Many of these organizations publish documentary and reference materials concerned with Sino-Japanese relations in general and trade relations in particular. A collection of documents published by the Diet Members' League, and a White Paper on Trade between Japan and Communist China prepared by the Japan-China Exporters and Importers Association (**769** and **770**) have been included in this section as being illustrative of this kind of material. (Other representative publications, not included in the present section, include There Are No Two Chinas, a record of the visit to Communist China by a Delegation of the National Conference for the Restoration of Diplomatic Relations with Communist China; a White Paper on Sino-Japanese relations in the light of the Japan-U.S. Security Treaty, by the same organization; and records of fishery conferences between the two countries, by the Japan-China Fishery Conference.)

In this context, reference should be made to the chapters covering handbooks, directories and chronologies for a number of items carrying data on the Japan-Mainland trade, and to the relevant Japanese periodicals in Chapter XXI.

766 Shih-chieh chih-shih ch'u-pan she 世界知識出版社 (World Knowledge Publishing House). *Jih-pen wen-t'i wen-chien hui-pien* 日本問題文件彙編 (Collected Documents on the Japanese Question). Peking: Shih-chieh chih-shih ch'u-pan she, 1955—. Irregular.

> Volume 1 contains a selection of important documents concerning Japan from 1942 to 1954, arranged in four main categories: (1) eleven basic documents, including joint Sino-Soviet statements concerning Japan; (2) thirty-five relevant documents of the Chinese Communist Party and other 'democratic'

parties up to 1949, and of the Chinese Communist government up to 1954; (3) thirty-five documents regarding Soviet-Japanese relations; and (4) four documents about Japan that emerged from world, Pacific and Asian peace congresses in 1951 and 1952.

Volume 2 (published in 1958) covers the years 1955–1957, and deals more exclusively with Sino-Japanese relations, arranged in seven main categories: (1) Sino-Japanese political relations, (2) Overseas Chinese and Overseas Japanese, (3) Japanese war criminals, (4) trade, (5) the fishing industry, (6) peace movements, (7) 'friendly relations of the two peoples'. There are 125 documents.

Volume 3 (published in 1961) comprises 148 documents covering the years 1958–1960 inclusive, and focuses on Sino-Japanese relations in general and the United States-Japan Security Treaty of 1960 in particular. The volume is arranged in seven main categories: (1) Mao Tse-tung's speeches; (2) reports by Chou En-lai and statements of the Ministry of Foreign Affairs on Japan; (3) statements, communiqués, etc., issued by the governments of Communist China and Japan, and by prominent citizens of both countries; (4) statements concerning Chinese Communist support of the Japanese people's 'righteous struggle'; (5) *Jen-min jih-pao* editorials and other commentaries; (6) proclamations and resolutions issued by international organizations concerning nuclear warfare; and (7) official Soviet statements and memoranda to the Japanese government concerning United States-Japanese relations. The appendix contains a complete translation of the United States-Japan Security Treaty and the related notes, memoranda, etc., exchanged between the two governments.

Volume 4 (published in 1963) covers the period from 1961 through 1962.

In all volumes the documents are arranged chronologically within each category. None of the volumes are indexed.

A basic source for the study of Japanese-Chinese Communist relations and the attitude of Peking toward Japan and its relations with the United States.

767 Japan, Gaimushō, Ajiakyoku, Chūgokuka 日本外務省アジア局 中國課 (Japan, Ministry of Foreign Affairs, Bureau of Asian Affairs, China Section). *Chūkyō tainichi shuyō genron shū* 中共對日主要言論集 (Collection of Principal Chinese Communist Pronouncements on Japan). Tokyo, Vol. 1—, 1955—. Annual.

A compilation of important Chinese Communist policy statements on Japan, based on official Chinese publications and on the monitoring of Radio Peking. Beginning with the third volume, the documents are classified by subject (normalization of Japanese-Chinese diplomatic relations, nuclear weapons, etc.). Appended to each volume is a comprehensive chronological list of Chinese pronouncements on Japan. Entries provide title, date, source, and a brief annotation (an asterisk indicates texts reproduced in the main section of the volume). Since only the more important statements appear in the text, the appendix serves as a guide to further study of the subject.

Volumes 2 and 3 also contain a number of statements and unofficial agreements concluded between the Peking government and private Japanese organizations. Volume 5 has a similar appendix covering the visit of the Japanese Socialist leader Asanuma to Peking.

Volumes published thus far are listed below:

VOLUME NUMBER	DATE OF PUBLICATION	PERIOD COVERED	PAGINATION	NUMBER OF DOCUMENTS
1	1955	Dec. 1952–Mar. 1955	243	43
2	1956	Apr. 1955–Mar. 1956	217	42
3	1958	Apr. 1956–Jul. 1958	241	73
4	1959	Aug. 1958–Mar. 1959	225	66
5	1960	Apr. 1959–Jan. 1960	201	77
6	1961	Feb. 1960–Jan. 1961	305	113
7	1962	Feb. 1961–Jan. 1962	320	93
8	1963	Feb.-Dec. 1962	232	71
9	1964	Jan. -Dec. 1963	232	86

For the period prior to 1953, see next entry.

Limited distribution. An important compilation. See also preceding entry.

768 Japan, Gaimushō, Ajiakyoku, Dai 2-ka 日本外務省アジア局第二課 (Japan, Ministry of Foreign Affairs, Bureau of Asian Affairs, Second Section). *Chūkyō jūyō bunken shū—Taiheiyō sensō shūryōji yori 1952 nen made* 中共重要文献集 ——太平洋戰爭終了時より1952年迄
(Collection of Important Chinese Communist Documents—From the Time of the Conclusion of the Pacific War to 1952). Tokyo, 1952. 181p.

A collection of twenty-seven basic documents and statements by Chinese Communist government, party and military leaders with brief annotations, covering the period January 1946 to January 1952. No index. Limited distribution.

769 Nitchū Bōeki Sokushin Giin Remmei 日中貿易促進議員連盟 (Diet Members' League for the Promotion of Trade Between Japan and [Communist] China). *Nitchū kankei shiryō shū* 日中關係資料集
(Collection of Documents on Relations Between Japan and [Communist] China). Enlarged and revised edition. Tokyo, 1961. 342p.

A collection of documents bearing on relations between Japan and Communist China. Included are texts of treaties, statements, memoranda, non-governmental agreements, records of conversations, letters, etc., for the period 1949–1961. A chronology for the same period appears on pp. 247-330 (see **400**). A number of charts on foreign relations and trade are appended. Limited distribution.

A convenient compilation of the more important documents on Sino-Japanese relations.

770 **Nitchū Yushutsunyū Kumiai** 日中輸出入組合 (Japan-China Exporters and Importers Association). *Nitchū bōeki hakusho* 日中貿易白書 (White Paper on Trade Between Japan and [Communist] China). Tokyo: Daidō Shoin 大同書院, 1958. 150p.

A paper published on the occasion of the rupture of trade relations between Japan and Communist China over the 'flag incident' (1958). The appendix contains a number of treaties and agreements, and provides statistics on Communist China's economy and foreign trade in general and Sino-Japanese trade relations in particular.

771 **Chūgoku Sōgō Kenkyūkai** 中國綜合研究會 (Joint Study Group on China). *Chūkyō no jittai to Nitchū shin kankei no arikata* 中共の實態と日中新關係の在り方 (The Actual Situation in Communist China and What the New Relationship Between Japan and China Should Be). Tokyo, No. 1—, 1956—. Irregular.

A series of 100-to 350-page reports of study group meetings issued approximately twice a year (thirteen volumes appeared through February 1964). The Chūgoku Sōgō Kenkyūkai consists of some fifteen leading specialists on contemporary China from the universities, government, press, National Diet Library, business concerns and the Liberal-Democratic Party, who meet to discuss a variety of topics on Japan's relationship to Communist China. Research topics have included the Taiwan straits situation, the Chinese communes, Communist China's attitude toward the United Nations as well as toward Japan, Japanese trade with Communist China, etc. The research reports contain the papers presented and the discussions thereof, as well as documentary material in the appendices. The latter in one issue included, for example, the communiqués, speeches, and other documentary material related to a mission of the Japan Socialist Party to Communist China.

Limited distribution.

772 **Chung-kuo jen-min wai-chiao hsüeh-hui** 中國人民外交學會 (The Chinese People's Institute of Foreign Affairs). *Oppose the Revival of Japanese Militarism (A Selection of Important Documents and Commentaries)*. Peking: Foreign Languages Press, 1960. 192p.

A translation of *Fan-tui Jih-pen chün-kuo chu-i ti fu-huo* 反對日本軍國主義 的復活, comprising official Chinese Communist statements and *Jen-min jih-pao* editorials published between August 15, 1951 and January 24, 1960 concerning Japan in general, and the United States-Japan mutual cooperation and security treaty in particular. Most of the articles are translated in full; those which are extracted are so indicated. The documents are listed chronologically by date.

773 **Support the Just Struggle of the Japanese People Against the Japan-U.S. Treaty of Military Alliance.** Peking: Foreign Languages Press, 1960. 148p.

A collection of speeches made at a mass rally held on May 9, 1960 in Peking 'in support of the Japanese people's opposition to the Japan-U.S. Treaty of Military Alliance'; two statements by Mao Tse-tung; and some twenty editorials and commentaries from *Jen-min jih-pao* and *Hung-ch'i* on the subject.

d. *Soviet Union*

The most authoritative collection of documents on Soviet-Chinese relations for the 1917–1959 period is the first entry below, published in Moscow. No comparable collection has been issued from Peking. Also useful is the compilation by the U.S. State Department (second entry) on the relations of the two countries for the years 1950–1956, which identifies a few agreements not listed in the Soviet compilation.

The deterioration of Sino-Soviet relations since the late 1950's was not explicitly reflected in the available Soviet and Communist Chinese documentation until the end of 1962 and early 1963, when a stream of editorials in the People's Daily and in the Red Flag obliquely hinted at the basic differences between the two 'fraternal' parties. Open denunciations finally appeared in the June 14, 1963 letter of the Chinese Communist Party and the July 14 open letter of the Communist Party of the Soviet Union. Fuel was added to the fire on July 25 with the signing of the partial nuclear test-ban treaty in Moscow. Parallel with accusations and counter-accusations relating to the nuclear test-ban treaty, the Chinese Communist Party announced that it would answer the Soviet letter of July 14 with an eleven-part reply, the first instalment of which appeared early in September. In the meantime, a collection of anti-Chinese material from the Soviet press had been collected and published in book form in Peking in February 1964. (A list of published documents on the Sino-Soviet dispute emanating from Peking and in English is appended at the end of this section. The English-language weekly *New Times*, published in Moscow, and the *Current Digest of the Soviet Press* provide the relevant Soviet documentation.)

Sino-Soviet relations in general, and the unfolding of the intra-bloc conflict in recent years, have held a powerful attraction for scholars and others in the non-Communist world. In the past several years this subject has generated a good deal of scholarly activity, resulting in such publications as Donald S. Zagoria's *The Sino-Soviet Conflict, 1956–1961* (Princeton University Press, 1962); *Unity and Contradiction: Major Aspects of Sino-Soviet Relations*, papers presented to the Third Sovietological Conference held at Lake Kawaguchi (Japan) in 1960 and edited by Kurt London (New York: Praeger, 1962); Chin Szu-k'ai's *Communist China's Relations with the Soviet Union, 1949–1957* and Peter Mayer's *Sino-Soviet Relations Since the Death of Stalin*, both published in the Communist China Problem Research Series of the Union Research Institute (see **1565** and **1566**); Edward Crankshaw's *The New Cold War: Moscow v. Pekin* (Baltimore, Md.: Penguin Books, 1963); Klaus Mehnert's *Peking and Moscow* (New York: Putnam's, 1963); David Floyd's *Mao Against Khrushchev: A Short History of the Sino-Soviet Conflict* (New York: Praeger, 1963); William E. Griffith's *The Sino-Soviet Rift* (The M.I.T. Press, 1964); and Harry Schwartz' *Tsars, Mandarins, and Commissars; A History of Chinese-Russian Relations* (Philadelphia, Pa.: Lippincott, 1964).

In addition to these largely descriptive and analytical works, several documentary volumes on Sino-Soviet relations have also appeared and are described in this section. They include the collections by Hudson *et al.*, Dallin, and Berton, as well as the semi-documentary works of Floyd and Griffith mentioned above. Not included in this section, but deserving of mention, is Dennis J. Doolin's *Territorial Claims in the Sino-Soviet Conflict: Documents and Analysis* (Stanford: The Hoover Institution, 1965). Together these documentary compilations provide full coverage of the Sino-Soviet split since 1956.

Reference should also be made to the calendar of Soviet treaties described in Chapter III (**201**), the chronologies of Sino-Soviet relations (**402** and **403**), and the bibliographies on the same subject (**138–140**). The organs of the Soviet-Chinese and the Chinese-Soviet friendship associations are listed in Part Four (**875, 937** and **1212**).

774 **Kurdiukov, I. F., Nikiforov, V. N., and Perevertailo, A. S., eds.** *Sovetsko-kitaiskie otnosheniia, 1917–1957—Sbornik dokumentov*
(Soviet-Chinese Relations, 1917–1957—A Collection of Documents). Moscow: Izdatel'stvo vostochnoi literatury, 1959. 467p.

A collection of 259 treaties, agreements, notes, communications, cables, speeches, letters, etc., some published for the first time. Coverage extends from 1917 through 1957 (and, to some extent, 1958), and the materials are arranged chronologically. The documents (pp. 31–430) are prededed by an introduction and followed by a chronology (pp. 433–448, see **402**). Personal name index.

The most comprehensive compilation of its kind in any language.

775 **[U.S. Department of State, External Research Division.]**
Reported Agreements between the U.S.S.R. and Communist China. [Washington, D.C., 1956.] 95p.

A compilation of the texts of some forty agreements concluded in the period February 7, 1950–April 7, 1956, based on information available as of June 21, 1956. The volume also contains a calendar listing sixty-eight agreements reported to have been concluded between the Soviet Union and Communist China. Calendar entries include, when available, information on date and place of signature, and a brief description of treaty provisions. Mimeographed.

776 **Sladkovskii, M. I.** *Ocherki ekonomicheskikh otnoshenii S.S.S.R. s Kitaem*
(Economic Relations of the U.S.S.R. with China). Moscow: Vneshtorgizdat, 1957. 455p.

A survey of Russo-Chinese relations with an emphasis on economic and trade relations from the seventeenth century through 1955. The last chapter is devoted to the economic relations of the U.S.S.R. and Communist China. The book contains a number of useful appendices: (1) a statistical table of Russo-Chinese trade from 1697 through 1955; (2) a chronology of the most important events in the history of Russo-Chinese economic relations, 1618–1956; (3) a bibliography of predominantly Russian-language publications on the subject, with a few Chinese and English titles, pp. 367–372; (4) texts of treaties, conventions and other agreements concluded between Russia and China from 1689 to April 1956. No index.

777 Hudson, G. F., Lowenthal, Richard, and MacFarquhar, Roderick.
The Sino-Soviet Dispute. London: The China Quarterly, 1961. 227p.

Documentation and analysis of the dispute between Moscow and Peking over global policies. A general introduction on the background of the dispute by G. F. Hudson is accompanied by an analysis of the course of the dispute during 1960 by Richard Lowenthal, based on his article, 'Diplomacy and Revolution: The Dialectics of a Dispute,' *The China Quarterly*, January–March 1961 (including a long note clarifying the economic issues that affect Peking-Moscow relations). The bulk of the book, however, is given over to the reproduction, either in full or in extract form, of twenty-eight documents with an analysis by Roderick MacFarquhar, beginning with Khrushchev's address to the C.P.S.U.'s Twentieth Congress in February 1956 and concluding with a N.C.N.A. dispatch of January 20, 1961 on the Chinese Communist Party resolution on the Moscow Conference of November 1960. Two 'inside' reports from the Indian magazine *Link* are reproduced in an appendix—one on the Chinese position, the other on that of the Soviet Union.

An extremely useful reference work.

778 Dallin, Alexander, ed.
Diversity in International Communism; A Documentary Record, 1961–1963. New York: Columbia University Press, 1963. 867p.

About one-quarter of the book is given over to documentation emanating from or concerning the Chinese Communist Party. See especially Chapter 3, 'The Chinese Position', pp. 200–296 and Chapter 10, 'From Calm to Crisis (April, 1962–April, 1963)', pp. 650–828.

779 Floyd, David.
Mao Against Khrushchev: A Short History of the Sino-Soviet Conflict. New York: Praeger, 1963. 456p.

The second part of the book (pp. 209–444) is devoted to a chronology of documents and significant events, largely postwar and especially for the period of December 1962 to July 1963. The chronology contains extensive excerpts from speeches, articles, official papers and party statements emanating not only from Moscow and Peking, but also from other Communist parties.

780 Griffith, William E.
Albania and the Sino-Soviet Rift. Cambridge, Mass.: The M.I.T. Press, 1963. 423p.

A little over one-half of the book is given over to pertinent documentation covering the period 1960 through November 1962.

781 Griffith, William E.
The Sino-Soviet Rift. Cambridge, Mass.: The M.I.T. Press, 1964. 493p.

A continuation of the preceding entry, with about half of its contents given over to documentation covering the period March through November 1963.

782 Berton, Peter, comp.
The Chinese-Russian Dialogue of 1963; A Collection of Letters Exchanged Between the Communist Parties of China and the Soviet Union and Related Documents. Los Angeles: University of Southern California, School of International Relations, 1963. 295p.

A collection of pertinent party and governmental statements, resolutions, letters, communiqués, editorials, commentaries, and other documents emanating largely from Moscow and Peking, but also from Hanoi, Pyongyang, Havana, and elsewhere. This volume provides the essential documentation for the Sino-Soviet dispute for the period from March to November 1963. A 16-page chronology of Sino-Soviet relations and related events, June 1949–November 1963 is appended (see **403**). Mimeographed. Further volumes are under preparation.

783 Ch'üan shih-chieh wu-ch'an che lien-ho ch'i-lai fan-tui wo-men ti kung-t'ung ti-jen 全世界無產者聯合起來反對我們的共同敵人
(Workers of All Countries Unite, Oppose Our Common Enemy). Peking: Jen-min ch'u-pan she 人民出版社, 1963. 353p.

Editorials and other documents from the People's Daily and the Red Flag covering the period December 1962–March 1963.

784 Kuan-yü kuo-chi kung-ch'an chui-i yün-tung tsung lu-hsien ti chien-i ho yu-kuan wen-chien 關於國際共產主義運動總路線的建議和有關文件
(A Proposal Concerning the General Line of the International Communist Movement and Related Documents). Peking: Jen-min ch'u-pan she 人民出版社, 1963. 213p.

A collection of letters and statements by the C.C.P. and C.P.S.U., editorials from the People's Daily and other documents for the period March–July 1963.

785 Ch'üan shih-chieh jen-min t'uan-chieh ch'i-lai wei cheng-ch'ü ch'üan-mien ch'e-ti kan-ching chien-chüeh ti chin-chih ho hsiao-hui ho wu-ch'i erh tou-cheng 全世界人民團結起來爲爭取全面澈底乾淨堅決地禁止和銷毀核武器而鬥爭
(People of the World, Unite! For the Complete, Thorough, Total and Resolute Prohibition and Destruction of Nuclear Weapons). Peking: Jen-min ch'u-pan she 人民出版社, 1963. 172p.

Statement of the Chinese Communist government of July 31, 1963 on the partial test-ban treaty and related documents.

786 Sino-Soviet Alliance—Mighty Bulwark of World Peace. Peking: Foreign Languages Press, 1960. 49p.

A translation of *Chung-Su t'ung-meng shih shih-chieh ho-p'ing ti ch'iang-ta pao-lei* 中蘇同盟是世界和平的強大堡壘, which includes six important documents on Sino-Soviet relations, comprising greetings exchanged between Communist China and the Soviet Union on the tenth anniversary of the signing of the Sino-Soviet Treaty of Friendship, Alliance and Mutual Assistance, and speeches and articles by Chen Yi, Kuo Mo-jo and Soong Ching-ling. A *Jen-min jih-pao* editorial of February 14, 1960 on the same subject is also included.

See also Teng Hsiao-ping, *The Great Unity of the Chinese People and the Great Unity of the Peoples of the World* (Peking: Foreign Languages Press, 1959), 17p., written for *Pravda* in celebration of the tenth anniversary of the Chinese People's Republic.

787 Support the Just Stand of the Soviet Union and Oppose U.S. Imperialism's Wrecking of the Four-Power Conference of Government Heads. Peking: Foreign Languages Press, 1960. 32p.

A translation of *Chih-ch'ih Su-lien cheng-i li-ch'ang fan-tui Mei ti-kuo chu-i p'o-huai ssu-kuo shou-nao hui-i* 支持蘇聯正義立場反對美帝國主義破壞四國首腦會議, which contains five Chinese Communist statements on the Paris Summit Conference in 1960 and the U-2 incident.

788 The Historical Experience of the Dictatorship of the Proletariat. Peking: Foreign Languages Press, 1959. 64p.

789 Long Live Leninism. Peking: Foreign Languages Press, 1960. 106p.

790 Workers of All Countries Unite, Oppose Our Common Enemy. Peking: Foreign Languages Press, December 1962. 27p.

791 **The Differences Between Comrade Togliatti and Us.** Peking: Foreign Languages Press, December 1962. 48p.

792 **Leninism and Modern Revisionism.** Peking: Foreign Languages Press, January 1963. 20p.

793 **Let Us Unite on the Basis of the Moscow Declaration and the Moscow Statement.** Peking: Foreign Languages Press, January 1963. 35p.

794 **Whence the Differences?—A Reply to Thorez and Other Comrades.** Peking: Foreign Languages Press, February 1963. 36p.

795 **In Refutation of Modern Revisionism.** Enlarged edition. Peking: Foreign Languages Press, February 1963. 141p.

796 **A Comment on the Statement of the Communist Party of the U.S.A.** Peking: Foreign Languages Press, March 1963. 18p.

797 **A Mirror for Revisionists.** Peking: Foreign Languages Press, March 1963. 12p.

798 **More on the Differences Between Comrade Togliatti and Us—Some Important Problems of Leninism in the Contemporary World.** Peking: Foreign Languages Press, March 1963. 199p.

799 **A Proposal Concerning the General Line of the International Communist Movement.** Peking: Foreign Languages Press, June 1963. 114p.

800 **The Struggle Between Two Lines at the Moscow World Congress of Women.** Peking: Foreign Languages Press, 1963. 61p.

801 **People of the World, Unite! For the Complete, Thorough, Total and Resolute Prohibition and Destruction of Nuclear Weapons!** Peking: Foreign Languages Press, 1963. 208p.

802 **The Origin and Development of the Differences Between the Leadership of the Communist Party of the Soviet Union and Ourselves.** Peking: Foreign Languages Press, September 1963. 70p.

803 **On the Question of Stalin.** Peking: Foreign Languages Press, September 1963. 23p.

804 Is Yugoslavia a Socialist Country? Peking: Foreign Languages Press, September 1963. 48p.

805 Apologists of Neo-Colonialism. Peking: Foreign Languages Press, October 1963. 37p.

806 Two Different Lines on the Question of War and Peace. Peking: Foreign Languages Press, November 1963. 38p.

806a The Truth About How the Leaders of the C.P.S.U. Have Allied Themselves with India Against China. Peking: Foreign Languages Press, November 1963. 50p.

807 Peaceful Coexistence—Two Diametrically Opposed Policies. Peking: Foreign Languages Press, December 1963. 70p.

808 The Leaders of the C.P.S.U. Are the Greatest Splitters of Our Times. Peking: Foreign Languages Press, February 1964. 63p.

809 The Proletarian Revolution and Khrushchov's Revisionism. Peking: Foreign Languages Press, April 1964. 67p.

809a On Khrushchov's Phoney Communism and its Historical Lessons for the World. Peking: Foreign Languages Press, July 1964. 112p.

809b Seven Letters Exchanged Between the Central Committee of the Communist Party of China and the Communist Party of the Soviet Union, February–May, 1964. Peking: Foreign Languages Press, 1964. 76p.

809c Letter of the Central Committee of the Communist Party of China in Reply to the Letter of the Central Committee of the Communist Party of the Soviet Union Dated June 15, 1964. Peking: Foreign Languages Press, 1964. 50p.

809d Letter of the Central Committee of the Communist Party of China in Reply to the Letter of the Central Committee of the Communist Party of the Soviet Union Dated July 30, 1964. Peking: Foreign Languages Press, 1964. 20p.

Most of the preceding unannotated entries have also appeared in the *Peking Review,* and in a single-volume collection entitled *Kuan-yü kuo-chi kung-ch'an chu-i yün-tung tsung lu-hsien ti lun-chan*—*The Polemic on the General Line of the International Communist Movement* (Peking: Jen-min ch'u-pan she, 1965), 631p. A 586-page English-language edition of the latter appeared in the same year.

e. India (Including the Tibetan Question)

Published documents, white papers and reports provide fairly substantial documentation on the Sino-Indian border dispute. The major sources—both Indian and Chinese—are listed in this section. In this connection, the reader is advised to consult the notes and bibliography in P. C. Chakravarti, *India's China Policy* (Bloomington, Ind.: Indiana University Press, 1962) and the *Peking Review*, Nos. 47/48, (November 30, 1962), for a set of six reference maps used by Communist China to support its claim. The same issue also contains a statement of the Chinese Communist government made on November 22, 1962, announcing the cease-fire and withdrawal of its troops, as well as a lengthly letter to leaders of Asian and African countries by Chou En-lai presenting the Chinese side in the dispute.

For collections of Nehru's speeches on the border dispute, see *Prime Minister on Sino-Indian Relations* and *Prime Minister on Chinese Aggression* published by the Indian Ministry of External Affairs in 1961 (2 vols.) and 1963 (118p.) respectively, as well as the Ministry's monthly *Foreign Affairs Record*. The reader is also referred to bibliographies and a chronology on the Sino-Indian dispute (see **142** and **404** respectively).

On the Tibetan question, in addition to the collection of documents listed below, see a chronology of Tibet, 1949–1959 (**397**), which also includes a number of selected documents. The section on Tibet in the 1959 People's Handbook likewise carries a number of additional documents. See also *Reports on Tibet and the Sino-Indian Border Issue*, a semi-documentary study published by the U.S. Information Service in Hong Kong in 1960.

810 **Documents on the Sino-Indian Boundary Question.** Peking: Foreign Languages Press, 1960. 143p.

A translation of *Chung-Yin pien-chieh wen-t'i wen-chien chi* 中印邊界問題文件集 providing the entire exchange of diplomatic correspondence on the Sino-Indian border dispute between Communist China and India from September 1959 to February 1960.

811 **Selected Documents on Sino-Indian Relations (December 1961–May 1962).** Peking: Foreign Languages Press, 1962. 79p.

A translation of *Chung-Yin kuan-hsi wen-chien hsüan-chi* 中印關係文件選輯, serving as a continuation of the preceding entry and bringing the collection of official documents on the Sino-Indian boundary dispute up to May 1962. Fifteen Chinese and Indian documents have been selected for this volume, which also contains a sketch map of the border and an appendix providing an abbreviated version of the *Report of the Officials of the Governments of India and the People's Republic of China on the Boundary Question* (see **814**).

812 The Sino-Indian Boundary Question. Enlarged Edition. Peking: Foreign Languages Press, Nov. 1962. 134p. 14 maps.

Contains two Chinese government statements, two of Chou En-lai's letters (one to Prime Minister Nehru and the other to the leaders of Asian and African countries), a note from the Ministry of Foreign Affairs to the Indian Embassy in Peking, and a *Jen-min jih-pao* editorial. Two of these documents date from November-December 1959, while the rest are from the October-November 1962 period.

813 India, Ministry of External Affairs.
White Paper: Notes, Memoranda and Letters Exchanged and Agreements Signed Between the Governments of India and China. New Delhi: Government of India, Vol. 1—, 1959—.

A collection of official Indian and Chinese documents on Chinese Communist activities in Tibet and on the Sino-Indian border disputes. Ten volumes have been published through 1964. A summary of contents follows:

VOLUME NO.	PERIOD COVERED	DATE OF PUBLICATION
1	1954–1959	1959
2	Sep.-Nov. 1959	1959
3	Nov. 1959–Mar. 1960	1960
4	Mar.-Nov. 1960	1960
5	Nov. 1960–Nov. 1961	1961
6	Nov. 1961–Jul. 1962	1962
7	Jul. 1962–Oct. 1962	1962
8	Oct. 1962–Jan. 1963	1963
9	Jan.-Jul. 1963	1963
10	Jul. 1963–Jan. 1964	1964

A basic source. See also the next entry.

814 India, Ministry of External Affairs.
Report of the Officials of the Governments of India and the People's Republic of China on the Boundary Question. New Delhi: Government of India, 1961. 342; 213p.

Contains the texts of two separate reports—Chinese and Indian—drawn up by representatives of the two countries who met in Delhi, Peking, and Rangoon in 1960 to examine the available historical evidence relating to the Sino-Indian boundary.

An indispensable source. The concluding chapter (110p.) and a thirteen-page summary of the report have been issued by the Ministry of External Affairs as separate reprints.

See also Indian Society of International Law, *The Sino-Indian Boundary: Texts of Treaties, Agreements and Certain Exchange of Notes Relating to the Sino-Indian Boundary* (New Delhi, 1962), and a special issue of *International Studies, Quarterly Journal of the Indian School of International Studies*, Vol. 5, Nos. 1-2 (July–October 1963), entitled 'Chinese Aggression and India'.

815 Jen-min ch'u-pan she 人民出版社 (People's Publishing House). *Kuan-yü Hsi-tsang wen-t'i* 關於西藏問題 (Concerning the Question of Tibet). Peking: Jen-min ch'u-pan she, 1959. 220p.

A collection of Chinese Communist documents on the Tibetan Revolt, issued between March and May 1959. The volume incorporates Indian Communist documents and statements by Nehru. For a translation of most of the Chinese documents, see *Concerning the Question of Tibet* (Peking: Foreign Languages Press, 1959), 275p.

For a compilation of one hundred documents (translated and annotated) originating in the period 1950–1962 inclusive, see Ling Nai-min, ed., *Tibetan Sourcebook* (Hong Kong: Union Research Institute, 1964), 487p.

816 Sen, Chanakya, comp. and ed.
Tibet Disappears: A Documentary History of Tibet's International Status, the Great Rebellion and its Aftermath. Bombay: Asia Publishing House, 1960. 474p.

A collection of treaties, conventions, agreements, diplomatic notes, letters, speeches and other documents largely concerning the events in Tibet in 1959 and their effect upon Sino-Indian relations. Coverage of speeches by Nehru and other Indian leaders, parliamentary resolutions, etc., is particularly good.

In spite of a number of errors and discrepancies in the connecting text, the volume is valuable as a collection of basic documents.

See also Gunottam Purushottam Hutheesing, *Tibet Fights for Freedom; the Story of the March 1959 Uprising as Recorded in Documents, Dispatches, Eye-Witness Accounts and World-Wide Reactions: A White Book* (Foreword by the Dalai Lama), (Bombay: Orient Longmans for the Indian Committee for Cultural Freedom, 1961), 241p.

f. Other Countries

The following section comprises entries on Communist China's relations with Nepal, Vietnam, Laos, Cambodia, Burma, Turkey, the Arab countries, Africa, Cuba, and Asian-African conferences. For additional documentary materials on Peking's relations with the above-mentioned countries as well as others, reference is made to the 'General' section at the beginning of this chapter. Particular reference should also be made to the section on foreign affairs in the various editions of the People's Handbook, which provides policy statements, declarations and other important documents.

See also the semi-documentary studies entitled *Sino-Indonesian Relations* prepared by the United States Information Service in Hong Kong, which also include chronologies (volume covering 1950–1959 published in 1960; and the period January 1960–April 1961, in 1961).

817 Chung-kuo jen-min wai-chiao hsüeh-hui 中國人民外交學會 (The Chinese People's Institute of Foreign Affairs).
New Development in Friendly Relations Between China and Nepal. Peking: Foreign Languages Press, 1960. 92p.

A translation of *Chung-Ni yu-hao kuan-hsi ti hsin fa-chan* 中尼友好關係的新發展, containing official documents on the Sino-Nepalese boundary question, economic and general relations (including the texts of the boundary treaty and the economic aid agreement signed on March 21, 1960 and the Treaty of Peace and Friendship signed on April 28, 1960). Included also are Chou En-lai's speeches and statements made on the occasion of his visits to Katmandu in March and April 1960, and two *Jen-min jih-pao* editorials hailing the signing of the treaties.

818 Shih-chieh chih-shih she 世界知識社 (World Knowledge Publishing House).
Yin-tu-chih-na wen-t'i wen-chien hui-pien 印度支那問題文件彙編
(Collected Documents on the Indo-China Question). Peking: Shih-chieh chih-shih ch'u-pan she, 1961. 3 vols.

A collection of documents including government statements, diplomatic correspondence and editorials on Vietnam, Laos and Cambodia. Volume 1 covers the period August 1945 to February 1959 and is divided into three parts: Pre-Geneva, the Geneva Conference, and post-Geneva. Volume 2 covers the period February 1959 to March 1960, and Volume 3 the period from April 1960 to April 1961. A fourth volume, covering the period April 1961 to May 1963 appeared in March 1964.
See also the following entry.

819 Shih-chieh chih-shih she 世界知識社 (World Knowledge Publishing House).
K'an, Lai-meng hu che-mien ching-tzu 看, 萊蒙湖這面鏡子
(Look Into the Mirror of Lake Geneva). Peking: Shih-chieh chih-shih ch'u-pan she, 1963. 152p.

A collection of thirty-five documents on the Laos Conference covering the period May 1961 to July 1962.
See also the 'Chronology of Communist Reports on Laos' in *Current Background*, No. 661 (September 13, 1961) covering the period May 1 to July 31, 1961 and No. 688 (August 21, 1962) for the July 28, 1961-July 23, 1962 period.

820 Concerning the Situation in Laos. Peking: Foreign Languages Press, 1959. 84p.

A collection of documents on the situation in Laos in 1959, containing statements of the Chinese Communist Foreign Ministry, Foreign Minister Chen Yi's letters to the co-chairmen of the Geneva Conference, editorials and commentaries on Laos from *Jen-min jih-pao*, and New China News Agency news reports.

821 **Chung-kuo jen-min wai-chiao hsüeh-hui** 中國人民外交學會 (Chinese People's Institute of Foreign Affairs).
A Victory for the Five Principles of Peaceful Co-Existence—Important Documents on the Settlement of the Sino-Burmese Boundary Question Through Friendly Negotiations and on the Development of Friendly Relations Between China and Burma. Peking: Foreign Languages Press, 1960. 57p.

Contains documents on Sino-Burmese relations from 1954 to January 1960, when the friendship and non-aggression pact between Communist China and Burma was signed and the Sino-Burmese boundary line settled. This is a translation of *Ho-p'ing kung-ch'u wu-hsiang yüan-tse ti sheng-li—Chung-Mien yu-hao hsieh-shang chieh-chüeh pien-chieh wen-t'i fa-chan yu-hao kuan-hsi ti chung-yao wen-chien* 和平共處五項原則的勝利——中緬友好協商解決邊界問題發展友好關係的重要文件.

822 **Support the Patriotic and Just Struggle of the Turkish People.** Peking: Foreign Languages Press, 1960. 28p.

A collection of speeches made at a mass rally held on May 4, 1960 in Peking in support of the 'patriotic and just struggle of the Turkish people', and two *Jen-min jih-pao* editorials on the subject.

823 **Chung-kuo jen-min wai-chiao hsüeh-hui** 中國人民外交學會 (Chinese People's Institute of Foreign Affairs).
China Supports the Arab People's Struggle for National Independence (A Selection of Important Documents). Peking: Foreign Languages Press, 1958. 242p.

A translation of *Chih-ch'ih A-la-po jen-min cheng-ch'ü min-tsu tu-li ti tou-cheng (wen-chien hsüan-chi)* 支持阿拉伯人民爭取民族獨立的鬥爭（文件選輯）. In four parts: Part 1 contains basic documents concerning Communist China's policy with respect to national independence movements (speeches by Mao Tse-tung, Chou En-lai, Chen Yi, and Liu Shao-ch'i made between 1950 and 1958); Part 2 provides important Chinese Communist documents on the Egyptian nationalization of the Suez Canal and the subsequent invasion of Egyptian territory by Anglo-French forces in 1956; Part 3 documents Communist China's relations with the Arab countries during the period following the Suez Canal conflict; and Part 4 is devoted to the Lebanese crisis and the Iraqi revolution of 1958. Appended to Parts 2, 3 and 4 are a number of *Jen-min jih-pao* editorials.

824 **Chung-kuo Fei-chou jen-min yu-hao hsieh-hui** 中國非洲人民友好協會 (Chinese-African Peoples' Friendship Association).
The Chinese People Resolutely Support the Just Struggle of the African People. Peking: Foreign Languages Press, 1961. 139p.

A translation of *Chung-kuo jen-min chien-chüeh chih-ch'ih Fei-chou jen-min ti cheng-i tou-cheng* 中國人民堅決支持非洲人民的正義鬥爭, containing official documents and *Jen-min jih-pao* editorials published in 1960 and 1961 on Africa. In five parts: Part 1 consists of speeches by Mao Tse-tung, Liu Shao-ch'i and Chou En-lai; Part 2 provides two speeches by Liao Cheng-chih 廖承志 and Liu Ning-I 劉寧一 on Afro-Asian solidarity (1961), and a speech by Liu Ch'ang-sheng 劉長勝, president of the Chinese-African Peoples' Friendship Association, at an Africa Rally in Peking in November 1960; Parts 3 and 4 are on the Congo and Algeria, respectively. Both of the last contain official statements and articles and editorials from the *Jen-min jih-pao*. Part 5 is given over to three *Jen-min jih-pao* editorials on Africa in general, dated November 28, 1960, April 2, 1961, and April 15, 1961.

See also Feng Chih-tan, *Glimpses of West Africa* (Peking: Foreign Languages Press, 1963), 119p. (an account of a visit by a delegation of the Chinese-African Peoples' Friendship Association to eight West African countries, including Guinea, Mali and Ghana).

825 **Shui-tu pu-neng tsu-tang Ku-pa jen-min ch'ien-chin** 誰都不能阻擋古巴人民前進
(Nobody Can Hinder the Advance of the Cuban People). Revised and enlarged edition. Peking: Shih-chieh chih-shih ch'u-pan she 世界知識出版社, 1962. 238p.

Sixty-seven statements, letters and other documents concerning the Cuban Crisis of October 1962.

826 **Support the Cuban and other Latin American People's Just Struggle Against U.S. Imperialism.** Peking: Foreign Languages Press, 1961. 185p.

A translation of *Chih-ch'ih Ku-pa ho La-ting Mei-chou ko-kuo jen-min fan-tui Mei ti-kuo chu-i ti tou-cheng* 支持古巴和拉丁美洲各國人民反對美帝國主義的鬥爭. The volume contains speeches by Mao Tse-tung, Chou En-lai, Chen Yi, Chu Teh, Kuo Mo-jo, P'eng Chen, and Chu T'u-nan 楚圖南, President of the China-Latin America Friendship Association, during the period March 3, 1959 to September 1961, and incorporates editorials and articles from *Jen-min jih-pao* and *Hung-ch'i* published between July 1960 and May 1961.

827 **Shih-chieh chih-shih she** 世界知識社 (World Knowledge Publishing House). *Ya-Fei hui-i wen-chien hsüan-chi* 亞非會議文件選輯
(Selected Documents of the Asian-African Conference). Peking: Shih-chieh chih-shih she, 1955. 118p.

A collection of important documents concerning the Bandung Conference, April 18-24, 1955, including Chou En-lai's speeches and report on the conference to the Standing Committee of the National People's Congress, etc. Two appendices. Appendix 1 provides the text of the treaty on dual nationality signed between Communist China and Indonesia on April 22, 1955 (with a supplementary exchange of notes dated June 3, 1955), together with Chou En-lai's speeches in Indonesia during the Bandung Conference. Appendix 2 reproduces five *Jen-min jih-pao* editorials on the conference.

For a translation of Chou En-lai's speeches, etc., See *China and the Asian-African Conference (Documents)*, (Peking: Foreign Languages Press, 1955), 81p.

828　**Ti-erh chieh Ya-Fei jen-min t'uan-chieh ta-hui wen-chien hui-pien**
第二屆亞非人民團結大會文件彙編
(Collected Documents of the Second Asian-African People's Solidarity Conference). Peking: Shih-chieh chih-shih ch'u-pan she 世界知識出版社, 1960. 320p.

Contains the manifesto, resolutions, reports and speeches (including those of Communist Chinese participants) emanating from the Second Afro-Asian People's Solidarity Conference held from April 11 to 15, 1960 at Conakry, Guinea, and attended by a delegation from the Chinese Committee for Afro-Asian Solidarity. The first conference was held in Cairo in 1958.

B. Republic of China

Compared with what has been published by the Government of the People's Republic on its foreign relations, little has been issued from the Nationalist government on Taiwan. This is perhaps all the more striking because the Republic of China, recognized by more countries than its Communist competitor, has enjoyed a far greater number of contacts in the international community.

The entries in this section are the basic sources on the foreign relations of Nationalist China. The first entry provides the most important treaties, agreements, etc., concluded during the period 1927–1957 and is kept up-to-date by the third entry, the Gazette of the Ministry of Foreign Affairs. The second entry is an unofficial English language compilation.

For additional documentary sources, one must consult both the Chinese and English-language editions of the *China Yearbook* (**239** and **240**), which carry detailed sections on foreign affairs (including the texts of the treaties concluded during the year under review in the English-language edition). Mention also might be made of the *Chung-yang jih-pao* (Central Daily News), the official organ of the Kuomintang (**938**), and the Bulletin of the Office of the President (**676**), both of which are important additional sources of documentary material on the subject.

829　**China, Wai-chiao pu** 中華民國 外交部 (China, Ministry of Foreign Affairs).　✓
Chung-wai t'iao-yüeh chi-pien 中外條約輯編 （中華民國十六年至四十六年）
(Treaties Between the Republic of China and Foreign States, 1927–1957).
Taipei, 1958. 892p.

A collection of more than 200 bilateral treaties and agreements signed and notes exchanged between China and foreign states from 1927 to 1957, roughly a quarter of which emerged in the period 1950–1957. Arrangement is alphabetical by country, and under each country by date. For the most part, both Chinese and English (or French) texts are given. The volume contains a calendar of included documents, in English and Chinese, providing in tabular form signatory, type of document, subject matter, dates of signature and entry into force, and page reference.

829a Chen, Yin-ching, comp.
Treaties and Agreements Between the Republic of China and Other Powers, 1929– 1954, Together with Certain International Documents Affecting the Interests of the Republic of China. Washington, D.C.: Sino-American Publishing Service, 1957. 491p.

A collection of over 130 treaties, agreements, conventions, and exchanges of notes between the Republic of China and foreign powers, over one-half of which were undertaken in the years 1945–1954. Arrangement is chronological, and all texts are given in the English language. A calendar of included documents provides in tabular form dates of signature and entry into force, signatory, type of document, subject matter and page reference. The volume concludes with a one-page index to treaty partners and main categories of treaty subject matter.

830 Wai-chiao pu kung-pao 外交部公報
(Gazette of the Ministry of Foreign Affairs). Nanking, Chungking, Taipei: Wai-chiao pu ch'ing-pao ssu 外交部情報司, Vol. 1, No. 1—, May 1928—. Bi-monthly.

Contains lists of appointments, dismissals and transfers of personnel in the Ministry of Foreign Affairs (dropped with Vol. 27, No. 11/12, January 1, 1963), pertinent governmental laws and regulations, and texts of treaties and agreements concluded with other countries. Included also in each issue are texts of important speeches by high government officials on current international affairs. Formerly published in Nanking and Chungking, the gazette resumed publication in Taipei with Volume 20, No. 1 (October 1955) as a monthly. Published bi-monthly since August 1956. No index.

PART FOUR

SELECTED SERIAL PUBLICATIONS

The periodical press has been the classic mode of expression of radical movements in modern history. The phenomenal rise of modern newspapers and periodicals in China since the turn of the twentieth century is an excellent case in point. Both the Kuomintang and the Chinese Communist Party, as well as a host of minor political parties in China, have skillfully utilized these communication media to try to reach the largest possible number of people to inform, to indoctrinate, to recruit. Because of this widespread reliance on the printed word as an organizational weapon, the Chinese periodical press has over the years come to assume a most important place in the documentation of the political, economic, social and cultural change in modern Chinese society. This is particularly true of the present time.

In the sections that follow, a number of newspapers and periodicals from the Mainland, Taiwan and Hong Kong have been included as a representative sample of the most important (and almost exclusively post-1949) publications. It should be noted, however, that while an attempt has been made to include all of the most important or representative publications, the selection inevitably has been influenced by the availability of materials in the United States, Taiwan, Hong Kong and Japan. Furthermore, the emphasis has been on national publications, and only a few provincial periodicals have been included. In addition to these Mainland, Taiwan, and Hong Kong publications, periodicals on China published elsewhere (in English, Japanese, Russian, and other languages) have been described, as have the most important series of translated Chinese materials (American Hong Kong Consulate General series, the Joint Publications Research Service reports, *Union Research Service*, etc.), and monitored radio broadcasts. The Part concludes with a list of series published by institutions in the United States and abroad which are devoted wholly or in part to contemporary China.

Some 445 titles have been annotated for this Part. In addition, an equal number in series are listed without annotations. Of the 445 annotated entries, about 160 are in Chinese, some 170 in English, some 90 in Japanese, 13 in Russian and 7 in other languages. Calculated by place of imprint, Mainland, Taiwan, Japanese and American publications each account for roughly a fifth of all entries listed and Hong Kong publications some 35, with the balance being Soviet and British publications, as well as those from other countries.

Most Mainland (and some Taiwan) periodicals carry their own annual indexes. Reference also should be made to periodical indexes described in Chapter III (**184** ff.). Indexes to, as well as translations from, individual newspapers and periodicals have been listed next to the titles in question, regardless of the fact that they may have been compiled in Japan, in Hong Kong or in the United States.

A comment on the overall organization of this Part is in order. Owing to the variety of the publications under survey, it was decided that materials can be more satisfactorily brought under control for reference purposes through listing by place of origin (Mainland China, Taiwan and Hong Kong). One hundred thirty additional periodicals concerned with China but published outside of the Mainland, Taiwan or Hong Kong are classified by language (English, Japanese, Russian, etc.) in Chapter XXI. Chapter XX is a 'catch-all' containing translations and radio monitoring services, irrespective of place of publication. For a detailed breakdown of this arbitrary scheme, consult the table of contents.

In addition to the titles included in this Part, annual publications are to be found in Chapters IV and V, and official gazettes in Part Three. Chapter II contains lists of newspapers and periodicals as do the yearbooks (Chapter IV) and library catalogs (Appendix A).

In conclusion, a word might be added about the accessibility of serial publications concerned with contemporary China. The serial holdings of the major libraries are being disseminated through union lists (see **1708** and **1709**), as well as through the *Union Card File of Oriental Vernacular Serials: Chinese, Japanese, and Korean*, now available from the Photoduplication Service of the Library of Congress. The Library of Congress is also engaged in the microfilming of selected Chinese-language newspapers and periodicals published in Mainland China, Taiwan, Hong Kong and the major centers of the Overseas Chinese, as well as of English-language translations of Chinese source material, such as the Hong Kong American Consulate General translation series, and further has prepared lists of Chinese local newspapers which are now available at its Orientalia Division.

CHAPTER XVII

MAINLAND PUBLICATIONS

All publishing activity and the dissemination of information in Communist China is controlled by the Chinese Communist Party. Next to radio broadcasting, the newspapers and periodicals form the most important link between the state and the masses and are impressive in their number. According to one survey, a total of 1,055 newspapers and some 1,334 periodicals were being published in Communist China as of January 1, 1960 (see **170** and **171**), although the 1959 People's Handbook lists only sixty-five newspapers and 465 periodicals as being of particular importance (the last year such a list appeared in the Handbook).

A significant aspect of Mainland publishing is that each newspaper and periodical is an organ of one or more organizations within the vast structure of the Chinese Communist state, although the link between a publication and its sponsoring organization is not always clear. In most cases, however, this relationship is either explicitly stated in the publication or identifiable by other means. Because the link between sponsor and publication in large measure accounts for the contents of the publication, an effort has been made in this Guide to establish this relationship whenever possible.

Included in the following sections are a number of selected Mainland newspapers, periodicals and a few news releases—a fair sample of the Mainland press (except local newspapers) available in the United States.

For lists of Chinese Communist newspapers and periodicals, see Chapter II and Wang Chi's *Mainland China Organizations of Higher Learning in Science and Technology and Their Publications: A Selected Guide* (**330**). A union list of Chinese Mainland periodicals available in the United States, Japan, Hong Kong and Great Britain may be found in G. Raymond Nunn, comp., *Chinese Periodicals: International Holdings, 1949–1960* (**1709**) and Bernadette Shih and Richard Snyder, comps., *International Union List of Communist Chinese Serials* (**1708**). Most of the newspapers and periodicals annotated here are indexed in the Index to Major Newspapers and Periodicals (**184**), which carries in every issue a list of newspapers and periodicals being indexed. Translations from the Mainland press and periodicals are listed in Chapter XX.

Professor Franklin W. Houn's *To Change a Nation, Propaganda and Indoctrination in Communist China* (New York: The Free Press, 1961), and Frederick T. C. Yu's *Mass Persuasion in Communist China* (New York: Frederick A. Praeger, 1964) both present an excellent description of the communications and propaganda systems on the China Mainland.

A. Newspapers

Six of the most important national newspapers have been selected for inclusion in this section. The combined coverage of these six papers provides a fairly complete picture of the Communist Party attitude with respect to economic, educational and social matters, as well as of the government's foreign policy. The newspapers are the *Jen-min jih-pao* (People's Daily, the organ of the Chinese Communist Party and the central government, first entry), the *Kuang-ming jih-pao* (the organ of the so-called 'democratic parties' specializing in reporting cultural, educational, legal and minority affairs, **836**), the *Ta-kung pao* (covering business, commerce and finance, **839**), the *Kung-jen jih-pao* (Worker's Daily, the organ of the All-China Federation of Trade Unions, **842**), the *Wen-hui pao* (having an emphasis on elementary and secondary education, **845**), and the *Chung-kuo ch'ing-nien pao* (China Youth Daily, the organ of the Chinese Young Communist League, **847**).

It would have been extremely useful to include also the leading provincial and local newspapers, but because of their general unavailability, this has not been done. (The Center for Research Libraries—formerly the Midwest Inter-Library Center— in Chicago has been designated as the depository of the entire microfilm collection of Chinese Communist newspapers and periodicals—including local newspapers— purchased from the Union Research Institute in Hong Kong. Lists of what has been received are now available from the Center. The Center for Chinese Studies of the University of California [Berkeley] and the East-West Center of the University of Hawaii have also purchased the complete collection of microfilms from the U.R.I. and other centers have purchased parts of it.)

All of the six papers included here publish their own indexes. These indexes, however, are at best only rough guides and far from what one is accustomed to seeing in the index to *The New York Times*. (Whereas the *Times* index lists over thirty items for each full page of text, the People's Daily provides only seven or eight.) Other indexes to Mainland newspapers are listed in Chapter III, the most important of which is the Index to Major Newspapers and Periodicals (**184**). Particular reference should also be made to the Index to Editorials of the People's Daily, 1949–1958, which is indispensable for the use of the most important Mainland daily (**833**).

Since the Mainland newspapers constitute one of the most authoritative sources for the study of Chinese Communist policies and actions, extensive translations from its pages—especially of its editorials—have been made by the various agencies of the United States Government. The two most important sources are the translations of the Hong Kong American Consulate General and the Joint Publications Research Service (described in Chapter XX). In addition, from 1961 to 1962 the J.P.R.S. provided systematic translations of selections from each of the first four newspapers in serial form (e.g., *Translations from Ta-kung pao*). For convenience, the six newspapers are listed here accompanied by their indexes and translations.

831   Jen-min jih-pao 人民日報
(People's Daily). Shih-chia-chuang 石家莊 Peking, No. 1—, June 15, 1948—.

The official organ of the Central Committee of the Chinese Communist Party, the four to six-page *Jen-min jih-pao* reports on both national and international affairs, and sets the tone for the rest of the country's press. Nos. 1–269 were published in Shih-chia-chuang; the Peking edition began publication on March 15, 1949 with No. 270. There is a separate index (see next entry).

For a collection of selected editorials, see **570**. See also **833** for an index to editorials, 1949–1958. Articles from the *Jen-min jih-pao* are regularly translated in the *Survey of China Mainland Press* (**1038**), the *Union Research Service* (**1065**), and the J.P.R.S. *Selected Translations from Jen-min jih-pao*. The latter provided the most comprehensive coverage from March 1961 to May 1962 (see **835**). Selected materials from the People's Daily on specific subjects are periodically published in special collections. See, for example, the series on agriculture, *Jen-min jih-pao nung-yeh k'o-hsüeh wen-hsüan* 人民日報農業科學文選 (Peking, 1963—).

It should be noted that between May 15, 1946 and April 30, 1948 another *Jen-min jih-pao*, the predecessor to the current edition, was published in Han-tan 邯鄲 (Nos. 1–44, May 15–June 27, 1946) and Wu-an 武安 (Nos. 45–602, July 1, 1946–April 30, 1948). Also, prior to the publication of the present *Jen-min jih-pao* in Peking, still another newspaper of the same name was published in that city from February 2 to March 14, 1949 (Nos. 1–41). The latter's name was changed to *Pei-p'ing chieh-fang pao* 北平解放報 (Peiping Liberation Daily) on March 15, 1949, concurrently with the move of the Shih-chia-chuang *Jen-min jih-pao* to Peking. The Peiping Liberation Daily continued publication through April 24, 1949 (Nos. 42–82), at which time publication was presumably suspended.

The People's Daily is the most important newspaper published on the Mainland.

832 Jen-min jih-pao so-yin 人民日報索引
(Index to People's Daily). Peking: Jen-min jih-pao, January (?) 1951—. Monthly.

A monthly index published since 1951. Prior to the July 1958 issue, it was arranged by an unidentified decimal classification system under the following topical headings: philosophy (added since July 1956); social and political affairs (predominant in the index, including Communism, international relations, economic, legal, military, and social and cultural affairs); language; natural sciences; medicine, technology and agriculture; the arts, recreation and athletics; literature; history, geography and biography; and general (covers editorials, articles by *Jen-min jih-pao* Observers, extracts of editorials and articles from the local press, etc.).

Beginning with the July 1958 issue, the arrangement of the index has been improved by the utilization of the 'Classification System for Medium and Small-Size Libraries' 中小型圖書館圖書分類表 under the following headings: Marxism and Leninism; philosophy; history; economic affairs; political and social affairs (still the major emphasis of the index); law; military affairs; culture and education; language; literature; the arts; natural sciences (general); mathematics, physics and chemistry; biological sciences; medicine and hygiene; agricultural technology; industrial technology; chemical industry; light industry and handicraft industry; architecture and construction; transportation and communications; and general (covers editorials, articles by *Jen-min jih-pao* Observers, extracts of editorials and articles from the local press, letters to the editor, editor's comments, etc.).

An index to the 1948, 1949 and 1950 issues was compiled and published in Peking in 1961, and recently reprinted in Hong Kong.

833 Jen-min jih-pao, Kuo-nei tzu-liao tsu 人民日報國內資料組 (People's Daily, Domestic Reference Materials Section). *Jen-min jih-pao she-lun so-yin, 1949–1958* 人民日報社論索引, 1949–1958

(Index to Editorials of the People's Daily, 1949–1958). Peking: Jen-min jih-pao, 1959. 108p.

An index to all the editorials of the *Jen-min jih-pao* published between January 4, 1949 and December 20, 1958. In three parts: a chronological index, a subject index, and an alphabetical *P'in-yin* index to titles of selected editorials. An indispensable basic reference.

Chūgoku geppō 中國月報 (Monthly Report on China, **1120**), published by the China Section of the Japanese Foreign Ministry, carries in each issue a list of *Jen-min jih-pao* editorials for the preceding month.

See also next entry.

834 **'Jimmin nippō shuyō rombun sakuin'** 人民日報主要論文索引 (Index to Important Articles in the People's Daily), *Ajia keizai jumpō* アジア 經濟旬報 (Ten-Day Report on Asian Economy), Tokyo, Nos. 337–372 (October 1957–September 1958).

A continuation of the Index to Important Articles in Principal Chinese Newspapers and Periodicals (**190**), but limited only to *Jen-min jih-pao*. Each issue covers editorials appearing during a period of about six weeks prior to publication of the index.

835 **U.S. Joint Publications Research Service.** *Selected Translations from Jen-min jih-pao.* Washington, D.C., Nos. 1–67; June 1961–July 1962, April 1963—. Irregular.

Translations of selected articles from the People's Daily (see above). Mimeographed.

The following numbers of the J.P.R.S. reports are special issues of this title:

NO.	J.P.R.S. NO.	SOURCE SPAN	DATE OF PUBLICATION	U.S.G.P.O. MONTHLY CATALOG NO.
1	9367	Mar. 6–18, 1961	6– 6–61	1961–15478
2	9398	Mar. 19–27, 1961	6–19–61	15501
3	9454	Mar. 28–31, 1961	6–20–61	15537
4	9469	Apr. 5–8, 1961	6–26–61	15543
5	9491	Apr. 9–11, 1961	6–26–61	15558
6	9506	Apr. 12–15, 1961	7– 3–61	15572
7	9539	Apr. 16–19, 1961	7–20–61	15587
8	9549	Apr. 1–4, 20–21, 1961	7–20–61	15594
9	9561	Apr. 22–26, 1961	7–12–61	15601
10	9584	Apr. 27–30, 1961	7–25–61	15612
11	9620	Apr. 25, May 1–3, 1961	7–25–61	15627
12	9642	May 4–5, 1961	7–27–61	15633
13	9666	May 6–9, 1961	8– 7–61	15643
14	9668	May 10–11, 1961	8– 6–61	15644
15	9669	May 12–15, 1961	8–20–61	17512
16	9684	May 16–17, 1961	8– 1–61	15647
17	9716	May 8–22, 1961	8– 2–61	15657

NO.	J.P.R.S. NO.	SOURCE SPAN	DATE OF PUBLICATION	U.S.G.P.O. MONTHLY CATALOG NO.
18	9739	May 23–27, 1961	8– 7–61	15660
19	9750	May 28, Jun. 2, 1961	8–17–61	17513
20	9760	Jun. 3–6, 1961	8– 4–61	15664
21	9813	Jun. 7–9, 1961	8–14–61	1961–17522
22	9814	May 31, Jun. 10–12, 1961	8–14–61	17523
23	9930	May 19, Jun. 13–18, 1961	8–24–61	19699
24	10020	Jun. 19–21, 1961	8–31–61	19710
25	10021	Jun. 22–23, 1961	8–31–61	19711
26	10044	Jun. 24–28, 1961	9– 5–61	19717
27	10191	Jun. 29–Jul. 6, 1961	9–19–61	19751
28	10152	Jul. 7–9, 1961	9–14–61	19738
29	10151	Jul. 12–18, 1961	9–21–61	19737
30	10190	Jul. 19–23, 1961	9–20–61	19750
31	10353	Jul. 10–Aug. 6, 1961	10–6–61	21041
32	10431	Jul. 31–Aug. 14, 1961	10–12–61	21072
33	10483	Aug. 18–24, 1961	10–14–61	21086
34	10559	Aug. 3–19, 1961	10–19–61	1962– 1122
35	10660	Aug. 17–25, 1961	10–25–61	1188
36	11057	Aug. 26–30, 1961	11–14–61	not listed
37	11058	Aug. 31–Sep. 7, 1961	11–16–61	1447
38	11143	Sep. 8–13, 1961	11–22–61	1497
39	11311	Sep. 14–21, 1961	12– 1–61	2962
40	11209	Sep. 22–29, 1961	11–27–61	1516
41	11352	Sep. 30–Oct. 8, 1961	12– 6–61	2988
42	11646	Oct. 10–13, 1961	12–28–61	3153
43	11647	Oct. 14–20, 1961	12–28–61	3154
44	11889	Oct. 15–22, 1961	1–11–62	5849
45	11969	Oct. 23–30, 1961	1–15–62	5906
46	12029	Oct. 31–Nov. 9, 1961	1–18–62	5951
47	12040	Nov. 10–15, 1961	1–19–62	5961
48	12158	Nov. 15–21, 1961	1–25–62	6056
49	12389	Nov. 20–25, 1961	2– 8–62	8000
50	12430	Nov. 26–Dec. 4, 1961	2–12–62	8034
51	12484	Dec. 5–12, 1961	2–15–62	8079
52	12431	Dec. 6–14, 1961	2–12–62	8035
53	12563	Dec. 15–18, 1961	2–19–62	8135
54	12511	Dec. 19–24, 1961	2–20–62	8101
55	12533	Dec. 27–30, 1961	2–16–62	8113
56	12586	Dec. 25, 1961–Jan. 10, 1962	2–20–62	8154
57	12605	Jan. 3–14, 1962	2–21–62	8163
58	12668	Jan. 9–17, 1962	2–28–62	8199
59	12629	Jan. 18–21, 1962	2–23–62	8176
60	12993	Jan. 22–Feb. 7, 1962	3–15–62	10065
61	13222	Feb. 1–25, 1962	3–28–62	10249
62	13676	Feb. 15–Mar. 16, 1962	5– 7–62	12269
63	13700	Mar. 20–31, 1962	5– 9–62	12285
64	13992	Apr. 6–24, 1962	6– 4–62	14243
65	14059	Apr. 25–May 5, 1962	6– 8–62	not listed
66	14114	May 8–16, 1962	6–14–62	14330
67	14327	May 14–17, 1962	7– 2–62	15900

No further issues published in this series. However, beginning in April, 1963, translations from the People's Daily began to appear from time to time as part of another J.P.R.S. series, *Translations on International Communist Developments* (T.I.C.D.) subtitled 'Articles from *Jen-min jih-pao*'.

The following numbers of the J.P.R.S. reports are special issues of this subseries:

T.I.C.D. NO.	J.P.R.S. NO.	DATE OF PUBLICATION	U.S.G.P.O. MONTHLY CATALOG NO.
408	18655	4–11–63	1963– 9014
429	19249	5–17–63	12339
464	20194	7–16–63	15828
473	20485	8– 2–63	16119
483	20724	8–20–63	17666
490	20843	8–29–63	17785
495	21015	9–11–63	17957

836 Kuang-ming jih-pao 光明日報
(Kuang-ming Daily). Peking, No. 1—, June 16, 1949—.

A four-page daily, presumably published by the 'democratic parties', specializing in reporting cultural and educational affairs, political and legal matters, minority affairs, and the activities of these parties. Index published separately (see next entry).

From March 1961 to May 1962 the J.P.R.S. *Translations from Kuang-ming jih-pao* (see **838**) provided the most comprehensive coverage of this newspaper in translation. The *Survey of China Mainland Press* (**1038**) and the *Union Research Service* (**1065**) are also important sources for translations from this newspaper.

One of the most important Mainland newspapers.

837 Kuang-ming jih-pao so-yin 光明日報索引
(Index to Kuang-ming Daily). Peking: Kuang-ming jih-pao, November (?) 1952—. Monthly.

A monthly index, published since 1952. Prior to the January 1957 issue, it was arranged by an unidentified decimal system under the following topical headings: Marxism and Leninism; philosophy; social sciences (the major emphasis of the index); economic affairs; military affairs; law; culture and education; language; literature and art; history, geography and biography; natural sciences; medicine and hygiene; engineering and technology; agriculture, animal husbandry, marine products and forestry; and general (covers editorials, features, editor's comments, etc.).

Beginning with the January 1957 issue, the decimal numbering system was dropped. The current arrangement, somewhat simplified and improved, is under the following headings: Marxism and Leninism; philosophy; social and political affairs (still predominant part in the index); economic construction;

military affairs; law; cultural affairs; education; literature and art; language; science and technology; medicine and hygiene; agriculture, animal husbandry and marine products; history and biography; geography; and general (covers the same topics as before).

838 **U.S. Joint Publications Research Service.**
Translations from Kuang-ming jih-pao. Washington, D.C., Nos. 1–33, June 1961–July 1962. Irregular.

Translations of selected articles from *Kuang-ming jih-pao* (see above). Mimeographed.

The following numbers of the J.P.R.S. reports are special issues of this title:

NO.	J.P.R.S. NO.	SOURCE SPAN	DATE OF PUBLICATION	U.S.G.P.O. MONTHLY CATALOG NO.
1	4738	Mar. 15–31, 1961	Jun. 29, 1961	1961–12875
2				
3	4819	Apr. 2–May 1, 1961	Jul. 31, 1961	15051
4				
5	4844	Apr. 17–24, 1961	Aug 4, 1961	15056
6	4861	May 3-8, 1961	Aug 11, 1961	17390
7	4938	Feb. 21–Jun. 12, 1961	Aug. 28, 1961	17418
8	4937	May 17–Jun. 26, 1961	Aug. 31, 1961	17417
9	4963	Jun. 7–Jul. 11, 1961	Sep. 11, 1961	19513
10	10309	Jul. 16–25, 1961	Sep. 28, 1961	19783
11	10896	Jul. 27–Aug. 18, 1961	Oct. 31, 1961	1962– 1359
12	11034	Aug. 21–Sep. 5, 1961	Nov. 8, 1961	1436
13	11359	Sep. 13–20, 1961	Nov. 30, 1961	2992
14	11670	Sep. 21–30, 1961	Dec. 15, 1961	3171
15	11720	Oct. 3–18, 1961	Dec. 26, 1961	3201
16	11803	Oct. 19–22, 1961	Dec. 29, 1961	5795
17	11922	Oct. 22–Nov. 10, 1961	Jan. 9, 1962	5873
18	12278	Nov. 10–20, 1961	Jan. 25, 1962	7932
19	12331	Nov. 21–Dec. 3, 1961	Jan. 31, 1962	6162
20	12472	Dec. 4–8, 1961	Feb. 8, 1962	8068
21	12524	Dec. 10–29, 1961	Feb. 14, 1962	8107
22	12692	Dec. 30, 1961–Jan. 4, 1962	Feb. 23, 1962	8209
23	12839	Jan. 3–19, 1962	Feb. 28, 1962	9942
24	13039	Jan. 16–Feb. 1, 1962	Mar. 16, 1962	10107
25	13143	Feb. 8–18, 1962	Mar. 23, 1962	10192
26	13330	Feb. 19–25, 1962	Mar. 30, 1962	10316
27	13430	Feb. 26–Mar. 12, 1962	Apr. 9, 1962	12080
28	13531	Mar. 13–17, 1962	Apr. 18, 1962	12163
29	13713	Mar. 19–Apr. 1, 1962	May 7, 1962	12293
30	13808	Mar. 25–Apr. 15, 1962	May 15, 1962	14071
31	13885	Apr. 2–24, 1962	May 25, 1962	14145
32	14168	Apr. 23–May 13, 1962	Jun. 15, 1962	15760
33	14321	May 14–27, 1962	Jul. 2, 1962	15899

839 Ta-kung pao 大公報
L'impartial. Tientsin, Peking, No. 1—, June 17, 1902—.

One of the independent newspapers most influential in China before 1949. Since the Communist take-over, the Tientsin *Ta-kung pao* (a daily of four pages) has been restricted primarily to coverage of business, commerce and finance. It was moved to Peking on October 1, 1956. Publishes a selective index (see next entry). The *Survey of China Mainland Press* (**1038**) and the *Union Research Service* (**1065**) provide translations from the paper. From March 1961 to May 1962, the most comprehensive source is the J.P.R.S. *Translations from Ta-kung pao* (see **841**).

840 Ta-kung pao yao-mu so-yin 大公報要目索引
(Index to Important Items in *Ta-kung pao*). Peking: Ta-kung pao, January 1956—. Monthly.

An index to selected articles in the *Ta-kung pao* published since 1956(?), arranged basically under the following topical headings: political and social affairs; foreign relations; Five-Year Plan; finance and trade; industry; agriculture; transportation and communications; culture and education; international relations; Soviet Union; Asia; Africa; Australia; Europe; The Americas; laws, regulations and documents; editorials and essays; features and pictorials; cartoons and illustrations; and reference materials. Other topics of current interest such as 'General Line,' 'Reconstruction of Privately-Owned Enterprises,' etc., have also been included in the index.

841 U.S. Joint Publications Research Service.
Translations from Ta-kung pao (Peiping). Washington, D.C., Nos. 1–49, August 1961–July 1962. Irregular.

Translations of selected articles from the Peking *Ta-kung pao* (see above). Mimeographed.
The following numbers of the J.P.R.S. reports are special issues of this title:

NO.	J.P.R.S. NO.	SOURCE SPAN	DATE OF PUBLICATION	U.S.G.P.O. MONTHLY CATALOG NO.
1	8636	Mar. 16–30, 1961	Aug. 3, 1961	1961–15143
2	8681	Mar. 31–Apr. 9, 1961	Aug. 3, 1961	15171
3	8786	Apr. 10–17, 1961	Aug. 24, 1961	17469
4	8834	Apr. 18–25, 1961	Sep. 6, 1961	19565
5	8947	Apr. 26–May 1, 1961	Sep. 25, 1961	19611
6	8953	May 3–9, 1961	Sep. 27, 1961	19612
7	8995	May 10–16, 1961	Oct. 5, 1961	19630
8	10369	May 17–23, 1961	Oct. 11, 1961	21050
9	10374	May 24–29, 1961	Oct. 10, 1961	21052
10	10325	May 30–Jun. 4, 1961	Oct. 5, 1961	21024
11	10544	Jun. 5–12, 1961	Oct. 18, 1961	1962– 1114
12	10365	Jun. 13–19, 1961	Oct. 11, 1961	1961–21047
13	10563	Jun. 20–26, 1961	Oct. 20, 1961	21112

NO.	J.P.R.S. NO.	SOURCE SPAN	DATE OF PUBLICATION	U.S.G.P.O. MONTHLY CATALOG NO.
14	10566	Jul. 4–9, 1961	Oct. 18, 1961	1962– 1127
15	10564	Jun. 26, Jul. 5–12, 1961	Oct. 19, 1961	1125
16	10511	Jun. 23–Jul. 3, 1961	Oct. 18, 1961	1961–21097
17	10723	Jul. 14–20, 1961	Oct. 27, 1961	1962– 1236
18	10745	Jul. 21–26, 1961	Oct. 27, 1961	1247
19	10720	Aug. 21–25, 1961	Oct. 25, 1961	1234
20	10886	Jul. 27–Aug. 13, 1961	Nov. 6, 1961	1352
21	11029	Jul. 28–Aug. 19, 1961	Nov. 14, 1961	1434
22	11051	Aug. 27–Sep. 7, 1961	Nov. 14, 1961	
23	11020	Sep. 15–21, 1961	Nov. 13, 1961	1426
24	11084	Aug. 4–24, 1961	Nov. 17, 1961	1466
25	11234	Aug. 30–Sep. 10, 1961	Nov. 28, 1961	2946
26	11433	Aug. 1–Oct. 1, 1961	Dec. 7, 1961	3030
27	11552	Jul. 27–Sep. 29, 1961	Dec. 18, 1961	3098
28	11768	Aug. 31–Oct. 8, 1961	Jan. 4, 1962	5780
29	11839	Oct. 9–21, 1961	Jan. 9, 1962	5814
30	12136	Oct. 17–28, 1961	Jan. 26, 1962	6038
31	12249	Nov. 16–Dec. 3, 1961	Feb. 1, 1962	6125
32	12287	Oct. 29–Nov. 15, 1961	Feb. 2, 1962	7936
33	12496	Nov. 18–Dec. 10, 1961	Feb. 15, 1962	8088
34	12592	Dec. 4–24, 1961	Feb. 21, 1962	8157
35	12778	Dec. 26–Jan. 14, 1962	Mar. 5, 1962	8257
36	12958	Jan 8–26, 1962	Mar. 14, 1962	10034
37	13076	Jan. 22–25, 1962	Mar. 21, 1962	10139
38	13120	Jan. 20–Feb. 15, 1962	Mar. 23, 1962	10171
39	13210	Feb. 14–23, 1962	Mar. 29, 1962	10242
40	13346	Feb. 27–Mar. 12, 1962	Apr. 5, 1962	10324
41	13550	Mar. 14–21, 1962	Apr. 25, 1962	12179
42	13637	Mar. 26–Apr. 8, 1962	May 3, 1962	12245
43	13830	Apr. 9–22, 1962	May 22, 1962	14092
44	13955	Apr. 23–25, 1962	Jun. 1, 1962	14208
45	14121	Apr. 26–30, 1962	Jun. 14, 1962	14332
46	14247	May 1–5, 1962	Jun. 25, 1962	15833
47	14480	May 7–13, 1962	Jul. 16, 1962	15951
48	14516	May 14–20, 1962	Jul. 18, 1962	15964
49	14581	May 21–27, 1962	Jul. 25, 1962	17855

842 Kung-jen jih-pao 工人日報
(Worker's Daily). Peking, No. 1—, July 15, 1949—.

Kung-jen jih-pao, an official organ of the All-China Federation of Trade Unions 中華全國總工會 is a two to four-page daily newspaper that concerns itself with the trade union movement, labor conditions, etc. Separate index (see next entry). See also other organs of the Federation, *Chung-kuo kung-jen* 中國工人 (Chinese Worker, **871**) and *The Chinese Trade Unions* (**927**).

For translations of articles from this newspaper, see *J.P.R.S. Translations from Kung-jen jih-pao* (**844**), the *Survey of China Mainland Press* (**1038**), and the *Union Research Service* (**1065**).

One of the most important Mainland newspapers.

843 Kung-jen jih-pao so-yin 工人日報索引
(Index to Worker's Daily). Peking: Kung-jen jih-pao, January 1956 (?)—.
Monthly.

An index to the Worker's Daily published monthly since 1956 (?). Classification system varies slightly from time to time, but the basic arrangement is as follows: Marxism and Leninism (including articles by and on Mao Tse-tung); politics and government; military affairs; economic affairs; labor and labor movement; culture, education, science and hygiene; foreign relations; international affairs; editorials, comments, and selected editorials of *Jen-min jih-pao;* features; and letters to the editor.

844 U.S. Joint Publications Research Service. *Translations from Kung-jen jih-pao.*
Washington, D.C., Nos. 1–28, June 1961–July 1962. Irregular.

Translations of selected articles from the Worker's Daily (see above). Mimeographed.
The following numbers of the J.P.R.S. reports are special issues of this title:

NO.	J.P.R.S. NO.	SOURCE SPAN	DATE OF PUBLICATION	U.S.G.P.O. MONTHLY CATALOG NO.
1				
2	4748	Mar. 19–May 1, 1961	Jun. 30, 1961	1961–12881
3				
4	4843	Mar. 18–May 16, 1961	Aug. 4, 1961	15055
5				
6				
7	4890	May 9–Jun. 30, 1961	Aug 17, 1961	17397
8	4923	Apr. 13–May 24, 1961	Aug. 28, 1961	17410
9	4936	May 25–Jul. 16, 1961	Aug. 31, 1961	17416
10	10237	Mar. 21–Jul. 21, 1961	Sep. 25, 1961	19766
11	10490	Jul. 22–30, 1961	Oct. 10, 1961	21091
12	10631	Aug. 1–19, 1961	Oct. 17, 1961	1962– 1166
13	10895	Aug. 22–Sep. 1, 1961	Oct. 31, 1961	1358
14	11188	Sep. 2–26, 1961	Nov. 22, 1961	2924
15	11364	Sep. 27–Oct. 15, 1961	Nov. 30, 1961	2994
16	11719	Oct. 17–28, 1961	Dec. 26, 1961	3200
17	12123	Oct. 31–Nov. 19, 1961	Jan. 19, 1962	7900
18	12277	Nov. 21–Dec. 3, 1961	Jan 25, 1962	6144
19	12332	Dec. 5–9, 1961	Jan. 31, 1962	6163
20	12651	Dec. 10–24, 1961	Feb. 15, 1962	8189
21	12691	Dec. 26, 1961–Jan. 11, 1962	Feb. 23, 1962	8208
22	12909	Jan. 4–26, 1962	Mar. 9, 1962	9991
23	13038	Jan. 27–Feb. 1, 1962	Mar. 16, 1962	10106
24	13142	Feb. 1–15, 1962	Mar. 23, 1962	10191
25	13834	Apr. 4–21, 1962	May 18, 1962	14096
26	13875	Apr. 24, 1962	May 24, 1962	14136
27	14079	May 8–12, 1962	Jun. 8, 1962	not listed
28	14320	May 15–22, 1962	Jul. 2, 1962	15898

845 Wen-hui pao 文滙報
(Wen-hui Daily). Shanghai. No. 1—, 1945 (?)—. Daily.

A four-page daily newspaper having an emphasis on elementary and secondary education. Index is published separately (see next entry). Its editorials and articles are sometimes translated in the *Survey of China Mainland Press* (**1038**) and the *Union Research Service* (**1065**).

846 Wen-hui pao so-yin 文滙報索引
(Index to Wen-hui Daily). Shanghai: Wen-hui pao, 1957 (?)—. Monthly.

An index of about twenty pages to the Wen-hui Daily arranged under the following headings: (1) Marxism and Leninism (including works by and on Mao Tse-tung); (2) philosophy; (3) social and political affairs; (4) economic affairs; (5) military affairs; (6) legal affairs; (7) cultural and educational affairs; (8) literature and fine arts; (9) language and philology; (10) history; (11) geography; (12) science and technology; (13) medicine and hygiene; (14) engineering; (15) agriculture, marine products and animal husbandry; and (16) general. Feature sections are also indexed. Beginning with the January 1959 issue, a chronology for the indexed month as published in the Daily is included.

847 Chung-kuo ch'ing-nien pao 中國青年報
(China Youth Daily). Peking, No. 1—, April 27, 1951—. Three times a week through 1955; daily (except Mondays) thereafter.

The China Youth Daily, a newspaper of four pages, is an official organ of the Chinese Communist Youth League 中國共產主義青年團 (known as the Chinese New Democratic Youth League 中國新民主主義青年團 from 1949 to 1957). Emphasis is placed on the youth movement and its activities. Separate index (see next entry). See also another organ of the League, *Chung-kuo ch'ing-nien* 中國青年 (Chinese Youth, **868**).

848 Chung-kuo ch'ing-nien pao so-yin 中國青年報索引
(Index to China Youth Daily). Peking: Chung-kuo ch'ing-nien pao, July 1951—. Quarterly.

An index to the China Youth Daily, from 1951 to 1955; a monthly since January 1956. The index to the first nineteen issues is published on one sheet. The classification system varies but generally includes the following categories: general (Marxism, Leninism and works by and on Mao Tse-tung), political and social affairs, economic affairs, culture and education, 'study and conduct of life', history and geography, literature and the arts, foreign relations of Communist China, international relations, letters to the editor (added since March 1958), editorials and comments.

B. News Releases

The *Chung-kuo hsin-wen* 中國新聞 (China News) and the *Hsinhua News Agency Release* are extremely useful supplements to the Mainland newspapers. Though largely similar in contents, the Chinese and the English-language news releases are not identical.

See also American radio monitoring of Peking newscasts described in Chapter XX (**1071** ff.).

The Center for Research Libraries—formerly the Midwest Inter-Library Center— has about 100 reels of microfilm containing the *New China News Agency Releases* in both Chinese and English for the period May 1953 to December 1961.

849 Hsinhua News Agency Release. Peking: Hsinhua News Agency, April 21, 1949—.

The daily releases (averaging twelve pages per day) consist mainly of short news items, selected *Jen-min jih-pao* editorials, etc. Occasional supplements are published. Successively issued by the New China News Agency, the China Information Bureau of the Press Administration, and the Hsinhua News Agency, the publication appeared under the title *Daily News Release* during the period April 21, 1949–December 31, 1955, inclusive. Printed and issued in monthly paper-bound volumes to August 31, 1957; mimeographed thereafter. Beginning September 1, 1957, foreign subscribers were asked to obtain the *Hsinhua News Agency Release* from the Agency's branch offices in Hong Kong (see next entry) and Prague. With the deterioration of Communist China's relations with Czechoslovakia in the summer of 1963, the Prague office of the Agency was closed and its subscriptions transferred to Hong Kong.

850 Daily News Release. Hong Kong: New China News Agency, May 25, 1948—.

The Hong Kong edition of the Hsinhua News Agency Release (see preceding entry). Mimeographed.

851 Chung-kuo hsin-wen 中國新聞

(China News). Canton: Chung-kuo hsin-wen she 中國新聞社, 1954—.

A daily release in Chinese (averaging twelve pages) issued by the China News Service, similar to **849**.

C. Periodicals

I. CHINESE-LANGUAGE

As was mentioned previously, over a thousand periodicals are being published on the Mainland, of which over four hundred are considered to be of particular importance. Selected for inclusion in this section, however, are only some fifty titles judged to be the most important or representative publications of the Communist Party and government organs, including those of affiliated mass organizations, publications for the general public, as well as scholarly publications in each of the major disciplines and a sample of university journals. (An exception is made in the highly specialized field of science and technology, where only a few titles of general interest are listed). As in the case of the newspapers, indexes to and translations from individual publications are listed with the periodicals themselves, such as, for example, the J.P.R.S. translations from and its index to the Red Flag.

Among Communist Party periodicals, *Hung-ch'i* (Red Flag, **885**), the organ of the Central Committee, is undoubtedly the most authoritative. Others listed in this section include *Hsüeh-hsi* (Study, **884**), *Cheng-chih hsüeh-hsi* (Political Studies, **853**) and *Chih-pu sheng-huo* (Party-Branch Life, **862**), issued in Tientsin. The last is given as an example of similar publications of the same title published by other party branches throughout the country.

A number of important organs of government agencies are also to be found here. Among those included are *Chi-hua yü t'ung-chi* (Planning and Statistics, **856**), the joint organ of the State Planning Commission and the State Statistical Bureau; *Chung-kuo nung-pao* (Chinese Agricultural Bulletin, **873**), official organ of the Ministry of Agriculture; *Jen-min chiao-t'ung* (People's Communications, **888**), organ of the Ministry of Communications; *Jen-min chiao-yü* (People's Education, **889**), organ of the Ministry of Education; *Chieh-fang chün pao* (Liberation Army News, **861**); *Wen-wu* (Cultural Relics, **918**), organ of the Cultural Relics Bureau of the Ministry of Culture; and *Ch'iao-wu pao* (Bulletin of Overseas Chinese Affairs, **859**), organ of the Overseas Chinese Affairs Commission. (The Gazette of the State Council and the Gazette of the Standing Committee of the National People's Congress are described in Chapter XIII; see **634** and **643**).

Almost all of the mass organizations maintain their official organs, and the most important ones are listed in this section. They are *Chung-kuo ch'ing-nien* (Chinese Youth, **868**), organ of the Chinese Communist Youth League; *Chung-kuo fu-nü* (Women of China, **870**), published by the All-China Federation of Women; *Chung-kuo kung-jen* (Chinese Worker, **871**), organ of the All-China Federation of Trade Unions; *Hsien-tai fo-hsüeh* (Modern Buddhism, **880**), published by the Buddhist Association of China; and *Jen-min wen-hsüeh* (People's Literature, **891**), official organ of the All-China Federation of Literary and Art Circles. (See also the next section for English-language publications issued by some of these same organizations.)

The sample of scholarly periodicals included here represents a variety of disciplines and fields irrespective of whether or not their subject matter concerns contemporary China. Such publications are included because they reflect the Chinese Communist Party line on the subject, be it ancient history, philosophy, or fine arts. Some of the important titles are *Che-hsüeh yen-chiu* (Philosophical Studies, **852**), *Ching-chi yen-chiu* (Economic Studies, **863**), *Cheng-fa yen-chiu* (Studies in Government and Law, **854**), *Li-shih yen-chiu* (Historical Studies, **897**), *Ti-li hsüeh-pao—Acta Geographica Sinica*, **908**, *Min-tsu yen-chiu* (Studies on National Minorities, **901**), *T'u-shu kuan hsüeh t'ung-hsün* (Library Science Bulletin, **912**), and, in view of the importance of the language reform and literacy campaigns, *Chung-kuo yü-wen* (Chinese Language, **874**) and *Wen-tzu kai-ko* (Language Reform, **917**). In addition, three university journals are given as samples: Journal of Peking University—Humanities (**903**), Wuhan University Journal of Humanities (**919**), and *Universitatis Amoiensis: Acta Scientiarum Socialum* (**878**).

In the field of science and technology only *K'o-hsüeh t'ung-pao—Scientia* (**894**), a journal of general interest, is listed. (Three English-language scientific periodicals published on the Mainland are described in the next section; see **932** ff.) It should be noted that a number of periodicals such as *Chung kung-yeh t'ung-hsün* (Bulletin of Heavy Industry, **866**) also carry articles of a technical nature.

Perhaps the most important single periodical published on the Mainland is the *Hsin-hua pan-yüeh-k'an* (New China Semi-Monthly, **882**), comprehensive in its coverage of official documents dealing with international and, in particular, domestic affairs. Much of it appeared in translation in *Communist China Digest* published by the Joint Publications Research Service (see **1052**) and in the translation series issued by the American Consulate General in Hong Kong (**1038** ff.). Unfortunately, this publication has not been available for some time.

Special mention also should be made of the *Kung-tso t'ung-hsün* (Bulletin of Activities, **895**), a secret military journal published by the General Political Department of the People's Liberation Army. Although only twenty-nine issues of this journal are available, its unique contents make it one of the most important documents for the study of Communist China.

Some of the periodicals listed in this section—as indicated in the annotations—carry their own indexes. In addition, reference must be made to the Index to Major Periodicals and Newspapers (**184**) and other indexes, as well as to the *Index to Learned Chinese Periodicals* compiled by the East Asian Library, Columbia University (Boston: G. K. Hall & Co., 1963), which provides an author and subject guide to thirteen Chinese journals, most of them published by major academic institutions in Mainland China from 1923 to 1954.

The reader is also referred to the next section, which covers English-language periodicals published on the Mainland, as well as to the translations from these periodicals described in Chapter XX.

Finally, it might be noted that some 160 Mainland Chinese-language periodicals in the social sciences and humanities published since October 1959 are in the process of being assembled for microfilming at the Library of Congress.

852 Che-hsüeh yen-chiu 哲學研究

(Philosophical Studies). Peking: K'o-hsüeh ch'u-pan she 科學出版社, 1955 No. 1—, May 1955—. Monthly.

A scholarly journal published by the Institute of Philosophy of the Chinese Academy of Sciences 中國科學院哲學研究所 and devoted to the discussion of dialectical materialism and historical materialism and to the criticism of idealism and pragmatism. Published at irregular intervals through 1960, a bi-monthly in 1961, and a monthly thereafter. Annual cumulative table of contents.

853 Cheng-chih hsüeh-hsi 政治學習
(Political Studies). Peking: T'ung-su tu-wu ch'u-pan she 通俗讀物出版社,
1955 No. 1—, January 1955—. Bi-monthly.

An elementary theoretical journal in the field of politics designed to assist
cadres having only limited education and working in rural areas. In general, the
articles included are intended to explain and interpret government and party
policies as well as to provide a basic understanding of political theory from the
Marxist-Leninist standpoint. Published as a monthly from 1955 to 1958 inclusive. Cumulative subject index for every twelve issues since 1958.

854 Cheng-fa yen-chiu 政法研究
(Studies in Government and Law). Peking: Fa-lü ch'u-pan she 法律出版社,
1954 No. 1—, May 1954—. Quarterly.

Published jointly by the Political Science and Law Association of China
中國政治法律學會 and the Institute of Legal Studies of the Chinese Academy
of Sciences 中國科學院法學研究所, *Cheng-fa yen-chiu* is a theoretical journal
of Marxist-Leninist orientation in the fields of political science and law, with
primary emphasis on the latter. It contains articles on Chinese Communist law
and legal system, as well as critiques and analyses of Western law and international law (some translated from Russian and other languages). Book reviews
of legal publications are included, as are news items on legal societies and
legal education in Communist China. Published as a bi-monthly prior to 1961
No. 1. Annual index arranged under broad subject categories in the December
issue of each year.

An important publication.

855 Chi-hua ching-chi 計劃經濟
(Planned Economy). Peking: Chi-hua t'ung-chi tsa-chih she 計劃統計雜誌社,
1955 No. 1–1958 No. 12, January 1955–December 1958. Monthly.

A joint official organ of the State Planning Commission 國家計劃委員會 and
the State Economic Commission 國家經濟委員會, containing theoretical articles
on economic planning, as well as articles concerning the Chinese Communist
economy in general, and reviews of methods and actual planning experience in
particular. Documents are frequently included. An annual subject index appears
in the December issue.

Publication suspended with the No. 12 issue of 1958 (December 1958).
United with *T'ung-chi kung-tso* 統計工作 (Statistical Work, **914**) in January
1959 to form *Chi-hua yü t'ung-chi* 計劃與統計 (Planning and Statistics, see next
entry).

856 Chi-hua yü t'ung-chi 計劃與統計
(Planning and Statistics). Peking: Chi-hua t'ung-chi tsa-chih she 計劃統計
雜誌社, 1959 No. 1—, January 1959—. Monthly.

Superseding *Chi-hua ching-chi* (see preceding entry) and *T'ung-chi kung-tso*, this publication is the joint official organ of the State Planning Commission and the State Statistical Bureau 國家統計局. The journal publishes official documents concerning economic planning and statistical work (regulations, resolutions, directives, etc.), discussions of problems encountered in the execution of various projects, and economic and statistical data accompanied by analysis.

857 Ch'i-yeh k'uai-chi 企業會計
(Enterprise Accounting). Peking: Ts'ai-cheng ch'u-pan she 財政出版社, 1952 No. 1— (No. 1—), January 1952—. Semi-monthly.

A specialized journal devoted to accounting and auditing, containing government regulations and articles on accounting theories, systems and methods, together with discussions of experiences and problems encountered in actual operations in various enterprises. Published as a monthly under the title *Kung-yeh k'uai-chi* 工業會計 (Industrial Accounting) from 1952 to 1958, inclusive. The journal assumed its present title with the January issue of 1959 and began publication as a semi-monthly. Since then attention has been increasingly given to accounting theory and practice, etc., with respect to the communes.
Annual subject index.

858 Chiao-hsüeh yü yen-chiu 教學與研究
(Teaching and Research). Peking: Chung-kuo jen-min ta-hsüeh 中國人民大學, No. 1—, May 1953—. Monthly.

A journal devoted to the social sciences generally, published by the Chinese People's University. Regularly publishes articles on matters concerning teaching and curriculum, as well as critiques on 'right-wing revisionist' theories and attitudes allegedly held by certain leading educators, writers and university professors. Published as an 'internal publication' prior to 1954. Annual subject index in the December issue of each year.

859 Ch'iao-wu pao 僑務報
(Bulletin of Overseas Chinese Affairs). Peking: Ch'iao-wu pao she 僑務報社, 1956 No. 1—, October 1956—. Bi-monthly.

An official publication of the Overseas Chinese Affairs Commission 華僑事務委員會, the bulletin publishes government policy statements, directives, etc., concerning the Overseas Chinese, including interpretations of regulations and rules. Included also are articles on the lives and work of returned Chinese nationals, and reports by cadres engaged in work with the Overseas Chinese. Published as a monthly until the end of 1960. An annual subject index appears in the December issue of each year.

860 Chieh-fang chün hua-pao 解放軍畫報
(Liberation Army Pictorial). Peking: Chung-kuo jen-min chieh-fang chün tsung cheng-chih pu 中國人民 解放軍 總政治部, No. 1—, February 1951—. Semimonthly.

Published by the General Political Department of the People's Liberation Army, the pictorial is designed for domestic consumption to acquaint the Chinese people with developments in the various branches of the armed forces. In addition, it serves as a popular visual instrument for the indoctrination of armed forces personnel. Published as a monthly until July 1958.

Much less important than the Liberation Army News (next entry), which is a primary source for the study of military affairs of Communist China.

861 Chieh-fang chün pao 解放軍報
(Liberation Army News). Peking: Chung-kuo jen-min chieh-fang chün tsung cheng-chih pu 中國人民 解放軍 總政治部, No. 1–20 (?), September–December 1955; No. 1—, January 1956—. Daily since 1958 (?).

The official organ of the People's Liberation Army, published by its General Political Department. The paper carries news items on the Chinese Communist armed forces, together with articles intended primarily for purposes of indoctrination. Literary pieces on the Liberation Army as well as the writings of armed forces personnel also appear in its pages.

Some twenty issues of a four-page experimental semi-weekly edition appeared in the period September 28–December 23, 1955. The regular edition began publication January 1, 1956 with No. 1. Published in six pages, the paper was issued three times a week until 1958 (?) when it became a daily. The News is the most valuable source for the study of Chinese Communist military affairs, but unfortunately it has not been available in quantity anywhere in the Western world.

Two more publications of the People's Liberation Army deserve mention: *Chieh-fang chün chan-shih* 解放軍戰士 (The Liberation Army Warriors), a semi-monthly published since June 1955, and *Chieh-fang chün wen-i* 解放軍文藝 (Liberation Army Literature and Art), a monthly published since June 1951.

See also **895**.

862 Chih-pu sheng-huo 支部生活
(Party-Branch Life). Tientsin: Tien-ching chih-shih shu-tien 天津知識書店, 1950 No. 1— (No. 1—), June (?) 1950—. Semi-monthly.

A popular publication edited by the Tientsin Municipal Committee of the Chinese Communist Party, designed primarily for mass indoctrination. Articles are written in simple language, accompanied by illustrations. Similar publications of the same title are issued by other municipal and provincial committees. No index.

863 **Ching-chi yen-chiu** 經濟研究

(Economic Studies). Peking: K'o-hsüeh ch'u-pan she 科學出版社, 1955
No. 1— (No. 1—), April 1955—. Monthly.

A scholarly journal of Marxist-Leninist orientation in the field of economics,
published by the Institute of Economics of the Chinese Academy of Sciences
中國科學院經濟研究所. Recent issues have devoted more space to theoretical
articles on specific issues in Communist China's economic development.
Critiques of capitalism appear frequently. Published as a bi-monthly prior to
No. 1 (1959). An annual subject index appears in the December issue of each
year. For translations, see next entry.

The most important journal in the field of economic theory.

864 **U.S. Joint Publications Research Service.**
Translations from Ching-chi yen-chiu (Economic Studies). Washington, D.C.,
July 1962—. Irregular.

Translations from *Ching-chi yen-chiu* (see preceding entry). Mimeographed.
The following numbers of the J.P.R.S. reports are special issues of this title:

CHING-CHI YEN-CHIU NO.		J.P.R.S. NO.	DATE OF PUBLICATION	U.S.G.P.O. MONTHLY CATALOG NO.
1961	8	16093	11- 8-62	1962–23918
	11	15942	10-30-62	23775
	12	16038	11- 6-62	23866
1962	1	16033	11- 5-62	23862
	2	14387	7- 5-62	15932
	2 (sic)	15910	10-29-62	23744
	4	14371	7- 3-62	15927
	5	16065	11- 6-62	23893
	6	16066	11- 6-62	23894
	7	15819	10-22-62	23656
	9	17095	1-11-63	1963- 2897
	10	16978	1- 4-63	2786
Dec. 1962–Jan. 1963		18715	4-18-63	10416
1963	2	18684	4-12-63	10385
	3	19343	5-22-63	12433
	4	19551	6- 4-63	12641
	5	20182	7-16-63	15816
	6	20893	9- 3-63	17835
Errata			11- 8-63	1964- 884
	7	20979	9- 9-63	1963-17921
	8	21447	10-14-63	19749
	9	22040	11-26-63	1964- 1294
	10	22557	12-31-63	2925
	11	22946	1-28-64	5260
	12	23276	2-18-64	7052

865 Ch'u-pan hsiao-hsi 出版消息
(Publishing News). Peking: Hsin-hua shu-tien 新華書店, June 1958—.
Weekly.

A four to six-page bibliographical tabloid newspaper published by the
Peking branch of Hsin-hua bookstore. Page 1 is usually devoted to surveys of
politically important books, such as those on Marxism-Leninism, works by
Chinese Communist leaders, and documentary materials on congresses, conferences and the like. The newspaper also includes periodic plans of publishing
houses. The middle pages of the newspaper list new non-periodical publications
for the previous week, arranged under (1) new books, (2) second and other
editions, and (3) books in press. The books are further grouped according to
the classification scheme of the Chinese People's University (see **1757**), and in
each case a full bibliographical citation is provided. The last page usually
carries reviews of new books for librarians, party cadres, and other interested
personnel. *Ch'u-pan hsiao-hsi* appeared three times a month from June through
October 1958.

The newspaper, important as a national bibliography, serves additionally
as a guide to books considered to be politically significant by the Chinese
Communist Party. The periodical was not available for examination.

866 Chung kung-yeh t'ung-hsün 重工業通訊
(Bulletin of Heavy Industry). Peking: Chung kung-yeh ch'u-pan she
重工業出版社, 1953 No. 1— (No. 1—), January 1953—. Three times a
month.

An official organ of the Ministry of Heavy Industry, containing both descriptive and technical articles and government regulations and directives.

867 Chung-kuo ch'ing kung-yeh 中國輕工業
(Light Industry of China). Peking: Kung-yeh ch'u-pan she 工業出版社, 1950
No. 1—, October 1950—. Semi-monthly.

An official publication of the Ministry of Light Industry, providing comprehensive coverage on the development of Communist China's light industry
(including both technical and non-technical articles), government regulations
and directives, and—since 1958—a special section on light industrial development in the communes. Published as a monthly prior to 1954 No. 2. No
index.

868 Chung-kuo ch'ing-nien 中國青年
(Chinese Youth). Peking: Chung-kuo ch'ing-nien ch'u-pan she 中國青年出版社,
No. 1—, December 1948—. Semi-monthly.

An official organ of the Chinese Communist Youth League 中國共產主義青年團
(known as the Chinese New Democratic Youth League 中國新民主主義青年團

from 1949 to 1957). The contents of the journal range from the theoretical to the popular, and include informative articles on Communist-led youth and student activities prior to 1949. Documents relating to the Youth League frequently appear in its pages.

Chung-kuo ch'ing-nien was published in Shanghai from 1923 to 1927 and again in Yenan from 1939 until the capture of the city by Nationalist forces in 1947.

869 Chung-kuo fang-chih 中國紡織
(Chinese Textiles). Peking: Fang-chih kung-yeh ch'u-pan she 紡織工業出版社, 1950 No. 1— (No. 1—), June 1950—. Three times a month.

An official publication of the Ministry of Textile Industry. Contents are largely technical, but official directives, policy statements and production statistics frequently appear in its pages. Published as a monthly from 1950 to 1951 inclusive, a semi-monthly until 1959, and every ten days thereafter.

870 Chung-kuo fu-nü 中國婦女
(Women of China). Peking: Chung-kuo fu-nü she 中國婦女社, No. 1—, July 1959—. Monthly.

The official organ of the All-China Women's Federation 中華人民共和國全國婦女聯合會, containing popular articles on the status of women in Communist China and abroad. Official documents such as the proceedings of the successive congresses of the Federation are also published in its pages. Published under the title *Hsin Chung-kuo fu-nü* 新中國婦女 (Women of New China) from July 1949 to December 1955, and as a semi-monthly from 1955 to 1960 inclusive. Separate subject index for each year.

See also *Women of China* (**936**).

871 Chung-kuo kung-jen 中國工人
(Chinese Worker). Peking: Kung-jen ch'u-pan she 工人出版社, 1956 No. 1—, January 1956—. Semi-monthly.

An official organ of the All-China Federation of Trade Unions 中華全國總工會, containing popular articles on labor conditions; short stories, poetry, etc., by workers; official regulations and directives; and reminiscences of personal experiences in the Chinese Communist movement prior to 1949. Annual cumulative table of contents arranged by subject.

This publication was formed by the merger of two semi-monthlies: *Kung-jen* 工人 (Workers), Nos. 1–83 (January 1952–December 1955) and *Hsüeh wen-hua* 學文化 (Study Culture!), Nos. 1–116 (March 1951–December 1955). Another monthly publication entitled *Chung-kuo kung-jen* was also published in Peking from February 1950 to June 1951 (16 issues).

872 Chung-kuo kung-yeh 中國工業
(Chinese Industry). Shanghai: Chung-kuo kung-yeh yüeh-k'an she 中國工業
月刊社, Vol. 1, No. 1—, April 1949—. Monthly.

A general periodical on Communist China's industrial development, including
articles on planning, management and technology.

873 Chung-kuo nung-pao 中國農報
(Chinese Agricultural Bulletin). Peking: Nung-yeh tsa-chih she 農業雜誌社,
Vol. 1, No. 1—, May 1950—. Semi-monthly.

An official publication of the Ministry of Agriculture of Communist China
carrying reports on agricultural conferences and agricultural developments,
and technical articles on planting, seeds, soil, fertilizer, irrigation, animal
husbandry, veterinary medicine, agricultural implements, etc. Since 1958 an
increasing number of articles have appeared on the agricultural development
of the communes. News items on agricultural developments in the Communist
bloc countries are also published from time to time. A large number of the
articles are written by government researchers.

874 Chung-kuo yü-wen 中國語文
(Chinese Language). Peking: Jen-min chiao-yü ch'u-pan she 人民教育出版社,
1952 No. 1— (No. 1—), July 1952—. Monthly.

A scholarly journal of Chinese linguistics and philology. Articles on Chinese
language reform and teaching also appear in its pages. Subject index in the
December issue of each year.

875 Chung-Su yu-hao 中蘇友好
(Chinese-Soviet Friendship). Peking: Chung-Su yu-hao hsieh-hui tsung-hui
中蘇友好協會總會, Vol. 1, No. 1–Vol. 4, No. 14, November 1, 1949–August
25, 1952. Monthly.

The organ of the headquarters of the Sino-Soviet Friendship Association in
Peking. Superseded by *Chung-Su yu-hao pao* 中蘇友好報 (Chinese-Soviet
Friendship Newspaper) on October 5, 1952. Published three times a month
until 1953 (?). Available issues indicate that it was published twice a week on
Wednesdays and Saturdays after 1956. The latest available issue is dated March
30, 1957. Provincial branch offices of the Friendship Association also have
published their own organs for local cadres. No publications of the Friendship
Association are believed to be coming out at the present time.

876 Chung-yang ho-tso t'ung-hsün 中央合作通訊
(Central Bulletin of Cooperatives). Peking: Ch'üan-kuo kung-hsiao ho-tso
tsung-she 全國供銷合作總社, 1951 No. [1]—, April 1951—. Monthly.

A joint official bulletin of the All-China Federation of Supply and Marketing cooperatives and the Ministry of Trade, containing government regulations and policy statements, local survey reports, articles on the problems of the organization and operation of cooperatives and on the problems of procurement, as well as statistical data on agricultural and commercial products.

877 Hsi-chü yen-chiu 戲劇研究
(Studies in Drama). Peking: Chung-kuo hsi-chü ch'u-pan she 中國戲劇出版社, 1959 No. 1—, February 1959—. Bi-monthly.

The official organ of the Union of Chinese Drama Workers 中國戲劇家協會 superseding *Hsi-chü lun-ts'ung* 戲劇論叢 (Collections of Essays on Drama) and *Hsi-ch'ü yen-chiu* 戲曲研究 (Studies in Drama), published since 1957. It contains articles on the theory and technique of both Western-style drama and traditional Chinese opera. The No. 4 issue of 1959 is a special issue on the tenth anniversary of the establishment of the People's Republic of China, containing reviews of various aspects of the development of traditional and modern Chinese theater during the ten-year period 1949–1959.

878 Hsia-men ta-hsüeh hsüeh-pao: She-hui k'o-hsüeh 厦門大學學報：社會科學
Universitatis Amoiensis: Acta Scientiarum Socialum. Amoy: Hsia-men ta-hsüeh yen-chiu pu 厦門大學研究部, 1956 No. 1—, January 1956—. Irregular.

A scholarly journal in the social sciences published by the University of Amoy.

879 Hsiao-hsüeh chiao-shih 小學教師
(Primary Schoolteacher). Peking: Jen-min chiao-yü ch'u-pan she 人民教育出版社, 1952 No. 1–1956 No. 3 (Nos. 1–42), October 1952–March 1956. Monthly.

A journal designed primarily to assist elementary school teachers in their teaching assignments. The section on 'Teaching Experiences' is useful for the light it sheds on educational problems in local communities. Official documents are included occasionally. Publication ceased with the No. 3 issue of 1956 (March 1956).

880 Hsien-tai fo-hsüeh 現代佛學
(Modern Buddhism). Peking: Chung-kuo fo-chiao hsieh-hui hsüeh-hsi wei-yüan hui 中國佛教協會學習委員會, 1950 No. 1— (No. 1—), September 1950—. Monthly.

The official organ of the Buddhist Association of China. In addition to articles on Buddhism, official policy statements on religion and news items of the activities of the association are published from time to time. No. 6 issue of 1959 is a special issue on the Tibetan revolt. An English table of contents appears in each issue. Annual subject index.

881 Hsin chien-she 新建設
(New Construction). Peking: Kuang-ming jih-pao she 光明日報社, Vol. 1, No.
1— (No. 1—), September 1949—. Monthly.

A general periodical devoted to scholarly articles in the fields of the social
sciences and humanities from the standpoint of Marxism-Leninism. The
editorial board originally included people such as Fei Hsiao-t'ung 費孝通,
Ch'ien Tuan-sheng 錢端升, Ch'u An-p'ing 儲安平, and other leading non-
Communist intellectuals, but publication of this journal is now entirely under
Chinese Communist Party and government control. A large number of articles
attacking Ma Yin-ch'u 馬寅初, Feng Yu-lan 馮友蘭, and Liang Sou-ming 梁漱溟,
are found in its pages. Published semi-monthly prior to Vol. 3, No. 1 (October
1950). Annual subject index (previously published semi-annually).

An important journal for gauging the intellectual climate in Communist China.

882 Hsin-hua pan-yüeh-k'an 新華半月刊
(New China Semi-Monthly). Peking: Hsin-hua pan-yüeh-k'an she 新華半月刊社,
1949—.

Published monthly from November 1949 to December 1955 under the title
Hsin-hua yüeh-pao 新華月報, this periodical contains Chinese Communist policy
statements on international and national affairs and reports on domestic political,
economic, social and cultural conditions. Each issue also carries a chronology
of national and international events of significance during the preceding month.
(For a translation of this section since 1958, see *Communist China Digest*, **1052**.)
Beginning with Vol. 3, No. 4 (February 1951), an index to selected articles on
political, economic, social, cultural, and international affairs in leading Chinese
newspapers and periodicals has also been included.

The most important periodical published in Communist China. The title
reverted to *Hsin-hua yüeh-pao* (New China Monthly) in 1962.

883 Hsin kuan-ch'a 新觀察
(New Observer). Peking: Hsin kuan-ch'a tsa-chih she 新觀察雜誌社, Vol. 1,
No. 1— (No. 1—), July 1950—. Semi-monthly.

Started as a general periodical on Communist China edited by a group of
leading non-Communist intellectuals such as Fei Hsiao-t'ung 費孝通, P'an
Kuang-tan 潘光旦 and others, *Hsin kuan-ch'a* has come under government
control and is largely devoted to literature and the creative arts, although the
subject matter remains political in content. A 'Political Commentary' section
appears in each issue. The publication is now profusely illustrated and contains
a number of cartoons.

Annual subject index published separately.

884 Hsüeh-hsi 學習
(Study). Peking: Hsüeh-hsi tsa-chih she 學習雜誌社, No. 1–No. 145, September
1949–October 1958. Semi-monthly.

A theoretical journal on Marxism-Leninism and its application to the internal development of Communist China for the cadres, middle school students and other 'intellectual youth' (articles on foreign relations are only occasionally included). Published as a monthly prior to No. 1 (1957). Annual subject index appears in the final issue of each year.

885   Hung-ch'i 紅旗
(Red Flag). Peking: Hung-ch'i tsa-chih she 紅旗雜誌社, 1958 No. 1— (No. 1—), June 1958—. Semi-monthly.

The official organ of the Central Committee of the Chinese Communist Party. Most editorials and some of the more important articles are regularly translated into English and published in the *Peking Review* (see **930**), and the American Consulate General translations (**1038**ff.). Full translation of issues beginning with the August 1, 1960 issue are available in *Translations from 'Hung-ch'i'* (**887**). Semi-annual subject index. See also the J.P.R.S. index (next entry).

Hung-ch'i is the most important theoretical journal of the Chinese Communist Party.

886   U.S. Joint Publications Research Service.
[Index to *Hung-ch'i*], *Communist China Digest*, No. 75, J.P.R.S. 16,161, November 13, 1962, 107p. (U.S.G.P.O. Monthly Catalog, 1963, No. 700).

This issue of the *Communist China Digest* is an index to all available translations from *Hung-ch'i* (Red Flag) extending coverage from the first issue in June 1958 through the twelfth issue of 1962 (June). In six parts: (1) a chronological index by issue, (2) an author index, (3) an index to editorials, (4) an index to commentaries, (5) an index to editorials reprinted from other theoretical journals, and (6) an index to articles attributed to various organizations. Full bibliographical information is provided for entries in all six parts. Most translations have appeared in the J.P.R.S. reports; some are taken from the *Extracts from China Mainland Magazines* (E.C.M.M.) of the American Consulate General in Hong Kong, and a few from the *Union Research Service*. (It should be noted that full translations of *Hung-ch'i* began only with the August 1, 1960 issue.)
An indispensable guide.

887   U.S. Joint Publications Research Service.
Translations from Hung-ch'i (Red Flag). Washington, D.C., March 1959—. Irregular.

Translations of articles from Red Flag (see above). Previously published under the title *Articles from the Chinese Communist Theoretical Journal 'Hung-ch'i'*. Full translation began with the August 1, 1960 issue (J.P.R.S. No. 3929, September 16, 1960). Mimeographed.
The following numbers of the J.P.R.S. reports are special issues of this title:

HUNG-CH'I NO.		DATE	J.P.R.S. NO.	DATE OF PUBLICATION	U.S.G.P.O. MONTHLY CATALOG NO.
		Jun.–Aug. 1958	7837	4–21–61	1962– 5498
		Sep. 1958	9181	5– 9–61	1961–15357
		Oct. 1958	9182	5– 9–61	15358
		Nov.–Dec. 1958	7836	5–17–61	11159
	14	16 Dec. 1958	579D	3– 6–59	1959– 5016
(1,1959)	15	1 Jan. 1959	588D	3–13–59	6354A
(2)	16	16 Jan. 1959	1629	5–25–59	9236
(3)	17	1 Feb. 1959	648D	4–13–59	9161
(4)	18	16 Feb. 1959	706D	5– 4–59	9176
(5)	19	1 Mar. 1959	708D	5– 8–59	9178
(6)	20	16 Mar. 1959	715D	5–14–59	9180
(5–8)	19–22	Mar.–Apr. 1959	4820	7–31–61	1961–17376
(7)	21	1 Apr. 1959	745D	6– 4–59	1959– 9193
(8)	22	16 Apr. 1959	758D	6–11–59	10235
(9)	23	1 May 1959	795D	7– 3–59	not listed
(10)	24	16 May 1959	844D	7–29–59	12889
(10–16)	24–30	May–Aug. 1959	4972	9–12–61	1961–19516
(11)	25	1 Jun. 1959	872D	8–11–59	1959–14810
(12)	26	16 Jun. 1959	908D	9–11–59	14840
(13)	27	1 Jul. 1959	917D	9–15–59	16516
(14)	28	16 Jul. 1959	942D	9–29–59	16538
(15)	29	1 Aug. 1959	971D	10–14–59	17543
(16)	30	16 Aug. 1959	989D	10–23–59	17558
(17)	31	1 Sep. 1959	1004D	11– 9–59	1960– 781
(18)	32	16 Sep. 1959	1057D	11–27–59	834
(19)	33	1 Oct. 1959	1013D	11–16–59	791
(20)	34	16 Oct. 1959	1067D	12–15–59	843
(21)	35	1 Nov. 1959	1098D	1– 4–60	1924
(22)	36	16 Nov. 1959	1168D	2–12–60	5639
(23)	37	1 Dec. 1959	3046	3– 4–60	5592
(24)	38	16 Dec. 1959	3060	3–11–60	5604
(2, 5, 12, 14)	40, 43, 50, 52	Jan., Mar., Jun., Jul. 1960	8476	6–19–61	1961–13335
(3, 1960)	41	1 Feb. 1960	3169	4–15–60	1960– 7230
(4)	42	16 Feb. 1960	3214	5– 4–60	8630
(6)	44	16 Mar. 1960	3730	8–18–60	15634
(7)	45	1 May 1960	3623	7–28–60	14320
(8)	46	16 Apr. 1960	3591	7–26–60	14295
(9)	47	1 May 1960	3901	9–13–60	
(10)	48	16 May 1960	3977	9–28–60	17236
(11)	49	1 Jun. 1960	3814	9– 1–60	15683
(12)	50	16 Jun. 1960	6010	9–27–60	17639
(13)	51	1 Jul. 1960	3920	9–20–60	17290
(15)	53	1 Aug. 1960	3929	9–16–60	17297
(16)	54	16 Aug. 1960	6077	10–12–60	18911
(17)	55	1 Sep. 1960	6112	10–17–60	18929
(18)	56	16 Sep. 1960	6184	10–31–60	18973
(19)	57	1 Oct. 1960	6276	11–21–60	1961– 1067
(20–21)	58–59	1 Nov. 1960	6471	12–22–60	2292
(22)	60	16 Nov. 1960	6700	2– 3–61	4561
(23)	61	1 Dec. 1960	6848	3– 6–61	7834

HUNG-CH'I NO.		DATE	J.P.R.S. NO.	DATE OF PUBLICATION	U.S.G.P.O. MONTHLY CATALOG NO.
(24)	62	16 Dec. 1960	8009	3–30–61	1961–12986
(1, 1961)	63	1 Jan. 1961	8003	4– 3–61	12982
(2)	64	16 Jan. 1961	8094	4–15–61	13055
(3–4)	65–66	1 Feb. 1961	8123	4–20–61	13081
(5)	67	1 Mar. 1961	8480	6–23–61	13338
(6)	68	16 Mar. 1961	8682	8– 3–61	15172
(7)	69	1 Apr. 1961	8759	8–16–61	17450
(8)	70	16 Apr. 1961	8828	9– 7–61	19561
(9–10)	71–72	5 May 1961	8880	9–14–61	19577
(11)	73	1 Jun. 1961	8960	9–29–61	19615
(12)	74	16 Jun. 1961	10440	10–13–61	21073
(13)	75	1 Jul. 1961	8992	10– 5–61	19629
(14)	76	16 Jul. 1961	10582	10–18–61	21113
(15–16)	77–78	10 Aug. 1961	10382	8–10–61	21055
(17)	79	1 Sep. 1961	11021	11–10–61	1962– 1427
(18)	80	16 Sep. 1961	11050	11–16–61	2896
(19)	81	1 Oct. 1961	11326	12– 4–61	2971
(20)	82	16 Oct. 1961	11516	12–14–61	3075
(21–22)	83–84	10 Nov. 1961	11953	1–15–62	5894
(23)	85	1 Dec. 1961	12404	2– 9–62	8011
(24)	86	16 Dec. 1961	12440	2–12–62	8044
(1, 1962)	87	1 Jan. 1962	12782	3– 5–62	8260
(2)	88	16 Jan. 1962	12970	3–15–62	10046
(3–4)	89–90	10 Feb. 1962	13347	4– 5–62	12039
(5)	91	1 Mar. 1962	13615	5– 1–62	12231
(6)	92	16 Mar. 1962	13683	5– 8–62	12273
(7)	93	1 Apr. 1962	13723	5–11–62	12301
(8–9)	94–95	25 Apr. 1962	13903	5–29–62	14162

HUNG-CH'I NO.	J.P.R.S. NO.	DATE OF PUBLICATION	U.S.G.P.O. MONTHLY CATALOG NO.
(10)	14549	7–23–62	1962–17824
(11)	14431	7–11–62	17745
(12)	14595	7–25–62	17868
(13)	14703	8– 2–62	17963
(14)	14827	8–13–62	18079
(15–16)	15027	8–29–62	19784
(17)	15492	9–28–62	22127
(18)	15745	10–17–62	22368
(19)	16165	11–13–62	1963– 704
(20)	16602	12–10–62	1113
(21)	16685	12–14–62	1144
(22)	16985	1– 4–63	2793
(23–24)	17164	1–16–63	2962
(1, 1963)	17543	2– 8–63	5407
(2)	18205	3–19–63	8564
(3–4)	18343	3–25–63	8702
(5)	18848	4–23–63	10549
(6)	19024	4–30–63	10725

HUNG-CH'I NO.	J.P.R.S. NO.	DATE OF PUBLICATION	U.S.G.P.O. MONTHLY CATALOG NO.
(7–8)	19317	5–20–63	1963–12407
(8)	21374	10– 8–63	19676
(9)	19446	5–28–63	12536
(10–11)	19838	6–25–63	14238
(12)*	{20025	{7– 3–63	14427
	20149	7–12–63	15783
(13–14)	21008	9–10–63	17950
(15)	21223	9–26–63	19525
(16)	21153	9–19–63	19455
(17)	21559	10–22–63	20851
(19)	21561	10–22–63	20853
(20)	21877	11–14–63	1964– 1131
(21)	22177	12– 6–63	2545
(22)	22660	1– 9–64	4974
(23)	23075	2– 4–64	5389
(24)	22903	1–27–64	5217

* Not issued in this series, but as No. 96 of the *Communist China Digest* and No. 462 of the *Translations on International Communist Developments*.

888 Jen-min chiao-t'ung 人民交通

(People's Communications). Peking: Chung-yang jen-min cheng-fu chiao-t'ung pu 中央人民政府交通部, Vol. 1, No. 1—, June 1950—. Semi-monthly.

The official organ of the Ministry of Communications of Communist China, containing both technical and non-technical articles on transportation as well as government regulations, directives, etc. Published as a monthly prior to 1955.

889 Jen-min chiao-yü 人民教育

(People's Education). Peking: Jen-min chiao-yü ch'u-pan she 人民教育出版社, 1950 No. 1— (No. 1—), May 1950—. Semi-monthly.

The official organ of the Ministry of Education of Communist China. Government directives, regulations, etc., concerning education and the proceedings of educational conferences appear regularly in its pages, in addition to articles dealing with teaching methods, teacher training, school management, and other related subjects. Publication was suspended with issue No. 10 of 1957 (October 1957), and was resumed with No. 4 of 1958 (April 1958) on a semi-monthly basis. (It was published as a monthly prior to that date.) Subject index (some published annually and some semi-annually).

890 Jen-min shui-wu 人民稅務

(People's Taxation). Peking: Ts'ai-cheng ch'u-pan she 財政出版社, 1951 No. 1–1958 No. 15 (Nos. 1–192), January 1951–December 1958. Semi-monthly.

The official organ of the Bureau of Taxation of the Ministry of Finance, *Jen-min shui-wu* carried government regulations and official policy statements on tax affairs as well as articles discussing administrative problems and theoretical matters. A total of 192 issues were published from 1951 to 1958 inclusive, and in January 1959 the journal was absorbed by *Ts'ai-cheng* 財政 (Finance) (see **909**).

891 Jen-min wen-hsüeh 人民文學
(People's Literature). Peking: Jen-min wen-hsüeh ch'u-pan she 人民文學出版社, 1949 No. 1— (No. 1—), October 1949—. Monthly.

The official organ of the All-China Federation of Literary and Art Circles 中國文學藝術界聯合會, publishing new works by the members of the federation, including some of the most prominent writers. Literary criticism and interpretative articles on individual authors, published in the earlier issues, no longer appear in its pages. Absorbed *Wen-i hsüeh-hsi* 文藝學習 (Literary Studies) at the end of 1957. See the index to this journal for the years 1949–1959, published in Japan (next entry).

892 Aiura, Takashi 相浦杲. '"Jimmin bungaku" shosai shōsetsu, sambun, hōkoku ichiran hyō' 人民文學所載小說, 散文, 報告一覽表
(A List of Fiction, Prose Writings and Reports in 'People's Literature'), *Osaka Gaikokugo Daigaku gakuhō.* 大阪外國語大學學報 *Journal of Osaka University of Foreign Studies*, Osaka, No. 9 (1961), pp. 93–145.

A publication of the University's Seminar on Chinese Literature. Contains 947 items arranged by the date of appearance in the monthly 'People's Literature' beginning with the first issue in October 1949 through November 1959. Each entry lists the title, genre (novel, report, etc.), author, a short summary of the contents and remarks. A very convenient guide in spite of the absence of an index.

893 K'ao-ku hsüeh-pao 考古學報
(The Chinese Journal of Archeology). Peking: K'o-hsüeh ch'u-pan she 科學出版社, No. 1—, 1939 (?)—. Quarterly.

Published by the Institute of Archeology of the Chinese Academy of Sciences 中國科學院考古研究所 since 1952 (?), *K'ao-ku hsüeh-pao* carries archeological survey and excavation reports (with photographs and illustrations), as well as scholarly research papers. Tables of contents appear in Chinese, Russian and English. Starting in 1959, each article is accompanied by a summary in either English or Russian. The annual index is arranged under two sections: 'Archeological Surveys and Excavations', and 'Others', which also have appeared in Russian and English since 1959.

894 K'o-hsüeh t'ung-pao 科學通報
Scientia. Peking: K'o-hsüeh ch'u-pan she 科學出版社, Vol. 1, No. 1—, May 1950—. Monthly.

One of the leading scientific journals published in Communist China by the Academy of Sciences. In addition to scientific papers (mostly by known scientists), it also publishes government directives relating to scientific research, reports on scientific meetings, and book reviews. Published as a semi-monthly from 1957 to 1959 inclusive. Tables of contents in Chinese, Russian, and English. Annual classified index by broad subject categories.

895 Kung-tso t'ung-hsün 工作通訊

(Bulletin of Activities). Peking: Chung-kuo jen-min chieh-fang chün tsung cheng-chih pu 中國人民解放軍總政治部. Nos. 1–30, January–August 1961. Irregular.

Published by the General Political Department of the Chinese People's Liberation Army, this military journal succeeds the *Pa-i tsa-chih* 八一雜誌 (August 1st Magazine). It is an irregular (in terms of frequency) secret journal for internal purposes, designed for the use of party cadres at and above the regimental level. The present series does not contain No. 9, which has been classified as 'top secret', available only down to the divisional level and to the party committee of equivalent status.

Some of the documents contained in the journal may be regarded in effect as 'executive orders', bearing a terse inscription at the very beginning that 'no separate communication will be issued'. Others often carry a special indorsement by Mao Tse-tung, or by some other Chinese Communist leader, such as Marshal Lin Piao, Minister of National Defense. The significance of these secret military papers appears to lie in the fact that their contents transcend the scope of what usually falls within the jurisdiction of the military authorities. In addition to their rich coverage of military affairs, they deal with almost every major politico-ideological development and socio-economic issue then prevailing in Communist China. Furthermore, the available issues cover one of the most crucial periods, 1960–1961, of the Chinese People's Republic, when it was confronted with serious economic difficulties and widespread social discontent following the Great Leap Forward movement and severe natural disasters.

Microfilm or Xerox copies of this journal are available for purchase from the Photoduplication Service of the Library of Congress, Washingon 25, D.C. A translation of the entire series, under the editorship of J. Chester Cheng, entitled *The Politics of the Chinese Red Army*, was published by the Hoover Institution (776 p.).

896 Lao-tung 勞働

(Labor). Peking: Chung-hua jen-min kung-ho kuo, Lao-tung pu 中華人民共和國勞働部 (People's Republic of China, Ministry of Labor), 1954 (?) No. 1—, 1954 (?)—. Monthly.

The official organ of the Ministry of Labor of Communist China. It regularly publishes articles on a wide range of labor problems including the utilization and training of labor, wages, incentives, safety measures, factory management, etc. Published as a semi-monthly between January 1957 and June 1962. Annual subject index to major articles.

897　Li-shih yen-chiu 歷史研究
(Historical Studies). Peking: K'o-hsüeh ch'u-pan she 科學出版社, 1954 No. 1— (No. 1—), February 1954—. Bi-monthly.

A leading historical journal published by the Institute of History of the Chinese Academy of Sciences 中國科學院歷史研究所 (Chief editor: Yin Ta 尹達). It contains articles on historiography and Chinese history, and, on occasion, articles on the history of other countries. Notes on current historical research in Communist China and abroad, as well as on important foreign publications, also appear. Published as a bi-monthly from 1954 to 1955 inclusive, and as a monthly from January 1956 to May 1960, the Journal reverted to bi-monthly publication from the No. 6 issue of 1960 (June 1960). Tables of contents in Chinese, Russian, and English. Annual subject index.

898　Min-chien wen-hsüeh 民間文學
(Folk Literature). Peking: Jen-min wen-hsüeh ch'u-pan she 人民文學出版社, 1955 No. 1— (No. 1—), April 1955—. Bi-monthly.

Edited by the China Folklore Research Association 中國民間文藝研究會, this publication contains legends, folk songs, fairy tales, fables, etc., as well as articles on the study of Chinese folklore. Most of the material published is collected from among the minority groups. Published as a monthly prior to 1962. No index.

899　Min-tsu t'uan-chieh 民族團結
(Solidarity of National Minorities). Peking: Min-tsu ch'u-pan she 民族出版社, 1957 No. 1— (No. 1—), October 1957—. Monthly.

An illustrated popular publication containing articles on the life and status of national minority groups in the various autonomous regions of Communist China, including official statements on policy.

For translations of selected articles from this periodical, see next entry.

900　U.S. Joint Publications Research Service.
Articles from the Chinese Communist Periodical 'Min-tsu t'uan-chieh'. Washington, D.C., May 1959–March 1960. Irregular.

Translations of selected articles from *Min-tsu t'uan-chieh* (see preceding entry). Mimeographed.

The following numbers of the J.P.R.S. reports are special issues of this title:

MIN-TSU T'UAN-CHIEH NO.	J.P.R.S. NO.	DATE OF PUBLICATION	U.S.G.P.O. MONTHLY CATALOG NO.
No. 6, 1958	1551	5–11–59	1959– 9219
No. 7, 1958	1662	7– 6–58	9243
No. 10, 1958	1005		not listed
No. 11, 1958	1719	6–24–59	10342
No. 12, 1958	1563	5–18–59	9224
No. 2, 1959	740D	5–30–59	9191
No.	860D	8–11–59	12901
No. 7, 1959	998D	11– 4–59	17561
No. 8, 9, 1959	1144D	2– 5–60	1960– 3999
No. 10, 1959	3001	2–22–60	5554
No. 11, 12, 1959	3130	3–31–60	7207
	10550	10–13–61	1961–21108
	15540	10– 2–62	1962–22173

901 Min-tsu yen-chiu 民族研究

(Studies on National Minorities). Peking: Min-tsu ch'u-pan she 民族出版社, 1956 No. 1— (No. 1—), January 1956—. Monthly.

A scholarly journal published by the Institute of Ethnology of the Chinese Academy of Sciences 中國科學院民族研究所 devoted to the study of national minority groups. Originally published under the title *Min-tsu wen-t'i i-ts'ung* 民族問題譯叢 (Translations of Articles on Ethnography), from January 1956 to August 1958. It has been published under the present title since September 1958, when it was expanded to include articles on the Marxist theory of nationalities, the history and present status of nationality groups in Communist China (and their languages), official Chinese Communist policies toward minority groups, and translations of articles published in the Soviet Union and other Soviet bloc countries on ethnography. Tables of contents in Chinese, Russian, and English.

For selected translations from this journal, see next entry.

902 U.S. Joint Publications Research Service.

Articles from the Chinese Communist Periodical 'Min-tsu yen-chiu'. Washington, D.C., July 1959–March 1960. Irregular.

Translation of selected articles from *Min-tsu yen-chiu* (see preceding entry). Mimeographed.

The following numbers of the J.P.R.S. reports are special issues of this title:

MIN-TSU YEN-CHIU NO.	J.P.R.S. NO.	DATE OF PUBLICATION	U.S.G.P.O. MONTHLY CATALOG NO.
No. 3, 1958	848D	7–31–59	1959–12892
No. 4, 1958	879D	8–18–59	14817
No. 1, 1959	871D	8–14–59	14809
No. 3, 1959	843D	7–27–59	12888
No. 4, 1959	862D	8–17–59	14804
No. 7, 1959	998D	11– 4–59	17561
No. 8, 9, 1959	1144D	2– 5–60	1960– 3999
No. 10, 1959	3001	2–22–60	5554
No. 11, 1959	3130	3–31–60	7207

903 Pei-ching ta-hsüeh hsüeh pao: Jen-wen k'o-hsüeh 北京大學學報：人文科學
(Journal of Peking University: Humanities). Peking: Pei-ching ta-hsüeh, 1955
No. 1— (No. 1—), July 1955—. Quarterly.

A scholarly journal edited by Chien Po-tsan 翦伯贊 and published by the
Peking University. Tables of contents in Chinese, Russian and English appear
in each issue. Annual subject index.

904 Shih-chieh chih-shih 世界知識
(World Knowledge). Shanghai, Peking: Shih-chieh chih-shih she, Vol. 1, No.
1—, September 1934—. Semi-monthly.

A leading periodical on international relations, *Shih-chieh chih-shih* is one of
the very few pre-1949 publications in China which continued in existence after
1949. Originally published by the Sheng-huo shu-tien 生活書店 (Life Publishing Company) under the editorship of Hu Yü-chih 胡愈之 (now one of
the vice ministers of culture of Communist China), the periodical has been
published successively in Shanghai (1937–1938), Hankow (1938), and Hong
Kong (1938–1941). Publication was suspended between January 1942 and
August 1945, resumed in September 1945 in Shanghai, and in Peking in May
1950 (Vol. 21, No. 17). Published as a weekly between 1946 and December 1952.
An annual subject index has appeared in recent years.

The articles contained in *Shih-chieh chih-shih* have been consistently critical
of the West in general, and of imperialism and colonialism in particular.

905 Shih-k'an 詩刊
(Poetry). Peking: Jen-min wen-hsüeh ch'u-pan she 人民文學出版社, 1957 No.
1— (No. 1—), January 1957—. Monthly.

A specialized publication devoted to modern Chinese poetry, including
original works, translations and theoretical discussions. Poems in traditional
literary style are published occasionally. Tsang K'o-chia 臧克家 is the chief
editor. No index.

906 Shih-p'in kung-yeh 食品工業
(Food Industry). Peking: Ch'ing kung-yeh ch'u-pan she 輕工業出版社, 1957
No. 1— (No. 1—), January 1957—. Semi-monthly.

An official publication of the Ministry of Light Industry, containing government regulations and directives pertaining to food processing, as well as technical
reports and articles on management (especially in the communes since 1958).
The journal was published as a monthly prior to 1959, at which time it absorbed
the following three 'internal publications' also issued by the Ministry of Light
Industry: *Jang-tsao chien-hsün* 釀造簡訊 (Brewing News), *T'ang-yeh chien-hsün*
糖業簡訊 (Sugar Industry News), and *Yen-ts'ao kung-yeh chien-hsün* 烟草工業簡訊
(Tobacco Industry News).

907 Ti-li chih-shih 地理知識

(Geographical Knowledge). Nanking, Peking: K'o-hsüeh ch'u-pan she 科學出版社, Vol. 1, No. 1—, January 1950—. Monthly.

Edited jointly by the Institute of Geography of the Chinese Academy of Sciences 中國科學院地理研究所 and the Chinese Geographical Society 中國地理學會, *Ti-li chih-shih* contains articles on the human and physical geography of China, together with maps, book reviews and photographs. Articles on the instruction of geography in the schools appear in its pages, and, in general, the journal provides much information on construction projects (e.g., railways, plants, dams, etc.). Between the years 1953 and 1958 inclusive, there was provided a one-page bi-monthly index to geographical literature in Chinese Communist periodicals. Annual subject index.

908 Ti-li hsüeh-pao 地理學報

Acta Geographica Sinica. Nanking, Chungking, Peking: K'o-hsüeh ch'u-pan she 科學出版社, Vol. 1, No. 1—, September 1934—. Quarterly.

The official publication of the Chinese Geographical Society, *Acta Geographica Sinica* carries primarily articles on China's physical and economic geography and geology. It has been successively published in Nanking, Chungking, and Peking. Issued as a quarterly through Volume 4 (1934–1937), the journal appeared annually from Volume 5 to Volume 14 (1938–1947), and again as a quarterly from Volume 15 (1948) to the present time. Recent issues carry a combined Russian-English table of contents in addition to that in Chinese. Some articles are accompanied by English or Russian summaries. An annual cumulative table of contents since 1949 (?).

909 Ts'ai-cheng 財政

(Finance). Peking: Ts'ai-cheng ch'u-pan she 財政出版社, 1956 No. 1— (No. 1—), October 1956—. Semi-monthly.

Originally issued to publicize government financial policies and to provide a medium for the discussion of administrative experiences and theoretical questions. *Ts'ai-cheng* absorbed *Jen-min shui-wu* 人民稅務 (People's Taxation; see **890**) in January 1959, and expanded its coverage to include financial management in various enterprises and businesses, financial management in the communes, and tax affairs. Published as a monthly prior to the No. 9 issue of 1958. Annual subject index.

910 Tu-shu 讀書

(Book Readers). Peking, No. 1—, July 1955—. Semi-monthly.

Superseded *Tu-shu yüeh-pao* 讀書月報 (Book Readers Monthly) in April 1958. A bibliographical journal for the general public, containing book reviews, review articles and publication news (both Mainland and overseas). A list of new publications, arranged according to topical categories, appears in each issue.

911   T'u-shu kuan 圖書館

(Libraries). Peking: Pei-ching t'u-shu kuan 北京圖書館, 1961(?) No. 1—, 1961(?)—. Quarterly.

Supersedes the next entry. Intended for librarians working in universities, technical institutes, and special libraries, it contains articles on both library administration and technical organization, book reviews, reports on biblio-graphical work in progress in various Chinese libraries. In addition to coverage of library activities in China, the journal carries news briefs on foreign libraries (mostly Russian and East European). Annual cumulative index in last issue of each year.

The leading library journal in Communist China, published by the National Library of Peking.

912   T'u-shu kuan hsüeh t'ung-hsün 圖書館學通訊

(Library Science Bulletin). Peking: Pei-ching t'u-shu kuan 北京圖書館, 1957 No. 1–1961 (?), April 1957–1961 (?).

The predecessor to the preceding entry. Published as a bi-monthly prior to January 1959, the journal was issued as an 'internal publication' in 1957. A subject index to all 1957 and 1958 issues is available in the No. 6 issue of 1958 (December 1958).

913   T'u-shu kuan kung-tso 圖書館工作

(Library Work). Peking: Pei-ching t'u-shu kuan 北京圖書館, 1955 No. 1—, February 1955—. Monthly.

A library journal published by the National Library of Peking primarily for those working in school libraries and libraries in rural areas, in factory libraries and in public libraries up to the *hsien* (縣) level, and in other 'mass' libraries. The journal publishes reports on the activities and problems of these institutions, and frequently includes articles on librarianship and bibliography. Publication has been on a bi-monthly basis from 1955 to 1956 inclusive. Annual subject index in the December issue of each year.

For more advanced professional publications, see the preceding entries.

914   T'ung-chi kung-tso 統計工作

(Statistical Work). Peking: Chi-hua t'ung-chi tsa-chih she 計劃統計雜誌社, 1957 No. 1–1958 No. 24, January 1957–December 1958. Semi-monthly.

The official organ of the State Statistical Bureau 國家統計局, containing official documents concerning statistical work in Communist China (regulations, reports, data, etc.), as well as case studies, discussions of specific problems and methods, book reviews, and related information designed primarily for the guidance of cadres engaged in statistical work. Superseding the next entry, this publication was merged with *Chi-hua ching-chi* 計劃經濟 (Planned Economy; see **855**) to become *Chi-hua yü t'ung-chi* 計劃與統計 (Planning and Statistics) as of January 1959 (**856**).

915 **T'ung-chi kung-tso t'ung-hsün** 統計工作通訊
(Statistical Work Bulletin). Peking: Chi-hua t'ung-chi tsa-chih she 計劃統計雜誌社, 1954 No. 1–1956 No. 24, April 1954–December 1956. Semi-monthly.

An official publication of the State Statistical Bureau 國家統計局 containing theoretical articles on statistics, official statistical data and reports, local surveys, etc. Twenty-four issues were published (as a monthly in 1955 and 1956).
Superseded by the preceding entry.

916 **T'ung-chi yen-chiu** 統計研究
(Statistical Studies). Peking: T'ung-chi ch'u-pan she 統計出版社, Nos. 1–9, January–September 1958. Monthly.

Contains theoretical articles on statistics, official articles on statistics, official documents and reports on statistical work, and discussions of specific case studies. Nine issues were published (index in No. 9). The journal was absorbed by *T'ung-chi kung-tso* 統計工作 (Statistical Work) in October 1958 (see **914**).

917 **Wen-tzu kai-ko** 文字改革
(Language Reform). Peking: Wen-tzu kai-ko ch'u-pan she 文字改革出版社, 1956 No. 1— (No. 1—), August 1956—. Monthly.

Formerly published under the title *P'in-yin* 拼音 (Romanization), August 1956–July 1957, *Wen-tzu kai-ko* was designed to be a forum for the discussion of the technical implications of the new romanization system sponsored by the Chinese Communist government. Since August 1957 it has appeared under the present title, and the coverage has been expanded to include articles on the simplification of the Chinese characters, and the popularization of the teaching and use of Mandarin. Government decrees as well as reports on conferences on language reform also frequently are published.
Published as a semi-monthly from August 1958 to 1961 inclusive. Annual subject index.

918 **Wen-wu** 文物
(Cultural Relics). Peking: Wen-wu ch'u-pan she 文物出版社, 1950 No. 1— (No. 1—), January 1950—. Monthly.

The official publication of the Cultural Relics Bureau of the Ministry of Culture 文化部文物局, *Wen-wu* publishes archeological survey and excavation reports, descriptive articles on discoveries, reports on museums, and descriptions of historical documents relating to the Chinese Communist movement. Published under the title *Wen-wu ts'an-k'ao tzu-liao* 文物參考資料 (Reference Materials on Cultural Relics) from 1950 to 1958 inclusive. Profusely illustrated. Annual subject index.

919   **Wu-Han ta-hsüeh jen-wen k'o-hsüeh hsüeh-pao** 武漢大學人文科學學報 (Wuhan University Journal of Humanities). Wuhan: Wu-Han ta-hsüeh, 1956 No. 1— (No. 1—), May (?) 1956—. Irregular.

A general scholarly journal published by the Wuhan University. The following are special issues for 1959: Nos. 3 and 7 (library science); No. 4 (history); No. 5 (economics); No. 6 (language and literature).

920   **Yin-yüeh yen-chiu** 音樂研究
(Studies in Music). Peking: Yin-yüeh ch'u-pan she 音樂出版社, 1958 No. 1— (No. 1—), February 1958—. Bi-monthly.

The leading music journal in Communist China. While it does not publish actual scores, it does include articles on theory, technique, and instruments, musical criticism, and studies on traditional Chinese music (including Chinese opera). Book reviews and news of musical activities frequently appear in its pages. Annual subject index.

2. ENGLISH LANGUAGE

This section contains a fairly complete alphabetical listing of current as well as defunct English-language periodicals from the Mainland. The most important single periodical is the *Peking Review* (successor to the *China Digest* and *People's China*, **930**) which interprets for the English-speaking world the official Chinese Communist viewpoint on international as well as domestic affairs. The journal regularly carries translations of leading editorials and articles published in the main party organs, the People's Daily and Red Flag in particular.

Several of the titles included in this section are organs of mass organizations published for foreign consumption, such as *Evergreen* (**929**) and *Chinese Youth Bulletin* (**928**), published by the All-China Youth Federation and the All-China Students' Federation, respectively; *Women of China* (**936**), issued by the All-China Women's Federation; and *The Chinese Trade Unions* (**927**) by the All-China Federation of Trade Unions. Noteworthy also is the monthly *Chinese Literature* (**926**). Less useful are the popular propaganda magazines, such as *China Pictorial* or *China Reconstructs* (**922** and **923**).

Included here also are two scientific publications of general interest: *Scientia Sinica* and *Science Record* (**935** and **934**). *The Science Abstracts of China* (**932**) is accompanied, for convenience, by the *KWIC Index* to that publication prepared at the Massachusetts Institute of Technology (**933**).

Not listed here are the various publications of the Communist Chinese diplomatic missions, such as *China Today* (India), or *Bulletin d'Information* (Switzerland).

Foreign Trade of the People's Republic of China is described in Chapter VI (**321**).

921 China Digest. Hong Kong, Vol. 1, No. 1–Vol. 7, No. 9, December 31, 1946–February 1, 1950. Fortnightly.

The predecessor of *People's China* (see **931**), published from December 31, 1946 to February 1, 1950, on a fortnightly basis.

922 China Pictorial. Peking, No. 1—, January 1951—. Semi-monthly.

A Chinese Communist popular illustrated magazine published currently in eighteen languages. Monthly through 1958; semi-monthly from 1959.

923 China Reconstructs. Peking, No. 1—, January/February 1952—. Monthly.

Published by the China Welfare Institute on a bi-monthly basis through 1954, monthly since January 1955, *China Reconstructs* contains illustrated articles on conditions in Mainland China, chiefly for foreign consumption. Supplements and annual index. Numbering: 1–6, January/February–November/December 1952; No. 1–6, January/February–November/December 1953; Vol. 3, No. 1–January/February 1954—.

924 China Weekly Review. Shanghai: Millard Publishing Company, Vols. 1–124, 1917–1953.

Published weekly through Vol. 118, No. 10 (August 5, 1950), the periodical became the *China Monthly Review* with Vol. 119, No. 1 (September, 1950). Of particular interest are the following regular features: 'Who's Who in China' (one biographical sketch), 'People in the News', 'Events in Brief', 'What Chinese Papers Say', and 'Chinese Magazine Roundup'.

The foreign-owned publishing company also issued translations from the Chinese press (see **1069** and **1070**), as well as the *Monthly Report*, a resumé and analysis of political, military and economic developments in China (Vol. 1, September 1946 to Vol. 8, 1950).

925 China's Sports. Peking: 1957 (?)—. Bi-monthly.

A bi-monthly sports magazine. Each issue consists of about thirty-two pages, profusely illustrated.

926 Chinese Literature. Peking, 1951—. Monthly.

A monthly edited by Mao Tun, carrying stories, poems, prose and literary criticism. Also publishes regularly selections from the old classics and pieces of modern Chinese literature written since 1919.

927 The Chinese Trade Unions. [Peking]: All-China Federation of Trade Unions, 1951—. Monthly.

The official organ of the All-China Federation of Trade Unions published in English, reporting on labor conditions and the trade union movement on the Mainland.

928 Chinese Youth Bulletin. Peking: All-China Youth Federation and All-China Students' Federation, Vol. 1, No. 1—, 1958 (?)—. Irregular.

A two to four-page official publication of the All-China Youth Federation and All-China Students' Federation in Peking. The *Bulletin* reports current youth and student activities in Communist China, and occasionally includes a supplement devoted to official policy statements on current affairs. The contents of the *Bulletin* are similar to, though less comprehensive than, those of *Evergreen* (see next entry). Volumes 1 and 2 were published under title *Information Bulletin*.

929 Evergreen. Peking, 1957—. Bi-monthly.

An official publication of the All-China Youth Federation and All-China Students' Federation. Contains occasional translations of documents.

930 Peking Review. Peking, Vol. 1, No. 1—, March 4, 1958—. Weekly.

A weekly magazine containing articles on current developments in Communist China and Chinese Communist views on international affairs. Also publishes translations of important articles, editorials, and documents from the *Jen-min jih-pao* (People's Daily) and *Hung-ch'i* (Red Flag). Superseded *People's China* (see next entry). Semi-annual subject index.

The most important English-language periodical published on the Mainland.

931 People's China. Peking, January 1, 1950–December 16, 1957. Semi-monthly.

A semi-monthly predecessor of the *Peking Review* (see preceding entry). Numbering: Vol. 1, No. 1–Vol. 4, No. 12 (January 1, 1950–December 16, 1951); 1952 No. 1–1957 No. 24 (January 1, 1952–December 16, 1957). Supersedes *China Digest* (see **921**). Subject index.

932 Science Abstracts of China. Peking: Chung-kuo k'o-hsüeh yüan, K'o-hsüeh chi-shu ch'ing-pao yen-chiu so 中國科學院 科學技術情報研究所 (Chinese Academy of Sciences, Institute of Scientific and Technical Information), October 1958—. Bi-monthly.

Issued in five separate series: biological sciences, chemistry and chemical technology, earth sciences, mathematical and physical sciences, and technical sciences. Each series is further divided into subsections by subject. The abstracts are in English, and are accompanied by complete bibliographical information, together with Chinese characters for the author, title, and journal references. Publications of the *Abstracts* is believed to have ceased. For an index to the *Abstracts*, see next entry.

933 Massachusetts Institute of Technology Libraries.
KWIC Index to the Science Abstracts of China. First edition. Cambridge, Mass.,
1960. 154p.

An index to the *Science Abstracts of China* (see preceding entry).

This index, prepared by computer for the Symposium on the Sciences of
Communist China held by the American Association for the Advancement of
Science in December 1960, is a key word and author index to all issues of the
Science Abstracts of China available in the United States. It provides reference
to 3,300 current Communist scientific and technical papers.

In three parts: (1) an alphabetical listing of key words-in-context for each
significant word that appears in the titles of the papers abstracted in the *Science
Abstracts of China;* (2) a listing by author of all items including full title, source
and bibliographic data (plus the romanization of the Chinese journal title, a
notation for locating the English abstracts in the *Science Abstracts of China* and a
notation for the M.I.T. Library holdings); (3) an index of the authors of papers
included in the publication along with the codes for the entries in the bibliography.

The most comprehensive index of its kind.

934 Science Record. Peking: K'o-hsüeh ch'u-pan she 科學出版社, Vol. 1, No.
1—, 1957—. Monthly.

Articles in English, Russian, French and German on scientific research
conducted in Mainland China in the natural and physical sciences, and technology. In general the material is less technical than that appearing in the *Scientia
Sinica* (see next entry). There is also a Chinese edition of this publication,
K'o-hsüeh chi-lu 科學紀錄. An earlier series was published between 1942 and
1952 (?).

935 Scientia Sinica. Peking: K'o-hsüeh ch'u-pan she 科學出版社, Vol. 1, No.
1—, 1952—. Monthly.

A monthly compilation of advanced papers on scientific and technological
research in Mainland China, edited by the Bureau of Compilation and Translation of the Chinese Academy of Sciences. Most of the articles are in English;
some are in Russian, French or German.

936 Women of China. Peking, 1952—. Bi-monthly.

A bi-monthly magazine of about 40 pages with illustrations, published by the
All-China Women's Federation, containing articles on the status and role of
women in Communist China.

3. OTHER LANGUAGES

From the Foreign Languages Press in Peking comes a ceaseless flow of publications—
including periodicals—in some eighteen languages, among them such familiar titles

as *China Pictorial* and *China Reconstructs*, the English-language editions of which have been described in the preceding section. The Japanese edition of *People's China* (*Jimmin Chūgoku*), first published in Peking and subsequently transferred to Tokyo, is described along with the other Japanese-language periodicals in Chapter XXI (**1150**).

Inasmuch as this Guide is directed primarily at an English-speaking public, it does not list the periodicals published in Peking in foreign languages other than English. An exception was made in the case of Russian-language periodicals, because of the importance of Sino-Soviet relations, and the organ of the Sino-Soviet Friendship Association is listed below. (The Chinese-language Soviet counterpart published in Moscow by the Society of Soviet-Chinese Friendship is described in Chapter XXI, **1212**.)

937 Druzhba

(Friendship). Peking: Chung-Su yu-hao hsieh-hui 中蘇友好協會, Nos. 1–145 (?), October 1957–July 1960. Weekly.

The Russian-language organ of the Sino-Soviet Friendship Association. It absorbed the newspaper of the same title (published from April 15, 1955 to October 1, 1957) and *Narodnyi Kitai* (People's China), the bi-weekly Russian-language edition of *People's China* published by the Foreign Languages Press in Peking from November 1950 to September 1957. The distribution of *Druzhba* in the Soviet Union was abruptly suspended in July 1960, following the worsening of relations between the Communist parties of China and the Soviet Union at the Bucharest Conference in June 1960.

CHAPTER XVIII

TAIWAN PUBLICATIONS

Following the retrocession of Formosa to China at the end of the Second World War, the new Chinese Nationalist administration faced the necessity of replacing Japanese with Chinese as the national language. The most efficient road to this end was the development of the mass communications media—newspapers, periodicals and radio—but in the early postwar years very few newspapers and periodicals were published in Taiwan. This situation changed over night with the removal of the seat of the Nationalist government from the Mainland to Taipei in 1949. The day-to-day publications associated with a functioning government (central, provincial and local) began to proliferate. The Kuomintang stepped up its large-scale publishing activity for information, indoctrination and propaganda purposes. The affiliated mass organizations, like their counterparts on the Mainland, began to publish their official organs. The two million people who came with the government to Taiwan sought new sources of information, and to fill this need many publications, including literary journals, significantly swelled the total periodicals output. Thus, from some 150 periodicals (excluding government gazettes) registered with the Ministry of Interior in 1950, the total number of periodicals published in 1963 had become almost seven hundred.

According to the 1963–1964 English edition of the *China Yearbook*, a total of twenty-eight Chinese-language and two English-language newspapers were being published as of June 1963. Of these newspapers and periodicals a number of the most important and representative titles in both Chinese and English are selected for inclusion in this chapter. Official gazettes such as *Tsung-t'ung fu kung-pao* (Bulletin of the Office of the President, **676**) and *Wai-chiao pu kung-pao* (Gazette of the Ministry of Foreign Affairs, **830**) are described in the appropriate chapters of the documentary Part Three.

For comprehensive listings of titles, see the Chinese edition of the *China Yearbook* (**239**), the Journalism Yearbook of the Republic of China (**247**) and the 1954 Chinese Periodicals Yearbook (**248**). Reference is also made to the *Directory of the Cultural Organizations of the Republic of China* (**341**).

In addition to the regular newspapers and periodicals, this chapter also has a special section containing a number of Chinese and English-language periodicals and serial compilations concerned exclusively with the Mainland.

A. NEWSPAPERS

I. CHINESE-LANGUAGE

Included in the next two sections are five major Chinese and the two English-language newspapers currently published in Taiwan. The *Chung-yang jih-pao—Central Daily News* (first entry) is the most important, being the organ of the Kuomintang and the Nationalist government. The *T'ai-wan hsin-sheng pao* (Taiwan New Life Daily, second entry), an official organ of the Taiwan Provincial Government, concentrates on local news. The *Lien-ho pao—United Daily News* (**940**) appeals to the intellectuals and has a significant following, while the *Chen-hsin hsin-wen pao* (Financial and Economic News, **941**) is a reputable financial daily. The *Kung-lun pao—Public Opinion Daily News* (**942**) is a privately owned independent publication, as are the two English-language newspapers, *China Post* and *China News*, both catering to the foreign community. It might be noted, parenthetically, that the Library of Congress has been filming the files of *Chung-yang jih-pao* and the *T'ai-wan hsin-sheng pao* since 1950.

The Journalism Yearbook of the Republic of China provides short descriptions of the history of each paper, as does the Chinese edition of the *China Yearbook*. The 1962 edition of the latter also contains a list of all newspapers published in Taiwan. All of the Chinese-language newspapers listed in this section as well as the *Chung-hua jih-pao* (China Daily News, **696**) since 1962 have been indexed in the *Classified Index to Chinese Newspapers* (see **194a**).

Some of the more important editorials and articles appearing in the following and other major newspapers and periodicals in Taiwan are translated for the *Press and Publications Summary* published by the United States Information Service in Taipei (see **1074**).

938   Chung-yang jih-pao 中央日報

Central Daily News. Nanking, Chungking, Taipei, No. 1—, February 1, 1929—.

The official organ of the Kuomintang, the four-page *Central Daily News* (international airmail edition) carries both national and international news, official documents, and a number of supplements. Originally published in Nanking, it was moved to Chungking in September 1938. Publication continued at Chungking until September 10, 1945, at which time the newspaper moved back to Nanking. Publication on the Mainland ceased on April 23, 1949, when the Communist forces took the city. The Taipei edition was launched prior to that, on March 12, 1949, with continuous numbering. No index.

An indispensable source for the study of Nationalist China.

939   T'ai-wan hsin-sheng pao 臺灣新生報

(Taiwan New Life Daily). Taipei, No. 1—, October 25, 1945—.

The official organ of the Taiwan Provincial Government, *Hsin-sheng pao* was the first newspaper published by the Chinese government following the retrocession of Taiwan to the Republic of China, succeeding the Japanese-language *Taiwan shimpō* 臺灣新報. The eight-page daily is devoted primarily to local news. No index.

940   Lien-ho pao 聯合報

United Daily News. Taipei, No. 1—, September 16, 1951—.

An amalgamation of three privately owned newspapers: the *Ch'üan-min jih-pao* 全民日報 (All People's Daily), the *Min-tsu pao* 民族報 (The Nation), and the

Ching-chi shih-pao 經濟時報 (Economic Times). The independent eight-page *Lien-ho pao* has a slight emphasis on cultural and educational affairs, and carries a daily literary supplement, and an entertainment page. No index.

941 Cheng-hsin hsin-wen pao 徵信新聞報
(Financial and Economic News). Taipei, No. 1—, October 2, 1950—. Daily.

Originally published as a mimeographed sheet, the *Cheng-hsin hsin-wen pao* has grown into a regular four-page daily newspaper devoted to the reporting of economic and financial news and market quotations. No index.

942 Kung-lun pao 公論報
Public Opinion Daily News. Taipei, No. 1—, October 25, 1947—.

An independent newspaper originally owned by a native Taiwanese, the *Kung-lun pao* has expanded from a two-page to an eight-page daily. It carries mostly local news; and prior to its reorganization in 1961, it was highly critical editorially of the Nationalist government. No index.

2. ENGLISH-LANGUAGE

943 China Post. Taipei, No. 1—, September 3, 1952—.

The privately owned six-page *China Post*, one of the two English-language newspapers published in Taiwan primarily for the foreign community (the other is *China News*, see next entry), carries both national and international news, and publishes a special colored supplement four times a year. No index.

944 China News. Taipei, No. 1—, June 6, 1949—.

The *China News*, one of the two English-language newspapers published in Taiwan primarily for the foreign community (the other is *China Post*, see preceding entry), carries both national and international news. In mimeographed form until July 1, 1960, when it began to appear in a printed edition in four pages. The paper is privately owned, but a number of staff members are affiliated with the Kuomintang. No index.

B. PERIODICALS

1. CHINESE-LANGUAGE

As mentioned above, nearly seven hundred Chinese-language periodicals are being published in Taiwan. Included here are thirty-seven which are important or representative titles dealing in one way or another with the contemporary period. Thus, important publications of only historical interest, such as the *Chuan-chi wen-hsüeh* (Biographical Literature), or those dealing with traditional Chinese studies, such as

Ta-lu tsa-chih (The Mainland Magazine), *Wen-shih-che hsüeh-pao* (Bulletin of the College of Arts, National Taiwan University) and similar publications of the Academia Sinica, are not included.

The periodicals described below fall into a number of categories: publications for the general public, semi-official publications of the various branches of the government (official gazettes are listed in Part Three), organs of political parties and mass organizations, economic journals, literary publications, and scholarly journals.

Perhaps the chief distinguishing characteristic of Taiwan periodicals when compared with those published on the Mainland is the abundance of magazines for the general public. Only a few of these are listed here: *Cheng-lun chou-k'an—China Critic* (**945**), *Chung-kuo i-chou—China Newsweek* (**954**), *Hsin shih-tai—New Age* (**964**), and *Tzu-yu Chung-kuo—Free China* (**979**).

Among the semi-official publications of the government as well as periodicals in the fields of government, politics and law, titles such as the following are included: *Chung-kuo nei-cheng* (Domestic Affairs of China, **956**); *Min-chu hsien-cheng—The Democratic Constitutionalist* (**969**); *Chung-kuo ti-fang tzu-chih* (Chinese Local Government, **957**); *Chung-kuo hai-chün—Chinese Navy* (**953**) and *Chung-kuo ti k'ung-chün— Chinese Air Force* (**958**); *Min-chu ch'ao—Current Democracy* (**968**) and *Hsin Chung-kuo p'ing-lun—New China Review* (**963**), the official organs of the two factions of the Youth Party; *Chung-hua fu-nü—China's Women* (**951**), the official organ of the Chinese Women's Anti-Aggression League headed by Madame Chiang Kai-shek; and *Ch'iao-wu yüeh-pao* (Overseas Chinese Affairs Monthly, **946**), an official publication of the Overseas Chinese Affairs Commission.

In the economic field, the leading journal is *T'ai-wan yin-hang chi-k'an* (Bank of Taiwan Quarterly, **975**), although its coverage is limited to Taiwan's economy. Other important periodicals include *T'u-ti kai-ko—Land Reform Monthly* (**978**), which carried articles on the highly successful land reform program in Taiwan; *Ts'ai-cheng ching-chi yüeh-k'an—The Financial and Economic Monthly* (**977**); *Chung-kuo ching-chi —The China Economist* (**952**), and *Kung-shang yüeh-k'an—The Industry and Commerce Monthly* (**966**), an organ of the Association of Industry and Commerce.

Two titles each are included in the fields of education and literature: *Chiao-yü yü wen-hua—Education and Culture* (**947**), *T'ai-wan chiao-yü—Taiwan Education Review* (**973**), *Wen-hsüeh tsa-chih—Literary Review* (**980**) and *Wen-t'an* (Literary Forum, **981**). One title of general interest in the field of science, *K'o-hsüeh chiao-yü—Science Education* (**965**), appears here, as do three academic journals: *The Tsing Hua Journal of Chinese Studies* (**949**), *The National Chengchi University Journal* (**967**), and the *Journal of Social Science*, published by the College of Law of the National Taiwan University (**970**).

For more comprehensive listing of periodical titles published in Taiwan, consult the Chinese edition of the *China Yearbook* (**239**) and the *Chung-hua min-kuo tsa-chih nien-chien* (Chinese Periodicals Yearbook, **248**). The latter provides background information on the periodicals published as of 1954 and also carries an index to the periodicals. Two other important periodical indexes to Taiwan periodicals are the *Chung-wen ch'i-k'an lun-wen fen-lei so-yin—Classified Index to Chinese Periodicals* (see **192**), compiled by the National Taiwan University Library, and the *Ch'i-k'an lun-wen* *so-yin—Chinese Periodicals Index* (**193**), prepared by the National War College Library. Selected translations of editorial comments from some of the periodicals listed in this section are available in the *Press and Translations Summary* published by the United States Information Service in Taipei (see **1074**).

Government-sponsored periodical publications concerned exclusively with Mainland China (both in Chinese and in English) are listed in special sections below.

945 Cheng-lun chou-k'an 政論週刊
China Critic. Taipei: Chung-kuo hsin-wen ch'u-pan she 中國新聞出版社, Nos. 1–185, May 1953–August 1958. Weekly.

A general periodical published successively under the titles *San-min chu-i pan-yüeh-k'an* 三民主義半月刊 (Three People's Principles Semi-Monthly), Nos. 1–40, May 1953–December 1954; *Chu-i yü kuo-ts'e* 主義與國策 (Principles and National Policy), Nos. 41–77, January 1955–July 1956; and *Cheng-lun chou-k'an* 政論週刊 (China Critic Weekly), Nos. 78–185, July 1956–August 1958. Publication is believed to have ceased with No. 185. Indexed in the *Classified Index to Chinese Periodicals* (Nos. 1–76 only); see **192**.

946 Ch'iao-wu yüeh-pao 僑務月報
(Overseas Chinese Affairs Monthly). Taipei: Ch'iao-wu yüeh-pao she 僑務月報社, No. 1—, July 1952—. Monthly.

An official publication of the Overseas Chinese Affairs Commission of the Republic of China, *Ch'iao-wu yüeh-pao* publishes reports on the activities of the Chinese residing in foreign countries as well as those who have returned to Taiwan (especially students). Official policies and regulations concerning the Overseas Chinese are regularly published, as are anti-Communist articles on conditions on the Mainland. No index.

947 Chiao-yü yü wen-hua 教育與文化
Education and Culture. Taipei: Chiao-yü yü wen-hua chou-k'an she 教育與文化週刊社, Vol. 1, No. 1— (No. 1—), June 1950—. Semi-monthly.

A general education periodical containing articles (including translations) on educational theory and practice, and domestic and foreign educational and cultural activities. Published under the title *Chiao-yü t'ung-hsün* 教育通訊 (Educational Bulletin) from June 1950 through December 1954. No index. A semi-official publication.

948 Ching-min tao-pao 警民導報
Police and People Gazette. Taipei: Ching-min tao-pao she, No. 1—, August 1949—. Three times a month.

Contains articles (including translations) on police work in general and police administration and police problems in Taiwan in particular. Reports on Taiwan police activities are included in each issue, as are interpretations of police regulations. The earlier issues also included pertinent laws and regulations affecting the work of the police. No index.

949 Ch'ing-hua hsüeh-pao 清華學報
Tsing Hua Journal of Chinese Studies. Taipei: Ch'ing-hua hsüeh-pao she 清華學報社, New Series Vol. 1, No. 1—, June 1956—. Annual.

The *Journal*, one of the leading scholarly publications in Taiwan, is similar to the old series published by Tsing Hua University in Peiping in its emphasis on the humanities and social sciences. Articles are written in both Chinese and English (many by Chinese scholars now residing in the United States); Chinese articles are accompanied by English abstracts and vice versa. An English table of contents appears in each isuse. Indexed in the *Classified Index to Chinese Periodicals* (see **192**).

950 Chün-fa chuan-k'an 軍法專刊
The Military Law Journal. Taipei, Vol. 1, No. 1—, May 1, 1952—. Monthly.

Carries texts of current military laws and regulations, interpretations, court decisions, and similar legal materials. Annual subject index.

951 Chung-hua fu-nü 中華婦女
China's Women. Taipei: Chung-hua fu-nü fan-kung k'ang-O lien-ho hui 中華婦女反共抗俄聯合會, Vol. 1, No. 1—, July 1950—. Monthly.

The official organ of the Chinese Women's Anti-Aggression League. It regularly carries reports of the activities of the League in addition to short stories and matters of interest to women, such as family, hygiene, etc. No index.

952 Chung-kuo ching-chi 中國經濟
The China Economist. Taipei: Chung-kuo ching-chi yüeh-k'an she 中國經濟月刊社, No. 1—, October 1950—. Monthly.

Contains articles on economic theory and domestic and foreign economic conditions. Included in each issue are news briefs concerning economic activity in Taiwan and abroad, as well as Taiwan economic statistics. Indexed in the *Classified Index to Chinese Periodicals* (see **192**). A private publication.

953 Chung-kuo hai-chün 中國海軍
Chinese Navy. Nanking, Taipei: Chung-kuo hai-chün yüeh-k'an she 中國海軍月刊社, Vol. 1, No. 1—, March 1947—. Monthly.

A semi-official publication of the Chinese Navy containing reports on the activities and development of the Chinese Navy, personal narratives concerning engagements with Chinese Communist naval forces in the Formosa Straits, and technical articles (mostly translations) on naval engineering. Published in Nanking between 1947 and 1949; in Taipei starting with Vol. 3, No. 1 (January 1950). Photographs. No index.

954 **Chung-kuo i-chou** 中國一週
China Newsweek. Taipei: Chung-kuo hsin-wen ch'u-pan kung-ssu 中國新聞 出版公司, No. 1—, May 1950—. Weekly.

A semi-official popular magazine, general in scope, with a slight emphasis on China's cultural heritage. Events in Taiwan and the Mainland are covered in brief news reports. No published index. A card-file index to this periodical from its first issue is available at the library of the National Taiwan University.

955 **Chung-kuo lao-kung** 中國勞工
(China Labor). Taipei: Chung-kuo lao-kung ch'u-pan she 中國勞工出版社, No. 1—, November 1950—. Semi-monthly.

A popular periodical principally devoted to the discussion of and reporting on labor conditions in Taiwan. Government policies and the proceedings of labor conferences are frequently included. Coverage is also extended to labor conditions in foreign countries, especially those in the United States. No index.

956 **Chung-kuo nei-cheng** 中國內政
(Domestic Affairs of China). Taipei: Chung-kuo nei-cheng she 中國內政社 Vol. 1, No. 1—, January 1951—. Monthly.

A semi-official publication of the Ministry of Interior, *Chung-kuo nei-cheng* carries articles on the domestic policies of the Republic of China and of other countries, with an emphasis on social conditions. Reports on political activities in Taiwan at the *hsien* and municipal levels are frequently included. Published in each issue is a special documents section containing relevant laws and regulations (and interpretations), official lists of books licensed for publication, drugs licensed for sale, etc. No index.

957 **Chung-kuo ti-fang tzu-chih** 中國地方自治
Chinese Local Government. Taipei: Chung-kuo ti-fang tzu-chih yüeh-k'an she 中國地方自治月刊社, Vol. 1, No. 1— (No. 1—), June 1953—. Monthly.

The official organ of the Chinese Society for the Study of Local Self-Government 中國地方自治學會 carrying articles on the theory and organization of local government, with special emphasis on the status and problems of self-government in Taiwan. Published semi-monthly from Vol. 1 through Vol. 11 (June 1953–January 1959). No index except for the volumes bound by the publisher. A semi-official publication.

958 Chung-kuo ti k'ung-chün 中國的空軍
Chinese Air Force. Taipei: Chung-kuo ti k'ung-chün ch'u-pan she 中國的空軍
出版社, No. 1—, January 1938—. Monthly.

A semi-official publication of the Chinese Air Force carrying reports on the
activities and development of the C.A.F., biographical sketches of prominent
personnel, personal accounts of air battles, and occasional technical articles on
aeronautics, both original and translated. Published successively in Hankow,
Chengtu, and Nanking prior to 1949, when publication was suspended, to be
resumed in January 1950 in Taipei. Photographs. No index.

959 Chung-kuo t'u-shu kuan hsüeh-hui hui-pao 中國圖書館學會會報
Bulletin of the Library Association of China. Taipei: Chung-kuo t'u-shu kuan
hsüeh-hui, No. 1—, 1953(?)—. Irregular.

The official bulletin of the Library Association of China, containing articles
on library administration, technical services, library education, and Chinese
bibliography, as well as reports on various university and public libraries in
Taiwan. The *Bulletin* also covers the activities of the association. Chinese and
English tables of contents. Issues after No. 3 are indexed in the *Classified Index
to Chinese Periodicals* (see **192**).

960 Fa-ling yüeh-k'an 法令月刊
The Law Monthly. Taipei, Vol. 1, No. 1—, October 1950—.

Publishes regularly the most recent laws and statutes, digests, interpretations,
and court decisions. Averages twenty-eight pages per issue. Semi-annual subject
index.

An indispensable reference for the study of Taiwan's legal system.

961 Fa-lü p'ing-lun 法律評論
(The Law Review). Peiping, Taipei: Ch'ao-yang ta-hsüeh fa-lü p'ing-lun she
朝陽大學法律評論社, No. 1—, July 1923—. Monthly.

Contains articles on jurisprudence and other aspects of law, both Chinese and
foreign. Texts of important laws, statutes, and regulations, as well as court
decisions and interpretations, also are published regularly. The publication of
the *Review* was twice suspended (from 1937 to 1946 and from 1949 to 1951),
and resumed in June 1951 in Taipei. Not indexed except in the case of some
of the volumes bound by the publisher.

The Ch'ao-yang University, which publishes this journal, is primarily a
legal training institute originally located in Peiping.

962 Ho-tso ching-chi 合作經濟
Co-operative Economic Review. Taipei: Ho-tso ching-chi yüeh-k'an she
合作經濟月刊社, Vol. 1, No. 1—, July 1950—. Monthly.

Contains articles on the theory and practice of cooperatives with particular emphasis on the role of the cooperatives in Taiwan's economy. Experiences and problems encountered in the cooperative movement in Taiwan receive regular attention. Published frequently are translations of reports on cooperative enterprises in foreign countries. Annual subject index. A private publication.

963 Hsin Chung-kuo p'ing-lun 新中國評論
New China Review. Taipei: Hsin Chung-kuo p'ing-lun yüeh-k'an she 新中國 評論月刊社, Vol. 1, No. 1—, November 1950—. Monthly.

An official organ of one of the two factions of the Youth Party in Taiwan. (see also *Min-chu ch'ao*, **968**). Contents are general in scope, including articles on conditions in Taiwan and on the Mainland, as well as on the policies and programs of the Youth Party. No index.

964 Hsin shih-tai 新時代
New Age. Taipei: Hsin shih-tai tsa-chih she 新時代雜誌社, Vol. 1, No. 1—, January 1961—. Monthly.

One of the latest additions to the list of periodicals published in Taiwan, *New Age* is a general magazine with regular articles on Taiwan and current international affairs. The articles on modern Chinese history and personal memoirs (including interviews) are of particular interest to students of the history of modern China. Annual topical index. Also indexed in the *Classified Index to Chinese Periodicals* (see **192**).

965 K'o-hsüeh chiao-yü 科學教育
Science Education. Taipei: Chung-kuo tzu-jan k'o-hsüeh ts'u-chin hui 中國自然 科學促進會, Vol. 1, No. 1—, March 1955—. Monthly.

An official publication of the Chinese Association for the Advancement of Natural Science, *Science Education* seeks to promote scientific training and research in Taiwan. It publishes research results, translations of works by foreign authors, scientific news items, and news of the activities of the association. Issued as a bi-monthly prior to Vol. 5, No. 5 (August 1959). An English table of contents also was added thereafter. Indexed in the *Classified Index to Chinese Periodicals* (see **192**).

966 Kung-shang yüeh-k'an 工商月刊
The Industry and Commerce Monthly. Taipei: Chung-hua min-kuo kung-shang hsieh-chin hui 中華民國工商協進會, Vol. 1, No. 1—, August 1953—. Monthly.

The organ of the Association of Industry and Commerce of China, carrying reports on economic activities in Taiwan, as well as articles on industrial and commercial developments in foreign countries. Selections of laws and regulations and a chronology of economic activities in Taiwan for the preceding month are published in each issue. No index. A semi-official publication.

967 Kuo-li cheng-chih ta-hsüeh hsüeh-pao 國立政治大學學報
The National Chengchi University Journal. Taipei: Kuo-li cheng-chih ta-hsüeh,
No. 1—, May 1960—. Semi-annual.

A general scholarly journal devoted to traditional Chinese studies, carrying
only occasional articles of current interest. An English table of contents is
provided. Indexed in the *Classified Index to Chinese Periodicals* (see **192**).

968 Min-chu ch'ao 民主潮
Current Democracy. Taipei: Min-chu ch'ao she, Vol. 1, No. 1—, October 1950—.
Semi-monthly.

An official organ of one of the factions of the Youth Party, published in
Taiwan. Its contents are similar to those of the other Youth Party publication,
Hsin Chung-kuo p'ing-lun 新中國評論 (see **963**). A special supplement was
published on December 2, 1950, on the occasion of the twenty-seventh anniversary of the founding of the party, and Vol. 1, No. 16 (May 25, 1951) was a special
issue in memory of Ts'eng Ch'i 曾琦, one of the founders of the Youth Party.
Published as a monthly prior to Vol. 4, No. 1 (March, 1954).

969 Min-chu hsien-cheng 民主憲政
The Democratic Constitutionalist. Taipei: Min-chu hsien-cheng tsa-chih she
民主憲政雜誌社, Vol. 1, No. 1—, March 1951—. Semi-monthly.

Published by a group of members of the Legislative Yuan, *The Democratic
Constitutionalist* is devoted principally to discussions of legislative issues in
Taiwan. Articles on current international affairs—including Communist
China—occasionally appear in its pages. No index.

970 She-hui k'o-hsüeh lun-ts'ung 社會科學論叢
Journal of Social Science. Taipei: T'ai-wan ta-hsüeh fa-hsüeh yüan 臺灣大學法
學院, Vol. 1—, April 1950—. Annual.

A leading journal devoted to the social sciences and law, with an emphasis
on traditional Chinese studies, published by the College of Law of the National
Taiwan University. A special appendix containing Taipei economic statistical
data compiled by the Econometrics Study Group has appeared regularly in
every issue since 1952. A cumulative table of contents for Nos. 1–7 is available
in Volume 8. The *Journal* is indexed in the *Classified Index to Chinese Periodicals*
(see **192**).

971 Shih yü ch'ao 時與潮
Time and Tide. Taipei: Shih yü ch'ao she, No. 1—, December 1959—. Weekly.

A popular magazine on international affairs, with a slight emphasis on problems of Communism. Occasional articles are devoted to Taiwan. Carries no
index, but some articles are indexed in the *Chinese Periodicals Index* published
by the National War College in Taipei (see **193**).

972 Shui-wu hsün-k'an 稅務旬刊

Tax Affairs. Taipei: Shui-wu hsün-k'an she, No. 1—, October 1951—. Three times a month.

Contains theoretical articles on taxation, texts of tax laws, interpretations and digests, statistics, and other pertinent data relating to tax affairs in Taiwan. A topical index is appended to certain of the volumes bound by the publisher.

973 T'ai-wan chiao-yü 臺灣教育

Taiwan Education Review. Taipei: T'ai-wan sheng chiao-yü hui 臺灣省教育會, No. 1—, January 1948—. Monthly.

Published by the Taiwan Educational Association, the *Taiwan Education Review* carries articles on various aspects of elementary and secondary education in Taiwan. Publication was suspended between the years 1949 and 1950 inclusive, resumed in January 1951 under the title *T'ai-wan sheng chiao-yü hui hui-wu t'ung-hsün* 臺灣省教育會會務通訊 (Bulletin of the Taiwan Educational Association). Twenty-four issues were published through 1952. Published under the original title after 1952. Annual topical index. A private publication.

974 T'ai-wan ching-chi yüeh-k'an 臺灣經濟月刊

(Taiwan Economic Monthly). Taipei: T'ai-wan ching-chi yüeh-k'an she, Vol. 1, No. 1—, April 1948—. Monthly.

Publishes articles on various aspects of Taiwan's industry, commerce, foreign trade, agriculture, and finance, accompanied by short commentaries on specific problems. An analytical report on a special enterprise or line of business appears in each issue. No index. A private publication.

975 T'ai-wan yin-hang chi-k'an 臺灣銀行季刊

(Bank of Taiwan Quarterly). Taipei: T'ai-wan yin-hang ching-chi yen-chiu shih 臺灣銀行經濟研究室, Vol. 1, No. 1—, June 1947—. Quarterly.

The leading economic journal dealing exclusively with the economy of Taiwan, edited and published by the Office of Economic Research of the Bank of Taiwan. In addition to scholarly articles, the following sections appear in each issue: 'Tai-wan ching-chi jih-chih' 臺灣經濟日誌 (Chronology of Economic Events in Taiwan, see **407**); 'T'ai-wan ching-chi fa-kuei' 臺灣經濟法規 (Economic Laws and Regulations of Taiwan, see **626**); and 'T'ai-wan ching-chi wen-hsien fen-lei mu-lu' 臺灣經濟文獻分類目錄 (A Topical Index to Economic Literature Concerning Taiwan, see **123**). Annual topical index; indexed also in the *Classified Index to Chinese Periodicals* (see **192**).

An invaluable publication.

976 Ti-fang tzu-chih 地方自治
(Local Self-Government). Taipei: Ti-fang tzu-chih she, Vol. 1, No. 1— (No. 1—), October 1948—. Semi-monthly.

The official organ of the Local Self-Government Association of Taiwan Province 臺灣省地方自治協會, carrying articles and reports on the condition and status of local government in Taiwan. Laws and regulations concerning local government are frequently published in its pages. Published weekly between April 1950 and July 1951. No index. A private publication.

977 Ts'ai-cheng ching-chi yüeh-k'an 財政經濟月刊
The Financial and Economic Monthly. Taipei: Ts'ai-cheng ching-chi ch'u-pan she 財政經濟出版社, Vol. 1, No. 1—, December 1950—. Monthly.

Sponsored by a group of university professors in Taiwan, *The Financial and Economic Monthly* is devoted to the discussion of financial and economic theory and the analysis of current economic and financial conditions in Taiwan. Included also are surveys of international market conditions, as well as financial and economic statistics. Contains an English table of contents. Indexed in the *Classified Index to Chinese Periodicals* (see **192**).

978 T'u-ti kai-ko 土地改革
Land Reform Monthly. Nanking, Taipei: T'u-ti kai-ko yüeh-k'an she 土地改革月刊社, Vol. 1, No. 1—, April 1948—. Monthly.

The official organ of the Chinese Land Reform Association 中國土地改革協會, carrying articles on the land reform program in Taiwan. Included also are land laws and regulations, as well as articles on land reform and agrarian problems in Communist China and other countries. Publication began in Nanking in April 1948 and was suspended in October of the same year after the publication of fifteen issues. Publication resumed in September 1951 in Taipei with Vol. 2 No. 1. Annual topical index.

979 Tzu-yu Chung-kuo 自由中國
Free China. Taipei: Tzu-yu Chung-kuo she, Vol. 1, No. 1–Vol. 23, No. 5, November 1949–September 1960. Semi-monthly.

Started by a group of prominent scholars in 1949, including the late Dr. Hu Shih, *Free China* became one of the most popular and influential magazines in Taiwan, Hong Kong, and other Southeast Asian countries. Mildly critical of the Nationalist government at the beginning, *Free China* became increasingly so in its editorial comments in the late 1950's until the time of its suppression and the arrest and imprisonment of its publisher Lei Chen 雷震 in September 1960. Indexed in the *Classified Index to Chinese Periodicals* (see **192**).

980 Wen-hsüeh tsa-chih 文學雜誌
Literary Review. Taipei: Wen-hsüeh tsa-chih she, Vol. 1, No. 1–Vol. 8, No. 6, September 1956–August 1960. Monthly.

A leading literary journal published in Taiwan from 1956 to 1960, containing articles on literary theory, history and criticism, original works and translations. No index.

981 Wen-t'an 文壇
(Literary Forum). Taipei: Wen-t'an she 文壇社, Vol. 1, No. 1—, June 1952—. Monthly.

A popular literary magazine, carrying mostly original works by writers in Taiwan. Articles on literary theory and criticism are also included. No index.

2. ENGLISH-LANGUAGE

Most of the titles included in this section concern conditions on Taiwan and are published primarily for foreign consumption. The *China Youth* (second entry), organ of the National Association of Youth Organizations of the Republic of China, has its counterpart on the Mainland in the *Chinese Youth Bulletin* (see **928**). *Free China Weekly* (**986**), a news digest of the Nationalist government, is issued in New York.

Four other English-language titles published in Taiwan but dealing exclusively with Mainland China are described separately below (**1014–1016a**).

982 China Today. Taipei: Institute of Chinese Culture, Vol. 1, No. 1—, January 1958—. Monthly.

A monthly news digest and feature report of some sixty pages. Special articles appear on developments in art, the economy, industry, education and science in Taiwan. Of general interest. Not indexed.

983 China Youth. Taipei: National Association of Youth Organizations of the Republic of China, Vol. 1, No. 1—, July 1957 (?)—. Monthly.

A four-page English-language publication, *China Youth* is the official organ of the Chung-hua min-kuo ch'ing-nien t'uan-t'i lien-ho hui 中華民國青年團體聯合會. Official policy statements and reports on youth activities on Taiwan regularly appear in its pages.

984 Free China and Asia. Taipei: The Asian Peoples' Anti-Communist League. Vol. 1, No. 1—, October 1954—. Monthly.

A monthly report (approximately twenty pages) of anti-Communist activities in the Republic of China, including comments on Chinese Communist activities on the Mainland. Published under the title *A.P.A.C.L., R.O.C. Bulletin*, Vol. 1, No. 1–Vol. 2, No. 10 (October 1954–December 1955). Assumed its present name with Vol. 3, No. 1 (January 1956). Not indexed. Strongly anti-Communist.

For a list of A.P.A.C.L. pamphlets, see **1580ff.**

985 Free China Review. Taipei, Vol. 1, No. 1—, April 1951—. Monthly.

A monthly publication (approximately sixty pages) containing reports on internal developments in Taiwan, occasional articles on Mainland China, regular sections on 'News from the Mainland', 'Chinese Press Opinion', 'Foreign Press Opinion', 'Book Reviews', and a chronology of events for the preceding month. Not indexed. Strongly anti-Communist.

986 Free China Weekly. New York: Chinese News Service. Vol. 1, No. 1—, August 8, 1950—. Weekly.

A news digest published every Tuesday by the Chinese News Service (an information agency of the Republic of China), including articles on developments in Taiwan together with frequent comment on conditions on the China Mainland. Prior to January 3, 1956, the digest appeared under the title *This Week in Free China*.

The Chinese News Service also issues from time to time a special news release, the first issue of which was dated March 2, 1950. No index.

987 Industry of Free China. Taipei: Industrial Development Commission and Economic Stabilization Board, Vol. 1, No. 1—, January 1954—. Monthly.

A bilingual publication (Chinese title: *Tzu-yu Chung-kuo chih kung-yeh* 自由中國之工業) of roughly 110 pages, concerned with the industrial development of Taiwan. Thirty-six cumulative statistical tables appear in each issue under the caption 'Taiwan Economic Statistics'. Index for Vols. 1–15, January 1954–December 1961.

988 T'ai-wan 臺灣
Taiwan Pictorial. Taichung: T'ai-wan sheng hsin-wen ch'u 臺灣省新聞處, No. 1—, November 1956—. Irregular.

A bilingual pictorial publication issued irregularly by the Department of Information, Taiwan Provincial Government. Devoted primarily to news of Taiwan's internal development, the magazine supersedes *T'ai-wan hua-k'an* 臺灣畫刊 *Taiwan Pictorial*, Nos. 1–42, July 1953–October 1956.

989 West and East. Taipei: Sino-American Cultural and Economic Association, Vol. 1, No. 1—, October 1956—. Monthly.

A bilingual publication (Chinese title: *Chung-Mei yüeh-k'an* 中美月刊) devoted to Sino-American cultural relations in general, and Chinese cultural heritage and traditions in particular. It occasionally contains articles on contemporary affairs. Vol. 7, No. 5 (May 1962) is a special issue on the refugee problem in Hong Kong.

C. COMPILATIONS CONCERNED WITH THE MAINLAND

1. CHINESE-LANGUAGE

The Kuomintang and the Chinese Nationalist government have been conducting extensive intelligence research on the Mainland. This activity has resulted in an impressive flow of published reports and other materials, ranging in their concerns from affairs at the national level (military matters, politics, government) to those at the local level (administrative changes, etc.). Certain non-classified publications are available for research in the United States as are, of course, the open sources. The quality of these materials varies. Some are analytical, others are purely descriptive. All are obviously strongly anti-Communist. Taiwan collections of Mainland documents are useful as accurate substitutes for the originals in cases where the latter are unavailable, their value being enhanced by careful compilation and convenient arrangement.

The principal research centers in Taiwan—and the primary sources of this kind of information—are the Sixth Section of the Central Committee of the Kuomintang, the Bureau of Intelligence of the Ministry of National Defense, the Bureau of Investigation of the Ministry of Justice, the Institute of International Relations, and the National War College.

Included here are the most important serial compilations issued by the various centers, together with collections they have issued of Chinese Communist documentary materials. Individual monographs and pamphlets are excluded. Certain of the entries in the present section could with equal justification have been placed elsewhere in this Guide, but because of the nature of the materials themselves and in order to facilitate their use, they appear here grouped mostly under their respective publishers. An exception has been made for directories, biographies, bibliographies and indexes which are described in the appropriate chapters in Parts One and Two.

Although most entries included in this section were originally prepared for limited distribution, they have recently been declassified and are available through the new Modern China Historical Materials Center, Box 1644, or the A.A.S. Chinese Materials and Research Aids Service Center, Box 22048, Taipei. The most important current titles are *Fei-ch'ing yen-chiu* (Bandit Intelligence Studies, first entry), *Fei-ch'ing yüeh-pao* (Bandit Intelligence Monthly, **991**), *Ta-lu fei-ch'ing chi-pao* (Mainland Bandit Intelligence Quarterly, **994**), and *Fei-ch'ing shu-p'ing* (Report and Analysis of Bandit Intelligence, **1003**). In general, these publications share a common emphasis, reporting conditions on the Mainland (based on Chinese Communist publications) and analyzing trends in Chinese Communist activities in domestic and international spheres. The appendices in *Fei-ch'ing yüeh-pao* and *Fei-ch'ing yen-chiu* are particularly useful, for they provide the most up-to-date information on such subjects as personnel changes, activities of prominent leaders, biographical sketches, important meetings, etc. It should be noted that the major obstacle to the use of this voluminous material is the lack of effective and current bibliographical control. With a few exceptions, the publications do not themselves carry indexes. Some are partially indexed in the various indexes and bibliographies compiled in Taiwan and listed in Part One of this Guide.

For a list of library catalogs issued by the various institutions mentioned in this section, see **1736** ff.

990 Fei-ch'ing yen-chiu 匪情研究
(Bandit Intelligence Studies). Taipei: Kuo-fang pu, Ch'ing-pao chü 國防部情
報局, Vol. 1, No. 1—, March 1958—. Irregular until the end of 1960;
monthly since January 1961.

A monthly publication (of some 125 pages) on Communist China, issued by the Bureau of Intelligence of the Ministry of National Defense, Republic of China. Each issue is divided into four parts: (1) analysis of activities (動態分析); (2) topical studies (專題研究); (3) surveys (調查專報); and (4) basic reference materials (基本資料).

Part 1 deals with current Chinese Communist activities. Part 2 is devoted to the analysis of Chinese Communist policies. Part 3 contains special reports (e.g., on transportation, autonomous regions, etc.). Part 4 is a collection of good reference materials, providing current personnel and position data and biographical sketches of leading party and government personalities. The personnel and position data are among the most recent available (see also next entry). These two features in Part 4 are found separately annotated in Chapters 6 and 7 (**302** and **360**), respectively. Vol. 2, No. 7 (October 15, 1959) is a special issue on Communist China, 1949–1959. Limited distribution.

991 Fei-ch'ing yüeh-pao 匪情月報
(Bandit Intelligence Monthly). Taipei: Fei-ch'ing yüeh-pao she, Vol. 1,
No. 1—, February 1958—.

A monthly survey (over 100 pages in length) of events in Communist China based on Chinese Communist sources. Articles in each issue are arranged under the following topics: (1) political affairs, (2) economic affairs, (3) party affairs, (4) cultural and educational affairs, (5) military affairs, (6) activities of prominent personalities, (7) chronology, (8) major conferences and meetings, (9) personnel, (10) a list of delegations sent abroad and foreign delegations visiting Communist China. Also a summary of contents. An annual subject index of titles in the first number of each volume.

This and the preceding entry represent two of the best publications of this kind in Taiwan. The information contained in categories 6 through 10 is the most recent available. These sections have been separately annotated elsewhere in the Guide (see **361, 388, 301** and **317**).

From 1954 to 1958 this publication was issued for limited distribution by the Bureau of Intelligence of the Ministry of National Defense (see preceding entry).

992 Wen-t'i yü yen-chiu 問題與研究

(Problems and Studies). Taipei: Kuo-chi kuan-hsi yen-chiu hui 國際關係研究會, Vol. 1, No. 1–Vol. 6, No. 5, April 1956–August 1961; Vol. 1, No. 1—, October 1961—. Monthly.

Published monthly by the Institute of International Relations in Taipei. Oriented primarily toward international affairs and world Communism, the journal publishes one or two articles on Communist China in every issue. Published for limited distribution prior to October 1961, at which time public distribution began (with a new numbering system, Vol. 1, No. 1). The new series carries in each issue a brief column on 'Chinese Communist Activities'. Index to Vols. 1 to 4 published separately; Index to Vol. 5 published in Vol. 5, No. 12 (March 1961); Index to Vol. 6, Nos. 1–5 published in Vol. 6, No. 5 (August 1961).

993 Chin-jih ta-lu 今日大陸

(Mainland Today). Taipei: Chin-jih ta-lu pien-chi wei-yüan hui 今日大陸 編輯委員會, No. 1—, January 1952—. Semi-monthly.

A semi-monthly devoted exclusively to reporting on Communist China for the general public. Monthly to No. 102 (December 1959). Averages thirty pages per issue. A typical issue might contain three or four analytical articles, a personal exposé by a refugee from the Mainland, letters from the Mainland, a chronology of the period since the last issue, photographs, etc. The analytical article may be written by members of the staff, by government experts, by academic figures or by persons outside of Taiwan (mostly Hong Kong, occasionally the United States). Sometimes full issues are devoted to a single subject.

The editor of this magazine was Li Pai-hung 李白虹, Deputy Director of the Sixth Section of the Central Committee of the Kuomintang. He has been replaced by an editorial board which continues to enjoy close relations with government and Kuomintang circles. The magazine maintains a small reference library and has, in addition, access to the collections of government libraries. It has a circulation of about 15,000 in Taiwan, 4,000 in other parts of Asia, and a few hundred in the United States. Partially indexed in the 1954 Chinese Periodicals Yearbook, pp. 135–138 (**248**) and *Chinese Periodicals Index*, Appendix (**193**).

994 Ta-lu fei-ch'ing chi-pao 大陸匪情季報

(Mainland Bandit Intelligence Quarterly). Taipei: Chung-kuo kuo-min tang, Chung-yang wei-yüan hui, Ti liu tsu 中國國民黨 中央委員會 第六組, Jan. 1960—.

Published formerly under the series title *Jen-shih ti-jen* (see next entry), the quarterly continues to be a cumulation of the *Chuan-t'i yen-chiu* series published by the Sixth Section of the Central Committee of the Kuomintang (see **997**). Starting with the April/June 1960 number, a quarterly chronology has been included in each issue. Limited distribution.

Ranks as one of the major current Taiwan publications concerned with the Mainland.

995 Jen-shih ti-jen 認識敵人

(Know Thy Enemy). Taipei: Chung-kuo kuo-min tang, Chung-yang wei-yüan hui, Ti liu tsu 中國國民黨 中央委員會 第六組, Vol. 1, No. 1–Vol. 8, No. 3, 1951–1959. Irregular.

A cumulated edition consisting primarily of the *Chuan-t'i yen-chiu* series published by the Sixth Section of the Central Committee of the Kuomintang (see **997**) and a companion publication to the *Kung-fei chung-yao tzu-liao hui-pien*, also published by the Sixth Section (see **998**). In addition to the *Chuan-t'i yen-chiu*, this series initially included reprints from two other publications: (1) *Fei-ch'ing fen-hsi hui-pien* 匪情分析彙編 (Bandit Intelligence Analysis Series), a collection of articles on Communist China originally published in the Taipei *Kai-tsao pan-yüeh-k'an* 改造半月刊 (Reconstruction Semi-Monthly), and (2) *Fei-ch'ing yen-chiu hui-pien* 匪情研究彙編 (Bandit Intelligence Research Series), another pamphlet series on Communist China published by the Sixth Section. Since January 1960 this series has been published quarterly under the new title *Ta-lu fei-ch'ing chi-pao* (Mainland Bandit Intelligence Quarterly; see preceding entry). Limited distribution.

996 Fei-ch'ing chou-pao 匪情週報

(Bandit Intelligence Weekly). Taipei: Chung-kuo kuo-min tang, Chung-yang wei-yüan hui, Ti liu tsu, 中國國民黨 中央委員會 第六組, February 1958–1960.

A weekly newsletter on Chinese Communist activities published by the Sixth Section of the Central Committee of the Kuomintang. A convenient guide for quick reference. Limited distribution.

997 Chuan-t'i yen-chiu 專題研究

(Monographic Studies). Taipei: Chung-kuo kuo-min tang, Chung-yang wei-yüan hui, Ti liu tsu 中國國民黨 中央委員會 第六組, 1951—. Weekly.

A weekly series on Communist China published since 1951 by the Sixth Section of the Central Committee of the Kuomintang. Each issue deals with some particular aspect of current Chinese Communist activities at home and abroad. Limited distribution.

998 Chung-kuo kuo-min tang, Chung-yang wei-yüan hui, Ti liu tsu 中國 國民黨 中央委員會 第六組 (Kuomintang, Central Committee, Sixth Section). *Kung-fei chung-yao tzu-liao hui-pien* 共匪重要資料彙編 (Collections of Important Communist Bandit Documents). Taipei: Chung-yang wen-wu kung-yin she 中央文物供應社, 1952. 10 vols.

A comprehensive collection of official Chinese Communist documents of the period 1949 to 1952 compiled from published and other sources. The work is divided into ten catagories: (1) international Communism and Chinese Communist foreign relations, (2) statements and speeches, (3) party affairs, (4) political and social affairs, (5) military affairs, (6) finance, (7) economic affairs, (8) land reform, (9) cultural and educational affairs, and (10) biography.

A supplement in six volumes was issued in 1953 under the title *Kung-fei chung-yao tzu-liao hui-pien hsü-pien* ... 續編, presenting documents issued to that date and covering the following topics: (1) international Communism, Chinese Communist foreign relations, and the Soviet Union, (2) statements and speeches, (3) party affairs, (4) political and military affairs, (5) financial and economic affairs, and (6) socio-cultural affairs. Limited distribution.

An important and useful source for the period covered.

999 Chung-kuo kuo-min tang, Chung-yang wei-yüan hui, Ti liu tsu 中國國民黨 中央委員會 第六組 (Kuomintang, Central Committee, Sixth Section). *Kung-fei chung-yao tzu-liao hui-pien* 共匪重要資料彙編 (Collections of Important Communist Bandit Documents). Taipei, No. 1—, January 15, 1960—. Semi-monthly.

Collections of Mainland documents of current interest, together with a brief summary of contents in each issue. Limited distribution. The type of material covered is similar to and equally as important as that contained in the preceding entry.

1000 Fei-ch'ing chou-pao 匪情週報 (Bandit Intelligence Weekly). Taipei: Nei-cheng pu, Tiao-ch'a chü 內政部 調查局, Nos. 1–18, February 9–June 8, 1951.

A publication of the Bureau of Investigation of the Ministry of Interior, Republic of China, covering political, party and military activities of Communist China. Mimeographed. Limited distribution.

Superseded by *Fei-ch'ing yüeh-pao* (see next entry).

1001 Fei-ch'ing yüeh-pao 匪情月報 (Bandit Intelligence Monthly). Taipei: Nei-cheng pu, Tiao-ch'a chü 中華民國 內政部 調查局, August 1952–March 1955.

Supersedes *Fei-ch'ing chou-pao* (see preceding entry). Similar contents. Superseded by *Fei-ch'ing ts'an-k'ao tzu-liao* (see next entry).

1002 China, Ssu-fa hsing-cheng pu, Tiao-ch'a chü 中華民國 司法行政部 調查局 (China, Ministry of Justice, Bureau of Investigation). *Fei-ch'ing ts'an-k'ao tzu-liao* 匪情參考資料 (Reference Materials on Bandit Situation). Taipei, May 1955–January 1958. 34 vols.

A monthly publication superseding *Fei-ch'ing yüeh-pao* (see preceding entry), containing articles on Chinese Communist activities during the preceding month. Organized into four main sections: politics and government, foreign relations, finance and economy, and culture and education. Each number has a brief summary of contents, a chronology of events of significance, and a list of important conferences and meetings which took place during the month under review (including information on the date and place of conference or meeting; person in charge; names of persons present; and a selective list of important resolutions passed).

Beginning with No. 10 (January 1956) a section on the activities of prominent Chinese Communist personalities also was included, comprising three parts: (1) a list of appointments, dismissals, and transfers, (2) a name list of committees, delegations, associations, etc., and (3) activities of prominent personalities. Limited distribution. Beginning in February 1958 the title was changed to *Fei-ch'ing shu-p'ing* (see next entry).

1003　China, Ssu-fa hsing-cheng pu, Tiao-ch'a chü 中華民國 司法行政部 調查局 (China, Ministry of Justice, Bureau of Investigation). *Fei-ch'ing shu-p'ing* 匪情述評 (Report and Analysis of Bandit Intelligence). Taipei, No. 1—, February 1958—.

Supersedes *Fei-ch'ing ts'an-k'ao tzu-liao* (see preceding entry). Comprehensive coverage and useful data.

1004　China, Ssu-fa hsing-cheng pu, Tiao-ch'a chü 中華民國 司法行政部 調查局 (China, Ministry of Justice, Bureau of Investigation). *Fei-ch'ing yen-chiu chuan-pao* 匪情研究專報 (Special Report on the Bandit Situation). Taipei, Nos. 1–63, 1952–1956; New Series No. 1—, 1956—.

A series of special monographic reports on Communist China. Nos. 23–63 (1954–1956) of the old series were also published in the *Fei-ch'ing chi-pen hsü-shu ts'ung-shu* 匪情基本叙述叢書 (Basic Reports on the Bandit Situation). The Library of the Bureau of Investigation maintains a hand-written catalog of all of the 171 pamphlets (Nos. 1–63; new series Nos. 1–108) issued from 1952 through November 1961.

1005　China, Nei-cheng pu, Tiao-ch'a chü 中華民國 內政部 調查局 (China, Ministry of Interior, Bureau of Investigation). *Chien-fei hsien-chuang hui-pien* 奸匪現狀彙編 (Survey of Puppet and Bandit Situation). Taipei, 1950. 12 vols.

A comprehensive survey of Communist China as of 1950, presented in twelve sections: (1) party work, (2) internal affairs and public security, (3) foreign relations and Overseas Chinese, (4) armed forces, (5) finance, (6) agriculture and land reform, (7) commerce and industry, (8) cultural and educational affairs, (9) transportation and communications, (10) judicial system, (11) minority groups, and (12) political parties. Limited distribution.

1006 China, Nei-cheng pu, Tiao-ch'a chü 中華民國 內政部 調查局 (China, Ministry of Interior, Bureau of Investigation). *San-nien fei-ch'ing* 三年匪情 (Bandit Intelligence, 1949–1953). Taipei, 1952–1953. 10 vols.

A survey of Chinese Communist activities from 1949 to the end of 1953 in ten parts: (1) military affairs, (2) administrative and political divisions, (3) finance and economic affairs, (4) agriculture, (5) education, (6) foreign relations, (7) labor, (8) judicial system, (9) transportation and communications, and (10) minority groups. Limited distribution.

1007 Ko-ming shih-chien yen-chiu yüan 革命實踐研究院 (National War College). *Ti-ch'ing yen-chiu ts'an-k'ao tzu-liao* 敵情研究參考資料 (Reference Materials for the Study of Enemy Intelligence). Taipei, 1949–1957. 20 vols.

A series of topical pamphlets (each some 100 pages in length) on such subjects as the Chinese Communist Party, the New Democracy, cadres education, the Twentieth Congress of the Communist Party of the Soviet Union, etc. Some pamphlets bear the imprint of Yang-ming shan chuang (Yangmingshan Institute). The first two of the series bear no date of publication. No pamphlets were published between 1951 and 1956.

1008 Yang-ming shan chuang 陽明山莊 (Yangmingshan Institute). *Ti-ch'ing p'i-p'an ts'ung-k'an* 敵情批判叢刊 (Collection of Critiques on Enemy Intelligence). Taipei, March 1950–March 1953.

A collection of pamphlets on Communist China, similar to the preceding entry.

1009 Yang-ming shan chuang 陽明山莊 (Yangmingshan Institute). *Ti-ch'ing yen-chiu ts'ung-k'an* 情敵研究叢刊 (Collection of Studies on Enemy Intelligence). Taipei, July–October 1951 and November 1958. 7 vols.

A series of seven pamphlets on Communist China's education, propaganda, etc.

1010 Yang-ming shan chuang 陽明山莊 (Yangmingshan Institute). *Fei-ch'ing chuan-t'i yen-chiu ts'ung-shu* 匪情專題研究叢書 (Bandit Intelligence Monographic Studies Series). Taipei, 1957–1958. 19 vols.

Contains nineteen monographic studies on Communist China. For abstracts of the first seventeen studies, see *Fei-ch'ing chuan-t'i yen-chiu ts'ung-shu t'i-yao* 匪情專題研究叢書提要 (Abstracts of the Bandit Intelligence Monographic Studies Series), (Taipei: Yang-ming shan chuang, 1957).

1011   China, Kuo-fang pu, Ti-erh t'ing 中華民國 國防部 第二廳 (China, Ministry
of National Defense, G–2). *Pei-p'ing wei tsu-chih chung-yao jen-yüan lu chi
fan-tung wen-chien hui-pien* 北平僞組織重要人員錄暨反動文件彙編
(A Personnel Directory and Collections of Subversive Documents of the
Peiping Puppet Regime). Taipei, 1950–1953. 17 vols.

The most comprehensive compilation of position data on leaders of Communist China and of Chinese Communist documents for the period October 1,
1949–1953. The documents are arranged by subject and include resolutions,
speeches, decrees, regulations, orders, instructions, editorials, etc. Separate
index to Volumes 1–5 published in August 1951 (44p.). Limited distribution.
A basic source.

1012   China, Hsing-cheng yüan, She-chi wei-yüan hui 中華民國 行政院 設計
委員會 (China, Executive Yuan, Planning Committee). *Fei-ch'ing yen-chiu
tzu-liao* 匪情研究資料
(Research Materials on Bandit Intelligence). Taipei, September 1952–July
1954. 13 vols.

A series of thirteen pamphlets on a variety of topics on Communist China
(land reform, minorities, the Three-Anti and Five-Anti campaigns, etc.).
Publication is believed to have ceased.

1013   China, Wai-chiao pu 中華民國 外交部 (China, Ministry of Foreign Affairs).
Fei-ch'ing hui-pien 匪情彙編
(Survey of Bandit Situation). Taipei, 1949–1950. 2 vols.

A collection of news dispatches and foreign radio broadcasts on Communist
China compiled by the Nationalist Ministry of Foreign Affairs. In three parts:
(1) Chinese Communist and Russian activities, (2) Chinese Communists in
Southeast Asia, and (3) conditions on the Mainland (divided into four sections:
economy, culture, politics, and anti-Communist movements). Limited
distribution.
Useful background information for the study of the period covered.

2. ENGLISH-LANGUAGE

Most of the English-language newspapers and periodicals published in Taiwan,
which are largely though not exclusively concerned with Taiwan, are to be found in
preceding sections.

Listed here are four Taiwan publications concerned with Mainland China, the
last entry representing the most recent addition. These English-language publications
supplement the twenty-odd Chinese-language compilations of Mainland data emanating from Taiwan and listed directly above.

1014 Asian Peoples' Anti-Communist League.
Charts About Chinese Communists on the Mainland, Series I—. Taipei, 1955—. Irregular.

Diagrams, graphic charts, and tables outlining Chinese Communist activities on the Mainland. Twelve issues had appeared to 1964.

1015 Free China Review.
China Mainland Today. Taipei, 1957. 3 vols. 58; 94; 108p.

A collection of eye-witness reports on conditions in Mainland China as reported in the Western press. In three volumes: Volume 1, 'Communist-Controlled China as Foreign Visitors See It'; Volume 2, 'Communist-Controlled China as Foreign Residents See It'; Volume 3, 'Communist-Controlled China as Foreign Missionaries See It'.
Strongly anti-Communist.

1016 Analysis of Current Chinese Communist Problems. Taipei: Institute of International Relations of the Republic of China, December 1962–September 1964. Monthly; 22 issues.

An anti-Communist monthly devoted to analysis of current Chinese Communist affairs. Each issue is given over to a special topic (e.g., 'Analyses of the Tenth Plenary Session of the Eighth Central Committee of the Chinese Communist Party'; 'Background and Perspective of the Peiping-New Delhi Conflict'; 'Petroleum Resources and Production in Mainland China'; 'On the Mainland Intelligentsia').

In October 1964 this periodical was superseded by *Issues and Studies: A Monthly Journal of World Affairs and Communist Problems*. A list of titles of all the twenty-two issues of *Analysis of Current Chinese Communist Problems* appears on the back cover of *Issues and Studies*, Vol. 1, No. 6.

1016a Chinese Communist Affairs: A Quarterly Review. Taipei: Institute of Political Research, Vol. 1, No. 1—, March 1964—. Quarterly.

A new fifty-page magazine edited by Pao Chin-an and devoted to the review of Mainland developments. The first issue contains four articles by leading scholars and specialists on the following topics: 'A Historical View of the Moscow-Peiping Schism', 'An Anaysis of Chou En-lai's African Tour', 'Anti-Communist Activities on the Chinese Mainland During 1963', and 'Combat Capabilities of the Peiping Regime'.

CHAPTER XIX

HONG KONG PUBLICATIONS

The British authorities forbid the Chinese resident in Hong Kong to engage in political activity on behalf of either the Communist or the Nationalist government. They do, nonetheless, license semi-official publications closely affiliated with Peking or Taipei. There are also a number of Hong Kong publications whose political affiliation lies somewhere in between.

According to the 1963 *Hong Kong Yearbook*, forty-one Chinese-language newspapers and 106 periodicals were published as of September 30, 1962. No complete listing of titles seems to be available, although a partial list is provided in the *Yearbook* (see **256**). Selected for inclusion in this chapter are three Chinese-language newspapers and eleven periodicals, including some of the more influential publications representing the pro-Communist, anti-Communist, and neutral viewpoints.

Also incorporated here are three English-language newspapers and five periodicals. Translations of the American Consulate General in Hong Kong and publications of the Union Research Institute are described in the next chapter, as well as in Chapter XXII. (The official *Daily News Release* of the New China News Agency, although issued in Hong Kong, is listed in the Mainland chapter, XVII; see **850**.)

Reference also might be made to the bibliography of social science periodicals and monograph series published in Hong Kong between 1950 and 1961 listed in Chapter II (**176**).

A. NEWSPAPERS

Of the forty-odd Chinese-language newspapers published in Hong Kong, the number of pro-Communist newspapers exceeds by a slight margin those of pro-Nationalist coloration. Included here as representative samples are the Hong Kong *Wen-hui pao* (Wen-hui Daily), a leading Communist newspaper (first entry); the *Hsiang-kang shih-pao* (The Hong Kong Times), a semi-official publication of the Kuomintang and the Nationalist government (second entry); and the *Ch'eng-pao—Sing Pao Daily News*, an independent and neutral publication which has in recent years attracted a large following, especially among white-collar workers and the middle class (**1019**). (It might be mentioned that the Library of Congress is currently filming the files of the following three Hong Kong newspapers: *Ta-kung pao* [since 1950], and *Kung-shang jih-pao* and *Wen-hui pao* [since 1954].)

Six pro-Nationalist newspapers, including the *Hsiang-kang shih-pao*, have been indexed since 1962 in the *Classified Index to Chinese Newspapers* compiled in Taiwan (see **194a**).

Reference should be made to the *Review of the Hong Kong Chinese Press* (see **1075**), published by the American Consulate General, which provided English-language translations until May 1961.

All three English-language newspapers are listed in the next section: the *South China Morning Post*, the *China Mail*, and the *Hong Kong Standard*.

1. CHINESE-LANGUAGE

1017 Wen-hui pao 文滙報
(Wen-hui Daily). Hong Kong, No. 1—, September 9, 1948—. Daily.

First published as an organ of the Chinese Democratic League, the *Wen-hui Daily* since shortly after 1949 has been controlled by the Chinese Communist Party. The eight-page paper is directed mostly toward the Hong Kong intelligentsia. No index.

1018 Hsiang-kang shih-pao 香港時報
(Hong Kong Times). Hong Kong, No. 1—, August 4, 1949—. Daily.

The Kuomintang organ in Hong Kong, the ten-page daily is designed primarily to counter Communist propaganda, and is directed toward the general public in Hong Kong. No index.

1019 Ch'eng pao 成報
Sing Pao Daily News. Hong Kong, No. 1—, 1939—. Daily.

An independent publication enjoying one of the largest circulations among all Chinese newspapers published in Hong Kong. The eight-page newspaper is directed toward what might be considered the Hong Kong 'middle class'. No index.

2. ENGLISH-LANGUAGE

1020 South China Morning Post. Hong Kong, No. 1—, 1881—. Daily.

One of the oldest newspapers now published in Hong Kong, the British-owned *South China Morning Post* is generally considered to be a semi-official publication representing the viewpoint of the Hong Kong government. In recent years each issue averages twenty-six pages. The Sunday edition bears the title *South China Sunday Post Herald*. An evening edition called *China Mail* (the oldest daily newspaper in the Colony, established circa 1845) is also published.

1021 Hong Kong Standard. Hong Kong, No. 1—, 1949—. Daily.

One of the newspapers published by the Sin Poh (Star News) Amalgamated, Ltd., owned by the Aw Boon Haw family. The paper usually runs to sixteen pages, and the Sunday edition includes the *Asia Magazine*. Editorially, it is slightly right of center.

B. PERIODICALS

1. CHINESE-LANGUAGE

Of the Chinese-language periodicals published in Hong Kong, eleven titles representative of those dealing with contemporary China have been selected for inclusion in this section. Except for the second entry, they are all anti-Communist. The *Lien-ho p'ing-lun* (United Voice Weekly, **1026**) is also anti-Kuomintang in its editorial position. The *Shih-tai p'i-p'ing* (*Modern Critique*, **1028**) is strongly anti-Communist, as is its sister publication *The Peking Informers*, a semi-monthly news sheet on Communist China, included in the next section on English-language periodicals (**1037**). Another publication, *Yüan-tung kuan-ch'a—Far East Observation*, is also noteworthy in that it is almost exclusively devoted to reports from refugee interviews (see **1032**).

The two periodical indexes published in Taiwan (**192** and **193**) also provide coverage of selected Hong Kong journals. Publications listed in this section and indexed in Taiwan have been so identified in the annotations.

1022 Chan-wang tsa-chih 展望雜誌
Look. Hong Kong, No. 1—, April 1958—. Monthly.

A general periodical (averaging twenty-four pages) carrying in each issue articles on Chinese Communist problems from an anti-Communist viewpoint.

1023 Ching-chi tao-pao 經濟導報
Economic Bulletin. Hong Kong: Ching-chi tao-pao she, No. 1—, January 1947—. Weekly.

Reports on economic conditions in Hong Kong, the China Mainland, Southeast Asia, and the world at large (with special emphasis on foreign economic policies of the United States). Statistical tables are frequently included. Separate subject index for Nos. 1–201 (1947–1950); quarterly index thereafter.

A pro-Communist publication.

1024 Chung-kuo p'ing-lun 中國評論
China Review Weekly. Hong Kong, No. 1—, April (?) 1962—.

An avowedly anti-Communist publication dealing with international relations, with major emphasis on Communism and Chinese Communist affairs.

1025 Hsin-wen t'ien-ti 新聞天地
Newsdom. Hong Kong: Hsin-wen t'ien-ti she, No. 1—, January 1945—. Weekly.

A popular news magazine featuring allegedly true behind-the-scene news items, and covering Taiwan, Mainland China and Hong Kong. The first seven issues were published in Chungking; issue Nos. 8–69 (September [?] 1945–May 1949) were published in Shanghai. Since issue No. 70 (June 1949) the magazine has been published in Hong Kong. An English edition of this magazine was issued between 1949 and 1951 under the title *Newsdom;* only twenty-six issues were published. No index.

1026 Lien-ho p'ing-lun 聯合評論
United Voice Weekly. Hong Kong [New York Air Edition,] No. 1—, December 1958—. Weekly.

An anti-Communist and anti-Kuomintang publication with contributions by Tso Shun-sheng 左舜生, Li Huang 李璜 and other members of the Youth Party now residing in Hong Kong. This weekly contains critical editorials and articles on current events on the Mainland and Taiwan, as well as reminiscences on episodes in the history of Republican China. Issue No. 1 of the New York air edition is actually the 16th issue of this publication. No index.

1027 Min-chu p'ing-lun 民主評論
The Democratic Review. Hong Kong: Min-chu p'ing-lun she, Vol. 1, No. 1—, June 1949—. Semi-monthly.

A general periodical dealing with the humanities and social sciences, with an emphasis on Chinese philosophy and culture and on current conditions on the Mainland. A special section entitled 'Chinese Communist Activities' has appeared regularly in each issue in recent years. Indexed in the *Classified Index to Chinese Periodicals* (see **192**).

Anti-Communist in orientation.

1028 Shih-tai p'i-p'ing 時代批評
Modern Critique. Hong Kong: Shih-tai p'i-p'ing she, Vol. 1, No. 1—, June 1938—. Semi-monthly.

Modern Critique, since resuming publication in Hong Kong in August 1958, has been devoted to the reporting and analysis of conditions on the China Mainland and in Southeast Asia. Articles on International Communism also frequently appear in its pages. No index except for the issues bound by the publisher. *Modern Critique* has twice suspended publication (January 1942–May 1947 and June 1949–July 1958). The pre-1949 issues were concerned mainly with China's internal political strife, and in general represented the views of the China Democratic League of which Chow Ching-wen, the editor, was once the Deputy Secretary-General. Chow is also the publisher of *The Peking Informers* (see **1037**).

The publication is strongly anti-Communist.

1029 T'ien-hsia 天下
(The World). Hong Kong, Vol. 1, No. 1—, June 1959—. Semi-monthly.

About half of the contents of this publication, averaging some thirty pages per issue, is devoted to Communist problems from an anti-Communist, pro-Kuomintang point of view.

1030 Tsu-kuo chou-k'an 祖國週刊
China Weekly. Hong Kong: Tsu-kuo chou-k'an she, Vol. 1, No. 1–Vol. 45, No. 13, January 1953–March 1964. Weekly.

Published by the Union Research Institute in Hong Kong, the *China Weekly* is devoted primarily to the reporting and analysis of conditions on Mainland China from an anti-Communist point of view. Articles on Taiwan, as well as on international relations, also frequently appear in its pages. Only the volumes bound by the publisher are indexed. Published under name *Tsu-kuo yüeh-k'an* 祖國月刊 since April 1964.

1031 Tzu-yu chen-hsien 自由陣綫
Freedom Front. Hong Kong: Tzu-yu chen-hsien she, Vol. 1, No. 1–Vol. 42, No. 8, December 1949–November 1959. Weekly.

A general anti-Communist periodical carrying articles on conditions in Mainland China and current international affairs. Publication is believed to have ceased with Vol. 42, No. 8. No index except for the volumes bound by the publisher.

1032 Yüan-tung kuan-ch'a 遠東觀察
Far East Observation. Hong Kong, No. 1—, May 1963—. Monthly.

About eighty per cent of the contents of this publication (averaging twenty-four pages per issue) is devoted to reports of refugee interviews, the balance being given over to Overseas Chinese affairs. Anti-Communist and pro-Kuomintang. Believed to have ceased publication.

2. ENGLISH-LANGUAGE

A number of scholarly English-language periodicals devoted to the study of Communist China are published in Hong Kong. The *China News Analysis* (**1034**) and the *Current Scene* (**1035**), both critically evaluating recent developments in Communist China, are deserving of special mention. (*Union Research Service* and the various translations issued by the American Consulate General—also significant contributions to the Communist China field—are described in the next chapter dealing with translations and compilations.)

This section contains five titles, all of which deal with Communist China; two also cover Taiwan and other areas in Asia.

1033 China Missionary Bulletin Shanghai, Hong Kong, Vol. 1, No. 1–Vol. 2, No. 6, March 1948–June 1949; Vol. 1, No. 1–Vol. 5, No. 6, September 1949–June/July 1953; Vol. 5, No. 7—, September 1953—. Ten issues per year.

Originally published under the auspices of the Catholic Central Bureau in Shanghai for Catholic missionaries in China, this publication contained a number of articles dealing with current developments on the Mainland, particularly in the fields of religion and education. In 1949 the editorial offices moved to Hong Kong. In September 1953, with Vol. 5, No. 7, the name of the periodical was changed to the *Mission Bulletin*, and in January 1960, with Vol. 12, No. 1, to *Asia*. The scope of the periodical gradually expanded to serve the needs of Catholic missionaries in East and Southeast Asia, from Korea to India. While articles on Mainland developments decreased, the journal began to carry articles on Taiwan and Hong Kong.

1034 China News Analysis. Hong Kong, No. 1—, August 25, 1953—. Weekly.

A weekly newsletter (forty-eight issues a year) of critical comment on recent developments in Communist China, published by Father Ladany, a Jesuit priest in Hong Kong. Based entirely on Chinese Communist sources and well footnoted. Contents of Nos. 1–145 are listed in No. 145, and subsequently in Nos. 249, 325, 450, and 525. Subject and name indexes in Nos. 28, 50, 75, and in each twenty-fifth issue.

An excellent publication.

1035 Current Scene—Developments in Mainland China. Hong Kong: The Green Pagoda Press, Vol. 1, No. 1—, May 1961—. Irregular.

Two to three issues, each approximately ten pages in length, appear every month. Each issue is given over to an article on Communist China, on topics ranging from current political, economic, and ideological developments to foreign relations and literature. Some issues are authored by recognized Western authorities on Communist China; others are devoted to interviews with recent escapees from the Mainland. Indexes to Vol. 1 (Nos. 1–34) and the first seventeen issues of Vol. 2 (July 1962–July 1963) appeared separately on July 5, 1962 and August 1, 1963, respectively. These indexes list all titles in order of appearance, followed by author and subject indexes.

Supersedes a mimeographed publication by the same title, 118 issues of which appeared from early 1959 to April 1961. A reprint of 65 of the 118 issues entitled *Current Scene—Reports on Communist China (October 1959–April 1961)* was published in 1961 (346p.). The volume contains the more lasting contributions—largely articles on current developments in Communist China (some based on interviews with refugees from the Mainland). Mimeographed. No index.

1036 Far Eastern Economic Review. Hong Kong, Vol. 1, No. 1—, October 1946—. Weekly.

Carries notes and editorials on Communist China in nearly every issue and furnishes trade statistics. Articles and comments on Communist China are based largely on the Chinese press and related sources. Semi-annual index. A useful publication.

See also the *Far Eastern Economic Review Yearbook* described in Chapter IV (**205**).

1037　The Peking Informers. Hong Kong: The Continental Research Institute, Vol. 1, No. 1—, September 1, 1960—. Semi-monthly.

A semi-monthly news sheet on Communist China edited by Chow Ching-wen, who also edits *Modern Critique* (see **1028**). Topical analysis, based on Chinese Communist sources, with footnotes. Mimeographed. Strongly anti-Communist.

CHAPTER XX

TRANSLATIONS AND MONITORING SERVICES

Fortunately for scholars working on contemporary China, there exists a large body of translated Chinese publications, especially newspaper and periodical articles. Most of this is in English, although a considerable amount of Chinese source material also has been translated into Japanese, Russian and other languages. (Since this Guide is primarily designed for the English-speaking public, translations from the Chinese into languages other than English have been omitted.) For translations other than serial publications, consult Part Three: Selected Documentary Materials.

Most of the material listed in this chapter, irrespective of its origin, is concerned with or emanates from Mainland China. The latter includes monitored radio broadcasts. A small section at the end covers translations of the Taiwan, Hong Kong, Japanese and Soviet press, the last two of which contain frequent articles on Communist China.

A. PUBLICATIONS CONCERNED WITH THE MAINLAND

Materials in this section are grouped for convenience under the Hong Kong American Consulate General Series, Joint Publications Research Service (the two largest bodies of translated Mainland data), other translation series and radio monitoring services.

Material originating on the China Mainland is listed in Chapter XVII, and collections of Mainland source material emanating from Taiwan in Chapter XVIII.

1. HONG KONG CONSULATE GENERAL SERIES

Prior to the appearance of the Joint Publications Research Service (J.P.R.S.) reports on Communist China in 1957 (see next section), the Hong Kong American Consulate General translation series was the most important single source of translated Mainland material. In terms of volume, the number of issues runs into the thousands and the number of pages into the hundreds of thousands.

At the present time, the following four translation series are being issued: *Survey of China Mainland Press* (S.C.M.P., first entry), *Selections from China Mainland Magazines* (S.C.M.M., second entry), *Current Background* (C.B., **1040**), and *Extracts from China Mainland Publications* (E.C.M.P., **1041**). The first two series cover newspapers and news releases, and periodicals, respectively. The latter two contain materials devoted to single events or topics.

Since 1956 the first three series have been brought under bibliographical control through the publication of a bi-monthly index (see **1043** in the Indexes subsection below). In order to provide some sort of guide to the material published prior to 1956, the Press Monitoring Unit of the American Consulate General prepared in April 1958 three indexes which cover the periods 1950–1952, 1953–1954, and 1955, respectively. These indexes are described following the regular on-going bi-monthly index (**1044–1046**).

The Consulate General also issued the *Review of Hong Kong Chinese Press* from 1946 to 1961 (**1075**) and the *Chinese Communist Propaganda Review* from 1951 to 1953 (see **1042**).

It might be noted that thirteen press summaries and related publications issued by U.S. consulates and U.S. Information Service offices in China during the period 1944–1950 have been filmed by the Library of Congress. For a list containing the titles and dates, see the *Newsletter of the Association for Asian Studies*, Vol. 9, No. 4 (May 1964), pp. 18–19.

1038 American Consulate General, Hong Kong.
Survey of China Mainland Press. Hong Kong, No. 1—, November 1, 1950—. Daily (approx.).

Each issue comprises some thirty to fifty legal-size pages and contains translations of New China News Agency (N.C.N.A.) press releases, translations of articles and editorials from major newspapers, and the texts of N.C.N.A. English-language releases. Items are selected to cover significant developments in both domestic and foreign affairs rather than to provide a cross section of the China Mainland press. (2,368 issues have appeared during the first ten years.) Mimeographed.

One of the basic sources of translated Mainland materials. Indexes to this and the succeeding publications are listed below.

1039 American Consulate General, Hong Kong.
Selections from China Mainland Magazines. Hong Kong, No. 1—, August 1, 1955—. Weekly (approx.).

The first 212 issues (to May 23, 1960) appeared under the title *Extracts from China Mainland Magazines* (E.C.M.M.). Each issue, normally thirty to forty legal-size pages, contains translations of five or six articles from periodicals such as *Chung-kuo nung-pao* 中國農報 (Agricultural Bulletin), *Jen-min chiao-yü* 人民教育 (People's Education), *Hsüeh-hsi* 學習 (Study), and *Ch'iao-wu pao* 僑務報 (Overseas Chinese Affairs Journal). The articles are translated in full. Mimeographed.

Indexes to this and to other publications of the Consulate General are described below.

1040 American Consulate General, Hong Kong.
Current Background. Hong Kong, No. 1—, June 1950—. Weekly (approx.).

Each issue, ranging from ten to twenty legal-size sheets in length, consists of a compilation of translations from Mainland China newspapers, magazines or press releases on a single major political or economic theme or event. For example, most of the pertinent documents on the meetings of the Chinese Communist Party, Young Communist League, the National People's Congress, and other political groups are brought together in separate issues of the publication.

The *Current Background* also presents periodically a chronology of major events in Communist China (see **386**). A listing of the titles of the first 613 numbers was issued separately in 1960 (51p.). A total of 619 issues appeared in the first ten years. Mimeographed.

Indexes to this and to preceding publications are described below.

1041 American Consulate General, Hong Kong.
Extracts from China Mainland Publications. No. 1—; April, 1962—. Irregular.

A new addition to the translation series issued by the American Consulate General in Hong Kong, the *E.C.M.P.* provides extracts from translations already published in the *Survey of China Mainland Press, Selections from China Mainland Magazines*, and *Current Background*. Each issue is devoted to a specific topic (e.g., 'Ethnic Minorities'), or several issues may form a series (e.g., Nos. 1–4, 'Attitudes and Policies Toward Non-Communist Countries'). A full bibliographical citiation is given for all extracts, providing the original source as well as the *S.C.M.P., S.C.M.M.*, or *C.B.* number, and two lists are provided identifying individuals quoted and showing the principal sources cited. Mimeographed.

An extremely useful compilation, the value of which lies in the fact that it draws together in one place material on a given subject scattered among the several Hong Kong Consulate publications.

1042 American Consulate General, Hong Kong.
Chinese Communist Propaganda Review. Hong Kong, Nos. 1–45, August 1951–August 1953. Bi-weekly.

A bi-weekly translation of articles from Chinese Communist newspapers, magazines, and propaganda handbooks, organized as follows: 'Propaganda Review', 'Theme and Contents', and 'Methods and Techniques'.

Indexes

1043 American Consulate General, Hong Kong.
Index to Survey of China Mainland Press, Selections from China Mainland Magazines, and Current Background. Hong Kong, No. 1—, March 15, 1956—. Bi-monthly.

A new series of bi-monthly indexes (120 to 150 pages in length) to the titles appearing in the *Survey of China Mainland Press, Selections from China Mainland Magazines* (formerly known as *Extracts from China Mainland Magazines*), and *Current Background*. Entries are listed under nine sections (with 78 major headings) as follows: (1) China—general, (2) central government—political, (3) political parties and public bodies, (4) question of Taiwan, (5) economic, (6) military, (7) education, culture, health, (8) domestic, (9) foreign. A key to the *Index* is included in No. 1, March 15, 1956 and also in No. 1, March 10, 1961. Mimeographed.

For an alphabetical listing of the categories used in the index, see the *Alphabetical Guide to the Index to Survey of China Mainland Press, Extracts from China Mainland Magazines and Current Background*, compiled by the East Asiatic Library of Columbia University (New York, 1958), 11p.

An indispensable tool.

See also the following three indexes for the 1950–1955 period.

1044 American Consulate General, Hong Kong.
Index to Survey of the China Mainland Press (November 1, 1950–December 31, 1952). Hong Kong, April 1958. 490p.

A compilation reproducing index sheets and index cards prepared informally by the Press Unit from November 1, 1950, the time at which the *Survey of the China Mainland Press* began publication, to December 31, 1952. Excluded are titles from the *Current Background* series, but some magazine titles are indexed, since *Extracts from China Mainland Magazines* did not exist as a separate publication until August, 1955.

The index covers titles, not contents. An article covering several subjects is usually listed only under the category of its title and is seldom cross-entered under other categories. Because the breakdown into categories is unsystematic, it is always necessary to consult the table of contents and the 'Feature' section which itemizes the most significant articles on all subjects, only some of which are cross-indexed. Some of the original index cards dealing with the Communist Party from April 1951 to July 1952 are missing and are excluded from the index (such omissions are generally noted). Earlier entries give as references only the issue number and the date, so that the table of contents of issue must be scanned to locate the article desired. Later entries give the page number as well. Entries appear under fourteen sections, with 147 headings, in the following order: (1) feature, (2) 'Anti-U.S. Campaign' (3) China's international relations, (4) culture, (5) economic items, (6) education, (7) labor, (8) military, (9) political, (10) regional administration, (11) religion, (12) social, (13) women, and (14) youth. The table of contents lists the sub-headings under each section. Mimeographed.

This index and the 1953–1954 index (see next entry) were compiled on an *ad hoc* basis, and each has its separate system of categories unrelated to other systems.

1045 American Consulate General, Hong Kong.
Index to the Publications of the Press Monitoring Unit, 1953–1954. Hong Kong, April 1958. 594p.

Incorporates two indexes prepared by the Press Unit: (1) the main index, which covers the *Survey of China Mainland Press* for the years 1953 and 1954, and (2) a supplementary index which covers the *Current Background* series from its first issue of June 13, 1950 through issue No. 310, dated January 17,

1955 (after which date the titles of articles in the *Current Background* series were entered in the main index to the *S.C.M.P.*).

Because this is an index to titles, not to contents, it is always necessary to consult the table of contents which covers the supplementary as well as the main index. The letters 'HK' refer to numbers of the *Review of the Hong Kong Chinese Press* which were entered in the *Index* for a brief period beginning in January 1953. The letters *CB* refer to *Current Background* material which was sometimes entered in both the main and suplementary indexes, and occasionally in the supplementary index only. 'Background Material' refers to certain items indexed but not generally distributed. Entries in the first part are arranged according to a decimal classification system under six sections (with 76 major headings) as follows: (100) China—internal, miscellaneous; (200) cultural and social affairs; (300) military; (400) economic; (500–600) regions; (700–800) China's international relations.

1046 American Consulate General, Hong Kong.
Index to Publications of the Press Monitoring Unit, 1955. Hong Kong, April 1958. 453p.

A compilation reproducing the Press Unit index for 1955, listing titles from the *Survey of China Mainland Press*, Nos. 963–1199 (January 7 to December 31, 1955), *Extracts from China Mainland Magazines*, Nos. 1–19 (August 15 to December 19, 1955), and *Current Background*, Nos. 311–372 (February 1 to December 28, 1955). The letters 'SU' refer to S.C.M.P. Supplements (for limited distribution). In listing titles from Supplements prior to No. 1111, no page numbers are given. In the case of some listings from the *Extracts* series, the figure in the second column represents the number of the magazine in which the original article appeared.

The table of contents is arranged according to a decimal system under nine sections (with 75 major headings) as follows: (100) China—general; (200) central government—political; (300) political parties and public bodies; (400) question of Taiwan; (500) economics; (600) military; (700) education, culture, health; (800) local—general; and (900) foreign—general.

(For details, see 'A Key to Index' in the first issue of *Index to Survey oj China Mainland Press, Extracts from China Mainland Magazines and Current Background 1956*.)

2. JOINT PUBLICATIONS RESEARCH SERVICE

The Joint Publications Research Service (J.P.R.S.) is a federal agency of the United States Government providing a centralized translation service for other American government departments and agencies. Since late 1957, source materials and other data on Communist China from Chinese Communist books, newspapers, and periodicals, as well as writings in Russian, Japanese, and other languages have been translated and issued either individually or in series (over 40,000 pages of translations of social science material on China were issued during fiscal year 1963 [July 1962–June 1963] alone). These supplement the translations issued by the American Consulate General in Hong Kong, and are an indispensable source of documentation.

Thirteen current and defunct series are listed in this section arranged roughly in the following order: general, political, military, economic, cultural, and scientific. In addition, the following J.P.R.S. series have been listed elsewhere in this Guide:

1) *Activities of Prominent Chinese Communist Personalities* (see **362**).

2) Translations from *Jen-min jih-pao* (**835**), *Kuang-ming jih-pao* (**838**), *Ta-kung pao* (**841**) and *Kung-jen jih-pao* (**844**) following the newspapers themselves in Chapter XVII.

3) Translations from *Hung-ch'i* (Red Flag, **887**), *Ching-chi yen-chiu* (Economic Studies, **864**), *Min-tsu t'uan-chieh* (Solidarity of Nationality Groups, **900**), and *Min-tsu yen-chiu* (Nationalities Studies, **902**)—likewise following the periodicals themselves in Chapter XVII.

All translations are available on microfilm or on photocopy from the Library of Congress. In addition, microfilms of all translations of material on China issued from 1957 to July 1960 and microfilms or Xerox copies of translations in the social sciences on China issued from July 1962 are available from Research & Microfilm Publications (P.O. Box 267, Annapolis, Maryland). (Original copies in mimeographed form on China in the social sciences were distributed directly to research institutions and libraries for the in-between two-year period ending June 1962.) Most (though not all) J.P.R.S. translations are listed in the *Monthly Catalog of U.S. Government Publications*, and they are also available in the microprint edition of Non-Depository U.S. Government Documents (issued by the Readex Microprint Corporation, 5 Union Square, New York, N.Y. 10003), which is arranged according to the *Monthly Catalog* number.

Beginning February 1963, direct distribution of mimeographed copies was reinstated by the J.P.R.S. with the following series available for subscription:

1) *Activities of Prominent Chinese Communist Personalities* (now defunct).

2) *Communist China Digest* (see **1052**).

3) *Translations on Communist China's*
   a) *Agriculture, Animal Husbandry, and Materials* (**1060**).
   b) *Industry, Mining, Fuels and Power* (**1061**).
   c) *Trade, Finance, Transportation and Communications* (**1062**).
   d) *Science and Technology* (**1064**).

4) *Translations of Political and Sociological Information on Communist China* (**1054**).

5) *Translations from Hung-ch'i (Red Flag)* and *Ching-chi yen-chiu* (Economic Studies).

For detailed information on the sales and subscription system in effect since February 1963 (with subsequent revisions), etc., see the *Catalog of Current Joint Publications Research Service Publications* (**1050**).

For a bibliography and index to all issues published through July 1960, and a bibliography of issues published since July 1962, see the first two entries listed below. (No bibliography is available for the period August 1960–June 1962.) Since most J.P.R.S. reports are listed in the *Monthly Catalog of U.S. Government Publications*, each December issue, which contains the cumulative index for the entire year, also can be of use. See also the monthly *Consolidated Translation Survey* (**1049**), which includes J.P.R.S. translations, as well as the bibliography of book-length J.P.R.S. reports (**1051**).

In addition to the bibliographical tools described below, it might be added that J.P.R.S. scientific and technical reports are also cataloged and subject-indexed in *Technical Translations*, which has been published semi-monthly since January 1959 by the Office of Technical Services (semi-annual indexes to the *Technical Translations* also are available).

Finally, it should be noted that not all J.P.R.S. translations emanating from China or concerning developments in China are issued in the China group of serials discussed and described in this section or elsewhere in this Guide. Certain Chinese translations are inserted into other J.P.R.S. serials, such as *Translations on International Communist Developments*, the Soviet, East European, Asian groups, and even such serials as *Translations on Cuba*.

It thus becomes clear that there is no comprehensive guide to the millions of pages of J.P.R.S. reports, and that the available tools provide only partial bibliographical control.

1047 Sorich, Richard, ed.
Contemporary China: A Bibliography of Reports on China Published by the United States Joint Publications Research Service. New York: Prepared for the Joint Committee on Contemporary China of the American Council of Learned Societies and the Social Science Research Council, 1961. 99p.

A bibliography containing all reports on China published by the Joint Publications Research Service from its inception in late 1957 through July 1960. The bibliography consists of three parts, each accompanied by a detailed explanatory note. Part 1 is the body of the bibliography, providing titles and contents of all J.P.R.S. reports on China within the scope of the present work and arranged numerically by J.P.R.S. number. Part 2 is a list of abbreviations for Chinese and non-Chinese serials occurring in the bibliographical citations of Part 1, and includes translations of serial titles and place of publication. Part 3 contains a subject index to reports cited in Part 1. There is also a separate list of index categories included to give an overview of the index subject classification scheme.

An invaluable reference tool for the use of a voluminous group of important translations not readily identifiable otherwise.

1048   Kyriak, Theodore E., comp.
China: A Bibliography and Guide to Contents of a Collection of United States Joint Publications Research Service Translations in the Social Sciences Emanating From Communist China. Annapolis: Research & Microfilm Publications, No. 1/3—, July/September 1962—. Monthly.

Covers J.P.R.S. translations in the social sciences concerning Communist China published since July 1962. The translations are arranged under three categories: serials, *ad hoc* translations, and book translations.

Under the first category, serials (the main body of the bibliography), the arrangement is first by title of serial (such as *Communist China Digest, Translations from Hung-ch'i,* etc.), and under each serial by the J.P.R.S. number. In the second and third categories, items are listed alphabetically by the English translated title. All entries in the bibliography are accompanied by a full contents note. There is a subject index and a cross-reference index, the latter listing the reports by J.P.R.S. number and providing the subject (or the serial title), and the location of the title in the bibliography and in the microfilm collection. The bibliography lacked the subject index until the November 1963 issue. Beginning with the April 1964 issue, scientific and technical translations are appended (with separate addenda covering the July 1963 to March 1964 period).

From Vol. 3, see *China and Asia (Exclusive of Near East): Bibliography— Index to U.S. J.P.R.S. Research Translations,* for a continuation of the above.

1049   U.S. Central Intelligence Agency, Foreign Documents Division.
Consolidated Translation Survey. No. 1—, 1958—. Monthly.

A list of English translations produced by the federal government, private industry, universities and research institutions, commercial translation organizations, foreign governments and private sources. Foreign documentary projects completed or started during the preceding month are also included.

Each issue is arranged by geographical area—the U.S.S.R., Eastern Europe, Western Europe, Africa, Middle East, Far East, Latin America and North America—and under each area within the following subject categories: economic, political, military, geographical, sociological, and biographical. Each subject category is further divided by language, and under language by periodical in alphabetical order. Scientific projects are grouped as a section regardless of geographical area. Each entry provides the title in English, author, foreign language title of source of material, date and data of publication, and publication identification of the completed project whenever available (e.g., the J.P.R.S. number). Material on China is translated not only from Chinese, Russian and Japanese, but also from Korean, Vietnamese, Mongolian, French, Spanish, Indonesian, Hebrew, Polish and other languages. Monthly author index.

Quinquennial Bibliography of Research Translations in English 1958–1962, Part I: The Social Sciences, and *Part II: Scientific and Technical,* based on the 1958–1962 issues of the *Consolidated Translation Survey,* are available on microfilm from Research & Microfilm Publications, Inc.

1050   U.S. Joint Publications Research Service.
Catalog of Current Joint Publications Research Service Publications. Washington, D.C., October 1963. 20p.

A brief introduction to the Joint Publications Research Service: the sales and subscription system in effect since February 1963 (with subsequent revisions); a list of various subscription categories, including serial report titles; the cataloging and indexing of current publications and back issues; and alternate sources for current J.P.R.S. publications. This pamphlet is expected to be revised from time to time.

1051   Research & Microfilm Publications, Inc.
A List of United States-J.P.R.S. Research Translations in the Social Sciences, 1957–1963. Annapolis, Md., 1963. 27p.

Most of this pamphlet, prepared for the 1963 annual meeting of the American Political Science Association, is given over to a list of titles in the scholarly book translation series of the Joint Publications Research Service. Over 100 titles are listed under China (pp. 17–23), most of them translations of Mainland works and of Soviet books on Communist China. The list of books is preceded by lists of current and backfile J.P.R.S. reports and J.P.R.S. bibliographies and catalogs.

1052   U.S. Joint Publications Research Service.
Communist China Digest. Washington, D.C. and New York, August 31, 1959—. Irregular.

Translations of extracts or summaries of current Mainland periodical and newspaper articles on political, economic, cultural, sociological, military, and international affairs. Nos. 1–45 of the *Digest* consist of two parts. A full translation of that section in the *Hsin-hua pan-yüeh-k'an* (New China Semi-Monthly, see **882**), which deals with significant national and international events, makes up Part 1. Part 2 is a miscellaneous section comprising extracts in English of selected articles from other Chinese Communist newspapers and periodicals.

Because of the discontinuation of overseas circulation of the *Hsin-hua pan-yüeh-k'an*, the division of the *Digest* into two parts ceased with issue No. 46. The general nature of the coverage of subject matter, however, has remained substantially the same. Each issue contains about 100 pages on the average, including, as a rule, an appendix entitled 'List of Translations on Communist China' which provides a listing with full bibliographical data of all J.P.R.S. translations published during the preceding months.

A very useful translation service.

The following numbers of the J.P.R.S. reports are in the *Communist China Digest*:

DIGEST NO.	J.P.R.S. NO.	DATE OF PUBLICATION	U.S.G.P.O. MONTHLY CATALOG NO.
1	892D	8–31–59	
2	933D	9–22–59	
3	957D	10–10–59	
4	979D	10–29–59	1960– 769
5	1014D	11–17–59	792
6	1059D	11–30–59	836
7	1081D	12– 6–59	1908
8	1106D	1–15–60	3963
9	1157D	2– 5–60	5628
10	3029	2–26–60	5570
11	3110	3–25–60	7189
12	3157	4–13–60	7223
13	3179	4–25–60	7235
14	3206	5– 2–60	8623
15	3285	5–25–60	8678
16	3349	6– 3–60	10106
17	3366	6– 6–60	10113
18	3421	6–21–60	11438
19	3520	7– 6–60	14239
20	3605	7–26–60	14307
21	3661	8– 8–60	14348
22	3725	8–18–60	15629
23	3781	8–29–60	15663
24	3834	7– 7–60	17231
25	6018	9–26–60	17642
26	6119	10–18–60	1961– 1000
27	6211	11– 8–60	1025
28	6375	12– 6–60	1106
29	6497	1– 3–61	2302
30	6660	1–30–61	4541
31	6703	2– 6–61	4563
32	6751	2–14–61	7763
33	6792	2–21–61	7794
34	6819	2–27–61	7815
35	6874	3– 7–61	7857
36	6928	3–14–61	9329
37	8071	4–10–61	13037
38	8116	4–18–61	13075
39	8308	5–19–61	13225

DIGEST NO.	J.P.R.S. NO.	DATE OF PUBLICATION	U.S.G.P.O. MONTHLY CATALOG NO.
40	8434	6– 9–61	1961–13310
41	8499	6–26–61	13353
42	8510	6–30–61	13361
43	8535	7– 5–61	13373
44	8737	8–16–61	17435
45	8767	8–21–61	17457
46	8978	9–29–61	19623
47	10372	10– 9–61	21051
48	10543	10–16–61	1962– 1113
49	11024	11–13–61	1430
50	11130	11–20–61	1495
51	11216	11–27–61	2941
52	11324	12– 4–61	2969
53	11590	12–20–61	3125
54	11957	1–15–62	5895
55	12238	1–31–62	6116
56	12591	2–21–62	8156
57	12988	3–16–62	10062
58	13133	3–26–62	10183
59	13460	4–16–62	12105
60	13547	4–25–62	not listed
61	13731	5–14–62	12303
62	13828	5–22–62	14090
63	14082	6–12–62	not listed
64	14122	6–15–62	14333
65	14482	7–16–62	15953
66	14533	7–20–62	15969
67	14913	8–21–62	19676
68	15010	8–28–62	19768
69	15445	9–24–62	22081
70	15515	9–28–62	22149
71	15657	10–11–62	22285
72	15726	10–16–62	22349
73	15998	11– 1–62	23827
74	16022	11– 5–62	23851
75	16161	11–13–62	1963– 700
76	16335	11–20–62	867
77	16579	12– 7–62	1096
78	16680	12–14–62	1140
79	16689	12–17–62	1145
80	16813	12–26–62	2625
81	16998	1– 7–63	2805
82	17206	1–21–63	5112
83	17663	2–15–63	6746
84	17700	2–18–63	6783
85	17853	2–27–63	6924
86	18217	3–19–63	8576
87	18254	3–20–63	8613
88	18664	4–11–63	10365
89	18712	4–16–63	10413
90	19116	5– 9–63	10817

DIGEST NO.	J.P.R.S. NO.	DATE OF PUBLICATION	U.S.G.P.O. MONTHLY CATALOG NO.
91	19221	5–16–63	1963–12311
92	19603	6– 7–63	12693
93	19670	6–12–63	12760
94	19694	6–14–63	14096
95	19843	6–25–63	14245
96	20025	7– 3–63	14427
97	20440	7–31–63	16074
98	20551	8– 8–63	16185
99	20563	8– 9–63	16197
100	21049	9–12–63	17991
101	21113	9–17–63	19415
102	21251	9–30–63	19553
103	21515	10–21–63	20807
104	21708	11– 2–63	1964– 962
105	21795	11– 8–63	1049
106	21860	11–14–63	1114
107	22216	12–10–63	2584
108	22244	12–12–63	2612
109	22301	12–16–63	2669
110	22402	12–20–63	2770

1053 **U.S. Joint Publications Research Service.**
Translations from Chinese Communist Periodicals. Washington, D.C., Nos. 1–17, October 1961–July 1962. Irregular.

Contains translations of articles selected from various Chinese Communist periodicals (source indicated). Coverage is not confined to any special field, and there is no apparent emphasis in either the selection of subjects or the arrangement of contents. A table of contents is provided for each issue. The publication varies in length from 25 to 200 pages. Mimeographed.

The following numbers of the J.P.R.S. reports are special issues of this title:

PUBLICATION NO.	J.P.R.S. NO.	DATE OF PUBLICATION	U.S.G.P.O. MONTHLY CATALOG NO.
1	10681	10–25–61	1962– 1205
2	11283	12– 2–61	2955
3	11333	12– 4–61	2978
4	11432	12– 7–61	3029
5	11506	12–12–61	3068
6	11784	1–30–62	5787
7	11809	1–22–62	5799
8	12066	1–22–62	5982
9	12180	1–29–62	6070
10	12594	2–21–62	8159
11	12760	3– 2–62	8246
12	12907	3–12–62	9989
13	13029	3–19–62	10098
14	13175	3–27–62	10218
15	13348	4– 5–62	10325
16	14045	6– 7–62	14290
17	14502	7–18–62	15960

1054 **U.S. Joint Publications Research Service.**
Translations of Political and Sociological Information on Communist China.
Washington, D.C., July 1962—. Irregular.

Contains summaries or translations of selected articles from Chinese Communist newspapers and periodicals on political and social developments on the Mainland. (See also the following three entries.) Mimeographed.

The following numbers of the J.P.R.S. reports are special issues of this title:

PUBLICATION NO.	J.P.R.S. NO.	DATE OF PUBLICATION	U.S.G.P.O. MONTHLY CATALOG NO.
1	14564	7-23-62	1962-17839
2	14691	8- 1-62	17953
3	14735	8- 6-62	17991
4	14751	8- 7-62	18007
5	14779	8- 9-62	18035
6	14852	8-15-62	19632
7	14917	8-21-62	19680
8	14980	8-27-62	19739
9	14983	8-27-62	19741
10	15003	8-28-62	19761
11	15168	9- 7-62	19914
12	15251	9-12-62	19994
13	15314	9-17-62	20013
14	15415	9-24-62	22053
15	15522	10- 1-62	22156
16	15527	10- 2-62	22160
17	15545	10- 3-62	22178
18	15630	10- 9-62	22259
19	15722	10-16-62	22346
20	15767	10-18-62	22389
21	15804	10-22-62	23642
22	15829	10-22-62	23666
23	15888	10-26-62	23723
24	15982	10-31-62	23812
25	16011	11- 2-62	23840
26	16106	11- 9-62	23924
27	16133	11-13-62	1963- 675
28	16249	11-19-62	783
29	16272	11-20-62	806
30	16433	11-30-62	962
31	16509	12- 4-62	1034
32	16583	12-10-62	1100
33	16658	12-13-62	2502
34	16697	12-17-62	2526
35	16732	12-17-62	2555
36	16752	12-18-62	2572
37	16825	12-26-62	2636
38	17047	1- 8-63	2851
39	17082	1-10-63	2884
40	17097	1-11-63	2899

PUBLICATION NO.	J.P.R.S. NO.	DATE OF PUBLICATION	U.S.G.P.O. MONTHLY CATALOG NO.
41	17122	1–14–63	1962– 2923
42	17196	1–18–63	2992
43	17230	1–22–63	5127
44	17291	1–24–63	5182
45	17336	1–29–63	5222
46	17346	1–29–63	5232
47	17442	2– 4–63	5321
48	17449	2– 4–63	5327
49	17460	2– 4–63	5338
50	17488	2– 5–63	5363
51	17561	2–11–63	5414
52	17601	2–12–63	6689
53	17634	2–14–63	6718
54	17660	2–15–63	6743
55	17733	2–19–63	6815
56	17758	2–20–63	6838
57	17766	2–21–63	6845
58	17858	2–27–63	6929
59	17867	2–28–63	6936
60	17935	3– 5–63	6998
61	17966	3– 6–63	7025
62	17991	3– 7–63	7047
63	18014	3– 7–63	7069
64	18079	3–12–63	7131
65	18158	3–15–63	8517
66	18283	3–22–63	8642
67	18308	3–25–63	8667
68	18344	3–25–63	8703
69	18368	3–26–63	8727
70	18373	3–26–63	8732
71	18393	3–27–63	8752
72	18454	3–31–63	8813
73	18470	4– 1–63	8829
74	18474	4– 1–63	8833
75	18535	4– 4–63	8894
76	18556	4– 4–63	1963– 8915
77	18597	4– 8–63	8956
78	18618	4– 9–63	8977
79	19139	5–10–63	10840
80	19175	5–14–63	10876
81	19378	5–24–63	12468
82	19550	6– 4–63	12640
83	19646	6–11–63	12736
84	19665	6–12–63	12755
85	19751	6–19–63	14153
86	19804	6–24–63	14206
87	19831	6–24–63	14233
88	19848	6–25–63	14250
89	19980	7– 1–63	14382
90	20021	7– 3–63	14423
91	20024	7– 3–63	14426

PUBLICATION NO.	J.P.R.S. NO.	DATE OF PUBLICATION	U.S.G.P.O. MONTHLY CATALOG NO.
92	20114	7–10–63	1963–15748
93	20125	7–11–63	15759
94	20295	7–22–63	15929
95	20326	7–24–63	15960
96	20439	7–31–63	16073
97	20689	8–19–63	17631
98	20859	8–30–63	17801
99	21017	9–11–63	17959
100	21074	9–13–63	19376
101	21259	9–30–63	19561
102	21339	10– 7–63	19641
103	21372	10– 8–63	19674
104	21379	10– 9–63	19681
105	21455	10–15–63	19757
106	21463	10–16–63	19765
107	21530	10–21–63	20822
108	21563	10–23–63	20855
109	21603	10–25–63	20895
110	21645	10–29–63	1964– 899
111	21658	10–30–63	912
112	21727	11– 5–63	981
113	21735	11– 5–63	989
114	21792	11– 8–63	1046
115	21846	11–13–63	1100
116	21859	11–14–63	1113
117	21884	11–15–63	1138
118	21935	11–20–63	1189
119	21969	11–21–63	1223
120	22027	11–25–63	1281
121	22043	11–26–63	1297
122	22053	11–27–63	1307
123	22066	11–29–63	1320
124	22088	12– 2–63	1342
125	22205	12–10–63	2573
126	22246	12–12–63	2614
129	22341	12–18–63	2709
130	22371	12–19–63	2739
131	22391	12–20–63	2759
132	22425	12–23–63	2793
133	22517	12–31–63	2885
134	22563	12–31–63	2931

1055 **U.S. Joint Publications Research Service.**
Translations from China's Political and Sociological Publications. Washington, D.C., September–October 1959. Irregular.

Within the general frame of politics and sociology, each issue, averaging fifty pages, is devoted to a special topic (party activities, nationalities and religion, etc.) and carries a table of contents, but no index. Mimeographed.

The following numbers of the J.P.R.S. reports are special issues of this title:

J.P.R.S. NO.	DATE OF PUBLICATION	U.S.G.P.O. MONTHLY CATALOG NO.
909D	9–11–59	1959–16509
941D	9–30–59	16537
984D	10–23–59	17554
1830	8– 4–59	13221
1842	8– 7–59	13229
1858	8–21–59	14886
1861	8–24–59	14889
1875	9– 2–59	16558
1932	10– 2–59	17592

A similar series of a general nature (no longer confined to any particular theme in any one issue) was published between October and December 1959 under the title *Selected Political and Sociological Translations on Communist China*.

J.P.R.S. NO.	DATE OF PUBLICATION	U.S.G.P.O. MONTHLY CATALOG NO.
1953	10–15–59	1959–17611
2011	11–17–59	1960– 902
2060	12– 7–59	937

1056 U.S. Joint Publications Research Service.
Translations of Political Articles from the China Mainland Press. Washington, D.C., April 1958–June 1959. Irregular.

Each issue, averaging 100 pages (with no apparent arrangement of contents), contains a table of contents, but no index.

The following numbers of the J.P.R.S. reports are special issues of this title:

J.P.R.S. NO.	DATE OF PUBLICATION	U.S.G.P.O. MONTHLY CATALOG NO.
101D	4–22–58	
187D	6– 2–58	
263D	8–22–58	
366D	11–12–58	1959– 556
463D	1– 6–59	1765
472D	1–13–59	3654
544D	2–17–59	4986
601D	3–17–59	6366
681D	4–24–59	9167
746D	6– 3–59	9194
796D	6–30–59	10249

1057 U.S. Joint Publications Research Service.
Political Information on Communist China—A Compilation of Translations. Washington, D.C., Nos. 1–28, January–October 1961. Irregular.

Translations of selected political articles taken from Chinese Communist publications. No apparent arrangement of contents. A table of contents is provided for each issue, but no index. The publication varies in length from 20 to 200 pages. Mimeographed.

The following numbers of the J.P.R.S. reports are special issues of this title:

PUBLICATION NO.	J.P.R.S. NO.	DATE OF PUBLICATION	U.S.G.P.O. MONTHLY CATALOG NO.
I	6657	1–30–61	1961– 4540
2	6960	3–22–61	9357
3	6936	3–16–61	9336
4	6953	3–20–61	9352
5	8013	4– 3–61	12989
6	8115	4–21–61	13074
7	8125	4–12–61	13083
8	8146	4–24–61	13100
9	8220	5– 3–61	13153
10	8249	5–12–61	13178
11	8262	5–15–61	13190
12	8344	5–26–61	13247
13	8293	5–18–61	13212
14	8312	5–24–61	13229
15	8408	5–31–61	13290
16	8409	5–26–61	13291
17	8410	5–31–61	13292
18	8418	6– 6–61	13300
19	8426	6– 9–61	13304
20	8547	7– 5–61	1962– 793
21	8552	7–12–61	1961–15102
22	8565	7–10–61	15105
23	8582	7–13–61	not listed
24	8609	7–26–61	15128
25	8666	8– 4–61	15164
26	8734	8–14–61	17432
27	8823	9– 3–61	17486
28	10506	10–16–61	1962– 1095

1058 **U.S. Joint Publications Research Service.**
Military Information on Communist China. Washington, D.C., May–July 1958. Irregular.

Based on the Chinese Communist press and the *Chieh-fang chün chan-shih* 解放軍戰士 (Liberation Army Warriors). Four issues were published: J.P.R.S. 47D (information unavailable); J.P.R.S. 125D (May 6, 1958, 25p.) covering the period from January 1956 to February 1957; J.P.R.S. 192 (January 28, 1958) with information taken from *Chieh-fang chün chan-shih*, Nos. 1–24, January–December 1956; J.P.R.S. 203D (July 1, 1958, 30p.) covering the period from January 1956 to January 1957.

The following J.P.R.S. reports, published under various titles, also contain military information on Communist China: (1) J.P.R.S. 764 and 767, June 18, 1959, 43p., and June 17, 1959, 43p. (U.S.G.P.O. Monthly Catalog, 1959, Nos. 10239 and 10240), *Translations of Articles from Peiping Chieh-fang chün pao* (解放軍報); (2) J.P.R.S. 1357, March 16, 1959, 31p. (1959–6471), *Articles from the Chinese Communist Newspaper Chieh-fang chün pao;* (3) J.P.R.S. 1687, June 9, 1959, 18p. (1959–10338), *Military Information from Chieh-fang chün pao;* (4) J.P.R.S. 1730, June 26, 1959, 49p. (1959–10343), *Selected Articles on Chinese Military Information from Chieh-fang chün pao;* (5) J.P.R.S. 4270, December 15, 1960, 47p. (1960–2140), *Selections from Shanghai Chieh-fang jih-pao;* and (6) J.P.R.S. 10680, October 24, 1961, 22p. (1962–1204), *Military Radio Communications, Communist China.*

1059 U.S. Joint Publications Research Service.
Economic Information on Communist China—A Compilation of Translations. Washington, D.C., Nos. 1–41, January–October 1961. Irregular.

Translations of selected economic articles taken from Chinese Communist publications. No apparent arrangement of contents. A table of contents is provided for each issue, but no index. The publication varies in length from 50 to 200 pages. Mimeographed.

The following numbers of the J.P.R.S. reports are special issues of this title:

PUBLICATION NO.	J.P.R.S. NO.	DATE OF PUBLICATION	U.S.G.P.O. MONTHLY CATALOG NO.
1	6627	1–24–61	1961– 4526
2	6781	2–23–61	7786
3	6866	3– 8–61	7849
4	6871	3– 8–61	7854
5	6951	3–17–61	9350
6	6952	3–20–61	9351
7	8014	4– 3–61	12990
8	8101	4–15–61	13062
9	8124	4–12–61	13082
10	8172	4–27–61	13116
11	8222	5– 3–61	13154
12	8227	5– 1–61	13159
13	8248	5–11–61	13177
14	8364	5–29–61	13260
15	8277	5–18–61	13202
16	8298	5– 9–61	13216
17	8310	5–23–61	13227
18	8311	5–23–61	13228
19	8345	5–25–61	13248
20	8398	5–31–61	13285
21	8399	5–31–61	13286
22	8400	5–31–61	13287

PUBLICATION NO.	J.P.R.S. NO.	DATE OF PUBLICATION	U.S.G.P.O. MONTHLY CATALOG NO.
23	8413	5-29-61	1961-13295
24	8414	5-25-61	13296
25	8415	6- 6-61	13297
26	8416	6-6-61	13298
27	8427	6- 9-61	13305
[28]	8429	6- 9-61	13307
29	8489	6-22-61	13344
30	8550	7-12-61	15100
31	8567	7-10-61	not listed
32	8581	7-13-61	15111
33	8608	7-26-61	15127
34	8617	7-21-61	15133
35	8694	8- 4-61	15179
[36]	8728	8-11-61	15196
37	8735	8-14-61	17433
38	8826	9- 1-61	19560
39	8928	9-25-61	20925
40			not listed
41	10507	10-16-61	1962- 1096

1060   U.S. Joint Publications Research Service.
Translations on Communist China's Agriculture, Animal Husbandry, and Materials.
Washington, D.C., No. 1—, July 1962—. Irregular.

Contains summaries or translations of selected articles on the subject from Chinese Communist publications (source indicated), arranged according to no apparent scheme. The publication, varying in length from 10 to over 100 pages, carries a table of contents. Mimeographed.

The following numbers of the J.P.R.S. reports are special issues of this title:

PUBLICATION NO.	J.P.R.S. NO.	DATE OF PUBLICATION	U.S.G.P.O. MONTHLY CATALOG NO.
1	14565	7-23-62	1962-17840
2	14690	8- 1-62	17952
3	14757	8- 7-62	18013
4	14844	8-14-62	19626
5	14998	8-27-62	19756
6	15112	9- 4-62	19859
7	15198	9-10-62	19943
8	15376		22014
9	15495	10- 1-62	22130
10	15778	10-18-62	22400
11	15884	10-25-62	23719
12	15904	10-26-62	23738
13	15937	10-30-62	23770
14	16097	11- 8-62	1963- 650

PUBLICATION NO.	J.P.R.S. NO.	DATE OF PUBLICATION	U.S.G.P.O. MONTHLY CATALOG NO.
15	16121	11– 9–62	1963– 665
16	16128	11–13–62	672
17	16385	11–27–62	915
18	16397	11–28–62	926
19	16506	12– 4–62	1031
20	16584	12–10–62	1101
21	16759	12–19–62	2578
22	16794	12–20–62	2608
23	16829	12–26–62	2640
24	16982	1– 4–63	2790
25	17030	1– 8–63	2835
26	17221		not listed
27	17502	2– 6–63	5376
28	17600	2–12–63	6688
29	17654	2–15–63	6737
30	17798	2–25–63	6871
31	17869	2–28–63	6938
32	18098	3–13–63	8457
33	18171	3–18–63	8530
34	18237	3–20–63	8596
35	18259	3–21–63	8618
36	18309	3–25–63	8668
37	18484	4– 2–63	8843
38	18623	4– 9–63	8982
39	18747	4–17–63	10448
40	18797	4–19–63	10498
41	18826	4–22–63	10527
42	18988	4–30–63	10689
43	19038	5– 6–63	10739
44	19297	5–21–63	12387
45	19306	5–21–63	12396
46	19589	6– 6–63	12679
47	19781	6–20–63	14183
48	19840	6–25–63	14242
49	19845	6–25–63	14247
50			not listed
51	20121	7–11–63	15755
52	20266	7–19–63	15900
53	20354	7–29–63	15988
54	20457	8– 1–63	16091
55	20483	8– 2–63	16117
56	20524	8– 7–63	16158
57	20815	8–27–63	17757
58	20845	8–29–63	17787
59	20963	9– 6–63	17905
60	21082	9–13–63	19384
61	21190	9–23–63	19492
62	21256	9–30–63	19558
63	21361	10– 8–63	19663
64	21397	10–10–63	19699
65	21456	10–15–63	19758

PUBLICATION NO.	J.P.R.S. NO.	DATE OF PUBLICATION	U.S.G.P.O. MONTHLY CATALOG NO.
66	21503	10–18–63	1963–20795
67	21598	10–25–63	20890
68	21657	10–30–63	1964– 911
69	21731	11– 5–63	985
70	21854	11–13–63	1108
71	21930	11–20–63	1184
72	21971	11–21–63	1225
73	22086	11–29–63	1340
74	22203	12–10–63	2571
75	22226	12–11–63	2594
76	22241	12–12–63	2609
77	22316	12–17–63	2684
78	22431	12–23–63	2799
79	22558	12–31–63	2926

1061 U.S. Joint Publications Research Service.
Translations on Communist China's Industry, Mining, Fuels and Power. Washington, D.C., No. 1—, July 1962—. Irregular.

Contains summaries or translations of selected articles on the subject from Chinese Communist publications (source indicated), arranged according to no apparent scheme. Each issue, ranging in length from 10 to over 100 pages, carries a table of contents. Mimeographed.

The following numbers of the J.P.R.S. reports are special issues of this title:

PUBLICATION NO.	J.P.R.S. NO.	DATE OF PUBLICATION	U.S.G.P.O. MONTHLY CATALOG NO.
1	14652	7–30–62	1962–17920
2	14712	8– 2–62	17970
3	14773	8– 9–62	18029
4	15014	8–28–62	19772
5	15197	9–10–62	19942
6	15281	9–17–62	21951
7	15418	9–24–62	22056
8	15547	10– 3–62	22180
9	15551	10– 3–62	22184
10	15766	10–18–62	22388
11	15873	10–24–62	23709
12	15959	10–30–62	23791
13	16098	11– 8–62	1963– 651
14	16384	11–27–62	914
15	16505	12– 4–62	1030
16	16585	12–10–62	1102
17	16730	12–17–62	2553
18	16890	12–28–62	2699
19	16984	1– 4–63	2792
20	17112	1–14–63	2913

PUBLICATION NO.	J.P.R.S. NO.	DATE OF PUBLICATION	U.S.G.P.O. MONTHLY CATALOG NO.
21	17656	2–15–63	1963– 6739
22	17797	2–25–63	6870
23	17988	3– 6–63	7044
24	18097	3–13–63	8456
25	18123	3–14–63	8482
26	18174	3–18–63	8533
27	18483	4– 2–63	8842
28	18624	4– 9–63	8983
29	18739	4–16–63	10440
30	19257	5–17–63	12347
31	19634	6–10–63	12724
32	19733	6–18–63	14135
33	19779	6–20–63	14181
34	20332	7–25–63	15966
35	20455	8– 1–63	16089
36	21080	9–13–63	19382
37	21258	9–30–63	19560
38	21365	10– 8–63	19667
39	21440	10–14–63	19742
40	21569	10–23–63	20861
41	21621	10–28–63	20913
42	21656	10–30–63	1964– 910
43	21848	11–13–63	1102
44	21959	11–20–63	1213
45	22085	11–29–63	1339
46	22235	12–11–63	2603
47	22243	12–12–63	2611
48	22355	12–18–63	2723
49	22419	12–23–63	2787
50	22561	12–31–63	2929

1062 U.S. Joint Publications Research Service.
Translations on Communist China's Trade, Finance, Transportation and Communications. Washington, D.C., No. 1—, July 1962—. Irregular.

Contains summaries or translations of selected articles on the subject from Chinese Communist publications (source indicated), arranged according to no apparent scheme. The publication, varying in length from 10 to over 100 pages, carries a table of contents. Mimeographed.

The following numbers of the J.P.R.S. reports are special issues of this title:

PUBLICATION NO.	J.P.R.S. NO.	DATE OF PUBLICATION	U.S.G.P.O. MONTHLY CATALOG NO.
1	14566	7–23–62	1962–17841
2	14575	7–24–62	17850
3	14625	7–27–62	17895
4	14714	8– 2–62	17972
5	14752	8– 7–62	18008

PUBLICATION NO.	J.P.R.S. NO.	DATE OF PUBLICATION	U.S.G.P.O. MONTHLY CATALOG NO.
6	14753	8– 7–62	1962–18009
7	14774	8– 9–62	18030
8	14809	8–13–62	18062
9	14887	8–17–62	19654
10	14928	8–22–62	19690
11	14955	8–24–62	19716
12	15065	8–31–62	19818
13	15196	9–10–62	19941
14	15375	9–21–62	22013
15	15490	9–28–62	22125
16	15521	10– 1–62	22155
17	15541	10– 2–62	22174
18	15582	10– 5–62	22213
19	15779	10–18–62	22401
20	15831	10–22–62	23668
21	15885	10–25–62	23720
22	15903	10–26–62	23737
23	15938	10–30–62	23771
24	15958	10–30–62	23790
25	16099	11– 8–62	1963– 652
26	16383	11–27–62	913
27	16508	12– 4–62	1033
28	16758	12–19–62	2577
29	16808	12–21–62	2621
30	16830	12–26–62	2641
31	17032	1– 8–63	2837
32	17084	1–10–63	2886
33	17501	2– 6–63	5375
34	17657	3–15–63	6740
35	17796	2–25–63	6869
36	17868	2–28–63	6937
37	17919	3– 4–63	6984
38	18040	3– 8–63	7092
39	18096	3–13–63	8455
40	18173	3–18–63	8532
41	18240	3–20–63	8599
42	18485	4– 2–63	8844
43	18625	4– 9–63	8984
44	18738	4–16–63	10439
45	18828	4–22–63	10529
46	19609	6–10–63	12699
47	19780	6–20–63	14182
48	19839	6–25–63	14241
49	19965	7– 1–63	14367
50	19976	7– 1–63	14378
51	20120	7–11–63	15754
52	20381	7–29–63	16015
53	20456	8– 1–63	16090
54	20555	8– 8–63	16189
55	20743	8–21–63	17685
56	20812	8–26–63	17754

PUBLICATION NO.	J.P.R.S. NO.	DATE OF PUBLICATION	U.S.G.P.O. MONTHLY CATALOG NO.
57	20874	8–30–63	1963–17816
58	20961	9– 6–63	17903
59	21072	9–13–63	19374
60	21160	9–19–63	19462
61	21186	9–23–63	19488
62	21364	10– 8–63	19666
63	21400	10–10–63	19702
64	21436	10–14–63	19738
65	21507	10–18–63	20799
66	21585	10–24–63	20877
67	21660	10–30–63	1964– 914
68	21685	10–31–63	939
69	21732	11– 5–63	986
70	21856	11–13–63	1110
71	21931	11–20–63	1185
72	21968	11–21–63	1222
73	22207	12–10–63	2575
74	22245	12–12–63	2613
75	22354	12–18–63	2722
76	22426	12–23–63	2794
77	22470	12–26–63	2838
78	22559	12–31–63	2927

1063 **U.S. Joint Publications Research Service.**
Sociological-Educational-Cultural Information on Communist China—A Compilation of Translations. Washington, D.C., Nos. 1–13, February–September 1961. Irregular.

Translations of selected sociological, educational and cultural articles taken from Chinese Communist publications. No apparent arrangement of contents. A table of contents is provided for each issue, but no index. The publication varies in length from 20 to 200 pages. Mimeographed.

The following numbers of the J.P.R.S. reports are special issues of this title:

PUBLICATION NO.	J.P.R.S. NO.	DATE OF PUBLICATION	U.S.G.P.O. MONTHLY CATALOG NO.
1	6728	2–14–61	1961– 4572
2	6872	3– 8–61	7855
3	8042	4– 7–61	13015
[4]	8061	4–10–61	13030
5	8205	4–24–61	13142
6	8211	5– 3–61	13147
7	8319	5–25–61	13232
8	8412	5–25–61	13294
9	8417	6– 6–61	13299
10	8551	7–12–61	15101
11	8566	7–10–61	13385
[12]	8729	8–11–61	15197
13	8933	9–25–61	19604

1064 **U.S. Joint Publications Research Service.**
Translations on Communist China's Science and Technology. Washington, D.C., July 1962—. Irregular.

Contains summaries or full translations of selected articles on science and technology in Communist China. Mimeographed.

The following numbers of the J.P.R.S. reports are special issues of this title:

PUBLICATION NO.	J.P.R.S. NO.	DATE OF PUBLICATION	U.S.G.P.O. MONTHLY CATALOG NO.
1	14545	7–20–62	1962–17820
2	14756	8– 7–62	18012
3	14834	8–14–62	18085
4	14854	8–15–62	18097
5	14920	8–22–62	18113
6	15305	9–17–62	21964
7	15526	10– 1–62	22159
8	15569	10– 5–62	22200
9	15590		22221
10	15710	10–15–62	22336
11	15846	10–23–62	23683
12	16094	11– 8–62	1963– 648
13	(no information)		
14	16659	12–13–62	2503
15	16761	12–19–62	2580
16	17165	1–16–63	2963
17	17197	1–18–63	2993
18	17277	1–24–63	5169
19	17684	2–18–63	6767
20	17848	2–27–63	6920
21	18023	3– 8–63	7075
22	18138	3–14–63	8497
23	18558	4– 4–63	8917
24	18588	4– 8–63	8947
25	18736	4–16–63	10437
26	18742	4–17–63	10443
27	18745	4–17–63	10446
28	18801	4–19–63	10502
29	18815	4–22–63	10516
30	18827	4–22–63	10528
31	18891	4–24–63	10592
32	18913	4–25–63	10614
33	18945	4–29–63	10646
34	19037	5– 6–63	10738
35	19258	5–17–63	12348
36	19302	5–21–63	12392
37	19523	5–31–63	12613
38	19907	6–27–63	14309
39	20006	7– 3–63	14408
40	20022	7– 3–63	14424
41	20166	7–15–63	15800

PUBLICATION NO.	J.P.R.S. NO.	DATE OF PUBLICATION	U.S.G.P.O. MONTHLY CATALOG NO.
42	20294	7–22–63	1963–15928
43	20339	7–25–63	15973
44	20362	7–29–63	15996
45	20434	7–31–63	16068
46	20569	8– 9–63	16203
47	20769	8–22–63	17711
48	21090	9–13–63	19392
49	21150	9–19–63	19452
50	21166	9–20–63	19468
51	21177	9–23–63	19479
52	21255	9–30–63	19557
53	21363	10– 8–63	19665
54	21435	10–14–63	19737
55	21478	10–17–63	20770
56	21587	10–24–63	20879
57	21661	10–30–63	1964– 915
58	21834	11–13–63	1088
59	21955	11–20–63	1209
60	21977	11–21–63	1231
61	22237	12–11–63	2605
62	22383	12–19–63	2751
63	22418	12–23–63	2786
64	22529	12–31–63	2897

3. UNION RESEARCH SERVICE AND OTHER TRANSLATION SERIES

The *Union Research Service* is another extremely useful translation service, complementing those issued by the American Consulate General in Hong Kong and the Joint Publications Research Service described in the preceding sections. In addition to the *U.R.S.*, this section also contains five other translation series, some unfortunately no longer in existence, but all representing important collections of translations from the Chinese press for the periods covered. The *Daily Translation Service* and the *Chinese Press Survey* (**1069** and **1070**) prepared by the publishers of *China Weekly Review* in Shanghai are particularly useful for the postwar period to early 1951.

1065   Union Research Service. Hong Kong: Union News Agency, Vol. 1, No. 1—, September 16, 1955—.

A translation series issued approximately nine times a month. Material is drawn from Chinese Communist periodicals and press, arranged topically and accompanied by a short editor's note. Each volume carries its own index. There is also an index to Vols. 1–26 (September 1955–March 1962) grouped under twenty-five general headings arranged alphabetically (agriculture, art and literature, commerce and trade, etc.), superseding others issued previously. Mimeographed.

An important translation service; especially useful for translations from local newspapers. The quality of the translations has improved in recent years.

The Union News Agency is an affiliate of the Union Research Institute.

1066 **China Record.** [London, n.p.], 1961 (?)–April 7, 1966. Weekly.

A weekly survey of developments in Communist China based on the Mainland press and radio. In four parts: summary, internal affairs, external affairs, and Communist bloc relations (with further subdivisions). Each issue averages eight to twelve legal-size pages. Mimeographed. Ceased publication as of April 7, 1966.

See also next entry.

1067 **China Topics.** [London, n.p.], 'Y.B.' No. 1—, 1961 [?]—. Irregular.

Documentation on specific current topics taken mainly from the Chinese Communist press and radio. In addition to a consecutive numbering system, each issue is also designated by a number in the subject-series (for example, Religion—No. 2, Agriculture—No. 5, etc.) Some 250 issues, ranging from two to fifteen legal-size pages have been published to early 1964. Mimeographed.

Lists of visitors to China and Chinese abroad are issued as supplements from time to time. These lists, covering several months, are divided by country and provide the name of the visitor, affiliation, date, and the occasion for the visit.

1068 **Weekly Report on Communist China.** Washington, D.C.: Central Intelligence Agency, Nos. 1–44, November 20 (?) 1959–September 23, 1960.

Translations of articles and news items from the Chinese Mainland press, with special emphasis on economic and political developments. The earlier issues of the report appeared at roughly ten-day intervals; later the interval between issues became more irregular and frequently shorter. The number of pages per issue varied from 15 to 100 pages. Publication ceased with No. 44, at which time its contents were incorporated into the J.P.R.S. reports (see preceding section). Especially useful for its coverage of the provincial press.

A complete file of the *Weekly Report* is available on microfilm with a printed *Guide to Contents* from Research & Microfilm Publications, Inc.

1069 **Daily Translation Service.** Shanghai: Millard Publishing Company, May 1946–June 1951 (?).

Selected translations from the Chinese press. Good coverage of the period.

See also next entry.

1070 **Chinese Press Survey.** Shanghai: Millard Publishing Company, Vol. 1, No. 1–Vol. 16, No. 4, November 1948–June 1951. Bi-weekly.

A supplement to the preceding entry, the survey is a translation service covering the more important articles appearing in Chinese newspapers and magazines.

Weekly Translation Service was published by the same company from February 1947 to March 1948 (Vol. 1, No. 1 to Vol. 2, No. 9).

4. RADIO MONITORING SERVICES

Of the four entries listed in this section, the reports of the Foreign Radio Broadcast Information Service (F.B.I.S.) contain the most comprehensive daily compilations of monitored radio broadcasts emanating from both Communist and Nationalist China (first entry).

1071 Daily Report, Foreign Radio Broadcasts. Washington, D.C., February 19, 1941—.

A digest of monitored foreign radio broadcasts, one section of which is devoted to the Far East and contains Peking newscasts. Successively issued by the Federal Communications Commission, the War Department, and, since October 11, 1949, by the Foreign Broadcast Information Service (F.B.I.S.), the *Daily Report* supplements the translations of the Hong Kong American Consulate General and has the advantage of being more current than the latter publications. No index. Limited distribution.

The F.B.I.S. also issues a number of separate series under the same title arranged by region (Far East, Latin America, etc.) The Far East series contains full transcriptions of radio broadcasts from all Far Eastern countries, including both Taiwan and Communist China.

1071a Summary of World Broadcasts. Reading, Berkshire: B.B.C. Monitoring Service, August 28, 1939—. Daily (except Sundays).

A digest of world-wide monitored broadcasts, one section of which deals with the Far East. From its inception through May 22, 1947, the *Summary* was entitled the *Daily Digest of World Broadcasts;* (Section Two covered the Far East); from May 23, 1947 to April 22, 1949, under the title *Summary of World Broadcasts*, First Series, the Far East was covered in Part Three, and from April 25, 1949 to April 14, 1959, in Part Five. The postwar series appeared weekly through August 21, 1952; semi-weekly through April 14, 1959; and daily (except Sundays) thereafter (Part Three covering the Far East). Far Eastern materials from the digests of Soviet and East European broadcasts will be found in Parts One and Two.

Supplements the preceding entry.

1072 U.S. Army, Broadcasting and Visual Activity, Pacific.
Communist Propaganda Trends. [Okinawa], No. 1—, 1953 (?)—. Weekly.

A survey of broadcasts emanating from Radios Moscow and Peking, Pyongyang, Hanoi and other Communist stations in Asia, each issue ranging from six to twelve pages in length. In three parts: 'Summary', 'The Week in Review', and 'Trends' (published monthly). Both the weekly summary and the monthly section on trends are one to two-page reviews of the highlights of Communist bloc broadcasts. The second part (the main body of the report) is divided by area and topic, (e.g., bloc relations, the Sino-Indian border dispute, Communist China-Ghana, Taiwan-U.S.-Mainland, etc.).

A conveniently arranged and concise weekly summary of Communist radio broadcasts in Asia, including Radio Peking.

1073 **Hsinhua (New China) News Agency Morsecast.** San Francisco: Radio Free Asia, April 4, 1952–April 28, 1953.

A radio monitoring service of Peking newcasts on national and international affairs (average twelve pages). Publication ceased after April 28, 1953.

B. Publications Concerned with Taiwan, Hong Kong, Japan and the Soviet Union

Most official American translations from the Chinese are focused on Mainland source material. The *Press and Publications Summary* published by the U.S.I.S. in Taipei, however, is an extremely important source of Taiwan newspaper and periodical material in translation (see first entry). A *Review of the Hong Kong Chinese Press* published since the end of the Second World War by the American Consulate General unfortunately was suspended in May 1961 (see second entry). The other entries in this section are translation series dealing with Japanese and Soviet newspapers and periodicals, included primarily because they provide a wealth of material on present-day China in general, and on its relations with Japan and the Soviet Union in particular.

For newspapers and periodicals published in Taiwan and Hong Kong, and in Japan and the Soviet Union, see Chapters XVIII, XIX, and XXI, respectively.

1074 **Press and Publications Summary.** Taipei: United States Information Service, August 18, 1955—. Daily (except holidays).

Carries verbatim or summary translations of Taiwan newspaper and magazine items regarding political, economic and social developments on Taiwan, selected primarily for their political significance. News also appearing in the local English-language press is generally omitted from the *P.P.S.* Some twenty pages in length. The newspapers covered are: *Chung-yang jih-pao* 中央日報, *Chung-hua jih-pao* 中華日報, *Hsin-sheng pao* 新生報, *Lien-ho pao* 聯合報, *Kung-lun pao* 公論報, *Cheng-hsin hsin-wen pao* 徵信新聞報, *Ch'ing-nien chan-shih pao* 青年戰士報, *Tzu-li wan-pao* 自立晚報, *Min-tzu wan-pao* 民族晚報, and *Ta-hua wan-pao* 大華晚報. Occasionally, items from *Hsin-wen pao* 新聞報 (Kaohsiung) and the Tainan edition of *Chung-hua jih-pao* 中華日報 also are included.

Magazines which are covered on a highly selective basis include *Chung-kuo i-chou* 中國一週, *Hsin-wen t'ien-ti* 新聞天地, *Min-chu ch'ao* 民主潮, *Min-chu Chung-kuo* 民主中國, *Min-chu hsien-cheng* 民主憲政, *Shih yü ch'ao* 時與潮, and others.

The *Press and Publications Summary (P.P.S.)* began on August 18, 1955, as a bi-weekly; as of the third issue on September 9, 1955, it became a weekly. Beginning March 20, 1956, it was published twice a week, and from September 9, 1958, the *P.P.S.* has been published every weekday except on official American and Chinese holidays. Mimeographed. Limited distribution.

Prior to the appearance of *Press and Publications Summary*, the U.S. Consulate General in Taipei issued the *Review of the Formosa Press*.

1075 Review of the Hong Kong Chinese Press. Hong Kong: American Consulate General, No. 1–No. 53/1961, June 1947–May 1961. Daily (approx.).

Prior to May 1950, appeared under the titles *Chinese Press Review* or *Review of Chinese Press*. Unnumbered typewritten issues for official use only were distributed from 1946 to June 1947. The *Review* was a resumé of editorial opinion and news summaries from both pro-Communist and pro-Nationalist newspapers published in Hong Kong, some four to eight legal-size pages in length. Two major topics regularly reported are Overseas Chinese affairs and trade union activities in Hong Kong. Mimeographed. Ceased publication with No. 53 (1961) in May of 1961.

1076 American Embassy, Tokyo, Translation Services Branch.
Daily Summary of Japanese Press. [Tokyo], May 1952—. Daily (except holidays).

A translation of significant articles appearing in the Japanese press. Articles on China appear regularly, particularly when occasioned by some important event—e.g., the signing of a trade agreement, a military crisis, or visits by Japanese delegations. Mimeographed.

See also next entries.

1077 Japanese Press Translations. Tokyo: Headquarters, U.S. Forces, Japan, Vol. 1, No. 1—, January 1963—. Daily (except Saturdays, Sundays and holidays).

Summaries of articles appearing in the major Japanese newspapers (two legal-size pages per issue). Mimeographed. Limited distribution.

1078 American Embassy, Tokyo, Translation Services Branch.
Summaries of Selected Japanese Magazines. [Tokyo], May 1952—. Weekly.

Contains summary translations of selected articles in Japanese periodicals, tables of contents of selected magazines with brief summaries of all articles, and translations of book reviews from weekly magazines. A number of articles deal with contemporary China and particularly with Japan's relations with Communist China.

1079 American Embassy, Tokyo, Translation Services Branch.
General Trend of Japanese Press. [Tokyo], February 1955–December 1958. Quarterly.

A review of the Japanese press arranged in three parts: domestic affairs; Japan's foreign relations; and international affairs, preceded by a section entitled, 'General Trend'. Japanese-Communist Chinese relations are treated in every issue.

The Embassy also puts out a monthly *Trend of Japanese Magazines*.

1080 Current Digest of the Soviet Press. New York: Joint Committee on Slavic Studies, Vol. 1, No. 1—, February 1949—. Weekly.

Selections from the Soviet press translated in full or condensed, and arranged by subject matter. Longer articles are listed in the 'Features' section; news items are included under 'News of the Week'. Articles on China can be located in the 'Far Eastern' subsection of the 'Foreign Affairs' section of the 'News of the Week'. Each issue also carries a weekly classified index to the two leading Soviet dailies, *Pravda* and *Izvestiia*, and a list of publications from which translations are made. Quarterly index.

Mention also might be made of the *Soviet Press Translations*, published bi-weekly (except August) by the Far Eastern and Russian Institute of the University of Washington from October 1946 to March 1953 (Vol. 1, No. 1 to Vol. 8, No. 6) with a yearly index arranged topically by country; the *Survey of the Soviet Press*, a 50–60 page mimeographed publication appearing since 1957; and *Current Soviet Documents*, a weekly translation service of official Soviet documentation published by Cross-Currents Press since 1963.

1081 Soviet Periodical Abstracts: Asia, Africa and Latin America. New York: Slavic Languages Research Institute, Vol. 1, No. 1—, 1961—. Quarterly.

An annotated bibliography of articles selected from Soviet periodicals and occasionally from newspapers. Includes all articles in *Aziia i Afrika segodnia* (Asia and Africa Today), *International Affairs* (Moscow), *Mirovaia ekonomika i mezhdunarodnye otnosheniia* (World Economics and International Relations), *Narody Azii i Afriki* (The Peoples of Asia and Africa), *Sovetskoe gosudarstvo i pravo* (Soviet State and Law), and *Voprosy istorii* (Problems of History). Coverage of other Soviet periodicals is selective.

Arrangement is as follows: general (subdivided into socialism and colonialism, formation of independent national states, and research and publications); Asia, Africa, and Latin America (consisting of general and country subsections). Each issue includes some ten to thirty articles on China, and the annotations vary from a few lines to a fairly lengthy summary. A list of sources gives the titles of periodicals under survey.

Vol. 1 appeared under the title *Selective Soviet Annotated Bibliographies: Asia, Africa and Latin America*, and was issued by the same organization under its original name of Soviet and East European Research and Translation Service.

1082 Great Britain, Department of Scientific and Industrial Research, Lending Library Unit.
LLU Translations Bulletin. London, January 1959—. Monthly.

A monthly superseding the *Translated Contents Lists of Russian Periodicals* published since 1949. Includes translations from Russian sources on scientific and technological developments on Mainland China.

CHAPTER XXI

ADDITIONAL PERIODICALS

This chapter brings together over 130 additional periodicals published in the United States, Japan, the Soviet Union and elsewhere and devoted wholly or in part to the study of China. The majority are in the Japanese language, reflecting the fact that, after Chinese and English, Japanese is the most important language for the study of modern China. For convenience, the chapter is organized by language, irrespective of country of publication.

A. English-Language

The twenty-four English-language journals, bulletins, and newsletters listed in this section supplement the English-language publications from the Mainland (such as the *Peking Review*, **930** in Chapter XVII), Taiwan (Chapter XVIII), and Hong Kong (*China News Analysis*, **1034**, *Current Scene*, **1035**, etc., in Chapter XIX), as well as those translations listed in the preceding chapter (the Hong Kong American Consulate General publications, J.P.R.S. reports, and so on). The entries appear in alphabetical order.

Not all periodicals listed in this section deal exclusively with China. Some cover Asia in general or parts of Asia, while others deal with Communism. All, however, contain articles on Communist China or Taiwan. The *Asian Survey*, *Pacific Affairs*, and *The Journal of Asian Studies* are too well known to need an introduction. For the study of Communist China the most important journal is *The China Quarterly* (**1093**), a relatively new publication issued in London. The editors of the *Quarterly* also put out a monthly mimeographed news sheet, *The China Bulletin* (**1091**). Likewise useful for the study of current developments in Mainland China is *Problems of Communism* (**1105**). Two of the entries included in this section are English-language publications of native Formosans (**1099** and **1100**).

Other English-language publications marginal for the study of contemporary China can be located through the annual 'Bibliography of Asian Studies' (**15**), which also provides an index to the more important articles appearing in some of the periodicals listed in this section.

1083 **Arts and Sciences in China.** London, Vol. 1, No. 1—, 1963—. Quarterly.

> A number of prominent scholars serve on the editorial board of this publication, the aim of which is to promote a better understanding of China. A selected list of books on China published since 1961 appeared in the third issue (July–September 1963), pp. 30–35.

1084 **Asian Affairs.** Tokyo: Asia Kyokai, Vol. 1, No. 1—, 1956—. Semi-annual.

> An English-language journal published by the Asia Association. Started as a quarterly in March 1956, *Asian Affairs* was discontinued with Vol. 3, No. 1 (March 1958). It resumed publication as a semi-annual in October 1959 with

Vol. 4, No. 1. Contains articles, commentaries and analyses by leading Japanese scholars, writers, government officials and journalists, and occasional articles and book reviews on contemporary China. Vol. 2, No. 1 (March 1957) was a special issue entitled, 'Prospects for New China'.

The Asia Association was established in 1954 with the support of Japanese business circles to promote friendly ties with Asian countries.

1085 Asian Recorder. New Delhi, Vol. 1, No. 1—, January 1955—. Weekly (consecutive pagination).

A weekly digest of Asian events containing news items, speeches and other material from the press, radio and government publications (with source indicated). Each issue, averaging twelve pages, is arranged by country listed in alphabetical order. Quarterly and annual indexes.

Good coverage of South Asian press and Communist China's relations with India, Pakistan, Burma and Ceylon.

1086 Asian Review. London: East India Association, New Series Vol. 1—, 1913—. Quarterly.

Incorporates the *Journal of the East India Association* and *The Asiatic Review* (the title of the magazine through Vol. 48, consecutive No. 176, October 1952; the present title was assumed with Vol. 49, consecutive No. 177, January 1953). Through 1963, 220 issues were published.

Asian Review contains frequent articles on Communist China and particularly on Peking's relations with South Asian countries.

1087 Asian Survey. Berkeley, Calif.: University of California, Institute of International Studies, Vol. 1, No. 1—, March 1961—. Monthly.

The successor to the *Far Eastern Survey* (see **1098**), the journal is concerned with Asian affairs and regularly includes brief articles on developments in contemporary China.

1088 The Bulletin. Tokyo: Gaikoku Chōsa Kenkyūjo 外國調查研究所, No. 1—, January 1961—. Irregular.

A bulletin containing digests and abstracts of Japanese books and articles on Communist China. Each issue is given over to a single topic such as people's communes, eye-witness accounts by Japanese visitors to the Mainland, and the Japanese left wing's view of the Sino-Soviet dispute. The bulletin is edited by Taijiro Ichikawa, formerly a member of the Japanese foreign service and later Chief of the International Exchange Division of the National Diet Library. It is published by the Institute of Foreign Studies, established by Kajima Morinosuke for the explicit purpose of studying Communist China. No. 8

(October 1963) is a 'List of Some Japanese Studies on China', 15p. Mimeographed. Kajima Morinosuke, president of Kajima Construction Company, is a former diplomat and an author of books on diplomatic history.

The institute also publishes *The Problems in the Eastern World* (see **1104**).

1089 **Central Asian Review.** London: Central Asian Research Centre, Vol. 1, No. 1—, 1953—. Quarterly.

Issued in association with the Soviet affairs study group of St. Antony's College (Oxford), the review covers cultural developments in Soviet Central Asia. In addition, the journal provides an analysis of Soviet publications on the countries adjacent to the Soviet Asian republics (Iran, Afghanistan, India, Pakistan, Tibet and Sinkiang). The journal comprises review articles, as well as a section entitled 'The Borderlands in the Soviet Press,' which incorporates reports on the border areas appearing in Soviet newspapers and periodicals for the previous three months.

The Centre also issues the *Bibliography of Recent Soviet Source Material on Soviet Central Asia and the Borderlands* as a semi-annual supplement (see **63**).

1090 **China Bulletin.** New York: National Council of the Churches of Christ, Far Eastern Office, Vol. 1, No. 1–No. 124, February 1947–February 1952, irregular; Vol. 2, No. 1–Vol. 12, No. 8, 1952–August 1962. Bi-weekly to March 1961; monthly thereafter.

The purpose of this periodical is to provide information about religious life in China (particularly Protestant Christianity), as well as education and medicine, which are subjects of particular concern to former China missionaries (e.g., Christian periodicals being published in China, hospital and medical work in China, church and school in China).

Subject index covering Vol. 1 to 8 (1947–1958). The first eight volumes are also available on one microfilm reel.

Superseded by *China Notes* (see **1092**).

1091 **The China Bulletin—Comment and Documentation.** London: The China Quarterly, No. 1—, October 1961—. Monthly.

A brief bulletin (four to six legal-size pages) issued by the editors of *The China Quarterly* (see **1093**) containing news and other items on China, largely based on Chinese Communist sources. Mimeographed.

1092 **China Notes.** New York: National Council of the Churches of Christ, Far Eastern Office, Vol. 1, No. 1—, September 1962—. Quarterly.

Superseded *China Bulletin* (see **1090**) in September 1962. One section of each quarterly issue provides information on Protestant Christianity in Communist China. Recent articles have included 'Buddhist and Muslim Activities', 'Further Light on Religious Freedom', 'Current Estimates of Confucius', 'Religion and Superstition', and 'How the Chinese Church has Changed in an Urban Setting'.

1093   The China Quarterly. London: Congress for Cultural Freedom, No. 1—, January/March 1960—. Quarterly.

Contains articles and book reviews on recent developments in Mainland China (and occasionally Taiwan) by specialists from a number of countries. The quarterly chronicle and documentation section (from five to thirty pages in length) provides a documented narrative of the major events of the preceding three months (i.e., internal political and economic developments, and foreign relations). Of late, articles on Communism in Asia have also appeared in its pages.

This is the most important English-language journal devoted to Communist China.

1094   China Trade and Economic Newsletter. London: British Council for the Promotion of International Trade, No. 1—, November 1955—. Monthly.

The newsletter is devoted to Communist China's foreign trade in general and British trade with Mainland China in particular (market conditions, trends, etc.). The articles are often based on reports and statements by firms or individuals directly involved in the trade. Commodity notes and Sino-British trade statistics are included in every issue.

See also the *Three-Monthly Economic Review: China, Hong Kong, North Korea* and the *Three-Monthly Economic Review: Japan, Formosa, South Korea* published by the Economist Intelligence Unit in London.

1095   Communist Affairs. Los Angeles: University of Southern California, Research Institute on Communist Strategy and Propaganda, Vol. 1, No. 1—, June 1962—. Bi-monthly.

A twenty-page review of developments in the Communist bloc, consisting of a background article, a section on developments and trends, quotations from the Communist press and publications, biographies of prominent Communist leaders, and book reviews. Primarily directed at the secondary school teacher and the non-specialist. Index to Vol. 1, Nos. 1–9 (June 1962–December 1963) in Vol. 2, No. 1 (January–February 1964).

1096   The Developing Economies. Tokyo: The Institute of Asian Economic Affairs, preliminary issues Nos. 1 and 2, 1962; Vol. 1, No. 1—, 1963—. Semi-annual.

An English-language publication of a Japanese semi-governmental research organization. See also its *Ajia keizai* (Asian Economic Affairs) in the next section (**1107**). The contents of the journal reflect the institute staff's strong interest in Communist China.

See also a symposium on Chinese studies in Japan which appeared in the second preliminary issue (September–December, 1962), pp. 57–98.

1097 **Far Eastern Affairs.** Oxford, No. 1—, 1957—. Irregular.

Collections of articles edited by Professor G. F. Hudson. Occasional articles on contemporary China (e.g., on the communes, cooperative farms, language reform, the Sino-Indian dispute, etc.).

The issues of *Far Eastern Affairs* form a part of *St. Antony's Papers:*

FAR EASTERN AFFAIRS NO.	ST ANTONY'S PAPERS NO.	DATE
1	2	1957
2	7	1960
3	14	1963

1098 **Far Eastern Survey.** New York: Institute of Pacific Relations, Vol. 1, No. 1– Vol. 30, No. 2; March 3, 1932–February 1961. Fortnightly.

A journal regularly containing brief articles and reviews on contemporary China, succeeded by the *Asian Survey* in 1961 (see **1087**).

1099 **Formosan Quarterly.** Tokyo: The Formosan Association, Vol. 1, No. 1—, July 1962—.

The English-language counterpart to *Taiwan Chinglian* 臺灣青年 *The Young Formosan* (see **1180**), a Japanese-language monthly published in Japan since 1960 by the Formosan Association. The first issue contains an index to the first sixteen issues of *Taiwan Chinglian* (1960–1962) and a one-page chronology (1945–1962) stressing Nationalist suppression of Formosans in Taiwan. With Vol. 2, No. 3 (February 1964), the publication became a bi-monthly and changed its title to *Independent Formosa*.

The journal, like its Japanese-language sister publication, is strongly anti-Nationalist and advocates an independent Taiwan.

See also next entry.

1100 **Ilha Formosa—A Quarterly Journal of Formosan Independence Movements.** Philadelphia, Pa.: United Formosans for Independence, Vol. 1, No. 1—, January 1963—. Quarterly.

An anti-Nationalist journal published by a group of native Taiwanese in the United States. Supersedes a bi-monthly newspaper of the same title.

1101 **The Journal of Asian Studies.** Ann Arbor, Mich.: The Association for Asian Studies, Inc., Vol. 1, No. 1—, November 1941—. Quarterly.

The official journal of the Association for Asian Studies (formerly The Far Eastern Association). Vol. 1–15 (1941–1956) were issued under the title *Far Eastern Quarterly*. The serial assumed its present name with Vol. 16, No. 1 (February 1957). Every fifth number comprises a bibliography (see **15**).

The Journal of Asian Studies is the principal American scholarly quarterly in the Asian field. Authoritative articles and reviews on contemporary China regularly appear in its pages.

1102 **New Orient: Journal for the Modern and Ancient Cultures of Asia and Africa.** Prague: Orbis Publishing House, February 1960—. Bi-monthly.

A richly illustrated popular journal published by the Czechoslovak Society for Eastern Studies, containing articles and book reviews by scholars on various aspects of Asian (including Chinese) history and archeology, art, music and theater, literature, language, ethnography, philosophy and religion, and travel accounts.

The journal is based on a Czech-language publication by the same title *(Nový Orient)* published by the Oriental Institute of the Czech Academy of Sciences (see **1208**) and contains regularly bibliographical information of interest to specialists.

1103 **Pacific Affairs.** Honolulu, New York, Vancouver, B.C.: Institute of Pacific Relations, May–December 1926 (unnumbered); Vol. 1, No. 1—, January 1927—. Quarterly.

A quarterly published from May 1926 to April 1928 under title *News Bulletin of the Institute of Pacific Relations, Pacific Affairs*. Contains from time to time articles and book reviews on contemporary China. The editorial office is now located in Vancouver.

1104 **Problems in the Eastern World.** Tokyo: Gaikoku Chōsa Kenkyūjo 外國調查研究所, No. 1—, November 1961—. Irregular.

A publication devoted to Communist China and issued by the Institute of Foreign Studies, which also publishes *The Bulletin* (see **1088**). Each issue is given over to a single topic, such as 'Technical Revolution in Red China's Agriculture', or a review of recent developments on the Mainland. Some twenty issues have appeared to spring 1964.

While *The Bulletin* comprises largely abstracts of Japanese work on Communist China, *Problems in the Eastern World* publishes the results of its own staff's investigations.

1105 **Problems of Communism.** Washington, D.C.: United States Information Agency, Vol. 1, No. 1—, February 1952—. Bi-monthly.

A journal devoted to the analysis of various aspects of world Communism, containing articles on Communist China and, in particular, Sino-Soviet relations.

1105a Review: A Journal for the Study of Communism and Communist Countries. Tokyo: The Ōa Kyōkai—Japan Association on Communist States in Europe and Asia, No. 1—, May 1964—.

The English-language organ of Ōa Kyōkai, the publishers of *Kyōsanken mondai—Communist Bloc Problems* (see **1161**). Two of the three articles in the first issue deal with Communist China.

B. JAPANESE-LANGUAGE

Japan leads the non-Chinese world in the amount of material produced on China, including the number of periodicals wholly or in part devoted to that country. For example, a bibliography of Japanese journals in the Oriental field, but largely concerned with China, lists over two hundred Japanese-language periodicals (excluding government-sponsored publications) published in Japan from 1945 to 1958 (see **177**).

The major publishers of Japanese periodicals in the contemporary China field include the various agencies of the Japanese government, semi-governmental research organizations, political groups and trade organizations, private research institutions sponsored by both pro- and anti-Communist organizations, news agencies, book dealers, and academic institutions. Eighty-eight of their periodicals are selected for inclusion in this section, covering the three major areas of interest: current political developments on the Chinese Mainland, economic affairs (particularly those relating to Japanese trade with Communist China), and scholarly humanistic research, especially in the field of Chinese language and literature. Because of frequent change of title and sponsoring organization, the periodicals are listed in straight alphabetical order with appropriate cross references. (A list at the end of these introductory remarks provides title changes of some of the more important publications.)

The two major Japanese governmental centers of research on China are the China Section of the Ministry of Foreign Affairs and the Cabinet Research Office. Their publications provide the most substantial coverage of current developments on the Mainland, and, to a lesser extent, in Taiwan. Biographical compilations, directories, chronologies and documentary collections published by these two centers have been described in other appropriate sections of this Guide. Only their periodical publications (both current and defunct) are listed in this section. Of these, *Chūgoku geppō* (Monthly Report on China, **1120**), issued by the Foreign Office, is the most authoritative compilation of current data, and is valuable for its coverage of foreign relations. *Chūkyō shiryō* (Communist China Documentation, **1143**) and *Chūkyō jōsei shūhō* (Weekly Report on Conditions in Communist China, **1140**), both issued by the Cabinet Research Office, are likewise very useful. The Public Security Investigation Agency (Kōan Chōsa Chō), the Japanese counterpart of the F.B.I., covers developments on the Mainland, particularly Chinese Communist broadcasts and activities directed towards Japan (see such titles as *Chūkyō tainichi dōkō geppō* [Monthly Report on Chinese Communist Activities Directed Towards Japan], **1144**).

In addition to conducting its own intensive research operations, the Japanese government subsidizes a number of semi-governmental research organizations. The business community also supports private research groups engaged in the study of the Communist bloc, especially China. The publications of these organizations are largely critical of Communism: *Chūgoku shiryō* (China Documentation, **1134**), a weekly mimeographed report of the International Friendship Club; *Junkan Kyokutō jōhō* (Far Eastern Intelligence—A Ten-Day Report, **1151**); *Tōa jiron* (East Asian Review, **1183**), by the Kazan Society; *Tairiku mondai* (Continental Problems, **1179**), by former Lieutenant-General Doi Akio, one of the Imperial Japanese Army's top experts on the Soviet Union who also served as an advisor to the Chinese Nationalist Army after the Second World War; *Soren kenkyū: Chūkyō Tōō* (Soviet Studies: Communist China and Eastern Europe, **1176**); and *Kyōsanken mondai—Communist Bloc Problems* (**1161**) and *Kokusai mondai* (International Problems, **1157**), the last two published by Foreign Ministry-sponsored organizations, both headed by retired diplomats.

In the area of Chinese economy and trade, pro-Communist publications predominate. The largest Japanese non-governmental research organization on China, the China Research Institute (Chūgoku Kenkyūjo), has taken the lead in publicizing the achievements of the Chinese Communists, and its publications betray its bias. The *Shin Chūgoku nenkan* (New China Yearbook, **216**) and other bibliographical and reference publications of the institute have been described in the first and second parts of the Guide. Over ten titles of the institute's periodical publications are described in this section, the most important of which are the *Ajia keizai jumpō* (Ten-Day Report on the Asian Economy, **1109**); *Chūgoku kenkyū geppō* (Monthly Research Report on China, **1131**), which comprises a series of monographs; and *Gendai Chūgoku* (Contemporary China, **1148**).

The Japan Association for the Promotion of International Trade, the Japan-China Exporters and Importers Association, and the Society for the Promotion of Trade Between Japan and China are quite frankly 'lobbying' for closer economic ties with Communist China, and their publications (*Kokusai bōeki* [International Trade], **1156**, *Nitchū bōeki kihō* [Japanese-Chinese Trade Quarterly], **1164**, and *Nitchū bōeki* [Japanese-Chinese Trade], **1163**, respectively) provide ample documentation of their activities. In this connection, mention must also be made of *Nihon to Chūgoku* (Japan and China, **1162**), organ of the Japan-China Friendship Association, and *Nitchū kokkō kaifuku nyūsu* (News on the Restoration of Diplomatic Relations Between Japan and China, **1166**), organ of the National Conference for Restoration of Diplomatic Relations Between Japan and [Communist] China, both important publications for the study of pro-Chinese Communist elements in Japan.

This section also lists two Mainland-sponsored periodicals—*Jimmin Chūgoku* (People's China, **1150**) and *Chūgoku gahō* (China Pictorial, **1119**); a press release of the Embassy of the Republic of China in Tokyo, *Chūka shūhō* (China Weekly, **1138**); and an anti-Chinese publication of Taiwanese exiles—*Taiwan Chinglian—The Young Formosan* (**1180**).

In addition to the two organizations promoting trade with Communist China, there are a number of commercial groups which issue daily or weekly bulletins containing news items of relevance to Japanese trade with the Mainland. Several of the better-established publications are listed. Among them are *Ajia tsūshin* (Asia Bulletin, **1113a**); *Chūgoku tsūshin* (China Bulletin—Trade Edition, **1137**); and *Tōzai bōeki tsūshin* (East-West Trade Bulletin, **1191**).

A number of Japanese news agencies from time to time also have issued special daily bulletins containing items pertaining to Mainland China. The two major Japanese news agencies, the Kyodo and Jiji, do not at the present time issue special China bulletins. Radio Press (R.P). News Agency, on the other hand, is very active in issuing monitored broadcasts series, a number of which are devoted entirely to Communist China. Deserving mention here are R.P. News (**1167**) and *Shūkan Chūgoku shiryō* (Weekly Documentation on China, **1175**).

Needless to say, left-wing organizations are not the only ones in Japan which are engaged in the study of Chinese Communist economic and trade policies. The East-West Trade Section of the Bureau of Economic Affairs of the Foreign Ministry regularly publishes the *Tōzai bōeki hangeppō* (East-West Trade Semi-Monthly, **1190**), while the semi-governmental Institute of Asian Economic Affairs issues *Ajia keizai* (Asian Economic Affairs, **1107**). Both contain data on the Chinese economy and trade.

Among Japanese university publications, the following four are devoted wholly or in part to the study of the Chinese economy: *Ajia kenkyū shiryō* (Asian Studies Data, **1112**), published by the Economic Research Institute of Osaka Municipal University; *Chūgoku keizai jōhō* (Information Bulletin on Chinese Economy, **1127**), by the Asian Economy Study Group at Kobe University; *Tōa keizai kenkyū* (Studies in East Asian Economy, **1184**), by the East Asian Economic Research Institute of Yamaguchi University; and *Kokusai Mondai Kenkyūjo kiyō—The Memoirs of [the] Institute of International Affairs* (**1158**), by the Institute of International Affairs of Aichi University (the last is not limited to the Chinese economy).

Research in the field of the humanities—largely the study of Chinese language and literature—occupies an honored place in the Japanese academic community. In the field of Chinese letters, mention must be made of the *Chūgoku bungakuhō—Journal of Chinese Literature* (**1115**) published by the Department of Chinese Language and Literature of Kyoto University, of *Chūgoku bungaku kenkyū* (Studies in Chinese Literature, **1116**) issued by the Department of Chinese Literature of Tokyo University, and of *Chūgoku gogaku* (**1122**), the leading journal devoted to the study of Chinese linguistics.

The Seminar on Modern China at the Tōyō Bunko has grown into a larger Center for Modern Chinese Studies. It publishes excellent bibliographical guides to Japanese academic work in this field. The publications of the Tōyō Bunko Seminar, and particularly of the recently launched *Kindai Chūgoku Kenkyū Sentā ihō* (Bulletin of the Center for Modern Chinese Studies, **1155**), are very important sources. Also noteworthy is *Ajia kenkyū—Asiatic Studies* (**1111**), organ of the Society for Asian Political and Economic Studies, which also produces a comprehensive yearbook on contemporary China (**202**).

Finally, mention should be made of two small publications of the two leading Japanese book dealers specializing in Chinese Communist materials: *Daian* (The

Daian Monthly, **1147**) and *Shohō* (Book News—Journal of Chinese Publications, **1171**). They are primarily trade journals containing useful lists of current Mainland publications as well as good bibliographical articles and indexes. The former also regularly publishes tables of contents of scholarly journals in a section entitled *Chūgoku kankei kokunai shuppan annai* (A Guide to Japanese Publications on China).

The Fairbank-Banno bibliography (see **41**) is a convenient starting point for assaying Japanese scholarly work on China. The bibliography of Kyoto University (**30**) provides excellent coverage of current scholarly output. The general *Japanese Periodicals Index—Zasshi kiji sakuin*—published by the National Diet Library, provides the key to the current Japanese periodical press.

Lists of Japanese periodicals are provided in Chapter II (**177** and **178**). Translations from the Japanese press and periodicals appear in Chapter XX (**1076–1079**).

Title Changes

1. *Chūken Bōeki Iinkai shiryō* and *Chūken Bōeki Iinkai tokuhō* (**1139**), 1947–1948
   Ajia keizai shiryō (**1110**), 1948–1949
   AJIA KEIZAI JUMPŌ (**1109**), 1949—

2. *Chūgoku kenkyū shiryō* (**1112**), 1955–1956
   Ajia keizai kenkyū shiryō (**1112**), 1956–1958
   AJIA KENKYŪ SHIRYŌ (**1112**), 1959—

3. *Chūgoku jumpō* (**1126**), 1947–1948
   Chūgoku hangeppō (**1123**), 1949–1951
   Tōa geppō (**1182**), 1951
   Chūgoku geppō (**1117**), 1951
   Chūgoku Chōsen geppō (**1117**), 1951–1952
   [*Sekai geppō* (**1169**), 1946–1958]
   CHŪGOKU GEPPŌ (**1120**), 1958—

4. *Chūgoku keizai nempō* (**1128**), 1953–1955
   Chūgoku keizai shiryō (**1129**), 1956–1960

5. *Chūgoku shiryō geppō* (**1135**), 1946–1947
   Chūgoku Kenkyūjo shohō (**1133**), 1947–1949
   Chūgoku shiryō geppō (**1135**), 1949–1960
   CHŪGOKU KENKYŪ GEPPŌ (**1131**), 1960—

6. *Chūgoku hyōron* (**1124**), 1946–1947
   Chūgoku kenkyū (**1130**), 1947–1952
   GENDAI CHŪGOKU (**1148**), 1953—

7. *Tenchijin* (**1181**), 1952–1956
   Kazan Kurabu kaishi (**1152**), 1957–1958
   TŌA JIRON (**1183**), 1959—

1106 Ajia bōeki アジア貿易
(Asian Trade). Tokyo: Ajia Bōeki Tsūshinsha アジア貿易通信社, No. 1—,
May 1961—. Daily (except Sundays and holidays).

A ten-page report on Japanese trade with the Communist bloc published by
a brother of Kamiyama Shigeo, one of the prominent members of the Japanese
Communist Party. For several years prior to the publication of *Ajia bōeki*, he
published *Jiritsu keizai tokushin—bōeki ban* 自立經濟特信——貿易版 (Special
Bulletin on Self-Sustaining Economy—Trade Edition). Mimeographed.

1107 Ajia keizai アジア經濟
(Asian Economic Affairs). Tokyo: Ajia Keizai Kenkyūjo アジア經濟研究所,
Vol. 1, No. 1—, May 1960—. Monthly.

The organ of the Institute of Asian Economic Affairs, a semi-governmental
research organization created for the study of economic development in Asia
and Africa, and of Japanese trade with these areas. The journal, which was
published on a bi-monthly basis through 1961, contains scholarly articles,
surveys, news commentaries, a documentary section, biographies of Asian
leaders, book reviews, bibliographical and reference sections, an 'Asian
Chronology', and reports on the Institute's activities and publications. Considerable material on Communist China and Overseas Chinese appears regularly
in the various departments of the journal. Table of contents in English. Indexed
in *Japanese Periodicals Index*.

In 1962, the Institute began publication of a periodical entitled *The Developing Economies* which makes available in English some of the materials contained
in *Ajia keizai* (see **1096**).

1108 Ajia keizai geppō アジア經濟月報
(Asian Economic Monthly). Tokyo: Gaimushō, Keizaikyoku, Ajiaka 外務省
經濟局アジア課, No. 1—, 1951—. Monthly.

A monthly report on economic problems in Asia prepared by the staff of the
Asia section, Bureau of Economic Affairs of the Japanese Foreign Ministry.
From a quarter to a third of the contents of the journal is devoted to Communist
China and Taiwan.

See also *Tōzai bōeki hangeppō* (East-West Trade Semi-Monthly, **1190**).

1109 Ajia keizai junpō アジア經濟旬報
(Ten-Day Report on the Asian Economy). Tokyo: Chūgoku Kenkyūjo 中國
研究所, No. 53—, October 1949—. Three times a month.

With No. 53 *Ajia keizai shiryō* アジア經濟資料 (Materials on the Asian
Economy), published by the Trade Committee of the China Research Institute,
was renamed *Ajia keizai junpō* and began appearing regularly three times a
month. In April 1962 the publication celebrated its 500th issue. The contents

include signed articles, documentary material, a chronology on Asia (see **394**), bibliographical surveys and indexes, reports on library acquisitions of the Institute, surveys of scholarly activities in the contemporary China field, news items, statistical data, and accounts of Japanese visitors to China. Although entitled a report on Asian economy, the bulk of this 40–50 page report is based on Chinese Mainland newspapers and periodicals, and deals with Mainland China.

Certain of the indexes and bibliographical surveys merit special mention: surveys of research in the fields of Chinese economics, politics, law, culture and education; bibliographies in the fields of Chinese politics and law; index to important articles in principal Chinese newspapers and periodicals (see **190**); the index to important articles in *Jen-min jih-pao* (**834**); indexes to other newspapers and periodicals; the index to materials on the people's communes (**128**); a list of 360 Chinese-language bibliographies, indexes and catalogs published from 1949 to 1959 (**3**); the index to pronouncements in the field of agriculture by the delegates to the National Congress; and the index to the Official Gazette of the State Council.

Issue No. 500 (pp. 23–50) contains a classified index to issue Nos. 310–500 (January 1957 to February 1962). Two indexes for the first and second half of 1956 and one for 1955 were also published as supplements.

Subscription limited to members of the China Research Institute. Mimeographed. Indexed in *Japanese Periodicals Index*.

A convenient source of Mainland data.

1110 Ajia keizai shiryō アジア經濟資料
(Materials on the Asian Economy). Tokyo: Chūgoku Kenkyūjo 中國研究所, Nos. 37–52, October 1948–September (?) 1949. Irregular.

A 20–45 page publication of the China Research Institute created as a result of a merger of the monthly *Chūken Bōeki Iinkai shiryō* 中研貿易委員會資料 (Materials of the China Research Institute's Trade Committee) and the semi-monthly *Chūken Bōeki Iinkai tokuhō* 中研貿易委員會特報 (Special Report of the China Research Institute's Trade Committee), and continued after No. 52 (September 15, 1949) as *Ajia keizai jumpō* アジア經濟旬報 (Ten-Day Report on the Asian Economy; see preceding entry). Consecutive numbering for all three publications.

Roughly half of the contents of the sixteen issues of the bulletin are devoted to the Chinese economy. No index.

1111 Ajia kenkyū アジア研究
Asiatic Studies. Tokyo: Ajia Seikei Gakkai アジア政經學會, Vol. 1, No. 1—, 1954—. Quarterly.

The organ of the Society for Asian Political and Economic Studies, containing scholarly articles and book reviews with a heavy emphasis on political and economic developments in China and Southeast Asia. Vol. 3, No. 1 is a special issue devoted to Communist China (322p.). Other issues contain many solid articles on Chinese Communism. English-language table of contents. Index to Vols. 1 through 5 in Vol. 6, No. 1 (pp. 85–103) arranged by type of material (articles, documentation, book reviews, etc.) listed in order of appearance by issue and followed by an author's index. Indexed in *Japanese Periodicals Index*.

1112 **Ajia kenkyū shiryō** アジア研究資料
(Asian Studies Data). Osaka: Ōsaka Shiritsu Daigaku, Keizai Kenkyūjo 大阪市立大學經濟研究所, Nos. 1–11, May 1955–March 1957; No. 1—, March 1959—. Irregular.

The organ of the Economic Research Institute, Osaka Municipal University. The first eight issues of the old series were published under the title *Chūgoku kenkyū shiryō* 中國研究資料 (Chinese Studies Data), and Nos. 9–11 (September 1956–March 1957) as *Ajia keizai kenkyū shiryō* アジア經濟研究資料 (Asian Economic Studies Data). Faculty interest in China is responsible for the preponderant attention given to the Chinese economy. Indexed in *Japanese Periodicals Index*.

1113 **Ajia mondai** アジア問題
Asian Affairs. Tokyo: Ajia Kyōkai アジア協會, Vol. 1, No. 1–Vol. 3, No. 6 (Nos. 1–17), 1952(?)–1954; Vol. 1, No. 1–Vol. 8, No. 3 (Nos. 18–60), September 1954–March 1958. Monthly.

A journal published by the Asia Association, each issue of which is given over to a special topic—e.g., trade between East and West in Asia; the new phase of China's reconstruction (Vol. 6, No. 1, January 1957); Communist China's five-year plan (Vol. 3, No. 2, August 1955), etc. A table of contents in English is provided.

The first seventeen issues (numbered separately) were published by Ajia Mondai Chōsakai アジア問題調査會 (Association for Asian Problems) before its amalgamation with the Asia Association. With No. 61, *Ajia mondai* was superseded by *Ajia Kyōkai shi* アジア協會誌 (Bulletin of the Asia Association), which was renamed *Kaigai gijutsu kyōryoku* (Overseas Technical Cooperation) in September 1960. Indexed in *Japanese Periodicals Index*.

1113a **Ajia tsūshin** 亞細亞通信
(Asia Bulletin). Tokyo: Ajia Tsūshinsha, No. 1—, November 1950—. Daily.

A bulletin containing New China News Agency releases, as well as other documentation from the Mainland, North Korea and North Vietnam. The Asia News Service, formerly known as the China News Service (Chūgoku Tsūshinsha 中國通信社), also puts out the daily *ANS sokuhō* ANS 速報 (ANS Flash Bulletin). Mimeographed.

1114 Chōsa geppō 調査月報
(Monthly Research Report). Tokyo: Naikaku Kambō, Naikaku Chōsashitsu
內閣官房內閣調查室, No. 1—, 1956—. Monthly.

An eighty-page monthly report by the Cabinet Research Office containing
several unsigned articles, as well as documentary material and a chronology.
The Communist bloc countries—especially Communist China—are emphasized.
The chronology for the previous month is presented in three columns: domestic
problems, international problems (not involving Japan), and diplomatic
problems. Limited distribution. No index. Indexed in *Japanese Periodicals
Index*.

1115 Chūgoku bungakuhō 中國文學報
Journal of Chinese Literature. Kyoto: Kyōto Daigaku, Bungakubu, Chūgoku
Gogaku Chūgoku Bungaku Kenkyūshitsu 京都大學文學部中國語學中國文學
研究室, Vol. 1—, 1954—. Semi-annual.

A scholarly journal devoted to the study of Chinese literature, published by
the Department of Chinese Language and Literature at Kyoto University.
The journal contains articles largely on classical and modern literature, but
occasional articles cover current literary developments on the Mainland,
including accounts of literary controversies.

Also publishes book reviews and a bibliography of books and articles on
Chinese literature published in Japan, China and the West (see **90**). English
summaries of articles are provided. Indexed in *Japanese Periodicals Index*.

1116 Chūgoku bungaku kenkyū 中國文學研究
(Studies in Chinese Literature). Tokyo: Chūgoku Bungaku no Kai 中國文學
の會, No. 1—, 1961—. Irregular.

A journal of the Society for the Study of Chinese Literature, Department of
Chinese Literature, Tokyo University, containing articles on modern Chinese
literature and recent literary developments on the Mainland. The first issue
includes a bibliography of the works of the late Yü Ta-fu 郁達夫, one of the
well-known literary figures of twentieth-century China (pp. 1–29).

1117 Chūgoku Chōsen geppō 中國朝鮮月報
(Monthly Report on China and Korea). Tokyo: Gaimushō, Ajiakyoku 外務省
アジア局, Vol. 1, No. 1–Vol. 2, No. 5, December 1951–December 1952.

A report on China and Korea prepared by specialists in the Ministry of
Foreign Affairs, superseding *Tōa geppō* 東亞月報 (Monthly Report on East
Asia). The first issue (December 1951) appeared under the title *Chūgoku geppō*
中國月報 (Monthly Report on China). Limited distribution.

1118 Chūgoku dokuritsu tsūshin 中國獨立通信
(Chinese Independent Bulletin). Tokyo: Chūgoku Mondai Kenkyūjo 中國
問題研究所, Nos. 1–20, December 1961–November 1962. Irregular.

A ten-page bulletin published in Japan by T'an Chüeh-chen 譚覺眞. Based
largely on the Mainland and Hong Kong press, it contained items of interest
to Japanese readers. Mimeographed.

1119 Chūgoku gahō 中國畫報
(China Pictorial). Peking: Jen-min hua-pao she, January 1954—. Semi-
monthly.

A Japanese-language edition of *Jen-min hua-pao* (China Pictorial), a magazine
published in Peking glorifying the achievements of the Chinese People's
Republic. Excellent illustrations, some of which are in color. Appeared monthly
from 1954 to 1957.

1120 Chūgoku geppō 中國月報
(Monthly Report on China). Tokyo: Gaimushō, Ajiakyoku, Chūgokuka 外務省
アジア局中國課, No. 1—, April 1958—. Monthly.

A 100 to 200-page report on Communist and Nationalist China prepared by
the China Section of the Foreign Ministry. Based on the monitoring of Radio
Peking, as well as Chinese newspapers and periodicals, the information included
in the report is listed (with source indicated) under foreign relations, politics,
military affairs, economics, and cultural affairs for Taiwan, the Mainland,
and Outer Mongolia. Since 1960, important articles, resolutions and other
documentary materials have been appended. The appendices also include a list
of visitors to and from Communist China, and a list of *Jen-min jih-pao* editorials,
both for the preceding month. The list of visitors is divided into incoming and
outgoing, and then by country, giving the names of the chief delegates and
prominent members of the delegation, number of members, period of stay,
and remarks (e.g., the sponsoring organization). Limited distribution.

Authoritative coverage of political and diplomatic developments in Communist China.

1121 Chūgokugo 中國語
(Chinese Language). Tokyo: Hokushinsha 北辰社, Vol. 1, No. 1—, 1959—.
Monthly.

A monthly journal for students of Chinese edited by Professor Kuraishi
Takeshirō of Tokyo University. Contains articles on such topics as Chinese
language reform, and pedagogical materials such as texts of Japanese radio
broadcasts in Chinese.

1122 Chūgoku gogaku 中國語學

(Chinese Linguistics). Kyoto, Osaka, Tokyo: Chūgoku Gogaku Kenkyūkai 中國語學研究會, Nos. 1–37, March 1947–October 1950; No. 1—, January 1951—. Monthly.

A publication (16 to 24 pages in length) of the Society for the Study of Chinese Linguistics, prepared under the supervision of Professor Kuraishi Takeshirō, one of Japan's leading scholars in the field. Nos. 1 to 33 of the new series appeared under the title *Chūgoku Gogaku Kenkyūkai hō* 中國語學研究會報 (Journal of the Society for the Study of Chinese Linguistics) January 1951 to the end of 1954. With No. 34 (January 1955), the journal reverted to its original title. Indexed in *Japanese Periodicals Index*.

This is the only important Japanese journal devoted to the scholarly study of Chinese linguistics.

1123 Chūgoku hangeppō 中國半月報

(Semi-Monthly Report on China). Tokyo: Tōa Jijō Chōsakai 東亞事情調査會, Nos. 1–40 (?), January (?) 1949–May 1951.

A 30 to 50-page mimeographed report on China, superseding *Chūgoku jumpō* 中國旬報 (Ten-Day Report on China), prepared by the China specialists in the Ministry of Foreign Affairs. The report contains a general review of Chinese affairs for the period under survey and numerous news items (with source indicated) classified under politics, economy and international relations. A three to four-page chronology for the preceding two weeks is appended to each issue.

A limited-distribution edition of the same publication was issued simultaneously by the First Section of the Research Bureau of the Foreign Ministry.

Chūgoku hangeppō was superseded by *Tōa geppō* 東亞月報 (Monthly Report on East Asia, **1182**).

1124 Chūgoku hyōron 中國評論

(China Review). Tokyo: Nihon Hyōronsha 日本評論社, Nos. 1–6, 1946–1947. Monthly.

The first periodical publication of the China Research Institute and the predecessor to *Chūgoku kenkyū* 中國研究—— The [sic] *China Research* (see **1130**).

1125 Chūgoku jijō 中國事情

(Chinese Affairs). Tokyo: Nihon Chūgoku Yūkō Kyōkai 日本中國友好協會, Nos. 1–39, January 1950–June 1953. Monthly.

A monthly journal (some thirty-four pages in length) devoted to current political, economic and cultural developments in Communist China, published by the Japan-[Communist] China Friendship Association. Incorporates articles, news from the Mainland, translations of contemporary Chinese literature, songs, etc.

1126 Chūgoku jumpō 中國旬報

(Ten-Day Report on China). Tokyo: Gaimushō, Chōsakyoku 外務省調査局,
Nos. 1–45, October 1947–December 1948).

A mimeographed report on China prepared by the China Section of the
Research Bureau of the Foreign Ministry. Superseded by *Chūgoku hangeppō*
中國半月報 (Semi-Monthly Report on China; see **1123**).

1127 Chūgoku keizai jōhō 中國經濟情報

(Information Bulletin on Chinese Economy). Kobe: Kōbe Daigaku, Keizai
Keiei Kenkyūjo, Ajia Keizai Kenkyū Iinkai 神戸大學經濟經營研究所アジア
經濟研究委員會, Vol. 1, No. 1—, 1950—. Monthly.

Began publication as an informal eight-page mimeographed semi-monthly
bulletin prepared by the Asian Economy Study Group at the Research Institute
for Economics and Business Administration, Kobe University, and contained
news items (with indication of source) arranged according to broad divisions
of the Chinese economy (finance, foreign trade, agriculture, transportation,
etc.).

Since March 1954 (Vol. 4, No. 1; consecutive No. 90), the bulletin has been
jointly sponsored with the China Study Committee of the Kansai Branch of
the Japan Institute of Pacific Relations. It was expanded in size to some
twenty printed pages and published on a monthly basis. The journal contains
articles, translations, documentary materials and economic news from both
the Mainland and Taiwan, and is based on Chinese newspapers from the
Mainland, Taiwan and Hong Kong. No index.

1128 Chūgoku keizai nempō, 1952-1955 中國經濟年報

(China Economic Annual, 1952–1955). Tokyo: Ōtsuki Shoten 大月書店,
Nos. 1–12, 1953–1955.

A journal devoted to Chinese Communist economic problems and economic
development, compiled by the China Research Institute. Each issue carries a
detailed chronology of economic developments, and translations of Chinese
Communist documents frequently appear in its pages.

No. 1, published in 1953, covers the period January to December 1952.
Beginning with No. 2, the coverage is quarterly (from January–March 1953
through July–September 1955). No. 7 is sub-titled *Chūgoku sōran* 中國綜覽
(China Handbook). Subject and name indexes.

Superseded by *Chūgoku keizai shiryō* 中國經濟資料 (Chinese Economic
Data; see next entry).

1129 Chūgoku keizai shiryō 中國經濟資料

(Chinese Economic Data). Tokyo: Chūgoku Kenkyūjo 中國研究所, 1956–
March 1960. Quarterly.

A journal published by the China Research Institute superseding *Chūgoku keizai nempō* 中國經濟年報 (China Economic Annual; see preceding entry). Indexed in *Japanese Periodicals Index*.

1130   Chūgoku kenkyū 中國研究
The [sic] *China Research*. Tokyo: Nihon Hyōronsha 日本評論社, June 1947–September 1952. 16 issues; irregular.

The organ of Chūgoku Kenkyūjo (China Research Institute) covering political, economic and cultural developments on the Mainland through articles, documents and book reviews. The journal (about 100 pages in length) regularly listed new books on China, and gave attention to developments in academic and research circles concerned with China. Contained, in addition, good bibliographical and reference articles, such as that on the postwar translation of Chinese books in Japan, and a chronology of educational and cultural developments on the Mainland (see **396**).

Announced as a quarterly, the journal actually appeared at irregular intervals, averaging from two to five issues yearly. A general table of contents to the first five issues of the magazine appeared in No. 6 (p. 95), arranged according to type of material (articles, book reviews, etc.). An English table of contents was provided beginning with No. 10.

Issue Nos. 14–16 were published by Gendai Chūgoku Gakkai 現代中國學會 (Association for the Study of Contemporary China), organized by the Institute. Superseded the monthly *Chūgoku hyōron* 中國評論 (China Review) and was in turn superseded by *Gendai Chūgoku* 現代中國 (Contemporary China; see **1148**).

1131   Chūgoku kenkyū geppō 中國研究月報
(Monthly Research Report on China). Tokyo: Chūgoku Kenkyūjo, No. 146—, April 1960—. Monthly.

A continuation of *Chūgoku shiryō geppō* 中國資料月報 (Monthly Report on Chinese Sources; see **1135**) published by the China Research Institute, this series of monographs covers a variety of topics concerning Communist China, authored by China specialists, mostly staff members of the institute. Some recent issues have dealt with such topics as public health, the five-year plans, Chinese Communist policy toward Japan, the budget, heavy industry, Japanese-Chinese trade agreements, the people's communes, electrification and other aspects of the Mainland economy. Indexed in *Japanese Periodicals Index*.

1132   Chūgoku Kenkyūjo kiyō 中國研究所紀要
The Memoirs of the China Research Institute. Tokyo: Chūgoku Kenkyūjo 中國研究所, Vol. 1—, 1961—. Irregular.

A collection of articles primarily on contemporary China, although some are concerned with the history of Chinese Communism, Chinese language, etc. Volume 2, published in 1963, is sub-titled *Chūgoku kindaika to Nihon* (Japan and the Modernization of China), 240p.

1133 Chūgoku Kenkyūjo shohō 中國研究所所報
(Bulletin of the China Research Institute). Tokyo: Chūgoku Kenkyūjo, Nos. 1–22, March 1947–August 1949. Irregular.

A mimeographed publication of the China Research Institute, the *Chūgoku Kenkyūjo shohō* contains articles and documents on Communist China, as well as reports on the activity of the Institute and acquisitions in the China field (including Western books).
Superseded *Chūgoku shiryō geppō* 中國資料月報 (Monthly Report on Chinese Sources; see **1135**) for the period March 1947–August 1949 (Nos. 1–22). Beginning with No. 23 (October 1949), the publication reverted to its original name.

1134 Chūgoku shiryō 中國資料
(China Documentation). Tokyo: Kokusai Zenrin Kurabu, Ajia Shiryōshitsu 國際善隣倶樂部アジア資料室, No. 244—, May 1961—. Three times a month.

A ten to thirty-page report containing two or three articles in each issue on current developments in China, published by the Office of Asian Documentation, International Friendship Club. No sources indicated as a rule. Mimeographed. Limited distribution.
Superseded (with No. 244) *Kōkusai Zenrin Kurabu Ajia Shiryōshitsu shiryō* (Report of the Office of Asian Documentation, International Friendship Club; see **1159**).
The International Friendship Club is a conservative organization.

1135 Chūgoku shiryō geppō 中國資料月報
(Monthly Report on Chinese Sources). Tokyo: Chūgoku Kenkyūjo 中國研究所, Nos. 1–4, November 1946–March 1947; Nos. 23–145, October 1949–March 1960. Monthly.

Published initially as a mimeographed fifty-page monthly bulletin containing translations of Chinese sources, the periodical was renamed *Chūgoku Kenkyūjo shohō* 中國研究所所報 (Bulletin of the China Research Institute; see **1133**) after four issues so as to avoid censorship by the occupation authorities. In October 1949, the bulletin reverted to its original title (maintaining the numerical sequence, however) and was reorganized into a monthly series of topical monographs on such subjects as the foreign trade of Communist China, the attitude of the Chinese People's Republic toward the Japanese peace treaty, Chinese-Soviet economic relations, women in new China, the five-year plan, socialist competition in China, Chinese-language textbooks in new China, the Geneva Conference and the position of China, etc. One issue is given over to a collection of agreements concluded between Communist China and foreign countries (see **754**). Roughly half of the monographs deal with economic problems and the other half with political, social, and cultural matters.

The publication has appeared in printed form since February 1952 (No. 49). With No. 146, the title of this periodical was changed to *Chūgoku kenkyū geppō* 中國研究月報 (Monthly Research Report on China; see **1131**). A list of titles from No. 23 to No. 104 appears in *Jūnen no ayumi* 十年のあゆみ (Ten Years of the China Research Institute), pp. 25–30. A dozen or so of the most recent titles are usually listed on the inside back cover. Indexed in *Japanese Periodicals Index*.

1136 Chūgoku sōgō shiryō 中國綜合資料
(Comprehensive Collection of Chinese Data). Tokyo: Chūgoku Shiryō Chōsakai 中國資料調查會, No. 1—, 1962—. Semi-weekly.

A 30–40 page report containing translations of editorials and news items from Communist China (North Vietnam and North Korea are also included). Mimeographed.

1137 Chūgoku tsūshin—Bōeki ban 中國通信——貿易版
(China Bulletin—Trade Edition). Tokyo: Chūgoku Tsūshinsha 中國通信社, No. 1—, 1954—. Daily (except Saturdays, Sundays and holidays).

A four to eight-page report on Japanese trade with Communist China, the Soviet Union and, to a lesser extent, with other European and Asian countries of the Communist bloc. Fairly objective coverage, based in part on information supplied by Japanese companies engaged in trade with the Soviet bloc. Mimeographed.

1138 Chūka shūhō 中華週報
(China Weekly). Tokyo: Chūka Minkoku Chūnichi Taishikan 中華民國駐日大使館, No. 1—, August 1959—. Weekly.

A sixteen-page illustrated press release of the Embassy of the Republic of China in Tokyo containing news items, editorials, etc. For a similar publication issued in New York by the Chinese Nationalist government, see *Free China Weekly* (**986**).

1139 Chūken Bōeki Iinkai tokuhō 中研貿易委員會特報
(Special Bulletin of the China Research Institute's Trade Committee). Tokyo: Chūgoku Kenkyūjo 中國研究所, Nos. 1–36, June 1947–October 1948. Semi-monthly.

Merged with the monthly *Chūken Bōeki Iinkai shiryō* 中研貿易委員會資料 (Materials of the China Research Institute's Trade Committee) to form *Ajia keizai shiryō* アジア經濟資料 (Materials on the Asian Economy), which, in turn, gave way to *Ajia keizai jumpō* アジア經濟旬報 (Ten-Day Report on the Asian Economy, **1109**) in October 1949. All three are publications of the China Research Institute.

1140 **Chūkyō jōsei shūhō** 中共情勢週報
(Weekly Report on Conditions in Communist China). Tokyo: [Naikaku Kambō, Naikaku Chōsashitsu] 內閣官房內閣調查室, Nos. 1–164, November 1959–February 1963.

A weekly 10 to 25-page bulletin on current developments in Communist China issued by the Cabinet Research Office. Contains three or four items with commentaries, a 'Memo' section with news and a weekly summary of developments in China relating to Japan. An 18-page list of tables of contents of the issue Nos. 1–55 (November 30, 1959 to December 26, 1960) was issued separately in January 1961. Nos. 1 through 28 were issued under the title *Chūkyō bunai sokuhō* 中共部內速報 (Express Report on Communist China for Internal Distribution), a part of the series *Chūkyō shiryō—bunai sokuhō* 中共資料——部內速報 (Chinese Communist Data—Express Report for Internal Distribution). Mimeographed. Limited distribution.

Superseded by *Shōten—Kaigai kankei* 焦點——海外關係 (Focus—Overseas Affairs) in March 1963 (see **1172**).

1141 **Chūkyō kokunai no ippanteki dōkō** 中共國內の一般的動向
(General Trends in Communist China). Tokyo: Kōan Chōsa Chō 公安調查廳, October 1958–February 1960. Irregular.

A report prepared by the Public Security Investigation Agency, providing the background for the Agency's more specialized reports on Communist Chinese propaganda and activities directed towards Japan. Emphasis is on economic developments. Mimeographed. Limited distribution.

1142 **Chūkyō shimbun gekkan ronchō** 中共新聞月間論調
(Monthly Report on Chinese Communist Press Comments). Tokyo: Kōan Chōsa Chō 公安調查廳, September 1956–April 1960. Irregular.

A report on Communist Chinese newspaper coverage prepared for limited distribution by the Public Security Investigation Agency. Mimeographed.

1143 **Chūkyō shiryō** 中共資料
(Communist China Documentation). Tokyo: [Naikaku Kambō, Naikaku Chōsashitsu] 內閣官房內閣調查室, Nos. 1500–1627, December 1957–December 1962; Supplement No. 1—, November 1962—. Irregular.

A series of topical reports on Communist China prepared by the Cabinet Research Office. Each report contains a survey of the subject at hand (e.g., the people's communes, the cultural exchange program of Communist China, treaties concluded between Peking and North Korea, the visit of a Japanese delegation to Peking, etc.), and includes translations of relevant editorials, and other material.

One hundred and twenty-eight reports were published to December 1962 (frequency of publication varies from two days to three months). They vary in length from ten to 100 pages. Two lists of titles of these reports are available: Nos. 1500–1596 and Nos. 1597–1623. (Nos. 1–1499 were not published; numbering began arbitrarily with No. 1500.)

In addition, special supplements (mimeographed, 30–50p. in length) have appeared since November 1962. These supplements are divided into three sections: domestic, international and Sino-Japanese relations (the last again subdivided into press coverage and pronouncements on Japan, trade between Japan and Communist China, and exchange of persons between the two countries). The contents—editorials, news items—are based largely on Chinese Communist sources, including broadcasts, and are usually given in abstract form rather than in full translation.

In 1963 the reports were superseded by *Shōten—kaigai kankei* 焦點──海外關係 (Focus—Overseas Affairs); (see **1172**). The publication of the supplements continues. Mimeographed. Limited distribution.

1144 Chūkyō tainichi dōkō geppō 中共對日動向月報
(Monthly Report on Chinese Communist Activities Directed Toward Japan). Tokyo: Kōan Chōsa Chō 公安調査廳, May 1960–February 1963. Monthly.

A report prepared by the Public Security Investigation Agency on Chinese Communist activities directed toward Japan, including trade matters and exchange of persons. Complements the agency's report on Chinese Communist propaganda directed toward Japan (see next entry). Mimeographed. Limited distribution.

1145 Chūkyō tainichi senden hōsō geppō 中共對日宣傳放送月報
(Monthly Report on Chinese Communist Radio Propaganda Toward Japan). Tokyo: Kōan Chōsa Chō 公安調査廳, August 1957–March 1960. Irregular.

A mimeographed report issued as a sub-series of *Kōan chōsa shiryō* 公安調査資料 (Research Data on Public Security) by the Public Security Investigation Agency. Limited distribution.

1146 Chū-So jijō 中ソ事情
(Chinese and Soviet Affairs). Tokyo: Kokusai Jijō Kenkyūjo 國際事情研究所, No. 1—, March 1954—. Every two days.

Current information on Communist China and the Soviet Union issued by the Institute for the Study of International Affairs. The institute is in fact a part of the Japan Press Service Company (J.P.S.), which issues an English-language weekly, *Japan Press*, distributed in the Communist bloc and especially in Communist China. The company maintains particularly close relations with New China News Agency in Peking and serves as its source of information in Japan.

1147 Daian 大安
The Daian Monthly. Tokyo, Vol. 1, No. 1—, October 1955—. Monthly.

A forty-page monthly magazine published by the Daian Company, one of the largest Japanese importers of reading matter from Mainland China. Its contents include articles on various aspects of Chinese language, literature, history, and culture; surveys of significant Chinese publications; bibliographical surveys and guides; book reviews; annotated sales catalogs of Chinese and Japanese-language books on China (arranged by subject under language); annotated lists of Chinese books compiled by the International Book Store in Peking; publication news from Peking; a classified index to articles in Chinese periodicals; and bibliographies (on people's communes, of Japanese translations of Chinese works, etc.)

Three bibliographical survey series published in over twenty instalments each in the years 1958–1961 deserve separate mention: (1) 'Chūgoku kindai shi kenkyū no tebiki' 中國近代史研究の手引 (A Guide to the Study of Modern Chinese History); (2) 'Chūgoku bungaku shisō gogaku kihon shiryō kaidai' 中國文學思想語學基本資料解題 (A Guide to the Basic Sources on Chinese Literature, Thought and Linguistics); and (3) 'Chūgoku keizai kenkyū no tebiki' 中國經濟研究の手引 (A Guide to the Study of the Chinese Economy).

The following instalments are of particular interest: a guide to works by and on Chiang K'ai-shek (November 1959), Kuo Mo-jo (January 1960), Mao Tun (November 1958 and October 1959), Chao Shu-li (November and December 1959), 'The National Liberation War' (June 1959), and language reform (April 1959).

Subject index to Nos. 1–100 in No. 100 (Vol. 10, No. 3, March 1964), pp. 27–46.

Daian is a convenient guide to current Japanese publications on China, as well as to Chinese books available in Japan.

1148 Gendai Chūgoku 現代中國
(Contemporary China). Tokyo: Gendai Chūgoku Gakkai 現代中國學會, No. 17—, 1953—. Quarterly.

The organ of the Society of Contemporary China Research, superseding *Chūgoku kenkyū* 中國研究— *The* [sic] *China Research*, (see **1130**), published by the China Research Institute (Nos. 1–13) and by the Society (Nos. 14–16). Initially published as a monthly, the journal became a bi-monthly after August 1954, and a quarterly the year following. No index. Indexed in *Japanese Periodicals Index*.

The Society of Contemporary China Research was organized in 1951 by the China Research Institute in order to draw wider support from Japanese scholars specializing on modern China. In 1951–1953 the Society also issued a bulletin *(Gendai Chūgoku Gakkai hō)*.

1149   Jiji Tsūshin kyōsanken tokuhō 時事通信共產圈特報
(Jiji Press Agency's Special Report on the Communist Bloc). Tokyo: Jiji Tsūshinsha, Nos. 1–617, 1955 (?)–December 27, 1957. Four times a week.

A 30–40 page mimeographed bulletin subtitled *Tetsu no kāten no uchigawa kara* 鐵のカーテンの內側から (From Inside the Iron Curtain) devoted to news coverage of the Communist orbit. Based on the reports of the Jiji Press Agency's own team of correspondents, radio monitoring and other conventional news sources, the bulletin is available in mimeographed form as well as on teletype.

Between April 13, 1956 and October 30, 1957, the press agency also published eighty-five issues of a special report on the Communist bloc (*Kyōsanken tokubetsu jōhō* 共產圈特別情報). Issues No. 64–85 were published under the title *Jiji Tsūshin kyōsanken tokuhō tokubetsu jōhō*.

1150   Jimmin Chūgoku 人民中國
(People's China). Peking: Jen-min cheng-fu hsin-wen ch'u-pan she 人民政府新聞出版社, No. 1—, 1953—. Monthly.

The Japanese edition of *Jen-min Chung-kuo* published from June 1953 to October 1956 in Peking and from the November 1956 issue by Kyokutō Shoten in Tokyo. Averaging 70 to 90 pages, the journal is devoted to political, economic and cultural developments in Communist China but also includes specially prepared articles on Japan, Sino-Japanese relations and Japanese missions to the Mainland. No index.

1151   Junkan Kyokutō jōhō 旬刊極東情報
(Far Eastern Intelligence—A Ten-Day Report). Tokyo: Kyokutō Jijō Kenkyūkai 極東事情研究會, October 1958—. Three times a month.

Supersedes *Kyokutō tsūshin* 極東通信 (Far Eastern Information Bulletin; see **1160**).

1152   Kazan Kurabu kaishi 霞山俱樂部會誌
(Bulletin of the Kazan Club). Tokyo: Kazan Kurabu, Nos. 1–15, September 1957–November 1958. Monthly.

Successor to *Tenchijin* 天地人 (Heaven, Earth, Man) and predecessor of *Tōa jiron* 東亞時論 (East Asian Review; see **1181** and **1183**), *Kazan Kurabu kaishi* was the organ of the Kazan Club. Contains brief items on China in general and on Communist China in particular.

1153 Kindai Chūgoku kenkyū 近代中國研究
Studies on Modern China. Tokyo: Tōkyō Daigaku Shuppankai 東京大學出版會, Vol. 1—, 1958—. Irregular.

An organ of the Seminar on Modern China (Kindai Chūgoku Kenkyū Iinkai 近代中國研究委員會) containing scholarly articles on modern China and bibliographical compilations. In the five volumes published thus far, no articles have appeared dealing with contemporary problems. Bibliographical work includes a listing of the tables of contents of important Chinese periodicals, among them *Chin-tai shih tzu-liao* 近代史資料, a Mainland journal on historical sources, 1954–1958. Volume 4 contains a list of books published during the past century by and on important Chinese (see **77**).

1154 Kindai Chūgoku Kenkyū Iinkai hō 近代中國研究委員會報
(Bulletin of the Seminar on Modern China). Tokyo, 1956—. Irregular.

A newsletter distributed to the members of the seminar containing outlines of research reports presented by seminar members, accounts of the organization's activities and the activities of seminar members. The bulletin also includes an index to Japanese articles on modern China. Mimeographed.

In 1962 the Seminar on Modern China moved from the study of nineteenth and early twentieth century China to the study of contemporary China. Its name was accordingly changed to the Seminar on Twentieth Century China (the Japanese name remained the same).

See also next entry.

1155 Kindai Chūgoku Kenkyū Sentā ihō 近代中國研究センター彙報
(Bulletin of the Center for Modern Chinese Studies). Tokyo, No. 1—, January 1963—. Irregular.

The organ of the Center for Modern Chinese Studies at the Tōyō Bunko, this new 30–50 page publication contains surveys of Chinese studies in Japan and abroad, activities of the new center, lists of new accessions, special bilbiographies, chronologies, catalogs and other compilations of a bibliographical or reference nature. No. 3 of the Bulletin (September 1963) contains a checklist of the Chen Cheng Collection on the Kiangsi Soviet microfilmed by the Hoover Institution. An index to articles on China appearing in general Japanese magazines (based on the *Japanese Periodicals Index*) is scheduled to appear regularly.

An important source of bibliographical information on modern Chinese studies in Japan.

1156 Kokusai bōeki 國際貿易
(International Trade). Tokyo: Nihon Kokusai Bōeki Sokushin Kyōkai 日本
國際貿易促進協會, No. 1—, 1954—. Monthly.

The organ of the Japan Association for the Promotion of International
Trade, headed until recently by the late Yamamoto Kumaichi, wartime Vice-
Minister of Greater East Asia. Devoted to the promotion of trade with the
Communist bloc, the 30-page journal contains trade news items, documents,
speeches and a chronology of the association's activities. Table of contents in
Chinese, Russian, English and Japanese.

1157 Kokusai mondai 國際問題
(International Problems). Tokyo: Nihon Kokusai Mondai Kenkyūjo 日本國際
問題研究所, No. 1—, April 1960—. Monthly.

The organ of the Japan Institute for the Study of International Problems, an
auxiliary organization of the Ministry of Foreign Affairs. Contains signed articles
on international affairs, book reviews, diplomatic reminiscences, biographical
information, a chronology and news of academic research in the field. Articles
on contemporary China appear in its pages, and almost one entire issue
(No. 35, February 1963) was devoted to the Sino-Indian border dispute.

The institute also publishes a monograph series (*Kokusai mondai shiriizu*—
International Problems Series). Two of these volumes containing Chinese
Communist diplomatic documents are listed in Chapter XVI (see **753**).

1158 Kokusai Mondai Kenkyūjo kiyō 國際問題研究所紀要
The Memoirs of [the] Institute of International Affairs. Toyohashi: Aichi
Daigaku, Kokusai Mondai Kenkyūjo 愛知大學國際問題研究所, No. 1—,
1949 (?)—. Irregular.

A scholarly journal of international affairs with a strong emphasis on Communist China, published by the Institute of International Affairs, Aichi
University. The journal, which usually appears semi-annually, carries scholarly
articles, documentary materials, bibliographical surveys, and book reviews.
Several issues of the journal have been devoted to Communist China. A few
bibliographical articles from this journal (such as the bibliography on people's
communes, etc.) have been annotated and appear as separate entries in the
present work. Indexed in *Japanese Periodicals Index.*

In 1961 the institute began a systematic survey of current Japanese research
on Communist China, and the first annual bibliography appeared in No. 33
(see **37**). Through No. 25, the journal was known as *Kokusai seikei jijō* 國際政
經事情——*International Politics and Economic Journal.*

The journal's preoccupation with Communist China is in part explained
by the fact that Aichi University was established after the war to create teaching
positions for Japanese scholars repatriated from China and former Japanese
colonial areas. A substantial number of the faculty of Aichi University come
from Tōa Dōbun Shoin, a Japanese college of Chinese studies in Shanghai.

1159 Kokusai Zenrin Kurabu, Ajia Shiryōshitsu shiryō 國際善隣倶樂部アジア
資料室資料
(Report of the Office of Asian Documentation of the International Friendship
Club). Tokyo, Nos. 1–243, July 1954–April 1961. Irregular.

A report devoted largely to Communist China, prepared by a conservative
organization which also issues an annual on Communist China (see **223**).
Mimeographed. Starting with No. 244 (May 5, 1961) the report was renamed
Chūgoku shiryō (China Documentation; see **1134**).

1160 Kyokutō tsūshin 極東通信
(Far Eastern Information Bulletin). Tokyo: Kyokutō Jijō Kenkyūkai 極東事
情研究會, 1949—. Three times a month.

A news bulletin published by the Far Eastern Affairs Research Association.
Based on radio monitoring, news agency releases and newspapers, the bulletin
contains largely news of the Communist bloc, accompanied by editorial com-
ments. Roughly one-third of the contents is given over to Communist China.
In October 1958, its title changed to *Junkan Kyokutō jōhō* 旬刊極東情報 (Far
Eastern Intelligence—A Ten-Day Report).

The Far Eastern Affairs Research Association is a conservative organization
specializing in the coverage of the international Communist movement,
especially the Japanese Communist Party. It also produces mimeographed
monographic reports entitled *Kyokutō Jijō Kenkyūkai tokubetsu shiryō* 極東事
情研究會特別資料 (Special Reports of the Far Eastern Affairs Research
Association), a number of which are devoted to Communist China.

1161 Kyōsanken mondai 共産圈問題
Communist Bloc Problems. Tokyo: Ō-A Kyōkai 歐ア協會, Vol. 1, No. 1—,
1957—. Monthly.

A monthly review (issued quarterly for the first four volumes) published by
the Japan Association on Communist States in Europe and Asia, containing
scholarly and journalistic articles on the Communist countries, documentary
material, and reports on the activities of the association. Communist China
accounts for about a quarter of the contents of the journal (the bulk of each
issue is devoted to the Soviet Union). Some issues are largely or entirely devoted
to Communist China (e.g., Vol. 6, No. 7). From its inception until 1959,
Communist Bloc Problems was published under the title *Soren mondai* ソ連問題
(Soviet Problems) by the same organization, then called Soren Kenkyūsha
Kyōgikai ソ連研究者協議會 (Japan Institute for Soviet Research). Index to Vol.
1 through Vol. 5, No. 1 appears in Vol. 5, No. 2 (August 1961), arranged by
issue under the main departments of the journal (articles, book reviews, etc.). A
table of contents in English is provided. Indexed in *Japanese Periodicals Index*.

The Association is subsidized by the Japanese Foreign Ministry, and its
officers and directors include a number of retired diplomats.

1162   Nihon to Chūgoku 日本と中國
(Japan and China). Tokyo: Nihon Chūgoku Yūkō Kyōkai 日本中國友好協會,
No. 1—, 1950—. Three times a month.

A tabloid newspaper published by the Japan-[Communist] China Friendship
Association. Indexed in *Japanese Periodicals Index*.

Good coverage of Japanese missions to the Mainland, Communist Chinese
missions to Japan, and the activities of pro-Communist Chinese organizations
in Japan.

1163   Nitchū bōeki 日中貿易
(Japanese-Chinese Trade). Tokyo: Nitchū Bōeki Sokushinkai 日中貿易促進會,
1951—. Weekly.

An eight-page tabloid newspaper containing news items, articles and other
information on Japanese trade with Communist China published by the Society
for the Promotion of Trade between Japan and [Communist] China.

1164   Nitchū bōeki kihō 日中貿易季報
(Japanese-Chinese Trade Quarterly). Tokyo: Nitchū Yushutsunyū Kumiai
日中輸出入組合, Vol. 1, No. 1—, May 1956—. Irregular.

The organ of the Japan-[Communist] China Exporters and Importers
Association, covering Chinese Communist economic developments and Japanese
trade with the Mainland. Renamed *Tōzai bōeki hangeppō* 東西貿易半月報
(East-West Trade Semi-Monthly) in October 1960; *Nitchū Yushutsunyū
Kumiai nyūsu* (Japan-China Exporters and Importers Association News) in
December 1960 (with a new numbering system beginning with No. 1); and
Nitchū Yushutsunyū Kumiai jumpō (Ten-Day Report of the Japan-China
Exporters and Importers Association) in October 1962. Planned to appear
thrice monthly, this eight-page bulletin is issued about once a month on the
average. The frequent changes in title, format, frequency, etc., reflect the
unstable position of the association following the rupture of trade between
Japan and Communist China in 1958.

1165   Nitchū bunka 日中文化
(Japanese-Chinese Cultural Relations). Tokyo: Nitchū Hon'yaku Shuppan
Konwakai 日中翻譯出版懇話會, No. 1-41, 1950-1956. Irregular.

The organ, now defunct, of the Conference of Japanese-Chinese Translators
and Publishers, containing a number of short articles and items on Sino-
Japanese cultural relations, but lacking in substantial, scholarly articles. Of
particular importance were the occasional bibliographical surveys and the
current index to articles in Chinese newspapers and periodicals (see **189**).
The first thirty-six issues (roughly fifty pages in length per issue) were

published under the title *Nitchū hon'yaku shiryō tsūshin* 日中翻譯資料通信 (Bulletin of Chinese-Japanese Translated Materials). Beginning with No. 37 (December 1955) the title changed to *Nitchū bunka*.

The Conference of Japanese-Chinese Translators was organized in the autumn of 1950 by translators and publishers of Communist Chinese materials for the purpose of facilitating the translation and dissemination of such materials in Japan and of promoting Japanese-Chinese cultural relations.

1166 Nitchū kokkō kaifuku nyūsu 日中國交回復ニュース
(News on the Restoration of Diplomatic Relations between Japan and [Communist] China). Tokyo: Nitchū Kokkō Kaifuku Kokumin Kaigi 日中國交回復 國民會議, No. 1—, 1957—. Irregular.

The organ of the National Conference for the Restoration of Diplomatic Relations Between Japan and [Communist] China.

1167 R.P. nyūsu R P ニュース
(R.P. News). Tokyo: Rajio Puresu Tsūshinsha ラジオプレス (R.P.) 通信社, No. 1—, 1951—. Daily.

A daily 30 to 40-page news report on Communist China issued by the Radio Press (R.P.) News Agency, one of the most active organizations in the field. The Soviet Union and the Asian Communist countries are also covered. Nos. 1 to 879 were issued under the title *Rajio Puresu Chūgoku nyūsu* ラジオ プレス中國ニュース (Radio Press' China News) and Nos. 880–1483 under the title *R.P. Chūgoku nyūsu* R.P. 中國ニュース (R.P. China News).

The News Agency also issues a variety of publications, among which are *Shūkan Chūgoku shiryō* (Weekly Documentation of China; see **1175**); *Radio Peking* (twice daily in English); *Pekin hōsō dōkō shiryō* (Peking Broadcast Materials—monitoring Radio Peking's broadcasts directed towards the various provinces); *R.P. shiryō kaisetsu ban* (R.P. Documentation: Commentary Edition—a daily ten-page summary of broadcasts and editorials of Peking, Moscow, etc.); *Tokubetsu shiryō—Kyōsan tainichi hōsō* (Special Materials—Communist Broadcasts Towards Japan). Mimeographed.

1168 Rekishigaku kenkyū 歷史學研究
The Journal of Historical Studies. Tokyo: Aoki Shoten 青木書店, No. 1—, 1933—. Monthly.

The organ of the Marxist-oriented Rekishigaku Kenkyūkai (The Historical Science Society) containing scholarly articles, reviews, bibliographies and professional news. From the February 1954 issue (No. 168), the bibliographical section lists articles of interest to historians, arranged by publication (largely academic journals).

An annual supplement entitled *Rekishigaku no seika to kadai* 歴史學の成果 と課題 (The Results and Issues of Historical Science in Japan) was published by Iwanami Shoten 岩波書店 from 1950 (for the year 1949) to 1955 (for 1954). This 200-page volume contains separate signed articles surveying the fields of ancient, medieval and modern Japanese, Far Eastern (largely Chinese) and Western history for the preceding year, and a review of the more important Japanese literature on the same subject areas. Beginning with issue No. 2 for 1950, the supplement also included a classified bibliography of Japanese books and articles in all the above-mentioned historical fields from 1949 to 1954. Starting with 1956, the annual supplement was published as one of the regular issues of the journal (e.g., June 1956 for 1955; November 1957 for 1956, etc.). So as to avoid making any one issue too bulky, the bibliography was spread out over several issues. Discontinued after July 1958. Indexed in *Japanese Periodicals Index*.

1169 Sekai geppō 世界月報
(Monthly World Report). Tokyo: Gaimushō, Jōhō Bunkakyoku 外務省情報文 化局, Vol. 1, No. 1–Vol. 13, No. 3, 1946–1958. Monthly.

A monthly report prepared by staff specialists of the Ministry of Foreign Affairs and published by the Ministry's Bureau of Information and Cultural Affairs. Essentially devoted to political, diplomatic and economic developments throughout the world, the Report nonetheless devotes about one-quarter of its coverage to Communist China and Taiwan. The news items (with indication of source) for the preceding month are arranged under eight geographical divisions ('international outlook', 'United Nations and international', the Americas, East Asia, etc.).

Through December 1948 (Vol. 3, No. 12), the publication was entitled *Saikin no kokusai jōsei* 最近の國際情勢 (Recent International Situation). Limited Distribution.

1170 Shigaku zasshi 史學雜誌
The Historical Journal of Japan. Tokyo: Shigakkai 史學會, Vol. 1, No. 1—, 1889—. Monthly.

The organ of the Historical Society of Japan, containing scholarly articles, notes, reviews and bibliographies. One issue of each volume (the May issue) is given over to survey articles on historical studies in Japan (*Rekishi gakkai— kaiko to tembō* 歴史學會——回顧と展望) on all periods of Japanese, Chinese and Western history, covering the preceding year. Four or five pages are always devoted to the field of modern and contemporary Chinese history.

Since the war, almost every issue has contained a bibliographical section listing articles of interest to historians in the journals received by the society (classified by issue of the journals under survey). In recent years, this section has been expanded to include books and articles, and is classified by historical field (i.e., Japanese, Oriental and Western) with additional chronological subdivisions (e.g., modern and contemporary China). The bibliography is not published as a unit; rather, each issue of the journal carries a section. English summaries of articles are provided. An annual index to the journal appears in the December issue (together with an English-language index since 1953).

To celebrate its sixtieth anniversary, the Society published *Shigaku bunken mokuroku* 史學文獻目錄 (Bibliography of Historical Materials), (1951, 204p.) covering books and articles on historical topics published in Japan from January 1946 to December 1950. Pages 87–88 and 117–120 list books and articles respectively on modern and contemporary China. Material on contemporary China also appears in the topical categories. Author index arranged according to the Japanese syllabary. Indexed in *Japanese Periodicals Index.*

1171 **Shohō—Chūgoku tosho no zasshi** 書報——中國圖書の雜誌
(Book News—Journal of Chinese Publications). Tokyo: Kyokutō Shoten 極東書店, No. 1—, April 1958—. Monthly.

A 40-page monthly magazine published by the Kyokutō Shoten (Far Eastern Book Sellers), one of the largest Japanese importers of foreign publications, including those of Mainland China and the Soviet Union. The magazine contains articles on various aspects of Chinese language, literature, history and current developments; surveys of Chinese publications; bibliographical surveys and book reviews; news and comments on Chinese studies abroad; reminiscences and travel accounts by Japanese visitors to Communist China; annotated sales catalogs of Chinese, Japanese, Russian and Western-language material on China (arranged by subject under language); and lists of Japanese-language publications from Peking. Noteworthy is a fifteen-instalment survey of postwar Japanese periodicals in the Chinese field (see **178**). Annual table of contents in the December or January issue.

A useful magazine for following current publications on China in all languages.

1172 **Shōten—Kaigai kankei** 焦點——海外關係
(Focus—Overseas Affairs). Tokyo: [Naikaku Kambō, Naikaku Chōsashitsu 內閣官房內閣調査室], No. 1—, March 1963—. Weekly.

A general report, published by the Cabinet Research Office, which supersedes *Chūkyō jōsei shūhō* 中共情勢週報 (Weekly Report on Conditions in Communist China), *Chūkyō shiryō* 中共資料 (Communist China Documentation) (see **1140** and **1143**), and similar reports covering other areas published by the same office. This report, roughly sixteen pages in length, is devoted to interpretation of trends in international affairs, with particular emphasis on Communist China, the Soviet Union and other countries of the Communist bloc. Mimeographed. Limited distribution.

1173 Shōwa dōjin 昭和同人
(Showa Comrade). Tokyo: Shōwa Dōjinkai, No. 1—, 1955—. Monthly.

The organ of the Showa Society, a group of persons associated in the prewar period with the now defunct Showa Research Institute. The journal, averaging thirty pages, contains many articles on Communist China (e.g., issues at stake in Sino-Soviet economic relations, the Mainland cotton industry, the democratization of the people's communes and the communization of state farms).

1174 Shuchō to kaisetsu 主張と解說
(Opinion and Comments). Tokyo: Sekai Minshu Kenkyūjo 世界民主研究所, Vol. 1, No. 1—, 1951—. Semi-monthly.

A publication of the Research Institute for World Democracy which is headed by Nabeyama Sadachika 鍋山貞親 and Kazama Jōkichi 風間丈吉, Moscow-trained ex-leaders of the Japanese Communist Party. The journal, averaging thirty-two pages, is designed to counteract Communist propaganda in the Japanese labor movement. Contains numerous articles on current Communist Chinese developments (e.g., recent trends in Chinese heavy industry, the Chinese Communist cadres' participation in manual labor, the Sino-Soviet dispute, and the Chinese image of the Japanese).

1175 Shūkan Chūgoku shiryō 週刊中國資料
(Weekly Documentation on China). Tokyo: Rajio Puresu (R.P.) Tsūshinsha フジオプレス (R.P.) 通信社, No. 1—, 1959—. Weekly.

A 30-page mimeographed report on Communist China issued by the Radio Press (R.P.) News Agency. Each issue, covering the preceding week, is arranged under the following headings: (1) Mainland material on or concerning Japan, (2) politics, (3) economics, (4) culture (education, science, sports, the arts), (5) editorials, commentaries, etc.
    See also *R. P. nyūsu* (**1167**).

1176 Soren kenkyū: Chūkyō Tōō ソ連研究 中共, 東歐
(Soviet Studies: Communist China and Eastern Europe). Tokyo: Soren Mondai Kenkyūkai ソ連問題研究會, Vol. 1, No. 1–Vol. 11, No. 8, 1952–1962. Monthly.

A monthly 80-page journal published by the Association for the Study of the Soviet Union, consisting largely of journalistic articles and documentary material on political and economic developments in the Soviet Union and, to a lesser degree, Communist China and the East European satellites. Among the features which appeared frequently in the journal were 'Developments in Communist China', and 'Prospects for Communist China'. Index in the April or May issue of each year.

1177 Tairiku 大陸

(The Continent). Tokyo: Tairikusha. Vol. 1, No. 1—, January 1950—. Monthly.

A journal of the organization of Japanese repatriates from Dairen (Manchuria) published from January 1950 to October 1951 under the title *Dairen* 大連 (some 30 pages in length). Contains information on conditions in Dairen under Communist control, the forced detention of Japanese technicians, and other items of interest to the group. As of March 1964, 148 issues had appeared. Mimeographed.

1178 Tairiku jumpō 大陸旬報

(The Continent: A Ten-Day Report). Tokyo: Tairiku Mondai Kenkyūjo 大陸問題研究所, No. 1—, 1958—.

A report on current developments in the Communist bloc. Consisting of news items, the coverage is essentially political and economic, with extensive utilization of charts and graphs.

More up-to-date coverage than *Tairiku mondai* (Continental Problems), published by the same organization (see next entry).

1179 Tairiku mondai 大陸問題

(Continental Problems). Tokyo: Tairiku Mondai Kenkyūjo 大陸問題研究所, Vol. 1, No. 1—, January 1952 —. Monthly.

A monthly 80-page journal published by the Continental Problems Research Institute devoted to the coverage of the political and military situation in and around the Soviet Union and Communist China. The journal's regular features include: 'Tidbits on Red China', and 'Data on Communist China'. Beginning with Vol. 9, No. 10 (1960), table of contents in English is provided. Index in the December issue.

The institute is staffed largely with former military officers, and its president is General Doi Akio 土居明夫, one of Japan's leading military experts on the Soviet Union, who served for several years after the war as a military adviser to the Chinese Nationalist government.

1180 Taiwan seinen—Taiwan Chinglian 臺灣青年

The Young Formosan. Tokyo: Taiwan Seinen Henshū Iinkai 臺灣青年編集委員會, No. 1—, 1960—. Bi-monthly.

A Japanese-language organ of the Formosan Association, containing articles, essays, book reviews, biographies of prominent Formosans and Nationalist Chinese, and a section on the Formosan dialect. Several special issues are devoted to the February 28th Incident (1947), the problem of Mainland Chinese in Taiwan, etc.

For an index of the first sixteen issues, see the first issue of *Formosan Quarterly*, the English-language counterpart to *Taiwan Chinglian*, pp. 21–26 (see **1099**).

The Formosan Association is an organization of native Formosans in Japan who aspire to an independent Formosa. Their views are reflected in the pages of their publication.

1181 Tenchijin 天地人
(Heaven, Earth, Man). Tokyo: Kazan Kurabu 霞山倶樂部, Vol. 1, No. 1–Vol. 5, No. 2, August 1952–April 1956. Quarterly.

An organ of the Kazan Club, containing articles on current developments in Asia, with particular emphasis on Chinese art, literature and history. Nos. 7 and 8 include two articles by Professor Hatano Tarō 波多野太郎 of Yokohama Municipal University on trends in Chinese scholarly circles, together with an annotated bibliography of some 150 significant books and articles in the fields of history and literature published in China between 1949 and 1953. From 30 to 80 pages in length.

The Kazan Club was organized in memory of Prince Konoye Atsumaro 近衛篤麿 (father of former Prime Minister Konoye and founder, in 1900, of Tōa Dōbun Shoin 東亞同文書院, a Japanese college in Shanghai). It has a membership drawn largely from the Japanese aristocracy, and its journal reflects the members' strong interest in Asia and, in particular, in China.

Superseded by *Kazan Kurabu kaishi* 霞山倶樂部會誌 (Bulletin of the Kazan Club; see **1152**) and *Tōa jiron* 東亞時論 (East Asian Review, **1183**).

1182 Tōa geppō 東亞月報
(Monthly Report on East Asia). Tokyo: Tōa Jijō Chōsakai 東亞事情調查會, Vol. 1, No. 1–Vol. 1, No. 5, June–October 1951.

A report on China prepared by the China specialists of the Foreign Ministry. Superseded *Chūgoku hangeppō* 中國半月報 (Semi-Monthly Report on China, **1123**) and, in December 1951, was in turn superseded by *Chūgoku Chōsen geppō* 中國朝鮮月報 (Monthly Report on China and Korea; see **1117**).

1183 Tōa jiron 東亞時論
(East Asian Review). Tokyo: Kazankai 霞山會, Vol. 1, No. 1—, 1959—. Monthly.

A 40 to 60-page organ of the Kazan Society (formerly the Kazan Club), the journal is almost entirely devoted to China in general and present-day China in particular. *Tōa jiron* is the successor to *Tenchijin* 天地人 (Heaven, Earth, Man) and *Kazan Kurabu kaishi* 霞山倶樂部會誌 (Bulletin of the Kazan Club); see **1181** and **1152**. Each issue carries a three to four-page section entitled 'Notes on Communist China', a news review for the preceding month.

1184 Tōa keizai kenkyū 東亞經濟研究
(Studies in East Asian Economy). Yamaguchi: Yamaguchi Daigaku, Tōa Keizai Kenkyūkai 山口大學東亞經濟研究會, Vol. 1, No. 1–Vol. 29, No. 2, 1917–1945; Vol. 1, No. 1–Vol. 5, No. 2, 1957–1961; Vol. 35, No. 1—, 1961—. Irregular.

A revival of a journal with the same title published at Yamaguchi University before the war. The university was at the time a higher commercial school with a long tradition of interest in problems of Sino-Japanese trade. At present the publication is the organ of the East Asian Economic Research Group at the same university. Because of the research interests of the faculty, the journal is largely devoted to the Chinese economy. Appears on the average twice yearly. Indexed in *Japanese Periodicals Index*.

1185 Tōhōgaku 東方學
Eastern Studies. Tokyo: Tōhō Gakkai 東方學會, No. 1—, 1951—. Irregular.

The organ of the Tōhō Gakkai (Institute of Eastern Culture) issued approximately twice a year (over twenty volumes during the first decade). Contains scholarly articles on pre-modern China and useful surveys of Chinese studies in various countries of the world. A good bibliographical section, *Books and Articles On Oriental Subjects Published in Japan* (see **38**). English-language table of contents. Index to Nos. 1–14 in *Tōhō Gakkai jūnen no ayumi* (Ten Years of the Institute of Eastern Culture), Tokyo, November 1957. Indexed in *Japanese Periodicals Index*.

1186 Tōyō bunka 東洋文化
Oriental Culture. Tokyo: Tōyō Gakkai 東洋學會, No. 1—, 1950—. Irregular.

Supersedes *Tōyō bunka kenkyū* 東洋文化研究 *The Oriental Culture Review* (see next entry), published by the Society of Oriental Culture at the Institute for Oriental Culture, Tokyo University. The journal contains scholarly articles with an emphasis on Chinese history and culture, including present-day China. Noteworthy also is the book review section. Several issues are devoted exclusively to China (e.g. No. 27, March 1959 on the people's communes). Some 100 pages in length, the journal is issued from two to four times a year. English-language table of contents is provided in each issue. An index to the first twenty-one issues appears in *Tōyō Bunka Kenkyūjo kiyō* 東洋文化研究所紀要 *(The Memoirs of the Institute for Oriental Culture)*, No. 12, pp. 88–93. Indexed in *Japanese Periodicals Index*.

1187 Tōyō bunka kenkyū 東洋文化研究
The Oriental Culture Review. Tokyo: Tōyō Gakkai 東洋學會, Nos. 1–11, October 1944–May 1949. Irregular.

The predecessor of *Tōyō bunka—Oriental Culture* (see preceding entry). The index to all eleven issues appears in *Tōyō Bunka Kenkyūjo kiyō*, No. 12, pp. 85–88. Indexed in *Japanese Periodicals Index*.

1188 Tōyō Bunka Kenkyūjo kiyō 東洋文化研究所紀要
The Memoirs of the Institute for Oriental Culture. Tokyo: Tōyō Bunka Kenkyūjo, No. 1—, 1943, 1951—. Irregular.

Scholarly articles and book reviews largely on traditional China, with occasional articles on the economic development of present-day China, the people's communes, contemporary Chinese literature, etc. Table of contents and summaries of articles in English. The journal is issued at irregular intervals (from one to four issues a year), averaging about two issues annually.

Index to the first eleven issues appears in a supplement to No. 12 entitled *Tōyō Bunka Kenkyūjo yōran* 東洋文化研究所要覽 (Handbook of the Institute for Oriental Culture), pp. 60–64. No. 15 contains the index to Nos. 12 through 14, and No. 19 the index to Nos. 15 through 18. Indexed in *Japanese Periodicals Index*.

1189 Tōyōshi kenkyū 東洋史研究
The Journal of Oriental Researches [sic]. Kyoto: Kyōto Daigaku, Tōyōshi Kenkyūkai 京都大學東洋史研究會, Vol. 1, No. 1–Vol. 8, No. 5/6, 1935–1944; Vol. 1, No. 1–Vol. 1, No. 5/6, 1944–1947; Vol. 10, No. 1—, 1947—. Quarterly.

A scholarly journal of the Society of Oriental Researches, Kyoto University, devoted largely to the study of traditional China. Coverage of the modern period was increased after the Second World War. Each issue carries a bibliography of articles in the Oriental field. Until 1954 the journal appeared on a bi-monthly basis (with the exception of the wartime and the immediate postwar period), quarterly thereafter. Indexed in *Japanese Periodicals Index*.

1190 Tōzai bōeki hangeppō 東西貿易半月報
(East-West Trade Semi-Monthly). Tokyo: Gaimushō, Keizaikyoku 外務省 經濟局, No. 1—, 1955 (?)—. Semi-monthly.

A 20–30 page publication of the East-West Trade Section of the Bureau of Economic Affairs, Ministry of Foreign Affairs. The journal contains both documents on and analytical surveys of trade between the Communist bloc and the West (including Japan), and intra-bloc trade relations. Roughly one-third of its contents are given over to Communist China's economy and trade. A yearly index lists articles in order of appearance under the main categories of the journal. Through February 1960 the journal was published under the title *Kyōsanken bōeki jōhō* 共産圈貿易情報 (Communist Bloc Trade Bulletin), and from March 1960 through March 1962 as *Tōzai bōeki jōhō* 東西貿易情報 (East-West Trade Bulletin).

See also *Ajia keizai geppō* (Asian Economic Monthly, **1108**).

1191 Tōzai bōeki tsūshin 東西貿易通信
(East-West Trade Bulletin). Tokyo: Tōzai Bōeki Tsūshinsha 東西貿易通信社,
No. 1—, May 1955—. Daily (except Sundays and holidays).

A ten-page report largely on trade with the Mainland, published by a group attempting to promote closer ties with Communist China. Documents also are included. Mimeographed.

1192 Zen'ei 前衛
(Vanguard). Tokyo: Nihon Kyōsantō, Chūō Iinkai 日本共産黨中央委員會,
Vol. 1, No. 1—, February 1946—. Monthly.

The official organ of the Central Committee of the Japanese Communist Party, containing articles on Communist China in general and the Chinese Communist Party in particular. Indexed in *Japanese Periodicals Index*.

Also useful, though to a lesser degree, is the Party's daily organ *Akahata* アカハタ (Red Flag).

C. RUSSIAN-LANGUAGE

In this section are collected twelve Russian-language journals and monograph series in the Oriental field published in the Soviet Union. (The few Russian-language journals published in Peking are listed in Chapter XVII, **937**. A Chinese-language Soviet counterpart *Su-Chung yu-hao* [Soviet-Chinese Friendship] is described in the next section, **1212**.)

As a result of the constant struggle of the Communist Party to push Soviet Orientalists towards the study of contemporary problems, the institutions of higher learning in the Asian field and their publications often undergo reorganizations and periodically change their names. Particular effort, therefore, has been made to make clear all changes of titles and of sponsoring institutions.

Only one Soviet journal is devoted entirely to the study of China—*Sovetskoe kitaevedenie* (Soviet Journal of Chinese Studies—published in 1958-1959, **1194**). Publication was discontinued after four issues. At the present time the Soviets publish only one scholarly periodical in the Oriental field—*Narody Azii i Afriki* (The Peoples of Asia and Africa, **1196**); one popular propagandistic periodical devoted to Asia and Africa, *Aziia i Afrika segodnia* (Asia and Africa Today, **1198**); and the short reports and transactions of the Institute of Asian Peoples, *Kratkie soobshcheniia* (**1199** and **1200**) and *Uchenye zapiski* (**1201** and **1202**), respectively. Material on China also appears in the more general transactions of Leningrad University (Oriental Studies Series, **1203**) and in the Transactions of the Department of Oriental Geography and Economics at the Institute of International Relations in Moscow (**1204**).

Reference should also be made to Skachkov's bibliography (**42**).

1193 Sovetskoe vostokovedenie
(Soviet Oriental Studies). Moscow: Izdatel'stvo Akademii Nauk S.S.S.R.,
1955 No. 1-1958 No. 6, 1955-1958. Bi-monthly.

The organ of the Institute of Oriental Studies of the Soviet Academy of Sciences, containing scholarly articles; documents; communications; surveys of scholarly activities in the Soviet Union, China and elsewhere; bibliographies; and book reviews of both Chinese books and periodicals. Coverage of the traditional, modern and contemporary periods embraces Chinese language, literature, art, history, politics, economics and foreign relations. Representative topics: the question of periodization of Chinese history, peasant rebellions, the successful Communist revolution, the influence of the Russian revolution upon the Chinese revolution, the May Fourth Movement, Sun Yat-sen, the five-year plans, and the critical evaluation of such writers as Lao She and Ai Ch'ing.

Bibliographies appearing in the journal include Western-language books on Asia accessioned by Moscow libraries in 1955–1956, and selected Soviet works in the Oriental field published from 1938 to 1953. Summaries of articles and tables of contents are provided in English. Index appears in No. 6 of each year.

In 1959 the journal merged with the Soviet Journal of Chinese Studies (*Sovetskoe kitaevedenie*) to form *Problemy Vostokovedeniia* (Problems of Oriental Studies; see below).

Another Soviet journal of Oriental studies with an identical title appeared irregularly from 1940 to 1949.

1194   Sovetskoe kitaevedenie
(Soviet Journal of Chinese Studies). Moscow: Izdatel'stvo Vostochnoi literatury, 1958 No. 1–1958 No. 4, 1958–1959.

The organ of the short-lived Institute of Chinese Studies of the Soviet Academy of Sciences, *Sovetskoe kitaevedenie* (ranging from 240 to 320 pages in length) contains scholarly articles, a documentary section, review articles and book reviews, bibliographies, surveys of Chinese studies in the Soviet Union and abroad, and a chronology of events in China. All aspects of traditional, modern and contemporary China are treated, and the topics range from language, literature, philosophy and art to political and economic developments and foreign relations of present-day China, with special emphasis on Sino-Soviet relations. The journal carried bibliographies of Soviet books and articles on China published in 1956 and 1957. Summaries of the main articles and the table of contents are provided in English, French, German and Chinese. An index to all four volumes appears in No. 4.

The Journal of Chinese Studies started out with much fanfare, including a congratulatory message from Kuo Mo-jo, the president of the Chinese Academy of Sciences, who also wrote the title of the journal in Chinese characters. What promised to be one of the world's most important scholarly journals in the China field was discontinued after four issues, reportedly because of Chinese demands for prepublication censorship.

The journal of Chinese Studies emerged from the general journal *Sovetskoe vostokovedenie* (Soviet Oriental Studies; see preceding entry), and was absorbed by the same journal, which on the occasion was renamed *Problemy vostokovedeniia* (Problems of Oriental Studies; see next entry). The Institute of Chinese Studies was likewise absorbed by the Institute of Oriental Studies, renamed the Institute of the Peoples of Asia.

1195 Problemy vostokovedeniia
(Problems of Oriental Studies). Moscow: Izdatel'stvo Akademii Nauk S.S.S.R., 1959 No. 1–1961 No. 1, March 1959–March 1961. Bi-monthly.

The official joint organ of the institutes of Oriental Studies and Chinese Studies, superseding *Sovetskoe vostokovedenie* (Soviet Oriental Studies) and *Sovetskoe kitaevedenie* (Soviet Journal of Chinese Studies; see preceding two entries).

Beginning with 1960 No. 2, the Institute on Africa joined in the sponsorship of the journal. When, in the same year, the Institute of Oriental Studies merged with the Institute of Chinese Studies to form the Institute of the Peoples of Asia, the journal became the joint organ of that institute and the Institute on Africa (beginning with 1960 No. 4). After 1962 No. 1, *Problemy vostokovedeniia* changed its name to *Narody Azii i Afriki* (The Peoples of Asia and Africa; see next entry) to reflect the growing emphasis on Africa.

For a description of the material on China appearing in the journal, see *Sovetskoe vostokovedenie* (Soviet Oriental Studies) above. Index in No. 6 of each year.

1196 Narody Azii i Afriki
(The Peoples of Asia and Africa). Moscow: Izdatel'stvo Akademii Nauk S.S.S.R., 1962 No. 2—, 1962—. Bi-monthly.

Beginning with 1962 No. 2, *Problemy Vostokovedeniia* (Problems of Oriental Studies; see preceding entry) was renamed The Peoples of Asia and Africa with the sub-title History, Economy, Culture. The contents of the journal have remained the same. After minor changes in organization, the material is now arranged under the following departments: contemporary problems; history; culture and language; review articles, book reviews and bibliographical notes; scientific life (the Oriental field in the Soviet Union and abroad); and personalia. (For a more complete description of the type of material on China appearing in the journal, see *Sovetskoe vostokovedenie* [Soviet Oriental Studies], **1193**). Index in No. 6 of each year.

The two institutes sponsoring *Narody Azii i Afriki* also publish a popular magazine *Aziia i Afrika segodnia* (Asia and Africa Today; see **1198**). Aside from the serial publication of monographs, *Narody Azii i Afriki* is at present the only scholarly Soviet periodical publication covering contemporary China.

1197 Sovremennyi Vostok

(Contemporary East). Moscow: Izdatel'stvo Vostochnoi literatury, 1957–February 1961. Monthly.

A popular illustrated 60-page monthly, containing articles on the history, culture and current political and economic developments in Asia and Africa, 'the struggle of the peoples of Asia and Africa for national liberation', activities of mass organizations and political parties, surveys, reports on scholarly developments in the field of Oriental studies, travel accounts in Asia and Africa, interviews with Asian and African leaders, reviews of the foreign press, book reviews, and translations from Asian literature. The journal carries a number of articles on Communist China, including translations of short stories by Chinese authors. Important documents are often appended as special supplements. The index for the year is issued separately, arranged by broad categories (editorials, art, interviews, bibliography, documentation, etc.), and alphabetically by author within these categories.

While presented as the 'Scientific, Social and Political Journal of the Institute of Oriental Studies, U.S.S.R. Academy of Sciences', the publication is essentially propagandistic in character.

Superseded by *Aziia i Afrika segodnia* (Asia and Africa Today) in March 1961. (See next entry).

1198 Aziia i Afrika segodnia

(Asia and Africa Today). Moscow: Izdanie Vostochnoi literatury, 1961 No. 3—, March 1961—. Monthly.

Supersedes *Sovremennyi Vostok* (see preceding entry), with consecutive numbering.

With more Soviet interest directed toward Africa, and because of the tensions which have arisen in Sino-Soviet relations, the contents of the journal are almost entirely devoted to Africa and provide little coverage on China. The makeup of the journal is very similar to that of its predecessor except for certain additional features (e.g., 'In the Last Colonies', and 'People and Events in the Soviet East', which paints a rose-colored picture of life in the Soviet Asian republics). Occasional chronologies of important events are included. The yearly index in the December issue is arranged in the same manner as the index to *Sovremennyi Vostok*. The index for 1961 covers the January and February issues of the journal, then still under the title of *Sovremennyi Vosotk*.

The journal is currently prepared under the joint auspices of the Institute of the Peoples of Asia and the Institute on Africa, both units of the Soviet Academy of Sciences.

1199 Akademiia Nauk S.S.S.R. (U.S.S.R. Academy of Sciences). *Kratkie soobshcheniia Instituta vostokovedeniia*

(Short Reports of the Institute of Oriental Studies). Moscow: Izdatel'stvo Vostochnoi literatury, Vols. 1–29, 31–38, 41; 1951–1960. Irregular.

A collection of short scholarly articles on the history, economy, languages and literature of Asian countries. Some of the articles are on China, and of these about half are on the contemporary period. One issue (Vol. 7, 1952) is devoted entirely to China. The journal also carries a documentary section, bio-bibliographies of leading Soviet Orientalists, book reviews, and a chronology of the activities of the institute.

See also next entry.

1200 **Akademiia Nauk S.S.S.R.** (U.S.S.R. Academy of Sciences). *Kratkie soobshcheniia Instituta narodov Azii*
(Short Reports of the Institute of the Peoples of Asia). Moscow: Izdatel'stvo vostochnoi literatury, Vols. 30, 39, 40, 42—; 1961—. Irregular.

In 1961, to reflect the change in name of the Institute of Oriental Studies to the Institute of the Peoples of Asia, the Short Reports of the Institute of Oriental Studies (*Kratkie soobshcheniia Instituta vostokovedeniia;* see preceding entry) were renamed Short Reports of the Institute of the Peoples of Asia (*Kratkie soobshcheniia Instituta narodov Azii*). The numbering of the volumes has remained consecutive, although the volumes are not published in strict numerical order (e.g., Vol. 30 appeared in 1961, Vol. 39 in 1963 and Vol. 41 in 1959).

The following volumes are devoted entirely to China:

Vol. 49 (1961): The Economy of the Chinese People's Republic, 124p.

Vol. 53 (1962): China, 116p.

Vol. 55 (1962): Modern and Contemporary History of China, 136p.

1201 **Akademiia Nauk S.S.S.R.** (U.S.S.R. Academy of Sciences). *Uchenye zapiski Instituta vostokovedeniia*
(Transactions of the Institute of Oriental Studies). Moscow-Leningrad, Vols. 1–21, 23–25; 1950–1960. Irregular.

Collections of scholarly articles on the history, economy, language, literature and foreign relations of Asian countries. The volumes, which range from 200 to over 500 pages in length, frequently are devoted to a single topic or a single country. The transactions contain a number of articles on contemporary China, some of which are collected in two special China issues (Vol. 2, 1951 and Vol. 11, 1955).

See also next entry.

1202 **Akademiia Nauk S.S.S.R.** (U.S.S.R. Academy of Sciences). *Uchenye zapiski Instituta narodov Azii*

(Transactions of the Institute of the Peoples of Asia). Vols. 22, 26—, 1960—. Irregular.

In 1960, to reflect the change in name of the Institute of Oriental Studies to the Institute of the Peoples of Asia, the transactions of the Institute of Oriental Studies (*Uchenye zapiski Instituta vostokovedeniia;* see preceding entry) were renamed Transactions of the Institute of the Peoples of Asia *(Uchenye zapiski Instituta narodov Azii)*. The numbering of the volumes has remained unchanged.

1203 Leningrad, Universitet, Vostochnyi fakul'tet (Leningrad University, Department of Oriental Studies). *Uchenye zapiski Leningradskogo universiteta; Seriia vostokovedcheskikh nauk*
(Transactions of Leningrad University; Oriental Studies Series). Leningrad, Vol. 1—, 1949—.

A subseries of the Transactions of Leningrad University. All of the transactions have their own titles and are numbered consecutively, in addition to which they are assigned additional numbering for the subseries. For example, *Iz istorii stran Dal'nego Vostoka i Indii* (Papers on the History of the Far East and India), published in 1955, is at the same time Vol. 183 of the General Series and Vol. 5 of the Oriental Series; *Istoriia i filologiia Kitaia* (History and Philology of China), 1959, is Vol. 281 and Vol. 10, respectively. Of the 304 volumes published to date, fourteen volumes are in the Oriental series, and a number of these contain scholarly articles on China.

Articles on China also appear in *Seriia istoricheskikh nauk* (Historical Series), *Seriia istorii, iazyka i literatury* (History, Language and Literature Series), etc.

1204 Moscow, Institut mezhdunarodnykh otnoshenii (Moscow, Institute of International Relations). *Uchenye zapiski kafedry geografii i ekonomiki stran Vostoka*
(Transactions of the Department of Oriental Geography and Economics). Moscow, No. 1—, 1956—. Irregular.

The first volumes, entitled *Voprosy ekonomiki stran Vostoka* (Economic Problems of Oriental Countries), are collections of articles by graduate students at the institute specializing in the economics of Asian countries, and book reviews and bibliographies. Of particular interest are the lists of books on Asian economy, geography, history and law in Russian and in foreign languages which have been acquired by Moscow libraries during the year or so preceding the publication of the issue. Books on China (including Chinese-language publications) represent over a quarter of all titles.

The Department of Oriental History of the institute likewise publishes its transactions, which contain articles on modern and contemporary China. (*Uchenye zapiski kafedry istorii stran Vostoka*, 1958—).

See also the transactions of the institute's Department of Foreign Languages of the Oriental Faculty (*Uchenye zapiski kafedry inostrannykh iazykov*, 1958—).

D. OTHER LANGUAGES

There are no special journals devoted exclusively to the study of modern and contemporary China other than those published in English, Japanese, and, of course Chinese. Czech, Polish, Hungarian and Rumanian journals do afford coverage to the broader Oriental field, and are included in this section.

For other Oriental journals, see the list of periodicals in the annual "Bibliography of Asian Studies" (**15**) and T. L. Yüan's *China in Western Literature* (**16**). The former also lists the more important articles appearing in some of these periodicals.

This section also contains an Italian Sinological journal, the Chinese-language magazine published by the Soviet-Chinese Friendship Association in Moscow (see last entry, **1212**), and the organ of the Franco-Chinese Friendship Association (first entry).

1205 Les cahiers Franco-Chinois

(Franco-Chinese Journal). Paris: Association des amitiés Franco-Chinoises, Nos. 1–15/16, 1959–1962. Quarterly.

The organ of the Franco-Chinese Friendship Association edited by Professor Jean Chesneaux, who also serves as the Secretary-General of the organization. Contains reports of visitors to China, articles on Communist China's achievements by Chinese and by pro-Communist foreign visitors, and occasional translations of Chinese scholarly articles. The journal also carried a running bibliography of French-language materials on China, not restricted to Communist literature (No. 1 contains the bibliography for 1958).

With the open break between Moscow and Peking, a rival, pro-Chinese organization (Comité d'initiative pour une association populaire Franco-Chinoise) began in December 1963 to publish a monthly *Bulletin d'information*.

1206 Cina

(China). Rome: Istituto Italiano per il Medio ed Estremo Oriente, No. 1—, 1956—. Irregular.

A Sinological journal published by the Italian Institute for the Middle and Far East containing, among other items, articles and book reviews on contemporary China (e.g., education and religion on the Mainland, the 1954 constitution, land reform, etc.). Each issue, beginning with No. 3, contains a book review section entitled 'Libri sulla Cina', and, in addition, beginning with No. 6, 'Bibliografia sulla Cina', a classified list of important publications and articles on China in European languages (including Italian).

Mention might also be made of *Quaderni di civilta cinese* (Notebook on Chinese Civilization) published since 1955 by the Italian-Chinese Cultural Institute in Milan.

1207 Archiv orientalní
(Oriental Archives). Prague, Vol. 1—, 1929—. Quarterly.

A scholarly journal of Oriental studies published by the Oriental Institute of the Academy of Sciences of Czechoslovakia. Contains articles in English, French, German and Russian on all aspects of Oriental studies (including Chinese history, language and literature), book reviews, bibliographical reviews, reports on activities of the institute, and surveys of Oriental studies (including Chinese) in Czechoslovakia, Rumania, Yugoslavia, etc. Supplements to the journal have included a classified 'Bibliography of Czechoslovak Oriental Studies for the Year'.

1208 Nový Orient
(The New Orient). Prague: Orientalní ustav, No. 1—, 1945—. Ten issues a year.

A richly illustrated popular magazine published by the Oriental Institute of the Czech Academy of Sciences to supplement its scholarly organ *Archiv orientalní* (see preceding entry). *Nový Orient* contains articles in Czech on the history, language, literature and culture of Oriental countries—especially China, India and the Near East; travel accounts, news of archeological expeditions; surveys of scholarly activity in the Oriental field in Czechoslovakia and abroad; translations of classical and contemporary Oriental authors and book reviews. Some issues are entirely devoted to China (e.g., 1953 No. 10). Bibliographical surveys cover such topics as 'Six Years of Cultural Exchange Between China and Czechoslovakia' (1955 No. 8); 'List of Czech Original and Translated Works in the Field of Oriental Studies Published in [year]'; 'Ten Years of Czechoslovak Oriental Studies' (1955 No. 5); 'Ten Years of Polish Studies' (1955 No. 6); 'Hungarian Oriental Studies' (1955 No. 5), etc.

1209 Przegla,d orientalistyczny
(Oriental Review). Warsaw: Polskie Towarzystwo Orientalistyczne, Nos. 1–4, 1949–1952 (annual); No. 1 (5)—, 1953—. Quarterly.

The organ of the Polish Oriental Society, containing original Polish works in the field, as well as translations from Oriental literature and news of the scholarly world. A classified bibliography of articles on Oriental subjects appearing in Polish journals (as well as special bibliographies—e.g., a bibliography of translations of modern Chinese literature into Polish) has appeared in recent issues of the review.

An Oriental Yearbook *(Rocznik orientalistyczny)* is also published in Poland, of which over twenty volumes have appeared thus far.

1210 Acta Orientalia Academiae Scientiarum Hungaricae. Budapest, Vol. 1—, 1950—. Three times a year.

A journal of the Philological and Literary Department of the Hungarian Academy of Sciences, containing articles on Turkish, Mongolian, Manchu, Chinese, Tibetan, Indian, Iranian and Semitic philology, culture, literature and history. Articles on China are largely in the field of linguistics (including the history of the Chinese language), contemporary Chinese folk art, and history. The journal also includes book reviews and reports on the latest developments in the field of Oriental studies in Hungary. Articles are in English, French, German or Russian.

1211 **Studia et acta orientalia.** Bucharest: Société des sciences historiques et philologiques de la R.P.R., Vol. 1 (1957)—, 1958—.

A journal of Oriental studies published by the Section on Oriental Studies of the Rumanian Society for Historical and Philological Sciences. The journal carries occasional articles (predominantly in French, sometimes in English) on Chinese language, literature and history.

1212 **Su-Chung yu-hao** 中蘇友好 **Sovetsko-kitaiskaia druzhba**
(Soviet-Chinese Friendship). Moscow: Su-lien Su-Chung yu-hao hsieh-hui 蘇聯蘇中友好協會, 1958 No. 1–1960 No. 30, January 1958–July 1960 (?). Weekly.

The organ of the Russian Society of Soviet-Chinese Friendship, containing articles, with illustrations, by Russian authors on the U.S.S.R. The counterpart to *Druzhba* (Friendship), published by the Sino-Soviet Friendship Association in Peking (see **937**), *Su-Chung yu-hao* is believed to have ceased publication in July 1960 following the deterioration of relations between the Chinese and Soviet Communist parties at the Bucharest Conference in June 1960.

CHAPTER XXII

SERIES

Books, pamphlets, articles, papers, reprints and special reports on contemporary China have emanated from a number of institutions—academic, governmental, semi-governmental and private in character—in the United States, Hong Kong, Taiwan and Japan. Collected in this chapter (largely without annotations) are more than 500 such publications which appeared as part of the respective institutions' general series or special series on China. Not all are scholarly; indeed, many are forthrightly polemical. Included at the end of the chapter is a selected list of special issues on China which have appeared in American periodicals.

Reference also should be made to the list of theses and dissertations on contemporary China in Appendix B.

A. AMERICAN UNIVERSITIES FIELD STAFF REPORTS ON CONTEMPORARY CHINA

The following list includes all pertinent A.U.F.S. Reports issued through June 1964 (the descriptive annotation accompanying each entry was provided by the A.U.F.S.). Reports issued thereafter can be located through the East Asia Series and Southeast Asia Series in forthcoming supplements to the *List of Publications* published annually and made available by the A.U.F.S., 366 Madison Avenue, New York, N.Y. 10017. The Reports also are listed in the Vertical File Index and the Public Affairs Information Service Index.

1213 **Barnett, A. Doak.** *General Background on China.* East Asia Series, Vol. 1, No. 1 (August 1952). 8p. (ADB-special-'52).

A paper prepared for the 1952-53 A.U.F.S. program of visits to member universities and colleges.

1214 ——. *'New Force' I—The Idea.* East Asia Series, Vol. 1, No. 2 (September 1952). 12p. (ADB-7-'52).

The ideology of refugee Chinese who accept neither the political philosophy of the Communists nor that of the Kuomintang.

1215 ——. *'New Force' II—The People.* East Asia Series, Vol. 1, No. 3 (September 1952). 10p. (ADB-8-'52).

A study of leaderless, partyless refugee dissidents groping for an organization.

1216 ——. *The Road to Collectivization.* East Asia Series, Vol. 1, No. 4 (October 1952). 14p. (ADB-9-'52).

Land reform and landlord liquidation as tactics of Chinese Communist policy.

1217 Barnett, A. Doak. *Conscript Labor and Public Works in Communist China.* East Asia Series, Vol. 1, No. 5 (October 1952). 9p. (ADB-10-'52).

An analysis of the role of forced labor in Communist China's rehabilitation program.

1218 ——. *Chinese Communist Propaganda Methods.* East Asia Series, Vol. 1, No. 6 (November 1952). 9p. (ADB-11-'52).

The structure, the media, and the methods used for shaping public opinion in Communist China.

1219 ——. *The Evolution of an Anti-Communist Chinese Youth—A Case Study.* East Asia Series, Vol. 2, No. 1 (March 1953). 7p. (ADB-special-'53).

The influence of education, family background and circumstance on one refugee.

1220 Ravenholt, Albert. *Christianity and the Chinese Communists.* East Asia Series, Vol. 2, No. 2 (October 1953). 19p. (AR-17-'53).

A study of the Communist campaign to neutralize Christian influences on the Chinese people.

1221 Barnett, A. Doak. *Five Policies Toward China.* East Asia Series, Vol. 2, No. 3 (November 1953). 14p. (ADB-1-'53).

A report on policy toward Communist China as expressed in Washington, London, Paris, Belgrade, and New Delhi.

1222 ——. *Chinese Communist Party—A Period of Consolidation.* East Asia Series, Vol. 2, No. 4 (December 1953). 8p. (ADB-2-'53).

A study of indications of problems of organization and morale within the Chinese Communist Party.

1223 ——. *Social Osmosis—Refugees in Hong Kong.* East Asia Series, Vol. 2, No. 5 (December 1953). 8p. (ADB-3-'53).

The Chinese family as a mechanism for refugee relief work.

1224 ——. *The Metamorphosis of Private Enterprise in Communist China.* East Asia Series, Vol. 3, No. 1 (January 1954). 7p. (ADB-1-'54).

Communist methodology in replacing private enterprise with state capitalism.

1225 ——. *Hong Kong and the China Trade.* East Asia Series, Vol. 3, No. 2 (February 1954). 34p. (ADB-2-'54).

An analysis of the impact of events in China on the economy of Hong Kong.

1226 ——. *Hsüeh Hsi—Weapon of Ideological Revolution in China.* East Asia Series, Vol. 3, No. 3 (March 1954). 14p. (ADB-3-'54).

Group psychology as a device for Communist indoctrination.

1227 Barnett, A. Doak. *What Mixture of Old and New?* East Asia Series, Vol. 3, No. 4 (March 1954). 6p. (ADB-4-'54).

An example of the survival of the family system among Westernized Chinese.

1228 ——. *Japanese Views on China.* East Asia Series, Vol. 3, No. 5 (April 1954). 10p. (ADB-5-'54).

A report on apparent Japanese reluctance to face up to the realities of Communism: a series of interviews.

1229 ——. *'Art of Mass Character'—Motion Pictures in Communist China.* East Asia Series, Vol. 3, No. 6 (May 1954). 8p. (ADB-6-'54).

The Chinese motion picture industry as a tool for Communist propaganda.

1230 ——. *Economic Development in Communist China: Finance and Capital Investment.* East Asia Series, Vol. 3, No. 7 (July 1954). 28p. (ADB-7-'54).

This report, together with Nos. 8, 9, and 15, covers the important aspects of Communist China's drive for economic development.

1231 ——. *Economic Development in Communist China: The Progress of Industrialization.* East Asia Series, Vol. 3, No. 8 (July 1954). 45p. (ADB-8-'54).

1232 ——. *Economic Development in Communist China: Agriculture and the Peasant.* East Asia Series, Vol. 3, No. 9 (August 1954). 26p. (ADB-9-'54).

1233 ——. *Who Is Hong Kong?* East Asia Series, Vol. 3, No. 10 (August 1954). 26p. (ADB-10-'54).

Brief case histories of twenty-six residents of Hong Kong.

1234 ——. *Tension off the China Coast.* East Asia Series, Vol. 3, No. 12 (October 1954). 10p. (ADB-11-'54).

A study of the situation on Quemoy and a comment on its political implications.

1235 ——. *Formosa: Political Potpourri.* East Asia Series, Vol. 3, No. 13 (October 1954), 7p. (ADB-12-'54).

Leadership patterns of the Chinese Nationalist Government and its problems of adjustment.

1236 ——. *The Economy of Formosa: Progress on a Treadmill.* East Asia Series, Vol. 3, No. 14 (October 1954). 11p. (ADB-13-'54).

Analysis shows that Formosa's economic gains are offset by the population increase and the military budget.

1237 ——. *Economic Development in Communist China: (Postscript): Increased Soviet Aid and a Few Unveiled 'State Secrets'.* East Asia Series, Vol. 3, No. 15 (October 1954). 4p. (ADB-14-'54).

1238   **Barnett, A. Doak.** *A Contest of Loyalties: Overseas Chinese in Thailand.* Southeast Asia Series, Vol. 2, No. 4 (December 1954). 23p. (ADB-15-'54).

A report on the position of Thailand's Chinese population; its problems in relation to Thailand and to China.

1239   ——. *Forced Labor in Communist China.* East Asia Series, Vol. 4, No. 1 (January 1955). 14p. (ADB-1-'55).

An analysis of existing data on conscript and prison labor.

1240   ——. *Chou En-lai at Bandung.* Southeast Asia Series, Vol. 4, No. 9 (May 1955). 15p. (ADB-4-'55).

A report on how Chou En-lai performed on behalf of Communist China at the Asian-African Conference.

1241   ——. *Asia and Africa in Session.*   Southeast Asia Series, Vol. 4, No. 11 (May 1955). 35p. (ADB-5-'55).

An observer's voluminous notes on the Asian-African Conference at Bandung.

1242   ——. *China's 'People's Democratic Dictatorship': Recent Political Trends in Communist China.* East Asia Series, Vol. 4, No. 2 (February 1955). 19p. (ADB-2-'55).

1243   ——. *Imprisonment of the Mind.* East Asia Series, Vol. 4, No. 3 (March 1955). 19p. (ADB-3-'55).

An interview with two Americans who were 'brainwashed' by the Chinese Communists.

1244   ——. *A Note on China.* East Asia Series, Vol. 4, No. 6 (July 1955). 12p. (ADB-special-'55).

A paper prepared for the 1955–56 A.U.F.S. program of visits to member universities and colleges.

1245   **Ravenholt, Albert.** *The Yellow River—Can the Communists Tame 'China's Sorrow'?* East Asia Series, Vol. 4, No. 9 (August 1955). 9p. (AR-9-'55).

A discussion of the Communist regime's flood control projects.

1246   **Hanna, Willard A.** *A Trip to Macao.* East Asia Series, Vol. 5, No. 1 (January 1956). 9p. (WAH-1-'56).

Comments on some aspects of the Portuguese colony that lies in the shadow of Communist China.

1247   ——. *Japan-Hong Kong-Indonesia Relationships.* East Asia Series, Vol. 5, No. 2 (January 1956). 14p. (WAH-2-'56).

A discussion of Japan's return to trade competition and of Indonesia's entry into the world market, as seen by an observer in Hong Kong.

1248 Hanna, Willard A. *Japan's Relations with Nationalist China.* East Asia Series, Vol. 5, No. 3 (February 1956). 17p. (WAH-3-'56).

Old animosities seem to be waning, but many problems beset Japanese-Chinese relations.

1249 ——. *Vestiges of Japanese Colonialism in Taiwan.* East Asia Series, Vol. 5, No. 5 (February 1956). 8p. (WAH-4-'56).

Impressions of a visitor who looked for evidences of Japan's fifty years of control.

1250 Ravenholt, Albert. *Formosa's Rural Revolution—A Unique Chinese and American Joint Achievement.* East Asia Series, Vol. 5, No. 7 (March 1956). 25p. (AR-3-'56).

A report on agricultural development under the Joint Commission on Rural Reconstruction.

1251 ——. *Chinese Comment on Rural Reconstruction.* East Asia Series, Vol. 5, No. 10 (May 1956). 6p. (AR-4-'56).

The Vice President of the Republic of China answers questions on the Joint Commission on Rural Reconstruction.

1252 Hanna, Willard A. *The Case of the Forty Million Missing Muslims.* Southeast Asia Series, Vol. 5, No. 15 (September 1956). 16p. (WAH-15-'56).

An Indonesian journalist visits China and concludes that Islam does not flourish there.

1253 ——. *Moscow Comes to Bung Karno—And So Does Peking.* Southeast Asia Series, Vol. 5, No. 20 (November 1956). 9p. (WAH-20-'56).

An account of Sukarno's visits to Russia and Communist China.

1254 ——. *Putting Three Best Feet Forward.* Southeast Asia Series, Vol. 5, No. 21 (December 1956). 9p. (WAH-21-'56).

The United States, Russia, and Communist China compete at the Jogjakarta Fair.

1255 Burton, Robert A. *A Handful of Powerful Men.* East Asia Series, Vol. 6, No. 7 (June 1958). 20p. (RAB-1-'58).

Personality studies of six leaders of Communist China.

1256 ——. *Self-Help, Chinese Style.* East Asia Series, Vol. 6, No. 9 (July 1958) 10p. (RAB-2-'58).

A detailed explanation of the operation of a *hui* and its importance to the middle and low-income segments of the Chinese population in Hong Kong.

1257 **Burton, Robert A.** *A Note on Communist China.* East Asia Series, Vol. 6, No. 12 (September 1958). 36p. (RAB-3-'58).

A paper, prepared for the 1958–59 A.U.F.S. program of visits to member universities and colleges, containing basic information on the country's geography, politics and economics.

1258 **Ravenholt, Albert.** *People's Communes.* East Asia Series, Vol. 6, No. 14 (October 1958). 15p. (AR-8-'58).

A study of the vast communalization program being instituted by the Chinese Communists.

1259 **Olson, Lawrence.** *'In Ten Years, In Fifty Years'.* East Asia Series, Vol. 6, No. 15 (October 1958). 11p. (LO-11-'58)

A review of Japanese official and public opinion regarding trade with Communist China.

1260 **Ravenholt, Albert.** *The Gods Must Go!* East Asia Series, Vol. 6, No. 16 (November 1958). 7p. (AR-9-'58).

The latest Communist step in remaking the Chinese personality: the destruction of the folk religion.

1261 ——. *Red China Beckons Its Neighbors.* East Asia Series, Vol. 7, No. 1 (January 1959). 28 p. (AR-1-'59).

An account, with pictures, of the journey of an unofficial group of Filipinos to and in Red China.

1262 **Burton, Robert A.** *The New Chinese in America.* East Asia Series, Vol. 7, No. 8 (August 1959). 12p. (RAB-1-'59).

Comments on the recent movement of Chinese to this country, their lives here, and the effect they are having on the established Chinese community.

1263 ——. *A Chinese Craftsman Under Three Regimes.* East Asia Series, Vol. 8, No. 1 (January 1960). 47p. (RAB-1-'60).

National characteristics and attitudes as revealed in the life story of a refugee.

1264 ——. *Stalking the Elusive Chinese in Russia.* East Asia Series, Vol. 8, No. 2 (March 1960). 22p. (RAB-2-'60).

A plan to interview Chinese residing in Russia yields negative results.

1265 **Ravenholt, Albert.** *Red China's Food Crisis.* East Asia Series, Vol. 9, No. 2 (January 1961). 14p. (AR-1-'61).

Communist agriculture crippled by massive revolutionary changes.

1266 **Ravenholt, Albert.** *The New Chinese 'Red' Catholic Church*. East Asia Series, Vol. 9, No. 3 (March 1961). 8p. (AR-2-'61).

A brief history of the Church in China before and after the Communist take-over.

1267 ——. *The Human Price of China's Disastrous Food Shortage*. East Asia Series, Vol. 10, No. 4 (May 1962). 12p. (AR-4-'62).

A refugee doctor describes his patients.

1268 ——. *Red China's Sagging Industry*. East Asia Series, Vol. 10, No. 5 (July 1962). 13p. (AR-5-'62).

Peking forfeits early modern great power prospects.

1269 **Hanna, Willard A.** *The Politics of Sport*. Southeast Asia Series, Vol. 10, No. 19 (October 1962). 13p. (WAH-15-62).

Indonesia as host to the 'Fourth Asian Games'.

1270 **Ravenholt, Albert.** *Feud Among the Red Mandarins*. East Asia Series, Vol. 11, No. 2 (February 1964). 10p. (AR-2-'64).

How Kao Kang and Jao Shu-shih challenged their comrades.

1271 **Olson, Lawrence.** *Japan's Relations with China: Some Recent Developments*. East Asia Series, Vol. 11, No. 4 (June 1964). 13p. (LO-3-'64).

The effect of French recognition of Communist China upon Japan.

B. University of California, Berkeley, Institute of International Studies, Center for Chinese Studies Reprint Series

1272 **Schurmann, H. F.** *Organization and Response in Communist China* (No. 1).

1273 **Scalapino R. A. and Schiffrin, Harold.** *Early Socialist Currents in the Chinese Revolutionary Movement* (No. 2).

1274 **Scalapino, Robert A.** *Communist China and Taiwan* (No. 3).

1275 **Li, Choh-ming.** *Economic Development* (No. 5).

1276 **Chen, S. H.** *Multiplicity in Uniformity: Poetry and the Great Leap Forward* (No. 6).

1277 **Schurmann, H. F.** *Organizational Principles of the Chinese Communists* (No. 7).

1278 **Levenson, Joseph R.** *Historical Significance* (No. 9).

1279 **Johnson, Chalmers A.** *An Intellectual Weed in the Socialist Garden: The Case of Ch'ien Tuan-sheng* (No. 11).

1280 **Schurmann, H. F.** *The Roots of Social Policy* (No. 12).

1281 **Brandt, Conrad.** *The French-Returned Elite in the Chinese Communist Party* (No. 13).

1282 **Scalapino, Robert A.** *Tradition and Transition in the Asian Policy of Communist China* (No. 14).

1283 **Li, Choh-ming.** *Statistics and Planning at the Hsien Level in Communist China* (No. 15).

1284 **Johnson, Chalmers A.** *Civilian Loyalties and Guerrilla Conflict* (No. 16).

1285 **Halpern, Abraham M.** *Communist China's Foreign Policy: The Recent Phase* (No. 17).

1286 **Scalapino, Robert A.** *Moscow, Peking and the Communist Parties of Asia* (No. 18).

1287 **Levenson, Joseph R.** *The Place of Confucius in Communist China* (No. 19).

1288 **Hsia, T. A.** *Twenty Years After the Yenan Forum* (No. 20).

1289 **Scalapino, Robert A.** *The Foreign Policy of the People's Republic of China* (No. 106).

1290 **Kallgren, Joyce.** *Nationalist China's Armed Forces* (No. 112).

1291 **Hsia, T. A.** *Demons in Paradise: The Chinese Images of Russia* (No. 115).

1292 **Schurmann, Franz.** *Economic Policy and Political Power in Communist China* (No. 116).

1293 **Townsend, James R.** *Democratic Management in the Rural Communes* (No. 124).

1294 **Hsia, T. A.** *Aspects of the Power of Darkness in Lu Hsun* (No. 125).

1295 **Scalapino, Robert A.** *The Sino-Soviet Conflict in Perspective* (No. 133).

1296 **Schurmann, Franz.** *China's 'New Economic Policy'—Transition or Beginning* (No. 134).

1297 **Li, Choh-ming.** *China's Industrial Development, 1958–64* (No. 136).

1298 **Scalapino, Robert.** *Sino-Soviet Competition in Africa* (No. 142).

C. University of California, Berkeley,
Current Chinese Language Project,
Studies in Chinese Communist Terminology

1299 **Li, Chi.** *General Trends of Chinese Linguistic Changes Under Communist Rule.* July 1956. 42p. (No. 1).

1300 **Li, Chi.** *Preliminary Study of Selected Terms.* July 1956. 24p. (No. 2).

1301 ——. *Part I, Literary and Colloquial Terms in New Usage. Part II, Terms Topped by Numerals.* April 1957. 51p. (No. 3).

1302 ——. *Part I, The Communist Term 'The Common Language' and Related Terms. Part II, Dialectical Terms in Common Usage. Part III, Literary and Colloquial Terms in New Usage* (continued). December 1957. 88p. (No. 4).

1303 ——. *The Use of Figurative Language in Communist China.* December 1958. 84p. (No. 5).

1304 ——. *'A Provisional System of Grammar for Teaching Chinese' with Introduction and Commentary.* June 1960. 204p. (No. 6).

1305 **Hsia, T. A.** *Metaphor, Myth, Ritual and the People's Commune.* June 1961. 60p. (No. 7).

1306 **Serruys, Paul L. M.** *Survey of the Chinese Language Reform and the Anti-Illiteracy Movement in Communist China.* February 1962. 208p. (No. 8).

1307 **Li, Chi.** *New Features in Chinese Grammatical Usage.* October 1962. 76p. (No. 9).

1308 **Hsia, T. A.** *A Terminology Study of the Hsia-Fang Movement.* September 1963. 68p. (No. 10).

1309 ——. *The Commune in Retreat as Evidenced in Terminology and Semantics.* September 1964. 91p. (No. 11).

D. FOREIGN POLICY ASSOCIATION HEADLINE SERIES ON CHINA

1310 **Rosinger, Lawrence K.** *Forging a New China,* January-February 1948. 64p. (HS No. 67).

1311 **Durdin, Tillman and Smith, Robert Aura.** *China and the World,* May-June 1953. 64p. (HS No. 99).

1312 **Seligman, Eustace and Walker, Richard L.** *Should the United States Change Its China Policy?* May-June 1958. 80p. (HS No. 129).

1313 **Durdin, Peggy.** *Mao's China,* July-August 1959. 64p. (HS No. 136).

1314 **Barnett, A. Doak.** *Communist China—Continuing Revolution,* May-June 1962. 60p. (HS No. 153).

1315 **Griffith, William E.** *World Communism Divided,* August 1964. 48p. (HS No. 166).

E. George Washington University,
Institute for Sino-Soviet Studies,
Books and Monographs Concerning Contemporary China

1. BOOKS

1316 **London, Kurt L.,** ed. *New Nations in a Divided World: The International Relations of the Afro-Asian States,* published for the Institute for Sino-Soviet Studies by Frederick A. Praeger, 1964. 336p.

1317 **Hinton, Harold C.** *Communist China in World Politics.* Boston: Houghton Mifflin, 1966. 527p.

2. MONOGRAPHS

1318 **Cheng, Chu-yuan.** *Economic Relations Between Peking and Moscow, 1949–1963,* published by Frederick A. Praeger for the Institute for Sino-Soviet Studies, 1964.

1319 **Huth, Arno G.** *Communications Media in the Communist Orbit,* to be published for the Institute for Sino-Soviet Studies, 1967.

1320 **Michael, Franz.** *The Sino-Soviet Conflict and the World Revolution,* to be published for the Institute for Sino-Soviet Studies, 1967.

1321 **Taylor, George E.** *U.S.-Chinese Relations Since 1949,* to be published for the Institute for Sino-Soviet Studies, 1967.

1322 **Simon, Sheldon.** *The Broken Triangle: Peking, Djakarta and the PKI.* To be published for the Institute for Sino-Soviet Studies, 1967.

1323 **Boyd, Robert G.** *Sino-Soviet Rivalry in Asia,* to be published for the Institute for Sino-Soviet Studies, 1967.

F. Harvard University,
Regional Studies Seminars, Papers on China

1324 **Arkush, R. David.** 'One of the Hundred Flowers: Wang Meng's "Young Newcomer",' Vol. 18 (1964), pp. 155–186.

1324a **Brandt, Conrad.** 'Agrarian Reform in Communist China Against the Background of the Marxist Tradition,' Vol. 1 (1947), pp. 243–288.

1324b **Butterfield, Fox.** 'The Legend of Sung Ching-shih: An Episode in Communist Historiography,' Vol. 18 (1964), pp. 129–154.

1325 **Chao, Kuo-chün.** 'Land Reform Methods in Communist China,' Vol. 5 (1950), pp. 107–174.

1326 Conant, Melvin A., Jr. 'JCRR: Problems of American Participation in the Sino-American Joint Commission on Rural Reconstruction', Vol. 6 (1952), pp. 45–74.

1327 Edwards, R. Randle. 'The Attitude of the People's Republic of China Toward International Law and the United Nations', Vol. 17 (1963), pp. 235–271.

1328 Goldman, Merle. 'Hu Feng's Conflict with the Communist Literary Authorities,' Vol. 11 (1957), pp. 149–191.

1329 Grieder, Jerome B. 'The Communist Critique of *Hung lou meng*', Vol. 10 (1956), pp. 142–168.

1330 Hawtin, Elise. 'The "Hundred Flowers Movement" and the Role of the Intellectual in China: Fei Hsiao-t'ung: A Case History', Vol. 12 (1958), pp. 147–198.

1331 Montell, Sherwin. 'The San-fan Wu-fan Movement in Communist China,' Vol. 8 (1954), pp. 136–196.

1332 Morrison, Esther. 'A Comparison of Kuomintang and Communist Modern History Textbooks,' Vol. 6 (1952), pp. 3–44.

1333 Moy, Clarence. 'Communist China's Use of the *Yang-ko*,' Vol. 6 (1952), pp. 112–148.

1334 ——. 'Kuo Mo-jo and the Creation Society,' Vol. 4 (1950), pp. 131–159.

1335 Nelson, William E. 'China's New Order: Centralization vs. Democracy in Local Government,' Vol. 1 (1947), pp. 175–208.

1336 Schwartz, Benjamin I. 'Marxist Doctrine in the Chinese Communist Movement,' Vol. 1 (1947), pp. 209–242.

G. THE HOOVER INSTITUTION PUBLICATIONS ON CONTEMPORARY CHINA
(See also N. Stanford University, Institute of Political Studies)

I. PUBLICATION SERIES (PS)

1337 Cheng, J. Chester, ed. *The Politics of the Chinese Red Army: A Translation of the Bulletin of Activities* (a translation of *Kung-tso t'ung-hsün*, published by the General Political Department of the Chinese People's Liberation Army, Nos. 1–30, January-August 1961). 1966. 776p. (PS 42). (See **895**.)

1338 North, Robert C. *Moscow and Chinese Communists*. Revised edition. Stanford University Press, 1963. 306p. (Hoover Institution Studies, Special Studies).

1339 **Rue, John.** *Mao Tse-tung in Opposition: 1927–1935.* Stanford University Press, 1966. 387p. (PS 48).

1340 **Wu, Yuan-li.** *Economic Development and the Use of Energy Resources in Communist China.* New York: Frederick A. Praeger, 1963. 280p. (PS 30).

1340a ——. *The Steel Industry in Communist China.* New York: Frederick A. Praeger, 1965. 340p. (PS 36).

1341 **Buck, John Lossing, Dawson, Owen L. and Wu, Yuan-li,** *Food and Agriculture in Communist China.* 1966. 171p. (PS 41).

1341a **Israel, John.** *Student Nationalism in China, 1927–1937.* Stanford University Press, 1966. 253p. (PS 46).

2. STUDIES SERIES (SS)

1342 **Doolin, Dennis J., ed.** *Communist China: The Politics of Student Opposition.* 1964. 70p. (SS 2).

1342a ——. *Territorial Claims in the Sino-Soviet Conflict: Documents and Analysis.* 1965. 77p. (SS 7).

1343 **Doolin, Dennis J. and North, Robert C.** *Communist China: The Party-State.* 1966. 68p. (SS 14).

1344 **North, Robert C.** *Kuomintang and Chinese Communist Elites.* 1952. 130p. (Series B: Elite Studies No.8).

3. BIBLIOGRAPHICAL SERIES (BS)

1345 **Berton, Peter and Wu, Eugene.** *Contemporary China: A Research Guide.* (Joint Committee on Contemporary China of the American Council of Learned Societies and the Social Science Research Council.) 1967.

1346 **Hsüeh, Chün-tu.** *The Chinese Communist Movement, 1937–1949.* 1962. 312p. (BS 11).

   A continuation of the author's bibliography, *The Chinese Communist Movement, 1921–1937,* 1960, 131p. (BS 8).

1347 **Israel, John.** *The Chinese Student Movement, 1927–1937: A Bibliographical Essay Based on the Resources of the Hoover Institution.* 1959. 22p. (BS 6).

1348 **Uchida, Naosaku.** *The Overseas Chinese: A Bibliographical Essay Based on the Resources of the Hoover Institution.* 1959 (second printing 1960). 134p. (BS 7). (See **137**).

1349 **Wu, Eugene.** *Leaders of Twentieth Century China: An Annotated Bibliography of Selected Chinese Biographical Works in The Hoover Library.* 1956. 106p. (BS 4). (See **76**).

H. Massachusetts Institute of Technology, Center for International Studies (CENIS), Papers and Books on Contemporary China

1350 **Borowitz, Albert.** *Fiction in Communist China.* June 1954. Summary, 5p. (Full text [124p.] available on loan from C.I.S. library.)

1351 **Chang, Kia-ngau.** *Inflationary Spiral: China, 1939–1950.* M.I.T. Press, 1958. 394p.

1352 **Chao, Kuo-chün.** *Land Policy of the Chinese Communist Party, 1921–1953.* 300p.

1353 ——. *The Mass Organizations in Communist China.* November 1953. 157p.

1354 ——. *Basic Level Elections and the Draft Constitution of Communist China.* 1954. 54p.

1355 **Dai, Shen-yu.** *Peking, Moscow, and the Communist Parties of Colonial Asia.* June 1954. Summary, 11p. (Full text [167p.] available on loan from C.I.S. library.)

1356 **Eckstein, Alexander.** *Conditions and Prospects for Economic Growth in Communist China.* July 1954. Summary, 25p. (Full text published in *World Politics*, Vol. 7, Nos. 1, 2, 3 [October 1954, January and April 1955].)

1357 **Griffith, William E.** *Albania and the Sino-Soviet Rift.* M.I.T. Press, 1963. 423p. (See **780.**)

1358 ——. *The Sino-Soviet Rift.* M.I.T. Press, 1964. 493p. (See **781.**)

1359 **Hatch, Richard W.** *News Out of Communist China.* Reprinted from *World Politics*, Vol. 8, No. 1 (October 1955), pp. 146–156.

1360 **Hollister, William W.** *China's Gross National Product and Social Accounts, 1950–1957.* New York: Free Press of Glencoe, 1958. 161p.

1361 **Hsia, Ronald.** *Economic Planning in Communist China.* May 1954. Summary, 12p. (Full text [90p.] available from the Institute of Pacific Relations.)

1362 ——. *The Role of Labor-Intensive Investment Projects in China's Capital Formation.* 1954. 103p.

1363 **Isaacs, Harold R.** *Scratches on Our Minds: American Images of China and India.* New York: John Day, 1958. 416p. Paperback edition: *Images of Asia: American Views of China and India.* New York: Capricorn Books, 1962. 416p.

1364 **Keesing, Donald B.** *Use of Top-Level Personnel by the Chinese Communist Government, 1949–1954.* December 1954. 71p.

1365 **Kierman, Frank A., Jr.** *The Chinese Communists in the Light of Chinese History.* June 1954. 44p.

1366 **Kierman, Frank A., Jr.** *The Chinese Intelligentsia and the Communists.* June 1954. 24p.

1367 ——. *The Fluke That Saved Formosa.* June 1954. 13p.

1368 **King, Vincent V. S.** *A General Study of the Channels of Communication Between Communist China and the Western World.* 1964. 94p.

1369 **Kun, Joseph C.** *Higher Education: Some Problems of Selection and Enrollment.* Reprinted from *The China Quarterly* (October–December 1961), pp. 135–148.

1370 ——. *Higher Educational Institutions of Communist China, 1953–1958: A Cumulative List.* (Appendix C of forthcoming study on selection and enrollment of students in Communist Chinese higher educational institutions.) December 1961. 48p.

1371 **Liu, Alan Ping-lin.** *Growth and Modernizing Function of Rural Radio in Communist China.* (Published in *Journalism Quarterly*, Vol. 41, No. 1 (Autumn 1964), pp. 573–577.)

1372 **McVey, Ruth T.** *The Development of the Indonesian Communist Party and Its Relations with the Soviet Union and the Chinese People's Republic.* May 1954. 97p.

1373 **Nivison, David S.** *Communist Ethics and Chinese Tradition.* November 1954. 83p.

1374 **Pye, Lucian W.** *Some Observations on the Political Behavior of Overseas Chinese.* June 1, 1954. 24p.

1375 **Rostow, W. W.** *A Comparison of Russian and Chinese Societies Under Communism.* January 1955. 25p. (Published in *World Politics*, Vol. 7, No. 4 [July 1955], as 'Russia and China under Communism.')

1376 **Rostow, W. W., et al.** *The Prospects for Communist China.* M.I.T. Press, 1954. 379p.

1377 **Schein, Edgar H.** *Brainwashing* (summary of book, *Coercive Persuasion*). December 1960. 37p.

1378 **Schwartz, Benjamin.** *China and the Soviet Theory of 'People's Democracy'.* 1954. 20p.

1379 **Solomon, Richard H.** *The Chinese Political Culture and Problems of Modernization.* December 1964. 32p.

1380 **Tsukahira, Toshio G.** *The Postwar Evolution of Communist Strategy in Japan.* November 1954. 89p.

1381 **Williams, Lea E.** *Overseas Chinese Nationalism: The Genesis of the Pan-Chinese Movement in Indonesia, 1900–1916.* New York: Free Press of Glencoe, 1960. 235p.

1382 Yang, C. K. *Chinese Family in Communist Revolution.* M.I.T. Press, 1959. 246p.

1383 ——. *A Chinese Village in Early Communist Transition.* M.I.T. Press, 1959. 284p.

I. University of Michigan, Occasional Papers and Reprints of the Center for Chinese Studies

1. Occasional Papers

1384 Chao, Kang. *Two Studies on Mainland China's Economy* (Occasional Paper No. 2): 'Yüan-Dollar Price Ratios in Communist China and the United States' and 'A Methodological Inquiry of the Official Indexes of Industrial Production in Communist China'.

2. Reprints

1385 Chao, Kang. *The Reliability of Industrial Output Data in Communist China* (Reprint No. 1).

1386 Eckstein, Alexander. *On China's Descending Spiral* (Reprint No. 2).

1387 Chao, Kang. *Indices of Industrial Output in Communist China* (Reprint No. 4).

J. National Council of the Churches of Christ in the U.S.A., Division of Foreign Missions, Publications on China of the Far Eastern Office

1388 Reports on Deputation of Australian Churchmen to Mainland China.

1389 China Consultation 1958.

1390 Ballou, Earle H., comp. and ed. *China Consultation 1960.*

1391 'U.S. Policy Toward China,' *Social Action*, March 1960.

1392 Bates, M. Searle, comp. and ed. *China Consultation 1962.*

1393 Jones, Francis P. *The Church in Communist China—A Protestant Appraisal.* New York: The Friendship Press, 1962. 180p.

1394 ——. 'Theological Thinking in the Chinese Protestant Church Under Communism,' *Religion in Life*, Autumn 1963.

1395 Merwin, Wallace C. and Jones, Francis P., comps. *Documents of the Three-Self Movement; Source Materials for the Study of the Protestant Church in Communist China.* 1963.

K. RAND CORPORATION STUDIES ON CONTEMPORARY CHINA

I. RAND BOOKS IN THE SOCIAL SCIENCES

1396 **Hsieh, A. L.** *Communist China's Strategy in the Nuclear Era.* Englewood Cliffs, N.J.: Prentice-Hall, 1962. 204p. R-346.

1397 **Liu, T. C. and Yeh, K. C.** *The Economy of the Chinese Mainland: National Income and Economic Development, 1933–1959.* Princeton University Press, 1963. 2 vols. (Vol. 1, AD 403682; Vol. 2, AD 403834). 974p.

Also published as RM-3519-PR.

1398 **Whiting, A. S.** *China Crosses the Yalu: The Decision to Enter the Korean War.* New York: Macmillan Co., 1960. 219p. R-356.

2. RESEARCH MEMORANDA (RM)

1399 **Halpern, A. M.** *The Chinese Communist Line on Neutralism.* 1960. 43p. RM-2657, AD 253001 (*The China Quarterly*, January–March 1961).

Also published as P-2026.

1400 **Hinton, H. C.** *Leaders of Communist China.* 1956. 314p. RM-1845.

Also published as P-1104.

1401 **Hoeffding, O.** *Sino-Soviet Economic Relations, 1958–1962.* 1963. 31p. RM-3787-PR, AD 412843 (*The Annals of the American Academy of Political and Social Science*, September 1963).

1402 **Hsia, Ronald.** *Government Acquisition of Agricultural Output in Mainland China, 1953–56.* 1958. 102p. RM-2207.

1403 **Hsieh, A. L.** *The Chinese Genie: Peking's Role in the Nuclear Test Ban Negotiations.* 1960. 26p. ('China, Russia and the Bomb,' *The New Leader*, October 17, 1960).

Also published as P-2022.

1404 ——. *Communist China's Military Doctrine and Strategy.* 1963. 38p. RM-3833-PR ('China's Secret Military Papers: Military Doctrine and Strategy,' *The China Quarterly*, April–June 1964).

1405 ——. *The Significance of Chinese Communist Treatment of Khrushchev's January 14 Speech on Strategy.* 1960. 21p. RM-2534.

1406 **Ikle, F. C.** *The Growth of China's Scientific and Technical Manpower.* 1957. 75p. RM-1893.

Also published as P-1104.

1407 **Mah, Feng-hwa.** *Communist China's Foreign Trade: Price Structure and Behavior, 1955–1959.* 1963. 141p. RM-3825-RC.

1408 **Scalapino, R. A.** *On the Trail of Chou En-lai.* 1964. 31p. RM-4061-PR.

1409 **Twammo, Chong.** *Production of Food Crops in Mainland China: Prewar and Postwar.* 1956. 84p. RM-1659.

1410 **Whiting, A. S.** *'Contradictions' in the Moscow-Peking Axis.* 1957. 66p. RM-1992 (*Journal of Politics*, February 1958).

Also published as P-1183.

1411 **Yeh, K. C.** *Communist China's Petroleum Situation.* 1962. 80p. RM-3160-PR.

1412 ——. *Electric Power Development in Mainland China: Prewar and Postwar.* 1956. 125p. RM-1821.

1413 **Young, G. B. W.** *Some Remarks on Scientific Achievements in Communist China.* 1962. 28p. RM-3077-PR.

3. PAPERS (P)

1414 **Clubb, O. E., Jr.** *The Effect of Chinese Nationalist Military Activities in Burma on Burmese Foreign Policy.* 1959. 64p. P-1595-RC.

1415 **Dinerstein, H. S.** *Sino-Soviet Conflict in Under-Developed Countries.* 1964. 26p. P-2857 (*Problems of Communism*, March-April 1964).

1416 **Dorrill, W. F.** *Political Research on Contemporary China: Some Problems and Opportunities.* 1964. 26p. P-2896.

1417 **Halpern, A. M.** *Between Plenums: A Second Look at the 1962 National People's Congress in China.* 1962. 20p. P-253 (*Asian Survey*, November 1962).

1418 ——. *Communist China's Demands on the World.* 1961. 29p. P-2382-1.

1419 ——. *Contemporary China as a Problem for Political Science.* 1962. 30p. P-2617 (*World Politics*, April 1963).

1420 ——. *The Foreign Policy Uses of the Chinese Revolutionary Model.* 1961. 28p. P-2230-1 (*The China Quarterly*, July-September 1961).

1421 ——. *Why Are the Chinese Nervous?* 1960. 26p. P-1987 ('Communist China and Peaceful Co-existence,' *The China Quarterly*, July-September 1960).

1422 **Halpern, J. M.** *The Role of the Chinese in Lao Society.* 1960. 40p. P-2161.

1423 **Hoeffding, O.** *Research on Communist China's Foreign Trade: Comments on Three Papers by Shun-hsin Chou, Robert F. Dornberger, and Feng-Hwa Mah.* 1963. 18p. P-2689-PR.

1424 ——. *Sino-Soviet Economic Relations in Recent Years.* 1960. 27p. P-2087. (*Ost-Europa Wirtschaft.* May 1961; K. L. London, ed., *Unity and Contradiction: Major Aspects of Sino-Soviet Relations* [New York: Praeger, 1962]).

1425 **Hsieh, A. L.** *Communist China and Nuclear Force.* 1963. 43p. P-2719 (R. N. Rosecrance, ed., *The Disperison of Nuclear Weapons: Strategy and Politics* [New York: Columbia University Press, 1964]).

1426 ——. *Communist China and Nuclear Warfare.* 1960. 20p. P-1894 (*The China Quarterly*, April-June 1960; *Survival*, July-August 1960).

1427 ——. *The Sino-Soviet Nuclear Dialogue: 1963.* 1964. 40p. P-2852 (*The Journal of Conflict Resolution*, June 1964; *Survival*, September 1964).

1428 **Kramish, Arnold.** *The Chinese People's Republic and the Bomb.* 1960. 7p. P-1950.

1429 **Langer, P. F.** *China and Japan.* 1963. 19p. P-2760 (*Current History*, September 1963).

1430 ——. *Independence or Subordination? The Japanese Communist Party Between Moscow and Peking.* 1962. 59p. P-2628 (A. D. Barnett, ed., *Communist Strategies in Asia: A Comprehensive Analysis of Governments and Parties* [New York: Frederick A. Praeger, 1963]).

1431 ——. 'Japan's Relations with China,' *Current History*, April 1964.

1432 ——. *Moscow, Peking and Japan: Views and Approaches.* 1960. 30p. P-2098 (K. L. London, ed., *Unity and Contradiction: Major Aspects of Sino-Soviet Relations* [New York: Frederick A. Praeger, 1962]).

1433 **Liu, Ta-chung.** *Structural Changes in the Economy of the Chinese Mainland, 1933 to 1952–1957.* 1959. 15p. P-1590 (*The American Economic Review*, May 1959).

1434 **Mah, Feng-hwa.** *The Financing of Public Investment in Communist China.* 1960. 53p. P-2031-RC (*The Journal of Asian Studies*, November 1961).

1435 **Moorsteen, R. H.** *An Economic Development of Strategic Significance in Communist China.* 1958. 5p. P-1578.

1436 ——. *Economic Prospects for Communist China.* 1958. 58p. P-1298 (*World Politics*, January 1959).

1437 **Mozingo, D. P.** *China's Relations with Asian Neighbors.* 1964. 16p. P-2947 (*Current History*, September 1964).

1438 **Remer, C. F.** *The Trade Agreements of Communist China.* 1961. 132p. P-2208.

1439 **Whiting, A. S.** *Conflict Resolution in the Sino-Soviet Alliance.* 1961. 33p. P-2029

1440 ——. *Dynamics of the Moscow-Peking Axis.* 1958. 29p. P-1447 (*The Annals of the American Academy of Political and Social Science*, January 1959).

1441 **Whiting, A. S.** *Sinkiang and Sino-Soviet Relations. 1960.* 20p. P-1953 (*The China Quarterly*, July-September 1960).

1442 ———. *The Sino-Soviet Alliance: How Durable?* 1959. 29p. P-1714 (*The New Leader*, October 14, 1959).

1443 **Wilson, D. A.** *China, Thailand and the Spirit of Bandung.* 1962. 97p. P-2607.

1444 **Wolf, Charles, Jr.** *The Uses and Limitations of Nuclear Deterrence in Asia.* 1964. 17p. P-2958.

1445 **Zagoria, D. S.** *Khrushchev's Attack on Albania and Sino-Soviet Relations.* 1961. 33p. P-2478-1 (*The China Quarterly*, October-December 1961).

1446 ———. *The Sino-Soviet Conflict and the West.* 1962. 30p. P-2595-1 (*Foreign Affairs*, October 1962).

1447 ———. *The Sino-Soviet Conflict Over the Transition to Communism.* 1961. 25p. P-2397 (*Survey*, October 1961).

1448 ———. *Some Comparisons Between the Russian and Chinese 'Models'.* 1962. 39p. P-2561 (A. D. Barnett, ed., *Communist Strategies in Asia: A Comprehensive Analysis of Governments and Parties*, [New York: Frederick A. Praeger, 1963]).

4. TRANSLATIONS (T)

1449 **Fong, J.** *On Problems Concerning the Legal Status of Outer Space.* 1961. 23p. T-141.

1450 **Schnitzer, E. W., tr.** *The Development of Chinese Communist Military Forces.* 1958. 8p. T-104 (*Wehrkunde*, October 1958).

L. PUBLICATIONS OF THE RESEARCH INSTITUTE ON THE SINO-SOVIET BLOC

1. MONOGRAPH SERIES

1451 **Tang, Peter S. H.** *Communist China as a Developmental Model for Underdeveloped Countries.* 1960. 111p. (MS No. 1).

1452 **Wraga, Richard.** *Integral Communism: A Program for Action.* 1961. 47p. (MS No. 2).

1453 **Tang, Peter S. H.** *The Training of Party Cadres in Communist China.* 1961. 44p. (MS No. 3).

1454 ———. *Russian Expansion Into the Maritime Province: The Contemporary Soviet and Chinese Communist Views.* 1962. 50p. (MS No. 4).

1455 **Tang, Peter S. H.** *The 22nd Congress of the Communist Party of the Soviet Union and Moscow-Tirana-Peking Relations.* 1962. 141p. (MS No. 7).

1456 ———. *The Chinese Communist Impact on Cuba.* 1962. 125p. (MS No. 12).

1457 **Grant, Natalie,** *Soviet Diplomatic Maneuvers: An Episode in History of the Far Eastern Republic.* 1962. 20p. (MS No. 15).

1458 **Tang, Peter S. H.** *The Chinese Communist Struggle Against Revisionism.* 1964. 50p. (MS No. 16).

2. PAMPHLET SERIES

1459 **Grant, Natalie.** *Communist Psychological Offensive: Distortions in the Translation of Official Documents.* 1961. 20p. (PS No. 1).

1460 **Tang, Peter S. H.** *The Commune System in Mainland China.* 1961. 41p. (PS No. 2).

1461 ———. *The Nature of Communist Strategy in Areas of Emerging Nations.* 1962. 32p. (PS No. 6).

3. BOOK SERIES

1462 **Tang, Peter S. H.** *Communist China Today: Volume I: Domestic and Foreign Policies.* Revised edition. 1961. 18; 745p. (BS No. 1).

1463 ———. *Communist China Today: Volume II: Documentary Analysis, Data, and Chronology.* Revised edition under preparation. (BS No. 2).

Originally published by Frederick A. Praeger in 1958. 137p. (See **393.**)

1464 ———. *Sino-Soviet Relations: Retrospect and Prospect.* Under preparation. (BS No. 3).

M. SOCIAL SCIENCE RESEARCH COUNCIL, COMMITTEE ON THE ECONOMY OF CHINA REPRINT SERIES

1465 **Kwang, Ching-wen.** *The Budgetary System of the People's Republic of China: A Preliminary Survey.* 1964 (No. 1).

1466 **Hoffman, Charles.** *Work Incentives in Communist China.* 1964 (No. 2).

1467 **Mah, Feng-hwa.** *The Terms of Sino-Soviet Trade.* 1964 (No. 3).

1468 **Chao, Kang and Mah, Feng-hwa.** *A Study of the Rouble-Yuan Exchange Rate.* 1964 (No. 4).

1468a **Hollister, William W.** *Capital Formation in Communist China.* 1964 (No. 5).

N. Stanford University, Institute of political Studies, Studies on Contemporary China

The following emerged from the work of two research groups in the institute, and are issued in two series: Studies in International Conflict and Integration, and Studies of the Communist System (presented here jointly). Working papers and internal reports have not been included.

1469 **Doolin, Dennis J.** 'The Revival of the 100 Flowers Campaign: 1961,' *The China Quarterly*, No. 8 (October-December 1961), pp. 34–41.

1469a **Holsti, Ole R.** 'East-West Conflict and Sino-Soviet Relations,' *The Journal oj Applied Behavioral Science*, Vol. 1 (April-May-June 1965), pp. 115–130.

1469b **McClelland, Charles A.** 'Decisional Opportunity and Political Controversy: The Quemoy Case,' *The Journal of Conflict Resolution*, Vol. 6, No. 3 (September 1962), pp. 201–213.

1469c **North, Robert C.** 'Sino-Soviet Alliance,' *The China Quarterly*, London, Vol. 1 (January-March 1960).

1469d ——. 'The Challenge of Communist China,' *World Politics*, Vol. 13, No. 1 (October 1960).

1469e ——. 'The Sino-Soviet Controversy,' *Current Scene*, Hong Kong, Vol. 1, No. 29 (April 5, 1962).

1469f ——. 'Soviet and Chinese Goal Values' in Kurt London, ed., *Unity and Contradiction* (New York: Frederick A. Praeger, 1962).

1469g ——. 'Two Revolutionary Models' in A. Doak Barnett, ed., *Communist Strategies in Asia* (New York: Frederick A. Praeger, 1963).

1469h ——. 'Communist China and the Population Problem' in Stuart Mudd, ed., *The Population Crisis and the Use of World Resources*, Vol 2, The World Academy of Art and Science (The Hague: Dr. W. Junk & Co., 1964).

1469i ——. *Chinese Communism: A History of Its Origins and Ideas*. (London: World University Library, 1966).

1469j **Triska, Jan F.** 'Stanford Studies of the Communist System: The Sino-Soviet Split,' *Background*, Vol. 8, No. 3 (November 1964), pp. 143–159.

1469k **Zaninovich, M. George.** *An Empirical Theory of State Response: The Sino-Soviet Case*. Stanford, Calif.: Studies in International Conflict and Integration, August 1964. 400p. Mimeographed (a revised edition of a Ph.D. dissertation [1964] entitled "An Operational Theory of Perceived Crisis").

O. General Electric Company, Santa Barbara, California, TEMPO Environmental Studies, The China Project

1470 Michael, F. *The Role of Communist China in International Affairs*, December 1958. 25p. (RM 58TMP-42).

1471 Krader, L. *The Economic Status of Communist China: 1965–1970*. December, 1958. 27p. (RM 58TMP-56).

1472 McClintock, C. G. *The Demography of the Asian 'Big Three'*. December 1958. 26p. (RM 58TMP-58).

1473 Berberet, J. A. *Science and Technology in Communist China*. December 1960. 157p. (RM 60TMP-72).

1474 North, R. C. *Possible Trends in Sino-Soviet International Relations*. December 1962. 65p. (RM 62TMP-73).

1475 Hsüeh, Chün-tu. *An Institutional Analysis of the Communist Rule in China*. December 1962. 49p. (RM 62TMP-73).

1476 Hsu, I. C. Y. *Reorganization of Higher Education in Communist China*. December 1962. 47p. (RM 62TMP-74).

1477 Wu, Y. L. *The Economic Impact of the Rise of Communist China*. December 1962. 52p. (RM 62TMP-77).

1478 Huang, L. J. *The Impact of the Commune on the Chinese Family*. December 1962. 56p. (RM 62TMP-78).

1479 Harner, E. L. *Middle School Education as a Tool of Power in Communist China*. December 1962. 56p. (RM 62TMP-79).

1480 Jansen, M. B. *Japan and Communist China in the Next Decade*. December 1962. 50p. (RM 62TMP-81).

1481 Schwartz, Benjamin. *Communist Ideology in China*. December 1962. 33p. (RM 62TMP-90).

1482 Berberet, J. A. *Science, Technology, and Peking's Planning Problems*. December 1962. 41p. (RM 62TMP-91).

1483 Harner, E. L. *Quality in Secondary Education in Communist China*. May 1963. 2p. (SP-232).

P. U.S. Department of State,
Bureau of Intelligence and Research, External Research Staff Publications on China

1. EXTERNAL RESEARCH PAPERS

1484 **The Thought of Mao Tse-tung,** *A Selected List of References to the Published Works and Statements Attributed to Mao Tse-tung and to the Literature on the Chinese Communist Leader*. 1962. 73p. (No. 138), (see **66**).

1485 **Nuclear Research and Technology in Communist China**—*A List of Monographs and Periodical and Newspaper Articles in the English Language on Atomic Energy Research and Technology in Communist China.* 1963. 7p. (No. 139), (see **159**).

1486 **Ethnic Minorities of Southern China,** *List of References in European Languages on Southern China and Adjoining Border-Lands.* 1963. 18p. (No. 140), (see **61**).

1487 **Bloc Policy Towards Underdeveloped Countries,** *Selective List of Publications on Soviet and Communist Chinese Policy Towards Representative Underdeveloped Countries.* 1963. 7p. (No. 144).

1488 **Scientific and Technical Manpower in Communist China,** *A Selective List of Books, Pamphlets and Periodical Articles in English, French and German on Scientific and Technical Manpower in Mainland China, Published Between 1953 and 1963.* 1964. 10p. (No. 148).

1489 **Schwarz, Henry G.** *Leadership Patterns in China's Frontier Regions.* 1964. 95p. (No. 149).

1490 **Education in Communist China,** *A Selective List of Books, Pamphlets and Periodical Articles on the State of Education in Mainland China, 1953–1963.* 1964. 10p. (No. 150).

1491 **A Background Reading List of Psychological Operations, with Special Emphasis on Communist China.** 1964. 26p. (No. 153).

2. POLICY RESEARCH STUDIES

1492 **Powell, Ralph L.** *Politico-Military Relationships in Communist China.* 1963. 21p.

1493 **Lewis, John Wilson.** *Chinese Communist Party Leadership and the Succession to Mao Tse-tung: An Appraisal of Tensions.* 1964. 35p.

Q. U.S. OFFICE OF EDUCATION PUBLICATIONS ON CHINA

1. BULLETIN SERIES

1494 **Barendsen, Robert D.** *Half-Work, Half-Study Schools in Communist China.* April 1964 (OE 14100). 56p. (Bulletin No. 24 [1964]).

1495 **Harper, Paul.** *Spare-Time Education for Workers in Communist China.* August 1964 (OE 14102). 29p. (No. 30 [1964]).

2. INFORMATION ON EDUCATION AROUND THE WORLD SERIES

1496 **Wong, Jennings L.** *Specializations in Higher Technological Education in Communist China.* May 1959 (OE-14034-13). 7p. (IEAW No. 13).

1497 **Chen, Theodore Hsi-en.** *The Popularization of Higher Education in Communist China.* August 1959 (OE-14002). 10p. (IEAW No. 24).

1498 **Barendsen, Robert D.** *Planned Reforms in the Primary and Secondary School System in Communist China.* August 1960 (OE-14034-45). 12p. (IEAW No. 45).

1499 **Cheng, J. Chester.** *Basic Principles Underlying the Chinese Communist Approach to Education.* January 1961 (OE-14034-51). 24p. (IEAW No. 51).

3. STUDIES IN COMPARATIVE EDUCATION SERIES

1500 **Chen, Theodore Hsi-en.** *Teacher Training in Communist China.* December 1960 (OE-14058). 49p.

1501 **Berrien, Marcia T. and Barendsen, Robert D.** *Education in Hong Kong.* May 1960 (OE-14049) 40p.

R. UNIVERSITY OF SOUTHERN CALIFORNIA, STUDIES IN CHINESE COMMUNISM, CHINESE DOCUMENTS PROJECT, HUMAN RESOURCES RESEARCH INSTITUTE

1502 **Chen, Wen-hui C.** *Chinese Communist Anti-Americanism and the Resist-America Aid-Korea Campaign.* 1955. 22p.

1503 ——. *The Family Revolution in Communist China.* 1955. 65p.

1504 ——. *Wartime 'Mass' Campaigns in Communist China: Official Country-wide 'Mass Movements' in Professed Support of the Korean War.* 1955. 14; 83p.

1505 **Chiu, Sin-ming.** *Some Basic Conceptions and Rules of Conduct of Chinese Communism (Initial Collation Towards the Conceptual and Operational Code of Chinese Communist Leaders).* 1955. 39p.

1506 **Ferris, Helen.** *The Christian Church in Communist China to 1952.* 1956. 11; 76p.

1507 **Ong, Shao-er.** *Agrarian Reform in Communist China to 1952.* 1955. 18; 61p.

1508 ——. *Chinese Farm Economy After Agrarian Reform.* 1955. 13; 32p.

1509 ——. *Labor Problems in Communist China.* 1955. 83p.

1510 **Wang, Charles K.** *The Control of Teachers in Communist China: A Socio-Political Study.* 1955. 61p.

1511 ——. *Reactions in Communist China: Analysis of Letters to Newspaper Editors* 1955. 11; 115p.

1512 **Wei, Henry.** *Courts and Police in Communist China to 1952.* 1955. 11; 65p.

1513 ——. *Mao Tse-tung's 'Lean-to-One-Side' Policy.* 1955. 12; 52p.

1514 Wei, Henry. *State and Government in Communist China: Their Ideological Basis and Statutory Pattern to the Spring of 1953.* 1955. 16; 56p.

1515 Yu, Frederick Te-chi. *The Propaganda Machine in Communist China, with Special Reference to Ideology, Policy, and Regulations as of 1952.* 1955. 13; 79p.

1516 ——. *The Strategy and Tactics of Chinese Communist Propaganda as of 1952.* 1955. 15; 70p.

UNPUBLISHED MANUSCRIPTS

1517 Chiu, Sin-ming. *The United States Through Four Chinese Communist Newspapers.*

1518 Ong, Shao-er. *Agricultural Taxation in Communist China.*

1519 Tang, Peter. *The Communist Party of China: Organization and Structure.*

1520 Yu, Frederick Te-chi. *The Top Leaders in Communist China.*

S. University of Southern California, Soviet-Asian Studies Center Publications

1. REPRINT SERIES

1521 Chen, Theodore Hsi-en. *Science, Scientists, and Politics in Communist China.* 1961 (No. 1).

1522 ——. *Education and Indoctrination in Red China.* 1961 (No. 2).

1523 ——. *Elementary Education in Communist China.* 1962 (No. 3).

1524 Yang, Richard F. S. *Industrial Workers in Chinese Communist Fiction.* 1963. (No. 4).

1525 Chen, Theodore Hsi-en. *Education and the Economic Failures in Communist China.* 1963 (No. 5).

2. MONOGRAPH SERIES

1526 Chen, Theodore Hsi-en. *The Chinese Communist Regime: A Documentary Study.* Vol. 1 and Vol. 2. Revised edition (see **572**).

1527 Pennington, Juliana and Marsh, Paul, comps. *The University of Southern California Doctoral Dissertations and Master's Theses on East and Southeast Asia, 1911–1964* (see **1881**).

T. University of Washington, Modern Chinese History Project Reprint Series

1528 Michael, Franz. *The Role of Law in Traditional, Nationalist and Communist China* (Reprint No. 1).

1529 Etō, Shinkichi. *Hai-lu-feng—The First Chinese Soviet Government* (No. 2).

1530 Laai, Yi-faai, Michael, Franz, and Sherman, John C. *The Use of Maps in Social Research: A Case Study in South China* (No. 3).

1531 Shih, Vincent Y. C. *A Talk with Hu Shih* (No. 4).

1532 Michael, Franz. *Khrushchev's Disloyal Opposition: Structural Change and Power Struggle in the Communist Bloc* (No. 5).

1533 Shih, Vincent Y. C. *Enthusiast and Escapist: Writers of the Older Generation* (No. 6).

1534 Wilhelm, Hellmut. *The Image of Youth and Age in Chinese Communist Literature* (No. 7).

1535 Hsia, T. A. *Heroes and Hero-Worship in Chinese Communist Fiction* (No. 8).

1536 Mah, Feng-hwa. *The Terms of Sino-Soviet Trade* (No. 13).

1537 Chao, Kang and Mah, Feng-hwa. *A Study of the Rouble-Yuan Exchange Rate* (No. 14).

1538 Shih, Vincent Y. C. *Mao Tun: The Critic* (No. 15).

1539 Bauer, Wolfgang. *Western Literature and Translation Work in Communist China* (No. 17).

U. UNION RESEARCH INSTITUTE (HONG KONG), COMMUNIST CHINA PROBLEM RESEARCH SERIES

1540 Fang, Shu. *Campaign of Party-Expansion of the Chinese Communist Party in 1952.* 1953. 48p. (CCPRS No. 1).

1541 Chung, Shih. *Higher Education in Communist China.* 1953. 108p. (No. 2).

1542 Hsin, Ying. *The Price Problems of Communist China.* 1954. 134p. (No. 3).

1543 ——. *The Foreign Trade of Communist China.* 1954. 144p. (No. 4).

1544 Cheng, Chu-yuan. *Monetary Affairs in Communist China.* 1954. 170p. (No. 5).

1545 Chi, Tung-wei. *Education for the Proletariat in Communist China.* 1954. 84p. (No. 6).

1546 Ting, Li. *Militia of Communist China.* 1954. 154p. (No. 7).

1547 Hsiao, Chi-jung. *Revenue and Disbursement of Communist China.* 1954. 128p. (No. 8).

1548 Cheng, Chu-yuan. *Anshan Steel Factory in Communist China.* 1955. 98p. (No. 9).

1549 Chao, Yung-seen. *Railways in Communist China.* 1955. 118p. (No. 10).

1550 Chao, Chung. *The Communist Program for Literature and Art in China.* 1955. 116p. (No. 11).

1551 Lu, Yu-sun. *Programs of Communist China for Overseas Chinese.* 1956. 92p. (No. 12).

1552 Chao, Chung and Yang, I-fan. *Students in Mainland China.* 1956. 156p. (No. 13).

1553 Cheng, Chu-yuan. *The China Mainland Market Under Communist Control.* 1956. 106p. (No. 14).

1554 Communist China, 1955. 1956. 246p. (No. 15).

1555 Yang, I-fan. *The Case of Hu Feng.* 1956. 182p. (No. 16).

1556 Shih, Ch'eng-chih. *People's Resistance in Mainland China 1950–1955.* 1956. 128p. (No. 17).

1557 Communist China, 1956. 1957. 282p. (No. 18).

1558 Cheng, Chu-yuan. *Income and Standard of Living in Mainland China.* 1957. 2 vols., 386p., (No. 19).

1559 Communist China, 1957. 1958. 376p. (No. 20).

1560 Johnson, Chalmers A. *Communist Policies Toward the Intellectual Class.* 1959. 140p. (No. 21).

1561 Chin, Calvin Suey Keu. *A Study of Chinese Dependence Upon the Soviet Union for Economic Development as a Factor in Communist China's Foreign Policy.* 1959. 194p. (No. 22).

1562 Knutson, Jeanne Nickell. *Outer Mongolia: A Study in Soviet Colonialism.* 1959. 194p. (No. 23).

1563 Communist China, 1958. 1959. 257p. (No. 24).

1564 Communist China, 1949–1959. 1961. 3 vols. 272; 219; 186p. (No. 25).

1565 Chin, Szu-k'ai. *Communist China's Relations with the Soviet Union, 1949–1957.* 1962. 162p. (No. 26).

1566 Mayer, Peter. *Sino-Soviet Relations Since the Death of Stalin.* 1962. 172p., Appendices (32; 89p.). (No. 27).

1567 Shih, Ch'eng-chih. *Urban Commune Experiments in Communist China.* 1962. 167p. (No. 28).

1568 **Communist China, 1960.** 1962. 2 vols. 273; 251p. (No. 29).

1569 **Shih, Ch'eng-chih.** *The Status of Science and Education in Communist China and a Comparison with That in USSR.* 1962. 89p. (No. 30).

1570 **Carin, Robert.** *River Control in Communist China.* 1962. 124p. Maps, chronology, and notes. (No. 31).

1571 **Communist China, 1961.** 1963. 2 vols., 224; 231p. (No. 32).

1572 **Carin, Robert.** *Irrigation Scheme in Communist China.* 1963. 366p. (No. 33).

1573 **Communist China, 1962.** 1963. 2 vols., 203; 186p. (No. 34).

V. Continental Research Institute (Hong Kong), Continental Research Series

1574 **Chow, Ching-wen.** *Between Khrushchev and Mao.* September 1960. 26p. (No. 1).

1575 ——. *Criticism on People's Commune.* December 1961. 50p. (No. 2).

1576 ——. *Chinese Communist Regime Trapped in Spiral Crises.* May 1962. 46p. (No. 3).

1577 ——. *Turbulent Exodus from Hunger.* September 1962. 42p. (No. 4).

1578 ——. *Communist Magic—United Front Operation.* December 1962. 22p. (No. 5).

1579 ——. *What We Must Know About Communists.* July 1963. 25p. (No. 6).

W. Publications of the Asian Peoples' Anti-Communist League (Taipei)

1580 **All Roads Lead to Freedom.** 1955. 3 vols.

1581 **An Analysis of Japan's Trade with Chinese Communists.** 1955. 34p.

1582 **Charts About Chinese Communism on the Mainland.** (Series I–XII completed to 1964).

1583 **Cheng, Hsüeh-chia.** *An Interpretation of the Purge of Kao and Jao in Chinese Communist Party.* 1955. 20p.

1584 **Communist Tyranny and People's Resistance on the Chinese Mainland in 1954.** 1955. 82p.

1585 **The Current Strategy and Tactics of International Communism.** 1955. 32p.

1586 **The Food Policy of the Chinese Communists.** 1955. 35p.

1587 The International Communist Conspiracy in Asia. 1955. 30p.

1588 Nehru's Illusion. 1955. 38p.

1589 Slave Labor Under the Chinese Communist Regime. 1955. 19p.

1590 Study of the Communist 'Peaceful Co-existence Conspiracy'. 1955. 54p.

1591 'Asia First' in Soviet Russia's Strategy for World Conquest. 1956. 37p.

1592 First Five Year Plan of the Chinese Communists. 1956. 46p.

1593 How to Combat Communism. 1956. 57p.

1594 Important Documents of the Second Asian Peoples' Anti-Communist Conference. 1956. 33p.

1595 Intrigues of Soviet Imperialists and Chinese Communists. 1956. 73p.

1596 Cheng, Hsüeh-chia. *The So-called Enlightened Despotism of Chinese Communists.* 1957. 125p.

1597 The Chinese Communist Agricultural Collectivization. 1957. 40p.

1598 Communist Menace to Asia. 1957. 45p.

1599 Development of the Chinese People's Anti-Communist Movement. 1957. 2 vols.

1600 Documents of the Asian Peoples' Anti-Communist League. 1957. 39p.

1601 How China Fights Communism. 1957. 49p.

1602 The Illicit Narcotic Trade of the Chinese Communists. 1957. 28p.

1603 Mao Tse-tung Can Never Be a Tito. 1957. 61p.

1604 The Overseas United Front of the Chinese Communists. 1957. 69p.

1605 Sung, W. M. *Outlook of Neutralism.* 1957. 49p.

1606 Cheng, Hsüeh-chia. *Why Do the Chinese Communists Serve as Vanguard Against Modern Revisionism.* 1958. 27p.

1607 Chinese Communist Judiciary, Police and Secret Service. 1958. 51p.

1608 Jen, Shan-shueh. *Escape from Hell.* 1958. 103p.

1609 Li, Chin-tsi. *What Is Behind the Chinese Communists' Program of Military Reorganization.* 1958. 70p.

1610 Mao Tse-tung and 'Let a Hundred Flowers Bloom and a Hundred Schools of Thought Contend' Campaign. 1958. 52p.

1611 New Development of the Asian Peoples' Anti-Communist Movement. 1958. 88p.

1612 The New Development of the Anti-Communist Revolution on the Chinese Mainland. 1958. 48p.

1613 New Moves by the Chinese Communists After the Moscow Conferences. 1958. 47p.

1614 Soviet Economic Aid to Underdeveloped Countries. 1958. 52p.

1615 Victory on Another Front: How Do We Eliminate Communist Infiltration and Subversive Activities on Taiwan? 1958. 53p.

1616 An Analytical Study of the Chinese Communists' 'People's Communes'. 1959. 102p.

1617 Cheng, Hsüeh-chia. *The People's Commune—Military Slavery Communism.* 1959. 67p.

1618 Chinese Communists' Trade Offensive. 1959. 60p.

1619 The Defense of Quemoy and the Free World. 1959. 53p.

1620 Life in the People's Commune. 1959. 77p.

1621 Shih, Yüan-ching. *'Peaceful Competition' or Threat of War.* 1959. 68p.

1622 The Tibet Revolution and the Free World. 1959. 42p.

1623 Yang-ming shan-chuang. *The People's Commune.* 1959. 24p.

1624 APACL—Its Growth and Outlook. 1960. 62p.

1625 Bankruptcy of 'Five Principles of Peace'. 1960. 23p.

1626 Cheng, Hsüeh-chia. *Whither Indonesia?* 1960. 108p.

1627 The Chinese Communist Political and Economic Activities in Southeast Asia. 1960. 18p.

1628 Factional Struggles Within the Chinese Communist Party. 1960. 88p.

1629 The Great Famine on the Chinese Mainland Under Communist Regime in 1960. 1960. 18p.

1630 Important Documents of the Asian Peoples' Anti-Communist League, 1954-1960. 1960. 74p.

1631 Kao, Hsiang-kao. *Ten Years of Chinese Communist Economy.* 1960. 103p.

1632 Li, T'ien-min. *The Retreat of People's Communes on the Chinese Mainland.* 1960. 73p.

1633 Tang, Chu-kuo. *The Student Anti-Communist Movement in Peiping.* 1960. 41p.

1634 Urban People's Communes—Today and Tomorrow. 1960. 45p.

1635 Communist China in Africa. 1961. 50p.

1636 Latin America's Red Peril. 1961. 36p.

1637 Shih, Yüan-ching. *The Relations Between Moscow and Peiping.* 1961. 61p.

1638 Cheng, Hsüeh-chia. *An Unprecedented Famine on the Chinese Mainland and the People's Communes.* 1961. 82p.

1639 Cheng, Tso-yüan. *Famine and Its Repercussion on the Chinese Mainland.* 1961. 24p.

1640 ———. *Chinese Communists' Infiltration Activities in South East Asia.* 1961. 57p.

1641 A Research on Mao Tse-tung's Thought of Military Insurrection. 1961. 94p.

1642 The 'Bumper Crops Farce'—Factual Survey of Mainland Agricultural Setbacks for the First Half of 1961. 1961. 69p.

1643 Li, T'ien-min. *Whither Goes the People's Commune.* 1961. 68p.

1644 Cheng, Hsüeh-chia. *Pure Capitalism or Communism—The Critique of CPSU Program—Part I.* 1961. 61p.

1645 ———. *Pure Capitalism or Communism—Part II.* 1962. 50p.

1646 Wan, Ya-kang. *World Revolution and Nationalism.* 1962. 74p.

1647 An Analysis of the Peiping Regime's Anti-US Campaign. 1962. 39p.

1648 Why Does Mao Tse-tung Want to Follow Leftist Line of Adventure? 1962. 32p.

1649 A Study of the Current Foreign and Domestic Policies of the Puppet Peiping Regime. 1962. 18p.

1650 A General Survey of Chinese Communist Rule. 1962. 53p.

1651 Cheng, Hsüeh-chia, *Hunger in Communist China—An Estimate of 1961 Food Production.* 1962. 80p.

1652 Famine as Told by Letters from the Chinese Mainland. 1962. 94p.

1653 China's Bitter Experiences with the Communists. 1962. 105p.

1654 Hsiang, Nai-kuang. *The Militia; A Thorn in the Peiping Regime's Side.* 1963. 21p.

1655 **A General Survey of Moscow-Peiping Relations.** 1963. 56p.

1656 **Li, T'ien-min.** *Can Agricultural Crises Be Averted by the Chinese Communists?* 1963. 78p.

1657 **Hwang, Tien-chien.** *Failures of Mao Tze-tung's Dictatorship 1949–1963, Part I.* 1963. 80p.

1658 ——. *Failures of Mao Tze-tung's Dictatorship 1949–1963, Part II.* 1963. 78p.

1659 **Wang, Sze-cheng.** *The Delicate Relationship Between Mao Tze-tung, Liu Shao-chi and Chow En-lai* [sic]. 1963. 24p.

1660 **Hwang, Tien-chien.** *Moscow-Peiping Relations and Khrushchev-Mao Struggle.* 1963. 78p.

1661 **Ho, Wen-hai.** *Chinese Communist Exploitation and Persecution of the Intelligentsia.* 1963. 60p.

1662 **Chinese Communist Expansion and Rivalry with the Soviet Union in Asia, Africa and Latin America.** 1964. 69p.

1663 **Impact of the Moscow-Peiping Schism on the World Situation.** 1964. 58p.

1664 **Kao, Hsiang-kao.** *Chinese Communist Foreign Trade and Diplomacy.* 1964. 82p.

1665 **Hwang, Tien-chien.** *Bitter Struggle of Chinese Communists in 1963.* 1964. 60p.

1666 **Communist Industry; Its Problems and Difficulties.** 1964. 71p.

1667 **An Analysis of the Communist 'Learning from the Liberation Army' Movement.** 1964. 64p.

X. Institute of Asian Economic Affairs
(Ajia Keizai Kenkyūjo, Tokyo), Research Reports on China

1668 **Ishikawa, Shigeru.** *Chūgoku keizai hatten no tōkeiteki kenkyū* (A Statistical Study of China's Economic Development). 3 vols. (Vol. 1, 1960, 270p.; Vol. 2, 1962, 324p.; Vol. 3, 1962, 306p.). (Chōsa kenkyū hōkoku sōsho [Research Report Series], Nos. 7, 20, 34).

1669 **Satō, Shin'ichirō.** *Chūgoku kyōsantō no nōgyō shūdanka seisaku* (Agricultural Collectivization Policies of the Chinese Communist Party). 2 vols. (Vol. 1, 1961, 384p.; Vol. 2, 1962, 350p.). (Ajia keizai kenkyū shiriizu [Asian Economic Research Series], Nos. 11, 28).

1670 **Okada, Yoshimasa,** *Chūgoku keizai kensetsu to kakyō* (China's Economic Construction and the Overseas Chinese). 1960. 110p. (Asian Economic Research Series, No. 6).

1671 **Miyashita, Tadao.** *Chūgoku no bōeki soshiki* (The Organization of China's Trade). 1961. 200p. (Asian Economic Research Series, No. 17).

1672 **Doi, Akira.** *Chūgoku jimmin kōsha no soshiki to kinō* (The Organization and Function of the Chinese People's Commune). 1961. 320p. (Research Report Series, No. 15).

1673 **Ichiko, Chūzō.** *Gendai Chūgoku no keizai* (The Economy of Contemporary China). 1962. 310p. (Bunken kaidai sōsho [Bibliographical Series], No. 3).

1674 **Amano, Motonosuke.** *Chūgoku no tochi kaikaku* (China's Agricultural Reform). 1962. 120p. (Asian Economic Research Series, No. 34).

1675 **Muramatsu, Yūji.** *Kaigai ni okeru saikin no Chūgoku kenkyū no jōkyō—Recent Research on China Abroad.* 1963. 155p. (Asian Economic Research Series, No. 45), (see **1796**).

1676 **Satō, Shin'ichirō.** *Nōgyō seisan gassakusha no soshiki kōzō* (The Organizational Structure of Agricultural Producers' Cooperatives). 1963. 198p. (Asian Economic Research Series, No. 41).

1677 ——. *Jimmin kōsha no soshiki kōzō* (The Organizational Structure of the People's Communes). 1964. 180p. (Asian Economic Research Series, No. 55).

1678 **Okazaki, Ayakoto.** *Chūgoku no tekkōgyō to kikai kōgyō no gijutsu suijun* (The Technological Level of Iron and Steel and Machinery Industries in China). 1964. 279p. (Kenkyū sankō shiryō [Research Reference Series], No. 29).

1679 **Akeno, Yoshio and Kojima, Reiitsu.** *Chūgoku no tekkōgyō to kikai* (The Iron and Steel, and Machinery Industries of China). 1964. (Research Reference Series, No. 58).

1680 **Yonezawa, Hideo.** *Chūgokū no keizai hatten to taigai bōeki* (China's Economic Development and Foreign Trade). 1964. 154p. (Research Reference Series, No. 62).

1681 **Chūgoku no denryoku, sekitan, bōshoku, seishi kōgyō** (China's Electrical Power, Coal, Spinning and Weaving, and Paper Manufacturing Industries). 1964. 187p. (Research Reference Series, No. 71).

1682 **Ishikawa, Shigeru.** *Chūgoku keizai no chōki tembō* (Long-Range Prospects of Chinese Economy). 1964. 334p. (Research Reference Series, No. 76).

Y. SPECIAL ISSUES ON CHINA

1683 **'Report on China'** (edited by H. Arthur Steiner), *The Annals of the American Academy of Political and Social Science*, Vol. 277 (September 1951).

1684 'Communist China,' *Current History*, Vol. 32, No. 185 (January 1957).

1685 'Communist China: A Special Report,' *New Republic*, May 13, 1957.

1686 'Communist China in World Politics,' *Journal of International Affairs*, Vol. 11, No. 2 (1957).

1687 'Communist China's Foreign Policy,' *Current History*, Vol. 33, No. 196 (December 1957).

1688 'Report on Communist China,' *Current History*, Vol. 35, No. 208 (December 1958).

1689 'Contemporary China and the Chinese' (edited by Howard L. Boorman), *The Annals of the American Academy of Political and Social Science*, Vol. 321 (January 1959).

1690 'Red China: A Special Issue—The First Ten Years,' *The Atlantic*, December 1959.

1691 'Communist China as a World Power,' *Current History*, Vol. 37, No. 220 (December 1959).

1692 'A Special Issue on China,' *Free World Forum*, Vol. 2, No. 3 (June 1960).

1693 'Communist China and Continuing Coexistence,' *Current History*, Vol. 39, No. 232 (December 1960).

1694 'Communist China in the World Community' (by H. Arthur Steiner), *International Conciliation*, No. 533 (May 1961).

1695 'Communist China: New World Power,' *Current History*, Vol. 41, No. 241 (September 1961).

1696 'Communist China, 1962,' *Current History*, Vol. 43, No. 253 (September 1962).

1697 'The Asian Triangle: China, India and Japan,' *Journal of International Affairs*, Vol. 17, No. 2 (1963).

1698 'Communist China and the Soviet Bloc,' *The Annals of the American Academy of Political and Social Science*, Vol. 349 (September 1963).

1699 'Communist China, 1963,' *Current History*, Vol. 45, No. 265 (September 1963).

1699a 'Special Number on Communist China,' *The Political Quarterly*, London, Vol. 35, No. 3 (July-September 1964).

1700 'China in the World Today,' *Current History*, Vol. 47, No. 277 (September 1964).

1700a 'The China Problem,' *Intercom*, Vol. 7, No. 1 (January-February 1965). Includes an annotated bibliography on China, pp. 59-72.

APPENDICES

APPENDIX A

RESEARCH LIBRARIES AND INSTITUTIONS: SURVEYS, DIRECTORIES, CATALOGS, AND REFERENCES

Appendix A brings together a number of surveys, directories, guides, handbooks and lists relevant to the field of contemporary Chinese studies, as well as union catalogs, catalogs of individual libraries and publishing houses, classification schemes and related bibliographical references. The appendix is organized on a geographical basis with separate sections on the United States; Taiwan, Hong Kong, and the Mainland; Japan; the Soviet Union; and other countries.

I. THE UNITED STATES

1701 Japan, Gaimushō, Ajiakyoku, Chūgokuka 日本外務省アジア局中國課 (Japan, Foreign Ministry, Bureau of Asian Affairs, China Section). *Beikoku ni okeru kindai Chūgoku kenkyū no genkyō* 米國における近代中國研究の現況 (A Survey of Current Studies on Modern China in the United States). Tokyo, 1963. 61p.

A brief survey of modern and contemporary Chinese studies in the United States. In three parts: (1) major developments since 1958 (the National Defense and Education Act, Ford Foundation grants, the Joint Committee on Contemporary China, and recent conferences); (2) a description of about twenty academic research and training programs (at Harvard, Columbia, Washington, etc.), including library resources and faculty publications; other activities (the Association for Asian Studies, the Council on Foreign Relations, the Library of Congress, the RAND Corporation, and government agencies).

This report was prepared by Dr. Shigeaki Uno of the China Section on his three-month trip to the United States in the fall of 1962. While there are a number of minor inaccuracies, this is the most recent survey giving an overall view of the modern, and particularly the contemporary, China field in the United States.

1702 Morehouse, Ward, ed.
American Institutions and Organizations Interested in Asia: A Reference Directory. Second edition. New York: Taplinger Publishing Co., 1961. 581p.

Describes the programs relating to Asia of some 1,000 American universities, religious and educational organizations, foundations, museums and libraries, scientific and professional societies, and other groups. Arranged alphabetically by name of institution, this volume is limited to current activities. The appendix contains two listings: (1) 'Asian Government, Diplomatic and Consular Offices and Information Services in the United States', (2) 'United States Government Diplomatic and Consular Offices and Information Services in Asia'. There is also an alphabetical index and a summary of activities described in the directory. The alphabetical index contains the following types of entries: institutions and organizations listed in the *Directory* (under their present, as well as former, names), departments, committees, or programs of the listed institutions and organizations when these are widely known under their own names; and all non-listed organizations cited in the body of the *Directory*.

1703   U. S. Department of State, Bureau of Intelligence and Research.
Foreign Affairs Research: Projects and Centers. Washington, D.C.: U.S. Government Printing Office, 1960. 153p. (External Research Report 44).

A revision of *Group Research Projects in Foreign Affairs and the Social Sciences* (published September 10, 1958, by the External Research Division), the present volume lists and describes 198 group research projects in the social sciences concerned with foreign areas and international relations, which are administered by an academic or research institution.

Compiled from information gathered by the External Research Division on the basis of published sources and correspondence with project directors and research scholars, the report is intended to show the scope and direction of current research efforts. Information provided for each project includes name of sponsoring institution, names of project director and principal researchers, funds, description of nature of project, recent publications, and study in preparation.

Eighty-nine projects are listed by subject matter or functional problem. The remainder are organized according to geographical area of primary concern, of which twenty-three deal specifically with East Asia, including six studies on Japan and nine on China, some of which are devoted to contemporary developments. There is an index by project director and an index by subject. A revised edition is under preparation.

1704   Moses, Larry, comp.
Language and Area Study Programs in American Universities. [Washington, D.C.]: Department of State, External Research Staff, 1964. 11; 162p.

Describes 153 programs offering graduate degrees for foreign language and area study, arranged regionally (Africa, Asia—General, East Asia, South and Southeast Asia, etc.). Contains information on over twenty programs concerned with China, in each case providing the name of the program, the name of the director and associated faculty, degrees offered, regional focus, number of language and area courses, library facilities, sources of outside support, national fellowships, and unique features. A representative sampling of twenty-three undergraduate programs is appended. Three indexes: undergraduate programs, by language, and by university.

This is a revision of the 1962 edition. In 1954, 1956, and 1959, this survey appeared as *Area Study Programs in American Universities*.

1705 **U. S. Department of State, External Research Division.**
External Research: A List of Studies Currently in Progress [on] East Asia, and
External Research: A List of Recently Completed Studies [on] East Asia.
Washington, D.C., 1952—.

Two in the series of semi-annual research lists based on the catalog of social science research on foreign areas and international affairs compiled by the External Research Division from information furnished by private scholars and graduate students throughout the United States.

The first External Research lists were published in January 1952, entitled *External Research Report: Research on . . .,* and included the titles of both recently completed and in-progress research projects on all countries of the world with the exception of the United States. Since 1954 the lists have been published semi-annually; research in progress is reported in the April lists and completed research in the lists for October. A separate list for research on China was published until 1958. Starting with the October 1958 issue (ER List No. 2.11), research on China has been reported in the External Research List for Far East (East Asia).

The ten lists published in the April and October series cover the following areas: (1) U.S.S.R. and Eastern Europe, (2) East Asia, (3) Southeast Asia and Southwest Pacific, (4) South Asia, (5) Western Europe, (6) Middle East, (7) Africa, (8) American Republics, (9) Great Britain and Canada, and (10) international affairs.

Coverage of China occupies from one-half to two-thirds of the East Asia issue. The Fall 1963-Winter 1964 list for East Asia (ER List No 2.21) reports the titles of 227 completed studies on China listed under the following subject headings: bibliography, communism, economics, education, foreign relations, geography, government and politics, history, language and literature, law, Overseas Chinese, philosophy and religion, population, press and propaganda, and social conditions. Each entry provides the author, affiliation, title, type of work (article, book, dissertation), completion date, and, in many cases, a descriptive note. No index.

A list of reports dealing in whole or in part with China follows:

August 1952 No. 22 Unpublished Research on China: Completed and in Progress
April 1963 No. 2.1 Unpublished Research on China: Completed and in Progress

April	1954	ERS 2·2	Research in Progress	China	Oct.	1954	ERS 2·3	Completed Research	China
,,	1955	2·4	,,	,,	,,	1955	2·5	,,	,,
,,	1956	2·6	,,	,,	,,	1956	2·7	,,	,,
,,	1957	2·8	,,	,,	,,	1957	2·9	,,	,,
,,	1958	2·10	,,	,,	,,	1958	2·11	,,	Far East
,,	1959	ER 2·12	,,	Far East	,,	1959	ER 2·13	,,	East Asia
,,	1960	2·14	,,	East Asia	,,	1960	2·15	,,	,,
,,	1961	2·16	,,	,,	,,	1961	2·17	,,	,,
Spring	1962	2·18	,,	,,	Fall	1962	2·19	,,	,,
,,	1963	2·20	,	,,	Fall	1963–			
					Winter	1964	2·21	,,	,,

Copies of the External Research Lists are sent regularly to many university libraries in the United States and to scholars engaged in social science research on foreign areas and international affairs. Requests for the lists should be directed to the External Research Staff, Department of State.

1706 Newsletter of the Association for Asian Studies. Ann Arbor, Michigan: The Association for Asian Studies, Vol. 1, No. 1—, 1955—. Quarterly.

The 'Area News: China' section of the *Newsletter* provides the details of the latest developments in the Chinese field in the United States, and occasionally abroad. Particularly useful for the readers of this Guide are the Bibliographic Notes feature of the China section and the section on Instructional Programs and Teaching Materials for publications of a non-commercial nature, as well as news of microfilming and other bibliographical projects at the Library of Congress and other institutions.

Since the December 1963 issue, the *Newsletter* also has carried a yearly list of dissertations in the Asian field.

1707 Nunn, G. Raymond and Tsien, Tsuen-hsiun.
'Far Eastern Resources in American Libraries', *The Library Quarterly*, Vol. 29, No. 1 (January 1959), pp. 27–42.

A general survey of American library resources on the Far East to 1959. Included are two tables showing (1) holdings of Far Eastern materials in American libraries; and (2) growth of Far Eastern collections in American libraries. Also a section on 'Subject Strengths and Specialities on China', with indications of general types of materials available at each library but no special mention of titles. The bibliography appended to this article lists publications (catalogs, accession lists, bibliographies, etc.) by various Far Eastern libraries in the United States.

A follow-up study by Professor Tsien was published in *The Library Quarterly*, Vol. 35 (October 1965), pp. 260–282.

1708 Shih, Bernadette P. N. and Snyder, Richard L., comps.
International Union List of Communist Chinese Serials, Scientific, Technical and Medical with Selected Social Science Titles. Cambridge, Mass.: Massachusetts Institute of Technology Libraries, 1963. [148p.]

In three parts. Part A contains 499 periodical titles in the fields of science, technology and medicine. Part B provides 100 selected titles in the social sciences and humanities. Part C records 273 unidentified titles and titles for which there are no known holdings. The entries for each title in the first two parts usually contain the following information: item number, romanized title (Wade-Giles and P'in-yin), Chinese title, Latin title (if any), English translated title, imprint (including beginning date and frequency), bibliographical history, and holdings. Information on holdings is given for eighteen

American libraries, three libraries each from Canada, Great Britain, and Japan, and for the Union Research Institute in Hong Kong. There are two indexes. The Chinese character title index is arranged by the number of strokes, and then by radical. The variant title index arranges the P'in-yin, Latin and translated titles alphabetically.

The *Union List* is the most up-to-date compilation of its kind now available. Although based on, and largely superseding, the next entry, the latter provides holdings information on more social science titles as of 1960.

1709 Nunn, G. Raymond, comp.
Chinese Periodicals, International Holdings, 1949–1960; Indexes and Supplements. Ann Arbor, Mich.: Association for Asian Studies, Committee on American Library Resources on the Far East, 1961. 2 vols.

The second and third of the Preliminary Data Papers on Communist China's publishing and information program. The data on holdings cover Chinese Communist periodicals in major American, British and Japanese research libraries as well as the Hong Kong Union Research Institute holdings. Bibliographical information for periodicals for which there are no known holdings is also included.

The main list (Data Paper 2) contains approximately 1,500 periodicals arranged alphabetically by title, and is based for the most part on reports from libraries, and not on first-hand inspection. There are a number of errors in the holdings statements.

The 'Indexes and Supplement' constitute Data Paper 3. It consists of two parts. The first contains three alphabetical title lists: Wade-Giles—P'in-yin; P'in-yin—Wade-Giles; and Latin—Wade-Giles. The second contains additions (the Library of Congress and the East Asiatic Libraries of Columbia University and of the University of California in Berkeley) and corrections to the information on holdings in Data Paper 2.

This list has been superseded largely by the preceding entry. See also Chapter II, 'Lists of Newspapers and Periodicals'.

1710 U.S. Library of Congress, Reference Department, Science and Technology Division.
Chinese Scientific and Technical Serial Publications in the Collections of the Library of Congress. Revised edition. Washington, D.C., 1961. 107p.

A list of Mainland serials in the field of science and technology compiled solely from titles in the Library of Congress. Includes a number of serials published in Taiwan, and in Hong Kong and elsewhere. A few serials published in China in Western languages are also listed. Alphabetically arranged by title (with English translation and Chinese characters) under broad subject headings (science, technology, agriculture, medicine, etc.) with subdivisions. Frequency, notes on title changes, and L.C. holdings are also included. No annotations.

Two alphabetical title indexes: (1) romanized titles (according to the Wade-Giles and the P'in-yin systems), and (2) Latin and English titles.

First edition was published in 1955.

1711 U.S. Department of Agriculture, Library.
Communist Chinese Periodicals in the Agricultural Sciences. Washington, D.C., 1960. 24p. (Library List No. 70).

A preliminary bibliography of 115 Chinese Communist periodicals on agriculture and related fields (excluding periodicals on agricultural economics, rural sociology and marketing) in the National Agricultural Library (formerly known as the U.S. Department of Agriculture Library). Titles are arranged according to the Wade-Giles system. Other bibliographical information includes frequency and place of publication, as well as the holdings of the U.S.D.A. Library. Notes indicate title changes and other pertinent data.

A revised edition was issued in 1963 including nineteen new titles and approximately 600 new issues.

See also *Communist Chinese Monographs in the U.S.D.A. Library* (**150**).

1712 U.S. National Library of Medicine.
Chinese Mainland Journals: Current NLM Holdings, January 1961. Washington, D.C.: U.S. Department of Health, Education, & Welfare, Public Health Service, 1961. 15p.

An alphabetical list of sixty-nine Chinese Mainland journals in the medical and biological sciences in the National Library of Medicine. Indicates also the holdings of the M.I.T. Library, the Library of Congress, the National Agricultural Library, and the Science Museum Library of the British Department of Scientific and Industrial Research. Arranged alphabetically by title (with titles in translation, Chinese characters and Latin alphabet following). Full bibliographical information is given where available, including frequency changes.

A revised list was issued in April 1963 to show additions through that date.

1713 The University of Chicago, Far Eastern Library.
Holdings of Chinese Mainland Periodicals, 1949–1963. Chicago, 1963. 14p.

A list of 118 Chinese Communist periodicals (including English-language titles published between 1949 and 1963 and available at the Far Eastern Library of the University of Chicago. Arranged alphabetically by romanized title (followed by Chinese characters and P'in-yin romanization), the entries list frequency, title changes, and holdings. A list (with holdings) of fifteen newspapers published on the Mainland and in Taiwan is appended. Mimeographed.

See also next entry.

1714 **University of Chicago, Far Eastern Library.**
List of Chinese Periodicals as of March 1, 1961. Chicago, 1961. 18p.

An alphabetical list of 318 serial titles, including yearbooks and newspapers, in the Far Eastern Library of the University of Chicago. Titles are also given in Chinese and in translation, and for each entry approximate holdings are indicated. The list contains eighty-seven post-1949 Mainland titles and forty-six for post-1945 Taiwan.

1715 **Cornell University Libraries.**
List of Current Chinese Periodicals Received from National Library of Peking. Ithaca, N.Y., 1963. 3p.

An alphabetical list of seventy-seven Chinese Communist periodicals in Chinese and English currently received by the Wason Collection at Cornell on exchange from the National Library of Peking. Chinese characters are provided for titles, but no information is given on holdings. Mimeographed.

1716 **Stanford University, Hoover Institution, East Asian Collection.**
Holdings of Chinese Mainland Periodicals. January 1960–June 1963. Stanford, Calif., 1963. 11p.

An alphabetical list of ninety-two Chinese Mainland periodicals (including English-language titles) published between January 1960 and June 1963, and available at the East Asian Collection of the Hoover Institution. Entries provide Chinese characters and holdings. A list of seven Mainland newspapers published during the same period is appended. Mimeographed.

1717 **Massachusetts Institute of Technology Libraries, Chinese Science Project.**
Current Holdings of Mainland Chinese Journals in the M.I.T. Libraries. Revised edition. Cambridge, Mass., 1963. 44p.

An alphabetical list of 198 Chinese Communist scientific and technical journals, arranged by the Wade-Giles system with Chinese characters, translated titles, and M.I.T. holdings. A variant title index and a subject index are provided at the end. Mimeographed. Supersedes three earlier listings.
This represents the most comprehensive collection of publications of this nature available in any American university.

1718 **University of Michigan, Asia Library.**
A List of Mainland China Periodicals Currently Received at Asia Library, January 1962–May 1963. Ann Arbor, Mich., 1963. 4p.

A list of fifty-six Chinese and English-language periodicals published in Communist China between January 1962 and May 1963 and available at the Asia Library of the University of Michigan. Arranged alphabetically by title with Chinese characters, the list specifies the last issue received and information on the cumulative total of receipts for the period covered. Mimeographed.

See also next entry.

1719 Hu, William C. C., comp.
Holdings of Chinese Journals of the Asia Library, University Library, University of Michigan. Ann Arbor, Mich.: University of Michigan, Asia Library, 1961. 41p.

Includes all periodicals, journals, newspapers, and monograph series, totaling approximately 325 titles. Entries are arranged alphabetically, incorporating information on frequency and date of first publication if available, and the holdings of the Asia Library.

1720 University of Washington, Far Eastern Library.
Periodical Issues Received on Exchange from the National Library of Peking. Seattle, Wash. [1963]. Irregular.

A two-page list providing information on current receipts of Chinese Mainland periodicals on exchange from the National Library of Peking. Arranged alphabetically by romanized title (without Chinese characters), the list gives issue numbers received in each shipment by date, together with cumulative receipt information. Three shipments are usually reported in each issue. Mimeographed.

1721 Yale University Library, East Asian Collections.
Periodical Issues Received on Exchange from the National Library of Peking. January 1962—. New Haven, Conn., 1963—. Monthly.

A monthly cumulative list of Chinese Communist periodicals received on exchange from the National Library of Peking by the East Asian Collections at Yale. The list, arranged alphabetically by title (giving only Chinese characters), contains some thirty-five titles (including English-language publications), and provides, in each issue, information on the monthly cumulative total of receipts. Mimeographed.

ADDITIONAL REFERENCES

1722 Beal, Edwin G., Jr. 'The Library of Congress and the Acquisition of Far Eastern Books and Materials', *The Journal of Asian Studies*, Vol. 15, No. 3 (May 1956), pp. 470–472.

1723 Quarterly Journal of Current Acquisitions of the Library of Congress, especially the annual reports of the Chinese Section.

1724   **Lindbeck, John M. H.** 'Research Materials on Communist China: United States Government Sources,' *The Journal of Asian Studies*, Vol. 18, No. 3 (May 1959), pp. 357–363.

1725   **Huff, Elizabeth.** 'Far Eastern Collections in the East Asiatic Library of the University of California,' *Far Eastern Quarterly*, Vol. 14, No. 3 (May 1955), pp. 443–446.

1726   **'Oriental Collection of the University of California at Los Angeles,'** *Far Eastern Quarterly*, Vol. 15, No. 2 (February 1956), pp. 326–327.

1727   **Tsien, T. H.** 'The Far Eastern Library of the University of Chicago', *Far Eastern Quarterly*, Vol. 15, No. 3 (May 1956), pp. 473–475.

1728   **'The Wason Collection on China and the Chinese, Cornell University,'** *Far Eastern Quarterly*, Vol. 15, No. 2 (February 1956), pp. 322–324.

1729   **Chiu, A. Kaiming.** 'The Harvard-Yenching Institute Library,' *Far Eastern Quarterly*, Vol. 14, No. 1 (November 1954), pp. 147–152.

1730   **Elisseeff, Serge.** 'The Chinese-Japanese Library of the Harvard-Yenching Institute,' *Harvard Library Bulletin*, No. 10 (Winter 1956), pp. 73–93.

1731   **'Far Eastern Collections in the Hoover Library, Stanford University,'** *Far Eastern Quarterly*, Vol. 14, No. 3 (May 1955), pp. 446–447.

1732   **Nunn, G. Raymond.** 'Far Eastern Collections in the General Library of the University of Michigan,' *Far Eastern Quarterly*, Vol. 13, No. 3 (May 1954), pp. 380–382.

1733   **'Chinese, Japanese and South Asia Collection of the University of Pennsylvania,'** *Far Eastern Quarterly*, Vol. 15, No. 2 (February 1956), pp. 324–326.

1734   **Krader, Ruth.** 'The Far Eastern Library, University of Washington,' *Far Eastern Quarterly*, Vol. 15, No. 4 (August 1956), pp. 656–658.

2. TAIWAN, HONG KONG, AND THE MAINLAND

I. TAIWAN

1735   **Chung-yang t'u-shu kuan** 中央圖書館 (National Central Library). *Handbook of Current Research Projects on the Republic of China*. Taipei, 1962. 200p.

The handbook provides data on about 400 current research projects undertaken by individuals in Taiwan. Research topics are arranged alphabetically by title under the following subject classifications: (1) general works, (2) philosophy, (3) political science, (4) economics, (5) education, (6) sociology and customs, (7) social science miscellanea, (8) philology and literature, (9) mathematics, (10) physics, (11) chemistry, (12) geology, (13) botany, (14) natural science miscellanea, (15) medicine, (16) agriculture, (17) applied science miscellanea, (18) history, and (19) historical science miscellanea. The following information is given under each title: author's name, academic degree and rank, names of affiliated department and institution, and an outline of the research project. The section on agriculture is the longest, having a total of 139 projects listed. The social sciences and humanities account for about 100 projects.

A informative handbook, but it carries no author index and it suffers from typographical errors and an inadequate subject classification. A second edition, containing 505 entries, was published in 1964 (288p.).

See also *Directory of the Cultural Organizations of the Republic of China* (341).

1736 **Ko-ming shih-chien yen-chiu yüan, T'u-shu tzu-liao shih** 革命實踐研究院 圖書資料室 (National War College, Library). *Fei-ch'ing ts'an-k'ao shu mu-lu* 匪情參考書目錄 (Catalog of Books on Bandit Information). Taipei, 1949–1955. Irregular.

A catalog consisting mainly of Mainland publications. Each entry gives call number, author, title, date of publication, publisher, and number of volumes when applicable. The last issue of the catalog was dated December 1955. Superseded by the next entry.

1737 **Kuo-fang yen-chiu yüan, T'u-shu kuan** 國防研究院 圖書館 (National War College, Library). *Kuo-fang yen-chiu yüan ti-ch'ing tzu-liao mu-lu* 國防研究院敵情資料目錄 (A Catalog of Reference Materials on Enemy Information in the National War College). Yangmingshan, 1959. 1 vol.

A catalog of publications (books, newspapers and periodicals) collected between 1949 and 1959 by the Library of the National War College in Taiwan, from and about Communist China. Has been kept current by the next entry. Mimeographed. Limited distribution.

1738 **Kuo-fang yen-chiu yüan, T'u-shu kuan** 國防研究院圖書館 (National War College, Library). *Ti-ch'ing tzu-liao shuang-yüeh mu-lu* 敵情資料雙月目錄 (Bi-monthly Catalog of Reference Materials on Enemy Information). Yangmingshan, 1959—.

A current bi-monthly catalog of materials on Mainland China in the library of the National War College, updating the preceding entry, with the same arrangement. Mimeographed. Limited distribution.

As in the case of the preceding volume, the current catalog is particularly useful for following Nationalist Government publications on Chinese Communist developments.

1739 **Kuo-chi kuan-hsi yen-chiu hui** 國際關係研究會 (Institute of International Relations). *Chung-wen t'u-shu mu-lu* 中文圖書目錄 (Catalog of Chinese Books). Taipei, No. 1—, 1958—. Annual.

An annual catalog of Chinese-language holdings in the library of the Institute of International Relations in Taipei. Title entries are arranged under ten subject groups (general, social sciences, etc.). Both Communist and non-Communist publications, almost all post-1949 imprints, are included.

1740 **China, Ssu-fa hsing-cheng pu, Tiao-ch'a chü** 中華民國 司法行政部 調查局 (China, Ministry of Justice, Bureau of Investigation). *Li-nien sou-ts'ang fei-pao mu-lu* 歷年蒐藏匪報目錄 (A Catalog of Bandit Newspapers). Taipei, 1960. 12p.

A mimeographed catalog of sixty-six Chinese Communist newspapers in the library of the Bureau of Investigation of the Ministry of Justice in Taipei. All are post-1949 publications except three: the *Chieh-fang jih-pao* 解放日報 (Sian, 1936–1937), the *Chieh-fang jih-pao* (Yenan, 1941–1946), and the *Hsin-hua jih-pao* 新華日報 (Chungking, 1938–1948). The Bureau of Investigation holdings are indicated.

1741 **China, Ssu-fa hsing-cheng pu, Tiao-ch'a chü** 中華民國 司法行政部 調查局 (China, Ministry of Justice, Bureau of Investigation). *Li-nien sou-ts'ang fei-wei ch'i-k'an mu-lu, Ti-i ts'e* 歷年蒐藏匪偽期刊目錄, 第一冊 (A Catalog of Bandit and Puppet Periodicals, Vol. 1). Taipei, 1960. 60p.

A list of some 300 Mainland journals (with holdings) in the Library of the Bureau of Investigation. Mimeographed. Limited distribution.

1742 **Chung-kuo kuo-min tang, Chung-yang wei-yüan hui, Ti liu tsu** 中國國民黨 中央委員會 第六組 (Kuomintang, Central Committee, Sixth Section). *Ti liu tsu t'u-shu tzu-liao fen-lei mu-lu ch'u-pien* 第六組圖書資料分類目錄初編 (A Classified Catalog of Materials in the Library of the Sixth Section—First Compilation). Taipei, 1957. 2 vols.

The first volume is a catalog of books divided into three parts: general books (Taiwan imprints), Mainland books and foreign books (subdivided into Japanese and Western). The second volume lists the holdings of Mainland, Taiwan and Hong Kong newspapers and periodicals, clipping files and studies of Mainland developments, subdivided into monographic studies and charts.

1743 **T'ai-wan sheng wen-hsien wei-yüan hui** 臺灣省文獻委員會 (Taiwan [Provincial] Commission of Historical Research). *T'ai-wan sheng wen-hsien wei-yüan hui t'u-shu mu-lu* 臺灣省文獻委員會圖書目錄 (Catalog of Books in the Collection of the Taiwan Provincial Commission of Historical Research). Taipei, Series 1, 1960. 289p.

A catalog of the Commission's Chinese and Japanese collections as of December 1959. In two parts: Part 1 (168 pages) consists of more than 2,600 entries for materials on Taiwan; Part 2 (121 pages) contains more than 1,900 items drawn from the general collection. In addition to books, the volume includes periodicals, reprints of articles, maps, rubbings, and other similar materials. Each entry provides a classification number, title, number of volumes, author, publisher, and date of publication.

The volume supersedes a previous catalog prepared in March 1956 which contains some titles in English, French, and Latin. Mimeographed.

1744 Wu, Hsiang-hsiang.
Available Materials and Research Work on Sino-Soviet Relations in Taiwan.
[Los Angeles: University of Southern California, 1959.] 8p. (School of International Relations, Soviet-Asian Relations Conference, Conference Report).

A brief survey of the archival and source material in the Academia Sinica, the library of the Bureau of Investigation, and other libraries in Taiwan, and a short report on current research. Mimeographed.

1745 Mote, Frederick W.
'Recent Publication in Taiwan', *The Journal of Asian Studies*, Vol. 17, No. 4 (August 1958), pp. 595–606.

A survey of publishing in Taiwan, including descriptions of five private publishing houses and several official and semi-official agencies, together with their recent publications. A separate section entitled 'Serials and Journals' discusses a dozen or so periodicals published in Taiwan in Chinese and in English.

1746 Rowe, David Nelson.
'Recent Acquisitions of Chinese Diplomatic Archives, Institute of Modern History, Academia Sinica, Taiwan, Republic of China,' *The Journal of Asian Studies*. Vol. 16, No. 3 (May 1957), pp. 489–494.

1747 Kuo, Ting-yee.
'Institute of Modern History, Academia Sinica,' *The Journal of Asian Studies*, Vol. 19, No. 4 (August 1960), pp. 495–497.

1748 ——. *Historical Research in Taiwan.* 1963. 14p. Mimeographed.

1749 'Institute of Modern History of Academia Sinica,' *Newsletter of the Association for Asian Studies*, Vol. 9, No. 1 (October 1963), pp. 20–23.

II. HONG KONG

1750 Union Research Institute.
Index to the Classified Files on Communist China Held by the Union Research Institute. Hong Kong, 1962. 10; 197p.

An index to the collection of clippings from Chinese Communist periodicals and newspapers compiled by the Union Research Institute, superseding the *Index to the Material on Communist China Held by the Union Research Institute* published in 1957. The *Index* is arranged under five major departments: general, political and social, military, financial and economic, and cultural and educational. Each department is elaborately subdivided, and all entries are assigned a classification or index number.

The original clippings are on file at the Union Research Institute in Hong Kong. A microfilm copy of these clippings as well as a microfilm copy of the entire volume file from which the clippings are taken are available on loan through the Center for Research Libraries (formerly known as the Midwest Inter-Library Center) in Chicago. Microfilm copies are also available at the East-West Center of the University of Hawaii and the Center for Chinese Studies of the University of California in Berkeley.

1751 Union Research Institute.
Catalogue of Mainland Chinese Magazines and Newspapers Held by the Union Research Institute. Hong Kong, 1962. 64; 116p.

Published in March 1962, the catalog includes periodicals and newspapers published in Communist China and acquired by the Union Research Institute as of the end of 1961. It supersedes a similar list published in 1957 as a supplement to the *Index to the Material on Communist China Held by the Union Research Institute*, and the *List of Mainland Chinese Magazines Contained in the Microfile of Union Research Institute, January 1961*. In two parts: Part 1, 'Mainland Chinese Magazines' (pp. M 1–64); Part 2, 'Mainland Chinese Newspapers' (pp. N 1–116). Entries in both parts are arranged alphabetically by romanized title, with translation, Chinese characters, frequency and U.R.I. holdings. A second edition was issued in July 1963 which brings the coverage through 1962.

1752 United States Information Service, Hong Kong, Research Library.
[List of Books in the U.S. Information Service Research Library. Hong Kong, 1962.] 42p.

Arranged alphabetically by title under the following sections: (1) China (historical China, Communist China, fiction, philosophy and religion); (2) Asia (general, Tibet, Malaya, Hong Kong, Taiwan, Japan, India); (3) Soviet Union; (4) miscellaneous; (5) reference books; and (6) Communist China's foreign-language publications (documents and reports, developments in Communist China, theoretical and political studies, Mao's works, education and literature, novels and stories, plays and operas, picture books). The listing in the last section is quite complete.

1753 Peace Book Company.
Complete Catalogue of Books from China (in English) 1964. Hong Kong, 1964. 42p.

A convenient listing of some 450 English-language items (with author and title also given in Chinese but without annotations) imported by the company from Communist China for sale in Hong Kong and elsewhere. While the purpose of this catalog is to promote sales, it nevertheless serves as a useful guide to Mainland publications as of early 1964.

More recent books are listed and annotated in *Book News*, published periodically by the same company.

III. MAINLAND

1754 **'Wo-kuo shih-nien lai ti t'u-shu kuan shih-yeh'** 我國十年來的圖書館事業 (Library Service in Our Country During the Last Ten Years) in *Pei-ching ta-hsüeh hsüeh-pao—Jen-wen k'o-hsüeh* 北京大學學報——人文科學 (Journal of Peking University—Humanities), 1959 No. 4, pp. 93–107. Translated into English and published in the *Union Research Service*, Vol. 19, Nos. 8 and 10 (April 26 and May 3, 1960).

1755 **Cheng, Chi.**
'Libraries in China Today,' *Libri*, Vol. 9, No. 2 (1959), pp. 105–110.

1756 **Rafikov, A.**
'In Chinese Libraries,' *Special Libraries*, Vol. 51, No. 10 (December 1960), pp. 527–532, or 'Libraries of China,' *LLU Translations Bulletin*, Vol. 2, No. 3 (March 1960), pp. 176–189.

Translations of an article by the Deputy Director of the Library of the Academy of Sciences of the U.S.S.R., written upon his return from a trip to China for the Soviet bibliographical journal *Bibliotekar*' (The Librarian), 1959 No. 9, pp. 47–51.

See also Mainland library journals (**911** ff.) and the section on library science in Chapter I (**147** ff.).

1757 **Chung-kuo jen-min ta-hsüeh, T'u-shu kuan** 中國人民大學 圖書館 (Chinese People's University, Library). *T'u-shu fen-lei fa* 圖書分類法 (Classification Scheme). Third edition, eighth printing. Peking: Chung-kuo jen-min ta-hsüeh ch'u-pan she 中國人民大學出版社, 1957. 736p.

The classification scheme—a decimal system—is arranged in seventeen classes: Marxism-Leninism and works by Mao Tse-tung; philosophy; dialectical materialism and historical materialism; social science and political science; economics, political economy, and economic policy; national defense and military affairs; state and law and jurisprudence; culture and education; fine arts; language and philology; literature; history and revolutionary history; geography and economic geography; natural sciences; medicine and health; engineering and technology, agricultural science, animal husbandry and fishery; reference works. A detailed stroke index arranged by subject.

This classification system is the one most widely used by libraries in Communist China. Also used in the cumulative national bibliography and the Index to Major Newspapers and Periodicals. The first edition appeared in 1953.

1758   Chung-kuo k'o-hsüeh yüan, T'u-shu kuan 中國科學院 圖書館 (Chinese Academy of Sciences, Library). *Chung-kuo k'o-hsüeh yüan t'u-shu kuan t'u-shu fen-lei fa* 中國科學院圖書館圖書分類法 (Classification Scheme of the Library of the Chinese Academy of Sciences). Peking: K'o-hsüeh ch'u-pan she 科學出版社, 1959. (First printing 1958.) 13; 259p.

A decimal system based on 'scientific Marxism-Leninism' and the practical needs of the libraries of the Chinese Academy of Sciences. In twenty-five classes: Marxism-Leninism, philosophy, social sciences (general), history and historical science, economics and economic science, politics and social conditions, state and law and jurisprudence, military art and science, culture and education, language and philology, literature, fine arts, religion and atheism, natural sciences (general), mathematics, mechanics, physics, chemistry, astronomy, geology, and geographical science, physiological science, medical science and health, agricultural science, science and technology, reference works. No index.

1759   Guozi Shudian 國際書店 (International Book Company). *Catalogue of Chinese Books Available in English.* Peking, 1960. 82p.

An annotated catalog covering some 300 books in English published on the Mainland up to 1960. The year of publication is not listed. Title index. More recent books are listed in *Publication News from China*, which usually annotates a number of recently published books.

The Guozi Shudian also publishes special catalogs from time to time, such as the *Catalogue of Mao Tse-tung's Theoretical Works on Literature and Art and Selections from Contemporary Chinese Literature* (1962), 40p., and *Book Catalogue: Works of Mao Tse-tung, Political Treatises, Documents, Books on International Affairs* (1963), 46p.

See also **1753**.

3. JAPAN

1760   Muramatsu, Yūji.
Japanese Studies of Contemporary China. Los Angeles: University of Southern California, 1959. 39p. (School of International Relations, Soviet-Asian Relations Conference, Report No. 7).

A survey of the origin and background of Japanese scholarly interest in China and Communism, accompanied by sections on training (Chinese language and study of modern China), library resources, research (academic institututions, government agencies, independent research centers, and professional, political, business and cultural organizations), publications, personnel resources and conclusions.

The section on library resources provides brief descriptions of some fifteen principal collections of Chinese materials in Japan. The section on research gives thumbnail sketches of some thirty-five research centers concerned with China. The appendices list some ninety China specialists classified by discipline and affiliation and contain bio-bibliographical sketches of eighteen representative scholars from each academic discipline, and researchers from the Foreign Ministry, the China Research Institute, the newspapers, etc. Except for recently established research centers such as the Institute of Asian Economic Affairs, the Japan Institute for the Study of International Problems sponsored by the Ministry of Foreign Affairs, and the Seminar on Twentieth-Century China at the Tōyō Bunko, the survey gives a full picture of modern Chinese studies in Japan. Mimeographed.

A Soviet view of 'Chinese Studies in Contemporary Japan' by S. L. Tikhvinskii appears as a supplement (see **1762**).

1761 **Banno, Masataka, et al.**
'Development of China Studies in Postwar Japan,' *The Developing Economies*, Preliminary Issue No. 2 (September-December 1962), pp. 57–98.

A collection of three articles on the subject with a foreword by Professor Banno. All three articles contain numerous citations to Japanese books and articles on China.

The first article, entitled 'China Study Institutions', by Akira Doi, provides brief descriptions of two academic associations and some fifteen research organizations and institutes wholly or in part concerned with Chinese affairs. It also contains a detailed table of contents of the 1962 edition of *Chūgoku seiji keizai sōran—Political and Economic Views on Present Day China* described in Chapter IV (**202**). The second article on political studies of modern China by Hiroharu Seki presents a picture of the prewar situation, postwar trends and future prospects. Professor Tadao Miyashita concerns himself with the development of studies on the Communist Chinese economy in postwar Japan. A list of about eighty Japanese specialists on the Chinese economy (along with the name of the institution with which each is affiliated and his field of interest) is appended. (An up-dated and revised version appeared in *Asian Studies in Japan*, published by the Society for Asian Political and Economic Studies in 1964, pp. 7–28.)

This is the latest survey of Japanese studies on China which partially updates the preceding entry.

1762 **Tikhvinskii, S. L.** 'Kitaevedenie v sovremennoi Iaponii'
(Chinese Studies in Contemporary Japan), *Sovetskoe kitaevedenie* (Soviet Journal of Chinese Studies), No. 1 (1958), pp. 223–229.

A brief survey of Chinese studies in Japan prepared by the director of the Soviet Institute of Chinese Studies in Moscow, based on the ten-year review of the activity of the China Research Institute and other institutional publications. The article covers a number of Japanese institutions, scholars and publications.

A translation of this article appears as a supplement to Muramatsu's *Japanese Studies of Contemporary China* (see **1760**).

1763 Vinogradova, T. V. 'Organizatsiia kitaevedeniia v Iaponii'
(The Structure of Chinese Studies in Japan), *Kratkie soobshcheniia Instituta narodov Azii* (Short Reports of the Institute of the Peoples of Asia), Vol. 66 (1963), pp. 126–139.

A general survey of prewar and postwar Chinese studies in Japan. Updates the information contained in the Tikhvinskii article (see preceding entry), stressing 'the penetration of the American dollar into the field of Chinese studies in Japan'.

1764 Enoki, Kazuo, ed.
Recent Trends of East Asian Studies in Japan with Bibliography. Tokyo: The Centre for East Asian Cultural Studies, 1962. 329p.

A survey of postwar trends in all branches of East Asian studies in Japan (including Chinese studies), augmented in each case by selected bibliographies of important publications. In twenty-one topical chapters: Chinese philosophy with an appendix on Chinese epigraphy; ethics; prehistory and archeology; Eastern history—largely Chinese history (pp. 111–140); geography; politics; law; economics; Chinese language (pp. 260–269); Chinese literature (pp. 309–322); etc.

1765 Chūgoku Kenkyūjo 中國研究所 (China Research Institute). *Jūnen no ayumi* 十年のあゆみ
(Ten Years of the China Research Institute). Tokyo, [1956]. 30p.

A brief history of the China Research Institute and its activities. All publications of the Institute (books as well as periodicals) and the titles of the monographic series *Chūgoku shiryō geppō* 中國資料月報 (Monthly Report on Chinese Sources) are listed in the appendix. Mimeographed. The Institute is the leading privately-supported Japanese research organization concerned with Communist China. The publications of the Institute betray a pro-Chinese Communist orientation.

1766 Tōyō Bunka Kenkyūjo yōran 東洋文化研究所要覽
(Handbook of the Institute for Oriental Culture). Tokyo, 1957. 110p.

A complete review of the objectives, history, organization, personnel, library resources, research activities and publications of the Institute for Oriental

Culture, Tokyo University, for the first fifteen years of its existence (November 1941 to 1957). The contents include a list of publications by the staff of the Institute (pp. 40–59); tables of contents of the first eleven issues of *Tōyō Bunka Kenkyūjo kiyō* 東洋文化研究所紀要 *The Memoirs of the Institute for Oriental Culture* (pp. 60–64); a list of the 323 Institute seminars conducted from January 1947 to July 1956 with the names of lecturers and dates (pp. 65–80); an index to the eleven issues of *Tōyō bunka kenkyū—The Oriental Culture Review* for 1944–1949 (pp. 85–88); an index to the first twenty-one issues of *Tōyō bunka—Oriental Culture* for 1950–1956 (pp. 88–93).

The volume originally appeared as a supplement to No. 12 of the *Memoirs*, which bore the title *Sōritsu jūgo shūnen kinen ronshū* 創立十五週年紀念論集 (Collection of Articles in Commemoration of the Fifteenth Anniversary of the Founding of the Institute). A similar handbook, compiled on the occasion of the tenth anniversary (51p.), was published in 1952, and, in addition, appeared as a supplement to No. 3 of the *Memoirs*.

See also *Kyōto Daigaku, Jimbun Kagaku Kenkyūjo yōran* 京都大學人文科學研究所要覽 (Handbook of the Research Institute for Humanistic Studies, Kyoto University), No. 1 (1951), Kyoto, 1952, 52p.; *Tōyō Bunko nempō—Shōwa 30-nendo* 東洋文庫年報——昭和三十年度 (The Tōyō Bunko Annual Report for 1955—) 1957—; and Andō Hikotarō 安藤彦太郎, 'Nihon ni okeru Chūgoku kenkyū to Waseda Daigaku' 日本における中國研究と早稻田大學 (Chinese Studies in Japan and Waseda University) in *Waseda seiji keizaigaku zasshi* 早稻田政治經濟學雜誌 (Waseda Journal of Politics and Economics), No. 10 (1962).

1767 Enoki, Kazuo, ed.
Research Institutes for Asian Studies in Japan. Tokyo: Centre for East Asian Cultural Studies, 1962. 110p. (Directories No. 1).

A directory of Japanese institutions in the Asian field based on *Zenkoku kenkyū kikan sōran* (全國研究機關綜覽 [General Survey of Research Institutions in Japan] published by the Japan Council for the Promotion of Science in 1959), as well as on the publications of the institutions concerned, and returned questionnaires. Lists ninety-six research institutes and museums classified under twelve categories (general, philosophy, political science and law, economics and business administration, etc.). For each institution the following information is provided: the name in romanization and in translation, address, name of the director, number of staff members, date of establishment, purpose, organization and major activities, a brief note on library facilities, and a list of publications. East Asian studies are emphasized in the description of major activities and publications. A selected classified list of fifty-one learned societies is appended.

A number of institutions and associations in the modern China field, such as China Research Institute (Chūgoku Kenkyūjo), the Tōyō Bunko, Society for Asian Political and Economic Studies (Ajia Seikei Gakkai), and Aichi University's Institute of International Affairs (Kokusai Mondai Kenkyūjo), are included.

1768   Japanese National Commission for UNESCO.
Directory of Researchers and Research Institutes on Oriental Studies in Japan.
Tokyo, 1957. 50p.

Covers Japanese research in the fields of Asian (including Japanese) history, archeology, literature, religion, philosophy, arts, ethnology and folklore, and lists a number of Japanese scholars in the Chinese field, including contemporary China.

In five parts: (1) universities—30 institutions; (2) research institutes—9; (3) libraries—11; (4) museums—11; (5) learned societies—60. Within each part the arrangement is in alphabetical order by name of institution. It should be noted that while university libraries and museums are listed under the appropriate university, most of the research institutes attached to universities are listed in the Research Institutes section.

The following data is provided: (a) for the universities, the address and a list of faculty members (arranged by department and within department according to rank), together with their fields of specialization; (b) for research institutes, also a brief history, purpose and publications; (c) for learned societies, address, purpose and publications.

1769   International House Library.
A Brief Guide to Japanese Library Resources. [Tokyo], 1960. 23p.

Largely devoted to the description of some forty governmental and academic libraries. In six parts: general, area studies, science and technology, medicine, bookstores, and museums. The following information is provided for the libraries: name in romanization, with Chinese characters and translation; address and telephone number; hours of service; and a brief note on history of the institution, its outstanding collections and fields of concentration. Mimeographed.

A revised edition, entitled *A List of Libraries and Museums*, was issued in 1962 (10p.).

See also another compilation of Miss Naomi Fukuda, Librarian of the International House: *List of Major Second-hand Book Stores in Tokyo*, revised edition (1962), 16p.

1770   Enoki, Kazuo, ed.
Japanese Researchers in Asian Studies. Tokyo: The Centre for East Asian Cultural Studies, 1963. 281p. (Directories No. 2).

Companion volume to *Research Institutes for Asian Studies in Japan* (see **1767**) containing personal information on about 4,000 individual research workers in the humanities and the social sciences on Asia, listed alphabetically according to the field of study (e.g., history—Japan, history—other Asian countries; law and politics; economy; language and literature—China; etc.).

Each entry provides the name (in romanization and Chinese characters); date of birth; academic degree, position and institution; year of graduation and alma mater; present address; and area of specialization. Alphabetical index of researchers. A list of some 450 academic institutions mentioned in the volume (with addresses and telephone numbers) is appended.

Covers more persons but provides fewer details than the survey conducted by the International House (see next entry).

1771 **Kokusai Kankei, Chiiki Kenkyū Genjō Chōsa Iinkai** 國際關係, 地域研究現狀調查委員會 (Committee for the Investigation of International Relations and Area Studies [in Japan]), comp. *Kokusai kankei oyobi chiiki kenkyū no genjō—chōsa hōkoku* 國際關係および地域研究の現狀──調查報告
(The Present Status of International Relations and Area Studies [in Japan]—A Survey Report). Tokyo: Kokusai Bunka Kaikan 國際文化會館, 1962. 43; 335p.

Supported by the Ford Foundation and conducted at the International House of Japan from 1958 to 1962, this survey is based on questionnaires sent out to some 900 scholars and over 100 universities, scholarly associations and research institutes. The introductory part consists of a quantitative analysis of international relations and area studies in Japan (with fourteen statistical tables); a list of thirty-nine universities and nine governmental and private research institutes and scholarly associations, providing information on their major research projects; and a list of the principal research resources of the libraries of forty-four universities and four research institutes. The body of the survey (pp. 1–226) contains data on some 900 scholars (arranged alphabetically), in each case giving date of birth; address; affiliation, including department and rank; alma mater; discipline and area of specialization; major publications; present research topics; courses taught; languages; and foreign study, travel and experience.

There are two indexes, one by discipline (international politics, international law, history, literature, etc.) and the other by area (Asia general, East Asia [including China], the Soviet Union, Latin America, etc.), each providing the name in romanization and characters, affiliation and rank, area of specialization, discipline, and page number.

The most comprehensive survey of its kind. Separate statistics are available for Chinese language proficiency, but none for Chinese studies.

1772 **Tōyō Bunko Tōyōgaku Infuomēshon-Sentā** 東洋文庫, 東洋學インフオメーション=センター (The Tōyō Bunko, The Information Center of Asian Studies), comp. *Nihon ni okeru Kanseki no shūshū—Kanseki kankei mokuroku shūsei*, 日本における漢籍の蒐集──漢籍關係目錄集成
Collections of Chinese Books in Japan—A Catalogue of Catalogues of Chinese Books in Public and Private Collections. Tokyo, 1961. 202; 10p. (Studies on Asia in Japan II).

A bibliography of 2,600 library catalogs, bibliographies, book exhibit catalogs and similar lists of Chinese books prepared in Japan from the Tokugawa period to June 1961. The entries include books and periodical articles wholly or partially listing Chinese books. The arrrangement is according to types of libraries (public libraries; libraries of government agencies, business companies, etc.; special libraries, including those in temples and shrines; university libraries, etc.) and types of lists (bibliographies, book exhibit catalogs). In each case full bibliographical citation is provided, including location symbols. Index to libraries at the end of the volume is arranged according to the Japanese syllabary.

This is the most comprehensive listing of catalogs and bibliographies of Chinese books, and has been prepared as a first step toward the compilation of a union catalog of Chinese books in Japan.

For a catalog of Chinese books at Kyoto University, see *Kyōto Daigaku, Jimbun Kagaku Kenkyūjo kanseki bunrui mokuroku* 京都大學人文科學研究所漢籍分類目錄 (Classified Catalog of Chinese Books at the Institute for Humanistic Studies, Kyoto University), 1963, in two volumes, the second being an index to authors and titles.

1773   **Tōhō Gakkai** 東方學會 (Institute of Eastern Culture). *Kin hyakunenrai Chūgoku bun bunken genzai shomoku* 近百年來中國文文獻現在書目 (Union List of Chinese Publications of the Last Hundred Years in Japan). Tokyo, 1957. 838p.

A union list of approximately twenty thousand Chinese books and periodicals (published between 1851 and 1954) housed in the National Diet Library, the Department of Chinese Literature and Philosophy of Tokyo University, the Institute for Oriental Culture of Tokyo University, and the Oriental Library (Tōyō Bunko 東洋文庫). Arranged by title according to the Japanese syllabary. Location symbols are supplied.

Appendix 1 (pp. 771–800) is a catalog of the library of the Seminar on Modern China, Tōyō Bunko, containing 720 titles on modern China. Appendix 2 (pp. 801–838) is a catalog of the Kamiyama Collection of the Department of Chinese Literature and Philosophy of Tokyo University, listing about 900 prewar Chinese publications. Mimeographed.

An up-to-date union catalog of twentieth century Chinese-language books in Japan is under preparation at the Tōyō Bunko for the Institute of Asian Economic Affairs.

1774   **Japan, Mombushō, Daigaku Gakujutsukyoku** 日本文部省大學學術局 (Japan, Ministry of Education, Bureau of Higher Education and Science). *Ajia chiiki sōgō kenkyū bunken mokuroku* アジア地域綜合研究文獻目錄 (Union List of Research Materials on Asia). Tokyo: Nihon Gakujutsu Shin-kōkai 日本學術振興會, Vol. 1—, 1959—. Irregular.

A list of books and pamphlets on Asia in Western European, Russian and Chinese languages acquired by eighteen research libraries including Chūgoku Kenkyūjo (China Research Institute), Tōyō Bunko, Tōyō Bunka Kenkyūjo, Kyoto University, and Aichi University.

Vol. 1 contains acquisitions reported to the Ministry of Education as of February 1959, while Vol. 5 lists those reported by November of 1962. The materials are divided into three language groups (Western European, Russian and Chinese languages), and within those groups by area and country. (Communist China and Taiwan are listed separately). Within the country category, entries are arranged according to the Nippon Decimal Classification and further alphabetically by author. Three alphabetical author's indexes: Western-languages, Russian, and Chinese (the latter arranged according to the Japanese pronunciation of the Chinese author's name).

1775 Tōyōgaku Bunken Sentā Renraku Kyōgikai 東洋學文獻センター連絡協議會 (Liaison Conference of Bibliographical Centers in the Field of Oriental Studies), comp. *Nihon bun, Chūgoku bun, Chōsen bun nado chikuji kankōbutsu mokuroku* 日本文, 中國文, 朝鮮文等逐次刊行物目錄 (A Catalog of Periodical Publications in Japanese, Chinese, Korean and other Languages). Tokyo: Tōyō Bunko 東洋文庫, March 1964. 178p.

A union catalog of Japanese, Chinese, Korean, Uighur, Tibetan and Mongol periodicals in the collections of the Tōyō Bunko (including the Seminar on Modern China), the Institute for Oriental Culture of Tokyo University, and the Research Institute for Humanistic Studies of Kyoto University. The catalog generally follows the pattern of the following entry (expanded to include Japanese, Korean and other publications) and extended to include the holdings to the end of 1962. Daily newspapers and yearbooks are excluded, but not journals published annually.

In three parts: Japanese periodicals (92p.), Chinese (66p.) and Korean. The appendix lists Uighur, Tibetan and Mongol periodicals. Stroke and P'in-yin indexes to Chinese titles. The arrangement in each part is by title according to the Japanese syllabary, with Chinese titles being listed according to their Japanese pronunciation (for example, *Hokukei* for Peking, *Shokai* for Shanghai). In addition to the title, each entry provides the editor, place of publication, publisher and the holdings of the four institutions.

1776 Kindai Chūgoku Kenkyū Iinkai 近代中國研究委員會 (Seminar on Modern China). *Nihon shuyō kenkyū kikan toshokan shozō Chūgokubun shimbun zasshi sōgō mokuroku* 日本主要研究機關圖書館所藏中國文新聞雜誌總合目錄 (Union List of Chinese-Language Newspapers and Periodicals in the Principal Japanese Research Libraries). Tokyo: Tōyō Bunko nai Kindai Chūgoku Kenkyū Iinkai 東洋文庫內近代中國研究委員會, 1959. 171p.

A union list of Chinese newspapers and periodicals (mostly post-1911 publications) published through the end of 1957, located in twenty-three Japanese university and research libraries, largely in the Tokyo area. Entries are arranged by title according to the Japanese pronunciation of the Chinese title in syllabic order, and provide title, frequency, place of publication, publisher and location symbols. Two indexes: (1) stroke and (2) alphabetic according to the Chinese pronunciation.

For more recent acquisitions of the Tōyō Bunko, see the next entries.

1777 **Kindai Chūgoku Kenkyū Iinkai** 近代中國研究委員會 (Seminar on Modern China). *Tōyō Bunko shinshū Chūgokubun shimbun zasshi mokuroku* 東洋文庫新收中國文新聞雜誌目錄

(List of Chinese-Language Newspapers and Periodicals Acquired by the Tōyō Bunko). Tokyo: Tōyō Bunko nai Kindai Chūgoku Kenkyū Iinkai 東洋文庫內近代中國研究委員會, 1961. 27p.

Updates the Tōyō Bunko holdings as given in the preceding entry for the period January 1958 to November 1961.

The list contains some 290 titles arranged, as in the previous volume, according to the Japanese syllabary and the Japanese pronunciation of the Chinese title. Entries provide title of the newspaper or periodical, newly acquired issue numbers and dates of publication. An errata sheet for the original Union List is appended. See also the next entries.

1778 **Kindai Chūgoku Kenkyū Sentā** 近代中國研究センター (Center for Modern Chinese Studies), comp. *Tōyō Bunko Kindai Chūgoku Kenkyūshitsu Chūbun tosho mokuroku* 東洋文庫近代中國研究室中文圖書目錄

(Catalog of Chinese Books in the Modern China Research Office of the Tōyō Bunko). Tokyo, 1965. 26; 207p.

A catalog of close to 5,000 Chinese books in the collection of the Seminar on Modern China, Tōyō Bunko, as of December 1963 (excluding books in Chinese binding and those in the general collection of the Tōyō Bunko). In two parts: (1) the catalog part arranged by author (pp. 1–166) providing complete bibliographical entry including size and call number; (2) title index (pp. 167–207). Both parts are arranged in Japanese syllabic order according to the Japanese reading of Chinese characters. Three indexes to Chinese characters: Wade-Giles, P'in-yin, and stroke count.

1779 **Kindai Chūgoku Kenkyū Sentā** 近代中國研究センター (Center for Modern Chinese Studies), comp. *Tōyō Bunko Kindai Chūgoku Kenkyūshitsu hōbun tosho mokuroku* 東洋文庫近代中國研究室邦文圖書目錄

(Catalog of Japanese Books in the Modern China Research Office of the Tōyō Bunko). Tokyo, July 1963. 204p.

A catalog of some 4,000 Japanese books on modern China in the collection of the Seminar on Modern China, Tōyō Bunko, as of December 1962 (a classified catalog of books on modern China throughout the Tōyō Bunko is under preparation). In two parts: (1) the catalog part arranged by author (pp. 1–143), providing complete bibliographical citation, including size and call number; (2) title index (pp. 145–204). Both parts are arranged according to the Japanese syllabary.

Tōyō Bunko Ōbun tosho mokuroku 東洋文庫歐文圖書目録 (Catalog of European-Language Books in the Toyo Bunko) covering acquisitions from November 1954 to March 1962 was published in 1962 (67p.).

1780 **Tōyō Bunko shinchaku tosho mokuroku** 東洋文庫新着圖書目録
(Catalog of New Acquisitions in the Tōyō Bunko). Tokyo: Tōyō Bunko Shiryōshitsu 東洋文庫資料室, No. 1—; 1960—. Quarterly.

An acquisitions report on Chinese, Japanese and Western books purchased by the Tōyō Bunko. Does not always appear at quarterly intervals.

See also *Kindai Chūgoku Kenkyū Sentā ihō* (Bulletin of the Center for Modern Chinese Studies, **1155**) for current acquisitions of the Seminar on Modern China.

1781 **Chūgoku Chōsen tosho sokuhō** 中國朝鮮圖書速報
Accession List: Chinese and Korean Language Publications. Tokyo: Kokuritsu Kokkai Toshokan 國立國會圖書館, No. 1—, 1956—. Irregular.

A mimeographed publication listing all the current acquisitions of the National Diet Library from China (Mainland and Taiwan) and North and South Korea. Arranged according to the Nippon Decimal Classification with full bibliographical citations, including the Library's call number. Issues of newly-received periodicals from China and Korea are listed in an appendix as they are received. Limited distribution.

Chinese-language acquisitions are also listed in the general yearly *Shūsho tsūhō* 收書通報 (Acquisitions List) published by the National Diet Library.

1782 **'Chūken toshokan ukeire tosho'** 中研圖書館受入圖書
(List of Accessions to the Library of China Research Institute), *Ajia keizai jumpō* アジア經濟旬報 (Ten-Day Report on Asian Economy).

An irregular feature of the journal appearing roughly once a month, listing the most recent Chinese, Japanese and Western-language acquisitions. Particularly useful for Chinese Mainland publications.

1783 **Torii, Hisayasu** 鳥居久靖. 'Kokunai kan tōhōshi nempyō—sengo no bu' 國內刊東方誌年表──戰後の部
(Chronology of Japanese Journals in the Oriental Field—Postwar), *Tenri Daigaku gakuhō*, 天理大學學報 (Journal of Tenri University), Tenri, Nara Prefecture, No. 27 (November 1958), pp. 115-126.

A companion article to the author's list of postwar Japanese periodicals in the Oriental field published in the preceding issue of the same journal (see **177**). Provides in chronological order the following information on some 200 Japanese postwar periodicals in the Oriental field: name of periodical, publisher or compiler and other bibliographical information, including the dates of the first and last issues.

ADDITIONAL REFERENCES

1784 **Japan, Economic Stabilization Board** (Keizai Antei Hombu, Kambō Chōsaka 經濟安定本部官房調查課). *Chūgoku kankei chōsa kikan yōran* 中國關係調查機關要覽 (Handbook of Research Organizations Concerned with China). Tokyo, 1947. 23p.

1785 **Yamamoto, Tatsuro.** 'Japan: Postwar Oriental Studies', *Far Eastern Quarterly*, Vol. 11, No. 1 (November 1951), pp. 118–119.

1786 **Jansen, Marius B.** 'Notes on Japanese Universities,' *Far Eastern Quarterly*, Vol. 12, No. 2 (February 1953), pp. 244–254.

1787 **Fujieda, Akira and Fairbank, Wilma.** 'Current Trends in Japanese Studies of China and Adjacent Areas,' *Far Eastern Quarterly*, Vol. 13, No. 1 (November 1953), pp. 37–47.

1788 **Honda, M. and Ceadel, E. B.** 'Post-war Japanese Research on the Far East (Excluding Japan),' *Asia Major*, New Series, Vol. 4, No. 1 (August 1954), pp. 103–148.

1789 **Berton, Peter, Langer, Paul and Swearingen, Rodger.** *Japanese Training and Research in the Russian Field.* Los Angeles, 1956. 266p. (Far Eastern and Russian Research Series, No. 1, School of International Relations, University of Southern California).

1790 **Etō, Shinkichi.** 'Asian Studies in Japan: Recent Trends,' *The Journal of Asian Studies*, Vol. 21, No. 1 (November 1961), pp. 125–133.

1791 **KDK Kōjimachi Institute** KDK 麴町研究所 (KDK Kōjimachi Kenkyūjo). *Nihon no kyōsanken kenkyū kikan to kenkyū dantai* 日本の共產圈研究機關と研究團體 (Japanese Institutions and Groups for the Study of the Communist Bloc). Tokyo, July 1964. 33p. Mimeographed.

1792 **Shakai Undō Chōsakai** 社會動運調查會 (Society for the Study of Social Movements). *Sayoku dantai jiten '64* 左翼團體事典 (The 1964 Handbook of Left-Wing Organizations). Tokyo: Musashi Shobō 武藏書房, 1963. 528; 10p.

1793 **Tōyō Bunko Tōyōgaku Infuomēshon-Sentā** 東洋文庫東洋學インフォメーション=センター (The Tōyō Bunko, The Information Center of Asian Studies). *Nihon no daigaku ni okeru Ajia jimbun, shakai kagaku kankei no kōgi—*

1958 nendo—Nihon ni okeru Ajia kenkyū no genjō chōsa I 日本の大學における
アジア人文社會科學關係の講義──1958年度──日本におけるアジア研究の
現狀調査 *Courses on Asia in the Humanities and Social Sciences Given in
Japanese Universities, 1958-59 Academic Year. Studies on Asia in Japan I.*
Tokyo, 1960. 24; 151; 17p.

1794 Chōsa kikan toshokan sōran 調查機關圖書館綜覽 *Directory of Research
Libraries.* Tokyo: Semmon Toshokan Kyōgikai, 1956. 17; 375; 76p.

See also the Fairbank-Banno guide (**41**).

4. THE SOVIET UNION

1795 Tveritinova, A. S., comp. *Vostokovednye fondy krupneishikh bibliotek Sovets-
kogo Soiuza*
(Oriental Collections of the Largest Libraries of the Soviet Union). Moscow:
Izdatel'stvo Vostochnoi Literatury, 1963. 239p.

A collection of articles describing the holdings of Oriental books, periodicals
and manuscripts in twelve major Soviet libraries: university libraries, state
public libraries, provincial research libraries, and the Academy of Sciences
libraries. In the case of the Moscow and Leningrad Libraries of the Institute
of the Peoples of Asia separate articles describe the various area collections,
including the following three: (1) Z. I. Gorbacheva and N. A. Petrov, 'Kitaiskii
fond' (Chinese Collection), pp. 26-29; (2) L. N. Men'shikov, 'Kitaiskie
rukopisi' (Chinese Manuscripts), pp. 51-53 (both located in the Leningrad
branch library); and (3) V. P. Zhuravleva and A. S. Kostiaeva, 'Sinologicheskaia
biblioteka Instituta Narodov Azii' (The Sinological Library of the Institute of
the Peoples of Asia [in Moscow]), pp. 101-109. Also worth mentioning are the
Chinese collections in the Lenin State Library, the State Library of Foreign
Literature, the State Library of Historical Literature, and the library of Moscow
University—all in Moscow; the Leningrad Public Library and the library of
the University of Leningrad.

The articles are very uneven and have not been uniformly structured. In
addition, a number of important research libraries have not been covered.
Nonetheless this publication represents the best overall survey of Chinese-
language and area collections in the Soviet Union. A very critical review of
this publication by Iu. E. Bregel' and B. L. Riftin appeared in the No. 1, 1964
issue of *Narody Azii i Afriki* (The Peoples of Asia and Africa), pp. 202-206.

1796 Muramatsu, Yūji 村松祐次. *Kaigai ni okeru saikin no Chūgoku kenkyū no
jōkyō* 海外における最近の中國研究の狀況
Recent Research on China Abroad. Tokyo: Ajia Keizai Kenkyūjo アジア經濟研
究所, 1963. 155p. (Ajia keizai kenkyū shiriizu, No. 45 [Asian Economic
Research Series, No. 45]).

A world survey of Chinese studies (excluding Japan), with the United States and the Soviet Union each occupying roughly one-third of the book. In five chapters: (1) recent trends in Chinese studies abroad; (2) the study of China in the United States; (2) the study of China in the Soviet Union; (3) the study of China in Great Britain, France, Germany and other countries; and (5) concluding remarks. The background and characteristics of Chinese studies are given for each area. The survey provides descriptions of some fifty governmental, academic and other research and training institutions, scholarly organizations and libraries. In addition, there are numerous bibliographical citations to pertinent publications in the Chinese field. Alphabetical personal name and general indexes.

Contains a good deal of information collected during the author's residence and travels in the United States and Europe in 1957–1960 and again in the fall of 1962.

1797 Swearingen, Rodger.
Soviet Training and Research on Asia. Los Angeles: University of Southern California, 1959. 24p. (School of International Relations, Soviet-Asian Relations Conference, Report No. 1).

A survey of Soviet training, research, library and personnel resources in the Asian field. The report contains descriptions of the programs of the Department of Oriental Studies, University of Leningrad; the Institute of Oriental Languages, University of Moscow; the Tashkent Institute of Oriental Studies; and the Institute of Oriental Studies (now called the Institute of the Peoples of Asia) of the U.S.S.R. Academy of Sciences, in Moscow; the Institute's Leningrad branch; the Institute of Chinese Studies in Moscow; the Lenin Library in Moscow. A list of other libraries is included along with a section on Soviet specialists and publications on Asia (including a separate page on China, p. 16). Mimeographed.

Preliminary version of this report appeared in the 'News of the Profession' *The Journal of Asian Studies*, Vol. 17, No. 3 (May 1958), pp. 515–537.

1798 Novaia sovetskaia i inostrannaia literatura po stranam Zarubezhnogo Vostoka
(New Soviet and Foreign Literature on the Countries of the Non-Soviet East). Moscow: Fundamental'naia biblioteka obshchestvennykh nauk AN SSSR, 1947–1959; 1960—. Monthly.

One of twenty-odd acquisitions bulletins published by the Fundamental Library of the Social Sciences of the Soviet Academy of Sciences in Moscow, this monthly lists materials in all languages on Asia and Africa received by the Fundamental Library, the Lenin Library, the State Library of Foreign Literature, the library of the Institute of World Economics and International Relations and the library of the Institute of the Peoples of Asia. It absorbed *Novye inostrannye knigi po vostokovedeniiu postupivshie v biblioteki SSSR* (New Foreign Books in the Oriental Field Accessioned by Soviet Libraries) published by the library of the Institute of Oriental Studies.

In nine parts: the writings of the founders of Marxism-Leninism on the countries of the Orient; Oriental studies; history and current developments; general works; the Near and Middle East; Africa; the Far East and Southeast Asia (each of the last three parts is subdivided into a general section, followed by country sections in alphabetical order); directories; bibliography; and foreign works on Soviet Asia.

The section on China is further subdivided by topic. The entries are given in the language of the work in question, except for Chinese-language items which, depending on the library reporting, are given either in Chinese characters with Russian transliteration or simply in Russian transliteration without Chinese characters. Titles are translated and a brief annotation provides information on the nature of the book or article and on the availability of bibliographical references. Over 100 books and articles in Chinese, Russian, English and other languages on China appear in each issue.

A very useful list for following the current Soviet scholarly output on China and the Chinese-language acquisitions of Soviet libraries.

1799 Svodnyi biulleten' novykh inostrannykh knig postupivshikh v biblioteki SSSR

(Joint Bulletin of New Foreign Books Accessioned by Soviet Libraries). Moscow: Vsesoiuznaia gosudarstvennaia biblioteka inostrannoi literatury, 1949—. Series A, 6 issues annually; Series B, 10 issues annually.

A combined accession list for foreign books received by 120 major Soviet libraries, classified by subject and published by the State Library of Foreign Literature. In two series: Series A—natural science, medicine, agriculture and technology, and Series B—the social sciences (philosophy, history, economics, law, linguistics, and literary and art criticism). Materials in Oriental languages, which account for roughly fifteen per cent of all the foreign books, are largely listed in Series B. Chinese-language books occupy first place among the Oriental materials. The entries provide Russian transliteration and translation accompanied by a brief annotation.

1800 Sovremennaia kitaiskaia literatura po obshchestvennym naukam

(Contemporary Chinese Literature in the Field of Social Sciences). Moscow: Fundamental'naia biblioteka obshchestvennykh nauk Akademii Nauk SSSR, No. 1—, 1953—. Bi-monthly.

Issued every other month (quarterly until December 1955) by the Fundamental Library of the Social Sciences of the Soviet Academy of Sciences in Moscow and by the library of the Academy of Sciences in Leningrad. The journal contains abstracts, review articles and bibliographical surveys of current

Chinese materials received in the Soviet Union in both the social sciences and the humanities (the title notwithstanding). From 1953 to 1955 the abstracting was largely limited to books (about 170), but after 1955 the abstracting of periodical literature increased sharply. Lists of books and periodicals received from China by the two libraries appear regularly in the appendix. Mimeographed.

1801 **Spisok knig i zhurnalov po vostokovedeniiu, poluchennykh Fundamental'noi bibliotekoi obshchestvennykh nauk AN SSSR**
(List of Books and Periodicals in the Field of Oriental Studies, Received by the Fundamental Library of the Social Sciences of the Academy of Sciences of the U.S.S.R.). Moscow: Fundamental'naia biblioteka obshchestvennykh nauk Akademii Nauk SSSR, 1948–1953. Irregular.

Ten to twenty-page pamphlets in Russian, Western and Oriental languages listing current acquisitions of the Fundamental Library of the Social Sciences of the Soviet Academy of Sciences in the Oriental field. Mimeographed.

ADDITIONAL REFERENCES

1802 **Aleksandrov, F.** *Biblioteki Moskvy* (Libraries of Moscow). Moscow, 1957.

1803 **Alekseeva, K. P.** 'Bibliograficheskaia rabota Fundamental'noi biblioteki obshchestvennykh nauk' (Bibliographical Work of the Fundamental Library of the Social Sciences), *Sovetskaia bibliografiia* (Soviet Bibliography), 1959 No. 1 (No. 53), pp. 76–81.

1804 **Berton, Peter.** 'Introduction,' *Soviet Works on China* (see **44**), pp. 11–53.

1805 **Golubeva, O. D.** 'Vostokovednye fondy Gosudarstvennoi publichnoi biblioteki im. M. E. Saltykova-Shchedrina v Leningrade' (Materials in the Field of Oriental Studies at the State Public Library Named for M. E. Saltykov-Shchedrin in Leningrad), *Sovetskoe vostokovedenie* (Soviet Oriental Studies), 1955 No. 4, pp. 148–150.

1806 **Gorbacheva, Z. I., Men'shikov, L. N., and Petrov, N. A.** 'Kitaevedenie v Leningrade za sorok let' (Forty Years of Chinese Studies in Leningrad), *Uchenye zapiski Instituta vostokovedeniia* (Transactions of the Institute of Oriental Studies), Vol. 25 (1960), pp. 82–101.

1807 **Hashimoto, Mantaro.** 'Chinese Language Studies in Soviet Russia' *Monographs on Chinese Language Teaching*, No. 1 (December 1961), 18p. (Yale University, Institute of Far Eastern Languages).

1808 **Horecky, Paul L.** *Libraries and Bibliographic Centers in the Soviet Union.* Indiana University Publications, Slavic and East European Series, Vol. 16 (1959). 287p.

1809 **Kovalev, E. F.** 'Izuchenie Kitaia v Sovetskom Soiuze' (The Study of China in the Soviet Union), *Sovetskoe vostokovedenie*, 1955 No. 3, pp. 158–162.

This is a report originally presented to the Twenty-Third International Congress of Orientalists held at Cambridge, England in 1954, and is also available in English in *International Congress of Orientalists, Twenty-Third, Papers* (Far East Section), pp. 83–93.

1810 **Kunin, V. V.** 'Kitaiskii i Kitaevedcheskii fond Vsesoiuznoi gosudarstvennoi biblioteki inostrannoi literatury' (Chinese and Sinological Collection of the All-Union State Library of Foreign Literature), *Sovetskoe kitaevedenie* (Soviet Journal of Chinese Studies), No. 2 (1958), pp. 205–207.

1811 **Lykova, S. A. and Trudoliubova, Z. F.** 'Kitaiskii fond Gosudarstvennoi publichnoi istoricheskoi biblioteki' (The Chinese Collection of the State Public Historical Library), *Sovetskoe kitaevedenie*, No. 2 (1958), pp. 207–208.

1812 **Maichel, Karol.** *Guide to Russian Reference Books*. Stanford, Calif.: Hoover Institution, 1962—. 7 vols.

See especially Vol. 1, 'General Bibliographies and Reference Works'.

1813 ——. 'Soviet Scientific Abstracting Journals,' *Special Libraries*. Vol. 50, No. 8 (October 1959), pp. 398–402.

1814 **Mancall, Mark.** Letter to John K. Fairbank from Leningrad, dated March 1, 1959, 7 p. Mimeographed.

1815 ——. 'The Twenty-First Party Congress and Soviet Orientalogy,' *The Journal of Asian Studies*. Vol. 19, No. 2 (February 1960), pp. 229–235.

1816 **Morley, James.** 'Some Important Soviet Organizations and Periodicals Devoted to the Study of the Modern History of Asia,' *The Journal of Asian Studies*, Vol. 16, No. 4 (August 1957), pp. 673–678.

1817 '**Ot redaktsii**' (From the Editorial Board), *Sovetskoe kitaevedenie*, No. 1 (1958), pp. 5–19.

A brief survey of Chinese studies in the Soviet Union for the past forty years.

1818 **Smolin, G. Ia.** 'Biblioteka Akademii nauk SSSR i Kitai' (The Library of the Academy of Sciences of the U.S.S.R. and China) in *Nauchnye i kul'turnye sviazi Biblioteki Akademii nauk SSSR so stranami zarubezhnogo Vostoka* (Scientific and Cultural Relations of the Library of the Academy of Sciences of the U.S.S.R. with the Countries of the Non-Soviet Orient). Moscow-Leningrad, 1957, pp. 9–28.

1819 ——. 'Kitaiskie fondy Biblioteki Akademii nauk SSSR' (The Chinese Collections of the Library of the Academy of Sciences of the U.S.S.R.), *Sovetskoe kitaevedenie*, No. 4 (1958), pp. 274–277.

1820   'Sokrovishchnitsa izdanii zarubezhnogo Vostoka' (A Treasure House of
       Publications of the Non-Soviet Orient), *Sovremennyi Vostok* (Contemporary
       East), 1960 No. 7, p. 55.
       Describes the Lenin Library.

1821   'V Fundamental'noi biblioteke obshchestvennykh nauk—Knigoobmen
       s Kitaiskoi Narodnoi Respublikoi' (At the Fundamental Library of the
       Social Sciences—Book Exchange with the Chinese People's Republic), *Vestnik
       Akademii nauk SSSR* (Bulletin of the Academy of Sciences of the U.S.S.R.)
       1954 No. 10 (October 1954), pp. 84–85.

1822   'Vostochnye fondy gosudarstvennoi publichnoi istoricheskoi biblio-
       teki' (The Oriental Collections of the State Public Historical Library),
       Sovetskoe vostokovedenie, 1956 No. 1, pp. 199–205.

1823   'Vostokovedenie v Leningradskom universitete' (Oriental Studies at
       the University of Leningrad), *Uchenye zapiski Leningradskogo universiteta*
       (Transactions of the Leningrad University), No. 296 (Oriental Studies Series,
       No. 13), 1960.

1824   **Zanegin, B. N.** 'O sobraniiakh kitaiskikh knig v bibliotekakh Rossii i SSSR'
       (Chinese Collections in the Libraries of Russia and the U.S.S.R.), *Vestnik
       istorii material'noi kul'tury* (Bulletin of the History of Material Culture), 1958
       No. 5 (No. 11), pp. 137–146.

See also sections C4 in Chapter I (pp. 28 ff.), and C in Chapter XXI (pp. 473 ff.).

5. OTHER COUNTRIES

1825   **Soviet-Asian Relations Conference, Conference Reports No. 1-15.** Los
       Angeles: University of Southern California, School of International Relations,
       1959. 15 papers.

       A collection of documents designed to serve as background papers for
   the Soviet-Asian Relations Conference held at the School of International
   Relations, University of Southern California, in June 1959. A number of the
   papers provide useful surveys of Chinese studies in various countries. Others,
   less useful for the purposes of the present work, do nevertheless deal with certain
   aspects of Chinese studies and deserve mention here. A selected list of the
   papers follows (those annotated separately are so indicated): *Soviet Training
   and Research on Asia* (Report No. 1, see **1797**); *Soviet Publications in the
   Asian Field (with Special Reference to China)* (Report 2, has been superseded
   by Peter Berton, comp., *Soviet Works on China*, see **44**); *United Kingdom
   Training and Research in the Russian and Asian Fields* (Report No. 3, see **1830**);
   German Training and Research in the Russian and Asian Fields (Report No. 4,
   Part 2, Far Eastern Studies in Germany); *French Training and Research in
   the Russian and Asian Fields* (Report No. 5, Part 2, East Asian Studies in
   France); *Japanese Studies of Contemporary China* (Report No. 7, see **1760**);

Korean Training and Research on Russia, China, and North Korea (Report No. 8, see **1876**); *Indian Training and Research on Russia and China* (Report No. 10, see **1874**); *Asian and Russian Studies in the United States* (Report No. 11, Part 1, 'Asian Studies in the United States); *American Research on Communist China (Political Problems)* (Report No 13); *United States Developments and Needs in the Soviet-Asian Field* (Report No. 14).

I. Western Europe—General

1826 Hervouet, Yves.
'Les bibliothèques chinoises d'Europe occidentale,' *Mélanges publiés par l'Institut des hautes études chinoises*, Paris, Vol. 1 (1957), pp. 451–511.

A survey of the forty principal Chinese collections (libraries, museums, etc.) in Western Europe (except Spain and Portugal) undertaken in 1954–55 under a grant from the Rockefeller Foundation by a French scholar, now a professor at the University of Bordeaux. Arrangement is by country (Great Britain—14 libraries, Belgium, Holland, Sweden, Denmark, West Germany—8, Switzerland, Austria, Italy and France—6), and in each case the author's description of the organization and principal holdings is followed by a section on existing catalogs.

While the libraries described cover pre-modern China, the article nevertheless deals with most of the major collections in which material on contemporary China may be found.

1827 Ceadel, E. B.
'Far Eastern Collections in Libraries in Great Britain, France, Holland and Germany,' *Asia Major*, New Series, Vol. 3, No. 2 (1952), pp. 213–222.

Brief survey of Western European collections in the Far Eastern field, covering a dozen libraries each in Great Britain and Germany, six in France and one in Holland. Except for those concerning Cambridge and the School of Oriental and African Studies in London, which are lengthy, the descriptions range from a line to a short paragraph.

1828 Hervouet, Y., ed.
Catalogue des périodiques Chinois dans les bibliothèques d'Europe. The Hague: Mouton & Co., 1958. 102p.

A union list of 600 Chinese periodicals in European libraries, including some post-1949 Mainland publications and some Taiwan journals published since 1945, arranged alphabetically by title.

II. Great Britain

1829 Grinstead, E. D., comp.
Chinese Periodicals in British Libraries, Handlist No. 1. London, [1962]. 41; 3; 8p.

A union catalog of the holdings of Chinese-language periodicals and newspapers in fourteen major university and institution libraries in Great Britain. The listing is comprehensive rather than exhaustive, some of the less important periodicals and newspapers having been omitted. The entries are arranged alphabetically by romanized title (no Chinese characters given), followed by the place of publication, the dates of available holdings, locations with holdings statement. Appendix A provides a list of science periodicals in the British Museum of Natural History. Appendix B is a list of Chinese scientific and technical periodicals published as of June 1962, available at the National Lending Library, all but two of which are post-1949 Mainland publications. Mimeographed on legal-size sheets.

A revised list bringing up the information through 1963 (arranged according to the P'in-yin transliteration and including Chinese characters) is under preparation. This will update and supplement the M.I.T. union list (see **1708**).

1830 Footman, David and Wheeler, G. E.
United Kingdom Training and Research in the Russian and Asian Fields. Los Angeles: University of Southern California, 1959. 28p. (School of International Relations, Soviet-Asian Relations Conference, Report No. 3).

A survey of Asian and Slavonic studies in the United Kingdom based on the 1947 report of the Scarbrough Commission (established to inquire into Slavonic, African and Asian Studies), materials from the University Grants Committee and other sources, prepared jointly by the head of the Soviet Affairs Study Group at Oxford and the director of the Central Asian Research Centre, London. Brief coverage is given to the origins of Oriental and Slavonic studies in Great Britain, developments since 1947, statistics on teaching posts and students, descriptions of the leading university programs, libraries (17 institutions), periodicals (13), research in progress, and bio-bibliographical notes on thirty-six British scholars in the Asian and Russian fields. Mimeographed.

1831 Bracken, J. R. 'The School of Oriental and African Studies, University of London,' *The Journal of Asian Studies*, Vol. 17, No. 1 (November 1957), pp. 175–183.

1832 Ceadel, E. B. 'Great Britain: Far Eastern Studies at the University of Cambridge,' *Far Eastern Quarterly*, Vol. 11, No. 4 (August 1952), pp. 517–522.

1833 ——. 'Indian and Far Eastern Studies at the University of Cambridge,' *The Journal of Asian Studies*, Vol. 17, No. 3 (May 1958), pp. 541–547.

1834 ——. 'A Survey of Oriental Studies in Great Britain,' *Far Eastern Quarterly*, Vol. 12, No. 3 (May 1953), pp. 383–391.

1835 Chesneaux, Jean and Lust, John. *Introduction aux études d'histoire contemporaine de Chine (1898–1949)*. Paris: Mouton, 1964. 128p. (Le Monde d'Outre-Mer, Passé et Présent, École Pratiques des Hautes Études, VIème Section).

1836 **Chinnery, J. D. and Russell, R.** 'Oriental Studies in British Universities,' *Universities Quarterly*, Vol. 14, No. 3 (June 1960), pp. 287–298.

1837 **Gardner, K. B., Grinstead, E. D. and Meredith-Owens, G. M.** 'The Department of Oriental Printed Books and Manuscripts of the British Museum,' *The Journal of Asian Studies*, Vol. 18, No. 2 (February 1959), pp. 310–318.

1838 **Irwin, Raymond and Staveley, Ronald.** *Libraries of London.* Second revised edition. 1961.

1839 **Pearson, J. D.** 'The Library of the School of Oriental and African Studies,' *The Journal of Asian Studies*, Vol. 17, No. 1 (November 1957), pp. 183–188.

1840 **Pike, Michael.** 'Far Eastern Studies in Britain,' *Asiatic Research Bulletin*, Seoul, No. 3 (February 1958), pp. 2–5.

1841 **University Grants Committee.** *Report of the Sub-Committee on Oriental, Slavonic, East European and African Studies.* London: Her Majesty's Stationery Office, 1961. 125p.

This is the Hayter Commission Report.

III. GERMANY

1842 **Mehnert, Klaus.** 'Soviet-Asian Studies in Germany,' *Conference Report No. 4, Soviet-Asian Relations Conference, University of Southern California*, Los Angeles, 1959, pp. 1–8.

1843 **Franke, Herbert.** 'Far Eastern Studies in Germany, *Conference Report No. 4, Soviet-Asian Relations Conference, University of Southern California*, Los Angeles, pp. 9–16. Also published in *The Journal of Asian Studies*, Vol. 18, No. 4 (August 1959), pp. 535–540.

1844 **Henle, Hans.** 'Chinese Studies in West Germany,' *Eastern Horizon*, Vol. 2, No. 1 (January 1962), pp. 21–25.

1845 **Grimm, Tilemann.** 'Far Eastern Studies in Germany,' *Asiatic Research Bulletin*, Seoul, No. 5 (April 1958), pp. 2–5.

1846 **Falkenstein, Adam, ed.** *Denkschrift zur Lage der Orientalistik* (A Memorandum on the State of Oriental Studies). Wiesbaden: Franz Steiner Verlag, 1960. 55p. Tables.

1847 **Franke, Wolfgang.** 'Probleme und heutiger Stand der China-Forschung in Deutschland' (Problems and the Present-Day State of China Research in Germany), *Moderne Welt*, 1 (1959/1960), pp. 409–429.

1848 ——. 'Die Entwicklung der Chinakunde in den letzten 50 Jahren' (The Development of China Studies During the Last Fifty Years), *Nachrichten der Gesellschaft für Natur- und Völkerkunde Ostasiens*, Vol. 72 (1952), pp. 8–18.

See also **54** and **55.**

IV. FRANCE

1849 **Demiéville, Paul.** 'Organization of East Asian Studies in France,' *The Journal of Asian Studies*, Vol. 18, No. 1 (November 1958), pp. 163–181.

See also **1205.**

V. NETHERLANDS

1850 **Hulsewe, A. F. P.** 'Chinese and Japanese Studies in Holland,' *The Journal of Asian Studies*, Vol. 17, No. 2 (February 1958), pp. 355–360.

VI. ITALY

1851 **Petech, Luciano.** 'Oriental Studies in Italy During the Last Ten Years,' *East and West*, 1 (1950–1951), pp. 3–5.

1852 **Tucci, Giuseppe.** 'Report on Far Eastern Studies in Italy,' *Far Eastern Quarterly*, Vol. 12, No. 1 (November 1952), pp. 107–109.

1853 **Zallio, Mario V.** 'Some Italian Books on Communist China,' *The Journal of Asian Studies*, Vol. 18, No. 1 (November 1958), pp. 126–130.

1854 **Special China supplement, 'La Cina d'oggi',** to Vol. 12, April 1956 issue of *Il Ponte* (Florence; La Nuova Italia), 727p.

See also **54a** and **1206.**

VII. CZECHOSLOVAKIA

1855 **Zbavitel, Dušan.** *Die Orientalistik in der Tschechoslowakei.* (Trans. from Czech by J. Fanta). Prague: Orbis, 1959. 80p.

An historical survey of Oriental studies in Czechoslovakia including postwar developments in the field. Information on training, research and publications is provided. Thirty-two tables. Also published in English, French and Russian.

1856 **Blaškovic, Josef.** 'Les buts, l'organisation et l'activité de l'école orientaliste Tschecoslovaque,' *Studia et Acta Orientalia*, Bucharest, Vol. 2, pp. 61–69.

1857 **Krebsova, Berta.** 'Chekosurobakia no Chūgoku kenkyū' (Chinese Studies in Czechoslovakia), *Shohō* (Book News), No 8 (1958), pp. 14–16.

1858 **Marek, Jan and Pokora, Tim.** 'Asian Studies in Czechoslovakia,' *The Journal of Asian Studies*, Vol. 22, No. 3 (May 1963), pp. 357–366.

1859 **Prušek, Jaroslav.** 'Deset let naší orientalistiky' (Ten Years of Our Oriental Studies), *Archiv Orientalni*, Vol. 23, No. 3 (1955), pp. 321–330.

1860 ——. 'Far Eastern Studies in Czechoslovakia,' *East Asian Cultural Studies*, Tokyo, Vol. 2, No. 1/2 (June 1962), pp. 52–56.

1861 **Prušek, Jaroslav.** 'Orientalische Studien in der Tschechoslowakei' (Oriental Studies in Czechoslovakia), *Wissenschaftliche Annalen* (Annals of Science), Vol. 5 (February 1956), pp. 126–135.

See also **56, 1102, 1207** and **1208.**

In addition, the Soviet journal *Narody Azii i Afriki* (The Peoples of Asia and Africa) and its predecessors often carry articles on developments in Czech Oriental studies.

VIII. POLAND

1862 **Kaluzinski, Stanislaw, et al.** 'Orientalistyka polska w okresie dwudziestolecia Polski ludowej' (Polish Oriental Studies During the Two Decades of People's Poland), *Przegląd orientalistyczny* (Oriental Review), 1964 No. 3 (No. 51), pp. 199–214.

1863 **Baskakov, N. and Luk'ianova, M.** 'Vostokovednye tsentry Pol'shi v 1954 g.' (Polish Centers of Oriental Studies), *Kratkie soobshcheniia Instituta vostokovedeniia* (Brief Reports of the Institute of Oriental Studies), No. 12 (1955), pp. 129–133.

1864 **Reychman, Jan, et. al.** 'Dix ans d'études orientales en Pologne Populaire' (Ten Years of Oriental Studies in People's Poland), *Rocznik orientalistyczny*, Vol. 20 (1956), pp. 7–14.

1865 **Tveritinova, A. S., ed.** *Soobshcheniia pol'skikh orientalistov* (Reports of Polish Orientalists). Moscow, 1961. (Zarubezhnoe vostokovedenie [Oriental Studies Abroad], Vol. 2), (Academy of Sciences of the U.S.S.R., Institute of the Peoples of Asia).

See also **57** and **1209.**

IX. RUMANIA

1866 **'Chronique d'activité de la section d'études orientales,'** *Studia et acta orientalia*, Vol. 1 (1958), pp. 398–401.

1867 **Constantin, G. I.** 'Kitaevedenie v Rumynskoi Narodnoi Respublike' (Chinese Studies in the Rumanian People's Republic), *Sovetskoe kitaevedenie* (Soviet Journal of Chinese Studies), No. 4 (1958), pp. 298–299.

1868 **Gubeglu, M.** 'Contributions roumaines aux études orientales,' *Archiv Orientálni*, Vol. 24, No. 3 (1956), pp. 454–475.

See also **1211.**

X. HUNGARY

1869 **Uray, C.** 'Raboty vengerskikh uchenykh po vostokovedeniiu v 1956–1957 godakh' (The Work of Hungarian Scholars in the Oriental Field in 1956–1957), *Problemy vostokovedeniia* (Problems of Oriental Studies), 1959 No. 1, pp. 144–152.

See also an article on Hungarian Oriental studies in *Novy Orient* (New Orient) Prague, 1955 No. 5; **53** and **1210.**

XI. Bulgaria

1870   Kabrda, J. [Oriental studies in Bulgaria], *Przegląd orientalistyczny*, 1956 No. 3 (No. 19).

1871   Cwetkowa, B. 'Sources et travaux de l'orientalisme bulgare,' *Annales-Economies, Société—Civilisations*, No. 6.

Updates the previous entry.

XII. Canada

1872   McLean, Ross.

Canada and Asia, A Survey on Canadian Resources for Participation in the UNESCO Major Project on the Mutual Appreciation of Eastern and Western Cultural Values. Ottawa: Canadian National Commission for UNESCO, 1959. 82p.

General information available on 'Materials and Institutions for Canadian-Asian Programs' in the universities, specialized institutions and agencies, and mass organizations (Chapter 3). The 'Appendices' (Chapter 4) contains a section on 'Canadian Publications of Interest in Asian Studies'. Of particular interest is the cumulative table of contents of the *International Journal*, Vols. 1–13 (No. 2), 1946–58, published by the Canadian Institute of International Affairs. A number of articles concern Communist China.

1873   Wang, Yi-t'ung.

'The P'u-pan Chinese Library at the University of British Columbia,' *Pacific Affairs*, Vol. 34 No. 1 (Spring 1961), pp. 101–111.

One of the leading Chinese collections in Canada, particularly strong on the pre-modern period.

XIII. India

1874   Dutt, Vidya Prakash.

Indian Training and Research on Russia and China. Los Angeles: University of Southern California, 1959. 8p. (School of International Relations, Soviet-Asian Relations Conference, Conference Report No. 10).

A short report prepared for the Conference by the head of the East Asian department at the Indian School of International Affairs, New Delhi. The paper contains a brief survey of the origin of Indian interest in China and Russia, a description of academic training (language, research, publications), government training programs, and a note on the non-official exchanges between India and Communist China, including a list of the more significant publications by Indian visitors to Communist China. Mimeographed.

1875   Fisher, Margaret W. and Bondurant, Joan V.

'Review Article: The Impact of Communist China on Visitors from India,' *Far Eastern Quarterly*, Vol. 15, No. 2 (February 1956), pp. 249–265.

A review of ten accounts published in 1952 and 1953 by Indian visitors to Communist China.

XIV. South Korea

1876 Zo, Kizun.
Korean Training and Research on Russia, China, and North Korea. Los Angeles: University of Southern California, 1959. 6p. (School of International Relations, Soviet-Asian Relations Conference, Conference Report No. 8).

A very brief report prepared for the Conference by the Deputy-Director of the Asiatic Research Center, Korea University in Seoul, covering the origin and background of Korean interest in Russia and Communist China, and the training now available for work in the field. The report also provides a list of the major academic centers, research projects, libraries, and a list of Korean specialists, primarily in the field of Chinese language and literature. Mimeographed.

XV. Australia

1877 Bielenstein, Hans. 'Oriental Studies in Australia,' *The Journal of Asian Studies*, Vol. 21, No. 2 (February 1962), pp. 257–261.

APPENDIX B

DISSERTATIONS AND THESES

It is perhaps not too much to say that unpublished Ph.D. dissertations and M.A. theses constitute a neglected treasure. In a field as complex and undeveloped as contemporary China, this body of scholarship should certainly not be overlooked. The contribution to knowledge made by such student research is perhaps nowhere better illustrated than in the Papers on China of Harvard University (see Chapter XXII). By way of rounding out the Guide, it seems, therefore, appropriate to conclude with a list of unpublished dissertations and theses.

This appendix is divided into two parts: (1) bibliographies of dissertations and theses, and (2) a list of dissertations and theses accepted by American universities dealing exclusively with post-1949 Mainland China and post-1945 Taiwan. This list is arranged by subject under four major categories: The People's Republic of China, the Republic of China, the Overseas Chinese, and China policy.

The nine bibliographies included in the first part are the only ones available. The first entry is the only general bibliography not restricted to a single institution, discipline or group of students. The remaining eight entries represent good sources for studies done at specific institutions (Columbia, Chicago, University of Southern California, and Syracuse), works by Chinese-born scholars, and dissertations in the fields of foreign education and foreign missions. These sources may be updated by using the *Dissertation Abstracts* published by University Microfilms (see Carl E. Orgren, 'Index to Dissertation Abstracts,' *College and Research Libraries*, July 1964, pp. 279–280); the *Newsletter of the Association for Asian Studies;* and the periodic lists compiled by the External Research Staff of the Department of State (see **1705**).

It should be noted that the roughly 340 titles (including some 130 doctoral dissertations) in the second part of this appendix are by no means an exhaustive listing, but they nonetheless represent most of the dissertations and theses on contemporary China done in the United States.

1. BIBLIOGRAPHIES OF DISSERTATIONS AND THESES

1878 Stucki, Curtis W., comp.
American Doctoral Dissertations on Asia, 1933–1962; Including Appendix of Master's Theses at Cornell University. Ithaca, N.Y.: Cornell University, 1963. 12; 204; 10p. (Cornell University, Department of Asian Studies, Southeast Asia Program, Data Paper No. 50).

Compiled from the Social Sciences and Humanities sections of *Doctoral Dissertations Accepted by American Universities* (1933–1955) and its successor, *Index to American Doctoral Dissertations* (1956–1962). This list includes over 600 titles on China, classified by discipline or subject (about a quarter of the dissertations are in the field of foreign relations; others are in history, economics, education, philosophy and religion, language and literature, sociology and anthropology, government and politics, etc.). The appendix lists 267 Master's theses on Asia (38 on China) accepted at Cornell University between the years 1933 and 1962. Titles available from University Microfilms are so indicated. Author index.

An earlier edition covers 1933–1958.

1879 Columbia University Libraries, East Asiatic Library.
Columbia University Master's Essays and Doctoral Dissertations on Asia, 1875–1956. New York, 1957. 96p.

A list of all titles of graduate work on Asia, arranged by subject within area and by author within subject, including works, heretofore not completely recorded in the library's Essay and Dissertation Office. The number of titles on China totals 542. The index at the end contains, in addition to authors, particular phases of subjects, biographies, some place and proper names.

An unpublished up-to-date list of essays and dissertations accepted by Columbia University after 1957 is available at the library.

1880 University of Chicago, Far Eastern Library.
The University of Chicago Doctoral Dissertations and Masters' Theses on Asia, 1894–1962. Chicago, 1962. 52p.

A list of 630 doctoral dissertations and M.A. theses completed at the University of Chicago from 1894 to the summer of 1962. Of the 630 titles, 247 are on China (73 dissertations and 174 theses), most of which deal with the pre-1949 period. Entries are arranged by country, and within each country-section by subject, and therein by author. The departments to which the dissertations and theses were submitted are not specified, but the volume does supply the dates of completion.

1881 Pennington, Juliana and Marsh, Paul, comps.
The University of Southern California Doctoral Dissertations and Master's Theses on East and Southeast Asia, 1911–1964. Los Angeles: University of Southern California, 1965. 54p.

A preliminary checklist of some 350 theses and dissertations on the Far East and Southeast Asia accepted at U.S.C. Of the total, about forty per cent are on China (one-half in the case of Ph.D.'s), but of these only a dozen deal with the post-1949 period. Arrangement is by subject under country (philosophy, religion and culture, history, international relations, government and politics, economics and commerce, education, etc.). Each entry provides the author, title, date of completion, pagination, department, degree and call number. Author index. Mimeographed.

1882   Hart, Donn V., comp.
*An Annotated Bibliography of Theses and Dissertations on Asia Accepted at
Syracuse University, 1907–1963.* Syracuse, N.Y.: Syracuse University Library,
1964. 46p.

Lists 161 Master's theses and doctoral dissertations on Asia accepted as of
late 1963 at Syracuse University (including those accepted at the adjacent
State University College of Forestry). Of the total, fifty deal with China, and
of these, less than ten concern themselves with the post-1949 period. The
entries accompanied by annotations are arranged by author in alphabetical
order. Combined subject and author index.

1883   Yüan, T'ung-li, comp.
A Guide to Doctoral Dissertations by Chinese Students in America, 1905–1960.
Washington, D.C.: Sino-American Cultural Society, Inc., 1961. 248p.

A list of 2,789 doctoral dissertations submitted by Chinese students and
accepted by American universities in the years 1905–1960 inclusive. A number
are concerned with recent developments in China. The dissertations are
arranged under two general headings: (1) the humanities and social, and
behavioral sciences, and (2) the physical, biological and engineering sciences.
Within each category, entries are listed alphabetically by author (Chinese
names are provided). There is also a short list (28 titles) of dissertations
accepted by Canadian universities. Two appendices contain the following:
(1) a list of the recipients of honorary degrees conferred by Chinese and
foreign institutions of higher learning, and (2) statistical tables of degrees
conferred, according to institution and field of study. Alphabetical index
by field of study.
     See also next entry.

1884   Yüan, T'ung-li, comp.
'Doctoral Dissertations By Chinese Students in Great Britain and Northern
Ireland, 1916–1961,' *Chinese Culture,* Vol. 4, No. 4 (March 1963), pp.
107–137.

A companion piece to the preceding entry, listing 344 doctoral dissertations
submitted by Chinese students and accepted by British universities in the
years 1916–1961 inclusive. Only a few deal with modern and contemporary
China. In two sections: (1) the humanities and social sciences (92 titles), and
(2) the biological and physical sciences, and engineering (252 titles). In each
section the entries are arranged alphabetically by author (Chinese characters
are provided). Two statistical tables: (1) distribution by institution, and (2)
distribution by major field of study.

1885 **Yüan, T'ung-li, comp.**
'A Guide to Doctoral Dissertations by Chinese Students in Continental Europe, 1907–1962 (1),' *Chinese Culture*, Vol. 5, No. 3 (March 1964), pp. 98–156; Vol. 5, No. 4 (June 1964), pp. 81–149; Vol. 6, No. 1 (October 1964), pp. 79-98.

1886 **Eells, Walter Crosby, ed.**
American Dissertations on Foreign Education. Washington, D.C.: National Education Association of the United States, Committee on International Relations, 1959. 39; 300p.

Lists 5,716 doctoral dissertations and Master's theses written at American universities and colleges, concerning education or educators in foreign countries and education of the foreign-born or persons of foreign ancestry in the United States, 1884–1958. Of the 517 works on Mainland China (the post-1949 period included), 149 are doctoral dissertations and 313 are Master's theses. An additional twenty-two dissertations and thirty-three theses concerned partially with Mainland China are listed in other sections. Those concerning the Republic of China since 1949 (one dissertation and two theses) are listed separately, as are those concerned with Hong Kong (one dissertation and one thesis). Works concerned only partially with education in Formosa (one dissertation and two theses) and Hong Kong (one dissertation) are listed in other sections of the volume. Entries are numbered consecutively. Full bibliographical information is provided for each entry (including the author's birth and death dates, when available) and its availability on microfilm. A general index and a separate author index.

The bibliography includes all titles on education listed in Curtis W. Stucki, comp., *American Doctoral Dissertations on Asia, 1933–1958* (see **1878**), and is supplemented by the three compilations of Dr. Yüan (see preceding entries) for works done after 1958.

1887 **Person, Laura, comp.**
Cumulative List of Doctoral Dissertations and Masters' Theses in Foreign Missions and Related Subjects as Reported by the Missionary Research Library in the Occasional Bulletin 1950 to 1960. New York: Missionary Research Library, 1961. 46p.

A list of some 150 doctoral dissertations and over 300 master's theses in the field of religion, missionary activity and related subjects, many of them done at theological seminaries. Arranged alphabetically by author under two divisions: doctoral dissertations and Master's theses. Some entries contain brief annotations, including references to *Dissertation Abstracts*. Index of institutions. Subject index. Mimeographed.

The December issue of the *Occasional Bulletin* from the Missionary Research Library is regularly a 'List of Theses in Foreign Missions and Related Subjects Accepted During the Academic Year . . . ,' arranged as the *Cumulative List*. Beyond 1960, therefore, the *Cumulative List* can be updated by using the December issues of the *Occasional Bulletin*.

2. A LIST OF DISSERTATIONS AND THESES ON CONTEMPORARY CHINA

I. People's Republic of China

A. General and Government

1. General, Government and Law

1888 **Andors, Stephen.** *The United Front of Communist China: Domestic and International Aspects.* Tufts University, 1962. 140p. (M.A.).

1889 **Buxbaum, David C.** *Preliminary Trends in the Development of the Legal Institutions of Communist China and the Nature of the Criminal Law.* University of Washington, 1963. 91p. (M.A.).

1890 **Chia, Jack Teh-tsao.** *The Red Regime in China—A Brief Analysis of Its History and Legal Structure.* Fordham University, 1952. 100p. (M.A.).

1891 **Chow, David T. W.** *Progress and Sacrifice Under the People's Republic of China.* University of Southern California, 1958. 123p. (M.A.).

1892 **Chu, Yung-hsin.** *The New Constitution and New Government of China.* Stanford University, 1949. 194p. (M.A.).

1893 **Gaudian, Robert Ronald.** *People's Republic of China, 1949–1959.* Georgetown University, 1959. 181p. (M.A.).

1893a **Greer, Robert Winchester.** *A Political Geography of the Gulf of Pohai Region.* Stanford University, 1958. 150p. (M.A.).

1894 **Hennelly, James Jerome.** *Communist Strategy in China.* St. John's University, 1960. 65p. (M.A.).

1895 **Hillam, Ray Cole.** *The Role of the Student in the Political History of Modern China.* George Washington University, 1958. 140p. (M.A.).

1896 **Madian, Marcia Dunn.** *The Marriage Law of Communist China, 1950–1953.* Columbia University, 1962. 102p. (M.A.), (East Asian Institute Certificate Essay).

1897 **Oksenberg, Michel C.** *The Structure of Field Administration in Rural China, 1955–1958.* Columbia University, 1963. 184p. (M.A.), (East Asian Institute Certificate Essay).

1898 **Pepper, Suzanne.** *Rural Government in Communist China: The Party-State Relationship at the Local Level.* University of Washington, 1963. 126p. (M.A.).

1899 **Shang, Ching-ting.** *A Study of the Chinese Communist Government.* Columbia University, 1953. 103p. (M.A.).

1900 **Thomas, Samuel B.** *The Government and Structure of the People's Republic of China: 1949–1950.* Columbia University, 1951. 64p. (M.A.), (East Asian Institute Certificate Essay).

2. National Minority Policy and Regional Administration

a. General

1901 **Heaton, Herald Grant.** *The Chinese Communist Policy Toward National Minority Groups: 1949–1954.* University of Washington, 1963. 171p. (M.A.).

b. Tibet
(See also the section on relations with India in I E, p. 571.)

1902 **Allen, John Louis.** *Chinese Communist Policy in Tibet.* University of California, Berkeley, 1963. 195p. (M.A.).

1903 **Clark, James J.** *Chinese Communist Administration in Tibet, 1950–1961.* Tufts University, 1962. 131p. (Honors Thesis).

1904 **Kargl, Raymond Charles.** *A Study of Sino-Tibetan Relations, 61 B.C.– 1952 A.D.* University of Southern California, 1953. 212p. (M.A.).

1905 **Nadell, Charles L.** *The Extent of China's Control Over Tibet.* New York University, 1963. 117p. (M.A.).

1906 **Rahul, R. Narayan.** *The Sino-Tibetan Agreement of 1951.* Columbia University, 1954. 53p. (M.A.).

c. Northeast and Northwest
(See also the section on relations with the Soviet Union in I E, p. 570.)

1907 **Hai, Badruddin W.** *Muslim Minority in China.* Columbia University, 1955. 153p. (M.A.).

1908 **Metzger, Thomas Albert.** *Communist Policy in Inner Mongolia, 1947–1957.* Georgetown University, 1959. 168p. (M.A.).

1909 **Murray, George J. A., Jr.** *Chinese Nationality Policy in Sinkiang, 1950–1960.* Columbia University, 1963. 116p. (M.A.).

1910 **SCHWARZ, Henry Guenter.** *Policies and Administration of Minority Areas in Northwest China and Inner Mongolia, 1949–1959.* University of Wisconsin, 1963. 692p. (Ph.D.).

1911 **STAUFFER, Robert B., Jr.** *Manchuria as a Political Entity: Government and Politics of a Major Region of China, Including Its Relations with China Proper.* University of Minnesota, 1955. 627p. (Ph.D.).

d. Southeast and Southwest

1912 **CHANG, Chi-jen.** *The Minority Groups of Yunnan and Chinese Political Expansion into Southeast Asia.* University of Michigan, 1956. 208p. (Ph.D.).

1913 **Cohen, Myron L.** *The Hakka or 'Guest People': Dialect as a Sociocultural Variable in Southeastern China.* Columbia University, 1963. 69p. (M.A.).

1914 **Pasternak, Burton.** *Continuity and Discontinuity in Chinese Policy Toward the Southwestern Tribes Since 1911.* Columbia University, 1962. 99p. (M.A.), (East Asian Institute Certificate Essay).

1915 **Pikelis, Anna Mary.** *Cultural Position of Independent Lolo of the Liang-Shan Area, Southwest China.* University of Chicago, 1956. 87p. (M.A.).

B. POLITICS

1. Ideology

1916 **Baum, Richard Dennis.** *The Nature and Function of Ideological and Political 'Super-Structure' in Communist China.* University of California, Berkeley, 1963. 153p. (M.A.).

1917 **CHAO, Paul Kwang-yi.** *Analysis of Marxist Doctrine on the Family with Testing Its Validity in Soviet Russia and Communist China.* New York University, 1963. 252p. (Ph.D.).

1918 **CHEN, Vincent.** *Mao Tse-tung's Communist Ideology on Revolution and War.* Yale University, 1957. 227p. (Ph.D.).

1919 **CHEN, Yung-ping.** *Chinese Political Thought: Mao Tse-tung and Liu Shao-ch'i.* University of Maryland, 1959. 156; 7p. (Ph.D.).

1920 **DAI, Shen-yu.** *Mao Tse-tung and Confucianism.* University of Pennsylvania, 1953. 456p. (Ph.D.).

1921 **Kim, Chong Bok.** *Various Aspects of Pragmatism in America and Its Application by Mao Tse-tung.* University of Maryland, 1961. 122p. (M.A.).

1922 **LOWE, Donald Ming-dah.** *The Idea of China in Marx, Lenin and Mao: A Study in Marxist Ideological Persistence and Transformation.* University of California, Berkeley, 1963. 339p. (Ph.D.).

1923 **MARSH, Susan S. Han.** *The Concept of the Proletariat in Chinese Communism.* University of Chicago, 1955. 156p. (Ph.D.).

1924 **Nagy, Juan G.** *The Phenomena of National Communist Deviation in Contemporary Historic Development.* University of California, Berkeley, 1951. 316p. (M.A.).

1925 **RUE, John Emery.** *Anti-Stalinist Bias in the Thought of Mao Tse-tung: A Study of the Origins of Maoism.* University of Minnesota, 1963. 606p. (Ph.D.).

1926 **Summers, Gilbert Lee.** *Communism in China: The Myth of Maoism.* George Washington University, 1963. 47p. (M.A.I.A.).

1927 **Tsai, Harry Do-ning.** *The 'New Democracy': Mao Tse-tung's Interpretation of Communism.* University of California, Berkeley, 1952. 124p. (M.A.).

1928 **Tsang, Yankee Pierre.** *The Sociological Implications of Mao Tse-tung's 'New Democracy'.* University of Southern California, 1952. 253p. (M.A.).

1929 **Weidenbaum, Rhoda S.** *The Career and Writings of Liu Shao-ch'i.* Columbia University, 1953. 86p. (M.A.).

1930 **Zelman, Annette Weinberg.** *Sun Yat-sen, Chiang Kai-shek and Mao Tse-tung on Nationalism and Imperialism.* Columbia University, 1963. 67p. (M.A.), (East Asian Institute Certificate Essay).

2. Chinese Communist Party

a. Organization

1931 **Carey, Catherine G.** *An Investigation into the Political Biographies of the Chinese Communist Politburo.* Columbia University, 1951. 137p. (M.A.).

1932 **Compton, Boyd Ross.** *Thought Discipline in the Chinese Communist Party.* University of Washington, 1951. 48p. (M.A.).

1933 **Fletcher, Merton Don.** *Communist Party Leadership and Organization in China, 1949–1962.* University of California, Berkeley, 1963. 136p. (M.A.).

1934 **Hsiao, Tsun.** *The Cadre System in Communist China.* University of California, Berkeley, 1960. 90p. (M.A.).

1935 **LEWIS, John Wilson.** *Chinese Communist Leadership Techniques.* University of California at Los Angeles, 1961. 409p. (Ph.D.).

1936 **PAK, Hyo Bom.** *The Power Structure of the Chinese Communist Party.* New York University, 1963. 301p. (Ph.D.).

1937 **Reiss, Annette.** *The Decision-Making Process of the Chinese Communist Party: With a View Toward the Degree of Local Autonomy.* University of California, Berkeley, 1963. 135p. (M.A.).

b. Policies

(See also **2118** and sections ID2, p. 566; IE2, p. 570; IE9, p. 573; IF, p. 574; IG, p. 575; and IH, p. 576.)

1938 **Anderson, Dara L.** *Burmese Communism and the Chinese Communist Party, 1948–1958.* Columbia University, 1963. 110p. (M.A.).

1939 **Carpenter, Francis Ross.** *The Peasant Policy of the Chinese Communists with Special Reference to the Post-World War II Era.* Stanford University, 1950. 158p. (M.A.).

1940 **DOOLIN, Dennis J.** *Chinese Communist Policies Toward the Chinese Intelligentsia: 1949–1963.* Stanford University, 1964. 242p. (Ph.D.).

1941 **Falkenheim, Victor C.** *Communist China's Population Policy.* Columbia University, 1964. 129p. (M.A.), (East Asian Institute Certificate Essay).

1942 **Francis, Albert Allen.** *Control of Labor in Communist China.* University of California, Berkeley, 1958. 198p. (M.A.).

1943 **GOLDMAN, Merle.** *The Literati and the Chinese Communist Party.* Harvard University, 1964. 2 vols. 643p. (Ph.D.).

1944 **Goldman, René.** *The Rectification Campaign of May-June 1957 and the Student Movement at Peking University.* Columbia University, 1962. 92p. (M.A.).

1945 **McGreevey, Margaret F.** *The Overseas Chinese and the Program on Overseas Chinese Affairs of the People's Republic of China, with Special Mention of Chinese in Indonesia.* Columbia University, 1958. 137p. (M.A.).

1946 **Rossabi, Morris.** *Chinese Communists and the Peasant Women, 1949–1962.* Columbia University, 1964. 154p. (M.A.).

1947 **SHA, Philip Shung-tse.** *The Bases and Tactics of the Anti-Vatican Movement in Communist China.* Georgetown University, 1960. 241p. (Ph.D.).

1948 **Smith, Leonard Lucien.** *Chinese Communist Policy and Propaganda: 1949– 1956.* Georgetown University, 1960. 230p. (M.A.).

1949 **Tan, Soo Fong.** *Chinese Communist Policy Towards Overseas Chinese in Southeast Asia, 1949–1960.* University of California, Berkeley, 1963. 249p. (M.A.).

1950 **THOMAS, Samuel B.** *The Doctrine and Strategy of the Chinese Communist Party: Domestic Aspects, 1945–1956.* Columbia University, 1964. 422p. (Ph.D.).

1951 **VAN SLYKE, Lyman P.** *Friends and Enemy: United Front and Its Place in Chinese Communist History.* University of California, Berkeley, 1964. 420p. (Ph.D.).

1952 **Wang, Minta C. H. C.** *A Study of the All China Federation of Labor.* Columbia University, 1953. 117p. (M.A.).

3. Other Political Parties

1953 **Archer, Barbara A.** *Minor Parties in Communist China.* Tufts University, 1963. 141p. (Honors Thesis).

1954 **Seymour, James D.** *Communist China's Bourgeois-Democratic Parties.* Columbia University, 1960. 133p. (M.A.).

C. ARMED FORCES

1955 **Babel, William T.** *Chinese Communist Military Doctrine and Capabilities.* American University, 1963. 112p. (M.A.).

1956 **BOBROW, Davis Bernard.** *Political and Economic Role of the Military in the Chinese Communist Movement, 1927–1959.* Massachusetts Institute of Technology, 1962. 2 vols. 779p. (Ph.D.).

1957 **CHIU, Sin-ming.** *A History of the Chinese Communist Army.* University of Southern California, 1958. 14; 352p. (Ph.D.).

1958 **CRONE, Ruth Beverly.** *An Inquiry Into a Possible Relationship Between Propaganda and the Fall of Shanghai, 1949.* New York University, 1960. 145p. (Ph.D.).

1959 **Cummings, Edward Joseph, Jr.** *The Red Chinese Navy and the Red Rift; Naval Implications of Peking-Moscow Differences.* George Washington University, 1963. 79p. (M.A.I.A.).

D. ECONOMY

(See also section IB2b, p. 563.)

1. Economic Development and Planning

1960 **Ante, Robert W.** *The Planned Redistribution of Economic Development in China Since 1949.* Columbia University, 1963. 164p. (M.A.).

1961 **CHANG, Ching Chi.** *China's Population: Its Past, Present, and Economic Implication.* New York University, 1962. 282p. (Ph.D.).

1962 **Cheng, Chu Yuan.** *The Structural Changes of Economy in Communist China.* Georgetown University, 1962. 193p. (M.A.).

1963 **Cutler, Henry Otis.** *The Population Explosion and Its Influence on Red China's Future Developments.* George Washington University, 1963. 71p. (M.A.I.A.).

1964 **Hoye, John Henry.** *Economic Problems and Trends of Communist China.* George Washington University, 1963. 57p. (M.A.I.A.).

1965 **PERKINS, Dwight H.** *Price Formation in Communist China.* Harvard University, 1963. 489p. (Ph.D.).

1966 **SCHRAN, Peter.** *The Structure of Income in Communist China.* University of California, Berkeley, 1961. 374p. (Ph.D.).

1967 **Smee, James Coleman.** *The Chinese Communist Ability to Develop as the World Economic Power.* George Washington University, 1961. 56p. (M.A.)

1968 **Sorich, Richard.** *Distribution in Communist China: Scope, Organization and Procedure of State Planning and Control.* Columbia University, 1962. 179p. (M.A.), (East Asian Institute Certificate Essay).

1969 **Ting, Anna L.** *The Role of Population Growth in China's Economic Development, 1949–1963.* Columbia University, 1964. 116p. (M.A.).

1970 Wang, George C. *The Economic Development of Socialist China, 1950–1960.* Columbia University, 1964. 106p. (M.A.).

1971 YEH, Kung-chia. *Capital Formation in Mainland China, 1931–36 and 1952–57.* Columbia University, 1964. 345p. (Ph.D.).

2. Agriculture and Land Reform

1972 Anderson, Bengt D. *Institutional Reorganization and Resource Mobilization in Agriculture in the People's Republic of China, 1950–58.* Columbia University, 1958. 135p. (M.A.).

1973 Chan, Ki-man. *The People's Communes of Communist China.* University of Ottawa, 1961. 93p. (M.A.).

1974 CHAO, Kuo-chün. *Land Policy of the Chinese Communist Party, 1921–1953.* Cornell University, 1954. 375p. (Ph.D.).

1975 Chen, Chao-chiung. *The Communist-led Land Reform in China.* University of Washington, 1954. 142p. (M.A.).

1976 Chen, Ho-chia. *Land Reform in Soviet Russia and Communist China.* Columbia University, 1951. 107p. (M.A.).

1977 CHOU, Ya-lun. *The Chinese Agrarian Problem and the Communist Reform.* University of Pennsylvania, 1951. 1 vol. (pagination varies). (Ph.D.).

1978 Cook, Richard H. *Chinese Agrarian Policy, 1949–54, in the Chinese and Soviet Interpretations.* Columbia University, 1954. 95p. (M.A.), (Russian Institute Certificate Essay).

1979 Degler, Stanley Elmer. *Agricultural Land Problems of Communist China.* George Washington University, 1957. 131p. (M.A.).

1980 Delany, Kevin F. X. *The Soviet Communes and the People's Communes of Communist China; A Comparison.* Columbia University, 1962. 144p. (M.A.).

1981 Gomez, Rudolph. *Major Agrarian Reform Policies of the Chinese Communists.* Stanford University, 1960. 80p. (M.A.).

1982 Gordon, James Duncan. *Population Problems and Policies in the Soviet Union and Communist China in Relation to Agricultural Resources.* University of Texas. 1962. 101p. (M.B.A.).

1983 Harrison, Eric J. *The Institutional Reorganization of Agriculture in Communist China, 1950–1956.* Columbia University, 1961. 93p. (M.A.), (East Asian Institute Certificate Essay).

1984 **Klein, Sidney.** *The Land Reform Policies of the Chinese Communist Party, 1928–52: An Economic Analysis and Evaluation.* Columbia University, 1954. 220p. (M.A.), (East Asian Institute Certificate Essay).

1985 **KLEIN, Sidney.** *The Pattern of Land Tenure Reform in East Asia After World War II.* Columbia University, 1956. 398p. (Ph.D.).

1986 **Larkin, Marlene Molly.** *Sociological Analysis of the Communes in Communist China.* University of Southern California, 1961. 114p. (M.A.).

1987 **Law, Willard E.** *The Chinese Peasant and His Relation to the Communist Movement in China.* Brigham Young University, 1953. 157p. (M.A.).

1988 **Lee, Dorothy Ya-shu.** *Chinese Communist Land Reform Practices.* Columbia University, 1950. 106p. (M.A.).

1989 **MITCHELL, William B.** *The Prospects for the Chinese Communist Yellow River Plan.* Columbia University, 1961. 141p. (Ph.D.).

1990 **Montee, Ralph Bruce.** *Agrarian Problems and Policies in China up to 1953.* University of California, Berkeley, 1961. 341p. (M.A.).

1991 **MOORE, William J.** *Ideology and Economic Development in China and India: A Study of Contrasting Political Approaches to the Problem of Agricultural Development, 1951–1961.* University of Redlands, 1963. 379p. (Ph.D.).

1992 **Noble, Naomi P.** *The Chinese Agrarian Problem and the Chinese Communist Reform.* University of Chicago, 1955. 81p. (M.A.).

1993 **Schaller, Martin K.** *The Producers Cooperative Phase in the Socialist Transformation of Agriculture in Communist China.* Columbia University, 1957. 131p. (M.A.).

1994 **Stover, Leon E.** *The Chinese Peasant and Communism.* Columbia University, 1952. 72p. (M.A.).

1995 **Titus, Kaoru M.** *The Changes in Ownership System of the People's Communes, August 1958 to August 1962.* Columbia University, 1963. 71p. (M.A.).

1996 **WANG, Te-hua.** *Land Reform in the People's Republic of China.* State University of Iowa, 1952. 229p. (Ph.D.).

1997 **Wissner, Faye D.** *The Chinese Communes: Sino-Soviet Conflict.* Columbia University, 1962. 85p. (M.A.).

3. Industry

1998 **CHAO, Kang.** *Indexes of Industrial Production of Communist China, 1949–1959.* University of Michigan, 1962. 286p. (Ph.D.).

1999 **FROST, Charles C.** *The Economic Development of Communist China's Machine-Building Industry: A Case Study in the Application of Soviet Development Doctrine to a Labor Surplus Economy.* Tufts University, 1961. 181p. (Ph.D.).

2000 **Gatterdam, Dwain Roger.** *The Socialization of Private Industry in Communist China, 1949–1956.* University of California, Berkeley, 1960. 126p. (M.A.).

2001 **GODARD, Walter R.** *Steel and Red China's Power Potential.* New York University, 1961. 508p. (Ph.D.).

2002 **Huang, Cheng-wang.** *Some Problems in the First Five-Year Plan in Communist China.* University of Washington, 1957. 92p. (M.A.).

2003 **LIANG, Leland Sung.** *Problems of the Cotton Manufacturer in China.* University of Pennsylvania, 1955. 202p. (Ph.D.).

2004 **Louie, Richard.** *Problems of Local Industry in Communist Chinese Economic Development.* University of Washington, 1963. 152p. (M.A.).

2005 **March, Andrew Lee.** *Studies in the Location of Iron-and-Steel and Machine-Building Industries, Mainland China, 1953–1957.* Syracuse University, 1959. 126p. (M.A.).

2006 **McDonell, Gavan John.** *Transport and Industrial Location in China (1949–1959).* Johns Hopkins University, 1961. 82p. (M.A.).

2007 **Pandit, Ramprasad D.** *Communist China's Industrial Development Under the First Five-Year Plan (1953–1957): Analysis and Appraisal.* University of Southern California, 1960. 151p. (M.A.).

2008 **Rosen, Richard Barry.** *The Soviet Role in Communist China's Heavy Industry Program, 1949–58.* Georgetown University, 1961. 113p. (M.A.).

4. Money and Finance

2009 **ECKLUND, George N.** *Taxation in Communist China, 1950–1959.* University of Minnesota, 1962. 211p. (Ph.D.).

2010 **MA, James Chao-seng.** *A Study of the People's Bank of China.* University of Texas, 1960. 182p. (Ph.D.).

2011 **MAH, Feng-hwa,** *The Financing of Public Investment in Communist China.* University of Michigan, 1959. 259p. (Ph.D.).

2012 **STARLIGHT, Lawrence Lee.** *Monetary and Fiscal Policies in Communist China, 1949–54.* Harvard University, 1956. 322p. (Ph.D.).

5. Foreign Trade

(See also IV—China Policy, p. 581.)

a. General

2013 **Jen, S. P.** *Communist China's Foreign Trade, 1949–1954.* University of California, Berkeley, 1954. 127p. (M.A.).

2014 **Laase, Paul L.** *The Foreign Trade of the People's Republic of China.* Tufts University, 1959. 224p. (M.A.).

2015 **Lao, Chia-hwa.** *The Foreign Trade of Communist China: An Analytical Study.* New York University, 1963. 126p. (M.A.).

2016 **MOK, Victor.** *The Foreign Trade of Communist China, 1949–1962.* Michigan State University, 1964. (Ph.D.).

2017 **WANG, Pe Sheng.** *Communist China's Foreign Trade and Its Relationship to Her National Income and Agricultural Production.* University of Washington, 1962. 266p. (D.B.A.).

2018 **Whitbeck, Everett E.** *A Survey of Sino-Soviet Trade from World War II to 1952, with Special Reference to Its Political Connotations.* American University, 1959. 124p. (M.I.S.).

b. Japan

(See also **2217.**)

2019 **Hutton, Robert W.** *Japanese Trade with the Soviet Union and Communist China, 1950–1960.* Columbia University, 1962. 114p. (M.A.).

2020 **Landman, Amos.** *Some Implications of Trade (or Lack of Trade) Between Communist China and Japan.* Columbia University, 1952. 153p. (M.A.).

2021 **Nishimiya, Hajime.** *A Study of Foreign Trade Relations Between China and Japan.* University of Southern California, 1953. 52p. (M.B.A.).

2022 **Richardson, Bradley M.** *The Development and Structure of Sino-Japanese Trade, 1950–58.* Columbia University, 1960. 160p. (M.A.)

2023 **Wendell, Larry H.** *Japan's Trade with Communist China.* Tufts University, 1960. 137p. (M.A.).

2024 **Yagi, Kuniyoshi.** *Some Aspects of Sino-Japanese Trade Relations in the Post-War Period: Limitations and Problems.* University of Denver, 1962. 171p. (M.A.).

E. FOREIGN RELATIONS

(See also section on Foreign Trade above and III—The Overseas Chinese, p. 577.)

1. General

2025 **AN, Tai Sung.** *Communist China and 'Peaceful Coexistence': An Analysis of Communist China's Foreign Policy.* University of Pennsylvania, 1963. 494p. (Ph.D.).

2026 **Chang, Raymond Jui-jong.** *Communist China's Foreign Policy Since 1949 as Reflected in Its Propaganda.* New York University, 1962. 109p. (M.A.).

2027 **Fullinwider, Peter Lansing.** *Communist China's Foreign Policy—A Study in Methodology.* George Washington University, 1963. 52p. (M.A.I.A.).

2028 **Jennings, Patrick Henry.** *The Foreign Relations of the Chinese Communist Party and the People's Republic of China.* University of Hawaii, 1953. 149p. (M.A.).

2029 **LEE, Oliver Minseem.** *National Interest and Ideology of Communist China's Foreign Policy.* University of Chicago, 1962. 281p. (Ph.D.).

2030 **Thomas, John N.** *The 'Elastic Bolshevik' Looks at the World: An Analysis of Some Major Foreign Policy Statements by Chou En-lai, 1954–1960.* Tufts University, 1962. 105p. (M.A.).

2. The Soviet Union

(See also **2018** and section IA2c, p. 561.)

2031 **Bridgeman, Gerald Ernest.** *Nationalism, Ideology, and Integration in the Sino-Soviet Alliance.* University of California, Berkeley, 1961. 114p. (M.A.).

2032 **Hedstrom, Carl E.** *Outer Mongolia: A Study of Soviet-Chinese Rivalry.* University of Pennsylvania, 1961. 118p. (M.A.).

2033 **Humphrey, Gay.** *The Sino-Soviet Alliance Through the Communist Press.* Columbia University, 1955. 97p. (M.A.).

2034 **Lieberman, Henry R.** *China versus Russia in Sinkiang (A Problem in Sino-Soviet Border Area 'Attachment').* Columbia University, 1950. 265p. (M.A.).

2035 **Mayer, Peter.** *Sino-Soviet Relations Since the Death of Stalin.* University of California, Berkeley, 1961. 357p. (M.A.). (See also **1566**.)

2036 **Pringsheim, Klaus H.** *The Sino-Soviet Friendship Association, October 1949–October 1951.* Columbia University, 1960. 224p. (M.A.).

2037 **Stockdale, James Bond.** *Taiwan and the Sino-Soviet Dispute.* Stanford University, 1962. 199p. (M.A.).

2038 **SU, Edward Shou-tsu.** *Sino-Russian Relations in Sinkiang: A Comparison of International Relationships Outside and Inside the Communist System.* Fordham University, 1962. 408p. (Ph.D.).

2039 **SUMMERS, Marvin Ruben.** *Chinese Communist Attitudes Toward the Soviet Union and Sino-Soviet Relations.* State University of Iowa, 1953. 230p. (Ph.D.).

2040 **Swearingen, A. Rodger.** *The Political and Ideological Relationship Between the Chinese Communist Party and the Soviet Union.* University of Southern California, 1948. 201p. (M.A.).

2041 **Tashjean, John Eugene.** *Where China and Russia Meet.* Georgetown University, 1958. 136p. (M.A.).

2042 **Tauscher, Robert Edward.** *Soviet-Chinese Communist Relations and Current Tensions.* George Washington University, 1963. 110p. (M.A.I.A.).

2043 **TSU, John B.** *Sino-Soviet Relations, 1945–52.* Fordham University, 1953. 2 vols. 487p. (Ph.D.).

2044 **ZAGORIA, Donald S.** *The Sino-Soviet Conflict, 1956–1961.* Columbia University, 1963. [Princeton University Press, 1962. 484p.] (Ph.D.).

3. The Communist Bloc

(See also **2062.**)

2045 **Greenblatt, Sidney L.** *The Impact of Sino-Yugoslav Relations on Chinese Communist-Bloc Relations, 1955–1958.* Columbia University, 1962. 73p. (M.A.), (East Asian Institute Certificate Essay).

2046 **Janczewski, George H.** *The Role of Communist China in the Polish Crisis of 1956–1957; A Preliminary Analysis.* Georgetown University, 1960. 135p. (M.A.).

2047 **Mitchell, Wyatt J.** *The Chinese Communist Attitude Toward Yugoslavia, 1948–59.* Columbia University, 1959. 179p. (M.A.).

2048 **Walker, Byron Paul.** *Chinese Criticisms of Yugoslavia, 1958–1961.* University of California, Berkeley, 1962. 129p. (M.A.).

4. India

(See also section on Tibet in IA, p. 561.)

2049 **Chang, Chin Bing.** *A Critical Review of the Relations Between Free India and Communist China, 1949–1954.* New York University, 1955. 116p. (M.A.)

2050 **CHAWLA, Sudershan.** *India, Russia, and China, 1947–1955: An Interpretation of the Indian Concept of National Interest.* Ohio State University, 1959. 304p. (Ph.D.).

2051 **Crum, Whitney Irving.** *Relations Between India and Communist China, 1949–1954.* University of Southern California, 1955. 202p., illus. (M.A.).

2052 **Dickinson, Martin Brownlow, Jr.** *Soviet and Chinese Relations With India.* Stanford University, 1961. 136p. (M.A.).

2053 **Friezer, Louis A.** *The Sino-Indian Border Conflicts.* Columbia University, 1964. 118p. (M.A.).

2054 **Giddens, Jackson A.** *Studies on Tibet. Part 2—Sino-Indian Relations with Special Reference to Tibet and the Tibetan Border Question, 1947–1960.* Tufts University, 1960. 70p. (M.A.).

2055 OSBORN, George Knox, III. *Sino-Indian Border Conflicts: Historical Background and Recent Developments.* Stanford University, 1963. 283p. (Ph.D.).

2056 Rao, Prabhavati Shrinivas. *Sino-India Border Issue.* University of California, Berkeley, 1960. 143p. (M.A.).

2057 ROSE, Leo Eugene. *The Role of Nepal and Tibet in Sino-Indian Relations.* University of California, Berkeley, 1960. 505p. (Ph.D.).

2058 SRIVASTAVA, Harishankar Prasad. *The India-China Boundary: A Study in Political Geography.* University of Florida, 1961. 170p. (Ph.D.).

2059 Weedon, John A. *Leadership in Asia—India or China.* American University, 1961. 236p. (M.A.).

2060 Wray, Carol Susann. *The Communist Threat to Nepal.* Georgetown University, 1961. 103p. (M.A.).

5. Hong Kong and Southeast Asia
(See also **1938**.)

2061 Chatate, Narayan M. *Sino-Burmese Border Dispute.* American University, 1962. 246p. (M.A.).

2062 CHEN, King. *China and the Democratic Republic of Vietnam (1945–1954).* The Pennsylvania State University, 1962. 326p. (Ph.D.).

2063 Du Cote, Robert A. *Communist China: Threat to Southeast Asia?* American University, 1963. 225p. (M.A.).

2064 Erickson, Philip. *Chinese Impact on Burmese Foreign Policy, 1949–1959.* Georgetown University, 1960. 104p. (M.A.).

2065 Hellmann, Donald Charles. *Burma-Communist China Relations, 1949–1958.* University of California, Berkeley, 1960. 103p. (M.A.).

2066 Jones, W. Craig. *The Communist Revolution in Vietnam: Internal Strategy and External Influence.* Brigham Young University, 1963. 160p. (M.A.)

2067 Lorenzo, May Kwan. *The Attitude of Communist China Toward Hong Kong.* University of Chicago, 1959. 65p. (M.A.).

2068 Noor, Gusti R. *Sino-Soviet Attitudes Towards Indonesia, 1950–55.* Columbia University, 1958. 97p. (M.A.).

6. Underdeveloped Countries

2069 CHANG, Yi-chun. *The Foreign Policy of Communist China in the Underdeveloped Areas.* Northwestern University, 1963. 191p. (Ph.D.).

2070 **Euben, J. Peter.** *Nationalist and Communist Chinese Foreign Policy in Asia, Africa, and Latin America.* University of California, Berkeley, 1964. 229p. (M.A.)

2071 **Saca, Mansur Khalil.** *Arab Reaction on Communist China and Communist Attitude Towards the Arabs.* University of California, Berkeley, 1961. 252p. (M.A.).

2072 **Van der Stoel, William.** *Communist China's Policy Towards the Afro-Asian Nations.* University of British Columbia, 1962. 161p. (M.A.)

2073 **Yin, Chi-wen.** *Communist China's Approach to Latin America.* Brigham Young University, 1964. 115p. (M.A.).

7. Japan

(See also section on Sino-Japanese Trade in ID5, p. 569.)

2074 **Pau, Yun-tong.** *Communist China and Japan: 1949–1960.* University of Massachusetts, 1964. 96p. (M.A.).

2075 **Urquhart, Joelle.** *Japanese Relations with Communist China, 1950–1958.* University of Pennsylvania, 1958. 82p. (M.A.)

8. United States

2076 **Kennedy, Thomas Laren.** *The Treatment of Americans in Red China Prior to the Korean War.* Georgetown University, 1961. 176p. (M.A.)

2077 **SMITH, Martha Jane.** *Key Symbols in U.S.S.R. and Chinese Propaganda to the U.S.A.* New York University, 1958. 295p. (Ph.D.).

9. The Korean War

2078 **BARENDSEN, Robert Dale.** *The Chinese Communist Germ Warfare Propaganda Campaign, 1952–53: A Case Study of the Use of Propaganda in Domestic and Foreign Policies.* Yale University, 1957. 352p. (Ph.D.).

2079 **Gilliland, William Shirley.** *Roots of Red China's Strategy in the Korean War.* Stanford University, 1960. 111p. (M.A.).

2080 **KIM, Myong Whai.** *Prisoners of War as a Major Problem of the Korean Armistice, 1953.* New York University, 1960. 323p. (Ph.D.)

2081 **Kolbenschlag, Richard P.** *The United States Air Force Tactical Reconnaissance in the Korean Conflict.* The Pennsylvania State University, 1963. 112p. (M.A.).

2082 **Milrod, Martin Oscar.** *Prisoners of War in Korea: The Impact of Communist Practice upon International Law.* Georgetown University, 1959. 207p. (M.A.).

2083 Rifkin, Sylvia. *The 1951 Resist-America—Aid-Korea Campaign in Communist China.* Columbia University, 1962. 120p. (M.A.), (East Asian Institute Certificate Essay).

10. United Nations

2084 Adams, Mervyn W. *Communist China and the United Nations: A Study of China's Developing Attitude Towards the U.N.'s Role in International Peace and Security.* Columbia University, 1964. 349p. (M.A.), (East Asian Institute Certificate Essay).

2085 APPLETON, Sheldon L. *The Question of Representation of China in the United Nations.* University of Minnesota, 1961. 389p. (Ph.D.).

2086 Brook, David. *The United Nations' Handling of the Chinese Representation Issue.* Columbia University, 1955. 103p. (M.A.).

2087 HUANG, William Yung-nien. *China's Role with Respect to Major Political and Security Questions Under Consideration by the United Nations.* University of Michigan, 1954. 826p. (Ph.D.).

2088 Lee, Oliver M. *Communist China's Representation in the United Nations.* University of Chicago, 1955. 106p. (M.A.).

2089 Long, Kathleen S. (Sister M. Stanislaus, O.P.). *An Analysis of the Claim of the People's Republic of China to Membership in the United Nations and Its Rejection by the United States.* St. John's University, 1964. 70p. (M.A.).

F. EDUCATION

(See also **1940, 1943, 1944**.)

2090 ARENS, Richard. *The Impact of Communism on Education in China, 1949–50.* University of Chicago, 1952. 255p. (Ph.D.).

2091 Chen, Anthony K. C. *The Philosophy of Education of Communist China as Applied to Secondary and Higher Education.* De Paul University, 1957. 149p. (M.A.).

2092 FRASER, Stewart Erskine. *Some Aspects of Higher Education in the People's Republic of China* (Part II: Selected Documents). University of Colorado, 1961. 476; 302p. (Ed.D.).

2093 Hsu, Constance Jen. *Development of Modern Education and Guidance Work in Chinese Secondary Schools and Organizing a Scientific Guidance Program.* Syracuse University, 1951. 105p. (M.A.).

2094 KIANG, Ying-cheng. *The Geography of Higher Education in China.* Columbia University, 1955. 299p. (Ph.D.).

2095 KONG, Shiu-loon. *A Critical Survey of Higher Education in the People's Republic of China During the Period 1949–1957.* University of Ottawa, 1960. 147p. (Ph.D.).

2096 **Lazen, Lillian Rae Caplan.** *The Education of the People's Republic of China* [sic]. Ohio State University, 1962. 162p. (M.A.).

2097 **LIN, En-chin.** *Educational Changes in China Since the Establishment of the People's Republic and Some Steps Leading to Them.* University of Pennsylvania, 1955. 131p. (Ed.D.).

2098 **LIN, Vincent Tsing Ching.** *Adult Education in People's Republic of China, 1950–1958.* University of California, Berkeley, 1963. 472p. (Ph.D.).

2099 **Newcomer, James R.** *On Political Control of the Academies of Science in the Soviet Union and China.* Columbia University, 1964. 164p. (M.A.), (East Asian Institute Certificate Essay).

2100 **Wang, Percy Hung-fang.** *Higher Education in Communist China.* University of Washington, 1953. 149p. (M.A.).

G. LITERATURE

(See also **1940, 1943.**)

2101 **ANDERSON, Colena M.** *Two Modern Chinese Women: Ping Hsin and Ting Ling.* Claremont Graduate School, 1954. 252p. (Ph.D.).

2102 **CHIN, Ai-li S.** *Interdependence of Roles in Transitional China: A Structural Analysis of Attitudes of Contemporary Chinese Literature.* Radcliffe College, 1951. 310p. (Ph.D.).

2103 **Elegant, Robert S.** *Confucius to Shelley to Marx. Kuo Mo-jo; A Critical Examination of His Opinions on the Nature of Literature, with Particular Reference to Its Function in Society.* Columbia University, 1950. 60p. (M.A.).

2104 **Feldman, Joan Jacobs.** *The Development of Mao Tun's Ideas of Literature.* Columbia University, 1950. 60p. (M.A.).

2105 **Forbes, Mary Ellen.** *The Social and Political Views of the Leading Modern Chinese Authors.* Cornell University, 1961. 236p. (M.A.).

2106 **Johnson, Paula.** *Yeh Shen-t'ao (Yeh Shao-chün), His Life and Literary Works—From 1894 Through 1963.* Columbia University, 1964. 112p. (M.A.), (East Asian Institute Certificate Essay).

2107 **LAMMERS, Raymond John.** *An Analysis of a Representative Sample of Plays Written and Used for Propagandistic Purposes by the Chinese Communists.* University of Minnesota, 1962. 223p. (Ph.D.).

2108 **LANG, Olga.** *Writer Pa Chin and His Time: Chinese Youth of the Transitional Period.* Columbia University, 1962. 490p. (Ph.D.).

2109 **McCaskey, Michael Joseph, Jr.** *The 1954 Controversy Over the 'Dream of the Red Chamber.'* Stanford University, 1960. 98p. (M.A.).

2110 **Ross, Timothy Arrowsmith.** *Ting Ling and Chinese Communist Literary Policy.* State University of Iowa, 1963. 131p. (M.A.).

H. RELIGION AND CULTURE

(See also **1947.**)

2111 **Faville, Donald David.** *Forced Culture Change in Communist China.* Stanford University, 1957. 197p. (M.A.).

2112 **GALLIGAN, David J.** *American Protestant Missions and Communist China, 1946–1950.* Rutgers University, 1952. 156p. (Ph.D.).

2113 **Huang, Nancy Lai-shen.** *Library Development in Communist China (1949–1962).* University of Chicago, 1964. 114p. (M.A.).

2114 **LACY, Creighton Boutelle.** *Protestant Missions in Communist China.* Yale University, 1953. 670p. (Ph.D.).

2115 **WINDEMILLER, Duane A.** *The Psychodynamics of Change in Religious Conversion and Communist Brainwashing with Particular Reference to the Eighteenth Century Evangelical Revival and the Chinese Thought Control Movement.* Boston University, 1960. 186p. (Ph.D.).

II. REPUBLIC OF CHINA

A. GOVERNMENT AND POLITICS

(See also **1930, 2037, 2070.**)

2116 **Chang, Archibald How.** *A Comparison of Sun Yat-sen's Constitutional Theories and the Current Constitution of the Republic of China.* Brigham Young University, 1964. 121p. (M.A.).

2117 **Chang, Tien-teh.** *The Development of a Position-Classification Plan in the Public Service in the Republic of China.* Columbia University, 1955. 90p. (M.A.).

2118 **Mallett, Richard D.** *Chinese Nationalist and Chinese Communist Party Relations, August 1945 to February 1947.* Columbia University, 1957. 250p. (M.A.).

2119 **Ruben, Bruce Lloyd.** *The Administrative Structure of the Government of the Republic of China.* University of Southern California, 1963. 283p. (M.A.).

2120 **WANG, Cheng.** *The Kuomintang: A Sociological Study of Demoralization.* Stanford University, 1953. 185p. (Ph.D.).

B. GEOGRAPHY AND DEMOGRAPHY

2121 **HSIEH, James Chiao-min.** *Successive Occupance Patterns in Taiwan.* Syracuse University, 1953. 417p. (Ph.D.).

2122 **Hsieh, Jean Kan.** *Typhoons: Origin, Routes, Speeds, and Their Effects on the Southeastern Coast of China and Taiwan.* Syracuse University, 1953. 145p. (M.A.).

2123 **YUAN, Dan Da-yuan.** *The Rural-Urban Continuum: A Demographic Case Study of Taiwan.* Brown University, 1964. 286p. (Ph.D.).

C. AGRICULTURE AND LAND REFORM

2124 **ATTERBURY, Marguerite.** *A Study of Some Phases of Chinese-American Cooperation in Promoting China's Agricultural Extension.* Columbia University, 1954. 401p. (Ph.D.).

2125 **Chang, Jen-hu.** *Agricultural Geography of Formosa.* Clark University, 1952. 86p. (M.A.).

2126 **CHAO, Ching Yuan.** *Dynamic and Nonlinear Programming for Optimum Farm Plans in Taiwan.* Iowa State University of Science and Technology, 1963. 146p. (Ph.D.).

2127 **Fan, Shuh-ching.** *The Economic Effects of Farm Land Reform to Farmers in Formosa, China.* Cornell University, 1957. 74p. (M.A.).

2128 **GALLIN, Bernard.** *Hsin Hsing: A Taiwanese Agricultural Village.* Cornell University, 1961. 741p. (Ph.D.).

2129 **HSIEH, Sam C.** *Rice and Sugar Cane Competition on Paddy Land in Central Taiwan.* University of Minnesota, 1957. 119p. (Ph.D.).

2130 **KAO, Charles Hsi-chung.** *The Role of the Agricultural Sector in Taiwan's Economic Development.* Michigan State University, 1964. 156p. (Ph.D.).

2131 **Kwoh, Min-hsieh.** *The Farmers' Associations Movement of Taiwan (Formosa).* Cornell University, 1957. 88p. (M.A.).

2132 **LIU, Wei-ping.** *An Economic Analysis of Taiwanian Agricultural Development Since 1950.* University of Minnesota, 1961. 149p. (Ph.D.).

2133 **Tan, Lynette P. C.** *The Contribution of Private Agencies in Rural Reconstruction in China.* Columbia University, 1952. 136p. (M.A.).

D. ECONOMY—GENERAL

2134 **Chen, Nai-ruenn.** *Formosa's National Income, Concepts, Estimation, Methods and Distribution.* University of Illinois, 1955. 59p. (M.A.).

2135 **Chien, Chih-hsing.** *Monetary System and Economic Growth of Taiwan.* University of Washington, 1958. 84p. (M.A.).

2136 **LI, Mabel K. W.** *The Tax System of Taiwan.* New York University, 1956. 2 vols. 470p. (Ph.D.).

2137 **Wu, Vivian S.** *America's Part in the Effort to Industrialize Taiwan Since the Removal of the Seat of the Chinese Nationalist Government to the Island.* Columbia University, 1955. 134p. (M.A.).

2138 **Young, Kan-hua.** *Capital Inflow and Economic Development: A Case Study of the Economy of Taiwan.* Columbia University, 1963. 126p. (M.A.).

E. EDUCATION AND RELIGION

2139 **Cheng, Lillian Li-ling.** *The Educational Program of the Chinese Nationalist Government in Formosa.* American University, 1953. 95p. (M.A.).

2140 **CHU, Godwin Chien.** *Culture, Personality and Persuasibility.* Stanford University, 1963. 170p. (Ph.D.).

2141 **FOSTER, Donald.** *Education as an Instrument of National Policy for Economic Development in the Republic of China.* Stanford University, 1962. 337p. (Ph.D.).

2142 **HUANG, Sophia Chang.** *A Comparison of Selected Values Among Formosan and American Adolescents.* Ohio State University, 1962. 191p. (Ph.D.).

2143 **Hwang, Shih-chen.** *Some Aspects of the Religion of the Ryūkyūs and Formosa: Ryūkyū Priestesses and Formosan Shamans.* Syracuse University, 1960. 87p. (M.A.).

2144 **Leung, Florence Yu.** *Application of Audio-Visual Aids to Secondary Education in Formosa: Problems and Possibilities.* American University, 1953. 66p. (M.A.).

2145 **LI, Anthony C.** *The History of Privately Controlled Higher Education in the Republic of China.* Catholic University, 1955. 315p. (Ed.D.).

2146 **LIANG, Shang Yung.** *Provisional Financing of Public Education in Taiwan, China: An Evaluation and a Proposed Plan.* University of Missouri, 1963. 325p. (Ed.D.).

2147 **Nee, Nelson Ven-chung.** *A Program of Vocational Industrial Education in Taiwan, Republic of China.* University of Tennessee, 1958. 117p. (M.A.).

2148 **NELSON, Wilbur Kenneth.** *Educational Goals in China with Emphasis on the Relationship of Public and Private Schools on Taiwan During the Period 1949–1962.* Claremont Graduate School, 1963. 197p. (Ph.D.).

2149 **RODD, William G.** *A Cross-Cultural Study of Taiwan Schools.* Western Reserve University, 1958. 351p. (Ph.D.).

2150 **Tzeng, Jenn.** *Charting Educational Philosophy for Free China.* De Paul University, 1956. 98p. (M.A.).

2151 **TZENG, Jenn.** *Taiwanian Vocational Education in Agriculture, 1945–1963.* Colorado State College, 1964. 193p. (Ed.D.).

III. The Overseas Chinese

(See also **1945, 1949.**)

A. GENERAL

2152 **LEICHTER, Hope J.** *Alternatives and Constraint in the Role of the Chinese Exile.* Radcliffe College, 1959. 261p. (Ph.D.).

B. UNITED STATES

2153 **HEYER, Virginia.** *Patterns of Social Organization in New York City's Chinatown.* Columbia University, 1953. 191p. (Ph.D.).

2154 **KAO, Lin-ying.** *Academic and Professional Attainments of Native Chinese Students Graduating from Teachers College, Columbia University, 1909–1950.* Columbia University, 1951. 153p. (Ed.D.).

2155 **LIU, Yung-szi.** *The Academic Achievement of Chinese Graduate Students at the University of Michigan (1907–1950).* University of Michigan, 1956. 169p. (Ph.D.).

In addition, there are a number of dissertations concerned with the Chinese in the United States not as an overseas community, nor as they relate to the Mainland or Taiwan, but rather as they relate to American society, mostly in sociological or psychological terms (e.g., *Alcohol and Culture: A Case Study of Drinking in a Chinese-American Community; The Chinese Laundryman: A Study of Social Isolation; Dating and Courtship Innovations of Chinese Students in America; A Study of the Heterosexual Social Life of Single Male Chinese Students in New York City*).

C. HONG KONG

2156 **BOXER, Baruch.** *Ocean Shipping in the Evolution of Hong Kong.* University of Chicago, 1962. 95p. (Ph.D.).

2157 **Chan, Yue-ping.** *A Study on 'Sing tao jih pao' and Its Position in Hong Kong Journalism.* University of Missouri, 1962. 127p. (M.A.).

2158 **Leung, Mei Lin.** *Music Education in the Schools in Hong Kong.* Claremont Graduate School, 1962. 90p. (M.A.).

2159 **POTTER, Jack.** *P'ing Shan: The Changing Economy of a Chinese Village in Hong Kong.* University of California, Berkeley, 1964. 401p. (Ph.D.).

2160 **TOM, Chiu Faat Joseph.** *Monetary Problems of an Entrepot: The Hong Kong Experience.* University of Chicago, 1963. 132p. (Ph.D.).

D. INDONESIA

2161 **Ellis, James William.** *The Influence of the Chinese Minority in the Political and Economic Affairs of the Republics of Indonesia and the Philippines.* Brigham Young University, 1964. 97p. (M.A.).

2162 **Lie, Joseph Aloysius Han Tie.** *The Chinese in Indonesia: A Study of Their Community Development and Problems.* Georgetown University, 1959. 157p. (M.A.).

2163 **RYAN, Edward J.** *The Value System of a Chinese Community in Java.* Harvard University, 1961. 166p. (Ph.D.).

2164 **Tan, Giok-lan.** *The Chinese Community in a Sundanese Town: A Study in Social and Cultural Accommodation.* Cornell University, 1961. 623p. (M.A.).

2165 **WILLMOTT, Donald Earl.** *Sociocultural Change Among the Chinese of Semarang, Indonesia.* Cornell University, 1958. 516p. (Ph.D.).

E. THAILAND

2166 **Chie, Paik-san.** *A Study of the Chinese Minority in Thailand.* American University, 1959. 114p. (M.A.).

2167 **COUGHLIN, Richard J.** *The Chinese in Bangkok.* Yale University, 1953. 633p. (Ph.D.).

2168 **DIBBLE, Charles Ryder.** *The Chinese in Thailand Against the Background of Chinese-Thai Relations.* Syracuse University, 1961. 546p. (Ph.D.).

2169 **SKINNER, G. William.** *A Study of Chinese Community Leadership in Bangkok, Together with an Historical Survey of Chinese Society in Thailand.* Cornell University, 1955. 842p. (Ph.D.).

F. MALAYSIA

2170 **BLAUT, James Morris.** *Chinese Market Gardening in Singapore: A Study in Functional Microgeography.* Louisiana State University, 1959. 424p. (Ph.D.).

2171 **FLEMING, John Ross.** *The Growth of the Chinese Church in the New Villages of the State of Johore, Malaya, 1950/60—A Study in the Communication of the Gospel to Chinese Converts.* Union Theological Seminary, 1962. 659p. (Th.D.).

2172 **FORTIER, David H.** *Culture Change Among Chinese Agricultural Settlers in British North Borneo.* Columbia University, 1964. 233p. (Ph.D.).

2173 **NYCE, Ray.** *The New Villages of Malaya: A Community Study.* The Hartford Seminary Foundation, 1962. 478p. (Ph.D.).

G. THE PHILIPPINES

(See also **2161**.)

2174 **AMYOT, Jacques.** *The Chinese Community of Manila: A Study of Adaptation of Chinese Familism to the Philippine Environment.* University of Chicago, 1960. 181p. (Ph.D.).

2175 **Shupe, Joseph B.** *The Chinese Minority Problem in the Philippines.* University of Maryland, 1963. 157p. (M.A.).

2176 **WEIGHTMANN, George H.** *The Philippine Chinese: A Cultural History of a Marginal Trading Community.* Cornell University, 1960. 477p. (Ph.D.).

H. OTHER COUNTRIES

2177 **CHANG, Ching-chieh.** *The Chinese in Latin America: A Preliminary Geographical Survey with Special Reference to Cuba and Jamaica.* University of Maryland, 1956. 194p. (Ph.D.).

2178 **JAN, George P.** *Nationality and the Treatment of Overseas Chinese in Southeast Asia.* New York University, 1960. 234p. (Ph.D.).

2179 **LUONG, Nhi-ky.** *The Chinese in Vietnam: A Study of Vietnamese-Chinese Relations with Special Attention to the Period 1862–1961.* University of Michigan, 1963. 218p. (Ph.D.).

IV. CHINA POLICY

(See also section IE, p. 569.)

A. GENERAL

2180 **Fielder, Virginia Berg.** *Formosa in Post-War International Politics.* University of California, Berkeley, 1951. 102p. (M.A.).

B. UNITED STATES

1. 1945–1950 Period

2181 **BABCOCK, Fenton.** *Issues of China Policy Before Congress, September 1945 to September 1949.* Yale University, 1956. 176p. (Ph.D.).

2182 **BARNETT, Irving.** *UNRRA in China: A Case Study in Financial Assistance for Economic Development (With Emphasis on Agricultural Programs).* Columbia University, 1956. 338p. (Ph.D.).

2183 **Bolnick, Maxwell N.** *Official Attitude of the United States Toward the Chinese Communists, 1944–1949.* Columbia University, 1951. 63p. (M.A.).

2184 **Gasster, Michael.** *United States Policy Toward China and the Mission of General George C. Marshall.* Columbia University, 1953. 152p. (M.A.).

2185 **Gibney, John Vandever.** *The China Policy of Secretary of State George C. Marshall.* Georgetown University, 1961. 125p. (M.A.).

2186 ——. *The Marshall Mission to China.* Georgetown University, 1961. 105p. (M.A.).

2187 **Jonas, Gilbert.** *American Aid to China as Part of a Policy, 1945–1949.* Columbia University, 1953. 165p. (M.A.), (East Asian Institute Certificate Essay).

2188 KENNEDY, Jesse C. *American Foreign Policy in China, 1937-1950: An Analysis of Why It Failed.* University of Chicago, 1962. 514p. (Ph.D.).

2189 LONG, F. M. S. Brother Ronald B. *The Role of American Diplomats in the Fall of China, 1941-1949.* St. John's University, 1961. 242p. (Ph.D.).

2190 McKenzie, Jane H. *China's Party Conflict and American Foreign Policy.* Claremont Graduate School, 1949. 197p. (M.A.).

2191 SHERRY, John C. *Aspects of American Policy Regarding the Unification of the Chinese Nationalist Government, 1944-1948.* Fordham University, 1956. 270p. (Ph.D.).

2192 SMITH, Cordell Audivell. *The Marshall Mission: Its Impact upon American Foreign Policy Toward China, 1945-1949.* University of Oklahoma, 1963. 294p. (Ph.D.).

2193 Tidd, J. Thomas. *The Formulation of United States Policy Toward China, 1945-50.* University of Denver, 1950. 163p. (M.A.).

2. Domestic Attitudes and Pressures

2194 DOUGHERTY, Patrick Thomas. *Catholic Opinion and United States Recognition Policy.* University of Missouri, 1963. 215p. (Ph.D.).

2195 Fallon, Patrick Martin. *The Committee of One Million Against the Admission of Communist China to the United Nations: A Case Study.* Georgetown University, 1961. 164p. (M.A.).

2196 HEDLEY, John Hollister. *The Truman Administration and the 'Loss' of China: A Study of Public Attitudes and the President's Policies from the Marshall Mission to the Attack on Korea.* University of Missouri, 1964. 229p. (Ph.D.).

2197 KOEN, Ross Y. *The China Lobby and the Formulation of American Far Eastern Policy, 1945-1952.* University of Florida, 1958. 434p. (Ph.D.).

2198 SKRETTING, John R. *Republican Attitudes Toward the Administration's China Policy, 1945-1949.* State University of Iowa, 1952. 204p. (Ph.D.).

3. Policy Towards Taiwan

2199 Bacon, Carol A. *America's Decision to Support Formosa, 1950.* Columbia University, 1962. 61p. (M.A.).

2200 Benge, Howard Beard. *U.S. Policy Towards Nationalist China.* George Washington University, 1961. (M.A.).

2201 **Harmon, Robert B.** *The Decisions by the United States to Support the Chinese Nationalist Government in Taiwan.* Brigham Young University, 1960. 112p. (M.A.)

2202 **XUTO, Manaspas.** *United States Relations with Formosa, 1850–1960.* Tufts University, 1961. 401p. (Ph.D.).

4. Problems of Recognition

2203 **Anderson, Oscar S., Jr.** *Communist China: Recognition or Non-Recognition.* George Washington University, 1963. 98p. (M.A.I.A.).

2204 **CHEN, Chiu-shan.** *American Recognition and Non-Recognition Policies in China: A Legal, Historical and Political Analysis.* Southern Illinois University, 1963. 353p. (Ph.D.).

2205 **DODGE, Dorothy R.** *Recognition of the Central People's Government of the People's Republic of China: Legal and Political Aspects, an Analysis of United States Recognition Policy as Seen in the China Case.* University of Minnesota, 1956. 637p. (Ph.D.).

2206 **Eismann, Bernard N.** *The Emergence of 'Two Chinas' in American Foreign Policy, 1950–1959.* Columbia University, 1959. 96p. (M.A.).

2207 **Johnson, Harold Scholl.** *Recognition in Law and Practice.* Syracuse University, 1957. 128p. (M.A.).

2208 **King, James Thomas, Jr.** *United States Policy of Recognition of the Communist Government of China.* Georgetown University, 1961. 126p. (M.A.).

2209 **Suh, Kyung Suk.** *American Recognition of Communist China.* Syracuse University, 1957. 124p. (M.A.).

5. Other Problems

2210 **CHANG, Yu Nan.** *American Security Problems in the Far East, 1950–1952.* University of Washington, 1954. 356p. (Ph.D.).

2211 **Chen, Shou-lien.** *The Taiwan Straits, 1949–58: Dilemma to American Policy Makers.* Columbia University, 1960. 73p. (M.A.).

2212 **CHUTASMIT, Suchati.** *The Experience of the United States and Its Allies in Controlling Trade with the Red Bloc.* Tufts University, 1961. 486p. (Ph.D.).

2213 **Lee, Ming T.** *The United States' Portrayal of Communist China; A Study of United States Propaganda.* New York University, 1962. 88p. (M.P.A.).

C. GREAT BRITAIN

2214 **Cox, W. Hupp.** *British Relations with Communist China.* University of Texas, 1954. 125p. (M.A.).

2215 **Hanson, Dean.** *British Recognition of Red China: Consequent Successes and Failures.* University of Southern California, 1957. 137p. (M.A.).

2216 **Min, Pyong Re.** *British Policy Toward Communist China, 1950–1961.* Syracuse University, 1963. 159p. (M.A.).

D. JAPAN

2217 **Rhee, Hang Y.** *The Role of the Development of Sino-Japanese Trade, 1950–1958: A Study of Economic Factors and Domestic Politics Affecting Japanese Policy Toward China.* Columbia University, 1963. 114p. (M.A.).

2218 **SUGIYAMA, Yasushi.** *Japan's Policies Towards Communist China, 1949–1963.* University of Maryland, 1964. 341p. (Ph.D.).

2219 **Yang, Alexander C.** *The Role of Japanese Business Groups in Japan's China Policy, May 1958–April 1962.* Columbia University, 1964. 110p. (M.A.), (East Asian Institute Certificate Essay).

E. INDIA

2220 **FEER, Mark C. I.** *India's China Policy, 1949–1954.* Tufts University, 1956. 278p. (Ph.D.).

2221 **Gopinath, Meledath.** *India's China Policy: A Critical Analysis.* Brigham Young University, 1964. 100p. (M.A.).

2222 **Jhaveri, Suresh Chandulal.** *India's Policy Towards Communist China, 1949–1953.* University of California, Berkeley, 1955. 108p. (M.A.).

2223 **SATYAPALAN, Chamavila Nilakantan.** *India's China Policy: The First Decade. An Analytical Interpretation.* University of Pennsylvania, 1964. 689p. (Ph.D.).

F. OTHER COUNTRIES

2224 **Jones, Joseph Edward.** *The Common Front: A Study of Soviet Policy in Relation to the Chinese National-Liberation Movement.* Georgetown University, 1963. 250p. (M.A.).

2225 **PETROV, Victor P.** *Manchuria as an Objective of Russian Foreign Policy.* American University, 1954. 373p. (Ph.D.).

2226 **Wagenberg, Ronald Harvey.** *Canada and Red China; Problems of Recognition.* Assumption University of Windsor, 1962. (M.A.).

INDEXES

INDEXES

SUBJECT INDEX

In view of the nature of many of the materials contained in this book (reference works, documentary compilations, periodicals, etc.), the broad range of subject matter surveyed, and the presence of a detailed table of contents and author-title index, the following subject index is keyed only to those materials devoted wholly to a given subject, and not to compilations in which a particular subject is only one of many. Thus, in locating references to marriage law, for example, the reader should consult not only the subject category 'Marriage law', but also such publication-type categories as 'Documentary compilations: laws and regulations'; and 'Periodicals: law'. The table of contents also will assist in finding appropriate categories of general publications.

Names of persons or organizations (including government agencies) are excluded from the subject index if they appear only in the context of authorship or sponsorship. In such instances, the author-title index should be consulted. An exception is made, however, when a country or its government organs appear themselves as subjects (e.g., 'China, research on'; or 'China, Republic of, National Assembly').

The terms 'Mainland' and 'Taiwan' used in subject headings are for purposes of word economy only. Their sole connotation is geographical. Where no designation is explicitly given, the publication in question is concerned with both the People's Republic of China and the Republic of China.

Bold-face figures refer to entries in this volume; light-face figures are page numbers.

A

Academia Sinica (Taipei): holdings of Chinese diplomatic archives, **1746**
Administrative divisions, Mainland: guides to, 185, **409, 414, 419–425**
Agrarian reform. *See* Agriculture and forestry, Mainland; Communes
Agriculture and forestry: dictionaries, **469, 470**; glossaries, **538–540**
Agriculture and forestry, Mainland: 289, **1216, 1232, 1265, 1267, 1268, 1324***a***, 1325, 1341, 1352, 1402, 1409, 1507, 1508, 1518, 1577, 1586, 1597, 1669, 1674, 1676, 1972–1997**; bibliographies of, 78, **150**; catalog of Mainland periodicals on, in U.S. Department of Agriculture Library, **1711**; documentary compilations, **591–595, 713–721**; handbook on, **227**; Mainland glossary on, **271**; Mainland newspapers on, translations of, **1060**; statistics, **269**; yearbooks on, **224, 225**
—Mainland periodicals on: **873, 876**; translations of, **1060**.
    See also Communes
Agriculture and forestry, Taiwan: **2124–2133**; bibliographies of, 78, **151, 152**; directory, **345**; documentary compilations, **736–738**; laws and regulations, documentary compilations of, Taiwan periodicals on, **978, 628**; statistics, **286–290**; yearbook, **252**. *See also* Rural Reconstruction, Joint Commission on
All-China Association of Musicians, Mainland, Second National Conference: documentary compilations, **746**

B

—Ministry of National Defense, Bureau of Intelligence: intelligence research of, 389
—National War College: intelligence research of, 389; library, holdings of, **1736–1738**
—serial publications: characteristics of, 335, 375, 378; newspaper and periodical publishing, 88–89
—statistics: Central Government, **272–275**; Provincial Government, **276–291**; Taipei Municipal Government, **292, 293.**
    See also Kuomintang; Newspapers, Taiwan; Periodicals, Taiwan; Reference works, general; *and* major subject headings, e.g., Agriculture and forestry, Taiwan; Foreign relations, Taiwan; Government and politics, Taiwan

China, library holdings on: in Canada, **1708, 1873**; in Great Britain, **1708, 1709, 1712, 1829, 1837, 1838**; in Hong Kong, **1708, 1709, 1750–1753**; in Japan, **4, 30, 1708, 1709, 1769, 1772–1783**; in Taiwan, **1736–1746**; in USSR, **1795, 1798–1803, 1805, 1808, 1810, 1811, 1814, 1818–1822, 1824**; in U.S., **1707–1734**; in Western Europe (general), **1826–1828.** *See also* individual entries for universities and governmental agencies

China, research on: **1416, 1475, 1675**; in Australia, **1877**; in Bulgaria, **1870, 1871**; in Canada, **1872**; in Czechoslovakia, **1207, 1208, 1855–1861**; in France, **1849**; in Germany, **1842–1848**; in Great Britain, **1830–1836, 1839–1841**; in Hungary, **1210, 1869**; in India, **1874, 1875**; in Italy, **1851–1854**; in Japan, **1154, 1155, 1158, 1760–1771, 1784–1794**; in Netherlands, **1850**; in Poland, **1209, 1862–1865**; in Rumania, **1866–1868**; in South Korea, **1876**; in Taiwan, **341, 1735**; in USSR, **473, 1193–1196, 1796, 1797, 1806–1809, 1813, 1815–1817, 1823**; in U.S., **1423, 1701, 1703, 1705.** *See also* Area study programs; Research libraries and institutions, publications of

China Association of Literature and Arts, Taiwan, **749**

China policy: **1221**; Canada, **2226**; Great Britain, **2214–2216**; India, **2220–2223**; Japan, **2217–2219**; USSR (*see* Sino-Soviet relations); U.S. **1312, 1391, 2181–2213**
—doctoral dissertations and M.A. theses on, **2180–2226**
    See also Foreign relations, Mainland

China Research Institute (Tokyo): 109–110, 314, **1765**; holdings, 3, 30

China Youth and Children's Corps, Mainland. *See* New Democratic Youth League

China Youth Anti-Communist and Salvation Corps, Taiwan: documentary compilations, **703**

Chinese Communism: **1469j**; bibliography of, **1346**; documentary compilations, 227, **572, 574, 575, 577**; Hong Kong periodical on, **1022**; and neutralism, **1399**
—history: bibliographies of, **80–82**; documentary compilations, **573, 578**

Chinese Communist Party: 263–264, **1222, 1272, 1277, 1281, 1286, 1331, 1339, 1344, 1365, 1453, 1469j, 1475, 1481, 1493, 1505, 1519, 1540, 1551, 1582, 1583, 1890, 1894, 1931–1952, 2028, 2118**; bibliography of, **1346**; directories to, **294–316**; documentary compilations, **650–662**; official organs of, **831, 862, 885–887.** *See also* Biographies

Chinese Federation of Labor, Taiwan, 280

Chinese language. *See* Language dictionaries

F

Forestry. *See* Agriculture and forestry
Formosan Association (Tokyo): organs of, in Japan, **1099, 1180**
Franco-Chinese Friendship Association (Paris), **1205**
Fukien Province: political and administrative personnel, directory of, **309**

G

Gazetteers, 182, 184, **414–418**
Geography, Mainland: **1530, 1893***a*, **2094**; dictionary of, **504**; Mainland periodicals on, **907, 908**, index to, **115**; Russian bibliography of, **51**
Geography, Taiwan: **2125**; bibliography of, **124**
Glossaries. *See* Dictionaries; Scientific and technical glossaries
Government and politics, Asia: Japanese periodical on, **1111**
Government and politics, Mainland: 254–255, **1235, 1242, 1272, 1273, 1280, 1292, 1331, 1335, 1342, 1347, 1364, 1379, 1430, 1475, 1489, 1492, 1510, 1514, 1521, 1529, 1552, 1556, 1578, 1888, 1894, 1895, 1897, 1900, 1956, 1991**; directories of, **294–320**; documentary compilations, **635**; handbooks on, **212–214, 217, 218, 220–222, 227–229**; Mainland periodicals on: **853, 854, 862**; translations of Mainland newspapers on, **1052, 1054–1057, 1066, 1068**; translations of Mainland periodicals on, **1052, 1054, 1055, 1057**; yearbooks on, **215, 217, 218, 223–225, 230** *See also* Chinese Communist Party; Hundred Flowers Movement; Ideology, Mainland; Mass organizations, Mainland; Minorities, Mainland, etc; *and* individual entries for conferences, congresses, organs
Government and politics, Taiwan: **2116–2120**; statistics, **274**; Taiwan periodicals on, **956, 957, 969, 976**
'Great Leap Forward,' 129, **1276**
Guides: to Mainland administrative divisions, 185–186, **409, 414, 419–425**; to Peking, **235**; to Shanghai, **236**

H

Hai-lu-feng, **1529**
Handbooks: general, 106, 109, **202, 203, 211**; on Hong Kong, 125, **257, 259**; on Mainland, 109, 110, **212–214, 217, 221, 222, 226–229, 231–236**; on Taiwan, 119–120, **241, 243***a*, **244, 255**. *See also* Yearbooks
Harvard University: Center for East Asian Studies, holdings of, **5**; Harvard-Yenching Library, holdings of, **1729, 1730**; Mainland periodicals, holdings of, **1708, 1709**
History (and historiography): **1278, 1324***b*, **1332**; bibliographies of, 46, **42, 78–84**; Mainland historical literature, production of, 46; Japanese periodicals on, **1168, 1170, 1185–1189**; Mainland periodicals on, **78, 79, 897**. *See also* Chinese Communism
Hong Kong: biographies, 173, **385, 1233**; directories, **259, 260**; materials published in, indexes to, 98, **192, 193, 194***a*; newspaper and periodical publishing, 88, 89, 398; serial publications on, 433, **1075**; relations with Japan and Indonesia, **1247**;

M

N

O

Public security, Mainland: laws and regulations, documentary compilations of, **612**
Publishing and printing. *See* Book publishing, Mainland; *and* various entries for
    Newspapers, Periodicals

Q

Quemoy: decisional analysis on, **1469***b*; political implications of, **1234**

R

Radio: monitoring services, serial publications of, 405, 432, **1066, 1067, 1071–1073.**
    See also Communications, Mainland; Communications, Taiwan
Radio Press (R.P.) News Agency, **1167**
Reference works, general, 105. *See also* specific types, e.g., Atlases; Biographies;
    Chronologies; Dictionaries; Directories; Encyclopedias
Refugees, Mainland: **1214, 1215, 1219, 1223, 1263**; Hong Kong periodical on, **1032**
Religion: Hong Kong periodical on, **1033**; and thought, bibliographies of, 55, **97, 98**
Religion, Mainland: **1033, 1220, 1260, 1388–1390, 1506, 2115**; Buddhism, Mainland
    periodical on, **880**; Catholicism, **1266, 1947**; Islam, **1252, 1907**; Protestantism,
    740, 1392–1395, 2114, 2121
Religion, Taiwan, **2143**. *See also* Chinese Moslem Association, Taiwan
Research Institute for World Democracy (Tokyo), **1174**
Research institutions:
    —Japan, 443–446
    —Taiwan: 389, 390; directory of, **341**
    See also China, research on; Research libraries and institutions, publications of
Research libraries and institutions, publications of: 518, **1825**; Australia, **1877**;
    Bulgaria, **1870, 1871**; Canada, **1872, 1873**; Czechoslovakia, **1855–1861**; France,
    1849, 1850; Germany, **1842–1848**; Great Britain, **1829–1841**; Hong Kong,
    1750–1753; Hungary, **1869**; India, **1874, 1875**; Italy, **1851–1854**; Japan, **1760–
    1794**; Mainland, **1754–1759**; Netherlands, **1850**; Poland, **1862–1865**; Rumania,
    1866–1868; South Korea, **1876**; Taiwan, **1735–1749**; USSR, **1795–1824**; U.S.,
    1701–1734; Western Europe (general), **1826–1828**. *See also* China, research on;
    Periodicals
Revisionism. *See* Ideology, Mainland
Rural Reconstruction, Joint Commission on. *See* Joint Commission on Rural
    Reconstruction

S

Science: Mainland periodicals on, **894, 932–935**; Taiwan periodical on, **965**
Science, Mainland: **1413, 1473, 1482, 1521, 1569**; bibliographies of, **51, 1485, 1488**;
    Mainland newspapers on, translations of, **1064**; Mainland periodicals on, transla-
    tions of, **1064**

Statistical compilations: 129; Mainland, 129, **264–271**; Taiwan, 132–133, **269–293.**
    See also Economics and statistics, Mainland; Economics and statistics, Taiwan
Student movement, Chinese: bibliography of, **1347**
Subject bibliographies. *See* Bibliographies, subject
Sun Yat-sen, **1930, 2116**; bibliographies of, **76**
Syracuse University: doctoral dissertations and M.A. theses, bibliography of, **1882**

T

Taipei: statistics, **292, 293**
Taiwan. *See* China, Republic of
Taiwan Provincial Administration, Republic of China: documentary compilations,
    684. *See also* Taiwan Provincial Government
Taiwan Provincial Assembly, Republic of China: 277–278; documentary compilations,
    689
Taiwan Provincial Commission of Historical Research: holdings, **1743**
Taiwan Provincial Government, Republic of China: 277–278, **685, 686**
Taiwan Provisional Provincial Assembly, Republic of China: 277–278; documentary
    compilations, **687, 688.** *See also* Taiwan Provincial Assembly
Taiwan question: documentary compilations, 309, 310, **757–760**
Taxation. *See* Finance and taxation, Mainland; Finance and taxation, Taiwan
Technology. *See* Science, technology and medicine; Scientific and technical glossaries
Technology, Mainland: **1340, 1340a, 1406, 1473, 1482, 1485, 1488, 1496, 1678,
    1998, 1999, 2001, 2007, 2008**; Mainland newspapers and periodicals on, **1064**;
    Russian bibliography of, **51.** *See also* Industry, Mainland; Science, Mainland
Theater, Mainland. *See* Drama, Mainland
Thought control. *See* "Brainwashing"
Three-Self Movement: documentary compilations, **740**
Tibet: **1902–1906, 2054, 2057**; chronology of events in, **397**; documentary com-
    pilations, **813, 815, 816**
Trade agreements, **1438.** *See also* Treaties and agreements
Trade and commerce, Hong Kong, **1225, 1247**
Trade and commerce, Mainland: **1407, 1423, 1424, 1438, 1671, 1680, 2013–2018**;
    dictionaries of, **469, 470, 472–475**; directories of, **322–327, 329**; documentary
    compilations, 294, **728–730**; laws and regulations, documentary compilations of,
    601, 602; Mainland periodical on, **876**; translations of Mainland newspapers and
    periodicals on, **1062**
—with Japan: 444–445, **1259, 1581, 2019–2024**; documentary compilations, **770**
—with USSR; *see* Sino-Soviet trade.
    See also Economy, Mainland
Trade and commerce, Taiwan: directories of, **339, 348**; laws and regulations, docu-
    mentary compilations of, **626, 627**; statistics, **284, 285.** *See also* Economy, Taiwan
Translations services: serial publications of, 405, 409–411, 430, **1038–1070**
Translations: bibliographies of, 85–86, **167–169.** *See also* Newspapers, Mainland;
    Periodicals, Mainland; Translation services

U

W

Y

AUTHOR-TITLE INDEX

Bold-face figures refer to entries in this volume; light-face figures are page numbers.

A

ANS sokuhō, Ajia Tsūshinsha, **1113***a*

APACL—Its Growth and Outlook, Asian Peoples' Anti-Communist League, **1624**

Academic Achievement of Chinese Graduate Students at the University of Michigan (1907–1950), The, Liu, Yung-szi, **2155**

Academic and Professional Attainments of Native Chinese Students Graduating from Teachers College, Columbia University, 1909–1950, Kao, Lin-ying, **2154**

Acta Orientalia Academiae Scientiarum Hungaricae, **1210**

Activities of Prominent Chinese Communist Personalities, U.S. Joint Publications Research Service, **362**, 410

Adams, Mervyn W., *Communist China and the United Nations: A Study of China's Developing Attitude Towards the U.N.'s Role in International Peace and Security*, **2084**

"Administrative Areas of Communist China," American Consulate General, Hong Kong, **420**

Administrative Structure of the Government of the Republic of China, The, Ruben, Bruce Lloyd, **2119**

Adult Education in People's Republic of China, 1950–1958, Lin, Vincent Tsing Ching, **2098**

Agrarian Policies of Mainland China: A Documentary Study (1949–1956), Chao, Kuo-chün, **111**

Agrarian Problems and Policies in China up to 1953, Montee, Ralph Bruce, **1990**

"Agrarian Reform in Communist China Against the Background of the Marxist Tradition," Brandt, Conrad, **1324***a*

Agrarian Reform in Communist China to 1952, Ong, Shao-er, **1507**

Agrarian Reform Law of the People's Republic of China (1950) and Other Relevant Documents, **591**

"Agreements Between Communist China and Foreign Countries, October 1949–December 1957," American Consulate General, Hong Kong, **200**

Agricultural Cooperation in China, Tung, Ta-lin, **715**

Agricultural Geography of Formosa, Chang, Jen-hu, **2125**

Agricultural Land Problems of Communist China, Degler, Stanley Elmer, **1979**

Agricultural Taxation in Communist China, Ong, Shao-er, **1518**

Ahmed, S. H., "Chronology of the Sino-Indian Border Dispute," **404**

Aichi Daigaku, Kokusai Mondai Kenkyūjo, *Chūka Jimmin Kyōwakoku hōrei mokuroku, 1949–1954 nen 6 gatsu*, **199**; *Kokusai Mondai Kenkyūjo kiyō*, **1158**; *Kokusai seikei jijō*, **1158**

Aichi University. *See* Aichi Daigaku

Aird, John S., *The Size, Composition, and Growth of the Population of Mainland China*, **120**

Aiura, Takashi, " 'Jimmin bungaku' shosai shōsetsu, sambun, hōkoku ichiran hyō," **892**

Ajia bōeki, Ajia Boeki Tsūshīnsha, **1106**

Ajia chiiki sōgō kenkyū bunken mokuroku, Japan, Mombushō, Daigaku Gakujutsukyoku, **1774**

Ajia keizai, Ajia Keizai Kenkyūjo, **1107**

Ajia keizai geppō, Japan, Gaimushō, Keizaikyoku, Ajiaka, **1108**

Ajia keizai jumpō, Chūgoku Kenkyūjo, **1109**; "Chūgoku hakkō shomoku ichiran hyō," **3**; "Chūken toshokan ukeire tosho," **1782**

Ajia keizai kenkyū shiryō, Osaka Shiritsu Daigaku Keizai Kenkyūjo, **1112**

Ajia Keizai Kenkyūjo, *Ajia keizai*, **1107**; *Chūgoku no denryoku, sekitan, bōshoku, seishi kōgyō*, **1681**

"Ajia keizai nisshi," *Ajia keizai jumpō*, **394**

Ajia keizai shiryō, Chūgoku Kenkyūjo, **1110**

Ajia kenkyū, Ajia Seikei Gakkai, **1111**

Ajia kenkyū shiryō, Osaka Shiritsu Daigaku Keizai Kenkyūjo, **1112**

Ajia Kenkyūjo, *1963 nemban Chūka Jimmin Kyōwakoku chihōbetsu soshiki jimmeihyō*, **299**; *1964 nemban Chūka Jimmin Kyōwakoku genshoku jimmei jiten*, **359**

Ajia Kyōkai, *Ajia Kyōkai shi*, **1113**; *Ajia mondai*, **1113**; *Kaigai gijutsu kyōryoku*, **1113**

Ajia Kyōkai shi, Ajia Kyōkai, **1113**

Ajia mondai, Ajia Kyōkai, **1113**

Ajia nenkan, Japan, Gaimushō, Ajiakyoku, **206**

Ajia ni kansuru shoshi mokuroku—jimbun kagaku, shakai kagaku, 1957 nendo, Tōyōgaku Infuōmēshon Sentā, **7**

Ajia rekishi jiten, Heibonsha, **208**

Ajia seiji keizai nenkan, Kokusai Nihon Kyōkai, **207**

Ajia Seikei Gakkai, *Ajia kenkyū*, **1111**; *Chūgoku seiji keizai sōran*, **202**; *Chūka Jimmin Kyōwakoku gaikō shiryō sōran*, **752**; "Gaikō nempyō," **398**

"Ajia seikei nisshi," *Ajia keizai jumpō*, **394**

Ajia tsūshin, Ajia Tsūshinsha, **1113***a*

Ajia Tsūshinsha, *ANS sokuhō*, **1113***a*; *Ajia tsūshin*, **1113***a*; *Chūgoku sangyō bōeki sōran*, **322**

Akademiia nauk S.S.S.R., *Kratkie soobshcheniia Instituta narodov Azii*, **1200**; *Kratkie soobshcheniia Instituta vostokovedeniia*, **1199**; *Uchenye zapiski Instituta narodov Azii*, **1202**; *Uchenye zapiski Instituta vostokovedeniia*, **1201**

"Chekosurobakia no Chūgoku kenkyū," Krebsova, Berta, **1857**

Chen, Anthony K. C., *The Philosophy of Education of Communist China as Applied to Secondary and Higher Education*, **2091**

Chen, Chao-chiung, *The Communist-Led Land Reform in China*, **1975**

Chen, Chiu-shan, *American Recognition and Non-Recognition Policies in China: A Legal, Historical and Political Analysis*, **2204**

Chen, Ho-chia, *Land Reform in Soviet Russia and Communist China*, **1976**

Chen, King, *China and the Democratic Republic of Vietnam (1945–1954)*, **2062**

Chen, Nai-ruenn, *The Economy of Mainland China, 1949–1963: A Bibliography of Materials in English*, **108**; *Formosa's National Income, Concepts, Estimation, Methods and Distribution*, **2134**

Chen, S. H., *Multiplicity in Uniformity: Poetry and the Great Leap Forward*, **1276**

Chen, Shou-lien, *The Taiwan Straits, 1949–58: Dilemma to American Policy Makers*, **2211**

Chen, Theodore Hsi-en, *The Chinese Communist Regime: A Documentary Study*, **572**, **1526**; *Education and Indoctrination in Red China*, **1522**; *Education and the Economic Failures in Communist China*, **1525**; *Elementary Education in Communist China*, **1523**; *The Popularization of Higher Education in Communist China*, **1497**; *Science, Scientists, and Politics in Communist China*, **1521**; *Teacher Training in Communist China*, **1500**; *Thought Reform of the Chinese Intellectuals*, **268**

Chen, Vincent, *Mao Tse-tung's Communist Ideology on Revolution and War*, **1918**

Chen, Wen-hui C., *Chinese Communist Anti-Americanism and the Resist-America Aid-Korea Campaign*, **1502**; *The Family Revolution in Communist China*, **1503**; *Wartime "Mass" Campaigns in Communist China: Official Country-Wide "Mass Movements" in Professed Support of the Korean War*, **1504**

Chen, Yin-ching, *Treaties and Agreements Between the Republic of China and Other Powers, 1929–1954, Together with Certain International Documents Affecting the Interests of the Republic of China*, **829a**

Chen, Yung-ping, *Chinese Political Thought: Mao Tse-tung and Liu Shao-ch'i*, **1919**

Ch'en, Ch'ang-hao, et al., *Russko-kitaiskii slovar'*, **461**

Ch'en, Cheng-hsiang, *T'ai-wan ching-chi ti-li wen-hsien so-yin*, **124**

Ch'en, Ch'eng, *Land Reform in Taiwan*, **736**

Ch'en, Ch'eng-chou, *T'ai-wan sheng hsien-hsing jen-shih fa-ling hui-pien*, **633**

Ch'en, Ch'üan, *"Ming Fang" hsüan-ts'ui*, **660**

Ch'en, Meng-hsien, *Chi-pen hua-hsüeh shu-yü tz'u-tien*, **497**

Ch'en, P'u-sheng, *Ssu-fa fa-ling p'an-chieh hui-pien*, **618**

Ch'en, T'ao, *Jih-Han tz'u-tien*, **463**

Cheng, Chi, "Libraries in China Today," **1755**

Cheng, Chu-yuan, *Anshan Steel Factory in Communist China*, **1548**; *The China Mainland Market Under Communist Control*, **1553**; *Communist China's Economy, 1949–1957; Structural Changes and Crisis*, **130**; *Economic Relations Between Peking and Moscow, 1949–1963*, **1318**; *Income and Standard of Living in Mainland China*, **1558**; *Monetary Affairs in Communist China*, **1544**; *The Structural Changes of Economy in Communist China*, **1962**

Cheng, Hsüeh-chia, *Whither Indonesia?*, **1626**; *Hunger in Communist China—An Estimate of 1961 Food Production*, **1651**; *An Interpretation of the Purge of Kao and Jao in Chinese Communist Party*, **1583**; *The People's Commune—Military Slavery Communism*, **1617**; *Pure Capitalism or Communism—Part II*, **1645**; *Pure Capitalism or Communism—The Critique of CPSU Program—Part I*, **1644**; *The So-Called Enlightened Despotism of Chinese Communists*, **1596**; *An Unprecedented Famine on the Chinese Mainland and the People's Communes*, **1638**; *Why Do the Chinese Communists Serve as Vanguard Against Modern Revisionism*, **1606**

Cheng, I-li, *Tsui-hsin hsiang-chieh Ying-Hua ta tz'u-tien*, **459**; *Ying-Hua ta tz'u-tien*, **459**

Cheng, J. Chester, *Basic Principles Underlying the Chinese Communist Approach to Education*, **1499**; *The Politics of the Chinese Red Army: A Translation of the Bulletin of Activities*, **1337**

Cheng, Lillian Li-ling, *The Educational Program of the Chinese Nationalist Government in Formosa*, **2139**

Cheng, S. and Feuerwerker, Albert, *Chinese Communist Studies of Modern Chinese History*, **79**

Cheng, Tse-kuang, *Wen-hua shih-yeh kuan-hsi fa-ling chih shih-yung*, **621**

Cheng, Tso-yüan, *Chinese Communists' Infiltration Activities in South East Asia*, **1640**; *Famine and Its Repercussion on the Chinese Mainland*, **1639**

Cheng, Yü-te, *Chung-kung jen-wu ch'ün-hsiang*, **370**

Cheng-chih hsüeh-hsi, T'ung-su tu-wu ch'u-pan she, **853**

Cheng-fa yen-chiu, Chung-kuo cheng-chih fa-lü hsüeh-hui, Chung-kuo k'o-hsüeh yüan fa-hsüeh yen-chiu so, **854**

Cheng-fu kung-tso pao-kao, 1950, Jen-min ch'u-pan she, **635**

Cheng-hsin hsin-wen pao, 61, **941**

Cheng-lun chou-k'an, Chung-kuo hsin-wen ch'u-pan she, **945**

Cheng-ming, Democratic League, **268**

Ch'eng pao, **1019**

Chennault, Anna, *Dictionary of New Simplified Chinese Characters*, **442**

Chesneaux, Jean, *Les cahiers Franco-Chinois*, **1205**

"Communist Chinese Claims Regarding Scientific Progress in the Last Decade, With Appended Bibliographical Notes," *Science News Letter,* **156**

Communist Chinese Monographs in the USDA Library, Kuo, Leslie T. C. and Schroeder, Peter B., **150**

Communist Chinese Periodicals in the Agricultural Sciences, U.S. Department of Agriculture, Library, **1711**

"Communist Critique of *Hung lou meng,* The," Grieder, Jerome B., **1329**

Communist Ethics and Chinese Tradition, Nivison, David S., **1373**

Communist Ideology in China, Schwartz, Benjamin, **1481**

Communist Industry: Its Problems and Difficulties, Asian People's Anti-Communist League, **1666**

Communist-Led Land Reform in China, The, Chen, Chao-chiung, **1975**

Communist Magic—United Front Operation, Chow, Ching-wen, **1578**

Communist Menace to Asia, Asian People's Anti-Communist League, **1598**

Communist Party Leadership and Organization in China, 1949–1962, Fletcher, Merton Don, **1933**

Communist Party of China, The: Organization and Structure, Tang, Peter, **1519**

Communist Policies Toward the Intellectual Class, Johnson, Chalmers A., **1560**

Communist Policy in Inner Mongolia, 1947–1957, Metzger, Thomas Albert, **1908**

Communist Program for Literature and Art in China, The, Chao, Chung, **1550**

Communist Propaganda Trends, U.S. Army, Broadcasting and Visual Activity, Pacific, **1072**

Communist Psychological Offensive: Distortions in the Translation of Official Documents, Grant, Natalie, **1459**

Communist Revolution in Vietnam, The: Internal Strategy and External Influence, Jones, W. Craig, **2066**

Communist Strategy in China, Hennelly, James Jerome, **1894**

Communist Threat to Nepal, The, Wray, Carol Susan, **2060**

Communist Tyranny and People's Resistance on the Chinese Mainland in 1954, Asian People's Anti-Communist League, **1584**

"Communists of the Chinese Revolution," North, Robert C., **373**

"Comparison of Kuomintang and Communist Modern History Textbooks, A," Morrison, Esther, **1332**

Comparison of Russian and Chinese Societies under Communism, A, Rostow, W. W., **1375**

Comparison of Selected Values Among Formosan and American Adolescents, A, Huang, Sophia Chang, **2142**

Comparison of Sun Yat-sen's Constitutional Theories and the Current Constitution of the Republic of China, A, Chang, Archibald How, **2116**

Complete Catalogue of Books from China (in English) 1964, Peace Book Company, **1753**

Complete Guide to Peking Streets and Alleys, U.S. Joint Publications Research Service, **235**

"Composition of the 1st National People's Congress," American Consulate General, Hong Kong, **315**

Compton, Boyd Ross, *Thought Discipline in the Chinese Communist Party,* **1932**

Conant, Melvin A., Jr., "JCRR: Problems of American Participation in the Sino-American Joint Commission on Rural Reconstruction," **1326**

Concept of the Proletariat in Chinese Communism, The, Marsh, Susan S. Han, **1923**

Concerning the Question of Tibet, Foreign Languages Press, **815**

Concerning the Situation in Laos, Foreign Languages Press, **820**

Conditions and Prospects for Economic Growth in Communist China, Eckstein, Alexander, **1356**

Conflict Resolution in the Sino-Soviet Alliance, Whiting, A. S., **1439**

Confucius to Shelley to Marx. Kuo Mo-jo; A Critical Examination of His Opinions on the Nature of Literature, With Particular Reference to Its Function in Society, Elegant, Robert S., **2103**

Conscript Labor and Public Works in Communist China, Barnett, A. Doak, **1217**

Consolidated Translation Survey, U.S. Central Intelligence Agency, Foreign Documents Division, **1049**

Constantin, G. I., "Kitaevedenie v Rumynskoi Narodnoi Respublike," **1867**

Contemporary China, Kirby, E. Stuart, **14**

Contemporary China: A Bibliography of Reports on China Published by the United States Joint Publications Research Service, Sorich, Richard, **1047**

"Contemporary China and the Chinese," *The Annals of the American Academy of Political and Social Science,* **1689**

Contemporary China as a Problem for Political Science, Halpern, A. M., **1419**

Contest of Loyalties, A: Overseas Chinese in Thailand, Barnett, A. Doak, **1238**

Continuity and Discontinuity in Chinese Policy Toward the Southwestern Tribes Since 1911, Pasternak, Burton, **1914**

"*Contradictions*" *in the Moscow-Peking Axis,* Whiting, A. S., **1410**

Contribution of Private Agencies in Rural Reconstruction in China, The, Tan, Lynette P. C., **2133**

"Contributions roumaines aux études orientales," Gubeglu, M., **1868**

D

Goldman, René, *The Rectification Campaign of May–June 1957 and the Student Movement at Peking University*, **1944**

Golubeva, O. D., "Vostokovednye fondy Gosudarstvennoi publichnoi biblioteki im. M. E. Saltykova-Shchedrina v Leningrade," **1805**

Gomez, Rudolph, *Major Agrarian Reform Policies of the Chinese Communists*, **1981**

Gopinath, Meledath, *India's China Policy: A Critical Analysis*, **2221**

Gorbacheva, Z. I., Men'shikov, L. N., and Petrov, N. A., "Kitaevedenie v Leningrade za sorok let," **1806**

Gordon, James Duncan, *Population Problems and Policies in the Soviet Union and Communist China in Relation to Agricultural Resources*, **1982**

Gotō Kimpei, "Postwar Japanese Studies on the Chinese Language," **89**

Gould, Sidney H., *Sciences in Communist China*, **155**

Government Acquisition of Agricultural Output in Mainland China, 1953–56, Hsia, Ronald, **1402**

Government and Structure of the People's Republic of China, The: 1949–1950, Thomas, Samuel B., **1900**

Grant, Natalie, *Communist Psychological Offensive: Distortions in the Translation of Official Documents*, **1459**; *Soviet Diplomatic Maneuvers: An Episode in History of the Far Eastern Republic*, **1457**

Great Britain, Department of Scientific and Industrial Research, Lending Library Unit, *LLU Translations Bulletin*, **1082**; *Translated Contents Lists of Russian Periodicals*, **1082**

"Great Britain: Far Eastern Studies at the University of Cambridge," Ceadel, E. B., **1832**

Great Debate on the Literary Front, A, Chou, Yang, **745**

Great Famine on the Chinese Mainland Under Communist Regime in 1960, The, Asian Peoples' Anti-Communist League, **1629**

Great Unity of the Chinese People and the Great Unity of the Peoples of the World, The, Teng, Hsiao-ping, **786**

Greenblatt, Sidney L., *The Impact of Sino-Yugoslav Relations on Chinese Communist-Bloc Relations, 1955–1958*, **2045**

Greer, Robert Winchester, *A Political Geography of the Gulf of Pohai Region*, **1893a**

Grieder, Jerome B., "The Communist Critique of *Hung lou meng*," **1329**

Griffith, William E., *Albania and the Sino-Soviet Rift*, **789**, **1357**; *The Sino-Soviet Rift*, 318, **781**, **1358**; *World Communism Divided*, **1315**

Grigor'ev, G. M., *Kratkii kitaisko-russkii slovar'*, **447**

Grimm, Tilemann, "Far Eastern Studies in Germany," **1845**

Grinstead, E. D., *Chinese Periodicals in British Libraries, Handlist No. 1*, **1829**

——Gardner, K. B. and Meredith-Owens, G. M., "The Department of Oriental Printed Books and Manuscripts of the British Museum," **1837**

Group Research Projects in Foreign Affairs and the Social Sciences, U.S. Department of State, Bureau of Intelligence and Research, External Research Division, **1703**

Growth and Modernizing Function of Rural Radio in Communist China, Liu, Alan Ping-lin, **1371**

Growth of China's Scientific and Technical Manpower, The, Ikle, F. C., **1406**

Growth of the Chinese Church in the New Villages of the State of Johore, Malaya, 1950/60, The—A Study in the Communication of the Gospel to Chinese Converts, Fleming, John Ross, **2171**

Gubeglu, M., "Contributions roumaines aux études orientales," **1868**

Guide to Chinese Communist Military and Political Terminology, A, Hanrahan, Gene Z., **479**

Guide to Doctoral Dissertations by Chinese Students in America, 1905–1960, A, Yüan, T'ung-li, **1883**

"Guide to Doctoral Dissertations by Chinese Students in Continental Europe, 1907–1962 (I), A," Yüan, T'ung-li, **1885**

Guide to Japanese Monographs and Japanese Studies on Manchuria, 1945–1960, U.S. Department of the Army, Office of Military History, **64**

Guide to New China, A, Foreign Languages Press, **213**

Guide to Russian Reference Books, Maichel, Karol, **1812**

Guide to the Writings of Mao Tse-tung in the East Asiatic Library, Columbia University Libraries, East Asiatic Library, **72**

Guozi Shudian, *Book Catalogue: Works of Mao Tse-tung, Political Treatises, Documents, Books on International Affairs*, **1759**; *Catalogue of Chinese Books Available in English*, **1759**; *Catalogue of Mao Tse-tung's Theoretical Works on Literature and Art and Selections from Contemporary Chinese Literature*, **1759**; *Chung-kuo pao-k'an mu-lu*, **173**

H

Hai, Badruddin W., *Muslim Minority in China*, **1907**

Hai-lu-feng—The First Chinese Soviet Government, Eto, Shinkichi, **1529**

Hai-wai ch'u-pan she, *Tzu-yu Chung-kuo ta chuan hsüeh-hsiao kai-lan*, **342**; *Tzu-yu Chung-kuo ta chung hsüeh-hsiao chien-chieh*, **343**

Hakka or "Guest People", The: Dialect as a Sociocultural Variable in Southeastern China, Cohen, Myron L., **1913**

Half-Work, Half-Study Schools in Communist China, Barendson, Robert D., **1494**

Halpern, Abraham M., *Between Plenums: A Second Look at the 1962 National People's Congress in China*, **1417**; *The Chinese Communist Line on Neutralism*, **1399**; "Communist China and Peaceful Co-existence," **1421**; *Communist*

I

L

M

S

T

Ta-hua Evening Post, *Tseng-ting T'ai-wan t'ung-lan*, 243

Ta-kung pao, 61, **398**, **839**

Ta-kung pao, *Jen-min shou-ts'e*, **212**; *Trade with China, A Practical Guide*, 321

Ta-kung pao ch'u-pan wei-yüan hui, *Hsin Shang-hai pien-lan*, 236

Ta-kung pao yao-mu so-yin, **840**

Ta-lu fei-ch'ing chi-pao, Chung-kuo kuo-min tang, Chung-yang wei-yüan hui, Ti liu tsu, **994**

Ta-lu fei-ch'ing nien-pao, 242

Ta-lu tsa-chih, 378

"Table of Contents of the 1959 People's Handbook," U.S. Joint Publications Research Service, 212

Taga, Akigorō and Yazawa, Toshihiko, *Chūgoku bunka shi Nihongo bunken mokuroku—kyōiku, kirisutokyō*, 101

Tai Chung Pou, *Ao-men kung-shang nien-chien*, 263; *Directório de Macau*, 263

Taipei, Chu-chi chü, *T'ai-pei shih jen-k'ou t'ung-chi*, 293; *T'ai-pei shih t'ung-chi yao-lan*, 292

Taipei, Government Information Office, *Selected Speeches and Messages of President Chiang Kai-shek*, **579**

T'ai-pei shih hsin-wen chi-che kung-hui, *Chung-hua min-kuo hsin-wen nien-chien*, 247

T'ai-pei shih jen-k'ou t'ung-chi, Taipei, Chu-chi chü, 293

T'ai-pei shih t'ung-chi yao-lan, Taipei, Chu-chi chü, 292

T'ai-pei shih wu-chia pien-tung fen-hsi pao-kao, Taiwan, Chu-chi ch'u, 284

Taira, Kazuhiko, "Chūgoku kenkyū shiryō mokuroku," **34**; *Chūka Jimmin Kyōwakoku hōrei sakuin, 1949 nen 10 gatsu–1953 nen 12 gatsu*, 196; "Hōbun gendai Chūgoku bunken mokuroku," 33

Tairiku, 1177

Tairiku jumpō, Tairiku Mondai Kenkyūjo, 1178

Tairiku mondai, Tairiku Mondai Kenkyūjo, 1179

Tairiku Mondai Kenkyūjo, *Tairiku jumpō*, 1178; *Tairiku mondai*, 1179

Taiwan, Chiao-t'ung ch'u, *Annual Statistical Data of Taiwan Communications and Transportation*, 279; *T'ai-wan sheng chiao-t'ung t'ung-chi hui-pao*, 279

Taiwan, Chiao-yü t'ing, Chu-chi shih, *T'ai-wan sheng chiao-yü t'ung-chi*, 278

Taiwan, Chien-she t'ing, *T'ai-wan sheng lao-kung t'ung-chi pao-kao*, 280

Taiwan, Ching-wu ch'u, Chuan-yüan shih, *Ching-ch'a fa-ling hui-pien*, 621

Taiwan, Chu-chi ch'u, *T'ai-pei shih wu-chia pien-tung fen-hsi pao-kao*, 284; *T'ai-wan sheng t'ung-chi yao-lan*, 276; *T'ai-wan wu-chia t'ung-chi yüeh-pao*, 284

Taiwan, Department of Publication of the Ministry of Interior, *Ch'u-pan shih-yeh teng-chi i-lan*, 346

Taiwan, Hsin-wen ch'u, *Hsin-wen shih-yeh chi-kou i-lan*, 346; *T'ai-wan ti chien-she*, 245; *T'ai-wan ti chien-she: Chung-hua min-kuo san-shih ssu nien chih wu-shih i nien*, 243a; *Taiwan, Ten Years of Progress*, 245

Taiwan, Hu-k'ou p'u-ch'a ch'u, *Chung-hua min-kuo hu-k'ou p'u-ch'a pao-kao shu*, 273

Taiwan, Kung-ch'an kuan-li ch'u, *T'ai-wan sheng kung-ch'an kuan-li fa-ling hui-pien*, 629

Taiwan, Liang-shih chü, *T'ung-chi shih, T'ai-wan liang-shih t'ung-chi yao-lan*, 287

Taiwan, Lin-yeh kuan-li chü, Chu-chi shih, *T'ai-wan lin-yeh t'ung-chi nien-pao*, 290

Taiwan, Mi-shu ch'u, *T'ai-wan sheng-cheng-fu shih-cheng pao-kao*, **686**

Taiwan, Min-cheng t'ing, Ti-cheng chü, *T'ai-wan sheng ti-cheng fa-ling chi-yao*, 628

Taiwan, Nung-lin t'ing, *T'ai-wan nung-yeh nien-pao*, 252; *T'ai-wan t'ang-yeh t'ung-chi*, 289

Taiwan, Nung-lin t'ing, Chien-yen chü, *Chien-yen t'ung-chi yao-lan*, 286

Taiwan, Nung-lin t'ing, Yü-yeh kuan-li ch'u, *T'ai-wan yü-yeh nien-pao*, 253

Taiwan, She-hui ch'u, *T'ai-wan sheng lao-kung sheng-huo k'ai-k'uang tiao-ch'a t'ung-chi pao-kao*, 281

Taiwan, Shui-li chü, *T'ai-wan sheng shui-li chü nien-pao*, 254

T'ai-wan, T'ai-wan sheng hsin-wen ch'u, **988**

Taiwan, Yen chiu kung-mai chü, Chu-chi shih, *T'ai-wan sheng yen-chiu shih-yeh k'ai-k'uang*, 288; *T'ai-wan sheng yen-chiu shih-yeh t'ung-chi nien-pao*, 288

Taiwan and the Sino-Soviet Dispute, Stockdale, James Bond, **2037**

Taiwan Buyer's Guide, 1962 Edition, China Productivity and Trade Center, 348

T'ai-wan chiao-yü, T'ai-wan sheng chiao-yü hui, 57, **973**

T'ai-wan chin-jung nien-pao, T'ai-wan yin-hang, Ching-chi yen-chiu shih, 250

"T'ai-wan ching-chi fa-kuei," T'ai-wan yin-hang, Ching-chi yen-chiu shih, **626**

"T'ai-wan ching-chi jih-chih," T'ai-wan yin-hang, Ching-chi yen-chiu shih, **407**

T'ai-wan ching-chi nien-pao, 242

T'ai-wan ching-chi ti-li wen-hsien so-yin, Ch'en, Cheng-hsiang, 124

"T'ai-wan ching-chi wen-hsien fen-lei so-yin," T'ai-wan yin-hang, Ching-chi yen-chiu shih, 123

T'ai-wan ching-chi yüeh-k'an, **974**

Taiwan Chinglian—Taiwan seinen, 1180

T'ai-wan hsin-sheng pao, 376, **939**

"T'ai-wan hsin-yin fa-lü shu-mu," Wang, Tse-yen, **106a**

U

Z